100

Hull-House entrance. Etching by Norah Hamilton.

YEARS

AT

HULL-

HOUSE

EDITED BY

MARY LYNN McCREE BRYAN

AND

ALLEN F. DAVIS

INDIANA UNIVERSITY PRESS   BLOOMINGTON & INDIANAPOLIS

The paper used in this publication meets the minimum requirements
of American National Standard for Information Sciences—Permanence of Paper
for Printed Library Materials, ANSI Z39.48-1984.

♾ ™

Manufactured in the United States of America

Library of Congress Cataloging-in-Publication Data

One hundred years at Hull-House / edited by Mary Lynn McCree Bryan and
Allen F. Davis.
    p.   cm.
    Rev., expanded ed. of: Eighty years at Hull-House. 1969.
    ISBN 0-253-31621-9 (alk. paper).—ISBN 0-253-20579-4 (pbk. : alk. paper)
    1. Hull House (Chicago, Ill.)—History. I. Bryan, Mary Lynn
McCree. II. Davis, Allen Freeman. III. Eighty years at
Hull-House. IV. Title: 100 years at Hull-House. V. Title: Years at
Hull-House.
HV4196.C4H74   1990
362.84′009773′11—dc20   88-46032
                                                  CIP

1 2 3 4 5   94 93 92 91 90

CONTENTS

MATURITY: 1914–1935   157

CONFUSION AND RECOVERY: 1935–1962   207

THE END AND A NEW BEGINNING: 1963–1989   275

AFTERWORD   323

PREFACE

Most people have heard of Hull-House and know that it is somehow connected with Jane Addams, but few appreciate its rich heritage and its involvement over one hundred years with movements and activities central to any understanding of the history of modern America. "Although its influence cannot be measured," historian Charles Beard wrote, "the guess may be hazarded that no other single institution of the period did as much to counteract the dogma of individualism and restore the social principle to thought about civilization." Robert Morss Lovett, writer and social commentator, announced: "The beginning of Miss Addams' and Miss Starr's residence among the poor of Chicago marks the beginning of the modern social movement in the United States." Founded in 1889 on the west side of Chicago, the settlement developed and changed over the years until it was forced to move in 1963 to make room for a new Chicago campus of the University of Illinois. But Hull-House continues to function today, operating a variety of programming in centers scattered throughout neighborhoods in the metropolitan area.

We read today of the urban crisis and of the horrors of poverty almost as if they were new phenomena, but from its beginning Hull-House confronted poverty, poor housing, disease, discouragement, and the other ills that flourished in the industrial city. Many contemporary social theorists decry the lack of a sense of community in our sprawling urban areas, but for many years, Hull-House workers have attacked the anonymity of the city and tried to restore a feeling of community in their shifting and volatile surroundings. They were not always successful in improving their neighborhoods, or in organizing the poor, but over the years many young men and women found encouragement and inspiration at Hull-House and were able to move up and out of that environment. Indeed the near west side of Chicago (with Hull-House as its focus), next to the lower east side of New York, has been the most significant portal through which thousands of immigrants have entered the mainstream of American life.

Perhaps more important than the neighborhood youngsters inspired by the early settlement programs were the young residents who spent a year or two or longer at Hull-House and went on to different jobs and duties with a changed social outlook. For example, Edith Saluda "Luda" Watson graduated from Rockford College in 1893 with a degree in music. She became a resident at Hull-House on February 29, 1896, and remained there until November 1899, when she married Frank Bartlett in Eau Claire, Wisconsin. She and her husband settled in Drummond, Wisconsin in 1900. Here she raised a family and lived until her death in 1966. "The greater part of the three and one-half years spent at Hull-House before my marriage was devoted to the organization of young people's clubs, so coming here with not much to do in a social way, I suggested a 'reading-sewing' club to some women," she wrote in a letter dated February 17, 1936, to the Wisconsin Federation of Women's Clubs. The Thursday Club had as its focus welfare work. She also conducted a Saturday afternoon sewing club for young girls aged thirteen to fifteen, and organized the Priscilla Club of village women, who met on Monday nights to discuss civic and cultural affairs. Luda Watson was active in the Wisconsin Federation of Women's Clubs and served as director of the Drummond school board for thirty years. Like so many others, she brought the philosophy and methods of settlement to her community and friends.

The impulse that led a generation of young college graduates to live and work in a settlement house is similar to the impulse that caused many bright young people to join the Peace Corps or a community organization project in the 1960s. Like those programs, Hull-House probably had a greater impact on the volunteers than on those they came to help. The many who were influenced over the years by the atmosphere of intellectual freedom and by the amazing group of people at the settlement reads like a twentieth-century *Who's Who,* and in itself is enough to ensure the importance of Hull-House in any account of recent history. There were Charles Beard, Philip Davis, George Hooker, Stuart Chase, William Chenery, William Hard, Ernest Crosby, LeRoy Scott, Robert Hunter, William English Walling, Robert Morss Lovett, Francis Hackett, Gerard Swope, Frances Perkins, Charlotte Perkins Gilman, Lewis Hine, Harriet Monroe, Paul Douglas, Walter Gifford, Mackenzie King, Ramsay MacDonald, Sidney Hillman, Jeannette Rankin, Robert Weaver—and this is just a sampling. A great many men were strongly influenced by Hull-House though they were never officially residents: John Dewey, Clarence Darrow, Harold Ickes, Frank Lloyd Wright, John Peter Altgeld, Henry Demarest Lloyd, Richard T. Ely, John Commons, and many more. Then, of course, there was the remarkable group of women who made Hull-House the vital and exciting place it was: Jane Addams, to be sure, and Ellen Starr, Florence Kelley, Julia Lathrop, Alice Hamilton, Alzina Stevens, Mary Kenney O'Sullivan, Grace and Edith Abbott, Adena Miller Rich, Louise deKoven Bowen, Jessie Binford, Sophonisba Breckinridge, Mary McDowell, and many others.

These men and women had an influence that spread far beyond the west side of Chicago. They left their mark on the movement to abolish child labor and to regulate and control the work of women. They tried to combat industrial disease, to promote parks and playgrounds and city planning. They were among the first to study the problems of the city systematically. They were leaders in the movement to improve housing, and they pioneered in working sympathetically with juvenile delinquents. They helped to introduce art into the schools and to spread the kindergarten movement, and they influenced the development of progressive education. They supported the fight of organized labor for recognition and worked for woman suffrage. They helped to influence and then to administer the programs of the New Deal and the Great Society. Indeed, to study the evolution of Hull-House over one hundred years is to be introduced to the liberal-progressive attempt to grapple with the problem of urban poverty and all its attendant ills.

But Hull-House was more than a reform outpost in the slums; it helped lead a cultural renaissance in Chicago. It was also an exciting place to visit and an intellectually stimulating place to live. Beatrice Webb, a visitor from England, discovered "one continuous intellectual and emotional ferment." John Dewey found it "a way of life—a companionship that had extended from the neighborhood to the world." Another former resident noticed how "Hull-House teemed with ideas, like a co-educational monastery crossed with, say, All Souls' at Oxford." And Henry Demarest Lloyd wrote: "It has nuns, but it is not a nunnery; it has monks, but it is not a monastery. What shall we call it? It is a most delightful place. I suspect it might easily make good its claim to be the best club in Chicago."

Hull-House has never been a static institution; it has changed with the times and with the fascinating people who have come and gone and made it always more than a group of buildings. It has witnessed several depressions and two major wars, not to count the minor ones. It has survived the death of its founder and the loss of its original settlement buildings and neighborhood, as well as reorganization as an association of facilities and programs in several different neighborhoods. It has seen the development of professional social work and the growth of the welfare state and has played a part in both movements. It stands now, at its hundredth year, among the oldest private welfare organizations in Chicago and is still struggling with the challenge of social injustice.

Hull-House has not been without its problems. There have been personality conflicts and disagreements over programs and priorities. There have been times, such as the years immediately after Jane Addams' death, when the settlement was racked with dissension and unsure of its purpose and direction. More recently, when the settlement became an association composed of separate affiliated centers, each with its own board and director, each developing its own program, each responding to the needs of its own neighborhood, the administration of the agency became even more complex and problematic, its image and identity in Chicago less certain. Financial worries have been constant. The settlement leaders occasionally displayed a paternalistic attitude toward the poor, or they sometimes erred in the other direction and admired the beauty and simplicity of poverty. The early Hull-House residents quite consciously tried to teach middle-class values to the immigrants. Though they did try to do things with, not for, their neighbors, they rarely allowed the poor to participate in planning settlement activities. As the years have passed, and especially since the War on Poverty programs of the 1960s, Hull-House has made special efforts to include its neighbors in planning and to employ them in programs in its various centers, not always successfully. Yet over the years, Hull-House has represented the best of the American liberal tradition and its attempt to solve the human problems of the city.

It is quite possible, of course, to survey the history of the past one hundred years and conclude that Hull-House and the entire progressive–New Deal–Great Society effort to solve the problems of urban America have failed. For example, one can examine the old Hull-House neighborhood on the near west side of Chicago. After Hull-House closed there in 1963, it was partly destroyed as a residential section by the development of the University of Illinois, and it is truncated by expressways. In a 1967 study, *The Social Order of the Slum*, Gerald D. Suttles made clear that the area suffered from many of the same ills found there in the 1890s—a high rate of crime and juvenile delinquency, poor housing, inadequate schools and recreational facilities, and racial and ethnic tensions that occasionally flared into violence and gang war. But the most obvious and depressing characteristic of the district was its provincialism. Surrounded by the signs of American affluence, the people who lived here were cut off, anonymous, and afraid. It was this very isolation of the poor from the rest of America (and the isolation of the affluent and well educated from the poor) that inspired Jane Addams to found Hull-House one hundred years ago. The settlement obviously had not solved the problem of isolation, nor had it alleviated that of poverty.

Ironically what survives of the old Hull-House neighborhood has been upgraded in the last twenty years. Houses once crowded with recent arrivals in America are now the homes of young professionals who find the area convenient to jobs and entertainment in the Loop and the near north side. But poverty and all its attendant ills continue to plague Chicago and the nation. In fact, William Julius Wilson in his 1987 book *The Truly Disadvantaged* argued that poverty, crime, and urban social problems have increased in the last two decades. The number of homicides in Chicago jumped from 195 in 1965 to 810 in 1970 to 970 in 1974 (still Chicago ranked fifth among major cities in murders). The number of people living in poverty in Chicago increased by 24 percent between 1970 and 1980 and has continued to rise in the 1980s. Neither Hull-House, the government, nor all the other social agencies seem to be able to solve the problem of the truly disadvantaged in America.

If the story of Hull-House over one hundred years is a story of failure, it is also a story of success. Many of the poor did find encouragement at the settlement and were able to move out of their neighborhoods, and many of the programs and reforms initiated at Hull-House improved working and living conditions in Chicago and America. The ultimate worth of the settlement and its attempts to deal with the overwhelming problems of the industrial city cannot be measured in one neighborhood or city, for the Hull-House influence permeated the entire social reform tradition in America. Both the successes and failures of Hull-House are well worth pondering today, as we gird ourselves once more to face the urban crisis.

We decided to write *Eighty Years at Hull-House* (the original edition of this book) one day in 1967 while observing tourists streaming through the restored version of Hull-House on the University of Illinois campus in Chicago. With the immediate neighborhood torn down and replaced with towering, antiseptic buildings, with well-organized exhibits and immaculately restored rooms replacing the hustle and bustle and dingy disarray of the original Hull-House, it was impossible even for the most perceptive of visitors to appreciate the purpose and meaning of the settlement. It was a story we thought worth telling.

We wrote *Eighty Years at Hull-House* at the end of Lyndon Johnson's Great Society, when some of the idealism of the early 1960s and the faith that one could build a better, more just world was already erroding. We did most of the research and writing of the book during the tumultuous year of 1968, which was marked by marches and protests against the war in Vietnam, as well as by the assassinations of Martin Luther King and Robert Kennedy, riots and looting in the cities, and the divisive scene at the national Democratic Party convention in Chicago, where police attacked and clubbed young demonstrators. We finished the book in the very early days of the presidency of Richard Nixon. Yet the tone of the first edition was basically optimistic. We wrote within the Progressive–New Deal, liberal tradition, and we had hope that the best of the Hull-House heritage could survive and would be remembered. Working on *One Hundred Years at Hull-House* in the early days of the George Bush administration, after eight years of Ronald Reagan's war on welfare and attacks on the progressive tradition of social justice, we are not as hopeful. But we still believe that the Hull-House reformers, in all their diversity over one hundred years, are worth studying. The Hull-House example, not only in politics and social reform, but also in art, literature, theater, and music and in the search for community within the city, defines much that is admirable in the American experience over the last century.

We have tried to communicate the excitement and the diversity of Hull-House and its changing neighborhoods by using the pictures, drawings, and the words of contemporary observers, residents of the settlement, and workers in the organization. This is not the complete story of Hull-House; we have had to be selective, and we have by choice given more weight to the first decade and a half of the twentieth century, when the settlement was at the peak of its reputation and influence. We have tried throughout to indicate the way the settlement and the neighborhood changed, and to record the conflicts and controversies, the failures along with the successes. We have tried to present a variety of opinions, but our own ideas and commitments have obviously influenced our choice of material.

In this edition we have retained most of what was in the original, but we have added an occasional piece, corrected a few errors, and brought introductions up-to-date. We conclude with a new chapter in which we try to indicate the traumatic changes that occurred as Hull-House spread out into the city and faced the overwhelming problems of the last twenty-five years. Within each selection we have retained the original spelling (except for obvious errors), capitalization, and punctuation. Though we have chosen to spell ''Hull-House'' in our own text the way Jane Addams did, in many selections it is spelled without a hyphen. We have used square brackets where we have inserted information or corrected errors and ellipsis points to indicate that we have omitted text in the original. Footnotes are those of the author of the selection unless identified by ''Eds.''

We would be remiss if we did not thank all of those that have contributed to the effort that has gone into this edition. Without the cooperation and assistance of Hull-House Association and particularly its director, Patricia Sharpe, it would have been extremely difficult to develop the history of the past twenty years of Hull-House. We are also grateful to Robert T. Adams, Nancy Slote, and Nancy Danker for their contributions. While we were able to copy, cut, and paste a great deal of the material for this book from *80 Years*, we thank Maree de Angury for typing, proofreading, and helping the editors to produce an organized manuscript of the whole book for submission to the publishers. We are grateful to all who gave us permission to include photographs, excerpts, letters, and drawings, and we hope they feel this finished work made their participation worthwhile.

Over the last six months the two of us have not met in person, working instead through long telephone conversations and sharing various versions of the text via express mail. Again, our most difficult task seemed to be meeting our publisher's deadline, and after twenty more years, we still remain friends.

MLB
AFD

Fayetteville, North Carolina
Philadelphia, Pennsylvania
February 1989

ACKNOWLEDGMENTS

Photographs and illustrations are used by permission of:

Chicago Historical Society, ICHi - 04285, p. 8; CRC - 143 - F, p. 72.
International Museum of Photography at George Eastman House, pp. 99–101.
Hull-House Association, Chicago, pp. 247, 251, 267, 277, 280, 284, 288, 291, 306, 311, 313, 319–321.
University of Illinois at Chicago:
   Department of Special Collections, The University Library: Photograph Collection, pp. 10, 14, 15, 24, 27, 32, 38, 41, 45, 46, 47, 50, 56, 66, 74, 75, 93, 97, 101, 107, 149, 165, 183, 185, 230, 243, 259, 260, 261; Wallace Kirkland Collection, pp. 79, 103, 133, 160, 171, 173, 175, 191, 193, 204, 208, 221, 226, 234, 236, 239, 270; Public Relations, p. 273.

Grateful acknowledgment is made to the following authors and publishers for permission to reprint copyrighted materials:

   The Atlantic Monthly, for ''The Devil Baby at Hull-House,'' *The Atlantic Monthly,* October 1916, pp. 441–448, © 1916; Jane Addams, as first published in *The Atlantic Monthly*; and ''Charlotte Carr—Settlement Lady,'' *The Atlantic Monthly,* December 1938, pp. 741–748, © 1938; Milton Mayer, as first published in *The Atlantic Monthly.* Reprinted with permission.

   Charles C. Thomas, Publishers, for Patricia L. Sharpe, Jane F. Connolly, Ruby L. Schmidt, and Marjorie A. Lundy, ''Outreach: Bringing Services to the Elderly Senior Centers of Metropolitan Chicago,'' from Richard E. Hardy and John G. Cull, eds., *Organization and Administration of Service Programs for the Older Adult,* 1974, pp. 51–58. Reprinted courtesy of Charles C. Thomas, Publishers, Springfield, Illinois.

   Chicago Historical Society, for Dewey Jones manuscript, Minutes of the March 15, 1939 meeting of the Executive Committee, Division on Education and Recreation, Welfare Council of Metropolitan Chicago, The Welfare Council of Metropolitan Chicago Papers, Box 145, Folder 1. Printed by permission.

Chicago Reader, Inc., for Grant Pick, "Neighborhood News: Is the CHA ready to try tenant management?" *Chicago Reader,* May 2, 1986. © 1986, Chicago Reader, Inc. Reprinted with permission.

Chicago Sun-Times, Inc., for Howard Vincent O'Brien, "All Things Considered," *Chicago Daily News,* January 11, 1943. Copyright ©. With permission of the Chicago Sun-Times, Inc., 1989.

Chicago Tribune Company, for Susan Lewis, "Unique Court Makes Differences to Victims of Domestic Violence," *Chicago Tribune,* November 10, 1985; and Stevenson O. Swanson, "The Failure of Uptown Housing Resource Center," *Chicago Tribune,* March 4, 1982. Copyrighted, Chicago Tribune Company, all rights reserved, used with permission.

Clayton F. Summy Co., for Eleanor Smith, *Hull-House Songs,* 1915, pp. 8–11. © 1915 Clayton F. Summy Co. All Rights Reserved. Used by permission.

Commonweal, for Eleanor Grace Clark, "Ellen Gates Starr, O. S. B. (1859–1940)," *Commonweal,* March 15, 1940, pp. 445–447. Reprinted with permission.

Doubleday, for excerpts from pp. 447–464 of Edmund Wilson, *The American Earthquake,* 1958. Copyright © 1958 by Edmund Wilson. Published by Doubleday, a division of Bantam, Doubleday, Dell Publishing Group, Inc. Reprinted with permission.

Richard Gosswiller, "Hull-House: A New Face," © 1947. Reprinted from *Chicago.*

W. Rush G. Hamilton, for Alice Hamilton, *Exploring the Dangerous Trades,* 1943, pp. 68–86; and Alice Hamilton to Agnes Hamilton, letters of October 13, 1897 and April 3, [1898], Hamilton Family Papers, Schlesinger Library, Radcliffe College. Printed with permission of W. Rush G. Hamilton.

Hull-House Association, Chicago, for selections from its records, including Paul B. Johnson, "Citizen Participation in Urban Renewal: The History of the Near West Side Planning Board and a Citizen Participation Project," 1960, pp. 3–16, 22–23; and Long Range Planning Committee, "Environmental Analysis Overview," 1983. Printed with permission of Hull-House Association.

Peter Jacobi, for his "Capital C, Small a," *New City,* June 15, 1965, pp. 5–9. Reprinted with permission of the author.

Macmillan Publishing Company, for Jane Addams, *Second Twenty Years at Hull-House,* 1930, pp. 140–143. Reprinted with permission of Macmillan Publishing Company. Copyright 1930, renewed © 1958 by John A. Brittain.

The New York Times, for Lloyd Lewis, "The House that Jane Addams Built," *The New York Times,* May 16, 1940 (magazine). Copyright © 1940 by The New York Times Company. Reprinted by permission.

Ralph G. Newman, for Sara L. Hart, *The Pleasure Is Mine: An Autobiography,* 1947, pp. 95–105. Reprinted with permission of Ralph G. Newman for Valentine-Newman, Publishers.

Northwestern University, School of Law, Journal of Criminal Law and Criminology, for John Landesco, "Memories of the 42 Gang," 23, *Journal of Criminal Law and Criminology,* 964, March 1933, pp. 967–980. Reprinted by special permission of Northwestern University, School of Law.

Pantheon Books, for Studs Terkel, *Division Street: America,* 1967, pp. 1–9. Copyright © 1967 by Studs Terkel. Reprinted by permission of Pantheon Books.

Philosophical Library, Publishers, for Philip Davis, *And Crown Thy Good,* 1952, pp. 85–93. Reprinted with permission of the Philosophical Library, Publishers.

Radcliffe College, The Schlesinger Library, for use of two letters of Alice Hamilton to Agnes Hamilton, October 13, 1897 and April 3, [1898], Hamilton Family Papers; and for excerpts from Mary Kenney, unpublished autobiographical manuscript.

Patricia L. Sharpe, for her "Contributions over 100 Years," manuscript, 1986. Printed by permission of the author.

Smith College, The Sophia Smith Collection, for letters from Ellen Gates Starr to Mary Blaisdell, May 18 and May 22, 1890, the Ellen Gates Starr Papers. Printed with permission.

Swarthmore College, Swarthmore College Peace Collection, for letters of Wallace L. DeWolf to Jane Addams, July 17, 1916, and Oscar Ludmann to Jane Addams, May 21, 1931, from the Jane Addams Papers. Printed by permission.

Time, Inc., for "Haunted Hull-House," *Time,* January 11, 1943, p. 82. Copyright 1943 Time Inc. All rights reserved. Reprinted by permission.

United Neighborhood Centers of America, Inc., for Elaine Switzer, "Four Years of Program Planning: A Report, 1945–1949," *Round Table,* March–April 1950, pp. 1–4. Reprinted by permission.

The University of Chicago Press, for excerpts from Edith Abbott, "Grace Abbott and Hull-House, 1908–1921," *Social Service Review,* September 1950, pp. 378–379, 384–385; December 1950, pp. 493–494. Copyright, The University of Chicago Press. Reprinted by permission.

University of Illinois at Chicago, The University Library, Special Collections Department, for the following, printed with permission from:

The Esther Loeb Kohn Papers, for Louise deKoven Bowen on the death of Jane Addams, manuscript, 1935.

The Adena Miller Rich Papers, for Louise deKoven Bowen to Adena Miller Rich, June 28, 1935, and Adena Miller Rich to Louise deKoven Bowen, July 9, 1935, letters; and "Head Residents Work during Transition since the Death of Miss Jane Addams," manuscript by Adena Miller Rich, March 15, 1937.

The Russell W. Ballard Papers, for Jessie Binford to Louise deKoven Bowen, July 23, 1943, letter; "An Evening at Hull-House," by Russell W. Ballard, 1945; mimeographed copies of letters of Nancy Craver, Charlene Dalpiza, Helen Z. Fedoryn, and the Debonairs, prepared to save Hull-House from destruction; and statement by Russell W. Ballard to the Committee on Housing and Planning of the Chicago City Council Public Housing, April 12, 1961.

University of Illinois, Urbana-Champaign, University Archives, for David D. Henry, remarks on January 23, 1964, at the ceremony dedicating the bust of Jane Addams, David D. Henry Papers, 1922–1984, Box 4. Printed with permission.

University of Wisconsin Press, for David A. Shannon, editor, *Beatrice Webb's American Diary, 1898,* © 1963, pp. 107–109. Reprinted with permission.

Robert C. Weaver, his *The Negro Ghetto,* 1948, pp. 191–196. Reprinted by permission of the author.

BEGINNINGS
1889–1900

ON SEPTEMBER 18, 1889, JANE ADDAMS AND ELLEN GATES STARR moved into an old, dilapidated mansion in the middle of a teeming immigrant neighborhood on the west side of Chicago, and Hull-House was born. The house had been built in 1856 for Charles J. Hull, an early Chicago real estate dealer and philanthropist. Once an elegant rural homestead, it had survived the Chicago Fire of 1871, had become in time a hospital, factory, apartment house, office building, even a furniture store, as it was engulfed by the shabby buildings of the booming city. It was still known in the neighborhood as ''Hull's House.'' After trying out a few other suggestions, the new residents decided to keep the old name.

What impulse led two well-educated young women like Jane Addams and Ellen Gates Starr to move into a poor section of a large city? The reasons are complex. Their action was part of a broad social movement that sought to solve the problems of an urban and industrial age, but personal factors were involved as well.

Jane Addams was born in 1860 in Cedarville, a small village in northern Illinois, not far from the Wisconsin border. Her father was a wealthy and influential businessman, miller, farmer, and politician. Although she was sickly as a child and had a slight curvature of the spine, Jane Addams had a normal, active, rural childhood. The Addams family, large and happy, was not unusual except that it was more prosperous than most small-town Midwestern families, and there were plenty of books available in the Addams home. Jane Addams was two and a half when her mother died. Almost seven years later her father remarried. His new wife, Anna Haldeman, was a widow. She brought two sons of her own to join the five Addams children, and a love and appreciation of culture, arts, and education.

In *Twenty Years at Hull-House* Jane Addams recalled a story, based on a family legend, that when she was seven she had gone with her father to nearby Freeport, Illinois, where for the first time she had seen real poverty. According to the story she declared that when she grew up she was going to have a large house, "but it would not be built among the other large houses, but right in the midst of horrid little houses like these." Some biographies of Addams have presented this story as evidence that she was a precocious child who had already decided at the age of seven to found Hull-House. But there is no truth to the legend; her decision to found Hull-House came much later and was more difficult to reach.

If there was anything that set the young Jane Addams apart from her Cedarville playmates it was her even temper and her strong determination to do something important with her life. She read widely, even compulsively; she also found time to roam the hills with her stepbrother George, who was about her age, and to play games with the village children. Her parents assumed that after completing the public school in Cedarville she would go to nearby Rockford Female Seminary like her sisters, then go abroad for a year to complete her education. But Jennie, as she was called at home, had read about the new and more prestigious women's colleges in the East—she announced that she was going to Smith. Her father insisted that she attend Rockford where he was a trustee. So in the fall of 1877 she found herself a college woman. Though she continued to talk about it, Jane Addams never transferred to Smith. She stayed at Rockford to graduate in 1881, returning the next year to receive one of the first bachelor's degrees awarded by the college.

The years at Rockford were crucial in Jane Addams' development. After the first weeks of temerity and homesickness, she gained confidence in her ability. She made friends and developed an intellectual companionship with other bright and ambitious young women. From the first, one of her best friends was Ellen Gates Starr, a petite, vivacious, and deeply spiritual girl from Durand, Illinois. After one year, when Ellen dropped out of college to teach school in Chicago, the two girls kept their relationship alive through long, devoted, and intellectually searching letters. There were other companions as well, for even as a college girl Jane Addams had a special ability for getting along with people. She became mediator, confidante, and friend to many of her fellow students. She was president and valedictorian of her class, editor of the school magazine and debater for Rockford during her senior year. Her college career was successful by any standard, but what did a women college graduate in 1881 do?

Jane Addams was well aware of her status as part of the first generation of college women. As one of them she felt a special obligation to get the best education possible and then to demonstrate through her use of it that women were worthy of the best. But what could she do? At Rockford the atmosphere was strongly religious; the seminary faculty and the president used pressure and persuasion to make the students accept an evangelical form of Christianity and become missionaries. Jane Addams resisted the pressure. She had grown up in a religious family and had always attended church and Sunday school, though like her father she had never joined a church. Finding it difficult to believe some features of orthodox Christianity, she quickly rejected the idea of becoming a missionary. Yet she worried about religion and confessed to Ellen Starr that if she could only get her thoughts on religion sorted out, "I could use my faculties and energy so much better and could do almost anything."

She also rejected the idea of becoming a teacher, another occupation then open to women. She thought teaching was a routine and bureaucratic profession which offered little opportunity for a significant contribution to society. She could have married and settled for the role of wife, mother, and homemaker; she was attractive and had at least two suitors whom she discouraged. To marry and raise a family was certainly an honorable undertaking for a woman. But the new college woman believed that one could not combine marriage and a career, and for Jane Addams there was never any question that a career was more important.

Her stepbrother Harry had studied medicine in Germany, her other stepbrother George was about to begin studying biology, and she had always liked science, so she decided to become a doctor. Anyhow, medicine was a field in which a woman could serve and make her mark. In the fall of 1881 she enrolled in the Women's Medical College in Philadelphia; but she soon discovered that she had little aptitude for medical studies. After a few months she became ill and gave up her attempt to become a physician.

For the next six years Jane Addams floundered around searching for a career and a purpose to her life. She became despondent and unsure of herself. The sudden death of her father during the summer after her graduation from college added to her depression, but it also left her with a legacy large enough to provide financial independence. While recuperating from an operation that successfully corrected her spinal curvature, she began to realize that her real problem was not a physical weakness, but finding something interesting and worthwhile on which to spend her strength and energy. She read constantly and began to study art and music. She was a companion for her stepmother and helped care for her sister Mary's children. Then, like so many other daughters of the well-to-do, she went to Europe. For twenty-two months she toured cathedrals and art galleries, took language lessons, kept a diary and wrote an elaborate stream of letters to family and friends. Occasionally she was disturbed—by a tour of the slums of east London, or the sight of girls working in a brewery in Bavaria—but in most ways she was an average American tourist, returning with no sense of purpose or commitment. Perhaps she didn't realize it, but she was gradually groping toward a solution for her future.

She spent two winters in Baltimore with her stepmother and stepbrother George, who was doing graduate work at Johns Hopkins University. She went to lectures, worked as a volunteer at the Johns Hopkins Colored Orphan Asylum, and observed other charities in the city. When she returned home she joined the Cedarville Presbyterian church, not so much a sign of religious commitment as of her feeling that the church as an institution was important to the community, and that one ought to belong. She was moving toward a social interpretation of Christianity where service would become more important than doctrine. But neither the church nor traditional charity answered Jane Addams' need to serve and to do something important.

In December 1887, she went to Europe again. This time she was accompanied by Ellen Gates Starr and by Sarah Anderson, an instructor at Rockford who had become a close friend of both women. They visited cathedrals and art galleries, and collected reproductions of art for Rockford College and for the school where Miss Starr taught. While in Spain in April 1888, the young women attended a bullfight which, in her autobiography, Jane Addams described as a virtual conversion experience which led directly to her decision to found Hull-House. Most historians have accepted her interpretation.

She sat through the killing of five bulls and several horses and remembered: "The sense that this was the last survival of all the glories of the amphitheater, the illusion that the riders on the caparisoned horses might have been knights of a tournament, or the matadores a slightly armed gladiator facing his martyrdom and all the rest of the obscure yet vivid associations of an historic survival, had carried me beyond the endurance of any of the rest of the party." When her companions chided her about being bloodthirsty, she recalled: "I had no defense to offer to their reproaches save that I had not thought much about the bloodshed; but in the evening the natural and inevitable reaction came, and in deep chagrin I felt myself tried and condemned, not only by this disgusting experience but by the entire moral situation which it revealed. It was suddenly made quite clear to me that I was lulling my conscience by a dreamer's scheme, that a mere paper reform had become a defense for continued idleness, and that I was making it a *raison d'être* for going on indefinitely with study and travel. It is easy to become the dupe of a deferred purpose, of the promise the future can never keep, and I had fallen into the meanest type of self-deception in making myself believe that all this was in preparation for great things to come. Nothing less than the moral reaction following the experience at a bullfight had been able to reveal to me that so far from following in the wake of a chariot of philanthropic fire, I had been tied to the tail of the veriest ox-cart of self seeking.''

According to her autobiographical account, the next morning she mentioned to Ellen Starr her scheme for living in the slums. Perhaps the bullfight did shock Jane Addams out of her years of preparation and begin the process that led to the founding of Hull-House, but there is nothing in her letters to her family at the time to indicate that she viewed the bullfight as a turning point in her life. In fact, she continued on through Spain and northern France, visiting cathedrals and museums as before. Sometime during the spring, however, she altered her itinerary in order to be in London for the World Centennial Conference of Foreign Missions which met early in June. It is interesting that she should seek out the missionaries that she had formerly rejected. ''I have become quite learned in foreign missions and ashamed of my former ignorance,'' she wrote her sister Alice.

In London it was not so much the talk of the opium trade in China and the liquor traffic on the Congo that fascinated her, but rather the mission work going on in the city itself. She read Walter Besant's novels, *Children of Gideon* and *All Sorts and Conditions of Men,* and visited his People's Palace; but, more important, she inspected Toynbee Hall, the pioneer university settlement founded four years before by Canon Samuel A. Barnett. ''It is a community for University men who live there, have their recreation and clubs and society all among the poor people, yet in the same style they would live in their own circle,'' she reported to her sister Alice. ''It is so free of 'professional doing good,' so unaffectedly sincere and so productive of good results in its classes and libraries so that it seems perfectly ideal.'' Here, not at the bullfight, was the real turning point. Here was the answer to the dilemma, a way to serve and yet to avoid the cloying paternalism, the ''professional doing good'' of organized charity and mission societies. Here was a way to help the poor and the disadvantaged while at the same time making use of all the carefully acquired culture, the knowledge of art, music, and history, she had collected with such persistence in college and in travels abroad.

Though she did not realize it, Jane Addams had been preparing intellectually for her visit to Toynbee Hall for some years. She had read John Ruskin, not only his art criticism, but also *Unto This Last,* the little book in which he indignantly attacked the evils of the industrial city and sketched out a reform program. She also knew of Ruskin's various projects to aid the workingman. She was familiar with Thomas Carlyle, Matthew Arnold, and the English Christian Socialists, all in their own way trying to confront the problems of an urban, industrial age and to create a spiritual reawakening for the workingman as well as for the college graduate. She had also read Leo Tolstoy's *My Religion* and *What to Do,* and had been fascinated by his attempt to live like a peasant in a remote village, repudiating wealth and position. For Jane Addams the visit to Toynbee Hall came as a culmination and climax to years of searching. Suddenly her vague scheme became concrete: she vowed to move into a poor section of Chicago on her return to America.

Jane Addams and Ellen Starr took an apartment in Chicago in January 1889, and began to look for support for their venture. They talked of their "scheme" to the Chicago Woman's Club, church groups, and even to the Woman's Christian Temperance Union. They had a difficult time explaining that their object was not to uplift the masses but to restore communications between classes, and that they were going to live in the slums as much to help themselves as to aid the poor. Some laughed and others ignored their requests for help, but a surprising number, including a few prominent and wealthy Chicago women, rallied to their cause.

It was Jane Addams who founded Hull-House, but without Ellen Starr it is doubtful that she would have been able to translate her ideas into action. Starr was passionately interested in art and music. Her tendency to be more emotional, more deeply religious, more committed to causes, helped balance Addams' calm, businesslike personality. She gave Jane Addams strength, confidence, and emotional support in the early, trying days. She also had a wide range of acquaintances in Chicago who proved useful in establishing the settlement.

Hull-House, founded in 1889, was the product of the experience and educational background of Jane Addams and Ellen Starr, but it was not unique. It borrowed something from Toynbee Hall in England, yet was part of an American movement that established more than four hundred social settlements in American cities by 1911. Nor was Hull-House the first settlement in the United States. Stanton Coit, also influenced by Toynbee Hall, had established Neighborhood Guild in New York in 1886, and in 1887 a group of Smith College graduates founded the College Settlement Association, which established a settlement in New York City barely a week before the opening of Hull-House. Jane Addams and Ellen Starr were unaware of the other American settlements when they made their decision to live in the slums. They soon learned of the New York experiments and quickly came to see their venture as part of a national movement, which indeed it was.

If Hull-House was not the first settlement in America, it soon became the most famous. Several articles describing Chicago's "Toynbee Hall experiment" appeared in magazines and newspapers even before the two young women were settled, and the publicity continued after 1889. By founding Hull-House, Jane Addams and Ellen Gates Starr struck a responsive chord. Other people were worried or felt guilty about the overcrowded tenements, about poverty, disease, and death in the cities, and Hull-House offered them a method of action, or a salve to their consciences, a way to participate without touching the filth. Many who read of the settlement approved; others volunteered to help, or came out of curiosity. Most were confused about the purpose of Hull-House. Some thought it was a mission to bring the message of Christianity to the poor; others believed it was a charity to distribute food and clothing with love and kindness to the downtrodden; still others assumed it was a kind of lodging house where the unfortunate could live for a time and learn cleanliness and other American manners. Years later some of the confusion about the purpose of the settlement remained. One of the frequent questions asked by curious visitors well into the twentieth century was, "Where do the poor live?" The "poor," of course, did not live in the settlement at all, for that was where the residents who came to "settle" among the "poor" stayed, and Hull-House was not a mission or charity or lodging house.

Jane Addams and Ellen Gates Starr hoped to be neighbors to the poor, sharing with them their plight and working with them to improve the neighborhood. Beyond that goal, Addams and Starr had few definite plans. They furnished the house, unpacked the pictures they had purchased in Europe and put them on the walls, invited their neighbors in, and began doing what they knew best—teaching, lecturing, and explaining their art objects. Starr organized a reading group to discuss George Eliot's *Romola*, and before long the two energetic young women had set up art exhibits. One of their primary tasks, they believed, was to bring an appreciation of beauty and great art to those forced to live in the drab and unattractive slums. Of the early activities at Hull-House, much was esoteric, even patronizing, but the founders were flexible and willing to change. There was need for a kindergarten, so they started one, and to interest the mothers of the children they organized homemakers' clubs and other social activities. They invited labor unions to meet at the house, organized a cooperative residence for working girls, and in 1893 started a music school.

From the very first months Hull-House attracted able and energetic residents and supporters. This remarkably talented and diverse group made the settlement an exciting and intellectually stimulating place, as well as a clearinghouse for different reform movements. First of all there were the women—strong-minded, well educated, and dedicated. Julia Lathrop, from Rockford, Illinois, a graduate of Vassar, a rigorous executive with a passion for research and a subtle sense of humor, came to Hull-House during the first year. Florence Kelley, daughter of a well-to-do Philadelphia family, who had studied at Cornell and the University of Zurich and had been converted to socialism, moved in at the end of 1891. Tough-minded and strong-willed, she more than any other resident forced Hull-House to take a stand on social issues. Alzina Stevens, a former labor leader, and Mary Kenney, a girl from the neighborhood who organized women into labor unions, added to the mix of personalities and backgrounds. Later Alice Hamilton, Grace and Edith Abbott, Sophonisba Breckinridge, Enella Benedict, Clara Landsberg, and many more joined the group. Strong women dominated Hull-House, but there were men, too. Edward Burchard was the first male resident, and George Hooker, the city planning expert, lived there for years. A great many others came for a short time, including historian Charles Beard, William Lyon Mackenzie King, who would one day be prime minister of Canada, and Gerard Swope, the future president of General Electric. The group shifted and changed; many came for a few years or even for a few months, then moved on. Almost everyone had a full-time job, paid room and board to Hull-House, and devoted spare time to settlement activities. Yet there was a sense of belonging to a group, of being dedicated to a cause that sometimes baffled the outside observer, especially the immigrant neighbor. Abraham Bisno, a labor leader and frequent visitor to the settlement, remarked, ''These people seldom sing, almost never dance, and their attitude toward each other carries no sign of their sex life.''

Bisno may not have noticed any indication of sex at Hull-House, but it was a place where many of the younger residents fell in love. Gerard Swope, for example, met his future wife, Mary Hill, at the settlement. More important, however, Hull-House was a place where women created an alternative lifestyle. Jane Addams, like more than half of the first generation of college women, never married. She could have lived with either of her married sisters, or at the family homestead, but she chose to live at Hull-House, which she always thought of as home. The settlement also became home for many other unmarried women. They usually had the privacy of a single room as well as the companionship of other women and the convenience of a common dining hall. When Ellen Starr and Jane Addams first moved to Hull-House they brought a housekeeper with them. Later there was more staff to relieve the professional women residents of domestic duties and free them to promote reform and write their books and articles. In addition to the model lodging house for dependent women and the Phalanx Club, a cooperative residence for men, there was a cooperative residence, the Jane Club, for working women. ''We have worked out during our years of residence a plan of living which may be called cooperative,'' Jane Addams wrote, ''for the families and individuals who rent Hull-House apartments have the use of the central kitchen and dining room as far as they care for them. . . . '' One of those who was influenced by the cooperative living arrangements was Charlotte Perkins Gilman. She spent a brief time at Hull-House in 1896 and was so impressed by the life-style that she later used the settlement as a model. Gilman suggested the need for apartment buildings without kitchens, but with a common dining hall and child care facilities to free women for professional careers.

More than the residents made up the Hull-House group. A great many people, most of whom lived in Chicago, contributed time, money, or expert advice to the settlement. Without them Hull-House would have floundered. Among a group of wealthy and dedicated Chicago women who gave both time and money, the most important were Louise deKoven Bowen and Mary Rozet Smith; there were also Anita McCormick Blaine, Mary Wilmarth, and Sara Hart. Helen Culver, who had inherited the original Hull-House building from Charles J. Hull, eventually gave it to Jane Addams together with most of the other property on which the settlement grew. A group of professional men aided the settlement in a variety of ways. Among them were scholars Henry Demarest Lloyd, John Dewey, Albion Small, and Charles Zueblin; ministers Jenkin Lloyd Jones and Graham Taylor (who founded Chicago Commons, a settlement of his own not far from Hull-House); and numerous lawyers, bankers, and businessmen, as well as labor leaders. As Hull-House developed it became involved with city problems, labor disputes, and reform campaigns in Chicago. Policy positions taken by the residents occasionally provoked angry reaction among outside supporters. At such times the organizational and mediating ability of pragmatic Jane Addams kept the settlement functioning. Over the years, one of the strengths of Hull-House was this very diversity of opinion and support; it kept the settlement flexible.

The physical facilities of Hull-House changed and developed during the settlement's first decade. When Jane Addams and Ellen Starr moved in, they occupied only the second floor of the old building and had the use of the drawing room on the first floor. By the next spring they were able to acquire a lease for the entire house. In 1891, after obtaining a four-year lease on the building, they erected the Butler Art Gallery on adjacent property to the south. It was a two-story structure which housed a branch of the public library, an art gallery, and had space for clubs and classes. When they received a seven-year lease in 1893, settlement leaders constructed a second building with a coffeehouse below and a gymnasium above. A third story was added on the original building, and Children's House, with rooms for kindergarten, nursery, and a music school, was erected when a twenty-five-year lease was negotiated in 1895. In 1896 a third story was added to the Butler Art Gallery to provide rooms for men in residence, and in 1898 a special building was erected for the Jane Club, the cooperative residence for working girls. A new coffeehouse, with a theater above it, was built in 1899 while the old coffeehouse and gymnasium were moved and remodeled. The new buildings were designed by Allen and Irving Pond, Chicago architects who were a part of the settlement group from the beginning. Hull-House was in a constant state of development and remodeling; like a medieval manor house, which it vaguely resembled in appearance, the settlement added a wing here or a section there, or changed the function of a room as the need arose.

Just as the physical appearance of the settlement changed over the first decade, so did its program and activities. Clubs, classes and lectures, art exhibits, and music instruction made up an important part of the program, which was always based on the needs of those the settlement meant to serve. When college extension courses and lectures on Greek art did not meet the educational requirements of many of the neighbors, the Hull-House leaders added basic instruction in English language and American government to aid the immigrant who was desperately trying to learn new American ways. At first there was a religious air about the settlement, complete with periodic evening prayers; but the Protestant emphasis soon disappeared as the residents sought to attract all kinds of people.

Although impractical and patronizing aspects of the settlement program remained, there was, during the first decade, an increasing involvement in the problems of the neighborhood and the city. While the activities of Florence Kelley, Alzina Stevens, and Julia Lathrop helped push the settlement toward research and reform, the depression of 1893 and the suffering it created also shocked the residents to action. The settlement group was horrified by the treatment of children in the neighborhood. They began a long battle for stringent regulation of child labor and for the abolition of the sweating system; they also opened the first public playground in Chicago in 1893. Many of the residents became expert social investigators, learning how to document with statistics their anger and concern. In the process they became pioneers in the development of urban sociology. They made elaborate studies of child labor, tenement conditions, ethnic groups, and wage rates in their neighborhood. All of this research, plus their informal knowledge of the neighborhood, led them naturally into politics, and in 1896 and again in 1898 they tried unsuccessfully to defeat the political boss in their ward.

By the turn of the century Hull-House had grown and developed until it was well known nationally. The residents had discovered that it was impossible to clean up one neighbor-

A typical street in the Hull-House neighborhood at the turn of the century.

hood without frequent trips to city hall, the state capital, and even to Washington. They accepted as part of the settlement goal the task of restoring the idea of a *neighborhood* to a crowded section of the city and making Hull-House a community center. But they also thought they had a wider responsibility. Jane Addams once remarked that she did not believe in "geographical salvation," and Hull-House, at least after the first few years, constantly spoke to a much wider area than its own ward and precinct. Hull-House became a neighborhood center whose constituency was the nation.

Jane Addams about the time Hull-House was founded.

First Days at Hull-House

Jane Addams

For nearly eighty years, people all over the world have discovered Hull-House through Jane Addams' autobiography, Twenty Years at Hull-House. *Its early chapters, first published as "Fifteen Years at Hull-House" in 1906 in* The Ladies Home Journal, *were revised and republished simultaneously in book form and in the* American Magazine *in 1910. The book was an immediate success and has continued to sell in a variety of foreign-language and English editions.*

The following selection from Twenty Years at Hull-House, *describing the early days at the settlement, is typical of Addams' writing at its best—simple, yet personal, and frequently illustrated with interesting anecdotes. Though "First Days at Hull-House" was written at least fifteen years after the events she described, Jane Addams managed to recapture some of the excitement and sense of adventure in finding the old mansion, which was to become the first Hull-House building, and in moving into the crowded, diverse neighborhood near the corner of Polk and Halsted. [Jane Addams,* Twenty Years at Hull-House *(New York, 1910), 91–112.]*

In our search for a vicinity in which to settle we went about with the officers of the compulsory education department, with city missionaries, and with the newspaper reporters whom I recall as a much older set of men than one ordinarily associates with that profession, or perhaps I was only sent out with the older ones on what they must all have considered a quixotic mission. One Sunday afternoon in the late winter a reporter took me to visit a so-called anarchist Sunday school, several of which were to be found on the northwest side of the city. The young man in charge was of the German student type, and his face flushed with enthusiasm as he led the children singing one of Koerner's* poems. The newspaper man, who did not understand German, asked me what abominable stuff they were singing, but he seemed dissatisfied with my translation of the simple words and darkly intimated that they were "deep ones," and had probably "fooled" me. When I replied that Koerner was an ardent German poet whose songs inspired his countrymen to resist the aggressions of Napoleon, and that his bound poems were found in the most respectable libraries, he looked at me rather askance, and I then and there had my first intimation that to treat a Chicago man, who is called an anarchist, as you would treat any other citizen, is to lay yourself open to deep suspicion.

Another Sunday afternoon in the early spring, on the way to a Bohemian mission in the carriage of one of its founders, we passed a fine old house standing well back from the street, surrounded on three sides by a broad piazza which was supported by wooden pillars of exceptionally pure Corinthian design and proportion. I was so attracted by the house that I set forth to visit it the very next day, but though I searched for it then and for several days after, I could not find it, and at length I most reluctantly gave up the search.

Three weeks later, with the advice of several of the oldest residents of Chicago, including the ex-mayor of the city, Colonel Mason,† who had from the first been a warm friend to our plans, we decided upon a location somewhere near the junction of Blue Island Avenue, Halsted Street, and Harrison Street. I was surprised and overjoyed on the very first day of our search for quarters to come upon the hospitable old house, the quest for which I had so recently abandoned. The house was of course rented, the lower part of it used for offices and storerooms in connection with a factory that stood back of it. However, after some difficulties were overcome, it proved to be possible to sublet the second floor and what had been the large drawing-room on the first floor.

The house had passed through many changes since it had been built in 1856 for the homestead of one of Chicago's pioneer citizens, Mr. Charles J. Hull, and although battered by its vicissitudes,

---

*Andreas Justinus Kerner (1786–1862).—Eds.
†Roswell B. Mason, mayor of Chicago, 1869–1871.—Eds.

was essentially sound. Before it had been occupied by the factory, it had sheltered a second-hand furniture store, and at one time the Little Sisters of the Poor had used it for a home for the aged. It had a half-skeptical reputation for a haunted attic, so far respected by the tenants living on the second floor that they always kept a large pitcher full of water on the attic stairs. Their explanation of this custom was so incoherent that I was sure it was a survival of the belief that a ghost could not cross running water, but perhaps that interpretation was only my eagerness for finding folklore.

The fine old house responded kindly to repairs, its wide hall and open fireplaces always insuring it a gracious aspect. Its generous owner, Miss Helen Culver,* in the following spring gave us a free leasehold of the entire house. . . . In those days the house stood between an undertaking establishment and a saloon. "Knight, Death, and the Devil," the three were called by a Chicago wit, and yet any mock heroics which might be implied by comparing the Settlement to a knight quickly dropped away under the genuine kindness and hearty welcome extended to us by the families living up and down the street.

We furnished the house as we would have furnished it were it in another part of the city, with the photographs and other impedimenta we had collected in Europe, and with a few bits of family mahogany. While all the new furniture which was bought was enduring in quality, we were careful to keep it in character with the fine old residence. Probably no young matron ever placed her own things in her own house with more pleasure than that with which we first furnished Hull-House. We believed that the Settlement may logically bring to its aid all those adjuncts which the cultivated man regards as good and suggestive of the best life of the past.

On the 18th of September, 1889, Miss Starr and I moved into it, with Miss Mary Keyser, who began by performing the housework, but who quickly developed into a very important factor in the life of the vicinity as well as in that of the household, and whose death five years later was most sincerely mourned by hundreds of our neigh-

*Helen Culver (1832–1925), business partner, cousin, and heir of Charles J. Hull (1827–1889), gave Hull-House most of the land on which the settlement was built and was also a lifelong supporter.—Eds.

bors. In our enthusiasm over "settling," the first night we forgot not only to lock but to close a side door opening on Polk Street, and were much pleased in the morning to find that we possessed a fine illustration of the honesty and kindliness of our new neighbors. . . .

Halsted Street has grown so familiar during twenty years of residence, that it is difficult to recall its gradual changes—the withdrawal of the more prosperous Irish and Germans, and the slow substitution of Russian Jews, Italians, and Greeks. A description of the street such as I gave in those early addresses still stands in my mind as sympathetic and correct.

> Halsted Street is thirty-two miles long, and one of the great thoroughfares of Chicago; Polk Street crosses it midway between the stockyards to the south and the ship-building yards on the north branch of the Chicago River. For the six miles between these two industries the street is lined with shops of butchers and grocers, with dingy and gorgeous saloons, and pretentious establishments for the sale of ready-made clothing. Polk Street, running west from Halsted Street, grows rapidly more prosperous; running a mile east to State Street, it grows steadily worse, and crosses a network of vice on the corners of Clark Street and Fifth Avenue. Hull-House once stood in the suburbs, but the city has steadily grown up around it and its site now has corners on three or four foreign colonies. Between Halsted Street and the river live about ten thousand Italians—Neapolitans, Sicilians, and Calabrians, with an occasional Lombard or Venetian. To the south on Twelfth Street are many Germans, and side streets are given over almost entirely to Polish and Russian Jews. Still farther south, these Jewish colonies merge into a huge Bohemian colony, so vast that Chicago ranks as the third Bohemian city in the world. To the northwest are many Canadian-French, clannish in spite of their long residence in America, and to the north are Irish and first-generation Americans. On the streets directly west and farther north are well-to-do English-speaking families, many of whom own their houses and have lived in the neighborhood for years; one man is still living in his old farmhouse.
>
> The policy of the public authorities of never taking an initiative, and always waiting to be urged to do their duty, is obviously fatal in a neighborhood where there is little initiative among the citizens. The idea underlying our self-government breaks down in such a ward. The streets are inexpressibly

dirty, the number of schools inadequate, sanitary legislation unenforced, the street lighting bad, the paving miserable and altogether lacking in the alleys and smaller streets, and the stables foul beyond description. Hundreds of houses are unconnected with the street sewer. The older and richer inhabitants seem anxious to move away as rapidly as they can afford it. They make room for newly arrived immigrants who are densely ignorant of civic duties. This substitution of the older inhabitants is accomplished industrially also, in the south and east quarters of the ward. The Jews and Italians do the finishing for the great clothing manufacturers, formerly done by Americans, Irish, and Germans, who refused to submit to the extremely low prices to which the sweating system has reduced their successors. As the design of the sweating system is the elimination of rent from the manufacture of clothing, the "outside work" is begun after the clothing leaves the cutter. An unscrupulous contractor regards no basement as too dark, no stable loft too foul, no rear shanty too provisional, no tenement room too small for his workroom, as these conditions imply low rental. Hence these shops abound in the worst of the foreign districts where the sweater easily finds his cheap basement and his home finishers. . . .

In the very first weeks of our residence Miss Starr started a reading party in George Eliot's "Romola," which was attended by a group of young women who followed the wonderful tale with unflagging interest. The weekly reading was held in our little upstairs dining room, and two members of the club came to dinner each week, not only that they might be received as guests, but that they might help us wash the dishes afterwards and so make the table ready for the stacks of Florentine photographs.

Our "first resident," as she gayly designated herself, was a charming old lady who gave five consecutive readings from Hawthorne to a most appreciative audience, interspersing the magic tales most delightfully with recollections of the elusive and fascinating author. Years before she had lived at Brook Farm as a pupil of the Ripleys,* and she came to us for ten days because she wished to live once more in an atmosphere where "ide-

alism ran high." We thus early found the type of class which through all the years has remained most popular—a combination of a social atmosphere with serious study.

Volunteers to the new undertaking came quickly; a charming young girl† conducted a kindergarten in the drawing-room, coming regularly every morning from her home in a distant part of the North Side of the city. . . . Her daily presence for the first two years made it quite impossible for us to become too solemn and self-conscious in our strenuous routine, for her mirth and buoyancy were irresistible, and her eager desire to share the life of the neighborhood never failed, although it was often put to a severe test. One day at luncheon she gayly recited her futile attempt to impress temperance principles upon the mind of an Italian mother, to whom she had returned a small daughter of five sent to the kindergarten "in quite a horrid state of intoxication" from the wine-soaked bread upon which she had breakfasted. The mother, with the gentle courtesy of a South Italian, listened politely to her graphic portrayal of the untimely end awaiting so immature a wine bibber; but long before the lecture was finished, quite unconscious of the incongruity, she hospitably set forth her best wines, and when her baffled guest refused one after the other, she disappeared, only to quickly return with a small dark glass of whiskey, saying reassuringly, "See, I have brought you the true American drink." The recital ended in seriocomic despair, with the rueful statement that "the impression I probably made upon her darkened mind was, that it is the American custom to breakfast children on bread soaked in whiskey instead of light Italian wine." . . .

The dozens of younger children who from the first came to Hull-House were organized into groups which were not quite classes and not quite clubs. The value of these groups consisted almost entirely in arousing a higher imagination and in giving the children the opportunity which they could not have in the crowded schools, for initiative and for independent social relationships. The public schools then contained little hand work of any sort, so that naturally any instruction which

*Her name was Mrs. Sedgewick. George Ripley (1802–1880), American literary critic and social reformer, founded the Brook Farm Institute of Agriculture and Education, an experiment in communal living, 1841–1847.—Eds.

†Jenny [Jennie] Dow (1867–1904), taught kindergarten at the settlement until she married William P. Harvey in 1893.—Eds.

The Hull-House kindergarten, begun in October 1889.

we provided for the children took the direction of this supplementary work. But it required a constant effort that the pressure of poverty itself should not defeat the educational aim. The Italian girls in the sewing classes would count that day lost when they could not carry home a garment, and the insistence that it should be neatly made seemed a super-refinement to those in dire need of clothing. . . .

In spite of these flourishing clubs for children early established at Hull-House, and the fact that our first organized undertaking was a kindergarten, we were very insistent that the Settlement should not be primarily for the children, and that it was absurd to suppose that grown people would not respond to opportunities for education and social life. Our enthusiastic kindergartner herself demonstrated this with an old woman of ninety, who, because she was left alone all day while her daughter cooked in a restaurant, had formed such a persistent habit of picking the plaster off the walls that one landlord after another refused to have her for a tenant. It required but a few weeks' time to teach her to make large paper chains, and gradually she was content to do it all day long, and in the end took quite as much pleasure in adorning the walls as she had formerly taken in demolishing them. Fortunately the landlord had never heard the æsthetic principle that the exposure of basic construction is more desirable than gaudy decoration. In course of time it was discovered that the old woman could speak Gælic, and when one or two grave professors came to see her, the neighborhood was filled with pride that such a wonder lived in their midst. To mitigate life for a woman of ninety was an unfailing refutation of the statement that the Settlement was designed for the young. . . .

In those early days we were often asked why we had come to live on Halsted Street when we could afford to live somewhere else. I remember one man who used to shake his head and say it was "the strangest thing he had met in his experience," but who was finally convinced that it was "not strange but natural." In time it came to seem natural to all of us that the Settlement should be there. If it is natural to feed the hungry and care for the sick, it is certainly natural to give pleasure to the young, comfort to the aged, and to minister to the deep-seated craving for social intercourse that all men feel. Whoever does it is rewarded by something which, if not gratitude, is at least spontaneous and vital and lacks that irksome sense of obligation with which a substantial benefit is too often acknowledged.

In addition to the neighbors who responded to the receptions and classes, we found those who were too battered and oppressed to care for them. To these, however, was left that susceptibility to the bare offices of humanity which raises such offices into a bond of fellowship.

From the first it seemed understood that we were ready to perform the humblest neighborhood services. We were asked to wash the newborn babies, and to prepare the dead for burial, to nurse the sick, and to "mind the children." . . .

. . . Perhaps these first days laid the simple human foundations which are certainly essential for continuous living among the poor: first, genuine preference for residence in an industrial quarter to any other part of the city, because it is interesting and makes the human appeal; and second, the conviction, in the words of Canon Barnett,* that the things which make men alike are finer and better than the things that keep them apart, and that these basic likenesses, if they are properly accentuated, easily transcend the less essential differences of race, language, creed and tradition.

Perhaps even in those first days we made a beginning toward that object which was afterwards stated in our charter: "To provide a center for a higher civic and social life; to institute and maintain educational and philanthropic enterprises, and to investigate and improve the conditions in the industrial districts of Chicago."

*Samuel A. Barnett (1844–1913), English clergyman who founded the first social settlement, Toynbee Hall, Whitechapel, London, and the one after which Hull-House was patterned.—Eds.

Two Women's Work, Tenements, and a Name

Nora Marks and Ellen Gates Starr

Hull-House and its residents were troubled during the early years by a steady stream of newspaper and magazine writers who discovered the settlement as a unique source for human interest stories. Though Jane Addams and Ellen Gates Starr welcomed publicity for their social experiment, they resented the tendency of many reporters to portray it as the product of sentimental do-gooders, dispensing charity with the zeal of missionaries. This was not their idea, nor was it the public image they hoped to create.

The following article was published on May 19, 1890, in the Chicago Tribune. *With Ellen Starr's letter to her sister, Mary Blaisdell, in which Ellen took Nora Marks to task for her interpretation of the settlement idea, it indicated some of the*

Ellen Gates Starr

early problems and some of the excitement and activity that surrounded Hull-House in its first months. Starr also offered an explanation for the name given the settlement and in the process revealed the quick wit and sensitive intelligence that made her an important influence at Hull-House. [Nora Marks, "Two Women's Work," Chicago Tribune, May 19, 1890; Ellen Gates Starr to Mary Blaisdell, May 18 and 22, 1890, Ellen Gates Starr Papers, The Sophia Smith Collection, Smith College.]

Two Women's Work

There was a social gathering at No. 335 South Halsted street* Saturday night that was not chronicled by the society reporter. South Halsted happenings are usually ignored in this Philistine fashion. But this was a notable event that deserves special mention and persuasion.

In my ramblings last week I discovered a letter of invitation addressed to

Mr. Agathno Harbaro,
Fruit Store, East Polk street,
Between the Alley and State street.

Inside the yellow envelope was a printed slip beginning "Mio Carissimo Amico" that warmly urged the recipient to come to see Le Signorine Jane Addams and Ellen Starr the evening of May 17 at No. 335 South Halsted street; to bring his family for a visit with American and Italian friends. Some hours were to be passed in "conversazione" and there would be a "concerto musicale," at which various distinguished maestros and dilettanti would entertain the company.

This unique invitation went on to say that the Misses Addams and Starr were of a distinguished family and that they had come to live among the children of Italy and desired their friendship. After a great deal more in this strain it was signed

Il vostro devotissimo Amico,
A. MASTRO-VALERIO. †

There is no doubt that Mastro-Valerio is a devoted friend of his fellow-countrymen. Mastro-Valerio is an humble editor on *L'Italia*, but he is also the Chicago Garibaldi who is trying to lead all the Italians out of the bondage of ignorance. The Signorine Starr and Addams have a good ally in Mastro-Valerio. He opened the door of No. 335 South Halsted street himself the eventful night, looking a Count Cavour, Garibaldi, and Leonardo da Vinci rolled into one.

"Mia carissima dianora!" he exclaimed in welcome, and ushered me right into a festa of Rome, held in the drawing-room of No. 335 South Halsted street, with Mastro-Valerio as master of ceremonies and the Misses Starr and Addams the central figures.

Agathno Harbaro had "brought his whole family"; as had Giovanni Vecchi and Valentino Riggio and all the padrones of South Clark street, the vendors and street-cleaners and fruit-dealers. They came in peasant dress, the American costume being good enough for only ordinary occasions. The women were bare-headed, except for a fanciful scarf from Rome or Florence; the babies wore earrings, and the men long locks and innocent expressions.

"Rosina," I said at random, holding out my arms to a red-frocked baby. My conjecture was right—her name was Rosina. So was the name of six others.

"Is this Rosina, too?"

"No; Teresina. Here is Rosina," pointing to an older child. It was a rosy, smiling young matron who sat with two brown-skinned babies on her lap. Her hair was finely braided and filled with silver pins. A lusty young man wearing earrings and long, shining hair had a marital arm about her.

Everybody was smiling, shaking hands, chattering, and gazing at ivory and gold walls, delicate etchings of old statues, and heads of madonnas. A

---

*Throughout the years, 800 South Halsted has become famous as the address of Hull-House; however, until a Chicago city ordinance of September 1909 was passed changing the street numbers on Halsted, the address of the settlement was 335 South Halsted.—Eds.

†In 1890, Alessandro Mastro-Valerio led a small group of Italian immigrants from the Hull-House neighborhood to southern Alabama, where they established the town of Daphne near Mobile. Valerio returned to Chicago to live at the settlement and participate in Hull-House and neighborhood activities for several years.—Eds.

photograph of Humbert and Marguerite* was on the mantel.

"Him no great man," said a grinning Italian.

"Well, who is?"

"Garibaldi, Cavour, the painter, and another—him—Washingtonio!" nodding his head vigorously. "La Signora told us about him. Neva heard before."

Rosina, the red-frocked one, was passed over heads to the upper end of the room, where some society people were sitting.

"Society people! We are all society people," interrupted Miss Starr, who had two Rosinas on her lap and was chattering something that sounded much like the American baby talk.

It was pretty free and easy anyhow. The Italians seemed to feel among friends. They unburdened their simple thoughts and reveled in simple pleasures. The undisguised family affection among them was something beautiful.

Presently there was singing in Italian. The program was as finely arranged as one of Mme. Patti's.† Then a violin solo with piano accompaniment, Mastro-Valerio acting as a music-rack for a Romeo.

The audience applauded heartily but judiciously and the performers all came back. There were more "conversazione" and music and then the guests said goodnight. Rosina cried, and Miss Addams, Miss Starr, and Mastro-Valerio shook everybody by the hand and asked all to come back.

I never saw anything quite like it. Here was a simple emigrant people invited to spend a social evening with cultivated Americans and enjoying it. What does it mean?

The Object Sought

It is part of a plan. It is a Toynbee Hall experiment in Chicago; a university settlement on South Halsted street living in touch with the uncultivated and under mutual obligations; a college, because there are classes; a club, because a number of people are banded together for social enjoyment. Just two young women—Miss Jane Addams and Miss Ellen Starr—got tired of keep-

ing their culture, and wealth, and social capacity to themselves, to be turned over and over among people who had enough anyhow. And down on South Halsted street were many people who had neither money, time, nor knowledge of how these things are done.

It is the beginning of the "People's Palace" of London; of Walter Besant's "Palace of Delight"; of "Toynbee Hall" in Whitechapel—a community where the exchange is equal. "All sorts and conditions of men" have a part in it and are instructed.

Miss Addams and Miss Starr got the inspiration first from one of those "waves of ideas" that become epidemic and get the Patent-Office mixed up. They didn't talk about it much, but went down to the desired locality, rented a dilapidated old house that was set back from the street and put it in order. The walls were made ivory and gold like the Auditorium;‡ there were Venuses with broken arms, Apollos, heads of Madonnas, art rugs, oak tables, china, silver, porcelain-lined baths, and the latest improved range. Then they went into the highways and byways for their guests.

This is a bill of fare for the week: The things they do, the amount of life and thought they set in motion, the practical happiness and help they bring the people with whom they live in touch and give a part in their esthetic, social, and intellectual life—literally in touch. These young women believe that all luxury is right that can be and is shared. They have taken their books, pictures, learning, gentle manner, esthetic taste—all—down to South Halsted street. This is how they are shared.

From 9 to 12 a kindergarten under the direction of Miss Dow is held in the long drawing-room. In the afternoon the kindergarten furniture is removed and the hall is devoted to the use of various clubs and classes. With its beautiful walls and pictures it is easily turned into a drawing-room with the addition of a rug and chairs.

Monday afternoon the drawing-room is filled with Italian girls who sew, play games, and dance, and the little ones cut out pictures and paste then in scrapbooks. Sometimes they take a bath when

---

*King and Queen of Italy, 1878–1900.—Eds.

†Adelina Patti (1843–1919), operatic coloratura soprano.—Eds.

‡The Auditorium Theater, a famous Chicago landmark, and a Louis Sullivan-Dankmar Adler architectural venture, was completed in 1889.—Eds.

they can be convinced of the beauty of the porcelain tubs, and clean clothes are talked about as a desideratum.

Every day the laundry is at the disposal of those who wish to make use of it.

Monday afternoon a club of young women meets and reads Romola, aided by pictures of Florence, contemporary art, and lectures by Miss Starr on Florentine artists. Mastro-Valerio talks about the Medici and Savonarola. Monday evening belongs to the French, who are reviewing the old salons of Paris. Music, conversation, and coffee form the excuse for a brilliant evening, with an occasional lecture on Marie Antoinette and kindred subjects.

Tuesday afternoon the Schoolboys' Club meets, gets books from the circulating library, and has reading aloud. At the same time a girls' cooking class is at work in the kitchen. In the evening the boys come back and have a lecture on what to do in emergencies, or simple chemical experiments. One class is reading Shakespeare and others not so far advanced are studying the three R's.

Wednesday evening the Workingmen's Discussion Club has the floor. The membership is already twenty-five, and many others who are interested attend. The Rev. Jenkin Lloyd Jones, Mr. H. D. Lloyd,* or some other well-known man delivers a short address, which is followed by the freest discussion on strikes, labor unions, the eight-hour question, child labor, etc.

Thursday afternoon Dr. Lelila Bedell† talks to the women on physiology and hygiene and how to raise healthy children, even near the Chicago River. A cooking class is also being instructed. Thursday evening the German population turns out en masse for a social evening of reading, music, and "cakes and ale."

Friday afternoon the Schoolgirls' Club comes in to sew, embroider, and cook, each taking home a book from the library. Friday evening the working girls come in to enjoy a lecture or concert, and

---

*Jenkin Lloyd Jones (1843–1918) was an independent minister, educator, and lecturer. Henry Demarest Lloyd (1847–1903), an American writer, was one of the first muckrakers, exposing misdeeds of railroads and Standard Oil. Both men were friends of Jane Addams and Hull-House.—Eds.

†Leila G. Bedell (d. 1914), a homeopathic physician associated with the Chicago Hospital for Women and Children, had been president of the Chicago Woman's Club, 1885–1886, and in 1890 was serving as one of its vice presidents.—Eds.

Saturday evening there is a typical Italian entertainment. Already they have celebrated Washington's birthday, witnessed a comedietta by the Circola Salvini, and been entertained by the Mandolin Club of the North Side.

These entertainments are crowded.

When I visited No. 335 South Halsted street Friday afternoon the play-room was full; five rooms were occupied by school girls who were sewing and listening to a young lady read from "Christmas Carols" or "Twice-Told Tales." A cooking class was turning out eggs in every style in the kitchen; the bath-room was occupied, and a heap of sand kept half a dozen diligent pie-makers busy. The long porch was filled with children who were arranging violets and buttercups into bouquets.

Lectures and concerts and classes and parties—work and play and social enjoyment. And then the life in the background—the daily contact of these opposite classes, the individual give and take that can not be measured except by posterity.

Future Plans

One of the most successful and enjoyable of the London Toynbee Hall experiments is the art exhibits in the "People's Palace." Before pictures go to the academy they come to the people. Ruskin encouraged this. Holman Hunt, Watts, Whistler, and Wilde talk it up so that it is fairly a cult. Bad pictures are being taken out of the shop windows, and for a penny Whitechapel can see "The Triumph of the Innocents" before St. James can pay a guinea for the same privilege.

Why not here?

There is a wide, bright livery stable at No. 331 South Halsted street that could be secured for a moderate rental. Skylights could be put in and the brick walls decorated. Then it could be a gallery for loan exhibits, a studio for instruction, a dance-hall.

"Why not?" says Miss Starr. "The worst thing about these crowded districts is the fact of there being no private places for dancing. Young people will dance. These people cannot do it in private houses—hence public balls. Why not a dance where the amusement could be indulged in innocently and without danger?"

It is expected, too, that a college-extension

German night at Hull-House, by Otto H. Bacher, a German-American artist. There were Italian and Irish nights at the settlement, too.

course on the plan of the university annex of Toynbee Hall will be realized. This has already been meditated by college women, and several men and women have volunteered to give instruction. For these things a small fee will be charged and this new movement is to be greater than any charity.

Tenements, and a Name

335 S. Halsted St.
May 18th: [18]90

Dear Mary [Blaisdell] . . .

For the last two days I have written for the press. We have staved off the press with varying success up to this time, but we learned that the Tribune & Journal intended to offer us up, & we decided to have a hand in it ourselves. I wrote a very good article, according to our idea, & the Tribune offered to "embody" it. That means that it will be put into nauty reporter's English. If they keep to the substance I shall be grateful. I think we managed the woman "Nora Marks" pretty well, gently directing her attention to the things we wished talked about, & directing it from delicate subjects of personal relationship. She was here last night—which was a brilliant Italian night—& I can say she will spend most of her energies on that. The Italians can't read it, & won't hear of it, so that is safe. If her article is good for anything, I will send it.

Sig. Valerio has issued a kind of manifesto in the form of a circular letter to Italians. He took this occasion of inviting them to the concert last night to make known to them several things—to explain the situation, in fact. This he sent to 228 Italians. The room was packed, & people were in the halls. It was a very good thing. Sometime when my right little finger & powers of composition are from these newspaper articles, I will translate it for you. Sig. V. has been very much depressed lately over the indifference & obstinacy of his countrymen, but his spirits were greatly raised last night. The sight was very interesting. There was a great many children, babies even & some of the women wore bright kerchiefs on their heads. The rich & vulgar Italians are taking to coming, sporting diamond crosses. I hope something will come of it. We put them on the back seats, & the peasants to the front. One of the ladies of the diamond cross recited a patriotic poem with great spirit. I missed it, being engaged in struggle with Nora Marks, on the other side of the house, but Jane says it was very spirited, & some of the people were quite moved. I was awfully glad the things went off so well. Poor Mr. V. had toiled so, & was so nervous.

22d. I went to S. Clark St. this morning to show tenement houses there to a youth of wealth who is inspired by the Holy Ghost to build model tenement houses. I don't mean that he professes his inspiration, but the source is undoubtedly no less. He is a callow youth in some respects, being, I should judge, not more than twenty-three or four years old, but a very serious & sensible one. Mr. Pond* says his father is rich, & that he himself commands money. He had been to London to investigate the model ones, but has evidently seen little of the worst ones; he was very much shocked by their conditions. We inspected water closets (so called) together, discussed them & disreputable parts of the city with freedom. People aren't as coy as they used to be. Many seem to be coming to the conclusion that if things aren't fit to be spoken of when necessary, they aren't fit to exist. This young man, Mr. Springer,† is going to consult some capitalists about forming a company for the erection of model tenements, keeping the average rent what it is now, & giving good quarters & the conveniences of civilization for it. It has been found that these tenements yield a reasonable income, these four & five percent. Mr. Springer's idea in this first enthusiasm was to give quarters free of rent, but he very reasonably concluded that it was better for people to pay a right & reasonable rent for their lodgings. As things stand now the people who own these wretched tenements get 14 & 15 percent on their money. If he (Mr. S.) can't get any capitalists to go into this novel philanthropy consisting of simple justice, he will at least put up a tenement himself. When one considers that he is young, & already thus illuminated his future career seems very promising.

The article in the Tribune was disgustingly vulgar & horrid. There were some consolations— she didn't call the neighborhood "slums" & she talked mostly about the Italians. I suppose the "salon" the gold & white walls & porcelain bath tubs will go for what it is worth if people have any sense. The worst thing was her saying at the end, of the college extension it will be greater than any charity. Why she wanted to slap it in the face by comparing it with a charity, I can't grasp. I will send you a paper.

Now comes the great item of news. Miss Culver has given us the house rent free for four years, amounting to $2880, & we have decided to call the house Hull-House. Connect these two facts in any delicate way that your refined imagination suggests. I basely observed that we were going to have "Castoria" on our pedestal for four years. Don't give this joke publicity, although I think it bright—for of course I pretend now that it seems to me the most natural & probable name imaginable, being the name by which it is already known to old residents & the neighborhood. Indeed, such awful names have been suggested that this one, though not musical, &, I fear causing restlessness & grief to the shade of Matthew Arnold, seems positively refreshing from the absence of nauseating qualities. It was growing very inconvenient not to have a name, &—it is very convenient to have four years rent. It may be necessary to explain my Castoria joke by stating, in case you don't know it, that the manufacturers of that article offered the nation a large sum (I have forgotten the amount) toward the pedestal of Liberty in exchange for the priviledge of having Castoria on it, in large letters, for a year. The government declined with dignity, it's a rich government, & can afford to be dignified. Besides, Liberty hadn't been previously known by that name, which makes a difference.

I will enclose, or send the Tribune article, though it is vilely vulgar. The programme is right—, in the main. . . .

Aff'ly,
ELLEN

*Probably Allen B. Pond (1858–1929), secretary of the Hull-House Board of Trustees, 1895–1929, who with his brother Irving K. (1857–1939), also an architect, designed most of the buildings added to the settlement.—Eds.
†Probably George Ward Springer (b. 1868), influential in real estate, insurance, and loan associations in Chicago during the first part of the twentieth century.—Eds.

Mary Kenney Is Invited In

Mary Kenney

From the beginning one of the most difficult tasks faced by the settlement workers at Hull-House was to convince their neighbors that they were not just upper-class club women on a lark in the slums. Mary Kenney's reaction was typical. In this fragment of her unpublished autobiography, this young Irish working girl, who had organized the first Book Binders' Union for women in Chicago, explained that at first she was suspicious of these well-to-do young women, but that she quickly began to realize they were really on her side. Mary Kenney not only brought her union meetings to Hull-House but also used the settlement as a base for organizing other women's unions and enlisting support for strikes. With the help of Addams and other Hull-House residents, in 1891 she established the Jane Club, a cooperative women's residence where girls with meager wages could live together without fear of eviction during the payless strike periods.

In 1892, when Mary Kenney was only twenty-eight, she became the first woman union organizer for the American Federation of Labor. She was also a deputy factory inspector and, with Florence Kelley and a few others, an important force in making Hull-House a strong supporter of organized labor. In 1893 Mary Kenney moved to Boston where she continued her organizing activity and married Jack O'Sullivan, a Boston labor leader. Ten years later she became one of the principal organizers of the National Woman's Trade Union League, whose Chicago branch was founded at Hull-House. [Mary Kenney, unpublished autobiographical manuscript, The Schlesinger Library on the History of Women in America, Radcliffe College.]

One day, while I was working at my trade, I received a letter from Miss Jane Addams. She invited me to Hull-House for dinner. She said she wanted me to meet some people from England who were interested in the labor movement. I had never heard of Miss Addams or Hull-House. I had no idea who she was.

I had been a member of a working girls' club and I was much disgusted with the talk of the group. It was always about outings. I thought that helping to get better wages was much more important. If you had good wages you could have your own outings. I left the club to give my time to work for trade organization.

I decided that I would not accept the invitation to Hull-House. No club people for me! At home I read Miss Addams' letter to Mother. She said, "Sure, Mary, you must go and see the lady. You can't judge without knowing her and she might be different from the other club women. It's condemning you are. You wouldn't like it if someone you didn't know condemned you."

When I went into Hull-House, I saw furnishings and large rooms different from anything I had

An alleyway near Hull-House. Etching by Hull-House resident Norah Hamilton.

ever seen before. With one look at the reception room, my first thought was, "If the Union could only meet here."

Miss Addams greeted me and introduced the guests from England and all the residents. My first impression was that they were all rich and not friends of the workers.

Small wages and the meagre way Mother and I had been living had been making me grow more and more class conscious. By my manner Miss Addams must have known that I wasn't very friendly. She asked me questions about our Trade Union. "Is there anything I can do to help your organization?" she said. I couldn't believe I had heard right. "Does she really want to help our Trade Union?" I asked myself. She said, "I would like to help. What can I do?" I answered, "There are many things we need. We haven't a good meeting place. We are meeting over a saloon on Clark Street and it is a dirty and noisy place, but we can't afford anything better." She said, "The Book Binders can meet here." I confided to her that, as I had passed through the large reception room, I had thought of what a wonderful meeting place it would make. "Can I help in any other way?" she said. I said we needed someone to distribute circulars. She said she would herself.

When I saw there was someone who cared enough to help us and to help us in our way, it was like having a new world opened up. I told Mother what had happened and how happy I was.

How grateful I was to have a mother that always understood.

Miss Addams not only had the circulars distributed, but paid for them. She asked us how we wanted to have them worded. She climbed stairs, high and narrow. Many of the entrances were in back alleys. There were signs to "Keep Out." She managed to see the workers at their noon hour, and invited them to classes and meetings at Hull-House.

Later, she asked me to come to Hull-House to live. Knowing Hull-House and what it stood for, I called it "heaven." My whole attitude toward life changed. I attended classes there. My first was in English. As a delegate to the Trades and Labor Assembly, I had been asked to serve on various committees. We had to draw up resolutions on many phases of life. While I was trying to do this work, I realized for the first time how handicapped I was

and how handicapped the children of other wage workers were that left school at fourteen.

Workers who attended classes at Hull-House were fortunate indeed. The teachers had such a high standard. We could feel their interest in us.

Miss Starr I quickly learned to love dearly. She had a sense of humor unequaled by anyone I'd ever known. At my first appearance in Hull-House, she seemed to sense my defiance and laughed. I was sensitive and I gave her a cold stare. When I went to live in Hull-House I tried to ignore Miss Starr, but she came to me, and after we talked things over, we became friends. It was a great privilege to have her for a friend. She was like an older sister. When I made mistakes, she "took me in hand," and she wasn't afraid to tell me just what she thought.

The organizations of wage workers and the executives of strike committees that met in the "Reception Room" at Hull-House were the Women's Book Binders Union I, the Shirt Maker's Union, Men and Women's Cloak Maker's Union, Cab Driver's Union, a gathering of representatives of the Retail Clerk Workers, the strike committees of the Garment Workers, and the Clothing Cutters. As official organizer of the American Federation of Labor I was chairman of these meetings, and it was our great fortune to have as speakers such men as Henry Demarest Lloyd, Clarence Darrow, and Ethelbert Stewart.* Miss Addams was always our helper and adviser.

One day Miss Addams said, "Mary, if you get the members for a cooperative boarding club, I will pay the first month's rent, and supply the furnishings. There's a vacant apartment on Ewing Steet." I knew what it would mean for working women to have a home near Hull-House. "I'll get the members," I said. Soon the apartment was ready, and at the end of the following week there were six members, with a cook and a general worker. We spent one evening each week discussing ways and means and management. The first business was the christening of our organization. We decided on the Jane Club. We had no rules or by-laws. We elected a president, who was also steward, and a treasurer, and we agreed to meet

*Ethelbert Stewart (1857–1936), writer, chief statistician at U.S. Children's Bureau, 1912–1913, and at the Bureau of Labor Statistics, 1913–1918.—Eds.

weekly. We had the great privilege of having Miss Addams and Miss Starr at our meetings. We voted to tax ourselves $3.00 each for weekly dues, which covered expenses for food, quarters, and service. When additional expense was necessary for supplies, each member was assessed fifty cents.

There were six apartments in the house. At the end of three months we occupied three of them with eighteen members. At the end of a year, we occupied all six. . . .

The social spirit was just as cooperative as the financial relationships. We enjoyed doing things together. While I was doing social and organization work, I had the opportunity of meeting a good many men, and if there was a dance or a ball we wanted to attend, I would tell an acquaintance that about twenty ''Janes'' would like to attend a certain ball and ask him to bring each an escort. Such fun in the introductions! And no choosing of a special girl, except for height. If a man was short, he tried to choose a short girl. Some of us were advocates of the union label and, as the young men entered and we took their hats, we looked to see if there was a union label inside. And we looked for the union labels on their cigars. In those days comparatively few men smoked cigarettes. All the Jane Club members were not interested in the union label, but they had the group spirit and they all shared in the sport.

Florence Kelley
Comes to Stay

Florence Kelley

Florence Kelley (1853–1932) was an important addition to the Hull-House group. ''No other man or woman whom I have ever heard so blended knowledge of facts, wit, satire, burning indignation, prophetic denunciation—all poured out at white heat in a voice varying from flute-like tones to deep organ tones,'' one of her friends remembered. Daughter of William D. Kelley, a Philadelphia judge and congressman who earned the nickname ''Pig-Iron'' from his insistent support of

high tariffs to protect the iron and steel industry, Kelley was educated at Cornell and at the University of Zurich. While in Europe she was converted to socialism, married a Russian physician, and translated one of Friedrich Engels' books into English. A few years later, when her marriage ended in divorce, she moved to Hull-House with her three young children. She was an expert social investigator, more radical than Jane Addams and most of the other residents, and she played a major role in making Hull-House a center for research and reform. Critical of some of the artistic and religious aspects of the settlement program, she forced the residents to become more concerned with the deplorable living conditions of the people in the neighborhood and the city. She was especially horrified by the acres of dreary tenements surrounding Hull-House, where thousands of women and children worked in dark, dank sweat shops on piles of heavy garments.

In 1893, Governor John Peter Altgeld appointed Florence Kelley Chief Factory Inspector for Illinois, a position she held for four years. She left Chicago for New York in 1899 to become Secretary of the National Consumers' League, but she returned to Hull-House frequently. Though she was aware of the problem before she came to Chicago, Florence Kelley's lifework, her crusade against child labor, began at Hull-House. The following article is from her own vivid account of those early years at the settlement. [Florence Kelley, ''I Go to Work,'' Survey (June 1, 1927), 271–274.]

On a snowy morning between Christmas 1891 and New Year's 1892, I arrived at Hull-House, Chicago, a little before breakfast time, and found there Henry Standing Bear, a Kickapoo Indian, waiting for the front door to be opened. It was Miss Addams who opened it, holding on her left arm a singularly unattractive, fat, pudgy baby belonging to the cook who was behindhand with breakfast. Miss Addams was a little hindered in her movements by a super-energetic kindergarten child, left by its mother while she went to a sweatshop for a bundle of cloaks to be finished.

We were welcomed as though we had been invited. We stayed, Henry Standing Bear as helper

Florence Kelley

human commentary upon Uncle Sam's treatment of his wards in the Nineties.

At breakfast on that eventful morning, there were present Ellen Gates Starr, friend of many years and fellow-founder of Hull-House with Jane Addams; Jennie Dow, a delightful young volunteer kindergartner, whose good sense and joyous good humor found for her unfailing daily reward for great physical exertion. She spent vast energy visiting the homes of her Italian pupils, persuading their mothers to remove at least two or three times during the winter their layers of dresses, and give them a thorough sponge-bath in the sympathetic and reassuring presence of their kindergartner, Mary Keyser, who had followed Miss Addams from the family home in Cedarville and throughout the remainder of her life relieved Miss Addams of all household care. This was a full-time professional job where such unforeseen arrivals as Henry Standing Bear's and mine were daily episodes in the place which Miss Addams' steadfast will has made and kept, through war and peace, a center of hospitality for people and for ideas.

Julia Lathrop, then recently appointed county visitor for Cook County for those dependent families who received outdoor relief in money or in kind, was mentioned as away for the holidays with her family at Rockford, Illinois. Miss Lathrop, later a member of the Illinois State Board of Charities and from 1912 to 1921 through its first nine creative years, chief of the Children's Bureau at Washington, was then and is now a pillar of Hull-House. Two others of the permanent group were Edward L. Burchard, for many years curator of the Field Museum; and Anna Farnsworth, an agreeable woman of leisure and means, happy to be hostess-on-call to some and all who appeared at the front door from breakfast until midnight seven days a week. That was before the squalid, recent social convention had been set up, according to which everyone, however abundant and well assured her income, must earn her own living or be censured as a parasite. Miss Farnsworth's gracious gifts of free time and abundant good-will for counselling perplexed immigrants, finding comfortable quarters for old people who could do a little work but not fend for themselves in the labor market, providing happy Saturdays in the parks for little groups of school children whose mothers

to the engineer several months, when he returned to his tribe; and I as a resident seven happy, active years until May 1, 1899, when I returned to New York City to enter upon the work in which I have since been engaged as secretary of the National Consumers' League.

I cannot remember ever again seeing Miss Addams hold a baby, but the first picture of her gently keeping the little Italian girl back from charging out into the snow, closing the door against the blast of wintry wind off Lake Michigan, and tranquilly welcoming these newcomers, is as clear today as it was at that moment.

Henry Standing Bear had been camping under a wooden sidewalk which surrounded a vacant lot in the neighborhood, with two or three members of his tribe. They had been precariously employed by a vendor of a hair improver, who had now gone into bankruptcy leaving his employees a melancholy Christmas holiday. Though a graduate of a government Indian school, he had been trained to no way of earning his living and was a dreadful worked away from home, were among the Settlement's early enrichments of the neighborhood life.

Reaching Hull-House that winter day was no small undertaking. The streets between car-track and curb were piled mountain high with coal-black frozen snow. The street cars, drawn by horses, were frequently blocked by a fallen horse harnessed to a heavily laden wagon. Whenever that happened, the long procession of vehicles stopped short until the horse was restored to its feet or, as sometimes occurred, was shot and lifted to the top of the snow, there to remain until the next thaw facilitated its removal.

Nor were these difficulties in the way of travel minimized by free use of the telephone. In all weathers and through all depths of snow and slush and sleet, we used to navigate across Halsted Street, the thirty-miles-long thoroughfare which Hull-House faced, to a drug store where we paid ten cents a call, stood throughout the process, and incidentally confided our business to the druggist and to any English-speaking neighbors who might happen in.

A superb embodiment of youth in the Mississippi Valley was Mary Kenney. Born in Keokuk, Iowa, of Irish immigrant parents, she had moved with her mother to a nearby brick tenement house, a distinguished three-story edifice in that region of drab one- and two-story frame cottages, in order to be a close neighbor to Hull-House and participate in its efforts to improve industrial conditions. Her volunteer work was with self-supporting, wage-earning young women whom she hoped to form into powerful, permanent trade unions. Tall, erect, broad-shouldered, with ruddy face and shining eyes, she carried hope and confidence whithersoever she went. Her rich Irish voice and friendly smile inspired men, women, and children alike to do what she wished. Her undertakings prospered and throve.

A highly skilled printer, she was employed by a company which gave preference to union employes. As a numberer she earned fourteen dollars a week, supporting herself and her lovely old mother on that wage. Hers was the initiative in making of the brick tenement a cooperative house for working girls known as the Jane Club, a large part of the success of which was for many years due to the gentle sweetness of Mrs. Kenney, who mothered the cooperators as though they had been her own.

Although this was an entirely self-governing undertaking, Miss Addams was elected year after year an honorary director, having underwritten the experiment from the beginning. Later a friend of the Settlement, as a first step towards an endowment, paid for a building planned for the convenience of the cooperators, the rent going to Hull-House. This became a model for the Eleanor Clubs and countless other cooperative home clubs for self-supporting women scattered over the great city and growing with its growth during the past quarter century.

My first activity, begun that week, was conducting for a few months a small experimental employment office for working girls and women. It was a tiny space in a corner of the building then adjoining Hull-House, occupied as a morgue and undertaking establishment by an Irish-American mentioned with respect in the neighborhood because he was rumored to have various cripples and two deaths to his credit.

It soon turned out that both employers and applicants for domestic work were too few in the Hull-House region to afford a basis for a self-supporting employment office. Yet finding work for people of every conceivable qualification, from high federal and state offices to rat-catching, forms a continuing chapter in the history of the House. But this has never been commercial.

In my first year at Hull-House, Carroll D. Wright, U.S. commissioner of commerce and labor, in charge of a federal study of the slums of great cities, entrusted me with the Chicago part of the enquiry. With a group of schedule men under my guidance, we canvassed a square mile extending from Hull-House on the west to State Street on the east, and several long blocks south. In this area we encountered people of eighteen nationalities.

Hull-House was, we soon discovered, surrounded in every direction by homework carried on under the sweating system. From the age of eighteen months few children able to sit in high chairs at tables were safe from being required to pull basting threads. In the Hull-House kindergarten children used with pleasure blunt, coarse needles for sewing bright silk into perforated outlines of horses, dogs, cats, parrots, and lesser-known creatures on cards. They did this in the intervals between singing, modeling and playing active games. At home they used equally coarse sharp needles for sewing buttons on garments. The contrast was a hideously painful one to witness, especially when the children fell asleep at their work in their homes.

Out of this enquiry, amplified by Hull-House residents and other volunteers, grew the volume published under the title Hull-House Maps and Papers. One map showed the distribution of the polyglot peoples. Another exhibited their incomes (taken by permission from the federal schedules) indicated in colors, ranging from gold which meant twenty dollars or more total a week for a family, to black which was five dollars or less total family income. There was precious little gold and a superabundance of black on the income map!

The discoveries as to home work under the sweating system thus recorded and charted in 1892 (that first year of my residence) led to the appointment at the opening of the legislature of 1893, of a legislative commission of enquiry into employment of women and children in manufacture, for which Mary Kenney and I volunteered as guides. Because we knew our neighborhood, we could and did show the commissioners sights that few legislators had then beheld; among them unparalleled congestion in frame cottages which looked decent enough, though drab and uninviting, under their thick coats of soft coal soot. One member of the Commission would never enter any sweatshop, but stood in the street while the others went in, explaining that he had young children and feared to carry them some infection.

This Commission had been intended as a sop to labor and a sinecure, a protracted junket to Chicago, for a number of rural legislators. Our overwhelming hospitality and devotion to the thoroughness and success of their investigation, by personally conducted visits to sweatshops, though irksome in the extreme to the lawgivers, ended in a report so compendious, so readable, so surprising that they presented it with pride to the legislature. We had offered it to them under the modest title, Memorandum for Legislative Commission of 1893. They renamed it. The subject was a new one in Chicago. For the press the sweating system was that winter a sensation. No one was yet blasé.

With backing from labor, from Hull-House, from the Henry Demarest Lloyds and their numberless friends, the Commission and the report carried almost without opposition a bill applying to manufacture, and prescribing a maximum working day not to exceed eight hours for women, girls, and children, together with child labor safeguards based on laws then existing in New York and Ohio, and quite advanced. There was a drastic requirement in the interest of the public health that tenement houses be searched for garments in process of manufacture, and goods found exposed in homes to contagious diseases be destroyed on the spot. Owners of goods produced under the sweating system were required to furnish to the inspectors on demand complete lists of names and addresses of both contractors and home workers.

The bill created a state factory inspection department on which was conferred power, with regard to tenement-made goods found on infected premises, unique in this country in 1893. Illinois changed, at a single stride, from no legislation restricting working hours in manufacture for men, women, or children, by day, by night, or by the week, to a maximum eight-hours day for girls and for women of all ages, in all branches of manufacture. . . .

When the new law took effect, and its usefulness depended upon the personnel prescribed in the text to enforce it, Governor Altgeld offered the position of chief inspector to Mr. Lloyd, who declined it and recommended me. I was accordingly made chief state inspector of factories, the first and so far as I know, the only woman to serve in that office in any state.

There had been suspiciously little opposition in the press or the legislature while our drastic bill was pending. It had passed both houses, and was signed by Governor Altgeld fairly early in the spring. Indeed the enactment of this measure, destined to be a milestone in the national history of our industry and our jurisprudence, was almost unnoticed. . . .

My appointment dated from July 12, 1893. The appropriation for a staff of twelve persons was $12,000 a year, to cover salaries, traveling expenses, printing, court costs, and rent of an office in Chicago. The salary scale was, for the Chief $1,500 a year; for the first assistant, also a woman, Alzina P. Stevens $1,000; and for each of the

Hull-House as it looked when Florence Kelley arrived. The Butler Art Gallery, built in 1891, is on the left.

ten deputies of whom six were men $720. Needless to say this had been voted by a legislature predominantly rural.

It was Governor Altgeld's definite intent to enforce to the uttermost limit this initial labor law throughout his term of office. He was a sombre figure; the relentless hardship of his experience as boy and youth had left him embittered against Fate, and against certain personal enemies, but infinitely tender towards the sufferings of childhood, old age, and poverty. He was an able, experienced lawyer, and his sense of justice had been outraged by the conduct of the trial of the Anarchists. Indeed, no one yet knows who threw the fatal bomb in the Haymarket riots. The men who were hanged were charged with conspiracy to do a deed of which no one has ever known the actual doer. All the evidence against them was circumstantial, and in this respect the trial is, so far as I know, still unique in the history of American jurisprudence, the only trial closely resembling it in any considerable degree being that of the Molly Maguires in the mining regions of Pennsylvania in the early seventies of the Nineteenth Century. To Governor Altgeld's mind the whole Illinois retributive procedure presented itself as terrorism.

To the personnel of the newly created department for safeguarding women and children who must earn their living in manufacture, Governor Altgeld showed convincingly a passionate desire to use every power conferred for the benefit of the most inexperienced and defenseless elements in industry in Illinois.

My first effort to apply the penalty for employing children below the age of sixteen years without the prescribed working paper, led me to the office of the district attorney for Cook County. This was a brisk young politician with no interest whatever in the new law and less in the fate of the persons for whose benefit it existed. The evidence in the case I laid before him was complete. An eleven-years-old boy, illegally engaged to gild cheap picture frames by means of a poisonous fluid, had lost the use of his right arm, which was paralyzed. There was no compensation law and no prohibition of work in hazardous occupations. There was only a penalty of twenty dollars for employing a child without the required certificate. The young official looked at me with impudent surprise and said in a tone of astonishment:

"Are you calculating on *my* taking this case?"

I said: "I thought you were the district attorney."

"Well," he said, "suppose I am. You bring me this evidence this week against some little two-by-six cheap picture-frame maker, and how do I know you won't bring me a suit against Marshall Field next week? Don't count on me. I'm overloaded. I wouldn't reach this case inside of two years, taking it in its order."

That day I registered as a student in the Law School of Northwestern University for the approaching fall term, and received in June 1894 a degree from that University whose graduates were automatically empowered to practice before the Supreme Court of Illinois. Credit was given for my reading law with Father in Washington in 1882, my study in Zurich, and one year in the senior class in Chicago. The lectures were given in the evening and did not interfere with my administrative work. . . .

Tenement House Manufacture

Florence Kelley

The Hull-House group, sickened by the horrors of the sweating system, worked hard for the passage of the Illinois Factory Act in 1893. With the aid of journalists, an occasional minister, and labor leaders, they lobbied in Springfield documenting their position with statistics and with true stories of human suffering. The reformers often overlooked the fact that many immigrant families desperately needed the income earned by their children to survive.

The 1893 act provided for periodic inspection of factories and tenement lofts but prohibited the employment of children under fourteen at night, or for more than eight hours during the day. There were many loopholes in the law, but it was a beginning. Florence Kelley, appointed chief factory inspector by Governor Altgeld, included in her competent staff Alzina P. Stevens, another Hull-House resident, as assistant inspector, and Mary Kenney as one of the deputy inspectors.

Immediately, the overwhelming task of regulating tenement manufacture was complicated by the smallpox epidemic which broke out in Chicago simultaneously with the depression of 1893 and the World's Fair. In her factory inspector's report of 1894, Mrs. Kelley described the tragedy she and her staff encountered. She suggested that the only solution to the disgrace of tenement manufacture was federal legislative control. But effective regulation of factory conditions was a long way off in 1893, and two years later, when the Illinois Supreme Court struck down the eight-hour provision of the factory act, most Hull-House residents felt their fight for the legislation had been for nothing. Though Altgeld's successor did not reappoint Florence Kelley in 1897, her reports survive as evidence of the misery she observed and worked to abolish. [Florence Kelley, Second Annual Report, Factory Inspectors of Illinois, for Year Ending December 15, 1894 *(Springfield, 1895), 28–30, 52–55, 57–59.]*

Small-pox in the Tenement Garment Shops of Chicago

. . . In the winter of 1893–4 the increase of smallpox in the tenement house districts in which garment manufacture prevails became so marked that on February 9th a circular letter was sent from this office to each of the 176 wholesale "manufacturers" and merchant tailors whose goods are made up in these districts, warning them of the existing and increasing danger of infection, and notifying them that Sections 1 and 2 of the Workshop law would be rigidly enforced for the protection of the purchasing public.

The Infected District

In April it became clear that while there was an occasional case of small-pox among the Scandinavian tailors on the North Side, the disease was overwhelmingly epidemic in the Polish and Bohemian district extending from Sixteenth street south to the river, and from May street westward to the city limits. In this district, in the months of April, May, and June, small-pox was found in 325 different tenement houses. In these houses the number of cases varied from 1 to 11 each.

Some Illustrative Cases

At 625 West Twenty-first street, on April 30, inspectors visited the shop of J. Kolka. This shop is in the rear of Kolka's living rooms, on the first floor. The entrance is by a side door, used also in going to the living rooms. The inspectors found Kolka and his wife with two men visitors in the shop, and 16 coats for Pfaelzer, Sutton & Co. in process of manufacture. The living rooms of the Kolka family were closed, and in process of fumigation; a 10-year-old son of Kolka died of small-pox on Saturday, April 28, after a week's illness, and was buried from the house on Sunday, April 29. The inspectors inquired when the last work has been returned to the firm. Mrs. Kolka, who attends to that part of the business, positively asserted that it was several weeks since they had had any work, except the 16 coats then on the premises; and that none had been returned since the boy was taken sick.

Pfaelzer, Sutton & Co. were notified of the infectious condition of the 16 coats on Kolka's premises, and promised not to accept the goods until said goods has been properly disinfected. The inspector repeated to them Mrs. Kolka's assurance that no goods had been returned since April 13, and requested them to ascertain from their books if this was correct. The books showed that Mrs. Kolka had returned 61 coats on April 23, while small-pox was in the house. The firm requested that these, also, might be disinfected, and agreed to keep them boxed away from other goods until this was done. It was nine days after this before these goods were disinfected, and the inspectors had no power to compel prompter action.

Manifestly, it cannot be maintained that the spread of infection through these 77 coats was prevented. The Kolka boy was ill a week before a physician was called, when the child was dying; and work upon the goods was carried on during that week. Before the report of the diagnosis reached the city board of health or this office, the child was dead and buried, and 61 coats had been returned to the manufacturer. From April 21, when the child was taken ill, to May 8, when the coats were finally fumigated, these garments had been serving as a medium for the conveyance of infection. They were worked upon by the parents (while they nursed their child) and were then in the wholesale house among stores of goods, awaiting fumigation.

At 691 Alport street there is a shop in the rear basement of a tenement house, the contractor, Joseph Triska, an employé of Cahn, Wampold & Co., living on the premises. On May 16 the inspector found the shop locked, and, looking through the window, ascertained that it was empty. There were then two cases of small-pox in the family of Triska; one daughter lay dead in the house, and another child had just been taken to the pest-house. The yellow card was on the door, and a policeman on guard. From a woman in the house the inspectors learned that goods had been removed from the shop that day. Neither the officer nor anyone else present knew who had removed the goods, nor by what authority, nor whither they had been taken. The cases of small-pox in the Triska family were not diagnosed as such till the

Sweating labor. Etching by Norah Hamilton.

night preceding this inspection, but the condition of the victims made it manifest that the disease must have been present some days before. How much clothing was manufactured and removed from the shop during that period the inspectors have no means of ascertaining.

There being small-pox, on May 12th, at 704 West Eighteenth street, inspectors visited the shop of David Schwartz, in the basement of the rear house. They found seven persons at work, and made an inventory of the goods in the shop, finding 125 children's cloaks for F. Siegel & Bros. in process of manufacture and in bundles. Two of the persons in the shop were unvaccinated. The shop was then closed. The inspectors, learning that there were ten families, 65 persons, living on this lot, proceeded to examine the arms of the persons then on the premises, 40 in all. Of these 40 persons they found only 18 vaccinated. In one family they found four children in different stages of the disease. One room was locked and darkened, and access to it could not be gained. Subsequently it was ascertained that there was small-pox there, also, and that there were eleven cases on the premises during the week of May 12–19. Could there be a more appalling example of the possibilities of tenement house manufacture than this case shows, with 65 people living on the premises, but 18 of them vaccinated, 11 cases of small-pox among them in a single week; and men and women coming from tenement houses in all directions to manufacture garments for children while the first five small-pox cases were running their course?

Danger of Infection Increased by Concealment

At 757 West Eighteenth street Mrs. Vrelna lives and works in rooms in the ground floor rear of a frame house. On the floor above, on May 31st, a woman with a newborn babe lay too ill of small-pox to be removed to the pest-house. The inspectors found no work in the possession of Mrs. Vrelna, who said that she had had none for three weeks. In her rooms the inspectors found a young girl whose face showed that she had recently recovered from small-pox. She lived in the ground floor front rooms of this house, adjacent to those of Mrs. Vrelna. This girl told the inspectors that she had been sick with small-pox eight weeks before, and had been well enough to be out for four

weeks; that no doctor was called for her, and no one outside of her family and a few neighbors knew of her sickness. She also said that while she was sick Mrs. Vrelna was finishing garments, and Mrs. Vrelna said that this was so. This successfully concealed case of small-pox with garment making going on in the adjoining rooms throughout the entire siege well illustrates the futility of attempted regulation of tenement house manufacture. Goods made up eight weeks before the danger of spreading contagion in them was known to any persons authorized to inspect them and the surroundings in which they were made had, long before the eight weeks had elapsed, passed through the hands of the contractor and the manufacturer, and may have carried contagion to unsuspecting purchasers. . . .

The table of places in which custom clothing was made in 1895, according to the lists furnished by 184 merchant tailors, shows that many of them are shops with a considerable number of employés; on premises in all ways like those on which ready-made clothing is made; i.e., tenement house premises. A great deal of custom tailor work is, however, given out to individual men and women, to be made in what are known in the trade as "back shops," and in the living rooms of the tailors. The back shop is a room rented by a number of working tailors, who pay rent together, but work each for himself, often each for a different merchant tailor. These shops are to be commended when they are in buildings not used for dwelling purposes, but they are frequently in tenement houses and sometimes over stables. The kitchen shop of the individual tailor is clean if his home is clean, and is usually free from the dangers that accompany overcrowding. The chief evil attending these shops is that they are scattered, and this isolation of the tailor destroys all hope of adequate inspection. The number of tailors thus employed is so great that no body of inspectors can know, day by day, whether their workshops are free from contagious disease.

That part of the garment manufacture of Illinois which is carried on in the 208 factories in Chicago can be kept under supervision as easily and effectively as any other process of manufacture. It is not impossible to give some supervision to the 1,715 contractors' shops, and to follow them as they move from place to place, although they shift about so rapidly that, by the end of another year 25 per cent of them will have been located in new quarters, and another 25 per cent will have been lost. The records of this office show that, in two and a half years, 254 tailors and clothing contractors on the North Side and in the First Ward of the city have dropped out of sight; and the disappearances from the "sweater" colonies in the southwest and northwest sections of the city have numbered 531.

It is clear, however, that even the 1,715 contractors' shops now known to us cannot be inspected often enough to render it safe for the public to purchase goods made up in them, while they are kept on premises where poverty continually breeds disease; and though any one given shop may be wholesome enough, yet no goods can be guaranteed non-infectious which have passed through it to the rooms of the poverty-stricken home finisher. Here, in the lowest depth of the conditions which tenement house manufacture fosters, lurks a danger to the community which no regulation can eradicate. From this danger nothing short of prohibition can protect the purchaser.

Tenement house manufacture is rapidly spreading in Chicago and entering a large variety of industries. Wherever the system enters, the trade becomes a sweated trade, carried on in the worst and most unwholesome premises, because it falls into the hands of the very poor. . . .

A Hull-House neighbor on her way home from the factory with her work.

Health of Employes

. . . Shops over sheds or stables, in basements or on upper floors of tenement houses, are not fit working places for men, women, and children.

Most of the places designated in this report as basements are low-ceiled, ill-lighted, unventilated rooms, below the street level; damp and cold in winter, hot and close in summer; foul at all times by reason of adjacent vaults or defective sewer connections. The term cellar would more accurately describe these shops. Their dampness entails rheumatism and their darkness injures the sight of the people who work in them. They never afford proper accommodations for the pressers, the fumes of whose gasoline stoves and charcoal heaters mingle with the mouldy smell of the walls and the stuffiness always found where a number of the very poor are crowded together.

In shops over sheds or stables the operatives receive from below the stench from the vaults or the accumulated stable refuse; from the rear, the effluvia of the garbage boxes and manure bins in the filthy, unpaved alleys; and from the front, the varied stenches of the tenement house yard, the dumping ground for all the families residing on the premises.

Shops on upper floors have no proper ventilation; are reached by narrow and filthy halls and unlighted wooden stairways; are cold in winter unless all fresh air is shut out, and hot in summer. If in old houses, they afford no sanitary arrangements beyond the vaults used by all tenants; if in modern tenements the drains are out of order, water for the closets does not rise to upper floors, and poisonous gases fill the shops. This defective water supply, the absence of fire escapes, and the presence of the pressers' stove greatly aggravate the danger of death by fire.

Shops on the middle floors are ill-lighted, ill-ventilated, and share the smells from the kitchens and drains of surrounding living rooms.

The group of workers in each shop is so small that they can take no effective measures for their own protection against long hours and bad sanitary conditions. Whatever is to be done to ameliorate these conditions must be done by legislation in the interest, not of the large body of garment workers only, but of the public health.

The Purchaser's Risk

. . . It is sometimes urged in defense of tenement house manufacture, that it affords cheaper garments than could be produced in any other way. This is a mere assertion, which cannot be proved until an experiment has been made in manufacture upon a large scale and in factories equipped with electricity or steam. Certainly in all other branches of industry cheapness has kept pace with the improvement of the plant and the increasing magnitude of the scale of production. But even if the assertion were true, the cheapness of the garments would be a poor compensation to the Nation for the continuous dissemination of disease, and the degradation of an industry employing tens of thousands of people.

The only other argument which is occasionally advanced in defense of the system of tenement house manufacture is, that it gives work to widows in their homes, and thus enables them to keep their children about them. Even if the widows in question earned a sufficient living for themselves and their children, the price paid for their prosperity, at the risk of the community, might be deemed exorbitant. It is, however, a fact that no tenement house garment maker earns a sufficient living for a family; least of all the widow whose house work and care of her children interrupt her sewing, and whose very necessities are exploited by the sweater in his doling out of her work and pay. The widow in her tenement room remains a pauper in spite of her best efforts; and its unhealthful surroundings make her one of the most dangerous

links in the chain of evils involved in this whole system.

There is no more reason for manufacture in tenement houses than there is for keeping cows there, a practice formerly common but now prohibited by reason of the changed condition of city life. There is no reason in Chicago, or in any Illinois city, for a bakery in a cellar. There is no reason for placing workshops in the midst of living rooms, in the most crowded tenement houses in the city. The custom is a survival of the old-fashioned house industries. It is possible only in those trades in which there is no plant, no highly developed machinery; but it is not inevitable even in these. It is certainly not inevitable that the cities of Illinois should repeat the experience which the purely local, geographical features of Manhattan Island have entailed upon New York City. Even less excuse can be found for Chicago than for her great competitor, whose island boundaries explain the concentration of manufacture in crowded tenement houses. For similar conditions in any city on the prairies of Illinois, there can be no excuse.

It cannot be too much emphasized that the difficulties in the way of successful regulation of tenement house manufacture are insuperable difficulties, by reason of the vast number of the shops and the shifting about of the workers. They are here today and gone tomorrow. It has been the chief occupation of a faithful and skilled inspector for two years to obtain lists of addresses of garment workers, but these lists require daily revision to keep them even approximately correct. After another year's experience the inspectors can only repeat, with renewed emphasis, the warning that halfway measures are extremely dangerous, because they lull the purchasing public into a false sense of security. To continue the toleration of manufacture in tenement houses, in the face of the epidemic of 1894, would argue the people of Illinois incapable of learning from experience. Every garment "season" shows anew the hopelessness of the attempt to protect the public health from dangers which are inherent in tenement manufacture and can be removed only by its abolition.

Since the epidemic of small-pox in Chicago, the impossibility of enforcing sanitary regulations in 25,000 workrooms is generally recognized. The point to aim at now, however, is not, as was attempted in the statute of 1893, the regulation of certain branches of garment manufacture alone, but the prohibition of the tenement house manufacture of candy, bread, butter, cigars, and all varieties of garments, including shoes. A sweeping prohibition of tenement house manufacture would go far to place the sweater's victims upon the same level of industrial surroundings as the workers in the factory trades. A law prohibiting the manufacture for sale of any article whatsoever in any tenement house would be a boon to thousands of tenants in Chicago, and would do more to cure the evils of the sweating system than any other measure which could be passed. Until this is enacted, all other local measures must remain attempts to keep the sweating system without any essential modification, but merely with a show of regulating it. It is impossible to keep the system and avoid its consequences.

Necessity for Federal Regulation

The conditions under which garments are manufactured are a matter of national interest. Vast quantities of garments made up in Chicago are sold and worn not only in all parts of Illinois, but throughout the west and southwest. In 1894, when small-pox was epidemic among the sweatshops in the Bohemian and Polish sections of the city, it was a matter of vital interest, on which action was taken by the Boards of Health in a number of States, that infectious goods should not be received from this State. This danger of sending infection from tenement house shops to other communities is always existent, though attention is not concentrated upon it at other times as it is during an epidemic. On the other hand, there are wholesalers and retailers of clothing in Illinois who do not manufacture here nor purchase of Illinois manufacturers. These have on hand, at all times, the product of eastern sweatshops among the goods which they offer for sale; and the eastern sweatshop is in no way better than the Chicago shop, its product is no more likely to be non-infected. The conditions which characterize the tenement shop are the same everywhere; and the purchasing public, warned by the press and enlightened by official reports from all the States which attempt to deal with this system of manufacture, is beginning to ask why it should be tolerated anywhere. . . .

Wage-Earning Children

Florence Kelley and Alzina P. Stevens

Nowhere were the evils of child labor more obvious than in the 19th Ward in which Hull-House was located. Underfed, raggedly clothed, unclean children worked fourteen to sixteen hours a day in various tenement industries where death and deformity were common. Settlement workers aroused by this social injustice sought to find ways to control and abolish it. To get the necessary information and statistics to back up their campaign to bring the American conscience to bear on the plight of these tenement children, the Hull-House residents conducted an extensive investigation in their neighborhood.

"Wage-Earning Children," a portion of which is republished here, was written from data collected by Florence Kelley and Alzina P. Stevens as Illinois factory inspectors. It was included in a volume of essays by Hull-House residents entitled Hull-House Maps and Papers, *published in 1895. This book, patterned after Charles Booth's* Life and Labour of the People of London *(first published in 1891 as* Labour and Life of the People*), was the first systematic attempt to describe immigrant communities in an American city. With information on several different Hull-House investigations, it contained elaborate multicolored maps depicting the results of a Hull-House door-to-door survey of neighborhood population in a third of a square mile near Hull-House. "The Italians, the Russian and Polish Jews, and the Bohemians lead in numbers and importance," the settlement workers explained. "The Irish control the polls; while the Germans, although they make up more than a third of Chicago's population, are not very numerous in this neighborhood; and the Scandinavians, who fill north-west Chicago, are a mere handful. Several Chinese in basement laundries, a dozen Arabians, about as many Greeks, a few Syrians, and seven Turks engaged in various occupations at the World's Fair give a cosmopolitan flavor to the region, but are comparatively inconsiderable in interest." Wage maps indicated*

Etching by Norah Hamilton.

income per dwelling place in the same area. Six different income categories ranging from $5 a week to "over twenty" were used. The settlement investigators found that most of their neighbors' earnings fell in the $5 to $10 range. The book also contained essays by Jane Addams and Ellen Starr, accounts of activities at the settlement, and studies of the Chicago ghetto, the Bohemian colony, and the Italian community.

Alzina P. Stevens (1849–1900) was well qualified to write on child labor. She had been forced to go to work at the age of thirteen in a textile mill in her native state of Maine. There she had lost two fingers from her right hand—a constant reminder to her of the danger of employing children in industry. She had moved west to Toledo where she was a proofreader, typesetter, and finally a correspondent for several newspapers. Before she

moved to Chicago and Hull-House in 1892, she had also been a labor leader and early member of the Knights of Labor. [Florence Kelley and Alzina P. Stevens, "Wage-Earning Children," Hull-House Maps and Papers (Crowell, 1895), 54–59, 61–65, 69–71, 73–76.]

The Nineteenth Ward of Chicago is perhaps the best district in all Illinois for a detailed study of child-labor, both because it contains many factories in which children are employed, and because it is the dwelling-place of wage-earning children engaged in all lines of activity.

The Ewing Street Italian colony furnishes a large contingent to the army of bootblacks and newsboys; lads who leave home at 2:30 A.M. to secure the first edition of the morning paper, selling each edition as it appears, and filling the intervals with blacking boots and tossing pennies, until, in the winter half of the year, they gather in the Polk Street Night-School, to doze in the warmth, or torture the teacher with the gamin tricks acquired by day. For them, school is "a lark," or a peaceful retreat from parental beatings and shrieking juniors at home during the bitter nights of the Chicago winter.

There is no body of self-supporting children more in need of effective care than these newsboys and bootblacks. They are ill-fed, ill-housed, ill-clothed, illiterate, and wholly untrained and unfitted for any occupation. The only useful thing they learn at their work in common with the children who learn in school is the rapid calculation of small sums in making change; and this does not go far enough to be of any practical value. In the absence of an effective compulsory school-attendance law, they should at least be required to obtain a license from the city; and the granting of this license should be in the hands of the Board of Education, and contingent upon a certain amount of day-school attendance accomplished.

In this ward dwells, also, a large body of cash-children, boys and girls. Their situation is illustrated by the Christmas experience of one of their number. A little girl, thirteen years of age, saw in an evening paper of December 23d last, an advertisement for six girls to work in one of the best-known candy stores, candidates to apply at seven o'clock the next morning, at a branch store on the West Side, one and a half miles from the child's home. To reach the place in time, she spent five cents of her lunch money for car-fare. Arriving, she found other children, while but one was wanted. She was engaged as the brightest of the group, and sent to a down-town branch of the establishment, at a distance of two and a quarter miles. This time she walked; then worked till midnight, paying for her dinner, and going without supper. She was paid fifty cents, and discharged with the explanation that she was only required for one day. No cars were running at that hour, and the little girl walked across the worst district of Chicago, to reach her home and her terrified mother at one o'clock on Christmas morning.* No

*Incidentally it is of interest that this firm was one of the most liberal givers of Christmas candy to the poor.

law was violated in this transaction, as mercantile establishments are not yet subject to the provisions of the factory act.

Fortunately the development of the pneumatic tube has begun to supersede the cash-children in the more respectable of the retail stores; and a movement for extending the workshop law to the mercantile establishments would, therefore, meet with less opposition now than at any previous time. The need for this legislation will be acknowledged by every person who will stand on any one of the main thoroughfares of Chicago on a morning between 6:30 and 7:30 o'clock, and watch the processions of puny children filing into the dry-goods emporiums to run, during nine or ten hours, and in holiday seasons twelve and thirteen hours, a day to the cry, "Cash!"

In the stores on the West Side, large numbers of young girls are employed thirteen hours a day throughout the week, and fifteen hours on Saturday; and all efforts of the clothing-clerks to shorten the working-time by trade-union methods have hitherto availed but little. While the feeble unions of garment-makers have addressed themselves to the legislature, and obtained a valuable initial measure of protection for the young garment-workers, the retail-clerks, depending upon public opinion and local ordinances, have accomplished little on behalf of the younger clothing-sellers.

In dealing with newsboys, bootblacks, and cash-children, we have been concerned with those who live in the nineteenth ward, and work perhaps there or perhaps elsewhere. We come now to the children who work in the factories of the nineteenth ward.

The largest number of children to be found in any one factory in Chicago is in a caramel works in this ward, where there are from one hundred and ten to two hundred little girls, four to twelve boys, and seventy to one hundred adults, according to the season of the year. The building is a six-story brick, well lighted, with good plumbing and fair ventilation. It has, however, no fire-escape, and a single wooden stair leading from floor to floor. In case of fire the inevitable fate of the children working on the two upper floors is too horrible to contemplate. The box factory is on the fifth floor, and the heaviest pressure of steam used in boiling the caramels is all on the top floor. The little girls sit closely packed at long tables, wrapping and packing the caramels. They are paid by the piece, and the number of pennies per thousand paid is just enough to attract the most ignorant and helpless children in the city. Previous to the passage of the factory law of 1893, it was the rule of this factory to work the children, for several weeks before the Christmas holidays, from 7 A.M. to 9 P.M., with twenty minutes for lunch, and no supper, a working week of eighty-two hours. As this overtime season coincided with the first term of the night-school, the children lost their one opportunity. Since the enactment of the factory law, their working week has consisted of six days of eight hours each; a reduction of thirty-four hours a week.

Health

It is a lamentable fact, well known to those who have investigated child-labor, that children are found in greatest number where the conditions of labor are most dangerous to life and health. Among the occupations in which children are most employed in Chicago, and which most endanger the health, are: The tobacco trade, nicotine poisoning finding as many victims among factory children as among the boys who are voluntary devotees of the weed, consumers of the deadly cigarette included; frame gilding, in which work a child's fingers are stiffened and throat disease is contracted; button-holing, machine-stitching, and hand-work in tailor or sweat shops, the machine-work producing spinal curvature, and for girls pelvic disorders also, while the unsanitary condition of the shops makes even hand-sewing dangerous; bakeries, where children slowly roast before the ovens; binderies, paper-box and paint factories, where arsenical paper, rotting paste, and the poison of the paints are injurious; boiler-plate works, cutlery works, and metal-stamping works, where the dust produces lung disease; the handling of hot metal, accidents; the hammering of plate, deafness. In addition to diseases incidental to trades, there are the conditions of bad sanitation and long hours, almost universal in the factories where children are employed. . . .

Of the reckless employment of children in injurious occupations the following are examples:—

Jaroslav Huptuk, a feeble-minded dwarf, whose affidavit shows him to be nearly sixteen years of age. This child weighed and measured almost exactly the same as a normal boy aged eight years and three months. Jaroslav can neither read nor write in any language, nor speak a consecutive sentence. Besides being dwarfed, he is so deformed as to be a monstrosity. Yet, with all these disqualifications for any kind of work, he has been employed for several years at an emery-wheel in a cutlery works in the nineteenth ward, finishing knife-blades and bone handles, until, in addition to his other misfortunes, he is now tuberculous. Dr. Holmes,* having examined this boy, pronounced him unfit for work of any kind. His mother appealed from this to a medical college, where, however, the examining physician not only refused the lad a medical certificate of physical fitness for work, but exhibited him to the students as a monstrosity worthy of careful observation.

The kind of grinding at which this boy was employed has been prohibited in England for minors since 1863, by reason of the prevalence of grinders' phthisis among those who begin the work young. And no boy, however free from Huptuk's individual disabilities, can grow up a strong man in this nineteenth ward cutlery, because no officer of the State can require the walls to be whitewashed, and the grinding and finishing rooms to be ventilated with suction pipes for withdrawing steel and bone dust from the atmosphere, as it is the duty of the English inspectors to do in English cutleries employing only adults.

Joseph Poderovsky, aged fourteen years, was found by a deputy inspector running a heavy buttonhole machine by foot-power at 204 West Taylor Street, in the shop of Michael Freeman. The child was required to report for examination, and pronounced by the examining physician, rachitic, and afflicted with a double lateral curvature of the spine. He was ordered discharged, and prohibited from working in any tailor-shop. A few days later he was found at work at the same machine. A warrant was sworn out for the arrest of the employer; but before it could be served the man left the State. This boy has a father in comfortable circumstances, and two adult able-bodied brothers.

*Dr. Bayard Holmes (1852–1924), professor of surgery at the University of Illinois Medical Department, candidate for mayor of Chicago on the Socialist party ticket in the 1890s.— Eds.

Children in the settlement front yard ca. 1893.

Bennie Kelman, Russian Jew, four years in Chicago, was found running a heavy sewing-machine by foot-power in a sweat-shop of the nineteenth ward where knee-pants are made. A health certificate was required, and the medical examination revealed a severe rupture. Careful questioning of the boy and his mother elicited the fact that he had been put to work in a boiler factory two years before, when just thirteen years old, and had injured himself lifting heavy masses of iron. Nothing had been done for the case; no one in the family spoke any English, or knew how help could be obtained. The sight test showed that the boy did not know his letters in English, though he said that he could read Jewish jargon. He was sent to the College of Physicians and Surgeons for treatment, and forbidden work. . . .

The following example of the reckless issuance of certificates is of interest here, the child being a resident of the nineteenth ward, employed in this ward, and receiving the certificates to be subsequently quoted from physicians living and practising in this ward:—

Annie Cihlar, a delicate-looking little girl, was found working at 144 West Taylor Street, in a badly ventilated tailor-shop, in a building in the rear of a city lot, with windows on alley, and a tenement house in front. The bad location and atmosphere of the shop, and the stooping position of the child over her work, led the inspector to demand a health certificate. Examination at the inspector's office revealed rachitis and an antero-posterior curvature of the spine, one shoulder an inch higher than the other, and the child de-

cidedly below the standard weight. Dr. Milligan*
indorsed upon the age affidavit: "It is my opinion
this child is physically incapable of working in any
tailor-shop." The employer was notified to discharge the child. A few days later she was found
at work in the same place, and the contractor produced the following certificate, written upon the
prescription blank of a physician in good and
regular standing: "This is to certify that I have
examined Annie Cihlar, and found her in a
physiological condition." A test case was made to
ascertain the value of the medical certificate
clause, and the judge decided that this certificate
was void, and imposed a fine upon the employer
for failing to obtain a certificate in accordance
with the wording of the law. The child then went
to another physician, and obtained the following
certificate: "To whom it may concern: This is to
certify that I have this day examined Annie Cihlar, and find her, in my opinion, healthy. She is
well-developed for her age; muscular system in
good condition; muscles are hard and solid; lungs
and heart are normal. The muscles of right side of
trunk are better developed than upon the left side,
which has a tendency to draw spine to that side. I
cannot find no desease [sic] of the spine." The
sweater, taught by experience, declined to re-en-
gage this child until this certificate was approved
by the inspector, and the inspector of course refused to approve it. . . .

The key to the child-labor question is the enforcement of school attendance to the age of sixteen, and the granting of such ample help to the
poorest of the working children as shall make our
public schools not class institutions, but in deed
and in truth the schools of the people, by the people, for the people. Only when every child is
known to be in school can there by any security
against the tenement-house labor of children in our
great cities.

The legislation needed is of the simplest but
most comprehensive description. We need to
have: (1) The minimum age for work fixed at sixteen; (2) School attendance made compulsory to
the same age; (3) Factory inspectors and truant officers, both men and women, equipped with ade-

quate salaries and travelling expenses, charged
with the duty of removing children from mill and
workshop, mine and store, and placing them at
school; (4) Ample provision for school accommodations; money supplied by the State through
the school authorities for the support of such
orphans, half-orphans, and children of the unemployed as are now kept out of school by destitu-
tion.

Where they are, the wage-earning children are
an unmitigated injury to themselves, to the community upon which they will later be burdens, and
to the trade which they demoralize. They learn
nothing valuable; they shorten the average of the
trade life, and they lower the standard of living of
the adults with whom they compete.

Art Work

Jane Addams

*Influenced by John Ruskin and William Mor-
ris, the Hull-House group believed that one way to
bring meaning and purpose into the drab lives of
their immigrant neighbors was to introduce them
to things of beauty, especially great art. To some
degree they were following the example set by the
prototype settlement Toynbee Hall in London. The
walls of Hull-House were crowded with reproductions of paintings, many purchased by Ellen Starr
and Jane Addams in Europe, and the first building
erected especially for Hull-House contained an art
gallery.*

*There is something pathetic about little immi-
grant girls hanging copies of Fra Angelico angels
on the dreary walls of their tenement rooms, and
about Miss Addams' conviction that the youngsters gained a heroic and historic impulse from
viewing art reproductions. Yet the early settlement
residents, for all their esoteric art exhibits and art
history classes, had captured a basic truth: the immigrants were hungry for a chance to see and create beautiful things. Ellen Starr, more than Jane
Addams, was the force behind the settlement's art
exhibits. She taught art history classes at Hull-*

*Dr. Josephine Milligan, a physician and settlement resi-
dent prior to 1895, was associated with the Illinois Factory Inspectors office.—Eds.

House and was the founder of the organization that became the Chicago Public School Art Society, which introduced art appreciation and instruction into public schools.

Ellen Starr also helped to organize the 1897 Easter Art Exhibit at Hull-House, which led, a few months later, to the founding of the Chicago Arts and Crafts Society. The Society's first president was another Hull-House resident, George Twose, an Englishman who taught woodworking at the settlement and was active in the theater program.

After the opening of the new Chicago Art Institute, Hull-House abandoned its art exhibits and gradually shifted its emphasis from art appreciation to instruction in art techniques. The men, women, and children who came to the settlement expressed their feelings through drawing, painting, sculpture, or crafts, and art remained a major part of the settlement program.

Enella Benedict (1858–1942), instructor at Chicago's Art Institute, founded the Hull-House Art School in 1893, was its director, and taught there until 1938. Among other artists associated with the settlement as residents and teachers were Leon Garland (1896–1941); Carl Linden (1869–1942), who painted a version of what Charles Hull's house looked like shortly after it was built, from a description provided by Hull's cousin, Helen Culver; Morris Topchevsky (1899–1947), a student of Diego Rivera; Emily Edwards (1888–1980), author of The Painted Walls of Mexico (1966); and Alice Kellogg Tyler (1866–1900), who created portraits of Addams and her friends and painted neighborhood people and scenes. Noted sculptor Lorado Taft (1860–1936) also lectured at the settlement. Michael Gamboney (1911–1986) and William Jacobs (d. ca. 1974) were neighborhood children who studied at the settlement. After attending the Art Institute of Chicago, they returned to teach art at Hull-House.

Jane Addams chose Norah Hamilton (1873–1945), sister of Alice, to illustrate Twenty Years at Hull-House (1910). Hamilton's etchings of the settlement and its area reveal the bleak jumble of the tenements and surrounding alleys as well as the vulnerability of the Hull-House neighbors almost better than the photographs that were the basis of some of her work. The present book contains several etchings by Hamilton, including her rendering of the Hull-House entrance, which serves as frontispiece. There is also a linoleum block print by William Jacobs. [Jane Addams, "The Art-Work Done by Hull-House, Chicago," Forum (July 1895), 614–617.]

The attempt of Hull-House to make the esthetic and artistic a vital influence in the lives of its neighbors, and a matter of permanent interest to them, inevitably took the form of a many-sided experiment. The direction of the effort naturally fell into the hands of Miss Starr, one of the founders of Hull-House, who not only feeds her own mind and finds her highest enjoyment in Art, but who believes that every soul has a right to be thus fed and solaced. The first furnishings of Hull-House were therefore pictures. They were hung upon all the wall spaces and were largely selected from photographs which the two original residents had the previous year together purchased in Europe.

From the first year Miss Starr has had large and enthusiastic classes in the "History of Art"; a number of the students have attended them consecutively for four years. There is abundant testimony that the lectures and pictures have quite changed the tone of their minds; for they have become, of course, perfectly familiar with the photographs of the best things, and have cared for them, not "as a means of culture," but as an expression of the highest human thought and perception. One of these has bought from her scanty earnings a number of classic works of art which will make her house really charming when she is married next fall, and more than that will be to her the same vital connection with the minds "who have transfigured human life," as a fine library is to the student who has time for constant reading. Within a short walk from Hull-House a little parlor has been completely transformed by the Fra Angelico over the mantel and the Luca della Robbias on the walls, from which walls the picture scarfs and paper flowers have fallen away. A few doors down the street a tiny bedroom has been changed from a place in which a fragile factory girl slept the sleep of the exhausted, into one where she "just loves to lie in bed and look at my pictures; it's so like Art Class."

A small circulating loan collection of pictures

has proved a satisfactory part of the attempt to make art a means of education. The collection numbers, at present, not more than seventy pictures, and very little more than one hundred dollars have been expended upon it. The pictures are for the most part photographs selected with great care, from choice things only, whether modern or old, and with a view to variety of appeal to the interest and taste of the borrowers. Some watercolor sketches have been given and lent, and the collection contains an Arundel print, and several colored prints of Fra Angelico's angels. The latter are so popular as to be engaged in advance. The loan and return of each picture is recorded, with the date, and the name and address of the borrower, upon a card. It is expected that the picture will be either exchanged or renewed at the end of two weeks. The borrowers frequently become attached to them, and prefer to keep the old one longer rather than to have a new one.

On the occasion of the death of a baby neighbor, the resident in charge of the pictures placed over the little one two colored Fra Angelico angels, in simple white and gold frames, with no certainty that they would be especially noticed or cared for. The tone of the room was entirely changed by them. Everybody spoke of them. The children said that the angels had come to take their sister, and that they were praying for the baby and singing to her. Some days after the mother asked timidly if she might buy the pictures and keep them in memory of the little one. A wax wreath encircling a coffin-plate hung in the room as a memorial of a child who had died before.

A member of the Hull-House Women's Club holds receptions of an informal kind to show her pictures to the children in her street. Another good mother, who is a graduate of the early Chicago high-schools, but who is battling with life against the odds too often found in a tenement-house, of a

Hull-House, including the art studio (on the left), was filled with reproductions of famous works of art.

drinking husband and ever increasing poverty, takes the pictures from the collection as she takes the books and lectures and social opportunities of Hull-House, not only as that which will sustain her own life, but as that which will enable her to realize for her children some of the things she dreamed out for them. The oldest one of her eight children saw the light in a pretty suburban house which she and the father, a promising State senator, had built. This mother borrowed Mrs. Jameson's ''Sacred and Legendary Art,'' and read the story of St. Genevieve to her children while they had Puvis de Chavannes's St. Genevieve pictures, and she took the Fra Angelico ''Paradise'' a second time because she thought it gave the children a pleasant idea of Heaven.

The first building erected for Hull-House contained a little art-exhibit room, carefully planned with a high, dark wainscoting and a north light, that fifty pictures might be exhibited to the best advantage. Since its opening it has had eight loan exhibits: five of oil paintings, one of old prints and engravings, one of water-colors, and another of such photographs as would be most helpful in the public schools. The total number of votes cast for the favorite picture at the last exhibit was 5,988. To quote from Miss Starr:

> An effort has been made in these exhibits to show only pictures which combine, to a considerable degree, an elevated tone with technical excellence, and at no time can a very large assortment of such pictures be obtained. There is an advantage on the side of a small exhibition carefully selected, especially to an untrained public. The confusion and fatigue of mind which a person of no trained powers of selection suffers in passing his eyes wearily over the assortment of good, bad and indifferent which the average picture exhibit presents, leaves him nothing with which to assimilate the good when he finds it, and his chances of finding it are small. Frequently recurring exhibitions of a few very choice pictures might do more toward educating the public taste of the locality in which they occur than many times the number less severely chosen and less often seen.

This leads to the ''Art in Schools'' movement, in which Miss Starr was the Chicago pioneer. With the means at her disposal she has been able to put a number of good pictures into each room of the school nearest to Hull-House. A society has since been inaugurated in connection with the Chicago Woman's Club that has for its object the decorating of all the public schools in the city.* Much has already been accomplished in tinting the walls and supplying the rooms with casts and pictures. The significance of the pictures are carefully explained to the children, and there is no doubt that the imagination receives a strong impulse toward the heroic and historic.

A Day at Hull-House

Dorothea Moore

Activities at Hull-House developed in response to the needs of the neighborhood, or occasionally because of the special talents of the residents. Daytime at the settlement was filled with women's clubs, kindergarten, and dozens of other activities. But at night Hull-House really came alive with large numbers of residents and neighbors who had full-time jobs during the day. As the schedule for 1895 indicates, lectures, clubs, and classes, everything from dancing to algebra to Dante occupied the evening hours.

In 1896, Dorothea Moore came to live at Hull-House as the bride of University of Chicago graduate student Ernest Carroll Moore. She taught physiology and acted as Addams' liaison with police stations, for the settlement was now a large and complex institution. The original building, with a new, full third story, was surrounded by an art gallery, a building for children's activities, a coffeehouse, and a gymnasium. In ''A Day at Hull-House,'' Dr. Moore described the bustling activity and rapid pace of life within the settlement. But this was only one side of Hull-House; through its residents and the programs in which they participated outside the settlement, the ideas and goals of Hull-House and its leaders reached out to affect education, housing, recreation, and even politics in Chicago and across the nation.

*The Chicago Public School Art Society.—Eds.

[Dorothea Moore, "A Day at Hull-House," American Journal of Sociology (March 1897), 629–632, 634–636, 638–640.]

The old house is almost submerged. With its hooded top story of fanciful brick, and its large flanking of additions to right and left, there remain but the long windows and wide doorway to hint of the aspect that was its own in the long-gone privacy of the estate of which it was an important and hospitable part in the quiet days before the invasion of crowd and hurry and competition. The house justly retains the name of its original owner.

These additions are more intrinsic than external—growing out of growing needs—and therefore present in themselves a kind of rough estimate or history of them. Thus, the most extensive area and the highest wall belong to the Children's Building, on the right flank, the corresponding smaller wing being used for lecture and class rooms, with dormitory space above. Following again the analogy of need, with the growth of the work came an extension of the commissary and economic bases, so that the coffeehouse, the model bakery and kitchen occupy a generous surface behind the central house, having appropriately above them the constant but not uncheerful noises of the gymnasium and club rooms for the men.

This can be but a suggestion of locality, for under the various roofs are harbored many variations of effort, placing themselves according to a natural convenience, and adding to themselves in slow accretions, much as the function adds its tool, the organ.

A few fortunate open spaces, bare or bricked as they are, defend the mass of buildings from the dread likeness to an institution. The playground porches of the Children's Building, where there are flowers up to the last moment, and the easy-

---

Evening Clubs and Classes...January 15, 1895.

MONDAY EVENING.

8.00	Lincoln Club	Miss Barnum	Lecture Hall.
7.00	Art History	Miss Starr	Dining Room.
8.00	Odyssey	Miss Starr	Dining Room.
7.00	German	Mr. McFadden	Library.
8.00	German	Mr. McFadden	Library.
7.30	Drawing	Miss Benedict	Studio.
7.00	Gymnastics (Men)	Mr. Pierson	Gymnasium.
8.00	Granite Club	Mr. Vanderlipp	Art Exhibit Room.
		Mr. Harding	
7.30	School Girls' Club	Miss Pratt	Miss Trowbridge's R'm.

TUESDAY EVENING.

8.00	Social Science Club	Dr. Brooks	Lecture Hall.
8.00	Henry Learned Club	Miss West	Dining Room.
7.00	Emerson Class	Mr. Arnold	Library.
8.00	Italo-American Club	Mr. Valerio	Art Exhibit Room.
7.30	English and Letter Writing	Miss Crain	Studio.
8.30	English and Letter Writing	Miss Crain	Studio.
7.00	Gymnastics (Women)	Miss Gyles	Gymnasium.
8.00	Mandolin Club	Members	Cottage.
7.30	Cash Girls' Club	Miss Fryar	Miss Trowbridge's R'm.

WEDNESDAY EVENING.

8.00	Anfreda Club	Miss Warner	Lecture Hall.
7.00	Dante	Miss Starr	Dining Room.
8.00	Shakespeare	Miss Crain	Dining Room.
8.00	Lexington Club	Mr. Will	Art Exhibit Room.
8.00	Young Citizens	Mr. Rosenthal	Studio.
7.00	Beginning Latin	Miss Zimmerman	Octagon.
8.00	Advanced Latin	Miss Young	Octagon.
7.30	Gymnastics (Men)	Mr. Pierson	Gymnasium.
8.00	Geometry	Miss Oakley	Laboratory.
8.00	Jolly Boys' Club	Miss Fryar	Miss Trowbridge's R'm.

THURSDAY EVENING.

8.00	Club Lectures		Lecture Hall.
7.00	Singing	Miss Smith	Dining Room.
8.00	Singing	Miss Smith	Dining Room.
7.00	German Needlework	Frl. Hannig	Library.
7.30	Parliamentary Law	Mrs. Lee	Art Exhibit Room.
8.00	Italian Class	Mr. Valerio	Studio.
8.00	Physics	Mrs. Blount	Laboratory.
7.30	Hull-House Glee Club	Miss Anderson	Miss Trowbridge's R'm.
8.00	Laurel Club	Miss Warner	Cottage.
8.00	Gen'l Entertainments	1 Y. P. Clubs	Gymnasium.
		2 Jane Club	
		3 Col. Ex.	
		4 Men's Club	

FRIDAY EVENING.

8.00	General Meetings	1 Civic Federation	Lecture Hall.
		2 M. C. Literary Sec.	
		3 Goodrich Alumnae Association	
		4 M. C. Literary Sec.	
8.00	German Reception	Mr. & Mrs. Goldmark	Dining Room.
8.00	English History	Miss Barton	Library.
7.30	Algebra	Mr. Monroe	Studio.
7.00	Beginning French	Miss Colvin	Art Exhibit Room.
8.00	Advanced French	Miss Colvin	Art Exhibit Room.
8.00	Choral Society	Mr. Tomlins	Gymnasium.
8.00	Mandolin Club	Members	Cottage.

SATURDAY EVENING

8.00	Dancing Class		Lecture Hall.
8.00	Italian Reception	Mr. Valerio	Dining Room.
8.00	Cloak Makers' Union (Women)		Art Exhibit Room.
7.00	Arithmetic	Mr. Chas. W. Mann	Studio.
8.00	Chemistry	Miss Hunt	Laboratory.
8.00	Dancing Class	Miss Browne	Gymnasium.

EVERY MORNING.

	Kindergarten	Miss Paine	Butler Gallery.
		Miss West	
		Miss Buckingham	
		Miss Eaton	

Schedule of events at Hull-House, 1895.

going aspect of the outside benches and their frequenters, help out the welcome.

The house has suffered a variety of nomenclature. To the children it is usually and comprehensively "the Kindergarten"; the Italian neighbors with their invincible poetry call it "la casa di Dio," while in spite of its own simply chosen name of a social settlement, to most of its immediate friends and to many at a remote distance it is the place "where Miss Addams lives"; for this name has come to have a generic meaning, and stands for a real presence to many who have no personal or visual knowledge of her.

To those who must have a definition of a thing whose being is essentially plastic, there is no better reply to be given than that of a young Englishman at a conference of good people. Upon being pestered for an exact statement he burst out with: "Why, hang it, madam, we settle." It is the personality of the "settlers" which determines the character of each group, and forms differ with their environment. The one necessary element is permanency. Individuals come and go; the attitude, the movement, the activity remain. Hull House itself is not unlike a rock of permanence, about which the tide of population flows and shifts and changes, bringing to it and taking away, altering it and wearing it into certain forms, but feeling it always firmly based, or as one of its neighbors expressed it "well grounded in the mud." This was at once a statement and a compliment.

About the house are its tributaries, some in material form and some visible only in spirit. Around the southern corner is a brick building, the home of the Jane Club, an active club of working women who in a life of five years have solved some of the most vexing questions of cooperative living to their own social and economic satisfaction.

Across the street to the north is the pleasant two-story frame building of the Phalanx Club, where the same plan of living, except for the cares of the kitchen, is carried on by the young men. Just north of this is the model lodging house for women, where any dependent woman may have the wise encouragement of a bed and a breakfast. Some thousand feet toward the river is the public playground, safely guarded by its iron fence and closed until after school hours. This piece of land, cursed by a bunch of miserable and criminal tenements and an absentee landlord, came finally by strange and picturesque ways into the hands of the settlement, and now clean and clear and wholesome, it has seen many a good time. May poles and singing children and flowers and music have surprised its sandy surface and in winter it gets a coating of ice for the skaters. And always it is the place where the crowded children may breathe and run and shout in safety. Away down toward the southeast and off to the northwest are large study clubs of young men and women whose literary life began under the roof of the house and who have outgrown her first care.

The public-library reading room on Blue Island avenue, the public baths a few blocks away, the popular lectures now being given in one of the public schools were initiated by the settlement. The decoration of public schoolrooms, which is so novel and lovely a thing, is now carried on by the Society of Art in Schools, of which Miss Starr was the founder and of which she is president.

And somewhere about, as one might say within calling distance, in little rooms at least warm and clean and rent free, are a dozen elderly women, for whom through one of its residents the house has laid forever the specter of the county poorhouse. Some, it is true, came to curse but remained to pray, and all preserve the freedom of the beneficiary relation by generous criticism or approval.

The day begins early with the paper carrier, who hides his impartial list of daily papers under the mat for safety. He meets the earliest working mother—or possibly father—who is bringing the baby to the crèche, where an average of twenty-five little ones are cared for every day. This means spending the day under wise supervision, with pictures and toys; it means bread and milk eaten at a tiny table in company; it means the neatness of a bath and the sweetness of a nap in a little white bed all to oneself; it means the big porch playground with bright red geraniums on its border, and an exciting squirrel and a placable parrot at the ends. So may these good hours of the waking day make all the others but a sleep and a forgetting.

Below the crèche is a larger room where the elder babies may play at serious kindergarten, al-

Hull-House as it looked from Halsted Street about 1897. On the left is a store with baled hay and feed stacked in front. In the center is the Butler Art Gallery with its new third-floor addition, built in 1896. At the far right is the Children's House, often referred to as the Smith Building, erected in 1895.

The first public playground in Chicago was started by Hull-House in 1893.

leviated by a sand-pile and a monstrous doll's house, and still above is the larger room for the older class.

By half-past seven o'clock the coffeehouse and bakery are well astir. In the latter, rosy "Annie" is turning out her quota of brown and white loaves, with a minor detail of pies and shining rolls. When the coffeehouse was opened, with its stained rafters, its fine photographs, and its rows of blue china mugs, it had a reflective visit from one of its neighbors. He looked it over thoroughly and without prejudice, and said decisively: "Yez kin hev de shovel gang or yez kin hev de office gang, but yez can't hev 'em both in the same room at the same toime." Time has shown the exactness of the statement. Its clientele, increasing with its

increasing efficiency, have selected themselves, and it is not the man in overalls who is the constant visitor, but the teacher, the clerk, and the smaller employer of the region. The laboring man sends his children for bread and soup and prepared food, but seldom comes himself, however well within his means the fare may be.

Here the residents of the house are served with a movable feast according to their uprisings. The quiet young inspector, whose work in the narrow alleys has changed them as by a daily miracle, is likely to be the first. Then come those who bear a divided burden; the factory inspector and her deputy, the librarian, the students, and the two schoolboys of the household. These are gone before those appear whose clubs and classes have

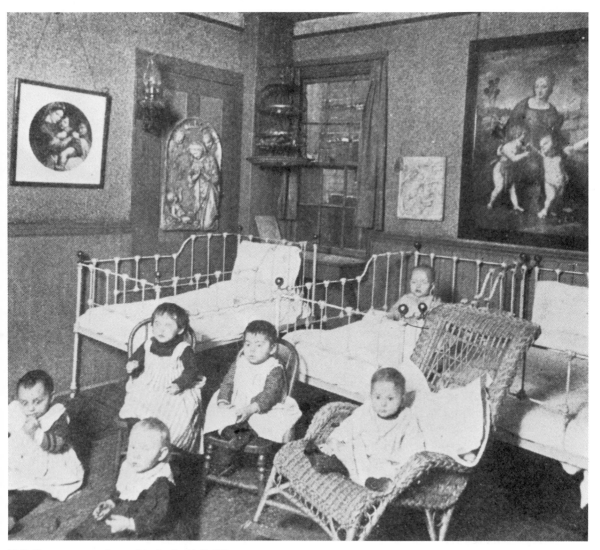

Hull-House nursery, located in the Smith Building.

kept them late the night before at the task of guide, philosopher, and friend.

From the coffeehouse are also served the luncheon and dinner for the house dining room, so that the family of twenty-four are placed in direct social and economic relations with the common kitchen, and the "belated industry" of private service is dispensed with. The domestic economy is all under one skilled management.

Leaving the coffeehouse by a covered way to the main building, one finds the large room on the right of the entrance already filled with applicants to the labor bureau for employment, or to the relief department for aid. The latter acts as a clearing house for organized aids except in the case of the friends with whom the house has summered and wintered. These receive help as freely as they would give in their turn.

Now the house is like some creature slowly awakening from sleep. It begins to put out its hands, touching, it is believed, with humility as well as hopefulness and trust the lives of those about it. By nine o'clock the visiting nurse may be seen packing her bag from her supply chest with the little mercies of lint and salve and baby food. The workers whose province lies outside, who see sick children, study racial needs through manners, foods, and customs, visit the police stations in search of the astray girl or boy, or minister to some special necessity, are beginning their rounds. In the octagon, which is a kind of open sanctuary, the heads of the house are attacking, with a patience born of long usage, the unmitigable mail of the morning.

By two in the afternoon the kindergarten training class is filling the largest room of the children's building, the lively and wide-awake session of the Woman's Club is at its climax, the gymnasium is mildly noisy with its afternoon classes of girls, and from far up in the upper story come sounds of the children's chorus.

The applicants for employment make way—with intervals for ventilation—to the children's sewing class which comes tumultuously from school. Here and there, in corners slightly secluded, are single pupils—a bright boy out of working hours getting up his Greek for college, an elderly Russian plodding slowly along some bit of English text, or an eager young Jew making the crooked ways of his letters straight—all this with assistance of someone in the house.

The six o'clock dinner hour brings the household and its guests together in the beautiful dining room. This is the meeting ground of the day. Here the generalizations of the over young are discouraged with kindness and qualifying facts; here are the all-experienced induced to reconsider and admit another fact of the great truth; here is the free play of the individual with enough of friction to stimulate and enough of the juice of humor to sweeten. Thus the social consciousness of the living house grows. There may be a very radical end or a very conservative middle at the long oval but there is always a fair field and fair play.

In this general life the private affairs of the residents become shadowy, yet mothers have been seen there plainly visiting their children; men have been known to come with motives not severely altruistic; there have actually been engagements, and to an interested friend from the far West who asked breathlessly, "Do they marry?" one might answer with truth, "Often, alas! often."

The leisurely last moments of the dinner hour are apt to be invaded by the classes, and from now on there is a riot of young people. The studious—and there are many—attend the Extension classes, which cover almost the entire ground of the teaching branches, ranging from clay modeling to psychology, from grammar to Dante, from embroidery to trigonometry. The younger and gayer crowd, the dancing and dramatic clubs, the gymnasium with its games and basketball, claim a share of all.

Each club, no matter how lightly social, has its own sober meeting once a month, when it listens to some lecture or informal talk. The club names range from the purely ornamental through the descriptive to the utilitarian. There is "The Violet," "The Study," and "The Fourth of July Mandolin." A favorite custom is to enshrine the name of some hero or heroine, local or general, whereby Henry Clay and Clara Barton appear in friendly competition.

The Penny Provident Bank, which opens at night from seven to eight, is an importation from New York. Supplies of bankbooks and stamps come from the parent institution, and there the deposits are finally redeemed. The system is one of great simplicity. The child exchanges his coin for a stout manilla book ruled in squares suitable for the stamp. This he signs with his name and address, receiving a stamp of the value of his coin. The money may be withdrawn at any time after it reaches the sum of fifty cents. Any impulse to reckless spending of a lesser sum is discouraged by the mulcting of five cents from the amount drawn. Visitors to the house find the bank, with its eager tangible depositors, full of vital interest; even more so, however, are the weekly meetings of the Social Science Club. These have gone on steadily for seven years and represent in an astonishing manner the "American spirit"

> That bids him flout the Law he makes,
> That bids him make the Law he flouts.

Speakers of every opinion and circumstance have come before this body, have said their say—not always undisputed, not always courteously received—until now the test of all real love of knowing can be put to it—for it seeks to make welcome not opinion but knowledge.

The lights linger in the gymnasium, which is also the theater and assembly room, but at midnight the kindly "special officer" sees them going out until all is dark. If some restless resident sits up with a problem, or wakens at every clanging car bell, he also waits to serve, for calls for the doctor or telegraph boys temper the night to the general average of the ward.

To speak of the external activities of the house; its holiday entertainments, its Sunday lectures and concerts, its summer vacation home and school, its lendings of pictures and books, its art exhibits, its maps and records, would be but an extension of its inner life. To describe its attitude toward the school, the saloon, and the church, to interpret its action in regard to strikes, arbitration, and municipal politics, would be to attempt its psychology. What has been here presented is the method alone.

Hull House stands not so much for a solution of problems as a place of exchange. The demands which are brought to it are varied enough. One man wants to be "shown the sense of poetry," another wants his wife "converted to the evangelical religion" for the sake of a peaceful fireside, and a third wants—just the patrol wagon. One mother leaves her baby "while she goes to the matinee," and another hopes to find her boy, arrested she knows not where, for what, or by whom. Often the effort put forth in return is unwise or inadequate, but the exchange is the vital thing. This is the heart of the movement. This is the reason of the settlement; the rest is pure facade. This only can destroy the artificial, and justify its life. It must help that direct human touch of richer with poorer, wise with simple, learned with untaught, dynamic with static which has for its aim the realization by all the children of their kinship with the great family.

The Social Value
of the Saloon

Ernest C. Moore

The early residents of Hull-House quickly became aware that the large number of saloons in their neighborhood posed a problem. By one count there was one for every twenty-six people in the ward, and three within fifty yards of Hull-House.

Settlement reformers saw the saloon as a gathering place for the street gang, the pimp, and the prostitute, as well as a den of temptation for the young and a center of political corruption. They had observed the effects of overindulgence on their neighbors and deplored them; but most of the settlement workers were not narrow prohibitionists. Earlier than most groups, they appreciated the social and economic reasons that often led a man to drink. They also saw that the saloon functioned as a social center for the community. Yet despite their appreciation of the social value of the saloon they tried desperately to find a substitute. One reason the settlement built a coffeehouse and gymnasium in 1893 was to promote an alternative meeting place for the neighborhood. Use of the gymnasium was divided between males and females, but it was reserved for the use of men at night. In addition, there were baths and a men's club room furnished with billiard and card tables. Soon after it was opened it had a membership of 150. The coffeehouse, which was enlarged in 1899, served food and non-alcoholic beverages. It became an important part of the settlement complex, but it never replaced the saloon.

This report on the social value of the saloon in the 19th Ward was done by Ernest C. Moore (1871–1955), a young researcher living at Hull-House while working toward a Ph.D. at the University of Chicago. After teaching at Harvard and Yale, Moore became instrumental in the growth and development of the University of California at Los Angeles, where he held several administrative positions including provost, vice-president, and president.

The fact that his essay was published in the American Journal of Sociology *is an indication of the close link between Hull-House and other settlements and the beginnings of professional, especially urban, sociology. Hull-House by 1897 was obviously a center for research as well as a place where one could find clubs and classes and kindergartens. [Ernest C. Moore, "The Social Value of the Saloon,"* American Journal of Sociology *(July 1897), 1–2, 4–12.]*

The nineteenth ward of Chicago according to the school census of 1896 has a population of

48,280. It is a workingman's district, and the population is typical of unskilled labor in general. The largest foreign elements in the ward are the Irish, German, Italian, and Bohemian, stated in the order of relative numerical strength. Of those of foreign parentage, about one-half are American born. As to moral condition, neither the extremes of vice nor of virtue are reached, while the general moral tone is rather healthful. It is believed that so far as population and worldly condition can be held to affect the saloon problem, the conditions of the nineteenth ward are typical of the problem in general. . . .

Primarily the saloon is a social center. Few will deny this. It is the workingman's club. Many of his leisure hours are spent here. In it he finds more of the things which approximate to luxury than he finds at home, almost more than he finds in any other public place in the ward. In winter the saloon is warm, in summer it is cool, at night it is brightly lighted, and it is always clean. More than that there are chairs and tables and papers and cards and lunch, and in many cases pool and billiards, while in some few well-equipped gymnasiums can be found which are free to patrons. What more does the workingman want for his club? He already has all that most clubs offer their members—papers and cards and food and drink and service—and being modest in his wants their quality satisfies him. But his demand for even these things is not fundamental, they are but means to his social expression. It is the society of his fellows that he seeks and must have.

To say that the saloon is the workingman's club does not answer a single objection which its opponents raise; one must first prove the necessity of workingmen's clubs and of the kind that the saloon represents. The common laborer works ten hours per day, his pay is small. In many cases his family is large, at best his food would not be found

A saloon near Hull-House.

sufficient for his gentler brother; add to this that his work is hard and his food poorly cooked, and the whole result will be a subnormal life. Given a human being, a center of life force, and among his first expressions will be a demand for society, nor does the family alone supply this want. History does not supply a single illustration of the self-sufficiency of the family. The social activity reaches beyond the immediate tie to the brother who is a brother only by courtesy. Social need outgrows the family and creates its own larger society, and this is what my workingman must do. He does not desert his family. He is not disloyal to them in seeking it, but he must find a larger circle in which to move. He must himself articulate in a larger life, and where shall he find it?

Does not the church offer what he seeks? In the first place four churches are somewhat inadequate to the needs of a population of 48,000, and yet if all places of worship in the ward, both Jewish and Gentile, be counted, four will be the net result. It is conceived that there is a difference between religious and social need—a difference between the organs of religious and social expression. The church is primarily devoted to worship. We seek *sociality,* and even a reconstructed church open seven days and nights in the week might fail to recognized our want. Indeed it may be questioned whether the church is called upon to note it. With us it does not, and our question remains unanswered.

But someone may say: ''Are there not clubs where he can go?'' No, and if there were they would offer conventions instead of freedom; must offer conventions of order of business, officers, etc., because of the inherent nature of clubs. The democratic element which is most essential—the absolute freedom to come and go and do as one pleases—cannot be incorporated into a club. But this reservation must be made, that in so far as the club expresses his vital interests, in the same measure does it become the institution which we seek. The trade union answers to this description. It is a much higher form of social expression than the saloon, and among its members it has supplanted the saloon in a large degree, but at present a very small percentage of workingmen belong to trade unions, and their demand for social expression is not thus supplied; yet the reformer's greatest hope lies along this line, while his energies are largely given to more futile forms of social service. Of other organizations created for the purpose of ministering to this social need, most have been failures. They have come from the outside, splendid schemes to impress men, but alas! not to express them. But they succeed only as they express the human energy which they seek to convert to better uses.

Four churches, a few trade unions, and impressive social forms cannot hope to meet the social needs of 48,000 people. Remember that there are no music halls or theaters beside. ''What else have they but the saloon,'' and to the saloon they go. It was created for this purpose and still functions to this want.

The saloonkeeper is the only man who keeps open house in the ward. It is his business to entertain. It does not matter that he does not select his guests; that convention is useless among them. In fact, his democracy is one element of his strength. His place is the common meeting ground of his neighbors—and he supplies the stimulus which renders social life possible; there is an accretion of intelligence that comes to him in his business. He hears the best stories. He is the first to get accurate information as to the latest political deals and social mysteries. The common talk of the day passes through his ears and he is known to retain that which is most interesting. He himself articulates in a larger social center composed of many social leaders like himself who, each representing his own following, together come to have a much larger power and place than the average citizen. My workingman is not too democratic to respect the ready intelligence, the power, and the better dress of the leader in his social center. They draw him to the saloon, and once there they continue to hold him. In addition the saloonkeeper trusts him for drinks—a debt of honor—yea more, he lends him money if in greater need. But the saloonkeeper is only one element in this analysis of attraction, and by no means the strongest. The desire to be with his fellows—the fascination which a comfortable room where men are has for him is more than he can resist; moreover, the things which these men are doing are enticing to him; they are thinking, vying with each other in conversation, in story telling, debate. Nothing of general or local interest transpires which they do not ''argue'' out. Their social stimulus is epitomized in the saloon.

It is center of learning, books, papers, and lecture hall to them, the clearing house for their common intelligence, the place where their philosophy of life is worked out and from which their political and social beliefs take their beginning. As an educational institution its power is very great and not to be scorned because skilled teachers are not present, for they teach themselves. Nay, verily, the apostle of the new education may welcome this as an illustration of education not divorced from social life by bonds of convention.

No one who is familiar with this life will deny the great educational value of the saloons, and this social expression, this freeing of human activity is rendered possible by the stimulant which the saloon offers. It stands not for social opportunity only. It affords also the conditions of sociality. "The first action of ethylic alcohol," says Dr. [Norman] Kerr, "is vascular relaxation, commonly called exhilaration or stimulation, when a glow of warmth spreads over the whole system, when the heart beats faster, when 'happy thoughts' crowd in upon the brain, when all seems life and light and joy, when everything without and within wears a roseate hue." The heart beats more rapidly—there is an exaltation of the mind, a freeing of emotional life, pleasurable ideas, rapid thought, unusual merriment. Is it not a social ideal—a condition in which each one would appear before his fellow? Only there are different ways of reaching it. The demanding power of individuals is here wanting. The stimulus of books, pictures, and good music is absent. The constant stimulus of purposive intelligence is denied—a thousand things which stimulate to swift and happy thought in other forms of society are entirely wanting here. But human energy, which is after all the primal social fact, demands an avenue of escape and finds its conditions in the best way it can.

Moreover this stimulus not only supplies immediate social need. It has all the value for present-day civilization that stimulants have ever had in the formation of history. It helps to preserve the idea which as yet cannot become an act, and failing in its function must otherwise die. Such, psychologists tell us, is the value of the stimulant—to free the individual from the consciousness of the limitation which prevents the realization of his ideal, and to preserve his ideal for him and for so-

ciety. It is here that the saloon gets its ultimate social value. The bacchanals were promoters of the Greek state, and the drinking of the Dark Ages contributed to the realization of the modern individual. Upon what beside shall the emotional life feed? or where shall it find its resting place of achievement, while the act itself is impossible save in the heightened activity of an exhilarated self? In this way it is believed that the saloon is aiding in the development of a higher form of society by preserving in its patrons a higher social hope. This is but a part of the social need to which it ministers, but by no means the least part.

There is another primal need which the saloon supplies and in most cases supplies well. It is a food-distributing center—a place where a hungry man can get as much as he wants to eat and drink for a small price. As a rule the food is notoriously good and the price notoriously cheap. And that air of poverty which unfailingly attends the cheap restaurant and finds its adequate expression in ragged and dirty table linen is here wanting. Instead polished oak tables are used and upon them reposes free an abundance such as to constantly surprise a depleted purse. That the saloon feeds thousands and feeds them well no one will deny who has passed the middle of the day there.

As to the physiological effects of the use of alcohol, the experiments conducted in the Yale laboratory, as they are reported in *Nature*, would seem to indicate that when the quantity of alcohol used is not in excess of 2 per cent of the digestive fluid, digestive activity is aided by its presence. "Whisky can be considered to impede the solvent action of the gastric juices only when taken immoderately and in intoxicating quantities." It is believed that a large part of the ordinary beer drinking contributes less than 2 per cent in alcohol to the whole digestive fluid—but the proof is almost inaccessible. Dr. Keeley* declares that "in the laboring man a certain quantity of alcohol will preserve the body weight with the same foot pounds of labor, and with a given quantity of food; and if these other things are equal the absence of the alcohol will require more food, or a decrease either in the labor or in the body weight." He con-

*Dr. Leslie E. Keeley (d. 1900) was the founder of the Keeley Institute, Dwight, Illinois, where his system for the treatment and cure of alcoholics and drug addicts, commonly known as the "Keeley Cure," was practiced.—Eds.

tends that its action is not to build up tissue but to prevent its breaking down. "It has an inhibitory action on cell metabolism." He adds: "I understand that these things are matters of demonstration, and that the everyday use of alcohol among laborers satisfactorily proves the value of the use and not the abuse of alcohol as a food—direct and indirect."

Such it is believed is the social value of the saloon. That it functions to certain social wants otherwise not supplied is our thesis. That its wares are poison is nowhere lost to sight, but that the poison appears in their abuse and not in their use is our contention. It is also admitted that social want is very inadequately supplied by the saloon. That a condition in which the idea can express itself in emotional terms only is essentially pathological. But it is believed that the saloon will continue to supply it as long as its opponents continue to wage a war of extermination against all that it represents, instead of wisely aiding social life to reach that plane where its present evils shall no longer be its accidents. The saloon is a thing come out of the organic life of the world, and it will give place only to a better form of social functioning. That a better form is possible to a fully conscious society no one can deny. When and what this form shall be remains for society's component units to declare. The presence of the saloon in an unorganized society is proof conclusive that society can wisely organize the need which it supplies.

It is hardly necessary to enlarge further upon the evils of the saloon in a protest against the predominance of one-sided statements in that very particular. They are many and grave, and cry out to society for proper consideration. But proper consideration involves a whole and not a half truth, and the whole truth involves its own power of proper action. In the absence of higher forms of social stimulus and larger social life, the saloon will continue to function in society, and for that great part of humanity which does not possess a more adequate form of social expression the words of Esdras will remain true: It is wine that "maketh the mind of the king and of the fatherless child to be all one, of the bondman and of the freeman, of the poor and of the rich. It turneth every thought into jollity and mirth, so that a man remembereth neither sorrow nor debt; and it maketh every heart glad."

Hull-House and the Ward Boss

Ray Stannard Baker

As the Hull-House reformers sought to improve life in their neighborhood, their social clubs, classes, and art exhibits aroused little controversy. But when they turned their attention to housing, education, and child labor problems, inevitably they became involved in politics. And politics in the 19th Ward meant Johnny ("de Pow") Powers, a shrewd and powerful Irish boss who was known as the "Prince of the Boodlers" in Chicago politics. The settlement workers became aware of his power and influence when he prevented construction of a new public school in the ward, and when their own investigation revealed that he was responsible for poor garbage collection in the ward because he used the job of garbage inspector as a political plum.

Hull-House residents concluded that they could make little progress toward improving conditions in the neighborhood until Powers was defeated, and so they decided to enter politics. Jane Addams and her associates encouraged the Hull-House Men's Club, which had been organized in 1893, to champion the settlement's cause against Johnny Powers. In 1895 the Hull-House organization actually elected a reform alderman, only to see him bribed by Powers and become one of the political boss's most loyal supporters.

Undismayed, the Hull-House group set out in 1896 to defeat Powers in his attempt to regain his aldermanic seat. They ran a well-organized campaign and learned a great deal about the realities of ward politics, but Powers won. Undaunted, two years later the Hull-House reformers tried once more to defeat the political boss. It was this campaign that Ray Stannard Baker (1870–1946), then a young journalist of twenty-eight, described in Outlook, *March 26, 1898. Baker, who sometimes wrote under the pseudonym David Grayson, later became one of America's leading journalists and the author of many books, including* Following the Color Line *and an eight-volume biography of*

Woodrow Wilson. [Ray Stannard Baker, "Hull-House and the Ward Boss," Outlook (March 26, 1898), 769–771.]

More than ordinary interest attaches to the struggle between "Johnny" Powers, the Democratic political king of Chicago, and the forces of reform, headed by Miss Jane Addams, of Hull House.

Powers is seeking re-election to the City Council from the notorious Nineteenth Ward, of which he has been the undisputed political boss for many years. Somewhat to his astonishment and consternation, the better element of the community in which he lives, spurred onward by the women of the Settlement, have organized a formidable combination which is fighting him with his own black record of misrepresentation and corruption. In times past he has opposed Hull House only by such secret means as the corrupt politician knows best how to wield, but now that he feels his throne tottering under him he has come out openly, threatening Miss Addams and her helpers with expulsion from his domain.

"Hull House," he declared angrily in a recent interview, "will be driven from the ward and its leaders will be forced to shut up shop."

Powers has been more than ordinarily successful as a ward boss. He is cool-headed, cunning, and wholly unscrupulous, and yet he possesses that effective gift known, for lack of a better name, as "good-fellowship" or "good-heartedness." Among his constituents he appears in his kingly aspects of unlimited power and benevolence. He impresses them with the primitive generosity which has turkeys to give away by thousands at Christmas-time, which elevates a faithful follower to a position on the city pay-roll in a single day, or discharges him with equal ease. He is the feudal lord who governs his retainers with open-handed liberality or crushes them to poverty as it suits his nearest purpose.

Among his colleagues in the Council he turns the other side of his character. He is shrewd and silent, planning his campaigns in some convenient wine-room, preferably his own, and letting other men do most of the speech-making and bring down upon themselves the abuse of the public. Imagine a short, stocky man with a flaring gray pompadour, a smooth-shaven face, rather heavy features and a restless eye, standing at the front of the Council Chamber with one finger aloft to catch the Mayor's eye, and you have a good picture of "Johnny" Powers. If he speaks, it is with a low and somewhat diffident voice with a distinct Hibernian twang, and yet every machine Democrat in the Council hangs on his words as the voicings of an oracle.

"Johnny" Powers has been interested in nearly every corrupt ordinance passed by the City Council for years. He has helped to give away millions of dollars' worth of franchises to street railway and gas companies. Often when the Mayor has vetoed his measures he has been prepared with a silent but significant two-thirds majority which voted without making any explanations. And no Alderman ever succeeded as he has done in getting his "heelers" and ward-workers on the city pay-rolls. At one time he boasted openly that he had no fewer than 2,600 men working in the various public departments of Chicago. Such a following, drawn from a single ward, will indicate what his power has been.

An Alderman's salary is only three dollars a week, but "Johnny" Powers has been able, with his partner [William "Billy"] O'Brien, who is also an Alderman, to purchase and maintain two large saloons in the downtown district of Chicago. He lives in a fine house—for his ward—and he is never without several aldermanic diamonds flashing about him. Only recently he was indicted by the Grand Jury for keeping a gambling-house. The proof was positive—it has been made many times before—and Powers did not deny the charge; he simply waved his hand and passed it off as a joke. And yet Powers is not a gambler himself, nor much of a drinker, and the "buttonhole men," who are helping him in his electioneering, tell what a kind and considerate husband and father he is.

In the present campaign Powers has even a stronger desire than usual to be elected. Yerkes,* the street-car magnate, will come before the next

*Charles Tyson Yerkes (1837–1905) came to Chicago in 1881. He had gained control of Chicago's street railway system by 1886.—Eds.

Council with ordinances asking for the extension of his franchises, now soon to expire, for another fifty years. Powers has been his willing coadjutor in the past, and he needs him more than ever in this coming crisis. Powers has skill and experience in assisting corrupt measures through the Council, and his place cannot be filled readily. Consequently, if he needs any "help" in his campaign, he knows where to get it.

The Nineteenth Ward is fertile soil for growing a ward boss. Its population consists of Italians, Polish and Russian Jews, Irish of the poorest class, and the offscourings of a dozen other nationalities. They live huddled together in ill-smelling houses, and few of the older people, many of whom are daylaborers, have any understanding of American institutions, or even of the English language. They are capable of being herded and driven by any one who is strong enough to wield the rod.

In this community Miss Addams quietly took up her residence more than ten years ago. She and a few helpers lived simply in an old brick mansion standing well back from the street, the remnant of a better day. Her first work was to make the acquaintance of the people around her, and to welcome them on terms of equality in her home. Presently she established a kindergarten, a gymnasium, evening classes, clubs for young people and clubs for old people, and a day nursery where working women might leave their children. As her work advanced she experienced the need of more room, and several buildings were added to the original brick Hull House, one being used as a branch of the public library, another containing a restaurant where wholesome food could be obtained at a moderate expense. Later she was instrumental in securing a free bath-house and public playgrounds for the children of the neighborhood. The public schools were overcrowded, there being at one time 3,000 less sittings than pupils, and that in a single ward. It was the duty of Alderman Powers, as the people's representative, to secure more schools, but he not only neglected to do this, but when Hull House circulated a petition, and had it approved by the School Board, the Council committee of which Powers's partner, O'Brien, was Chairman, quietly pigeonholed it, at the same time providing new schools in other wards where they were much less needed.

In all of these matters of public interest, which an Alderman is especially elected to advance, Powers has been a distinct impediment.

The streets and alleys of the ward were notoriously filthy, and the contractors habitually neglected them, not failing, however, to draw their regular payments from the city treasury. At last it fell to the women of Hull House to take the initiative. Miss Addams herself applied for the position of garbage inspector, and, to the astonishment of Powers and his retainers, received the appointment. Within two months the Nineteenth Ward was one of the cleanest in the city—and the contractors were squirming and complaining. Later, under the civil service rules, Miss Amanda Johnson, a resident of Hull House, became the regular inspector, Powers thereby losing one good place for a "heeler."

All this was in the nature of a daily object-lesson to the people of the ward, and in the course of ten years it made its deep impression even upon such clay. Italians and Jews and Irish have come to respect and trust the devoted women of Hull House, and to see wherein they are being betrayed by their chosen representative. Although political morality is hard to teach, especially to such alien pupils, "Johnny" Powers has not been slow to see that his ward, under the influence of Miss Addams and her helpers, is awakening to a realization of its rights.

A few weeks ago Powers appeared before the Civil Service Commission and demanded the discharge of Miss Johnson as garbage inspector, on the ground that she had been finding fault with his record as an Alderman and advising people of the ward to vote against him when he should appear as a candidate for re-election. The newspapers, one and all, declared against Powers, and the Commission found Miss Johnson entirely innocent of any attempt at electioneering, and, after commending her work, requested her to remain in office. But there is more than one way for a king to accomplish his purposes. The Council Finance Committee, of which Powers is Chairman, suddenly discovered the necessity of cutting down expenses, and promptly resolved to merge the Bureau of Street and Alley Cleaning with the regular Department of Streets. In this way Miss Johnson was deprived of her position, and her place was left to a Bohemian saloonkeeper named

Hull-House in 1898. Note the advertising the Coffee House–Gymnasium Building to the right.

Kostner, who was not even a civil service eligible—although he was a good friend to Powers.

In the meantime Hull House has been preparing to take the offensive. Miss Addams felt that after so many years of work she could exert enough influence to make a strong campaign against the corrupt reign of Powers, even if she could not beat him. She was encouraged by the large vote given at the last election to the reform ticket led by John Maynard Harlan,* and to the new primary law and to the civil service system— all encouraging signs of reform. Several largely attended meetings were held at Hull House, and, after much patient effort to unite all of the fac-

*Harlan (1864–1934), was a lawyer, Chicago alderman, 1896–1898, and Republican nominee for mayor of Chicago, 1897, 1905.—Eds.

tions, including the Republican party organization, Simeon Armstrong, a vigorous young Republican, was chosen for Powers's opponent. Women's clubs, Italian clubs, Irish clubs, and Jewish clubs were formed at once, and the campaign was opened with the vigor of enthusiasm. In his first speech Mr. Armstrong began his work of educating the people on the subject of boodle Aldermen with this pithy remark:

"A boodle Alderman does not take money from the rich and give it to the poor. Rather, he takes money from the rich and in return gives them the power to rob the poor."

But the cunning "Johnny" Powers was not to be outdone. He also formed women's clubs, and his speakers would not let the poor of the ward forget about the Christmas turkeys. Nor was it long before the reform element began to feel the might of Powers's kingship. Some of the business men of the ward who signed their names in support of Armstrong's candidacy dropped away suddenly and became Powers men. They were poor and in debt, and Powers had given a hint to a landlord here and a coal-dealer there, and they could not hope to survive if they rebelled. The ward is full of peddlers and small fruit merchants, each of whom holds a city license, without which he cannot ply his trade. Powers, the representative of the city, has but to threaten a revocation of a license and he has made a new supporter. Others believe that they are as much under Powers's control as if they were employees. They are ignorant foreigners, with centuries of tradition behind them which makes it impossible for them to understand that they are the masters and not the servants of public officers.

Powers has displayed his force even more openly. When John M. Harlan announced his intention of speaking in the Nineteenth Ward, Powers warned him that he would not be responsible for his safety. Harlan went, and Powers's rowdies began to make a disturbance, according to time-honored custom. Harlan, being a muscular man, invited a few of them up on the platform within reach of his fists—and that quieted them. Then he asked Powers some hard questions: Why is it necessary for the residents of the Nineteenth Ward to pay ten cents to get into some parts of the downtown district, when nearly every other part of the city is provided with five-cent fares? In eight years Chicago has expended more than $32,000,000 for street paving; with Powers at the head of the most important committee of the Council, why are not the streets of the Nineteenth Ward in better condition, and what has become of all this money?

These and other questions are having their effect. Powers himself shows it; he has been losing his temper, for the first time in a political campaign, and the opposition regards it as a favorable sign.

The fight is on. Powers controls all of the election machinery and the police, and he will stoop to any of the treacheries known to corrupt politics, but Hull House still hopes to accomplish his defeat. If it does not succeed, at least the residents of the ward will have had a stirring lesson in political morality, which will clear a way for success at another time.

✧ ✧ ✧

The Hull-House reformers went down to defeat again in 1898. Despite their all out efforts, the final totals read, Johnny Powers 5,450, Simeon Armstrong, the Hull-House candidate, 2,249. All was not lost, however, for out of this campaign and their previous forays into politics, Jane Addams and the Hull-House group gained a real understanding of their neighborhood and the combination of factors that allowed a man like Powers to rule. Addams analyzed the forces involved in city politics, while attacking Powers, in an address first delivered in Chicago in January 1898, and published in April 1898 in the International Journal of Ethics *under the ponderous title, "Ethical Survivals in Municipal Corruption." Her essay was one of the first attempts to understand the methods and motives of a city boss. Although she could not condone the corrupt acts of a man such as Powers, she was one of the first to realize that the boss was not all bad, that he provided real services to the people in his ward, and that he was elected not because he was corrupt but because in the eyes of his people he was a good and benevolent man.*

After their defeat in 1898 some of the Hull-House residents, especially Florence Kelley, wanted to continue the fight against Powers, but Jane Addams decided that it was more expedient to bypass Powers and exert pressure at city hall, in Springfield, and even in Washington. Though Hull-House remained interested in the politics of the neighborhood, the settlement never again assumed such an active political role.

Life at Hull-House

Alice Hamilton

Alice Hamilton (1869–1970) grew up in Fort Wayne, Indiana, one of four remarkable daughters in a moderately wealthy family. She went to Miss Porter's School in Farmington, Connecticut, then to the University of Michigan, to the University of Leipzig, and finally to the John Hopkins

University where she earned a medical degree. Dr. Hamilton came to Chicago in the fall of 1897 to take up her duties as a professor at Women's Medical School of Northwestern University. She chose to live at Hull-House because she had heard Jane Addams speak and thought the settlement would be an exciting place to live. She stayed until 1919, when she became the first woman ever to be appointed a professor at Harvard Medical School.

In these two letters, written to her cousin Agnes Hamilton (1868–1961), Hamilton captures some of the excitement, the fascinating people, the sense of community, even the personality conflict at the settlement. She also gives her version of the campaign against Johnny Powers. [Hamilton Family Papers, Schlesinger Library, Radcliffe College.]

Hull-House
Wednesday October 13*th* 1897

Dearest Agnes,

This is only a beginning, a faithful attempt, and perhaps if I am lucky it will succeed. It is my first free evening since so long ago that I can't remember. Last night Rachel came over and I lay off and rested while she talked to me. It was very nice and I loved to have her but I had planned to write to you. It was very forgiving of you to write to me again. Frankly I am awfully glad you didn't come back with me. Last week was interesting but not as interesting as I had expected, and this week I shouldn't have had any time at all for you. And I am not at all in the swim yet and could not go around and show you things as I could later on. No, January will be much, much better. As soon as I can I will ask Mrs. Kelley about your coming. You simply must take the first two weeks here, you know. Mrs. Kelley I am growing tremendously found of. She has made me very uncomfortable, however. Sunday evening she was talking to me and asking me if I thought the life here would be bad for me, and she added "I hope not, for I feel partly responsible for your coming. I urged Miss Addams very strongly to accept you." And when I asked why, she said "Oh well. I liked your cousins so much when I met them in Fort Wayne that I knew if you were anything like them we had better have you in Hull-House." Which of course

made me quite miserable. For of course I am not at all like you and if, as I think you wrote me, you and Katherine spoke to her about the sweating system and what things not to buy, then I am less like you than ever, for I don't even know whether I believe in not buying sweaters' clothes. So I sat there and felt like a miserable hypocrite and wished you were here to do the things they will expect me to do. Mrs. Kelley I find approachable and I can enjoy talking to her very much, but Miss Addams still rattles me, indeed more so all the time, and I am at my very worst with her. I really am quite school-girly in my relations with her; it is a remnant of youth which surprises me. I know when she comes into the room. I have pangs of idiotic jealousy toward the residents whom she is intimate with. She is—well she is quite perfect and I don't in the least mind raving over her to you, because by January fifth you will be just as bad as I, every bit.

This is a typical evening here. Here in the back parlour I am sitting at the table and opposite to me is Miss Johnson, who is the street-cleaning commissioner. She is having a most killing time interviewing an old Irishman who wants a job from the city. He has brought his wife with him and she is scolding him for saying he is sixty. She says he is only forty-five, although she insists he fought at Balaclava. Miss Johnson wants to know when his birthday comes, and his wife says "Say the fourth of July, it sounds well." Now they are having a fuss about his naturalization papers. He says he never had any, his wife says they were lost in the snow out in Utah when Brigham Young was dedicating the temple. At the other end of the table sits Miss Brockway, the sweet little girl who is engaged to Miss Addams' nephew. Mrs. Kelley is lying off on the sofa. In the front parlour are Mr. Deknatel and Mrs. Valerio. Mrs. Valerio speaks Italian and she and the man with the queer name— he is our mournful widower—are taking the names of the people who are registering for classes. Miss Addams is on the sofa with a very nice North End man, a friend of Miss Anderson's. They are looking over plans for an addition to the coffee-house. Miss Watson, Mr. Swope, Mr. Ball, Mr. Hooker, Miss Pitkin, Miss Gyles and all the others are managing classes and clubs in various rooms. In a few minutes a certain Dr. Blount is coming. It is a she-doctor and a socialist. I met her some time ago and she it is whom Miss Addams destines to help me in some scheme for the amelioration of the condition of the Italian "neighbors." Then at nine o'clock we are to have a residents' meeting, to divide up the duty of tending the door and showing people over the house.

Dr. Blount has just gone. We went up to Miss Addams' room and discussed a scheme which I haven't time to expound to-night. The chief part of it is that I needn't take any part in it till after Christmas. Meantime I am to take a class in Physiology and one in art anatomy. Do please help me with that last. Norah spoke of some lectures of Mr. Cox* which she said she would try to get for me when she was in New York, but I am sure she forgot. Do you suppose I could get them by writing to the Art League? And what book would be good?

---

*Those mentioned in the letter and not previously identified in the text or notes are:

Rachelle S. Yarros (1869–1946) was a physician and birth control activist who lived at Hull-House with her husband, Victor, from 1907 to 1927.

Katherine Hamilton (1862–1932), a cousin.

Amanda Johnson followed Jane Addams as garbage inspector for the Nineteenth Ward.

Wilfreda Brockway was a native of San Antonio, Texas, who taught at the Hull-House kindergarten. She married widower Frederick H. Deknatel.

John Linn (1872–1918), a nephew of Jane Addams, became an Episcopal clergyman and YMCA worker in France during World War I.

Frederick H. Deknatel, president of a small hardware manufacturing firm, became a resident at Hull-House after his first wife died. He worked with the boys clubs.

Amelie Robinson Mastro-Valerio, who taught French and Italian classes, was the wife of Alessandro Mastro-Valerio.

Probably Mary Anderson, who taught piano at Hull-House.

Edith Saluda Watson (1874–1966), called Luda, was a resident of the settlement for three years between 1896 and November 1899, when she married Frank Bartlett and went to live the remainder of her life in Drummond, Wisconsin.

Gerard Swope (1872–1957), resident who became president of General Electric, 1922–1939.

Frank H. Ball was director of manual training.

George E. Hooker (1861–1939) lived at Hull-House from shortly before 1900 until his death. A city planning expert, he was active in settlement attempts to improve its neighborhood.

May Pitkin taught evening classes and directed the relief bureau.

Rose Marie Gyles (1867–1949), a graduate of Rockford College, lived at Hull-House for 45 years and was responsible for women's sports and the gymnasium program. She also taught in public schools in the Chicago area.

Physician Anna Ellsworth Blount (b. 1872), wife of Hull-House resident, educator, and writer Ralph E. Blount (b. 1865). She lectured on social hygiene and medical subjects at Hull-House.

Kenyon Cox, a New York landscape and portrait painter.—Eds.

Norah insisted that all were iniquitous, but that was simply Mr. Cox' opinion. Last night I interviewed a nucleus of the Physiology class. It is not to be started unless six apply, and so far only four have: two nice-looking shop girls, a tired-looking middle-aged woman, and a fat Jew, who looks like an old-clothes man.

Well, here it is five minutes past nine, and I have reached my tenth sheet and haven't said one word about the Medical School. One would think it played a very small part in my life. Next time I'll tell you something about it.

It gives me a big tugging at the heart to think that Norry is on the ocean to-night. Write again soon do. Think of me as a lonely stranded heathen among many elect who scare her.

Very lovingly,
ALICE

Hull-House
Sunday April 3rd [1898]

My dearest Agnes,

I have such a delicious relieved feeling— Rachel Yarros has just telephoned me that they are invited to Dr. Carey's to dinner and so they cannot have me there to supper this evening. It is horrid to say that I feel relieved but I do. One needs good bracing December weather to make one feel up to Mr. Yarros, and in Spring time like this one longs for a little more vagueness and ramblingness and one gets cross and weary when a person insists on settling all questions at once in the hardest, most decided and positive way. I must go there to-morrow evening but to-morrow is a long way off and anyway we are going to see Frau Sorma in the "Doll's House." Perhaps by to-morrow I shall be rested. I have been dead tired for three days now. That campaign literature business was lengthy and dreadful. We began on Thursday in the afternoon, as soon as the new registration lists came in. I found Miss Gernon, Miss Brockway and Miss Bartlett at work when I came back, and the rest of us went at it right after dinner. All the first evening it was addressing envelopes. I found that I did two hundred and eighty in three hours. That kept up until late Friday night when the last of the twelve thousand was done. Then we adjourned to the dining-room and folded campaign literature. Mrs. Kelley and the men joined us at half past ten and we worked on till all hours of the night. Then Saturday morning we went at it again. A good many volunteers came in and of course Miss Addams insisted on working, though she is still on the sick list. We gave up the dining room to it and had lunch in the coffee-house and by half past four we really had finished and were the raggiest, flabbiest looking lot of people you ever saw. I had a Thomas concert on hand but I sent the ticket to Mary Hill and lay around on sofas and the longer I lay the tireder I grew. The poor men, however, really looked even more weary than we. Mr. Hill is on the last edge and Mr. Bruce looks like a wreck. While we were sitting around in the evening the big Powers' parade came by. It was Powers' last, supreme effort and was very imposing indeed. We all ran out to see it as it came down Polk street and turned north on Halsted. Of course we had run out with nothing around us, so the men had to lend us things and we stood all wrapped up on the corner and with our bare heads showed very plainly, I am afraid, that we came from Hull-House. First came the Father Mathew's cadets from the Jesuit church, the ones whom Powers uniformed two years ago. They say that he paid a thousand dollars to the church to have them march. He wanted Father Lambert to march at their head, but the reverend gentleman replied haughtily that he might hire the band, but he couldn't hire him. After them came the Cook County Democracy with Powers among them, all in Prince Alberts and silk hats and canes. Then a lot of carriages and then crowds on foot with banners and transparencies. One had ''No petticoat government for us,'' another had a picture of the House with the legend ''God bless the Hull-House.'' But the worst was a great long transparency with a picture of Mr. Hill at a window of the House dangling Mr. Armstrong at the end of a string. Mr. Murray and several others said that on the other side was a picture of Miss Addams tearing out Dr. Valerio's hair, but we didn't see it and I can't see the point of it anyhow. Except for cheering loudly for Powers as they passed the house nobody did anything much, indeed I think it was only small boys who yelled ''Down with Hull-House.'' Mr. Murray says that a good many mothers are very angry with Father Lambert for letting their boys who are Father Mathew's temperance boys march in a saloon-keeper's parade. To-day things seem very quiet. The men are all away, Miss Addams is lying down, Mrs. Stevens

type-writing and politics seem to have melted away for a little while.

A dreadful piece of news was broken to us to-day. Miss Gernon is going away for six months, going to Europe on five days' notice. What we are to do nobody knows. You can imagine what her going means. Somehow the house seems all upset. Mr. Hill goes away, and the Moores; Mr. Valerio comes in to stay in Miss Gernon's room, Miss Thomas moves down to one of the Moore's rooms, Miss Gyles to the other, Miss Howe into Miss Gyles' room, and Miss Watson comes back to take her room again. But you see, except for Miss Watson no worker comes into the house and we are left without Miss Gernon. I just wish you could come back. Miss Addams told me this morning that she was afraid they would have to keep a permanent toter in the house and pay her twenty-five a month until the Fall, but of course you couldn't stay in the city. Mrs. Stevens says that it is very trying having the Valerios in the house together, for they jar dreadfully and it makes a very strained, uncomfortable time for everybody. I feel forlorn about the changes. I wish things would stay as they have been.

It is Sunday afternoon and I haven't been out all day and I think I will put on my things and go for a ride on the grip,* as my back doesn't feel up to walking.

Miss Strong is ill and Mrs. Stevens has announced that she really cannot tote any more if she is to do any outside work and now with Miss Gernon going we really feel pretty despairing. Miss Addams is going away for a week after the campaign to rest, in Cedarville, which will be forlorn too.

Well I must go or I shall have no fresh air today. I send you our campaign literature and an amusing catechism which Miss Johnson brought in.

Lovingly,
ALICE

*Individuals and terms mentioned in this letter that have not been identified previously are:

Victor S. Yarros, journalist, lawyer, and Hull-House resident.

Maud Gernon lived at Hull-House from about 1895 to 1905, while she was a visitor for the Chicago Bureau of Charities. She served as director of the Drexel Club, a Hull-House young people's literary and social group, until it disbanded in

1902, and helped with various settlement investigations. She married fellow resident Charlie Yeomans.

Jessie Bartlett taught sloyd, a system of manual training in elementary woodwork originally developed in Sweden.

Theodore Thomas (1835–1905), conductor of the Chicago Symphony Orchestra.

Mary Dayton Hill was a student of John Dewey. She roomed with Alice Hamilton during part of her Hull-House residency and married fellow resident Gerard Swope in 1901.

William Hill taught economics at the University of Chicago and directed the settlement campaign against Alderman John Powers.

Andrew Alexander Bruce (1866–1934) was a Hull-House resident who had worked as an attorney for the Illinois State Board of Factory Inspectors. He became a professor of law at Northwestern University.

Father Mathew, a temperance advocate.

Aloysius A. Lambert, a Jesuit, was assistant pastor at Holy Family Church.

Simeon Armstrong the Hull-House candidate in the aldermanic election of 1898.

George Murray, a neighborhood policeman.

Elizabeth H. Thomas was secretary of the Dorcas Federal Labor Union, which met at Hull-House.

Gertrude Howe Britton (b. 1871) (Mrs. James Andrew) was director of the Hull-House kindergarten from 1897 to 1907, when she became involved in the work of the Juvenile Protective Association. She later became superintendent of the Chicago Heart Association.

Grip was slang for a cable car.—Eds.

A Fabian Visits Hull-House

Beatrice Webb

Hull-House even in the 1890s received international publicity and attracted visitors from around the world. Sometimes they came for a few hours, but often they stayed longer. William Stead, the British journalist; Aylmer Maude, the friend of Tolstoy and translator of his works; John Burns, the British labor leader; Prince Peter Kropotkin, the Russian anarchist; and Canon and Mrs. Samuel Barnett of Toynbee Hall were among early Hull-House visitors. In 1898, Sidney and Beatrice Webb stopped at the settlement during their whirlwind tour of the United States. The Webbs, a charming and gregarious couple, were leaders in the Fabian Socialist movement and co-authors of the History of Trade Unionism *and* Industrial Democracy, *the first major contributions in English on organized labor. They were about to embark on*

a study of local government that would run to fifteen volumes.

This excerpt from Beatrice Webb's (1858–1943) diary of her American trip recounted her reaction to the "continuous intellectual and emotional ferment" that was Hull-House. Though she was impressed by some aspects of the settlement, she discovered that it was no place for a rest or a gourmet meal. [Beatrice Webb, Beatrice Webb's American Diary, 1898, *edited by David A. Shannon (Madison, Wisc., 1963), 107–109.]*

On the Thursday, after our arrival at Chicago, we migrated . . . to Hull-House Settlement in the very heart of Chicago slums. Hull-House itself is a spacious mansion, with all its rooms opening, American fashion, into each other. There are no doors, or, more exactly, no *shut* doors: the residents wander from room to room, visitors wander here, there and everywhere; the whole ground floor is, in fact, one continuous passage leading nowhere in particular. The courtyard, in front of the house, is always filled with slum children. At the back, opening out of the kitchen, is a rough and ready restaurant. There is the usual scanty service; the front door being answered by the resident who happens, at that time, to be nearest to it.

The residents consist, in the main, of strong-minded energetic women, bustling about their various enterprises and professions, interspersed with earnest-faced self-subordinating and mild-mannered men who slide from room to room apologetically. One continuous intellectual and emotional ferment is the impression left on the visitor to Hull-House.

Miss Jane Addams, the Principal, is without doubt a remarkable woman, an interesting combination of the organiser, the enthusiast and the subtle observer of human characteristics. Her article in the *International Journal of Ethics*—"Ethical Survivals in Municipal Corruption" is an exact analysis of the forces of Tammany organisation and its root in human nature. She has a charming personality, gentle and dignified, shrewdly observant: above all she excels in persistency of purpose and unflinching courage. She has made Hull-House; and it is she who has created whatever spirit of reform exists in Chicago.

In the evening of our arrival we underwent a terrific ordeal. First an uncomfortable dinner, a large party served, higgledepiggledy. Then a stream of persons, labour, municipal, philanthropic, university, all those queer, well-intentioned or cranky individuals, who habitually centre round all settlements! Every individual among them must needs be introduced to us (a diabolical custom from which we have suffered greatly in America). Gradually the crowd pressed us into a large hall, with chairs for some hundreds and a small platform. From this place, Sidney and I were expected to orate to the assembly, on any topic we chose. We did our best, and they were so far entertained that they asked us innumerable questions.

For a right down exhausting business commend me to a dinner and a reception, preceding a lecture and a severe heckling. However, we seemed to give satisfaction.

The other days of our stay at Hull-House are so associated in my memory with sore throat and fever, with the dull heat of the slum, the unappetising food of the restaurant, the restless movements of the residents from room to room, the rides over impossible streets littered with unspeakable garbage, that they seem like one long bad dream lightened now and again by Miss Addams' charming grey eyes and gentle voice and graphic power of expression. We were so completely done up that we settled "to cut" the other cities we had hoped to investigate. . . .

CREATIVE YEARS
1900–1914

IN THE FIRST DECADE AND A HALF OF THE TWENTIETH
century, Hull-House reached the peak of its reputation and influence. Especially after
Twenty Years at Hull-House was published in 1910, Jane Addams became a national celeb-
rity and Hull-House a household word. A few criticized the settlement, and some still mis-
took it for a charity or a mission, but even these could not deny the influence of Hull-House
residents and graduates on the diverse social reform movements that reached a climax in
the years after 1900.

Hull-House continued to expand and change during this period. In 1902 the Hull-House
Apartment Building was completed with a Men's Club on the first floor. The Woman's
Club Building was erected in 1904, and by the next year the residents' dining hall had been
constructed. In 1906 the Boys' Club Building was finished, and in 1907 the Mary Crane
Nursery completed the complex of thirteen buildings which covered a large block and made
up Hull-House as it would remain until 1963. Two alleys bisected the block occupied by the
settlement, dividing its buildings into one large and two small groups. The maze of structures which bordered Halsted Street were all interconnected, though it took some experience
to negotiate the labyrinth of halls, corridors, and stairs without getting lost. A central heating plant, installed early in the century, served all the buildings, and a courtyard lent charm
and a parklike atmosphere to the rambling complex. The complicated and expensive task
of building, maintaining, and operating not only the buildings but the total settlement program was accomplished with funds provided chiefly through gifts, large and small.

As the settlement increased in size, so did the number of residents. Jane Addams, Ellen
Starr, Alice Hamilton, and Julia Lathrop remained the center of the group. Alzina P. Stevens died in 1900. Though Florence Kelley had moved to New York in 1899, she frequently
returned, as did Lathrop after she moved to Washington in 1912. Others came during these

years: Grace and Edith Abbott, Sophonisba Breckinridge, Francis Hackett, William Hard, Sidney Hillman, I. K. Friedman, and many more. The custom of all the residents eating together at the evening meal with Jane Addams presiding at the head of one of the long tables was continued, but size reduced informality. Still, despite its growth Hull-House was an exciting place to live, a place where one might meet a distinguished visitor, a statesman, writer, or scholar from almost anywhere in the world, a place to go after college or graduate school to meet other young men and women just getting started on careers in writing, or business, or city planning. It was a place to study people and to study the city. A few of the residents were beginning to work toward degrees in social work. The first professional schools in this field were organized early in the century, but most had no conception of social work as a profession; they were too busy trying to change the world.

Not everyone who came to Hull-House had a wonderful and rewarding experience. Mary E. Collson, for example, who was thirty years old and had been a Unitarian minister in Iowa, arrived at Hull-House during the hot summer of 1900. She had been hired to become Alzina Stevens's assistant as probation officer for the new Chicago Juvenile Court. Stevens died suddenly and Collson, with no experience, became the chief officer. The young juvenile delinquents she worked with were constantly getting into trouble; they lost their jobs, got arrested for stealing and were sent to reform school for violating their parole. For all of her efforts, Collson got paid only sixty dollars a month and much of that she had to return to the settlement for room and board.

As a new resident at the settlement she was assigned one of the least desirable rooms on the third floor, under the eaves. Her work space was a desk on the ground floor right in the middle of the steady stream of humanity that came to the settlement every day of the year. While the famous residents were attending conferences, giving lectures, or vacationing, Collson dealt every day and most nights with the reality of life in the slums. She witnessed child abuse, murder, drunkenness, and disease. She stuck it out for nearly a year before she collapsed one day at her desk. She had had enough of settlement work. Not everyone found life so difficult at Hull-House, but neither was it as wonderful as some of the memoirs suggest.

The clubs, classes, lectures, and investigations established during the first decade continued, but new programs and activities were continually added. The Labor Museum, which preserved and illustrated ancient and modern methods of textile, pottery, and food manufacture, was organized in 1900, and Ellen Starr's bookbindery began about the same time. The Hull-House Players came into their own with the construction of a new theater building, and the music school continued to expand. The Juvenile Protective Association and the Immigrants' Protective League, both housed within the Hull-House complex, sought to help those who were lost, floundering, or already in trouble. In 1912, Louise deKoven Bowen gave seventy-two acres of land near Waukegan, Illinois, with ten buildings, to Hull-House for a summer camp. The Bowen Country Club, as it was called, where residents and neighbors alike could escape some of the congestion and problems of the city, became a permanent year-round retreat. Despite the Country Club, most of the energy of the Hull-House group was spent in trying to solve the problems of the city, not to escape them.

While the settlement grew, the neighborhood also changed. The Bohemian colony formerly located near Hull-House moved further west and was replaced largely by Russian and Rumanian Jews. Even more dramatic was the sudden appearance, early in the century, of a large colony of Greeks. "We knew nothing of them until one night we observed the street and the saloon above us in Halsted Street were filled with them," a Hull-House resident told a reporter in 1902. "They were young men, and had arrived recently in search of work. Gradually they have assimilated with the Italians, with whom they seemed to fraternize."

The settlement residents who conducted a special study of their Greek colony between 1908 and 1909 kept careful charts of the shifting population in their neighborhood. They tried to understand and serve the new groups, yet many of the immigrants, especially the men, remained uninfluenced by the settlement.

The decade and a half after 1900 is often called the Progressive Era. It was a time of organization and reform in all areas of American life, a time when a number of reformers thought it was possible to create a better and more meaningful life for all the people. The Hull-House group were leaders in a wide variety of reform movements in Chicago and in the nation. They helped organize the first important survey of housing conditions in the city in 1901. Hull-House resident Robert Hunter directed the survey under the auspices of the City Homes Association and wrote the report which went a long way toward identifying the housing problems in Chicago.

Still confident they could improve life in the slums by working for social reform, Hull-House residents continued to gather information for their campaigns. They investigated the licensing and practices of midwives and discovered that of the 233 studied "only 30 per cent . . . had presumably received an adequate training, but the remainder were not obliged to produce any evidence of practical experience, merely to pass a state board examination. After the license was given, the work of the midwife was apparently under no control, very shocking conditions as to cleanliness being found." Dr. Alice Hamilton conducted a study of infant mortality among foreign-born parents and found that child mortality increased proportionally as the number of children in the family increased. Children's reading habits, the sale and use of cocaine by neighborhood youth, and the causes and prevention of truancy were among other investigations carried out by the Hull-House reformers.

Hull-House residents also played important roles in various attempts to create a more responsive government. They were still troubled by the presence of a corrupt political boss in their own ward, but in this period they tended to ignore or bypass him, seeking reform directly in city institutions. In 1903 a citywide attempt to win the municipal ownership of street railways for the city was based at Hull-House, but like so many other municipal reform attempts it failed. The Hull-House group were, however, responsible for stimulating the development of public playgrounds and recreation centers in the city. Jane Addams, Hull-House supporter Anita McCormick Blaine, Hull-House volunteer physician Cornelia DeBey, and former settlement resident Raymond Robins served on Mayor Edward Dunn's reform school board from 1905 until 1909 in hope of improving the city school system. In promoting reform in Chicago, Hull-House cooperated with the other settlements which had developed in the city (thirty-six by 1911), especially the University of Chicago Settlement in the stockyards district, and Chicago Commons and the Northwestern University Settlement, located not far from Hull-House.

On the national level, Hull-House residents and graduates played a leading role in organizing the National Women's Trade Union League and pressing for a national investigation of women and children in industry. They also helped organize the National Child Labor Committee in 1904, and were in part responsible for the establishment of the Children's Bureau in the U.S. Department of Labor in 1912, of which Julia Lathrop was first director. They pioneered in progressive education, the Americanization of immigrants, and the sympathetic and understanding treatment of juvenile delinquents. Indeed, few reform movements that sought to extend social justice in the Progressive Era did not have at least one Hull-House graduate or resident among its leaders. The Hull-House network, which extended far beyond the west side of Chicago and into the years after the Progressive Era, included some men, but was largely based on an extensive support system of women who worked together over the years on dozens of reform campaigns.

Several of the Hull-House group were very much involved in the Progressive party cam-

Hull-House and Halsted Street about 1915.

paign in 1912. They were not enthusiastic about Theodore Roosevelt, though he had visited the settlement on several occasions; but they believed the party represented their hopes for the future. They were especially enthralled by the Progressive platform, which they had had a part in drafting. It called for the improvement of housing conditions, prohibition of child labor, regulation of the employment of women, federal accident, old-age, and unemployment insurance, and votes for women. Louise Bowen, George Hooker, Edith and Grace Abbott, and many others took an active part in the campaign, while Jane Addams seconded the nomination of Theodore Roosevelt at the Chicago convention, wrote campaign essays, gave a series of campaign speeches, and was hailed as one of the leading Progressives in the country. The settlement workers had no hope for victory in 1912, but they believed the Progressives would win in 1916. When World War I and other factors led to the collapse of the Progressive dream, many of the settlement workers never quite recovered their faith and their optimism. They were disturbed, too, as they took a realistic look at all their hard work and organization over twenty years: they had not wiped out child labor and poverty, and they had not significantly improved housing.

Their disillusionment was at the time only partial. The Hull-House residents continued to work to improve life in their neighborhood, in Chicago, and in the nation; and on the eve of World War I, Hull-House remained a vital and forward-looking institution. But the greatness and vitality of Hull-House in the first decade and a half of the twentieth century, and the supreme confidence of its leaders that one could create a better world, would never be recaptured.

Hull-House—A Souvenir

Francis Hackett

Francis Hackett (1883–1962) was twenty-three years old in 1906 when he discovered Hull-House. He had arrived in America from Ireland when he was eighteen, and had worked as an office boy for a law firm in New York before coming to Chicago for a job as editorial writer on the Chicago Evening Post. *Later he became a successful literary critic for the* Evening Post *and the* New Republic, *the biographer of Henry VIII, and the author of several novels. In describing the process by which he became an American, Hackett said: "America dawned for me in a social settlement. It dawned for me as a civilization and a faith. . . . Till I knew a social settlement the American flag was still a flag on a circus-tent, a gay flag, but cheap. The cheapness of the United States was the message of quick-lunch and the boarding-house, of vaudeville and Coney Island and the Sunday newspaper, of the promenade on Broadway. In the social settlement I came on something entirely different. Here on the ash-heap of Chicago was a blossom of something besides success. The house was saturated in the perfume of the stock-yards, to make it sweet. A trolley-line ran by its bedroom windows to make it musical. It was thronged with Jews and Greeks and Italians and soulful visitors, to make it restful. It was inhabited by highstrung residents to make it easy. But it was the first place in all America where there came to me a sense of the intention of democracy, the first place where I found a flame by which the melting pot melts. I heard queer words about it. The men, I learned, were mollycoddles, and the women were sexually unemployed. The ruling class spoke of 'Unsettlement workers' with animosity, the socialists of a mealy-mouthed compromise. Yet in that strange haven of clear humanitarian faith I discovered what I suppose I had been seeking—the knowledge that America had a soul."*

In the following essay Hackett captured some of the excitement, enthusiasm, and purpose of Hull-House during the time when it was most suc-cessful and most exciting. [Francis Hackett, "Hull-House—A Souvenir," Survey (June 1, 1925), 275–279.]

When I went to live at Hull House in 1906, I did not really know it, and I was totally ignorant of settlement work as I was devoid of missionary spirit. I was torn at that time between the two impulses of wanting to know Chicago and wanting to escape from it, and I went to Hull House both for escape and for reconcilement.

I went there, as one always goes into a new experience, on the terms and in the light of the inappropriate things I already knew. Only very slowly did I frame for myself the kind of experience I was having. As I trusted myself to it gradually and suspiciously, and felt it give back more than it was receiving from me, I began to realize the peculiar quality of this strange American creation, its quality of goodness, of intelligence, of decent conscience, which filled Hull House almost to overflowing, and which renewed itself constantly from Miss Addams as a fountain is renewed.

To this day, meeting Miss Addams or her associates, the values of that year at Hull House take new shape and depth for me. In this way, later impressions mingling with the earlier, and feelings with facts, I want to give my picture of Hull House.

It is a picture, first of all, of being a resident grouped with other residents. The building in which we lived on Halsted Street did not fall back from the street. It was plump in the middle of the neighborhood, and yet it had a long semi-cloistral corridor and a grave, deep spacious reception hall which declared you were out of the world. We who came there on probation before we were accepted as residents could hardly help feeling it was a sort of withdrawn community. But in its being withdrawn it was anything but mystical or dogmatic. Its faith was humanism. It "warmed both hands before the fire of life." No newcomer could resist its ease, its tolerance, or its cordiality. The ferocious loneliness of Chicago in those early thin-skinned days made me reluctant to consider Hull House quite real, at first sight, and then made me enter into its community with thirsty zeal.

All, or nearly all, of the residents were employed outside the Settlement during the day, and many of them in work that was not "social work." At that time, for instance, I was literary editor of the Chicago Evening Post, Chicago's genteel evening paper. I followed Tiffany Blake as editor in the book department and writer of reviews and literary notes, and at the same time I succeeded Roswell Field, Eugene Field's brother, in writing editorials, my contribution being from twelve to fifteen a week. In addition, to give J. C. Shaffer* full value for his money, I worked up features such as Little Talks about Big People, etc. For these trivial services Mr. Shaffer paid me $23 a week, later hoisted to $28, and, in the course of five years, to $43. As my room and board at Hull House only came to $7 or $8, I had good cold reasons for being glad to live there, in a big, rather somber mission-furniture room. But, of course, I had duties at Hull House when I came back from the Evening Post. I had a weekly or bi-weekly class in English, trying to expound Shakespeare to young Russian Jewesses. I had a club of Irish boys, to whom I dispensed polysyllables and who were as much puzzled by me as I was by them. One evening a week I took the door, the easiest of all duties, and in some ways the most in contact with the neighborhood.

But it was contact with the residents, not with the neighborhood, which seemed to me more real at the beginning. We were a diverse group, mainly young, and meeting each other no more intimately than shipmates and messmates, outside the important residents. Yet my recollection is one of vivid and colored personalities that managed in some way to harmonize.

There were two sets in Hull House; we named them the Noble Set and the Frivolous Set, but I cannot imagine a diverse community in which there was less division or friction. We did not behave like business partners trying to round the corners of each other's silences, or like huddled intellectuals, or like rasping literary groups, or even like those theological seminaries and college faculties whose members develop vested interests and are full of gossip and spite. Our probation, I suppose, did result in a real selection. Certain thorny people were not admitted. We who were there, at any rate, were in harmony.

But this harmony did not root out differences. I can see the residents now, Miss Benedict in her effacing dress, like a Holbein print, her hands busy, her tongue silent. Fraulein,† big-boned and almost Mongolian-looking, with occasional positive utterance. Mrs. Britton, ample and active, her eyes quickly responsive and soft; articulate, very. Mr. Britton with a Raphaelic smile, big and brown and like a St. Bernard. Mr. George Hooker, steel-rimmed glasses, hair a little untidy, myopic, crammed with statistics on municipal ownership, unoiled, dry and good. Frank Hazenplug, almost unbearably aesthetic, dancing pliantly, hard at work in the Hull-House Theatre, painting, nailing, doing make-up, with a nervous giggle to hide his inarticulateness. Miss Nancrede, devotee of Henry James, skilled in vanishing from the successes she contrived, and disciplined as only the French can be disciplined. Von Borosini, the Austrian, native as the dawn, kindly and rambling, vague as the mist. Carl Linden the Swede, who

†The residents mentioned in this paragraph who have not been identified in previous text or notes are:

Fraulein is probably Amalie Hannig (b. 1868), a German woman who befriended Eleanor Smith when they both studied music in Germany. She joined Smith shortly after the settlement Music School opened in 1893, to teach piano.

Dr. James Andrew Britton (b. 1876) was a Chicago physician who lived with his wife, Gertrude Howe, at Hull-House and worked especially with those neighborhood people who suffered from tuberculosis.

Frank Hazenplug also taught metalwork, in addition to his work with Hull-House Theater.

Edith de Nancrede (1877–1936). As a young Chicago art teacher, she became a Hull-House resident in 1898 and spent the remainder of her life at the settlement working with young people in dance and dramatics.

Victor von Borosini, an Austrian by birth, was an educator. He lived at the settlement with his wife, Edith, who taught English classes there.

Charles Yeomans (1877–1959) became president of the Yeomans Pump Company of Chicago. He married resident Maud Gernon.

Edward Yeomans (b. 1866) was also associated with the Yeomans Pump Company of Chicago. He founded the Ojai School in Ojai, California.

Clara Landsberg (1873–1966) was in charge of adult education at Hull-House. She became a teacher at Byrn Mawr School in Baltimore.

Mary Rozet Smith (1868–1934) was Jane Addams' closest lifelong friend. She and her family were major financial supporters of the settlement even before 1895, when they built the Children's House for Hull-House.—Eds.

*John Charles Shaffer (1853–1943) was president and publisher of the *Chicago Evening Post* from 1901 until 1931.— Eds.

talked in a slow growl and brought with him the outdoor feeling, the stubborn fight, the unsentimentalism, the strong color, that he put into his paintings. Charlie Yeomans with eyes squeezed up when he laughed, solid worth, twinkling with humor yet subsiding into gloom. Miss Gernon, solid worth too, puzzled at life. Ned Yeomans, with a crackling laugh, full of the same Saxon manliness as Charlie, also an inchoate soul. Miss Alice Hamilton, clear as an etching, liberally intelligent, discerning, with a voice of such fine music that could only be matched by the candor of her eyes and the find hands. Miss Norah Hamilton, shy, sidelong, original, a Brontë, looking at one like a deer through the brake. Miss Clara [Landsberg], of Bryn Mawr vintage, valiant, tense, souffrante, at once impatient and remorseful, indefatigable and worn-out. Miss Mary Smith, wise, tolerant, unspoken. And, of course, Twose.

George Mortimer Randall Plantagenet Twose, or something of that sort. Him at any rate I shall sacrifice without decency. He was an Englishman who had a teaching job which sat very lightly on him. He gave one the impression of laughing at life and yet skipping away from it. He wanted above everything to be free, and at the same time to satisfy a conscience which had the disadvantages of being fastidious and social. But, of course, he concealed his conscience as he clothed his nakedness.

My room was next to his, up a short flight of stairs off the corridor, and right on Halsted Street. He had decorated his wall with great squares of tinfoil or silver paper out of tea chests, the whole side of the wall—it was peculiarly ghastly. He was painting a picture, an oil painting of olive trees near Athens, and it pleased him to change the foliage of this perennial picture according to the season of the year he was re-painting it.

He pooh-poohed Shaw. He pooh-poohed uplift. At the least sound of indignation he'd say, "Rats, it'll all be the same in a hundred years." He feared above all things to wear his heart on his sleeve. "You are bitterly young, aren't you?", he said to me, laughing his long laugh. I remembered that for months, being bitterly young. I got him to review "Hills and the Sea," by Belloc. He wrote his review on odd sheets of paper, a hopeless and disorderly scrawl, and one that did not capture the quality of Twose. It bored him. Formal, harnessed

effort bored him, but he effervesced in Hull House; he was incessantly useful and resourceful by stealth. "Oh, why do you do that, Miss Addams?" he'd query her, with an assurance that was always justified by his suggestion. He was counted on, by Miss Addams. He had that invaluable English sense of people which makes snobbishness in the majority of cases but a Borrow-like humanism in others. Twose had imagination for the lame and halt, he never flagged when it came to entertaining the dull, it was only the intimate young things he shied away from, set parties and set sentiments.

On his way home to England, seeing his native shores again, and visualizing his Set, he bundled up his evening clothes and pushed them through the porthole into the sea.

A very long-headed man, with a high bald forehead, twinkling eyes, a hoarsish cracked voice, a long yet gainly body, something of the capricious and something of the romantic Englishman.

Hull House was the only place in Chicago for a restive man like Twose, and Twose was excellent for Hull House. When they acted Shaw or Yeats, when they got up a dance, when people came who were interested in the Labor Museum, Twose rose to the occasion, an antidote to Noble Souls. But there were things he wouldn't do. The afternoon James Bryce arrived, Twose was making his own tea, and I could not get him to budge. The ambassador downstairs was important to "tote," but not as important as that.

With such persons as residents, Hull House was vibrant. To me, the literary bird of passage, they were not "copy," and yet after twenty years I can remember casual things they said. Ned Yeomans, quoting, "walking alone like the rhinoceros," and, of course, wishing he had a hide like a rhinoceros, which was in vain. Miss [Landsberg] commenting on George Eliot with scorn unfathomable, "Of course, she could say to Cross, 'I need you to tell me you love me, every hour.' It was just like that woman!"

This was far from social work, and I wonder now what Miss Addams thought about her residents. We were well behaved, we did our classes and so on, but we were not yoked oxen. I always had the feeling I did not do enough. Yet in Miss Addams there was no reproof. I can well remember how often, with residents passing through the room where people sat around the common table on occasion, Miss Addams would say, "Mr. Hooker! You can help us. What do you think . . ." Her attitude was, "you can help," and because she elicited goodwill in a common cause, that cause preoccupied the residents. In other groups where social idealism brings its practitioners very liberal funds, high prestige, and flattering publicity, the will-to-rule is likely to be stimulated, which in a hysterical period like the present leads to intrigue and politics and ends in the will-to-war. But this irony never confronted Hull House, where there was little prestige or publicity and no pay. The House not only recruited strong characters, it was excited about them.

In 1906 or 1907, I was told, "Miss Lathrop is coming! Miss Lathrop is coming!" as if it were an occasion for public rejoicing. I had never heard of Miss Lathrop; the name was a fashionable name in Chicago, and I thought this was much too fawning. I did not know Miss Julia Lathrop of Rockford, Illinois, who brought with her such force, such warmth, such an almost rouguish sense of the tragi-comedy of American politics. You felt she enjoyed the game, and through the game could bring into being the Children's Bureau or anything else, without losing sight for one moment of the big end she had in view. Her brown eyes, so sincere, but with a sparkle lurking in them, her slow redolent voice, her flavor of Illinois, gave her a richness which was valued by colleagues who had less vitality. Yet that almost Italian salience was only one kind of strength. There was a variety of strong character. The group that included Mrs. Kelley, Miss Lathrop, Dr. Hamilton, Miss Grace Abbott, and Miss Addams has made itself objectively important in the life of the American people.

In this impression of Hull House I record nothing of one of its founders, Miss Ellen Starr. It would be a pity to omit mention of one whose fearlessness, whose ardor for beauty, stirred many a young person to a new zeal—and a new appreciation of the difference between the best and its enemy, the good. But my own knowledge of her was slight, I remember most of all her fresh laughter, her passage with head thrown a little back, and a touch of whiteness at throat and wrists. And who could forget the pervading gentleness of Miss Waite*, or the buoyancy of Mrs. Pelham† or even the glimpse of such a gallant visitor as Raymond Robins.‡

The essential fact of Hull House, the dominant fact, was the presence of Miss Addams. This is strange because while one was living there Miss Addams was away a good deal of the time, and when she was there one did not have a great deal to do with her; yet Hull House, as one clearly felt at the time, was not an institution over which Miss Addams presided, it was Miss Addams, around whom an institution insisted on clustering.

However she might deprecate it, and no one was more skillful than Miss Addams in deprecation, we often said, "without her, it's—nothing."

A fine building, of course, and a fine group of people. A neighborhood that seethed with things to consider and do. But we returned to her personality for the overwhelming reason that our own personalities gained in value through contact with hers. She had the power to value human beings, to appreciate them, and to feel in terms of them. I do not mean to manipulate them in the fashion of a Disraeli, who, simulating that interest and that respect, twisted human beings around his jewelled finger. That is a trick to which human vanity lends itself and which innumerable public men employ, the Lloyd Georges and the Roosevelts, the makers of a "personal following." It is a trick which accounts for the inferiority of personal followings, but with Miss Addams it was not a trick, it was depersonal and disinterested. It really was her way of life. . . .

Hull House was American because it was international, and because it perceived that the nationalism of each immigrant was a treasure, a talent, which gave him a special value for the United States.

*Ella Raymond Waite (d. 1925) lived at the settlement from 1896 until her death. She taught embroidery and, for a number of years, managed the settlement summer camp program.—Eds.

†Laura Dainty Pelham (1845–1924), a retired actress who came to Hull-House about 1900 to successfully direct the Hull-House Players until her death in 1924.—Eds.

‡Raymond Robins (1873–1954) was an American social reformer, minister, and lawyer who in 1917 led the Red Cross expedition to the Soviet Union. He lived at the Chicago Commons settlement and was head resident of Northwestern University Settlement while taking part in reform campaigns in Chicago.—Eds.

We were flooded by nationalisms. How many nights did I not stay awake while the interminable whine of Greek folk-music came across Halsted Street to my exasperated ears. Had not Miss Addams gathered Greeks by the hundred to come to the Theatre during their unemployment so that English words could be taught to them in chorus and en masse. The Greeks to her were a Presence, a possibility no doubt of human suffering, but also a group that was suffused with reality for her, a group with a cluster of warm and ripened association. She felt the aura of Greece when she dealt with them. She had a heart for them, or rather an imagination for them, a grasp of their difficulties and their fractured loyalty.

And if the Greeks were neighbors, with their sharp profiles and sharper wits, the Italians were not less neighbors. An Italian family* lived in the House, the handsome matron who ran the coffee house, her seignorial husband who was an editor, and the two boys, one chiselled Latin and the other a ball of Nordic-Latin energy. But there was also the stream of Italian life from the neighborhood, the black eyes blazing out of immobile faces, the withered mothers, the gnarled fathers who seemed to carry with them the parched heat of a beating sun; and out of these indurated workers, these people made over by their toil into something like terra cotta itself, an occasional revelation of an inner life so hued by time, so fantastic and so tragically passionate that only a Miss Addams could find the clue to it. She has herself told the story of the Devil Baby that was torturing her neighbors, within sound of factory whistles.

In the crises of many lives, Hull House was an asylum. I recall late one night I went down to answer the door at Hull-House. Elsie Smith, Miss Addams' secretary, had arrived first, and she had let in an Italian woman. I shall not forget the crouching woman in the swathing shadows below, she had run away from a house of prostitution. I see Miss Smith in a long grey robe on the broad low stairs that led up to Miss Addams's room, her face with that look of stilly, starlike calmness, of self-collection, that it never lost. In the quietness the woman knew she was safe, and Miss Smith made plans with Miss Addams in a low tone.

The Irish did not come with quite the same

magnificent gesture as the Latins, who make a large free donation of their helplessness and who keep marvellous capacity for dramatic entry and surprise. A few Irish remained, to enliven the neighborhood. One afternoon I came back to Hull House to see crowds in the street, or rather a few torn wisps of a crowd that was scattering. In the House itself there was a sense that the worst had happened. Mrs. B., her brown eyes full of suppressed fire and her jaw set, looked forward to court. One of her Irish friends, apparently, had loosed the passion that was in him under the very walls of Hull House, had started a bloody and wondrous fight that was only halted by the arrival of the patrol-wagon. Still sweeping the air with blows and curses, the little bantam had been taken away to cool himself, leaving Hull House shaken and unhappy.

What shook it was not the normal householder's dismay over unruliness. It was the difficulty of doing the right thing that Miss Addams later expressed in The Spirit of Youth and the City Streets. Here was Youth, flashing, wrong-headed, turbulent. Hull House was on its side, and yet the young devil asked for the patrol-wagon! What could you do with him? His mother would be around, in a mood of despair that only Peter Dunne† could describe; what could *she* do with her firebrand?

One thing, at least, was done on the highly traditional occasion of St. Patrick's Day. Though many of the Irish who were once thick in the neighborhood had become better off and had moved away, they came back on St. Patrick's Night to a dance that showed Hull House at its most exciting.

For people like myself, who could dance in every way but with their feet, it still was a festivity. The preparations for it occupied weeks, the North Side helping, Crans Baldwin and B. Poole and others, and grave residents like Miss Benedict working like beavers, without a word. The music was daring, for that time, and the on-and-off lighting was a great feature nineteen years ago. But the main thing was the dance itself, which, in spite of its congestion and tropic warmth, had a way of seeming fresh and free, a way of seeming

---

*The Alessandro Mastro-Valerio family.—Eds.

†Finley Peter Dunne (1867–1936), American humorist, famous for his Irish-American dialogues with "Martin Dooley," a saloonkeeper.—Eds.

choral, and of releasing everyone into a hilarious mob. I suppose this can be done by any kind of group play, by mass, by revival meetings and by fighting. But Hull House did it for the Irish, and the North Side guests, with must and lighting, festoons, favors, streamers, and dancing.

No other nationality pulled off quite so glorious a stunt as the Irish, but Hull House had far deeper connections on the humanist side with the English and especially the Russians. In Chicago in 1906 there was some vagueness about Russia. A reporter from Hearst's Examiner came to see Miss Addams on her return from Europe, and when she told him that she had been in Russia and had visited Tolstoy, petrified her by saying, "That's fine. Now, who is this Tolstoy?" The Hull House Theatre fresco showed Leo Tolstoy at the plough, to which Miss Addams may have taken the reporter.

Russian Jews and Jewesses came in great numbers to the classes at Hull House, and had special leanings toward literature. Whenever Miss Ad-

dams got a hand-made tragedy, "The Tragedy of Julious Caesar," by an aspiring girl to whom Caesar was, as to Shakespeare, an incentive to blank verse, I had the privilege of reading the manuscript. I was even allowed to read Miss Addams's current book in proof, and to make suggestions. The skill with which she extricated herself from suggestions has always amazed me. After a whole night combing one of her paragraphs into an order that to my weary brain seemed superlative, I'd find that bit by bit, with perfect uncombativeness and humility, Miss Addams would have restored all the snarls. She liked them, they said what she had to say, and she was right.

Henry B. Fuller was of the Little Room group that included Edith Wyatt, I. K. Friedman, Irving Pond, Allen Pond, and other friends of Hull-House; as a fine literary critic he groaned a little because Miss Addams selected such vast titles. For example, Democracy and Social Ethics, or Newer Ideals of Peace. They are, in truth, inclu-

An immigrant neighborhood near Hull-House, about 1905.

sive titles, but Miss Addams's is an inclusive genius. One cannot talk to her for five minutes, one cannot watch her face—swept so often by shadows as far hills are swept by a shadow when a cloud moves across them and yet which live in a light of their own—without realizing that hers is the great gift of synthesis, of bringing things to unity, by "patience, subtlety, and breadth."

It is Sheldon of Dartmouth who defines the type of philosophy that "gains by yielding; its spirit is not aggressive, but meek; it rules by love rather than fear. Its code is that of non-resistance." But he makes the mistake of seeing the outcome as conservative and compromising. No, in Miss Addams, as in Fridthjof Nansen,* there is no mush of compromise. Their humanity is warm, clear, and free, but it is anything but soft. To be hard on herself is, indeed, just as much an instinct with Miss Addams as with Nansen. There have been times at Hull House when the disgracefulness of Miss Addams's hat has led to protest, and when her united friends have forced her to reform. Her asceticism, however, has been part of that self-scrutiny which is alive to what is due—to others. Like Nansen, again, one feels in her presence that to be an "other" is in itself a title to her recognition. Like him, she has included Turks, Greeks, Soviet, Reactionary. And, like him, she has asked for no passports nor installed an Ellis Island.

I do not say that she has not had twinges of conservatism. We had a baptism once at Hull-House, a kind of vegetarian baptism. I think Jenkin Lloyd Jones officiated, looking like a benign old Druid, and the baby was the progeny of the James Weber Linns.† I do not know whether they handed that well-behaved baby a white flower, but I have a vague recollection of the kindly patriarch's tickling the soles of the baby's feet and adjuring her—it was a her?—to walk in the paths of seemliness and righteousness. The name of God was avoided with a prudishness that delighted me. A baptism without God was so chic that I closed

my eyes to the anomaly of there being a baptism at all. But I remember Miss Addams looking a little lost, a little mournful and thoughtful, after the ceremony. She confessed it was rather "queer," to her sense. . . .

You could picture Miss Addams as a person solely of good works. I have been talking to her when, in answer to a ring at the door, she would let in a "bum" who wanted a cup of coffee. And she herself would lead him into the Coffee House, and, with her curious air of earnest pleading politeness, would say, "Mary, *would* you give this man a cup of coffee?" To the hobo, and to Miss Addams, nothing seemed more natural, but these incidents of humanity never meant that Hull House interposed mere charity between itself and the rough-and-tumble world.

Hull House lived in a bracing, not a mawkish, atmosphere. It met the world vigorously. . . .

Hull-House Basketball

Chicago Chronicle

Sports played a large part in the Hull-House program. For a time it seemed that the settlement was more famous in the Chicago community for its basketball team than for anything else. One reason for this notoriety was probably that the team was composed entirely of bloomer-wearing females. [Chicago Chronicle, May 25, 1902.]

Basket ball is more than a fad and a craze with the girls of Chicago. It has come to stay and grows more in favor every year. It has more than the fun of the thing to commend it to its devotees, for it not only affords good exercise and plenty of excellent sport but, what is much more in the eyes of its followers, conduces to beauty of form and gracefulness of carriage. And then it is a game girls can play. Football is too rough; baseball is an impossibility, for women never will learn to throw straight enough to become proficient in the na-

*Nansen was a Norwegian arctic explorer, scientist, statesman, and humanitarian who became famous between 1893 and 1896 for his attempt to reach the North Pole by drifting in the ice across the polar basin.—Eds.

†Linn (1876–1939) was a nephew of Jane Addams. His wife was Mary Howland Linn (1877–1951), and their first child was Elizabeth Howland (b. 1906).—Eds.

The Hull-House woman's basketball team.

tional game. But basket ball is different; it is not so rough as football, yet affords as much exercise; is not so exacting a game as baseball and still gives keenness to the intellect and develops presence of mind and self-control.

Of the numerous teams in Chicago, including those of the University of Chicago and Northwestern, that of Hull House is considered invincible. The team has never been defeated since the second year of its organization. . . . The regular game is played with five on a side, but in some gymnasiums six, seven, or eight may form the opposing forces. Costumes worn generally by the contestants are easy and comfortable, affording free play to the body and limbs. Navy blue flannel seems to be the favorite color and material, and when a bevy of girls clad in this picturesque garb

is running, jumping, and scrambling over a long waxed floor or upon a springy sward, the poses exhibited and the movements attained are graceful, beautiful, and beneficial to mind and body.

A Labor Museum

Marion Foster Washburne

Never static, the Hull-House program shifted and changed as the needs of the neighborhood developed, or as the residents altered their concep-

Ellen Gates Starr and Jane Addams having tea in the Labor Museum.

tions of those needs. The Labor Museum, established in 1900, was one example of the changing program.

From the beginning Hull-House had emphasized the importance of art; but the early exhibits and lectures on art history did not completely satisfy the art hunger of its immigrant neighbors. As the settlement workers looked around them they saw a great array of artistic talent and craft skill which the immigrants brought with them to America. They also saw a generation of young men and women, often employed in meaningless uncreative jobs, who had no appreciation of their parents' skills at weaving or spinning or making pottery. So Hull-House leaders, influenced by Ruskin and Morris, established the Labor Museum where they hoped to preserve the art associated with handicraft skill that seemed to be on the way to extinction in an urban, industrial age. They hoped, by employing some of the older skilled artisans as teachers, to restore some of the immigrants' pride and confidence in their ability while at the same time giving the younger generation, who were rebelling against the cultural background of their parents, some appreciation of that heritage. Hull-House residents also thought that by showing the history of the textile industry. or the process by which wheat was made into bread in different cultures, by teaching the ancient skills of pottery-making or wood carving, in short, by *showing the relationship between raw materials and finished products, they could instill a lost pride of workmanship and a respect for things of beauty.*

They did not always succeed in their goals, but for many people the Labor Museum was the favorite part of the settlement. Following are the impressions of a visiting journalist who inspected the Museum in 1904. [Marion Foster Washburne, "A Labor Museum," Craftsman *(September 1904), 570–579.]*

Steadfast amidst the clash of industrial warfare, true to the English tongue and the English better genius in the midst of a modern Babel, clean and wholesome on the edge of the Ghetto, serene among sweat-shops and saloons, in the very center of toiling Chicago, stands Hull-House. Originally, a fine old family mansion in the environs of the young city, it is now surrounded and well nigh buried out of sight by a group—almost a clutter—of related buildings, springing out of it like wings and tail. In one of these—in the fan-tail—is the Labor Museum, which I am going to tell about.

We came upon it through a long tunnel-like passage leading under the main house. It was evening, and the windows lining one wall of the passage looked down into the engine room, filled with dynamos and the steam heating apparatus. Even this business-like place, we noticed, contained two colored lithographs in cheerful gilt frames. The passage-way, with its walls stained red, opened at the far end upon an alley unlit except by reflections from the house. Across it, shone the lighted windows of the labor museum, and there a half-dozen street urchins were looking in. Swearing, twisting, pushing each other, using each other's backs and shoulders to obtain vantage-ground, clad in nondescript clothes, rough in manner, and of many nations, they looked in longingly from the cold alley where they lived, upon these glorified workshops which promised pleasantness and peace.

They slunk out of sight when they saw us, and, crossing the alley, we opened the door upon the humming activity of the wood and metal shops; for a shop this room is in appearance, much more than a museum. The big beams overhead, the

swinging rack for lumber, the tool cases lining one wall, the heavy benches and work tables, the vises, the mallets, the enameling and glazing furnaces, the sheets of cut and bent copper, the big jar for the acid bath, with a heap of sawdust beside it on which to wipe stained fingers, the battered table with a blowpipe at one end, spitting blue and yellow flames: all make up an interior not lacking in a certain grim picturesqueness. The general tone is brown, with a little relief where the cases of made articles: jugs, jars, candlesticks and lanterns, vases and boxes of enameled metal shine against the brown walls. A few pictures persist high up on the shelf running around the room, as an earnest of good intention. Some day, pictures will play, undoubtedly, as important a part in the decoration of this room as they do in the other rooms presently to be described. Indeed, the painting classes of Hull-House have already planned to place a frieze here, illustrating the history of wood, from the primeval forest to its use in manufacture. The place is filled with clamorous noise: the beating of copper, the gasping of blow-pipes, the pounding of hammers, the rough rasp of saws, the swish of planes, and the calls of the workers. The teachers alone and the bewildered visitors are silent, moving from group to group; some directing and others trying to comprehend this manifold activity. A young man with a long, dark, Italian face, and dressed in a workman's blouse, seems to be in charge. He is young Colorossi, we learn, nephew of the famous head of the art school of the same name in Paris. At the top of his lungs he tries to explain to us what he is doing and still more what he hopes to do.

The work in the shops saves some boys from clerkships, he says. It is a small attempt to stem the current steadily setting toward the cities and the work of the middlemen, and away from the industries and constructive hand-work. Numbers of his pupils are errand-boys, office-boys, and delivery-boys, who are earning a precarious living and learning very little which can permanently benefit them. They come here Saturday evenings and work; they learn to design a little; they gain some idea of a genuine beauty not based upon display; and they acquire a respect for good workmanship and good workmen. One of them recently gave up his place as office-boy, became apprenticed to a skilled metal worker, and is now in a fair way to master a paying and progressive trade. He and his companions at the Museum sell the product of their labor, and it is for this purpose that it is on exhibition in the cases. A small percentage of the selling price is returned to the House, although it is not as yet nearly enough to pay for the cost of the material and the use of the machinery. The sale of the work is encouraged more to hold the interest of the boys and to stimulate them to better craftsmanship than for any other reason.

When we first saw them, these boys were making sleds to be ready for the earliest snow-fall. It was evident from the way they handled the tools that they were new workers; nevertheless the sleds, made of rather heavy lumber, looked serviceable and not at all amateurish.

The direct object of such training may not be obvious to the casual observer, for it is plain that the boys have not time in these few hours of work a week to master even the beginnings of good carpentry. What does take place is what the visitor cannot see, although he may afterwards experience it himself. It is a change of mental attitude. The Museum stands for just this—for an attempt to change the common desire to make money into a desire to make useful things and to make them well. Moreover, because it is not immediately calculable, one must not underrate the practical advantage to the world at large of boys trained even to a slight understanding of mechanical possibilities. We may well remember that in the earliest steam engines a boy had to be at hand to open the steam valve at each stroke of the piston, and that it was one of them who, becoming tired of this monotonous task and wishing to run away to play, finally managed to connect the valve with the rest of the machinery. Who could have foretold what this touch of mechanical genius was to mean to the world?

But still, we do not see what it is that makes this a Museum. What is it more than a series of manual training shops? True, the groups of onlookers mark a characteristic difference. It is true also that ladies and gentlemen work here side by side with these neighborhood boys; but this may mean only that the manual training school has here been extended to embrace pupils of all ages and of all stages of ignorance—conventional, polite ignorance, as well as slum ignorance. And indeed, we shall find little in this room to declare to us the general object of the museum, which is to throw the light of history and of art upon modern industries. The historical object it has in common with all museums; the artistic object it possesses in common with all arts and crafts workshops; but the combination of the two ideals, and the concrete expression of them in the midst of a foreign population largely wrenched away from its hereditary occupations, is peculiar to Hull-House. As the curator, Miss Luther,* explains, "The word museum was purposely used in preference to the word school, both because the latter is distasteful to grown-up people from its association with childish tasks, and because the word museum still retains some fascination of the show. It may be easily observed that the spot which attracts most people at any exhibition, or fair, is the one where something is being done. So trivial a thing as a girl cleaning gloves, or a man polishing metal, will almost inevitably attract a crowd, who look on with absorbed interest. It was believed that the actual carrying forward of industrial processes, and the fact that the explanation of each process, or period, is complete in itself, would tend to make the teaching dramatic, and to overcome in a measure the disadvantage of irregular attendance. It was further believed, although perhaps it is difficult to demonstrate, that when the materials of daily life and contact remind the student of the subject of his lesson and its connections, it would hold his interest and feed his thought as abstract and unconnected study utterly fails to do. A constant effort, therefore, was made to keep the museum a labor museum in contradistinction to a commercial museum." . . .

. . . Here in the alcove of the wood and metal working rooms is a big vat of clay, a couple of potter's wheels, and a case of admirably modeled, glazed, and decorated pottery. Standing at the table is a clean old German kneading clay, his squat, bowed legs far apart, his body leaning forward, his long and powerful arms beating upon the clay like piston rods. He rolls it into a long cylinder and breaks it off with exactitude into a half dozen little lumps. As he carries it across the room, walking with a side-wise straddle, one sees that he is bent and twisted by his trade, conformed to his wheel.

*Jessie Luther (b. 1860), first curator of the Harbor Museum.—Eds.

Upon this he slaps his clay, and thrusting out a short leg, sets it whirling. Above the rough lump he folds his hands, and, in a minute, from that prayerful seclusion, the clay emerges rounded, smoothed, and slightly hollowed. His hands open, his thumbs work in; one almost sees him think through his skillful thumbs and forefingers: the other fingers lie close together and he moves the four as one. Like some mystery of organic nature, the clay rises, bends, becomes a vase. "Look at that thing grow!" an excited boy exclaims, forgetting the crowd of onlookers. "See it, see it!" The old potter rises, lifts the vase in his mitten-like hands and, bending, straddling sideways, his face unmoved, carries it tenderly to its place. . . .

The old potter has clapped another lump of clay upon the wheel, but we pass him, and go into the next little room, the printing-shop. There is not so very much to be seen here beyond the hand-press, the cases of type for hand setting, the examples upon the wall of old-fashioned block printing, the illuminated manuscripts, and the framed pages from the beautiful Kelmscott Chaucer. A good copy of John W. Alexander's frieze from the Congressional Library, representing the evolution of the book, hangs upon one wall, and below it is a series of four prints, Nordfeldt's* Wave, showing the stages through which a colored wood-cut must pass in order to reach completion.

This rooms brings to us no such feeling of surprise as do the others; perhaps because the book is, in fact, a fairly socialized instrument of progress. We take our public libraries for granted, expect to find books upon every cottage table, and our legislators even go so far as to buy them wholesale for the school-children of the State: a preposterous procedure, but one which excited little surprise. . . .

We must hurry through to the cooking-room. It is rather empty, just now, for no work is going on, but the room itself is interesting. In one corner is a big brick fireplace with old-fashioned and-irons and crane. From this latter hangs a copper tea-kettle, and below it is set an old-fashioned copper fire-pot. Brass porringers and kettles stand on the shelf above. A low window-seat to the right,

and a big table before it, covered with a blue and white homespun cloth, make one wish that one could go back at once to the old colonial days, and make apple dowdy and mulled cider in this picture-booky place. A dear little painted dresser stands next the window-seat, set out with old blue and white china; but an abrupt modern note is struck by the case of laboratory samples which hangs beside it. Here are bottles hermetically sealed, showing the amount of water in a pound of potatoes, the fat in a pound of butter, the proteid in cheese, the starch in wheat, the cellulose in beans, and the mineral matter in eggs.

In danger of regarding our stomachs with an uncomfortable degree of awe, we turn with relief to the series of pictures which show the planting, reaping, and marketing of food-stuffs, and rejoice in the colored panel in which a Dutch woman is taking butter and milk to market in a row-boat, past a big wind-mill with many other wind-mills in the distance, and all in a generous, yellow glow. Here is a fine old carved sideboard with more blue and white china on it—modern blue and white, alas! and not half so pretty as the old kind. And here, sheltered from dust, behind glass, are sheaves of corn, wheat, sugar-cane, oats, all manner of grains; farther on, we see stones used by the Indians for grinding corn, and above them a picture, showing a young squaw using them. Down through the middle of the room stretch long, ugly, but useful, modern demonstration tables with their gas-jets for cooking, their central racks for utensils, and behind them rows of yellow bowls and kitchen crockery. We sigh as we look and consider how little we know even of these foods upon which we live. "We civilized men and women," complains Kropotkin—and suddenly his complaint seems not at all unreasonable—"know everything, we have settled opinions upon everything, we take an interest in everything. We only know nothing about whence the bread comes which we eat, even though we pretend to know something about that subject as well; we do not know how it is grown, what pains it costs to those who grow it, what is being done to reduce their pains, what sort of feeders of our grand selves these men are. . . . We are more ignorant than savages in this respect, and we prevent our children from obtaining this sort of knowledge, even those of our children who would prefer it to the

---

*Bror Julius Olsson Nordfeldt (1878–1955) came to America from Sweden in 1891, was a painter, etcher, and wood engraver, and for a time, a resident of Hull-House.—Eds.

heaps of useless stuff with which they are crammed at school.''

But the next room, whirring with industry, induces us to yet another state of humility. It is a big room facing north, filled with a rich exhibit of textiles, largely loaned from the Field Columbian Museum. Great looms fill much of its floor space: a Jacquard loom with a piece of ingrain carpet on it; electric and fly-shuttle looms; a colonial loom on which homespun cloth is this moment being made. It is spun and woven here and sold at prices varying at from two to five dollars the yard. But, even at this price, so heavy is the cost of the raw material, of the labor, and of the cleaning and dyeing, that the industry is not commercially successful. Perhaps it might be made so, but this is not the concern of the Museum. It sells things, but its motive for being is not the desire to sell profitably. Nevertheless, there is a case full of work done here and for sale to the public. It contains hand-weaves of all sorts: rugs, towels, laces, embroideries, open-work, and baskets. The curator assures us that already the demand for pottery, metal work, wood-work, and textiles far exceeds the capacity of the various workers to fill the orders.

Above this show-case hangs a large engraving of Millet's "Spinner," which illustrates, among other things, the earliest method of spinning in France. There is a smaller picture of another "Spinner," in the painter's later and better manner, and a group of other pictures, representing spinning and weaving in all stages of development, under all skies, and with the workers costumed after all manner of national fashions. Mrs. Sweeney, a neighborhood woman, employed in keeping the museum clean, rolls her bare arms in her little red shoulder shawl and examines the pictures with me.

"This is an Irish lady spinnin', annyhow," she explains, pointing with a soaked forefinger. "Shure, I'd know her, big or little, in all the worrld."

Perhaps she overlooks a little the Kentucky spinners, whose picture hangs next, and disregards their blue and white quilt, which makes a background for the pictures; but, at least, she has seen the work of her own people under a new aspect: that is, with some historical perspective.

Here is a large wall case containing Navajo and Hindu handlooms: the East and the West cheek by jowl. A stocking loom stands next and bits of rare brocade and embroidery cover all available wall spaces. There are embroideries in gold and silk from Germany of the seventeenth century, beautiful Norwegian embroideries and fringes, Nuremberg and Italian embroideries, all manner of modern weaves, Mexican serapes, Venetian velvets from the fifteenth century, resplendent in gold, red, green, and yellow, upon a cloth-of-gold background, and even a framed fragment of mummy-wrapping. On a shelf, out of danger of collision, is an old Syrian spinning wheel. A woman of the neighborhood, finding that the House would appreciate such a wheel, sent to Syria for it. It was her grandmother's and is two hundred years old. The duties and cost of transportation amounted to forty-five dollars. . . .

. . . Miss Addams . . . hopes sometime to have the living workers in the Museum dressed in their national and historic costume, as they go about their work. This Italian woman, with big

Spinning in the Labor Museum.

gold ear-rings swinging against her dark and scrawny neck, patiently twirling the hand spindle hanging at her side, and skilfully drawing out the woolen thread with her long fingers, unconsciously carries out the idea. But the sweet-faced Irish woman near her, rocking the treadle of her spinning-wheel, with an invisible foot beneath a decent black skirt, her white Irish hands deftly twisting the thread, is altogether too respectable and modern to look her part. Her father was a famous broad-linen weaver, and she herself knows the process of linen-making from the breaking of the ground in order to sow the flax-seed, through the reaping, binding, spinning, weaving, and even dyeing, to the finished fabric. "But, shure, dear," she exclaims, "it is not your chemical dyeing at all, but the home-dyeing, that I know. We made the dyes ourselves from log-wood, and barks, and stuff we took out of the bogs of old Ireland. But one thing I will say for it: it never faded as your high-toned dyes do."

Presently she tells her story. "Yes, we all spun and wove in the old country. It is not many of them that keeps it up now, except perhaps an old granny in a tucked-away corner that does it for the love of it; but when I was young, we dressed in flannel and linen from the skin out, and grew it all and made it all ourselves."

"And how did you happen to come here?" I asked.

Her serene face darkens. "Never will I forgive them that misled us to it!" she exclaims. "There in the old country we had our comforts, our own bit of land, my man making a dollar and a quarter the day, Irish money; a blissid union of ten children and never a shoe wanting to the foot of one of them. O, wirra the day that we left!—I landed here with a baby in my arms—crippled—"

"Crippled? how?" I cried.

She passed the question. "Yes, crippled. She is a hump-back, dear, eleven by now, and none higher than my waist. The next to the baby had the spinal meningeetis soon after we landed and his reason fled; he has no mind since. The other eight were clinging to my skirts."

"And your husband? Is he dead?"

"No, worse luck! It is many a time I've wished he was. It is many a night I wish it now. He took to the strong drink."

"And what did you do?"

"I begged on the streets, dear. Oh, I can smile and laugh with the best when I am at work here, but there's something else in my heart." She turned to a young lady pupil, whom she was teaching to spin, unreeled the broken thread, mended it, and set it right with a skilful touch or two. "No, I ain't discouraged," she told the young lady, in her soft, smooth voice, "for discouraging won't do for a pupil. You'll spin, dear, but it'll take a deal o' practice." A minute more and she and Mrs. Sweeney are speaking the Gaelic together, and laughing like two children. She dances a quiet shuffle under her decent skirts. "And can I dance?" she asks. "It is a good old Irish breakdown dancer I was in my young days. You should see me do a reel and a jig." Her hidden feet nimbly shuffle and whisper on the wooden floor; her clean-washed eyes dance behind her spectacles. But in a moment she sits at her wheel again, quietly twirling and twisting the linen thread, working for the sodden husband at home, the little crippled girl who came by her injury so mysteriously, and the boy with his mind gone.

We feel that this living woman—this worker and victim and survivor—is the most precious thing that the Museum has shown us. Indeed, we suspect the founders of deliberate intention in placing her there, where she is not measured by petty, momentary standards, but by the laws which underlie human evolution. We catch a glimpse of the importance of her function in a historic industrial order; and while our minds leap to the new truth, our hearts thrill with a new sympathy.

Upstairs, in the auditorium of the House, these thoughts become more definite and these emotions strengthen to resolution; for there, crowded between eager listeners, who fill not only the three hundred fifty seats, but the stairway and the entire stage back of the speaker, we listen to one of a series of lectures on economic problems, a lecture which makes clear to us the connection between past and present. We get a broad view of labor conditions and their effect upon the mass of workers. Here is a significant list of the subjects that we find on the program: "Slave labor in the Roman Empire"; "From slavery to serfdom"; "The Guilds of the Middle Ages"; "Conditions of labor under the domestic system and under the factory"; "History of trades unions"; "Labor in competitive industries and in monopolistic ones.'' We listen also to a program of labor songs, rendered by the pupils of the Hull-House Music School, who sing to us an old Irish weaving song, a spinning song by Rheinberger, and finally a song composed for this purpose by Eleanor Smith.* The words were written by a sweat-shop worker, Morris Rosenfeld,† and the whole composition effects that difficult result: the interpretation by art of an existent condition. We are not surprised to learn that the Consumers' Leagues and other similar associations have urged the Music School to sing it before them, and have found it, so they say: ''Not only interpretative of an experience not remote from their own, but stirring and powerful in its moral appeal.''

*Eleanor Smith (1858–1936?) was the founder and, until her retirement in 1936, the head of the Hull-House Music School. ''The Sweat-Shop,'' was published in *Hull House Songs* by Eleanor Smith, [1915].—Eds.

†Morris Rosenfeld (1862–1923), a Russian poet born in Poland, was a tailor in New York city, 1866–1900.—Eds.

Stirred we are ourselves, as we squeeze slowly down the iron-stairs, elbowed by Hebrew, Greek, Finn, and Scot, feel the rush of the outside air upon our faces, and are thrust forth into the riotous city night. The crowded cable-cars clang their insistent way through the obstructing mass of vehicles; the dingy throng ebbs in and out of saloons and pawnshops; a 10–20–30 theatre hangs a glittering reminder of ''The Span of Life'' down the broken vista of the street, and we turn for a last look through the broad windows of the Museum. We, too, wistful children of a half-civilized state, look back through these windows into a warmed and lighted world of happy industry; and even while we shove and push for the best places, wish in our hearts that we were working within. The light and heat, even the joy of doing good work under right conditions, may be artificial and evanescent, but without, around us, all is struggle and clamor.

Children at Hull-House camps stayed at least one week. Camp Good Will, Evanston, Illinois, 1906.

Summer camps, called Country Club outings, were an important part of the Hull-House program from the 1890s. Camp Good Will, located in Evanston, Illinois, had a kitchen, dining hall, and sleeping quarters.

Hull-House Bookbindery

Ellen Gates Starr

Ellen Starr (1859–1940), co-founder of Hull-House, was the leading art expert at the settlement. She taught courses in art history and was largely responsible for the exhibits of watercolors, oils, etchings, and prints which were a part of the Hull-House program during the early years. Gradually she not only saw the anachronism of her projects, but also deplored the fact that she was only studying art secondhand. She was depressed by the process of industrialism which increasingly was separating those who worked with their minds from those who worked with their hands. It was important, she felt, for the workingman to have pride in his work, but it was also important for those who worked with their minds to do something artistic and skillful with their hands. She went to England, where she studied to become a bookbinder, and on her return, in 1899, she opened a bookbindery at the settlement. Years later, however, Miss Starr admitted the irony of her project. "If I had thought it through," she said, "I would have realized that I would be using my hands to create books that only the rich could buy."

The following from The Commons, *the monthly publication of Graham Taylor's settlement Chicago Commons, originally appeared as "A Note of Explanation" accompanying the May 1900 issue of the* Hull-House Bulletin. *The Bulletin, published monthly except during the summer and beginning in January 1896, was issued by Hull-House to advertise its activities to neighbors and the public, to promote cooperation in the efforts of various settlement clubs and societies, and to stimulate interest in public affairs. By 1902 the publication had become semiannual, and in 1906 the* Bulletin *became the* Hull-House Year Book, *an annual report of settlement activities and programs. [Ellen Gates Starr, "Hull-House Bookbindery,"* The Commons *(June 1900), 5–6.]*

People wonder, I suppose, why a resident of Hull House chose to bind books and what connection it has with the work or life of the House. I shall try to make this personal explanation as simply as possible.

Before I came to Hull House to live, and for some time afterward, I used to have classes and give lectures on the history of art. I partly earned my living in this way and partly did it for the pleasure of it. I used to enjoy interpreting to others, as far as I was able, the beautiful things which have been made in the past, and to think it did good. But after a time, living amidst a great deal that is ugly and ill-made in the present, and feeling how many people are forced to do so, even more than I, it began to seem to me not enough to talk about and explain beautiful and well-made things which have been done long ago. I began to feel that instead of talking, it would be a great deal better to make something myself, ever so little, thoroughly well, and beautiful of its kind. The influence of anything I could make would, to be sure, be very small, as I had no special talent for anything. But then, suppose that all the people who had no genius, in the ages when the most beautiful buildings, carving, books, silver and goldsmith's work, etc., was done, had fallen to talking about the work of past ages, and refused to do any work themselves, how much less we should have now to talk about or to enjoy.

Another thing I used to reflect upon was this: All modern life has been tending to separate the work of the mind and the work of the hands. One set of people work with their heads but produce nothing whatever with their hands. Another vast body work with their hands at very mechanical and uninteresting work, which does not in any way engage or develop the mind in its higher faculties. Both sets of people are living partial lives, not using all the powers God gave us, who certainly did not make half humanity with hands alone, and the other with only minds. To account for this tendency would require much space and much cleverness—more than I have. Suffice it to say that I believe it to be a wrong one, and that I do not think it necessary to submit to it. So then it became necessary for me, if I were to act as I believed, to learn to make something worth making, and to do it as thoroughly well as I was able. I thought of various things, and selected books, being interested in them from several points of view. I went to the man who, in my judgment, does the most beautiful bookbinding in the world at this time, was so fortunate as to be received as his pupil, and worked under him* for fifteen months, six hours or more every day, excepting a half holiday on Saturday. It is no light matter to learn a craft thoroughly, and if it is not thoroughly learned it does more harm than good. I promised my master that I would not teach or sell my work until he thought I might rightly do so. This was only sensible, since I had undertaken to set an example of good workmanship, in so far as I was able, and to produce something of a kind worth making.

I had thought, when I formed the intention of learning a craft, that I should teach it here at Hull-House on the basis of the extension classes and the manual training. I have not been able to do this for several reasons: the implements and material are expensive; the time required to accomplish anything is too long for those who only give an evening or two or three evenings a week, and the amount of personal attention required by beginners precludes the possibility of anything but a small class. I still hope to be able to instruct, thoroughly, a few who care to undertake the work in earnest, if there be any such, and who can arrange to give the necessary time. Meanwhile I earn my living, not by talking about other people's work— that I still do for pleasure—but by binding and ornamenting a few books as well as I can do it, and by teaching three private pupils as well as I can teach them. I cannot take a pupil for less than a year, nor more than three pupils at a time, tho more would like to learn. Indeed, the number of people who ask to be instructed shows that there is much thought of this question of learning to work with the hands, and seems to me a very good sign. It takes me a long time, sometimes two or three weeks, to bind a book as I have been taught to do it. Naturally, I only bind books which seem to me worthy to last. They are necessarily very expensive, and the people who most deserve to have choice books, choicely bound, cannot always or usually have them. That is to be regretted, but it is not the main question in doing any piece of work. The chief question is whether the piece of work itself is worth doing. Nobody cares very much for whom a guildsman of the middle ages did a bit of carving or smith's work, or for whom one of the Venetian binders bound a book. One sees these things in a museum and learns from each the lesson of its perfection in its degree and after its kind.

Please do not think that this means that I be-

HULL-HOUSE BULLETIN

PUBLISHED AT 335 SOUTH HALSTED STREET. TELEPHONE MONROE 70.

VOL. IV   AUTUMN, 1900   No. III

OBJECT OF HULL-HOUSE (as stated in its Charter): To provide a center for a higher civic and social life; to institute and maintain educational and philanthropic enterprises, and to investigate and improve the conditions in the industrial districts of Chicago.

PUBLIC ENTERTAINMENTS.

SUNDAY AFTERNOON CONCERTS--HULL-HOUSE AUDITORIUM 4.30 P. M.

November 18th—Singing and piano; in charge of Miss Large.

November 25th—Singing and piano; in charge of Miss Cameron.

December 2d—Singing, violin and piano.

December 9th—In charge of Miss Faulkner, who expects several of the "woodwind" players of the Chicago Orchestra. This woodwind music is very beautiful as well as interesting.

PUBLIC LECTURES.

Free lectures on the History of the World at the Hull-House Lecture Hall Monday evenings at 8 o'clock.

   I. THEORIES OF CREATION.

(a) Ancient............Nov. 5, Mr. Twose
(b) Modern.............Nov. 12, Mr. Twose

  II. ORIGIN OF THE EARTH AS DEMONSTRATED BY ASTRONOMY.

(a) The Universe........Nov. 19, Mr. Lemoyne
(b) Planets, Moon, Sun..Nov. 26, Mr. Lemoyne
(c) The Earth ....Dec. 3, Mr. Lemoyne

  III. LIFE UPON THE EARTH.

(a) Beginning of Plant and Animal
   Life.............Dec. 10, Mr. Yeomans
(b) Prehistoric Ages ....Dec. 17, Mr. Yeomans
(c) Appearance of Man..Jan. 7, Mr. Yeomans

  IV. AGE OF MAN.

(a) Waves of Immigration.Jan. 14 — Prof.
(b) Race Differences ......Jan. 14 — Frederick
(c) Development of Civilization ....Jan. 14 — Starr

TUESDAY EVENING LECTURE COURSE.

Under the management of The Federation of Social Justice, Hull-House Lecture Hall, 8 p. m.

LABOR MUSEUM IN OPERATION.

The Textile Department of the Labor Museum is open Saturday evenings at 8 p. m. on the second floor of the Butler Building. Actual weaving and spinning on exhibition.

ENTERTAINMENTS IN THE AUDITORIUM.

October 7th—Reception and Address. Mr. Joseph Jefferson.

October 25.—**Drexel Club** dance.

October 29th.—**Concert,** Woman's Club.

October 30th.—**Entertainment** and dance, Longfellow Club, Maxwell StreetSettlement.

November 1st.—**Neighborhood Party,** given by Hull-House Woman's Club. Shadow Plays, Recitations, Refreshments, Dancing.

November 2d.—**Men's Club** reception to lady friends.

November 18th—**Entertainment** for Italians by two Italian journalists, Sigs. Reiter and Galvani, consisting of songs, recitations and acrobatic feats. Admission 25 cents.

November 23d—**Lecture** before the Arts and Crafts Society by Mr. C. R. Ashbee, of Essex House, London.

November 24th.—**Lecture** under auspices of Woman's Club.

November 26th.—**Woman's Club** entertainment.

November 28th.—**Men's Club** reception.

December 6th.—**Drexel Club** play. Admission 15 cents. Box and Cox and "A Proposal Under Difficulties."

December 7th.—**Irving Club** play.

December 10th—**"A Mountain Pink."** A five-act romantic drama given by the Hull-House Dramatic Association, with Mrs. Fred Pelham (Laura Dainty) in her original character of Sincerity Weeks. Admission 25 cents. (For the benefit of the Hull-House organ fund.)

December 12th — **"A Mountain Pink."** Admission 25 cents.

December 13th.— **"A Mountain Pink."** Admission 25 cents.

December 20th.—**Entertainment** by Herzel Literary Society.

December 27th.—**Ladies' Night,** Men's Club.

December 28th.—**Play** by Goodrich Alumni, "Three Hats."

---

*T. J. Cobden-Sanderson, of the Doves Bindery in London.—Eds.

lieve my modest little books will be put into museums for future ages to wonder at. It only means that whatever good any handiwork of today can do must be done by showing forth the same pleasure in the well-doing of it which makes these things give pleasure to us now.

The Art and Craft of the Machine

Frank Lloyd Wright

Frank Lloyd Wright (1869–1959), the most famous and influential American architect of the twentieth century, graduated from the University of Wisconsin and moved to Chicago in 1889, the same year Hull-House was founded. He worked for the architectural firm of Adler and Sullivan and was strongly influenced by the work of Louis Sullivan. In 1894 he established his own architectural firm in Oak Park, Illinois, and began to build low-slung, rambling "prairie houses," designed to fit into the landscape and to make use of native stones and woods. Wright rebelled against the archaic eclecticism of his day, which built in "Colonial," "Renaissance," or "Italian Villa" style with no thought for the building material or the habits of the occupants.

Wright became acquainted with Hull-House soon after his arrival in Chicago, for his mother, Mrs. Russell Wright, was an early volunteer worker there and for a time took care of Florence Kelley's three children. Wright's uncle, Jenkin Lloyd Jones, a liberal Unitarian minister, was also a frequent visitor at Hull-House and a loyal ally of Jane Addams in her many reform campaigns. Wright himself was an interested observer of, though rarely a participant in, the settlement's activities. He must have been sympathetic to much of what he saw at Hull-House, for he was sensitive and humane and vitally concerned with perserving human values in the midst of a rapidly growing city. But he was critical of some of Hull-House's attempts to preserve handicrafts. On October 31, 1897, Wright addressed a group gathered at the

settlement to found the Chicago Society of Arts and Crafts. His topic, as reported in the Hull-House Bulletin, *November 1897, was "The Use of Machinery."*

The occasion for this version of the address, given at Hull-House, March 6, 1901, was a meeting of the Chicago Society of Arts and Crafts. Wright took the opportunity to attack most of the architecture in Chicago—and he might have included Hull-House, for the settlement, at least from some angles, had the look of an ancient English manor house. But the main thrust of Wright's address, which has become something of a classic, was to embrace the machine and modern technology, and to denounce the many followers of Ruskin and Morris who wanted to preserve human values by recapturing and preserving past art and handicraft. Wright, who has sometimes been called a romantic, and who certainly appreciated pastoral beauty and good workmanship, here calls for the acceptance of the machine and the twentieth century. He gave different versions of this address on a number of occasions through the years. This is the first known published version. [Frank Lloyd Wright, "The Art and Craft of the Machine," Cat-alogue of the Fourteenth Annual Exhibition of the Chicago Architectural Club, The Art Institute, *March 28 to April 15, 1901 (Chicago: The Chicago Architectural Club, 1901).]*

As we work along our various ways, there takes shape within us, in some sort, an ideal—something we are to become—some work to be done. This, I think, is denied to very few, and we begin really to live only when the thrill of this ideality moves us in what we will to accomplish. In the years which have been devoted in my own life to working out in stubborn materials a feeling for the beautiful, in the vortex of distorted complex conditions, a hope has grown stronger with the experience of each year, amounting now to a gradually deepening conviction that in the Machine lies the only future of art and craft—as I believe, a glorious future; that the Machine is, in fact, the metamorphosis of ancient art and craft; that we are at last face to face with the machine—the modern Sphinx—whose riddle the artist must solve if he would that art live—for his nature holds the key.

For one, I promise "whatever gods may be" to lend such energy and purpose as I may possess to help make that meaning plain; to return again and again to the task whenever and wherever need be; for this plain duty is thus relentlessly marked out for the artist in this, the Machine Age, although there is involved an adjustment to cherished gods, perplexing and painful in the extreme; the fire of many long-honored ideals shall go down to ashes to reappear, phoenix like, with new purposes.

The great ethics of the Machine are as yet, in the main, beyond the ken of the artist or student of sociology; but the artist mind may now approach the nature of this thing from experience, which has become the commonplace of his field, to suggest, in time, I hope, to prove, that the machine is capable of carrying to fruition high ideals in art—higher than the world has yet seen!

Disciples of William Morris cling to an opposite view. Yet William Morris himself deeply sensed the danger to art of the transforming force whose sign and symbol is the machine, and though of the new art we eagerly seek he sometimes despaired, he quickly renewed his hope.

He plainly foresaw that a blank in the fine arts would follow the inevitable abuse of new-found power, and threw himself body and soul into the work of bridging it over by bringing into our lives afresh the beauty of art as she had been, that the new art to come might not have dropped too many stitches nor have unraveled what would still be useful to her.

That he had abundant faith in the new art his every essay will testify.

That he miscalculated the machine does not matter. He did sublime work for it when he pleaded so well for the process of elimination its abuse had made necessary; when he fought the innate vulgarity of theocratic impulse in art as opposed to democratic; and when he preached the gospel of simplicity.

All artists love and honor William Morris.

He did the best in his time for art and will live in history as the great socialist, together with Ruskin, the great moralist: a significant fact worth thinking about, that the two great reformers of modern times professed the artist.

The machine these reformers protested, because the sort of luxury which is born of greed had usurped it and made of it a terrible engine of enslavement, deluging the civilized world with a murderous ubiquity, which plainly enough was the damnation of their art and craft.

It had not then advanced to the point which now so plainly indicates that it will surely and swiftly, by its own momentum, undo the mischief it has made, and the usurping vulgarians as well.

Nor was it so grown as to become apparent to William Morris, the grand democrat, that the machine was the great forerunner of democracy.

The ground plan of this thing is now grown to the point where the artist must take it up no longer as a protest: genius must progressively dominate the work of the contrivance it has created; to lend a useful hand in building afresh the "Fairness of the Earth."

That the Machine has dealt Art in the grand old sense a death-blow, none will deny.

The evidence is too substantial.

Art in the grand old sense—meaning Art in the sense of structural tradition, whose craft is fashioned upon the handicraft ideal, ancient or modern; an art wherein this form and that form as structural parts were laboriously joined in such a way as to beautifully emphasize the manner of the joining: the million and one ways of beautifully satisfying bare structural necessities, which have come down to us chiefly through the books as "Art."

For the purpose of suggesting hastily and therefore crudely wherein the machine has sapped the vitality of this art, let us assume Architecture in the old sense as a fitting representative of Traditional-art, and Printing as a fitting representation of the Machine.

What printing—the machine—has done for architecture—the fine art—will have been done in measure of time for all art immediately fashioned upon the early handicraft ideal.

With a masterful hand Victor Hugo, a noble lover and a great student of architecture, traces her fall in "Notre Dame."

The prophecy of Frollo, that "The book will kill the edifice," I remember was to me as a boy one of the grandest sad things of the world.

After seeking the origin and tracing the growth of architecture in superb fashion, showing how in the middle ages all the intellectual forces of the people converged to one point—architecture—he shows how, in the life of that time, whoever was born poet became an architect. All other arts simply obeyed and placed themselves under the discipline of architecture. They were the workmen of the great work. The architect, the poet, the master, summed up in his person the sculpture that carved his facades, painting which illuminated his walls and windows, music which set his bells to pealing and breathed into his organs—there was nothing which was not forced in order to make something of itself in that time, to come and frame itself in the edifice.

Thus down to the time of Gutenberg architecture is the principal writing—the universal writing of humanity.

In the great granite books begun by the Orient, continued by Greek and Roman antiquity, the middle ages wrote the last page.

So to enunciate here only summarily a process, it would require volumes to develop; down to the fifteenth century the chief register or humanity is architecture.

In the fifteenth century everything changes.

Human though discovers a mode of perpetuating itself, not only more resisting than architecture, but still more simple and easy.

Architecture is dethroned.

Gutenberg's letters of lead are about to supersede Orpheus' letters of stone.

The book is about to kill the edifice.

The invention of printing was the greatest event in history.

It was the first great machine, after the great city.

It is human thought stripping off one form and donning another.

Printed, thought is more imperishable than ever—it is volatile, indestructible.

As architecture it was solid; it is now alive; it passes from duration in point of time to immortality. . . .

So the organic process, of which the majestic decline of Architecture is only one case in point, has steadily gone on down to the present time, and still goes on, weakening the hold of the artist upon the people, drawing off from his rank poets and scientists until architecture is but a little, poor knowledge of archeology, and the average of art is reduced to the gasping poverty of imitative realism; until the whole letter of Tradition, the vast fabric of precedent, in the flesh, which has increasingly confused the art ideal while the machine has been growing to power, is a beautiful corpse from which the spirit has flown. The spirit that has flown is the spirit of the new art, but has failed the modern artist, for he has lost it for hundreds of years in his lust for the *letter,* the beautiful body of art made too available by the machine.

So the artist craft wanes.

Craft that will not see that human thought is stripping off one form and donning another, and artists are everywhere, whether catering to the leisure class of old England or ground beneath the heel of commercial abuse here in the great West, the unwilling symptoms of the inevitable, organic nature of the machine, they combat, the hell-smoke of the factories they scorn to understand.

And, invincible, triumphant, the machine goes on, gathering force and knitting the material necessities of mankind ever closer into a universal automatic fabric; the engine, the motor, and the battle-ship, the works of art of the century!

The Machine is Intellect mastering the drudgery of earth that the plastic art may live; that the margin of leisure and strength by which man's life upon the earth can be made beautiful, may immeasurably widen; its function ultimately to emancipate human expression!

It is a universal educator, surely raising the level of human intelligence, so carrying within itself the power to destroy, by its own momentum, the greed which in Morris' time and still in our own time turns it to a deadly engine of enslavement. The only comfort left the poor artist, sidetracked as he is, seemingly is a mean one; the thought that the very selfishness which man's early art idealized, now reduced to its lowest terms, is swiftly and surely destroying itself through the medium of the Machine.

The artist's present plight is a sad one, but may he truthfully say that society is less well off because Architecture, or even Art, as it was, is dead, and printing, or the Machine, lives? Every age has done its work, produced its art with the best tools or contrivances it knew, the tools most successful in saving the most precious thing in the world—human effort. Greece used the chattel slave as the essential tool of its art and civilization. This tool we have discarded, and we would refuse the return of Greek art upon the terms of its restoration, because we insist now upon a basis of Democracy.

Is it not more likely that the medium of artistic expression itself has broadened and changed until a new definition and new direction must be given the art activity of the future, and that the Machine has finally made for the artist, whether he will yet own it or not, a splendid distinction between the Art of old and the Art to come? A distinction made by the tool which frees human labor, lengthens and broadens the life of the simplest man, thereby the basis of the Democracy upon which we insist. . . .

The modern tall office building problem is one representative problem of the machine. The only rational solutions it has received in the world may be counted upon the fingers of one hand. The fact that a great portion of our ''architects'' and ''artists'' are shocked by them to the point of offense is as valid an objection as that of a child refusing wholesome food because his stomach becomes dyspeptic from over-much unwholesome pastry—albeit he be the cook himself.

We may object to the mannerism of these buildings, but we can take no exception to their manner nor hide from their evident truth.

The steel frame has been recognized as a legitimate basis for a simple, sincere clothing of plastic material that idealizes its purpose without structural pretense.

This principle has at last been recognized in architecture, and though the masters refuse to accept it as architecture at all, it is a glimmer in a darkened field—the first sane word that has been said in Art for the Machine.

The Art of old idealized a Structural Necessity—now rendered obsolete and unnatural by the Machine—and accomplished it through man's joy in the labor of his hands.

The new will weave for the necessities of mankind, which his Machine will have mastered, a robe of ideality no less truthful, but more poetical, with a rational freedom made possible by the machine, beside which the art of old will be as the sweet, plaintive wail of the pipe to the outpouring of full orchestra.

It will clothe Necessity with the living flesh of virile imagination, as the living flesh lends living grace to the hard and bony human skeleton.

The new will pass from the possession of kings and classes to the every-day lives of all—from duration in point of time to immortality. . . .

William Morris pleaded well for simplicity as the basis of all true art. Let us understand the significance to art of that word—SIMPLICITY—for it is vital to the Art of the Machine.

We may find, in place of the genuine thing we have striven for, an affectation of the naïve, which we should detest as we detest a full-grown woman with baby mannerisms.

English art is saturated with it, from the brand-new imitation of the old house that grew and rambled from period to period to the rain-tub standing beneath the eaves.

In fact, most simplicity following the doctrines of William Morris is a protest; as a protest, well enough; but the highest form of simplicity is not simple in the sense that the infant intelligence is simple—nor, for that matter, the side of a barn.

A natural revulsion of feeling leads us from the meaningless elaboration of to-day to lay too great stress on mere platitudes, quite as a clean sheet of paper is a relief after looking at a series of bad drawings—but simplicity is not merely a neutral or a negative quality.

Simplicity in art, rightly understood, is a synthetic, positive quality, in which we may see evidence of mind, breadth of scheme, wealth of detail, and withal a sense of completeness found in a tree or a flower. A work may have the delicacies of a rare orchid or the stanch fortitude of the oak, and still be simple. A thing to be simple needs only to be true to itself in organic sense.

With this ideal of simplicity, let us glance hastily at a few instances of the machine and see how it has been forced by false ideals to do violence to this simplicity; how it has made possible the highest simplicity, rightly understood and so used. As perhaps wood is most available of all homely materials and therefore, naturally, the most abused—let us glance at wood.

Machinery has been invented for no other purpose than to imitate, as close as possible, the wood-carving of the early ideal—with the immediate result that no ninety-nine cent piece of furniture is salable without some horrible botchwork meaning nothing unless it means that art and craft have combined to fix in the mind of the masses the old hand-carved chair as the *ne plus ultra* of the ideal.

The miserable, lumpy tribute to this perversion which Grand Rapids alone yields would mar the face of Art beyond repair; to say nothing of the elaborate and fussy joinery of posts, spindles, jig sawed beams and braces, butted and strutted, to outdo the sentimentality of the already overwrought antique product.

Thus is the wood-working industry glutted, except in rarest instances. The whole sentiment of early craft degenerated to a sentimentality having no longer decent significance nor commercial integrity; in fact all that is fussy, maudlin, and animal, basing its existence chiefly on vanity and ignorance.

Now let us learn from the Machine.

It teaches us that the beauty of wood lies first in its qualities as wood; no treatment that did not bring out these qualities all the time could be plastic, and therefore not appropriate—so not beautiful, the machine teaches us, if we have left it to the machine that certain simple forms and handling are suitable to bring out the beauty of wood and certain forms are not; that all wood-carving is apt to be a forcing of the material, an insult to its finer possibilities as a material having in itself intrinsically artistic properties, of which its beautiful markings is one, its texture another, its color a third.

The machine, by its wonderful cutting, shaping, smoothing, and repetitive capacity, has made it possible to so use it without waste that the poor as well as the rich may enjoy to-day beautiful surface treatments of clean, strong forms that the branch veneers of Sheraton and Chippendale only hinted at, with dire extravagance, and which the middle ages utterly ignored.

The machine has emancipated these beauties of nature in wood; made it possible to wipe out the mass of meaningless torture to which wood has been subjected since the world began, for it has been universally abused and maltreated by all peoples but the Japanese.

Rightly appreciated, is not this the very process of elimination for which Morris pleaded?

Not alone a protest, moreover, for the machine, considered only technically, if you please, has placed in artist hands the means of idealizing the true nature of wood harmoniously with man's spiritual and material needs, without waste, within reach of all.

And how fares the troop of old materials galvanized into new life by the Machine?

Our modern materials are these old materials in more plastic guise, rendered so by the Machine, itself creating the very quality needed in material to satisfy its own art equation.

We have seen in glancing at modern architecture how they fare at the hands of Art and Craft; divided and sub-divided in orderly sequence with rank and file of obedient retainers awaiting the master's behest.

Steel and iron, plastic cement and terra-cotta.

Who can sound the possibilities of this old material, burned clay, which the modern machine has rendered as sensitive to the creative brain as a dry plate to the lens—a marvelous simplifier? And this plastic covering material, cement, another simplifier, enabling the artist to clothe the structural frame with a simple, modestly beautiful robe where before he dragged in, as he does still drag, five different kinds of material to compose one little cottage, pettily arranging it in an aggregation supposed to be picturesque—as a matter of fact, millinery, to be warped and beaten by sun, wind, and rain into a variegated heap of trash.

There is the process of modern casting in metal—one of the perfected modern machines, capable of any form to which fluid will flow, to perpetuate the imagery of the most delicately poetic mind without let or hindrance—within reach of everyone, therefore insulted and outraged by the bungler forcing it to a degraded seat as his degenerate festival.

Multitudes of processes are expectantly awaiting the sympathetic interpretation of the master mind; the galvano-plastic and its electrical brethren, a prolific horde, now cheap fakirs imitating real bronzes and all manner of the antique, secretly damning it in their vitals.

Electro-glazing, a machine shunned because too cleanly and delicate for the clumsy hand of the traditional designer, who depends upon the mass and blur of leading to conceal his lack of touch.

That delicate thing, the lithograph—the prince of a whole reproductive province of processes—see what this process becomes in the hands of a master like Whistler. He has sounded but one note in the gamut of its possibilities, but that product is intrinsically true to the process, and as delicate as the butterfly's wing. Yet the most this particular machine did for us, until then in the hands of Art and Craft, was to give us a cheap, imitative effect of painting. . . .

Granting that a determined, dauntless body of artist material could be brought together with sufficient persistent enthusiasm to grapple with the Machine, would not some one be found who would provide the suitable experimental station (which is what the modern Arts and Crafts shop should be)—an experimental station that would represent in miniature the elements of this great pulsating web of the machine, where each pregnant process or significant tool in printing, lithography, galvano-electro processes, wood and steel working machinery, muffles and kilns would have its place and where the best young scientific blood could mingle with the best and truest artistic inspiration, to sound the depths of these things, to accord them the patient, sympathetic treatment that is their due?

Surely a thing like this would be worth while—to alleviate the insensate numbness of the poor fellows out in the cold, hard shops, who know not why nor understand, whose dutiful obedience is chained to botch work and bungler's ambition; surely this would be a practical means to make their dutiful obedience give us something we can all understand, and that will be as normal to the best of this machine age as a ray of light to the healthy eye; a real help in adjusting the *Man* to a true sense of his importance as a factor in society, though he does tend a machine.

Teach him that that machine is his best friend—will have widened the margin of his leisure until enlightenment shall bring him a further sense of the magnificent ground plan of progress in which he too justly plays his significant part.

If the art of the Greek, produced at such cost of human life, was so noble and enduring, what limit dare we now imagine to an Art based upon an adequate life for the individual?

The machine is his!

In due time it will come to him!

Meanwhile, who shall count the slain?

From where are the trained nurses in this industrial hospital to come if not from the modern arts and crafts? . . .

Upon this faith in Art as the organic heart quality of the scientific frame of things, I base a belief that we must look to the artist brain, of all brains, to grasp the significance to society of this thing we call the Machine, if that brain be not blinded, gagged, and bound by false tradition, the letter of precedent. For this thing we call Art is it not as prophetic as a primrose or an oak? Therefore, of the essence of this thing we call the Machine, which is no more or less than the principle of organic growth working irresistibly the Will of Life through the medium of Man.

Be gently lifted at nightfall to the top of a great down-town office building, and you may see how in the image of material man, at once his glory and menace, is this thing we call a city.

There beneath, grown up in a night, is the monster leviathan, stretching acre upon acre into the far distance. High overhead hangs the stagnant pall of its fetid breath, reddened with the light from its myriad eyes endlessly everywhere blinking. Ten thousand acres of cellular tissue, layer upon layer, the city's flesh, outspreads enmeshed by intricate network of veins and arteries, radiating into the gloom, and there with muffled, persistent roar, pulses and circulates as the blood in your veins, the ceaseless beat of the activity to whose necessities it all conforms.

Like to the sanitation of the human body is the drawing off of poisonous waste from the system of this enormous creature; absorbed first by the infinitely ramifying, thread-like ducts gathering at their sensitive terminals matter destructive to its life, hurrying it to millions of small intestines, to be collected in turn by larger, flowing to the great sewer, on to the drainage canal, and finally to the ocean.

This ten thousand acres of flesh-like tissue is again knit and inter-knit with a nervous system marvelously complete, delicate filiaments for hearing, knowing, almost feeling the pulse of its organism, acting upon the ligaments and tendons for motive impulse, in all flowing the impelling fluid of man's own life.

Its nerve ganglia!—The peerless Corliss tandems whirling their hundred ton fly-wheels, fed by gigantic rows of water tube boilers burning oil, a solitary man slowly pacing backward and forward, regulating here and there the little feed valves controlling the deafening roar of the flaming gas, while beyond, the incessant clicking, dropping, waiting—lifting, waiting, shifting of the governor gear controlling these modern Goliaths seems a visible brain in intelligent action, registered infallibly in the enormous magnets, purring in the giant embrace of great induction coils, generating the vital current meeting with instant response in the rolling cars on elevated tracks ten miles away, where the glare of the Bessemer steel converter makes a conflagration of the clouds.

More quietly still, whispering down the long, low rooms of factory buildings buried in the gloom beyond, range on range of stanch, beautifully perfected automatons, murmer contentedly with occasional click-clack, that would have the American manufacturing industry of five years ago by the throat to-day; manipulating steel as delicately as a mystical shuttle of the modern loom manipulates a silk thread in the shimmering pattern of a dainty gown.

And the heavy breathing, the murmuring, the clangor, and the roar!—how the voice of this monstrous thing, this greatest of machines, a great city, rises to proclaim the marvel of the units of its structure, the ghastly warning boom from the deep throats of vessels heavily seeking inlet to the waterway below, answered by the echoing clangor of the bridge bells growing nearer and more ominous as the vessel cuts momentarily the flow of the nearer artery, warning the current from the swinging bridge now closing on its stately passage, just in time to receive in a rush of steam, as a streak of light, the avalanche of blood and metal hurled across it and gone, roaring into the night on its glittering bands of steel, ever faithfully encircled by the slender magic lines tick-tapping its invincible protection.

Nearer, in the building ablaze with midnight activity, the wide white band streams into the marvel of the multiple press, receiving unerringly the indelible impression of the human hopes, joys, and fears throbbing in the pulse of this great activity, as infallibly as the gray matter of the human brain receives the impression of the senses, to come forth millions of neatly folded, perfected news sheets, teaming with vivid appeals to passions, good or evil; weaving a web of intercommunication so far reaching that distance becomes as nothing, the thought of one man in one corner of the earth one day visible to the naked eye of all

men the next; the doings of all the world reflected as in a glass, so marvelously sensitive this wide white band streaming endlessly from day to day becomes in the grasp of the multiple press.

If the pulse of activity in this great city, to which the tremor of the mammoth skeleton beneath our feet is but an awe-inspiring response, is thrilling, what of this prolific, silent obedience?

And the texture of the tissue of this great thing, this Forerunner of Democracy, the Machine, has been deposited particle by particle, in blind obedience to organic law, the law to which the great solar universe is but an obedient machine.

Thus is the thing into which the forces of Art are to breathe the thrill of ideality! A SOUL!

The Hull-House Players

Elsie F. Weil

By 1890, theater had begun at the settlement with the study of Shakespeare's plays. Before there was a theatre building, plays were performed in the drawingroom of the first settlement building and later in the gymnasium. The young people's clubs as well as adult groups put on dramatic productions. In 1903, a number of Greek immigrants living near the settlement staged the Ajax *of Sophocles and followed it with other ancient Greek plays. They felt pride in their national heritage and took great pleasure in educating the ignorant Americans. Lithuanians, Poles, and Russians also used the Hull-House stage to present plays in their native tongues. Jane Addams and the other Hull-House residents quickly realized the importance of the theatre as an educational institution and an agent for Americanization.*

Several amateur groups performed at the Hull-House Theatre, but the most important was the Hull-House Players, founded in 1900 as the Hull-House Dramatic Association under the direction of Laura Dainty Pelham, a former actress. This group, professional in quality though amateur in standing, achieved national and international rec-

ognition, and with the Neighborhood Theater in New York pioneered in the little-theater movement. Following is an account of the Hull-House Players' tour of Ireland in 1913. [Elsie F. Weil, ''The Hull-House Players,'' Theatre Magazine (September 1913), xix–xxii.]

✧ ✧ ✧

One day last month a very tanned and animated group of Thespians were seen again around their old stamping-grounds in Chicago. They were the Hull House Players, who had just returned from Europe. To many actors a trip abroad is a trifling incident of the summer vacation. Not so with the Hull House company. None of them had ever crossed the Atlantic before, most of them had never seen Broadway, and very few had done any travelling at all outside of the short trips made by the company to play in towns near Chicago.

THE HULL-HOUSE PLAYERS

Founded by LAURA DAINTY PELHAM

Will Present for the Benefit of

THE LAURA DAINTY PELHAM MEMORIAL FUND

THE SILVER BOX

By JOHN GALSWORTHY

WEDNESDAY, April 23rd, at 8:15 P. M.
THURSDAY, April 24th, at 8:15 P. M.
FRIDAY, April 25th, at 8:15 P. M.
SATURDAY, April 26th, at 8:15 P. M.
SATURDAY MATINEE, April 26th, 2:30 P. M.

Directed by Maurice J. Cooney.

ALL SEATS RESERVED.   TICKETS 75 CENTS.

Seats may be secured by mail or telephone from Mrs. Byron at Hull-House (Monroe 0070). Special dinners in the Coffee House as usual by order through Miss Hess (Monroe 2986).

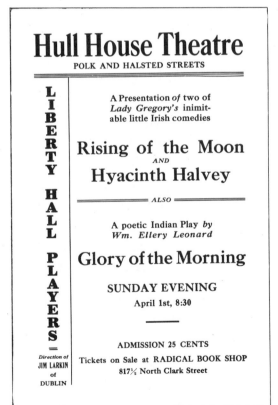

Hull House Theatre

POLK AND HALSTED STREETS

LIBERTY HALL PLAYERS

A Presentation *of* two of *Lady Gregory's* inimitable little Irish comedies

Rising of the Moon
AND
Hyacinth Halvey

= ALSO =

A poetic Indian Play *by Wm. Ellery Leonard*

Glory of the Morning

SUNDAY EVENING
April 1st, 8:30

———

ADMISSION 25 CENTS

Direction of **JIM LARKIN** *of* **DUBLIN**

Tickets on Sale at RADICAL BOOK SHOP
817½ North Clark Street

They had every reason to be proud of their ''grand tour,'' because they had earned the money it cost by the excellent performances they had given during the year. It was only a forty-two-day trip, but no one could make three thousand dollars stretch farther for fourteen people than Mrs. Laura Dainty Pelham, the director of the Hull House Players, or do more to insure their success. From the time they landed at Queenstown until they sailed for home from the Hague, they were royally entertained.* In Dublin they had tea with Lady Gregory and visited the Irish Players, with whom they had become fast friends during the latter's engagement in Chicago. They were the guests of honor at a reception given by the Lord Lieutenant and Lady Aberdeen, who placed at their disposal St. Patrick's Hall, of Dublin Castle, for a performance of ''By Products.'' They had lunch with the Countess of Warwick at Warwick

*Among those named in this paragraph are:
Lady Augusta Gregory (1852–1932) was an Irish playwright and one time director of the Abbey Theater, Dublin.
John Campbell Gordon (1847–1934) was Lord Lieutenant of Ireland, 1905–1915. His wife Ishbel (1857–1939) was president of Canning Town Women's Settlement, 1890–1939, and a feminist leader.
Frances Evelyn, Countess of Warwick (1861–1938), founded numerous British welfare organizations and was an active Socialist.
Sir Percy Alden (1865–1944) was a lecturer and writer on social and labor problems. —Eds.

Castle, were shown through the Houses of Parliament by Mr. Percy Alden, and in London lunched with John Galsworthy, who had met the players during a brief visit to Chicago.

Just before they went abroad, they gave a week of repertoire at Hull House, during which their many friends turned out to do them honor and speed them on their way. They gave "Kindling," "You Never Can Tell," "The Tragedy of Nan," "The Rising of the Moon" and "The Workhouse Ward," three one-act plays, "Marse Covington," by George Ade, "By Products," by Joseph Medill Patterson, and "Manacles," by H. K. Moderwell, and "The Pigeon."

It was at Mr. Galsworthy's own request that the Hull-House Players gave "The Pigeon." When he came to Chicago last year, he met Mrs. Pelham and became very much interested in her organization. He told her how delighted he was to have heard of their masterly production of his drama, "Justice." Mr. Galsworthy thought it was remarkable that this little company should bring out his play when other managers had been refusing to do so for over two years. He had a long talk with Frank Keough, Louis Alter, and Stuart Bailey, and said he was delighted with the work of the company. He suggested that they should do "The Pigeon," which play has been one of the most popular in their repertoire ever since.

The first performance of "The Pigeon" was given after it had been in rehearsal only four weeks, and as a result there occurred the slips characteristic of a first-night, even in the best professional companies. The lights flashed up in the wrong places and were extinguished at critical moments. The Pigeon's dressing-gown, which he draped around him after he had given his last pair of trousers to Ferrand, the French vagabond, was not quite long enough to guarantee the sobriety of the audience, and a chair had to be reached through the doorway by a thoughtful stage hand, who deplored the bareness of the studio. But these were only minor discrepancies, and Mrs. Pelham saw that they did not recur. Recent performances of the play have shown a real growth, and the prompter, that bugbear of all amateur organizations, was never in evidence again.

The Hull-House Players are not amateurs. They act with a finish and artistic precision, which, as one Chicago critic said, inflicts on them the penalty as well as the privilege of being considered professionals. They are not college students entering into dramatics as a sort of lark; they are not people of comparative leisure resorting to amateur acting to fill up part of their playtime. Rather they are hard-working young folks, who have plenty of troubles and worries, some of them with families to look after, and yet who come to their acting as to something that will freshen up the wilted aspect of life for them after the daily grind. Everyone must have some interest outside of the "bread alone" struggle to keep wholesome and happy. With some it is athletics, books, travelling, or cards. With these young people it is their acting, and they are satisfied to have it take up most of their spare time. They have two rehearsals a week, and just before a new production, all-day rehearsals on Sundays. Their connection with the company not only provides all their amusement, but a stimulating intellectual life for them as well. They have high ideals of life and society and prefer to present those plays that deal with the serious moral and social problems of the day, such as those of Shaw, Galsworthy, and Pinero.

Everyone connected with the organization works during the day. Mrs. Pelham, the director, is in her office from nine until six and devotes her evenings to her players. Louis Alter, one of the leading members of the company, is a cigar-maker; Stuart Bailey runs a little restaurant downtown; Frank Keough works in the office of a brewery, and Edward Sullivan in the office of a large corporation; Joseph Marsolais is a stereotyper; Debra McGrath, a schoolteacher, and Laura Thornton and Maud Smith, stenographers. Laura Criddle and Helen Silverman are employed in that most ancient of occupations, keeping house for their husbands. A. Rubenstein is in the feather business, and Paul Grauman is a photographer.

The Hull House Dramatic Association has been in existence eleven years, and of the original eleven members there are four remaining. Most of those who dropped out did so after the first year because they could not stand the pressure. The membership is limited to thirteen, and as none of the active members contemplate resigning, there seems little hope at present for those on the long waiting list. However, they often help out in emergencies. Charles McCormick, the president of the organization, Laura Thornton, the secretary,

Maud Smith, and Joseph Marsolais, have been in since the beginning; Miss McGrath comes next with ten years; then Alter, Keough, and Mrs. Silverman, nine years; Mrs. Criddle, eight; Bailey, three; and Grauman and Sullivan, two. Thus the players have really grown up together and have the delightfully informal and friendly attitude of a large family toward each other. The members were originally selected from the talented young people in the various social play clubs in existence at Hull House at the time.

One might marvel at the facility with which the company in "The Pigeon" mastered a dialect of which they have no personal knowledge, if one had not heard their delicious brogue in the Irish plays. In "The Pigeon," Mrs. Silverman as the flower girl, and Joseph Marsolais as the cabby, bring out the flavor of the London street jargon, and Stuart Bailey, who does not know a word of French, manages the broken dialect of the vagabond philosopher beautifully, and adds that distinct little flourish to his words so characteristic of the French speech.

In the Irish plays the company do the parts with an enchanting brogue and a delicious intonation. Of course, a number of the cast are Irish and fall naturally into the "spakin' of it." But the real source of inspiration is Mrs. Pelham herself. As Laura Dainty she was a great soubrette and famous in her specialty of Irish roles. . . .

Mrs. Pelham and her players were very proud of their success in the first play that had been written by a Hull House girl, Hilda Satt.* The play is called "The Walking Delegate," and is a dramatization of Leroy Scott's novel.

Miss Satt has lived most of her life in the neighborhood of Hull House. She was born of Russian-Jewish parents near Warsaw, and came to Chicago with her family in 1892. The young authoress has had a very busy young life. To the present writer during a rehearsal she explained with due cause for pride: "I went to work in a factory when I was thirteen years old, and I have been supporting myself ever since. I studied every night when I came home from work. When I was about sixteen I first came to Hull House. I joined a literary club and was the editor of a little paper we published, but it was the stimulus of coming to-

gether and exchanging opinions that helped me most.

"I have always been hungry for experiences of every type. I consider every employment an opportunity to reach out for new impressions, and I have often accepted a position at half the wages I was previously receiving for the sake of the novel experiences it would bring me. I expect to utilize all my experiences in my plays."

Miss Satt could not praise Hull House highly enough for all it had done for her. Like everyone else who has come in contact with Miss Addams, she worships her and has unconsciously absorbed the spirit of her ideals.

During the season that has just closed, the Hull-House Dramatic Association has added several new plays to their repertoire. Miss Illington† was very glad to loan them the manuscript of "Kindling," to be used only in Hull House, and they were very successful in this drama of the slums. They also worked hard to bring out the poetry of Masefield's "Tragedy of Nan," and its grim and bitter irony. Besides these, they gave three one-act plays, "Marse Covington," "By Products," and "Manacles."

Some idea of the standards they are aiming at may be obtained from a list of the plays they have appeared in from the beginning of the organization. They were the first company in Chicago to give Synge's "Riders to the Sea," and Lady Gregory's plays, "Devorgilla," "Grania," "The Workhouse Ward," "Spreading the News," and "Rising of the Moon," and also to give Gilbert's "Palace of Truth," Shaw's "You Never Can Tell," Masefield's "Tragedy of Nan," and Galsworthy's "Pigeon." They have presented "The Magistrate," "The Schoolmistress," "Trelawney of the Wells," and "The Amazons."

†Margaret Illington (1881–1934) became an actress on the American stage.—Eds.

*Hilda Satt Polacheck (1882–1967).—Eds.

Christmas at Hull-House

Amalie Hannig

Christmas at Hull-House was always special. The settlement residents encouraged ethnic festivals and the preservation of the old ways of celebrating holidays. It was a time of parties, dances, concerts, and dinners.

One of the most beautiful and famous Christmas presentations at the settlement was the "Tableaux" or "Living Pictures," which developed from the Christmas concert that Hull-House resident and Music School co-director Amalie Hannig (b. 1868) described in an article for the Ladies Home Journal, *December 1911. Scenes depicting the story of the birth of Christ were staged with neighborhood people in costumes. For many years these scenes, accompanied by a choir singing music describing the events taking place, and designed in the manner of Italian painters Fra Angelico and Botticelli, were directed by Edith de Nancrede. [Amalie Hannig, "Christmas at Hull-House,"* Ladies Home Journal *(December 1911), 31.]*

The activities at Hull-House cover a wide field at any time of the year. About nine thousand people come to us each week during the winter months. But when Christmas approaches Hull-House appears like a huge ant-hill where all the inhabitants are turning their efforts with great intensity into one channel—into making this particular Christmas better than any of its predecessors.

To begin with the small people: A Christmas play, performed by children for all the club children, is given in our theater, and the same performance is presented three times before different audiences of at least two hundred and fifty wide-eyed and breathless children each time, and when the performance is again twice repeated for their parents there is no loss of interest. It is difficult to find a suitable children's play that brings in good

old Santa Claus and a Christmas tree. But usually this is done by using a fairy tale that is elastic enough to admit a Christmas touch at the end.

If anybody happens to see our large drawing-room on the day before Christmas he will be inclined to believe that he has accidentally dropped into a grocery store. His nostrils, too, will be greeted by all the characteristic odors. Rows of market-baskets fill the middle of the large space. In one corner of the room stand barrels filled with chickens, sacks of potatoes and onions, boxes of various groceries—as coffee, tea, sugar—boxes of apples, oranges, and candy; another corner is stacked with small Christmas trees; and all these things send forth and mingle their particular odors. On large tables and on all available chairs packages containing warm, comfortable wearing apparel, dress goods or shoes, and an endless variety of toys are awaiting distribution. Soon many hands begin to sort and label, and by noon three hundred baskets are filled, varying according to the sizes of the families to whom they are addressed.

By the evening all baskets have disappeared; the little Christmas trees alone are still waiting. But at about nine o'clock a most delightful and mysterious activity begins. Each little tree, accompanied by candles, tinsels, and all sorts of fascinating decorations, is brought forth and carried to some household in our neighborhood where an expectant, smiling mother is ready and waiting. The children are safely asleep; the small, and for the most part very poor, dwelling is clean and shiny and shows itself at its best; a table is ready to receive the tree and the presents. Quickly the tree is trimmed and the candles are put on safe branches, and, after a friendly exchange of Christmas greetings, "Santa Claus" retires, leaving the rest to Mother. Back he goes to Hull-House to fetch another tree and place it in another home. Sometimes it happens that the last "Santa Claus" returns from his errand at about one or two o'clock in the morning. Twenty-eight trees were sent out last Christmas.

Some of us remember how on one Christmas Eve a tree and some presents were taken to an Irish mother who supported her six children and three of her dead sister's children by scrubbing day and night. Even on this evening she was not expected back in her three-roomed home until half-past twelve. When "Santa Claus" appeared at this late hour, loaded down with gifts for ten, he found six children sleeping peacefully in one bed—three at the foot and three at the top—in one room, and three others were in another room. Nine stockings were hanging up; and who would be surprised to learn that some of them showed holes so big that an orange was dropped in first so that other articles might not fall through? "Santa Claus" had to move on tiptoe, hardly daring to breathe, while he made his arrangements in the same room with the sleeping children.

Our Italian friends gladly receive the American "Santa Claus." Their homes are made to look festive and bright. The freshly scoured floor, still damp, is covered with newspapers, a little altar adorns the wall, the lamp of devotion is lighted, and when the little tree, gayly trimmed, stands on the floor before the altar the Virgin and Child seem to crown it with their blessed presence.

One feast at Hull-House fills hosts and guests alike with deep satisfaction. The Friendly Club, consisting of whole families of our people, come to a Christmas dinner, a real turkey dinner where everything is "grand" and "delicious." Here are parents and their children dining with a joy that might make the chief cook of a King envious. Such a precious fowl as a turkey is an event to all of the diners. Last year about two hundred and sixty guests were placed in our spacious coffee-house, and when thirty-five late comers found all seats occupied the children politely gave up their legitimate places to the older people and stood between the chairs.

An effort is made, however, to observe Christmas in such a way that it shall not consist solely of presents and dinners and parties, but that the spiritual side shall also be accentuated. Händel's "Messiah," rendered every year through the courtesy of a chorus from Evanston, has been a source of great pleasure to our neighbors, to those of the Christian faith and to many of our Jewish friends. Perhaps the most spontaneous celebration of the birth of Jesus finds expression in our own Christmas Concert, which has been given for eighteen years on the Sunday before Christmas. On this page is printed a recent program.

This concert consists of folk songs, carols and canons through which the people of many lands have for generations striven to express their joy

and devotion, and is rendered by young people of the many nationalities represented in the Hull-House neighborhood. Possibly it is the spirit of Christmas, possibly it is the influence of music which holds together the souls of these people, but certain it is that, although most of the songs are of a religious character, Russian and Polish Jewish children participate with the consent of their parents.

An eminent author who has made a study of immigrants, especially of the Jews, said after he had listened to one of these concerts: "It is wonderful to see people, who in Russia would have died rather than to speak the name of Christ, here singing these songs, and their families in the audience enjoying this music." Nobody who knows the principles of Hull-House will accuse us of trying to influence the religious convictions of our friends; but the fact that all these people are united in the true spirit of Christmas may perhaps be a genuine expression of "Peace on Earth and Good Will to Men."

This Christmas Carol was composed by one of the older pupils in the Music School, and, given for the first time at one of these concerts, was sung by a group of his younger brothers and sisters.

After the concert the children, with their families. take supper together in a spacious room lighted only by the tapers of a large Christmas tree. This "Music-School Tree" is always the same and unlike any of the others which flourish at Hull-House. It is a large fir tree which reaches

Christmas Carol

Harriett Monroe   Charles Cornish

Con espressione

1. Hear ye the tale! Long, long ago, Peace like a mantle Whiter than snow,
2. Ring the glad bells! There, thro'the night Came to the Shepherds Messengers bright,
3. Sing for the morn, When, love-beguiled, Princes and Shepherds Knelt to the Child,

Like a white man-tle Soft-er than snow, Wrapped the earth round
Came to poor shep-herds An-gels of light. High in the east,
When all the na-tions Worshiped a child. On-ly a babe,

When on the morn, Low in the man-ger A ba-by was born.
Flamed out a star, Sig-nal to wise men, Jour-ney-ing a-far.
Soft-ly at rest, Soothed by His-moth-er, Safe on her breast.

From the *Fourth Book of the Modern Music Series.*
Copyright, 1905, by Silver, Burdett & Company. By arrangement.

from floor to ceiling and is fastened to a secure stand. To the top is tied a star made of silver tinsel wound around a frame of strong wire. Many "icicles" of glass are attached to conspicuous branches, and a large number of candle-holders are fastened on so as to be almost invisible; the candle-holders are made of unpainted tin. Then we carefully spread soft fluffy asbestos or a new German non-combustible cotton over all the thicker and finer branches to make them look as if they were snow-covered. Twelve packages of plain silver-tinsel thread are also put on, starting at the top so that the tinsel covers the tree like a silver veil. The threads are laid on the branches almost singly and must not be in the least tangled. White candles are placed in the holders and holly is laid on the floor around the tree. After the candles have been lighted—beginning at the top—all lights in the room are turned out. There it stands in wonderful, mysterious, silent beauty, like the Spirit of Christmas, glittering softly in green, white, and silver.

This perhaps is the climax of our Christmas celebration, although the holiday week is full of all sorts of jollifications, ending with the "Old Settlers" party on New Year's Day.

A Traveling Photographer at Hull-House

Lewis Hine

Lewis Hine (1874–1940), the pioneer documentary photographer, was born in Oshkosh, Wisconsin. He worked at various jobs in his hometown before enrolling at the University of Chicago in 1900. During his year in Chicago he probably learned about Hull-House; he certainly met John Dewey, who was an active supporter of the settlement. In 1901 he moved to New York, where he became a teacher at the Ethical Culture School. He also studied sociology at Columbia University, and he taught himself photography.

Following the example of Jacob Riis, whose photographs of New York slums helped to promote housing reform, Hine understood the power of the documentary photograph to influence Americans and make them aware of urban problems. He became an expert at depicting the horrors of child labor and the human cost of industrialism. Working as a free-lance photographer, he was employed by the Child Welfare League, the National Consumers' League, and the Pittsburgh Survey before being hired full-time by the National Child Labor Committee in 1908, which paid him to document the plight of young boys and girls who worked in factories, on the farms, and in the streets.

In 1909, on one of his cross-country trips, Hine stopped at Hull-House, and he returned for brief stays during the next two years. Best known for his haunting portraits of children at work, these photographs taken of Hull-House activities, show another side of Hine's genius. Carefully posed and well controlled, they demonstrate his

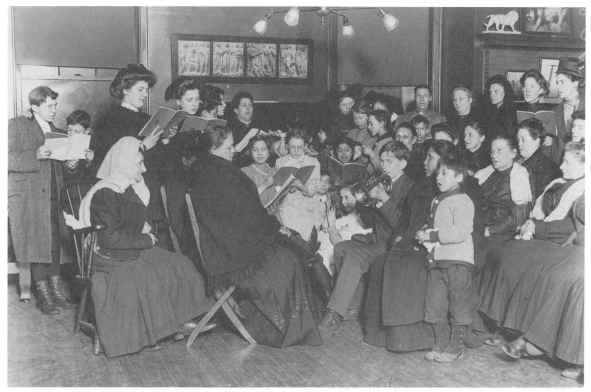

The singing class gathered in one of the club rooms at Hull-House, Chicago, 1910.—Hine. Friendly Club, originally composed of City Gardeners.—Hull-House Year Book, 1910.

Hull-House, Chicago, famous social settlement, where its Greek Wrestling Club lets off surplus energy. 1911.—Hine. A group of Greek Wrestlers, Hull-House Gymnasium.—Hull-House Year Book, 1910.

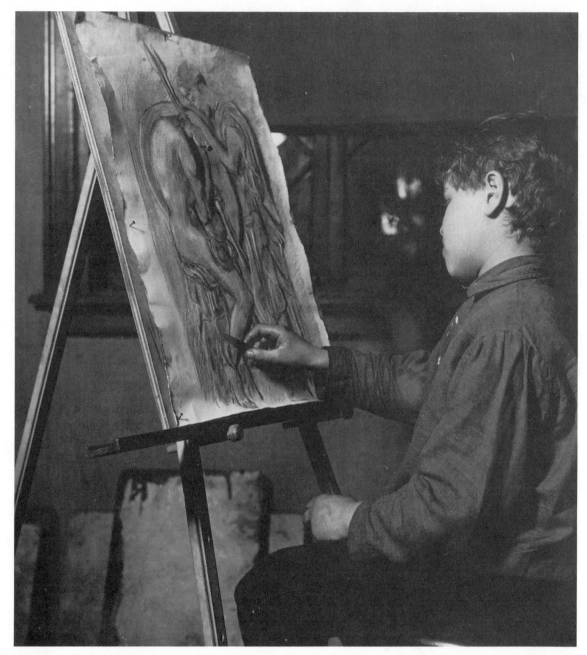

Hull-House Art Pupil.—Hine. In the Studio.—Hull-House Year Book, 1910.

ability to compose a picture and to make his subjects relax. They also reveal the cultural and recreational activities that drew people of all ages and ethnic backgrounds to the settlement.

In 1906, Hull-House published its first yearbook, identifying the residents and describing settlement programs and activities during 1906–1907. Despite the name, yearbooks were not published annually. The next to be issued was dated May 1, 1910. All of these photographs appear in it.

Two captions appear under each photograph: one attached by Hine, the other supplied by the Hull-House Year Book, May 1, 1910.

Hull-House Songs

Eleanor Smith

Music played an important role at Hull-House. Whether it was a group of residents and friends singing around the piano, Italians or Greeks singing a folk song which had never been written down, or a small boy practicing the violin, music often echoed through the settlement halls. Starting in 1893 Hull-House had a formal music school directed until 1935 by Eleanor Smith (b. 1858). Its purpose was "to give thorough musical instruction to those children showing the greatest apti-

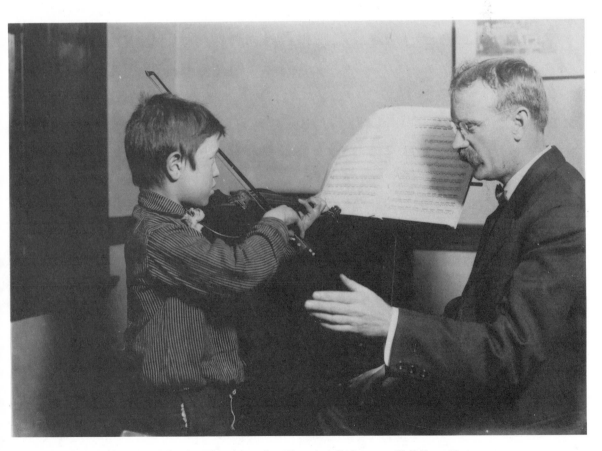

Hull-House, Refugee from Russia has his talent fostered.—Hine. A violin lesson.—Hull-House Year Book, 1910.

THE SHADOW CHILD

HARRIET MONROE

ELEANOR SMITH

Hull-House Music School students.

tude, and to foster in a much larger group the cultural aspects of a musical education.''

Smith was one of several Hull-House residents who composed music as well as taught it. She had been in charge of the Department of Vocal Music in the Cook County Normal School. While at Hull-House she joined the faculty of the Chicago Kindergarten College as a music teacher and authored a number of books of vocal music for children, among them the multi-volume Eleanor Smith Music Course, published by the American Book Company in the early 1900s. Five songs, with music by Eleanor Smith, were published in Hull-House Songs (1915) in celebration of the settlement's twenty-fifth anniversary. All of the songs were composed as part of the settlement's participation in campaigns associated with specific social issues. The ''Suffrage Song,'' for example, was a campaign song for the women's rights movement,

while ''The Land of the Noonday Night'' verbalized the unsafe and unhealthy conditions in mines. The song on page 102, with words by Harriet Monroe, was composed with the Hull-House crusade against child labor in mind. [Eleanor Smith, Hull-House Songs (Chicago, 1915), 8–11.]

The School as Social Center

John Dewey

Hull-House was an educational institution. Extending the advantages of a college education to the workingman was central to the original settlement idea. At one time the Hull-House faculty numbered thirty-five college-trained men and women. Early Hull-House publications show classes in arithmetic, geometry, algebra, Greek art, Ovid, Caesar, English composition, Shakespeare, American history, political economy, biology, and physiography. Each teacher is listed by name, college, and highest degree. There were also special lectures, such as those on "Charity Organization" by Seth Low, president of Columbia University; "The Conscience of the State" by Bayard Holmes, a Chicago physician; "Woman's Suffrage" by Susan B. Anthony; "Sir Thomas More" by Charles Zueblin of the University of Chicago; and "Epictetus" by John Dewey. But the settlement workers soon realized that another kind of educational fare would fill the more basic needs of most of their immigrant neighbors. They developed kindergartens for the children, homemaking classes for the women, vocational courses and eventually vocational guidance for the young people, and special courses in English, American history, and government for the foreign-born. They supplemented the narrow, stilted curriculum of the public schools, which had not adjusted to the rapidly developing urban, industrial environment, and they sought to improve the schools. "A settlement is a protest against a restricted view of education," Jane Addams remarked, and Hull-House became a leader in educational reform, especially in trying to relate education to the realities of urban life. Without quite realizing it, Hull-House became a pioneer in progressive education.

Hull-House residents had some success in improving the public schools in Chicago, but their major influence and contribution were their educational experiments. These were observed, accepted, and reported by a frequent Hull-House visitor, John Dewey (1859–1952), the leading educational philosopher in Chicago and America. Though Dewey gave an occasional lecture at Hull-House and served on the first board of trustees of the settlement, often he just dropped in to meet and talk to the interesting people who always seemed to gather there. His daughter, named after Jane Addams, once wrote, "Dewey's faith in democracy as a guiding force in education took on both a sharper and deeper meaning because of Hull-House and Jane Addams." The influence was mu-

tual, for the settlement workers learned a lot from the philosopher, especially about the implications of their daily actions.

Dewey was quick to praise the educational innovations at Hull-House. This essay, "The School as Social Center," was published in the National Education Association Proceedings for 1902. In it Dewey, in his typically involved and difficult-to-read style, viewed Hull-House as a model for what schools should become. [John Dewey, "The School as Social Center," Proceedings of the National Education Association (1902), 374–383.]

. . . I shall confine myself to the philosophy of the school as a social center . . . , but at same time I do not feel that the philosophical aspect of the matter is the urgent or important one. The pressing thing, the significant thing, is really to make the school a social center; that is a matter of practice, not of theory. . . .

The older idea of the school was that its primary concern was with the inculcation of certain facts and truths from the intellectual point of view, and the acquisition of certain forms of skill. When the school became public or common, this notion was broadened to include whatever would make the citizen a more capable and righteous voter and legislator; but it was still thought that this end would be reached along the line of intellectual instruction. To teach children the constitution of the United States, the nature and working of various parts of governmental machinery, from the nation thru the state and the county down to the township and the school district, to teach such things was thought to prepare the pupil for citizenship. And so some fifteen or twenty years ago, when the feeling arose that the schools were not doing all that they should be doing for our life as a whole, this consciousness expressed itself in a demand for a more thoro and extensive teaching of civics. To my mind the demand for the school as a social center bears the same ratio to the situation which confronts us today, as the movement for civics bore to the conditions of half a generation ago. We have awakened to deeper aspects of the question; we have seen that the machinery of governmental life is after all but a machinery, and depends for its rightness and efficiency upon underlying social and industrial causes. We have lost a good deal of our faith in the efficacy of purely intellectual instruction.

Some four specific developments may be mentioned as having a bearing upon the question of the school as a social center. The first of these is the much increased efficiency and ease of all the agencies that have to do with bringing people into contact with one another. Recent inventions have so multiplied and cheapened the means of transportation, and of the circulation of ideas and news thru books, magazines, and papers that it is no longer physically possible for one nationality, race, class, or sect to be kept apart from others, impervious to their wishes and beliefs. Cheap and rapid long-distance transportation has made America a meeting-place for all the peoples and tongues of the world. The centralization of industry has forced members of classes into the closest association with, and dependence upon, each other. Bigotry, intolerance, or even an unswerving faith in the superiority of one's own religious and political creed are much shaken when individuals are brought face to face with each other, or have the ideas of others continuously and forcibly placed before them. The congestion of our city life is only one aspect of the bringing of people together which modern inventions have induced.

That many dangers result from sudden dislocations of people from the surroundings—physical, industrial, and intellectual—to which they have become adapted; that great instability may accompany this sudden massing of heterogeneous peoples, goes without saying. On the other hand, these very agencies present instrumentalities of which advantage may be taken. The best as well as the worst of modern newspapers is a product. The organized public library with its facilities for reaching all classes of people is an effect. The popular assembly and lyceum is another. No educational system can be regarded as complete until it adopts into itself the various ways in which social and intellectual intercourse may be promoted; and employs them systematically, not only to counteract dangers which these same agencies are bringing with them, but so as to make them positive causes in raising the whole level of life.

Both the demand and the opportunity are in-

creased in our large cities by the commingling of classes and races. It is said that one ward in the city of Chicago has forty different languages represented in it. It is a well-known fact that some of the largest Irish, German, and Bohemian cities in the world are located in America, not in their own countries. The power of the public schools to assimilate different races to our own institutions, thru the education given to the younger generation, is doubtless one of the most remarkable exhibitions of vitality that the world has ever seen. But, after all, it leaves the older generation still untouched; and the assimilation of the younger can hardly be complete or certain as long as the homes of the parents remain comparatively unaffected. Indeed, wise observers in both New York and Chicago have recently sounded a note of alarm. They have called attention to the fact that in some respects the children are too rapidly, I will not say Americanized, but too rapidly de-nationalized. They lose the positive and conservative value of their own native traditions, their own native music, art, and literature. They do not get complete initiation into the customs of their new country, and so are frequently left floating and unstable between the two. They even learn to despise the dress, bearing, habits, language, and beliefs of their parents—many of which have more substance and worth than the superficial putting-on of the newly adopted habits. If I understand aright, one of the chief motives in the development of the new labor museum at Hull House has been to show the younger generation something of the skill and art and historic meaning in the industrial habits of the older generations—modes of spinning, weaving, metal working, etc., discarded in this country because there was no place for them in our industrial system. Many a child has awakened to an appreciation of admirable qualities hitherto unknown in his father or mother for whom he had begun to entertain a contempt. Many an association of local history and past national glory has been awakened to quicken and enrich the life of the family.

In the second place, along with the increasing intercourse and interaction, with all its dangers and opportunities, there has come a relaxation of the bonds of social discipline and control. I suppose none of us would be willing to believe that the movement away from dogmatism and fixed authority was anything but a movement in the right direction. But no one can view the loosening of the power of the older religious and social authorities, without deep concern. We may feel sure that in time independent judgment, with the individual freedom and responsibility that go with it, will more than make good the temporary losses. But meantime there is a temporary loss. Parental authority has much less influence in controlling the conduct of children. Reverence seems to decay on every side, and boisterousness and hoodlumism to increase. Flippancy toward parental and other forms of constituted authority waxes, while obedient orderliness wanes. The domestic ties themselves, as between husband and wife as well as in relation to children, lose something of their permanence and sanctity. The church, with its supernatural sanctions, its means of shaping the daily life of its adherents, finds its grasp slowly slipping away from it. We might as well frankly recognize that many of the old agencies for moralizing mankind, and of keeping them living decent, respectable, and orderly lives, are losing in efficiency— particularly, those agencies which rested for their force upon custom, tradition, and unquestioning acceptance. It is impossible for society to remain purely a passive spectator in the midst of such a scene. It must search for other agencies with which it may repair the loss, and which may produce the results which the former methods are failing to secure. Here, too, it is not enough for society to confine its work to children. However much they may need the disciplinary training of a widened and enlightened education, the older generation needs it also. Besides, time is short—very short for the average child in the average city school. The work is hardly more than begun there, and unless it is largely to go for naught, the community must find methods of supplementing it and carrying it further outside the regular school channels.

In the third place, the intellectual life, facts, and truths of knowledge are much more obviously and intimately connected with all other affairs of life than they ever have been at any previous period in the history of the world. Hence a purely and exclusively intellectual instruction means less than it ever meant before. And, again, the daily occupations and ordinary surroundings of life are much more in need of interpretation than ever they

have been before. We might almost say that once there was a time when learning related almost wholly to a world outside and beyond that of the daily concerns of life itself. To study physics, to learn German, to become acquainted with Chinese history, were elegant accomplishments, but more or less useless from the standpoint of daily life. In fact, it is just this sort of idea which the term "culture" still conveys to many minds. When learning was useful it was only to a comparatively small and particularly select class in the community. It was just something that the doctor or lawyer or clergyman needed in his particular calling, but so far away from and above the mass of mankind that it could only awaken their blind and submissive admiration. The recent public lament regarding the degradation of the teacher's calling is, to my mind, just a reminiscence of the time when to know enough to be a teacher was something which of itself set off the individual in a special class by himself. It fails to take account of the changes which have put knowledge in common circulation, and made it possible for every man to be a teacher in some respect unto his neighbor. . . .

The fourth point of demand and opportunity is the prolongation, under modern conditions, of continuous instruction. We have heard much of the significance of prolonged infancy in relation to education. It has become almost a part of our pedagogical creed that premature engagement in the serious vocations of life is detrimental to full growth. There is a corollary to this proposition which has not as yet received equal recognition. Only where social occupations are well defined, and of a pretty permanent type, can the period of instruction be cut short at any particular period. It is commonly recognized that a doctor or a lawyer must go on studying all his life if he is to be a successful man in his profession. The reason is obvious enough. Conditions about him are highly unstable; new problems present themselves; new facts obtrude. Previous study of law, no matter how thoro and accurate the study, did not provide for these new situations. Hence the need of continual study. There are still portions of [the] country where the lawyer practically prepares himself before he enters upon his professional career. All he has to do afterward is to perfect himself in certain finer points, and get greater skill in the manipulation of what he already knows. But these are the more backward and unprogressive sections, where change is gradual and infrequent, and so the individual prepared once is prepared always. . . .

The fourfold need, and the fourfold opportunity, which I have hastily sketched, defines to some extent the work of the school as a social center.

It must provide, at least, part of that training which is necessary to keep the individual properly adjusted to a rapidly changing environment. It must interpret to him the intellectual and social meaning of the work in which he is engaged: that is, must reveal its relations to the life and work of the world. It must make up to him in part for the decay of dogmatic and fixed methods of social discipline. It must supply him compensation for the loss of reverence and the influence of authority. And, finally, it must provide means for bringing people and their ideas and beliefs together, in such ways as will lessen friction and instability, and introduce deeper sympathy and wider understanding.

In what ways shall the school as a social center perform these various tasks? To answer this question in anything like detail is to pass from my allotted sphere of philosophy into that of practical execution. But it comes within the scope of a theoretical consideration to indicate certain general lines. First, there is mixing people up with each other; bringing them together under wholesome influences, and under conditions which will promote their getting acquainted with the best side of each other. I suppose whenever we are framing our ideals of the school as a social center, what we think of is particularly the better class of social settlements. What we want is to see the school, every public school, doing something of the same sort of work that is now done by a settlement or two scattered at wide distances thru the city. And we all know that the work of such an institution as Hull House has been primarily, not that of conveying intellectual instruction, but of being a social clearing-house. It is a place where ideas and beliefs may be exchanged, not merely in the arena of formal discussion—for argument alone breeds misunderstanding and fixes prejudice—but in ways where ideas are incarnated in human form and clothed with the winning grace of personal

life. Classes for study may be numerous, but all are regarded as modes of bringing people together, of doing away with barriers of caste, or class, or race, or type of experience that keep people from real communion with each other. . . .

In conclusion, we may say that the conception of the school as a social center is born of our entire democratic movement. Everywhere we see signs of the growing recognition that the community owes to each one of its members the fullest opportunity for development. Everywhere we see the growing recognition that the community life is defective and distorted excepting as it does thus care for all its constituent parts. This is no longer viewed as a matter of charity, but as a matter of justice—nay even of something higher and better than justice—a necessary phase of developing and growing life. Men will long dispute about material socialism, about socialism considered as a matter of distribution of the material resources of the community; but there is a socialism regarding which there can be no such dispute—socialism of the intelligence and of the spirit. To extend the range and the fullness of sharing in the intellectual and spiritual resources of the community is the very meaning of the community. Because the older type of education is not fully adequate to this task under changed conditions, we feel its lack and demand that the school shall become a social center. The school as a social center means the active

Maxwell Street scene. Linoleum block print by William Jacobs.

and organized promotion of this socialism of the intangible things of art, science, and other modes of social intercourse.

Hull-House Woman's Club Anthem

Jane Addams

Jane Addams liked to compose poems, especially for birthday parties or for special occasions at Hull-House. She had great talent and skill as a speaker and as a writer, but it is indeed fortunate that her reputation does not rest on her verse. With music written by Eleanor Smith, this particular offering became the anthem of the Hull-House Woman's Club. [Jane Addams, "A House Stands on a Busy Street," The Commons (April 1905), 225.]

A House Stands on a Busy Street

A house stands on a busy street,
  Its doors are opened wide,
To all who come it bids "Good cheer,"
  To some it says: "Abide."
Gathered within its friendly walls
  A club of women find
The joys of glad companionship,
  Contentment for the mind.

For they have learned what all must learn,
  That in life's hardest storm
The shelter we together build
  Is all that keeps us warm;
That fellowship is heaven-sent
  That it alone can free
The human heart from bitterness,
  And give it liberty.

Some hours they spend in quiet mood,
  On poet's wings up-borne,
They lose themselves in other's joys

Or weep with those who mourn.
Some hours by traveled mem'ry led
  To foreign lands they roam;
Some hours they bide beside the hearth
  And talk of things of home.

Some hours they sit 'neath music's spell,
  And when the air is rife
With all the magic of sweet sound,
  It heals the pang of life.
Some hours they dream with civic pride
  Of cities that shall be,
Within whose streets each citizen,
  Shall live life worthily.

Some hours they sew with tender thought,
  To keep one mem'ry green;
They talk of those whose lives are hard,
  Who suffer wrongs unseen.
They ever open wide their hearts
  To all who are oppressed,
And in life's strange perplexities
  They strive for what is best.

Hull-House Within and Without

Alice Hamilton

Dr. Alice Hamilton was an important addition to the Hull-House group. Slender and attractive, with a quick wit and a rapier-sharp mind, she had great sympathy and understanding for the immigrant women whom she tried to help, as well as for the society ladies who came to visit Hull-House and betrayed their prejudice. But most of all she was a scientist, whose passionate interest in the welfare of people and in research led her to become the American authority on industrial diseases.

In this excerpt from her autobiography, Exploring the Dangerous Trades, *Dr. Hamilton described some of the pathos and exhilaration of settlement life. Her descriptions of police brutality, press exaggeration, and unreasoned fear of radicals makes her account seem quite contemporary. [Alice Hamilton,* Exploring the Dangerous Trades *(Boston, 1943), 68–87.]*

Life at Hull-House was very simple so far as luxuries went, but it was full of beauty. Miss Addams and Miss Starr brought with them many charming furnishings, and whatever they bought had the two qualities of durability and beauty. Our food was inexpensive but dinner was served to us in a long, paneled dining room, lighted with chandeliers of Spanish wrought iron; breakfast in a charming little Coffeehouse built in imitation of an English inn. To me, the life there satisfied every longing, for companionship, for the excitement of new experiences, for constant intellectual stimulation, and for the sense of being caught up in a big movement which enlisted my enthusiastic loyalty.

My part in it was humble enough. At that time there were few of the social services which now we take as a matter of course. Hull-House had to have its own day nursery, kindergarten, public baths, playground, as well as all the other activities which settlements still carry on. There were no baby clinics, and, though I did not feel at all competent to treat sick babies, I did venture to open a well-baby clinic which very soon was taking in all the older brothers and sisters, up to eight years of age. Miss Addams let me use the shower-bath room in the basement of the gymnasium and provided a dozen little bathtubs, with soap and bathing towels, for most of the work of the "clinic" was bathing the children. Some of them came all sewed into their clothes for the winter, but I found I could get past the Italian mothers' dread of water if I followed the bath with an alcohol rub and anointing with olive oil. Then I gave what I had been taught was the best advice about feeding babies—nothing but milk till their teeth came. When I see the varied diet modern mothers give their babies, anything apparently from bacon to bananas, I realize that those Italian women knew what a baby needed far better than my Ann Arbor professor did. I cannot feel I did any harm, however, for my teachings had no effect. I remember a young mother who had brought her baby to me, showing me her fine specimen of a three-year-

old son, and telling me of his difficulties when he was a baby. "I gave him the breast and there was plenty of milk, but he cried all the time. Then one day I was frying eggs, and just to make him stop I gave him one and it went fine. The next day I was making cup cakes, and as soon as they were cool I gave him one, and after that I gave him just whatever we had and he got fat and didn't cry any more."

So now when I see an Italian boy sucking a slice of salami I feel quite serene. Garlic, we are told, is full of most valuable vitamins, and salami is full of garlic. Evidently, long before vitamins were discovered men decided that garlic was endowed with peculiarly beneficent properties. An elderly anarchist who used to come to Hull-House and talk to me about violent revolution and assassination (though I was sure he would not hurt a fly) underwent a radical conversion under a self-styled Hindu Mahatma, which led him to give up not only his revolutionary dreams but his way of life, so that he was changed to a shadow of his former self. He was instructed to plant his feet on the earth, lift his head to Heaven, say "I am divine," and eat nothing but garlic and popcorn. No better way could be devised for deflating a revolutionist.

Much more disquieting than the food habits was the recklessness of these Italian mothers toward contagious diseases. Perhaps fatalism is a better word. It was hard to argue with them because, after all, the results of exposure are so unpredictable, and so many cases occur without any known exposure. Once I was remonstrating with a woman who had deliberately taken her year-old baby into a room where there was a child with diphtheria, but instead of impressing her I shocked her sense of right and wrong.

"Do you think," she said, "that God would punish me for going in to help Maria with her sick child? No, He would rather punish me if I did not." I might have known her baby would not catch diphtheria. They never did when I said they would.

This woman was a worker of "white magic," which is the kind that cures sickness and brings good luck. It is valued among the Italians but not nearly so much as is "black magic," the kind practiced by witchmen and witchwomen who, in Italian, are called *il mago* or *la maga*—the same term that we use for the Three Wise Men. That sort

A one-room furnished apartment occupied by a woman and five children
in the Hull-House neighborhood.

of magic is always very secret; it is sought by un-successful lovers who pay as much as ten dollars for a love philter, by jealous lovers who want to cast a spell over a rival and make him or her waste away in a "consumption." Sometimes a woman will ask for a spell to be cast over a girl who has ensnared her son and whom she is willing to kill rather than accept as a daughter-in-law. One malignant old woman, who herself was a *maga,* sent a curse way over from her Calabrian village to West Polk Street, Chicago, which made her son's first-born baby pine away and die, just because he had married a girl who had no dowry. It was the young mother herself who told me about it, a girl born and brought up in Chicago, a product of the public school, but as firm in her belief as if she lived in Calabria. All the old woman had had to do, Cristina said, was to take a lemon and call it by the baby's name and stick a pin in it every day;

then, as the lemon slowly shriveled, the baby pined away.

Mostly, one needed more than a lemon—a doll was surer. A grief-stricken mother told me how she had lost her only son from what the doctors called consumption, but what was really black magic. A girl he had jilted bought a doll at the ten-cent store and stuck it full of pins, and when there was room for no more she threw it into Lake Michigan. The poor mother knew nothing of this till she visited a *mago* who told her that the only way to save her son was to find the doll and pull out the pins. Of course she could not find a doll in the Lake, and so her son died.

I asked another woman how one told a sickness that was just ordinary from one caused by black magic. "It's easy," she said. "If the doctor can cure you, it's a natural sickness, but if he can't do nothing for you, and the more medicine you take the worster you are, it's witching.'' Her husband and her oldest son had been ''witched'' by a malignant stepsister who was the daughter of a witch and had learned the art. Mike's blood was turned to water and he had strong fits, while Pasquale shook all over, ''even his teeth shook on him.'' ''How did she do it?'' I asked. ''For Mike, it was for death, so she put it in his wine, but for Pasquale it was only for sickness all his life long, so she put three hairs on his coat. He was lucky. He picked them off with his left hand. The *maga* said if he'd done it with his right hand, she couldn't have done nothing to save him.'' ''What did she do to unwitch them?'' I asked, full of curiosity. Feluccia hesitated. ''It's prayers,'' she said—''only not Christian prayers.'' Then, feeling my skepticism, she got up, folding her shawl about her. ''Everybody believes it,'' she said. ''Only Protestants don't, because Protestants don't know how to witch and they don't know how to unwitch.''

Life in a settlement does several things to you. Among others, it teaches you that education and culture have little to do with real wisdom, the wisdom that comes from life experience. You can never, thereafter, hear people speak of the ''masses,'' the ''ignorant voters,'' without feeling that if it were put up to you whether you would trust the fate of the country to ''the classes'' or to ''the masses,'' you would decide for the latter. But it also makes you distrust the sharp division which young radicals are always making between ''proletariat'' and ''petty bourgeoisie.'' (Why always ''petty''? Is the *haute bourgeoisie* more enlightened than the *petite?*) I have found plenty of typical, petty-bourgeois mentality in the same families that produced ardent Communists. If one's contact with the poor is only through their organizations, their clubs and trade-unions, one gets a very one-sided, distorted impression of the working class, which contains not only rebel youth but conservative middle age, not only the radical leader but his wife, who cares more for a nice flat and an electric refrigerator than for the emancipation of the workers. And if you follow for years the career of an ardent young radical you may find him slowly changing into a steady, conservative head of a family.

When I heard my wealthy friends speak of the spread of Bolshevism and the imminent danger of revolution, I would think of the families I knew, their devotion to their hard-won little properties, their reverence for property rights, their instinctive fear of change, their absorption in everyday life, and revolution seemed pretty remote. One evening young Upton Sinclair, who was living in Mary McDowell's Stockyards Settlement,* and writing *The Jungle,* told me with quiet conviction that the next President would be a Socialist. As I remember it, he proved to be McKinley.†

I think it is the undying hope of better times coming which keeps our poor from the desperation that drives men to revolt. A German immigrant once said to me: ''In the Old Country you know you are just what your father was and your grandfather, and your son will be the same; here you can go higher and he can go higher still.'' In the winter of 1914, when unemployment was very great and Chicago was full of drifting men from all over the Middle West, the French dramatist Brieux‡ came to Hull-House and I happened to be the one to ''tote'' him. (In Hull-House that is the convenient term for showing people over the House, and we speak also of ''toters'' and ''totees.'') M. Brieux said he wanted to see poor people, the really, abjectly poor. So I took him over to Bowen Hall, our largest auditorium, which we had thrown open to the unemployed and which was full of men, some in groups talking and smoking, some making coffee in a big boiler in the kitchen. ''Here you have our very poorest,'' I said—''men from all over the country who have had to leave their wives and children to the charities while they travel off in desperate search for work.'' He looked around the room, then he said, ''This is not poverty. This is sudden, temporary disaster. It is not what we French call *la misère.* These men are normal and they will go back to normal life again. In France we have people who for generations have not had enough to eat.''

In settlement life, as one comes to know simple people intimately, one loses one's contempt for the banal, the bromide, the cliché, because one hears them used with such complete sincerity. You cannot laugh at ''There's nothing like a mother's love'' when you hear it said by a widow who has

*University of Chicago Settlement.—Eds.
†Actually Theodore Roosevelt.—Eds.
‡Eugène Brieux (1858–1932).—Eds.

made up her mind to turn scrubwoman in a downtown office rather than send her child to an orphanage. When a young Irish girl said to me, "It would be selling my soul. I'd rather starve," the words did not sound melodramatic, for I knew that she was making the choice between working for eight dollars a week at the Fair* and following one of her friends into the luxury and idleness of a prostitute's life.

I used to go the the Friday-evening meetings of Mrs. Pelham's Friendly Club, made up of scrubwomen chiefly, and I would listen with real emotion when they sang, "Thou wilt still be adored, as this moment thou art, Let thy loveliness fade as it will. And around the dear ruin each wish of my heart, Shall entwine itself verdantly still." I could see the dreamy look in the "dear ruin's" eyes as she thought back to the days when "himself" was not an old drunken brute, but a gallant Irish lad whispering sweet promises. That a sense for fact was not lost in the sweetness of memory I realized when I heard one of them say, "My sister's got it good. Her old man's dead."

This sort of outspoken frankness sometimes startled me, but I came to see that it was only complete sincerity quite free from self-consciousness. A young Italian mother came to see me at the end of one of Chicago's most unendurable summers. Her baby had been sick for weeks, and night after night she had been up with him until she was exhausted. She said, "I'd look at him and think, 'My God, if you're going to die why don't you die?' " It was not hardhearted, it was only frank. The same thought might surely flash into the mind of any mother who was at the end of her strength, but she would push it back in horror. Antonia faced it without any shame; to her it was natural, but it did not make her stop pacing the floor with the baby.

In settlement life it is impossible not to see how deep and fundamental are the inequalities in our democratic country. That belief, so dear to Americans, that opportunity is open to all, that the exceptional child can rise to the highest position in the community if he will, may be true in politics, in business, even in the learned professions, but

*The Columbian Exposition of 1893, commemorating the four-hundredth anniversary of the discovery of America.— Eds.

certainly not in the arts. One of the saddest things in the lot of the poor is the crushing down of artistic talent. My sister Norah, who had art classes in Hull-House for several years, used to suffer again and again the grief of seeing some promising young artist, Italian or Mexican, or Bohemian, leave school for the barren monotony of factory work, too tired after hours of it to do anything creative, his gift wasted. Yet no one can deny the need in our country for those gifts which the immigrants from countries with a more highly developed artistic life could bring us. . . .

There were two things I acquired from my life at Hull-House which were certainly undesirable, and which, at long last, I have rid myself of: a deep suspicion and fear of the police and a hostility toward newspaper reporters. Both feelings had plenty of foundation in experience. Chicago's police were Tories in their political thinking, and they treated those they considered rebels against the social order with little consideration for the Bill of Rights. Also, though many were foreign-born, they despised the foreign-born of other nations. My first experience with the Chicago police came during my first year at Hull-House. At that time our neighborhood streets were lined with big, wooden garbage boxes, very convenient seats on a pleasant day. At the noon hour two Italian workmen were sitting talking on the one in front of their tenement when a Polish-born policeman told them to move on. The command was senseless; it was their garbage box, and they refused, whereupon he drew his revolver and shot them both. I came by a few moments later to find an angry mob of Italians storming our little playground house where the policeman had taken refuge (he was soon rescued by a patrol wagon), and the wounded men with their weeping wives waiting for the ambulance. One of them died in the County Hospital from a wound in the lungs.

This was so shocking a deed that we felt we could not let it be passed over in silence, as the Chief of Police had decided was best. When a delegation of Italians came to us to appeal for some sort of action we asked Clarence Darrow, then living not far from Hull-House, to bring charges against the Polish policeman, and we collected, in nickels and dimes, some four hundred dollars for a retaining fee. But nothing came of it. Darrow never pushed it: he explained that his role was that of defender, not prosecutor, and the policeman was not even suspended.

In our mass meetings the sight of an officer in uniform, instead of bringing a sense of security, would fill us with dread of some violent deed, not on the part of the audience, but of the police. There was a big meeting of Russians one evening, Mensheviks and Bolsheviks, gesticulating furiously and shouting at each other, but I knew nothing worse would happen if the police would let them alone. But a panicky resident had called up the Maxwell Street station and a group of burly Irish policemen gathered in a corner muttering to each other. I went up to them and said that it was only a discussion of two theories of government and I was sure it would end peacefully. "Lady," said one of them, "you people oughtn't to let bums like these come here. If I had my way they'd all be lined up against a wall at sunrise and shot." I lived through an hour of wretched suspense but luckily there was no chance for the use of police clubs and the meeting broke up without any incident.

But almost as much did I fear the newspaper reporter, and my fear was shared by all the residents of Hull-House. We knew that anything that went wrong at the House was a "story," and that ingenious twisting might turn the most innocent answer into a ridiculous or a damaging statement. And, of course, there was no redress. To write a protest only made matters worse by giving added publicity to the story. It was an unwritten rule that these gentry were not to be handled by anyone but Miss Addams or Miss Lathrop, a rule we were all thankful to follow. One of our worst experiences was over the Averbuch murder, a story that Miss Addams has told in her *Twenty Years*. Averbuch* was a young Russian Jew, an anarchist, who had been in this country only a short time. He went, on some errand never explained, to call upon the Chief of Police, who, when he saw a swarthy foreigner facing him, lost his head and emptied his revolver into the lad's body, most of the bullets entering from the back. Averbuch had no connection with Hull-House; he was studying English at another settlement, but Hull-House had more news value. The reporters came in swarms to in-

terview us and to prove that Hull-House was a nest of anarchism.

I learned then the deadly use the papers can make of the word "admit." Clara Landsberg, who was in charge of our adult education department, insisted that Averbuch was not among the students. "Would you have accepted him if he had applied and you knew he was an anarchist?" "Certainly," she said, "we do not ask anyone what his political theories are." But the reporter's words read: "Miss Landsberg admits that there are anarchists in the classes at Hull-House." Miss Addams was in bed with tonsillitis just then, and Julia Lathrop was away. I struggled in vain with a relentless young man and finally in despair took him up to Miss Addams. He listened to her in silence and then, blinking his colorless eyes behind his thick spectacles, he remarked, "I may as well tell you, Miss Addams, that I have orders from my paper to link Averbuch up with Hull-House and that is what I'm going to do."

It was the Averbuch case, by the way, which started a long friendship between Miss Addams and a young Chicago lawyer, Harold Ickes.† When she sought for a lawyer to take up the case, vindicate the young victim and bring to light the methods the police had made use of, she was refused by all the established, eminent lawyers. But one of them suggested that she try a young fellow who was known to have radical sympathies; she did, and Harold Ickes took the case. His effort was of value only as it served to show our terrified immigrant neighbors that there were still people in Chicago who believed in justice and freedom, and it did rescue from the hands of the police poor Olga Averbuch, the lad's elder sister, whom the police had tried to "third degree" into a confession of an anarchist plot. . . .

At Hull-House one got into the labor movement as a matter of course, without realizing how or when. As I look back I can remember a few startling experiences which must have pushed me farther along the way, but I cannot remember when I began to see the working world through the workers' eyes. One of these experiences came to me through an Italian girl whom I was helping with her English. Filomena was the eldest of a large

*Lazarus Averbuch (d. 1906).—Eds.

†Harold Ickes (1874–1952), Secretary of the Interior, 1933–1946.—Eds.

family and, as used to happen fairly often, she was sent over to this country to pave the way for the rest, to earn money for the family's passage. It was hard to understand an Italian family sending a young girl out into the world alone, especially when one saw how strictly she would be guarded as soon as her family arrived. Only a complete ignorance of what such a journey meant and of the difference between Chicago and a Calabrian village could explain it.

Filomena had but one purpose in life, to earn money. She worked in one of the great men's clothing factories and soon rose to the skilled job of making buttonholes on the lapels of men's dress suits. This was shortly before the great strike of 1910, Sidney Hillman's strike, and the work in the factories was let to subcontractors who acted as foremen and whose one idea was to push the work as much as possible. There was much talk of revolt among the girls in Filomena's department, but she told me she paid no attention to it, she stuck to her buttonholes and the girls called her a mean pace-maker.

Then one day the boss said to her, "How many needles of thread do you use in a day, Filomena?"

"About three hundred," she answered. "Why don't you take your needles home with you and thread them evenings?" he suggested. "You'd make a lot more if you did." Filomena was much impressed, she followed the suggestion, and that week she made more buttonholes than she had ever dreamed of. The foreman let all the other girls know what Filomena had drawn in her pay envelope, and one after another the girls began threading their needles at night. Then, when nearly all were doing this, he cut the pay so that they would make just what they had before. That was at last too much for Filomena; when the strike broke she went out with the others.

Another happening which is stamped on my memory concerns a young Irish girl of sixteen, gentle and shy, with the natural good breeding which one finds often among the poorest Irish and which makes one believe that they are right in saying that theirs was an old civilization when we Anglo-Saxons were still savages. Celia was a waitress in an all-night restaurant, for at that time a girl might work twelve hours a night seven nights in the week in Illinois. For her own protection I had her join the waitresses' union, and when her place

went on strike she took her turn picketing. Chicago police have never felt it part of their duty to observe the law toward strikers; violence, often needless and unprovoked, has been the rule. I felt personally responsible for Celia and made my way through the crowd outside the restaurant just in time to see her dragged along, unresisting, by a huge policeman and hustled with abusive words into a police van. We did get her off without a jail sentence but not till the next day.

Nobody who has not had to look on helplessly while servants of one's own government treat humble people with brutality can realize what rage it arouses, how all one's love and pride of country vanishes for the time being. Another time when this anger came over me was in the Kuppenheimer strike in Chicago. I do not remember the year but it must have been after 1915 for I know that I told Miss Addams I had seen nothing in occupied Belgium that so enraged me. Brutality in Belgium was the Germans' responsibility, brutality in Chicago was partly mine. I had undertaken to picket in that strike and had just reached a factory on the far West Side when I saw a little group of men running wildly in all directions. They were the pickets, thin, stoop-shouldered young Jews and Italians, and they were pursued by big thugs hired by the company, who struck and kicked them as they ran. A little knot of uniformed policemen, sent there to "keep law and order," looked on idly.

In the great Hart, Schaffner and Marx strike of 1910 I did not picket but went on a citizens' committee formed by Miss Addams, which met at Hull-House. She has told the story of that strike and how wisely it was settled, with a Joint Board of Arbitration composed of employers and employed with an impartial chairman, a method which has averted strikes ever since. Sidney Hillman emerged as leader of the new union. I met him in the course of the strike when Julia Lathrop and I called on him in his tiny hotel bedroom (I remember there was only one chair in it), a slender, very youthful-looking man, quiet and a bit shy, but very wise and steady.

Picketing in different strikes was no unusual job in those days. I used to volunteer for the early morning picket usually, because the police were much less in evidence then, and I was in mortal fear of having one of them seize me and drag me about. The fact of arrest was not as bad as the way it was done. But late one winter afternoon I found myself marching up and down in perfect safety because I was with Professor [William Gardner] Hale, head of the Latin Department of the University of Chicago. We were discussing the poems of Catullus, his favorite Latin poet. He was tall and very impressive, every inch a scholar and a gentleman, yet he could not understand why the police would not arrest him. "I am doing exactly what those poor fellows are doing," he said, "but they pay no attention to me." Of course the police had too much sense to provide such headlines for the papers.

Hull-House was the Mecca for many who came to Chicago in those days, for its fame had spread over the world with astonishing speed. It was said that Chicago had three *Sehenswürdigkeiten*—the University, the stockyards, and Hull-House. Some who came were radicals, Russian revolutionists, ranging from [Pavel Nikolayevich] Miliukoff, who worked for a parliamentary system based on the English, to Nikolai, who at his party's command had assassinated some high dignitary and then had escaped from his Siberian prison in an empty hogshead. There were Liberals and Socialists of the moderate English type—Patrick Geddes, John Morley, J. A. Hobson, Sidney and Beatrice Webb, H. G. Wells, John Burns. The last was impressive but a bit amusing, for when, after a long discussion on all the shortcomings of our political system, someone said helplessly, "Well, what ought we to do about it?" John Burns responded promptly, "What you need in this country is one hundred John Burnses." John Morley won my heart by the way in which he took our shamed acknowledgment of corruption in city politics. "We British are partly to blame," he said, "for a great many of your political bosses are Irish and we are responsible for the Irish attitude toward government—that it is a weapon to be used by the victor against the defeated." . . .

Aylmer Maude, the disciple and translator of Tolstoy, came to see us on his way back from Canada where he had settled that strange sect opposed to war and to civilization, the Dukhobors, using the royalties from Tolstoy's *Resurrection* to defray the expenses. Lord Robert Cecil* came after the

war, and so did Graham Wallas.† I remember a conversation between him and George Mead, professor of philosophy at the University of Chicago, and a devoted friend of Hull-House. Mr. Wallas had been reading some theses submitted by students of sociology for the Ph.D. degree. "Now look at these," he said, "careful, meticulously detailed studies of Chicago, of overcrowding, of housing, of recreation, but never once a bird's-eye view of the whole. Not one man ever stops to ask, 'Why have so big a city, anyway?' " Professor Mead protested, "But what use would that be? A student's ideas on such a subject are of no value. His careful collection of data is a real contribution." "Only to statistics," retorted Graham Wallas, "and you Americans have enough already. What you need is a wider outlook, a vision." . . .

Our English visitors sometimes surprised us by combining social radicalism with a total lack of democratic feeling, which to our way of thinking was most inconsistent. I remember a famous English Socialist who disapproved of our attempt at universal education up through the secondary schools. He believed that, after the essential primary grades, only gifted children should be helped to go farther. Another Fabian Socialist amused me very much when one morning I took him out into our neighborhood. He was talking eagerly about the need of vacation schools for London slum children as we stepped out into our courtyard, which was crowded with children waiting to go on a picnic in the country. He never saw them, at least not as slum children like those he was eager to help; he saw them only as obstacles in his way, and he pushed them aside impatiently as if they were so many chickens, all the time telling me about the pitiful children in London. I thought to myself, "You may love humanity, but you certainly do not love your fellow man." We found we could not always trust English radicals and Socialists to be nice to their American "comrades," when the latter were from an inferior social level, as most of them were, and we had some painful and embarrassing experiences when what

1885–1892, 1895–1902, Lord Cecil carried out such reforms as slum clearance and free public education.—Eds.

†Graham Wallas (1858–1932) was an English political scientist and lecturer at the London School of Economics.—Eds.

*As Prime Minister and Foreign Secretary of England,

was supposed to be a joyful meeting of kindred souls proved to be a meeting of the snubbers and the snubbed.

A great contrast to such visitors was Prince Peter Kropotkin, one of the most lovable persons I have ever met. He was a typical revolutionist of the early Russian type, an aristocrat who threw himself into the movement for emancipation of the masses out of a passionate love for his fellow man, and a longing for justice. His book, *Mutual Aid, a Factor of Evolution,* expounds a doctrine very different from that which now inspires Russian leaders, and he would be held in contempt by them as a sentimentalist; indeed that was true in his last years, after the Bolshevist revolution. I think he was as bitterly disappointed in the outcome of that revolution as was our other Russian revolutionary friend, Catherine Breshkovsky, but he never denounced it, as she did; that was not his way. He stayed some time with us at Hull-House, and we all came to love him, not only we who lived under the same roof but the crowds of Russian refugees who came to see him. No matter how down-and-out, how squalid even, a caller would be, Prince Kropotkin would give him a joyful welcome and kiss him on both cheeks.

It was most unfortunate that his visit to us came just a short time before the assassination of McKinley. That event woke up the dormant terror of anarchists which always lay close under the surface of Chicago's thinking and feeling, ever since the Haymarket riot. It was known that [Leon] Czolgosz, the assassin, had been in Chicago at the time when both Emma Goldman and Kropotkin were there, and a rumor started that he had met them and the plot had been of their making—Czolgosz had been their tool. Then the story came to involve Hull-House, which had been the scene of these secret, murderous meetings. We went through a bad time but chiefly at the hands of reporters; the police did not molest us. They did, however, make arrests right and left, of all who could be suspected of radical opinions.

It was at that moment, when the reputation of Hull-House was at its lowest point, that Raymond Robins, who was living at the Northwestern Settlement, came to beg Miss Addams to do something to help a group of Russian Jewish anarchists ("philosophical anarchists") who had been caught in the police dragnet and were being held in jail incommunicado, while the police sought for evidence that would link them to Czolgosz. Robins had been able to do nothing himself but he believed Miss Addams might persuade the mayor to let them have a lawyer and she might bring back some reassurance to their frightened families. Nobody who has not lived through one of Chicago's attacks of anti-radical hysteria can understand what courage it took to do this. It would have been easy to reason that her first duty was to Hull-House, that these anarchists had never been inside its doors, and that if she espoused their cause she would be injuring an institution which could succeed only if it had the confidence of the public. But that was never her way of thinking. She went to the mayor, Carter Harrison,* who told her that if she was ready to take the responsibility on her own shoulders, she might visit the prisoners and carry out their requests. She did, and of course she lived down the antagonism; Chicago came back to its senses and gave her again the warm admiration and help it always gave her in the long intervals between panics. . . .

*Carter Henry Harrison (1860–1953), mayor of Chicago, 1897–1905, 1911–1912.—Eds.

Ellen Gates Starr
and Labor

Eleanor Grace Clark

Ellen Gates Starr was frail and sensitive; she was artistic by nature and by training. Abhorring the dust that gathered on everything at Hull-House during the summer months, she could often be seen frantically dusting the furniture even though it was a futile task. At the settlement Miss Starr lectured on art history and spent long hours lovingly producing finely bound books in her own bookbindery. Yet there was no greater or more active defender of organized labor at Hull-House than Ellen Starr.

A number of the residents, including Jane Addams, were ardent supporters of organized labor, but instinctively disapproved of strikes and violence. Often they angered labor leaders because, in the name of arbitration, they appeared to sell out to management. Ellen Starr was different. When a strike broke out she was always in the picket line. On one occasion when she was arrested, she was defended by Harold Ickes, then a young Chicago lawyer. Ellen Starr's actions and her vocal defense of labor won her many friends among labor leaders in the city. The following is from a tribute by Eleanor Grace Clark (b. 1895) to Ellen Starr after her death. [Eleanor Grace Clark, "Ellen Gates Starr, O. S. B. (1859–1940)," Commonweal (March 15, 1940), 446–447.]

In her life-long labor for others, there is, perhaps, no more spectacular chapter than that which recounts her trade-union activities in Chicago. She was, in fact, one of the pioneers in the fostering of labor organization for women in this country. Early a member of the Women's Trade Union League, it was inevitable that Miss Starr should take an active part in the strikes where women were especially concerned. After having taken a sympathetic part in the textile strike of 1913, helping to secure a settlement in which the workers won sixty percent of their demands, she entered the 1914 Henrici Restaurant strike in deadly earnest. She elected to do picket duty in behalf of certain waitresses who had been, in Miss Starr's opinion, unjustly discharged. It was her experience "on the line" that induced her shortly to go the whole way with the girls, a wayfaring that led finally to her arrest and trial "for disorderly conduct." Describing the plight of the waitresses to the jury, Miss Starr won all fair minds to their side by declaring:

> Anyone who knows anything about the work of a waitress ought to feel sympathy with these girls. A girl will make possibly $12.00 a week on an average. This is counting their tips. [The Henrici girls received a weekly wage of $8.00.] And this average is bound to be most discouraging to the one whose average is below $12.00. If she makes a mistake with an order, or a customer is displeased with the order and sends it back, the waitress must pay for it and may not even have it for her own meal. Then she

> must pay thirty cents a day to her bus boy, and if she does not, she is bound not to get adequate service in the clearing of her tables and making them ready for the new customer. Besides this, she must pay five cents apiece for each apron she has laundered in the place.

Having stated so much to be true and verified by her own investigation, Miss Starr startled the jury by her ringing challenge: "Now, figure up just how much she can make, and when you have done that, figure up, if you can, how she can live on it."

At this trial Miss Starr was defended by "one Mr. Harold Ickes," then a rising young lawyer in Chicago. Mr. Ickes donated his services as his contribution to the cause of "fair labor conditions." The trial of so prominent a civic and social worker, who had been known and admired in Chicago for her good works for more than twenty-five years, naturally created a great sensation, and hence much favorable publicity for the strikers. Miss Starr was a very frail little woman, probably never weighing much over a hundred pounds; and her manners and speech were not only impeccable, but elegant, as indeed was everything else about her exquisite person. It was therefore a hilarious moment in the court-room when the officer who had arrested her declared that "she had attacked him with violence" and had "tried to frighten him" from the discharge of his duty (*i.e.*, from arresting the girls) by telling him to "leave them girls be!" Miss Starr's version of it was delivered to the jury, according to the newspaper accounts, "with a ready smile which was wholly and unswervingly on duty during all of her testimony." She testified as follows:

> I maintain the right of free speech. I maintain the right of organization for working people. I maintain the right of peaceful picketing, and I was there in front of Henrici's on March 2 to see fair play, to prevent brutality if I could by my presence, and to make formal protest against illegal arrest. All I said was, "As an American citizen, I protest against the arrest of these persons who are doing nothing contrary to the law." I did not jump into the air, or shake my fists about, as was charged, nor did I shout or make any commotion. I spoke in as even a tone as I could command. My act was a formal protest born of my sympathies and my desire to do what I believed was for the right. I said what I said

for the benefit of whomever it might concern. I should do so again if I felt so inclined.

And to be sure, she did feel so inclined again and again during the long strike of the Amalgamated Clothing Workers of America which took place the following year. On this occasion she was placed in charge of all the picketing activity. Since in this strike there were many factories, tailoring shops, and stores to be picketed, Miss Starr could not be everywhere at once "to protect" the workers from the violence of the police, particularly the "irregular police" and the hired sluggers. She therefore enlisted whole troops of her friends—doctors, lawyers, clergymen, and professors, as well as other social workers and residents at Hull-House. Among those who helped in the picketing were many sympathizers from the University of Chicago—Professor and Mrs. F. R. Lillie, Dr. Edward Ames, Dr. Edith Flint, Professor Hackett Newman, Dr. Alice Hamilton, and many others. Of course, the more prominent the names of social and civic and academic leaders she could enlist, the more favorable the publicity she gained for the strikers' cause. Indeed, Miss Starr turned over for this cause all the stones except the geological ones within her reach. In the final printed report of the strike, drawn up by Mr. Jacob Potofsky, the strike Secretary-Treasurer, he says:

> From outside individuals [*i.e.*, other than members of the Amalgamated] Ellen Gates Starr of Hull-House was the hardest worker I knew. Nothing was too hard for her; she gave and solicited funds, secured clothing, relief and shelter for individual families, was on the picket line, addressed meetings, wrote articles, interested others in our behalf. In a word, Miss Starr was one active in all phases of strike activities.

For her work in connection with this strike, Miss Starr was made an honorary life member of the Amalgamated, an association she valued to the end of her life.

An Anti–Hull-House Voice

Wallace L. DeWolf

Some people, including many who gave money to Hull-House projects, were not very happy with the settlement's support of organized labor. Included in that group was Wallace Leroy DeWolf (1854–1930), a lawyer and Chicago businessman, who in 1916 received a request to give money to the Bowen Country Club, the Hull-House summer camp. His reply follows. [Wallace L. DeWolf to Jane Addams, July 17, 1916, Jane Addams Papers, Swarthmore College Peace Collection.]

July 17, 1916

Dear Miss Addams:

Your letter, asking for a contribution for Hull-House for the entertainment of children at your country place, is at hand. I very much regret that for such a worthy object I do not feel inclined to respond. If Hull-House would confine its activity to work like this, it should meet the approval and support of all good citizens, but to my mind it has been so thoroughly unionized that it has lost its usefulness and has become a detriment and harm to the community as a whole.

In 1903 I was president of the Kellogg Switchboard and Supply Co., and for several months we had a serious strike in your immediate neighborhood. Without taking the trouble to investigate the causes of the strike, I felt that the strikers received sympathy and support from Hull-House. If you have not forgotten, I wish to recall to your mind the fact that you called upon me in regard to the strike, and tried to obtain a settlement, but the terms which you suggested were impossible, and while I appreciated your motive, the terms suggested by you were impracticable and impossible, and nothing in a practical way came of the interview.

Since that time I have carefully watched the attitude and sentiment of Hull-House on strikes and union labor, and must say that I do not approve of the same. In taking up the cause of union labor I believe you have gone far afield from your original purpose, and have done a vast amount of harm. I was particularly impressed with the attitude of Helen [sic] Starr in connection with the strike of waitresses and the attempts made by unions to discredit Judge Holdom and Judge Baldwin* for issuing injunctions in labor cases. These two judges have been the only judges who had the courage to issue injunctions in labor cases, and all of their orders have been sustained and approved by the courts of last resort. To discredit such men as these, even by implication, is positively wrong and is detrimental to the best interests of society and the community. Many instances of graft on the part of labor leaders must have come to the attention of Hull-House, and the recent conviction of a number of leaders of unions is evidence of the way in which many of them are conducted. When Judge Holdom and Judge Baldwin were up for re-election I noticed automobiles traveling through the streets of the down town district calling attention to the fact that these two judges had issued injunctions in labor cases, and one of them stated that they had prevented poor waitresses from getting $8 per week. If Hull-House has not stood for this sort of thing, I am not aware of it.

From Hull-House we have heard commendations of the unions and their acts by members of the Hull-House staff and its residents. It seems to me that it is time we heard something from Hull-House on the other side of this question, although as far as I am concerned, it seems to me that it would be better if Hull-House had nothing to do with these questions. If Hull-House is to continue its usefulness, it seems to me that it should divorce itself from politics, religion, employers' associations, and trade unions. Until this time arrives I do not think that Hull-House is entitled to the support of the community.

Yours very truly,
WALLACE L. DEWOLF

*Probably Jesse Holdom (1851–1930) and Jesse A. Baldwin (b. 1854), Appellate Court judges in 1916.—Eds.

The Working Girl's Song

Harriet Monroe

Harriet Monroe (1860–1936) was the founder of Poetry: A Magazine of Verse, *discoverer of Carl Sandburg and Vachel Lindsay, early publisher of Ezra Pound, and patron saint of the new American poetry of realism and imagery. A resident of Hull-House for a brief time, all her life she remained a friend and supporter of the settlement. She wrote poems in support of settlement goals and crusades. Some were put to music by Eleanor Smith, director of the Hull-House Music School and the composer with whom Miss Monroe collaborated on the operetta ''The Trolls' Holiday,'' often performed at Hull-House.*

This poem, praising the working girl, was read at the Chicago Conference of the National Women's Trade Union League in 1908. The League, founded in 1903 at the urging of William English Walling and Mary Kenney O'Sullivan, both graduates of Hull-House, sought to encourage the participation of women in trade unions and to foster cooperation between those women who had to work and those who did not. The Chicago branch of the League met regularly at Hull-House. [Harriet Monroe, ''The Working Girl's Song,'' Life and Labor (August 1912), 236.]

Sisters of the whirling wheel
  Are we all day;
Builders of a house of steel
  On Time's highway,
Giving bravely, hour by hour,
All we have of youth and power.

Oh, lords of the house we rear,
  Hear us, hear!
Green are the fields in May-time,
Grant us our love-time, play-time.
Short is the day and dear.

Fingers fly and engines boom
  The livelong day,
Through far fields when roses bloom

The soft winds play.
Vast the work is—sound and true
Be the tower we build for you!

Oh, lords of the house we rear,
   Hear us, hear!
Green are the fields in May-time,
Grant us our love-time, play-time.
Short is the day and dear.

Ours the future is—we face
   The whole world's needs.
In our hearts the coming race
   For life's joy pleads.
As you make us—slaves or free—
So the men unborn shall be.

Oh, lords of the house we rear,
   Hear us, hear!
Green are the fields in May-time,
Grant us our love-time, play-time.
Short is the day and dear.

Hull-House, Irreligious and Socialistic

Chicago Chronicle

Hull-House was often attacked and criticized by those who thought it harbored radicals and preached socialism or anarchism. This editorial from the Chicago Chronicle, *a newspaper which periodically attacked Hull-House, was typical. This piece also echoed the frequent charge of many religious groups that Hull-House was anti-religious. [*Chicago Chronicle, *September 16, 1903.]*

The fact that Hull house conducts its great work for the uplifting of humanity without religious teaching of any kind will be news to many people who as Christians or as members of Christian organizations have given support to that enterprise.

Whether religious or irreligious, Hull house

would not properly merit criticism from the secular press were it not for the fact that while ignoring religion it appears to embrace socialism—a theory which is and always has been at war with religion.

Last week it harbored for a time and gave audience to EUGENE V. DEBS, a socialist and revolutionist, who improved the opportunity to declare that KARL MARX was a greater man than THOMAS JEFFERSON and one whose philosophy might more safely be followed.

When it is remembered that KARL MARX was also irreligious and that the first thing contemplated by his scheme of social regeneration and political revolution was the destruction of religion, it is possible that some of the admirers of Hull house will be able to see a connection between its banishment of religion and the favor which its shows to socialists and socialism.

Just how KARL MARX viewed this subject is shown by the following extract from one of his books—an extract which furnishes a key to his revolutionary system: "The idea of God is the keystone of perverted civilization. The true root of liberty, of equality, of culture, is atheism."

Prince KRAPOTKIN [*sic*], whose portrait is a conspicuous embellishment of Hull house, is a Russian anarchist whose writings and speeches show that he subscribes to all this and more. Having dethroned God and annihilated religion, he would destroy the churches and disperse their congregations.

If Hull house finds it inconvenient to carry on its work in the slums with any religious connections—if religious doctrine of any kind would be likely to repel the people whom its activities reach—there is reason to ask if a work which must of necessity be inimical to religion is worth while.

A good many people fail to appreciate the fact that socialism is as much a partisan or sectarian doctrine as is to be found in the platform of a political party or in the confession of a church.

Enterprises in sociology which are so completely disassociated from partisanship as to have no avowed religious or political character certainly stultify themselves when they embrace socialism and anarchy, which, so far as their deluded followers are concerned, are religion and politics combined.

Hull house is planted in a community made up largely of foreigners who have had little instruc-

Hull-House neighborhood. Etching by Norah Hamilton.

who had worked in settlement houses in Boston while a student at Harvard, had high praise for Hull-House but criticized the settlement's and vice commission's overreaction to the white slave trade and prostitution.

Lippmann in 1913 was still a socialist, but he was groping toward a more conservative position. He saw Hull-House as a utopian experiment which he felt the world would not follow. Yet most settlement workers would have agreed with the basic thesis of his book—that politics must satisfy human wants, not abstract political concepts. [Walter Lippmann, A Preface to Politics *(New York, 1913), 150–55.]*

tion in Americanism. The fact that they there receive lessons in socialism such as are given in Russia and Germany will not help them to grasp American ideas or to become good citizens.

To whatever extent Hull house propagates socialism it confirms in them a bad habit of thought, the effects of which may be looked for later on when the recipients pass from the atmosphere of that establishment to the influence of agitators and revolutionists.

Well-Meaning but Unmeaning

Walter Lippmann

While some criticized Hull-House for being too radical, others, notably the socialists, single-taxers, and other political radicals, attacked the settlement for trying to "patch up" the American system rather than working for basic changes. Walter Lippmann (1889–1974), in A Preface to Politics, *written when he was only three years out of college, included Hull-House with various vice and crime commissions as futile attempts to solve urban problems. Each, he said, attacked the symptoms not the cause of society's ills. Yet Lippmann,*

. . . Whoever has visited Hull House can see for himself the earnest effort Miss Addams has made to treat sex with dignity and joy. For Hull House differs from most settlements in that it is full of pictures, of colors, and of curios. The atmosphere is light; you feel none of that moral oppression which hangs over the usual settlement as over a gathering of missionaries. Miss Addams has not only made Hull House a beautiful place; she has stocked it with curious and interesting objects. The theater, the museum, the crafts and the arts, games and dances—they are some of those "other methods of expression which lust can seek." It is no accident that Hull House is the most successful settlement in America.

Yet who does not feel its isolation in that brutal city? A little Athens in a vast barbarism—you wonder how much of Chicago Hull House can civilize. As you walk those grim streets and look into the stifling houses, or picture the relentless stockyards, the conviction that vice and its misery cannot be transmuted by policemen and Morals Commissions, the feeling that spying and inspecting and prosecuting will not drain the marsh becomes a certainty. You want to shout at the forcible moralizer: "so long as you acquiesce in the degradation of your city, so long as work remains nothing but ill-paid drudgery and every instinct of joy is mocked by dirt and cheapness and brutality—just so long will your efforts be fruitless, yes even though you raid and prosecute, even though you make Comstock* the Czar of Chicago.''

But Hull House cannot remake Chicago. A few hundred lives can be changed, and for the rest it is a guide to the imagination. Like all utopias, it cannot succeed, but it may point the way to success. If Hull House is unable to civilize Chicago, it at least shows Chicago and America what a civilization might be like. Friendly, where our cities are friendless, beautiful, where they are ugly; sociable and open, where our daily life is furtive; work a craft; art a participation—it is in miniature the goal of statesmanship. If Chicago were like Hull House, we say to ourselves, then vice would be no problem—it would dwindle, what was left would be the Falstaff in us all, and only a spiritual anemia could worry over that jolly and redeeming coarseness.

What stands between Chicago and civilization? No one can doubt that to abolish prostitution means to abolish the slum and the dirty alley, to stop overwork, underpay, the sweating and the torturing monotony of business, to breathe a new life into education, ventilate society with frankness, and fill life with play and art, with games, with passions which hold and suffuse the imagination.

It is a revolutionary task, and like all real revolutions it will not be done in a day or a decade because someone orders it to be done. A change in the whole quality of life is something that neither the policeman's club nor an insurrectionary raid can achieve. If you want a revolution that shall really matter in human life—and what sane man can help desiring it?—you must look to the infinitely complicated results of the dynamic movements in society. These revolutions require a rare combination of personal audacity and social patience. The best agents of such a revolution are men who are bold in their plans because they realize how deep and enormous is the task. . . .

You can have a Hull House established by private initiative and maintained by individual genius, just as you had planters who freed their slaves or as you have employers today who humanize their factories. But the fine example is not readily imitated when industrial forces fight against it. So

*Anthony Comstock (1844–1915), vice vigilante and head of the New York Society for the Suppression of Vice.—Eds.

even if the Commission had drawn splendid plans for housing, work conditions, education, and play it would have done only part of the task of statesmanship. We should then know what to do, but not how to get it done.

An ideal suspended in a vacuum is ineffective: it must point a dynamic current. Only then does it gather power, only then does it enter into life. . . .

Radicals Attack Hull-House

New York Call

The New York Call, *a socialist newspaper, took a more consistent radical position in denouncing what it considered the few accomplishments and the futile reform efforts of Jane Addams and Hull-House. Of the two editorials that follow, the first was written on the occasion of a speech by Miss Addams to a group of ministers, the second when she seconded the nomination of Theodore Roosevelt for President at the Progressive party convention in 1912. [''An Oft-Told Tale,''* New York Call, *April 25, 1912; ''The Lamb Tags on to the Lion,''* New York Call, *August 11, 1912.]*

An Oft-Told Tale

There is much truth in the statement that what are known as ''good'' people are very often tiresome. Most of them have contracted the habit of ''vain repetition,'' which now, as in the days of Christ, passes current for righteousness.

We confess that when we hear for the millionth time the statement that ''the church must take hold of the 'social evil' and stamp it out of existence,'' or words to that effect, it makes us very tired.

Just why our ''good'' people should keep on with the eternal reiteration of this flatulent phrase is difficult to understand except on the hypothesis that righteousness is usually developed at the expense of brains.

Here, for instance, is Miss Jane Addams, the well-known Chicago reformer, addressing the Christian Conservation Congress on this subject at Carnegie Hall, and repeating over and over again what she and thousands of other reformers have repeated weekly perhaps for the last thirty years.

And how was it received? With indifference? Not at all. With "tremendous applause" instead. And the press, what did it do? Did it reprimand Miss Addams for too plain speaking? Did it declare she had "gone too far"? Not at all. It declared she was all right. She didn't "mince words." It commended her therefore.

What will be the result? Will "the church" start out and do what Miss Addams says it should do? Is the "social evil" going to be "stamped out" at last? No, it isn't.

Perhaps it might be more charitable and at the same time a just recognition of Miss Addams' good intentions to answer, "Let us wait and see."

Patience is a virtue, to be sure, but it is possible to exhaust it. We have been waiting year in and year out for this thing to happen, but it hasn't happened. We have listened to Miss Addams in particular for the last twenty years, and a host of other reformers repeating week in and week out this very statement; we have seen innumerable "crusades" suggested, organized, and financed for this purpose, but what has come of it all? Nothing.

Miss Addams is an excellent and well-meaning woman. In fact, "gentle Jane is as good as gold." For her good intentions and desire to elevate humanity we have the sincerest respect. She has given her life and her fortune to this work. If the self-sacrifice of an individual could accomplish anything of value, her work should have told effectively. But what has her effort accomplished? We will not say it has accomplished nothing. Some of her handiwork remains, but what does it amount to? A speck in an ocean of misery, suffering, and poverty. And none know it better than Miss Jane Addams when she casts a retrospective glance at her life-work and compares it with the existing and ever swelling volume of evil conditions which she sought to remove. . . .

The Lamb Tags on to the Lion

In the strange political conjunction of the Gentle Jane Addams of Hull House with the Roaring Bull Moose of Oyster Bay, there is very much more than a mere additional confirmation of the increasing entrance of woman into political life. Miss Addams has been in politics of a small and quiet kind for many years, and apparently detested the noisy and explosive features of that interesting game. In seconding the nomination of the Turbulent One she has certainly made a wide departure from her heretofore calm and placid course, and to all appearances burned behind her many convenient little bridges which in the olden days secured her safe retreat after frequent little excursions into the wild and savage wastes of small radicalism.

Well do we remember those peaceful evenings at Hull House when some well-known, rampant, rip-snorting Socialist was invited to address the assemblage of timid reformers, and how the grim-visaged warrior of the red revolution always had his wrinkled front smoothed down by the mollifying little artifices of the Gentle Jane as a preliminary to his appearance on the platform.

No matter how resolutely the fighting man had determined to fright the souls of fearful reform adversaries, he found it a difficult, if not impossible, task to hand it to them raw and straight as he had intended, once Jane had got through with him. She could always, without actually saying so, manage to leave the impression that it was very bad manners to make a noise and scare timid people, and the would-be fire-eater usually found himself roaring as gently as any sucking dove instead of making the Hull House welkin ring as he had originally resolved. Jane had a curious little way of her own of clipping claws and extracting fangs in those days, and she and all her associates detested noise of all sorts, especially political, to all appearances, more than anything else in the world. And now she has hooked up with the Biggest Noise of all, and actually nominated him for the Presidency, and seemed not only to tolerate the yelling and general uproar but to actually enjoy it. Perhaps the only explanation is that after all the Socialists couldn't roar loud enough and she has been waiting all these years for Theodore the Thunderer to take the center of the stage. . . .

Immigrants at Hull-House

Edith Abbott

Hull-House, 1908–1921,'' *Social Service Review* *(September 1950), 378–379, 384–385; (December 1950), 493–494.]*

Grace (1878–1939) and Edith (1876–1957) Abbott came to live at Hull-House in 1908. Born in a small Nebraska town and students at the University of Nebraska, the two sisters became not only important members of the Hull-House group but leaders in a wide variety of social reform movements. Edith, who earned a Ph.D. from the University of Chicago, wrote many books, including Women in Industry *(1910) and* The Tenements of Chicago *(1931), on which she collaborated with Sophonisba P. Breckinridge (1866–1948), another Hull-House resident. She was also a faculty member at the University of Chicago for forty years and Dean of the School of Social Service Administration (formerly the School of Civics and Philanthropy, started by Graham Taylor) from 1924 until 1942. She lived at Hull-House for more than eighteen years.*

Grace Abbott published a two-volume study, The Child and the State *(1938), but she was less a scholar and more an activist than her sister. She was also director of the Immigrants' Protective League, which was located at Hull-House. The League sought to ease the adjustment of newcomers to America; it established waiting rooms at railroad stations, where multi-lingual men and women helped recent arrivals find their relatives or friends. The League investigated employment agencies, immigrant banks, and evening schools in an attempt to prevent fraud and to help improve the process of Americanization. Grace Abbott also devoted a large part of her time to the crusade against child labor, and she became director of the child labor division of the U.S. Children's Bureau during World War I. She was promoted to the position of director of the Children's Bureau on the retirement of Julia Lathrop in 1921, and occupied that post until 1934.*

The following account of Grace Abbott's work with immigrants at Hull-House, and the Immigrants' Protective League was written by her sister Edith. [Edith Abbott, ''Grace Abbott and

Hull House and the old West Side were full of newly arrived immigrants when Grace and I went to live there in 1908; we seemed to be surrounded by great tenement areas which have now given way to the factories and stores that have come with the business invasion.

Chicago at that time was the rushing, growing metropolis of the West, but the crowded streets about the House with their strange foreign signs and foreign-looking shops that were often very shabby and untidy seemed strangely unrelated to the great, prosperous city that was called the ''Queen of the West.''

The foreign colonies were well established, and there were Italians in front of us and to the right of us; and to the left a large Greek colony. There was a Bulgarian colony a few blocks west of Halsted Street and along to the north that had almost no women; but large numbers of fine Bulgarian men seemed to have emigrated—and they were pitiful when they were unemployed. Then you came to the old Ghetto as you followed Hull House a few blocks to the south, where the Maxwell Street Market with its competing pushcarts heaped with shoes, stockings, potatoes, onions, old clothes, new clothes, dishes, pots and pans, and food for the Sunday trade was as picturesque as it was insanitary.

I remember the story Grace told when she came back late one night from one of the small mean streets in the old Ghetto, where a League* visitor had taken her to see a Russian-Jewish girl dying of tuberculosis. The girl had come to live with a cousin on Liberty Street. ''Such a beautiful name—Liberty Street!'' the dying girl said mournfully. ''I thought to see wide beautiful street with something grand—like Statue of Liberty.'' She could not believe at first that the narrow little street with its drab frame houses was the Liberty Street of which she had dreamed. Then she got a job in a tailor shop—''Sew men's pants all day,'' but the shop was crowded, noisy, steaming in

*Immigrants' Protective League.—Eds.

summer, freezing in winter. Although she had paid back the money borrowed to come to America, she had not been able to send for her family. "Sick—maybe die and never help them," was her tragic story. The poor frame house where she lived with a kind immigrant family was also crowded, confused, and none too clean, but there seemed to be no way of making the poor girl more comfortable or hopeful, and she died soon after Grace saw her.

The Greeks were our nearest neighbors, and many of them came to the House for classes and clubs. The Greek immigrants at that time were mostly young men working for money to bring over their relatives. The Hull House residents and club leaders organized Greek clubs of various kinds and Greek dances, when there were so few Greek women that the women residents, young and old, were called in to "help the Greeks dance."

Some of the Greek children were our good friends, but Grace did not like the way the teachers changed their names at school. A little boy named Dionysios said one day, "Now you must call me Jim. At school I am Jim." As we expressed surprise, he added, "I took that name because my Greek name was too hard for my teacher." He had a little sister Estesthea, called Nellie by her teacher "because she doesn't like my Greek name." There were two little Hungarian girls named Janina and Kasamira, whose names at school had been changed to Jennie and Cassie. Even their mother seemed quite willing to adopt the new names. "The girls say they like better the American names," she explained when we showed our disappointment over the change.

The older immigrants often changed their names themselves. A Greek named Spiros appeared one night and said, "Now, I am Mike. I want American name." Grace was interested in a nice Slovak girl whom we called Anna Mokata. One night she said to Grace a little shyly, "I come to tell you I change my name."

"Oh," said Grace, "you haven't been married?"

"Oh, no, no," said Anna, "but I changed name. Mokata is now Strauss, because I want American name. I am Anna Strauss! You like my American name, Miss Abbott?" . . .

Just what the new Immigrants' Protective League was to do no one knew exactly. Miss Breckinridge had become interested through the Women's Trade Union League in the immigrant girls who came over here alone and were trying to earn money to send back to their families or to bring some of them to this country. They were willing to work for very low wages, and it was difficult to bring these non-English-speaking girls into the unions. This problem of the unaccompanied girls proved to be challenging; but nothing that ought to be done seemed impossible to Miss Breckinridge! This time she was sure that a special organization would take care of the situation. The girls were often successful and found friends from their own country with whom to live. But some of them were tragically unfortunate. However, there were many appeals made to the new League by the men as well as by the women workers.

Employment Agencies

Soon after she went to Hull House, Grace found that the new immigrants were being exploited by the private employment agencies and that the immigrant workers were rarely placed by the public employment offices maintained by the state of Illinois. The three state employment offices in Chicago usually placed what they called the "white" workers, or "American hoboes," and they left the immigrants to be placed at very high fees by the private agencies which were all along Canal Street and the near-by streets, an area called the "slave market." Grace collected the facts and published the results of a study of "The Chicago Employment Agency and the Immigrant Worker." The immigrants who had to get jobs through the private employment agencies were charged what the agents thought they could get, and, worst of all, they often paid for jobs that did not exist. That is, even after they had paid large fees, they were shipped out to places where there was no work or they were given work that lasted only a few days and then were left stranded at places remote from the city labor markets.

Grace studied the better employment agency laws in other states, and her demand for a new Illinois law led to her work in Springfield, when the legislature assembled in the first part of the following year, for the control of private employment agencies. She was successful in getting the new and better law in 1909.

But even after the new Employment Agency law was passed, there were still opportunities for exploiting the immigrants who wanted a job. One spring (1914) some Albanians appealed to her for help in recovering money they had paid for jobs that they did not get. Their story was that a Greek who had a candy store had offered to get work, on a new railroad station which was being built, for their group of forty-two Albanians if they would pay $420, or ten dollars for each job. But the men had been out of work most of the winter, and they did not have the money. However, one old Albanian in the group was able to put in $100 and took care of ten of them, and they borrowed $250 from a man who ran the bakery. The other seven had a little money and borrowed a little. But, when they had paid their fees, they were not given the promised jobs and were just told to wait. But after waiting and hoping, they finally became worried and came to Grace. She found the Greek who had got the money and who was still running the candy store. But he complained that the man he knew who could get the jobs at the new station had taken the money but had then gone off with it. So the Greek said, "What could I do?" He was reported to the state inspector of employment agencies and was arrested for conducting an employment agency without a license. But the case went to court before a judge who seemed to be both incompetent and biased. This judge, who "didn't trust foreigners," let the Greek off because he had no employment agency sign on his store, and therefore, the judge said, he couldn't be charged with running an agency without a license; and the judge also said that the Albanians were Mohammedans, not Christians, and "didn't know the meaning of an oath," so that they lost their case and what was to them a large sum of money.

Then she had nine Rumanians who paid an Italian agent ten dollars each and twenty-two Armenians who paid the same agent twelve dollars each for jobs in Ottawa, Illinois. The men "shipped out" but found no jobs. The chief of police of Ottawa telegraphed the state inspector, who got out a warrant for the Italian who had taken their money. But the case dragged along in the courts for nearly two years, and then the men were only repaid in part. . . .

There seemed to be a great many "lost immigrant girls" in Chicago—girls who were traveling alone, who were reported to have been put on the proper train for Chicago by federal inspectors at Ellis Island, and who never reached Chicago. What became of them? Sometimes a girl got off by mistake at the wrong station.

Sometimes the girl had had an address that no one could read or an American address that had been badly translated into a foreign language and then badly translated back again until it was meaningless.

Grace finally planned to have the names of all immigrant girls coming alone to Chicago sent to the League by the Ellis Island authorities. She thought that, if the League could visit these girls soon after they reached Chicago, they might be helped in various ways. The numbers visited gradually became very large, and during the five years before the first World War she received the names of 26,909 immigrant women and girls destined for the Chicago area. In a period of eighteen months, more than two thousand young Polish women and girls, most of them not yet twenty years old, had come to Chicago and had been visited by someone from Grace's office who spoke Polish. Of these girls, only 81 had parents in this country, and 626 came to "cousins" and "friends." Grace found these so-called "friends" had sometimes never known the girls at home. But when the difficulties of a journey to America were being considered, someone would suggest that the girl could stay during the first few weeks after she arrived with a friend's brother, cousin, or neighbor who had already gone to the United States. Grace found that the "friends" and relatives, even when the girl came to an uncle or an aunt, were so absorbed in their own problems that they showed little interest in the girl after she had found a job and got a place to board. A girl of seventeen came to an uncle on the North Side of Chicago, who took her over to the Stock Yards area twelve miles away. She found work in the neighborhood and got a place to board, and the uncle then left her to shift for herself. When the girl was in trouble six months later, she had no idea where the uncle lived and had no one to whom she could turn for advice and help. . . .

Grace had not been long at Hull House and the Immigrants' Protective League before she became a vigorous supporter of liberal immigration policies, and she was in demand as a speaker in behalf of the so-called "new immigration." She was convinced that the immigrants from southern and eastern Europe made good citizens, and she urged that our ports should be kept open for the men and women who were trying to escape from the hardships of the life in Europe. She believed in the old tradition of the right of asylum in America, and there were some old lines about Castle Garden that she always liked:

> There's freedom at thy gates and rest
> For earth's downtrodden and oppressed,
> A shelter for the hunted head,
> For the starved laborer toil and bread.

Studying the history of immigration, she knew that the objections raised against the new immigration had all been heard once against the Irish, the Scandinavians, and the Germans—the groups which were later called "the old immigration" and accepted as "desirable." Early in January, 1912, she went to Washington to testify before a congressional committee which had under consideration the adoption of the literacy test for the restriction of immigration. Henry Cabot Lodge, who was relentless in his opposition to immigration, had been one of the earliest advocates of a literacy restriction clause in the immigration law. Grover Cleveland had vetoed a provision for a literacy test in 1897, but its advocates refused to give up. Grace's statement before the House committee shows how clearly in her three and one-half years at Hull House she had worked out the reasons why liberal immigration policies should be followed. In her testimony she said: "I constantly meet the objection that the newly arrived immigrant is distinctly different from the older immigrants. People had no fear that the Scandinavian, the German, and the older western European immigrants could not be assimilated, they tell us now. This was not always the case, however, and the changed attitude of mind is largely due to the fact that the older immigrant has been here long enough to make good."

She went on to say to a congressman who questioned her: "You and I have had an opportunity to find out by personal experience that there are Germans who succeed and Germans who fail in almost everything they undertake, that there are Germans who are public-spirited and Germans who are selfishly interested only in their own advancement. In other words, there are good Germans and dishonest Germans." That is, she thought we had learned to judge the older immigrants as individuals instead of as nationality groups. But the new immigrants, the Slovaks, the Poles, the Lithuanians, the Italians, the Russian Jews, and all the others, whom most of our people did not know, were on very insufficient evidence called "undesirable." The average American, she said, knew few Greeks, Bulgarians, or Lithuanians. However, she pointed out that those who came in close daily contact with the newer immigrants found that they were men and women like the rest of us—some good and some undesirable—and that it was unfair to discriminate against them as a national group.

Grace's plan for what she called a "domestic immigration policy" would have provided for the federal government to give advice and help to the immigrants when they were admitted, instead of concentrating on debarment and deportation, and she urged greater attention to the better distribution of immigrants and adequate protective services. She thought that it was important to "develop those agencies designed to protect the immigrant against exploitation and to insure his proper Americanization."

Masked Ball at Hull-House

Judson Grenell

As part of their efforts to make the various immigrant groups feel at home in Chicago and at the settlement, the Hull-House reformers encouraged them to put on dances and festivals and to preserve other native customs. Addams and her associates knew that such affairs not only helped the older generation feel less homesick, but also encouraged the second generation, who tended to rebel against everything foreign, to realize that the old ways of their parents were not to be laughed at and rejected. Frequently the boisterous and rollicking dances and festivals made some of the straight-laced American settlement workers a little nervous, but many learned to take part, as this description of an Italian dance indicates. This account, extracted from a letter, appeared in the Detroit News *in 1903. It is interesting to compare it with Nora Marks's account of Italian night at the settlement which appears earlier in this book. [Judson Grenell, "Masked Ball in Hull-House,"* Detroit News, *March 8, 1903.]*

Judson Grenell of Chicago, in a letter to an acquaintance, speaks of attending a "masked ball" in Hull House, etc., and he adds:

"No, Jane Addams didn't dance at the masked ball at the Hull House, the other evening. The fact is, I didn't dance myself, but I had hanging on my arm, during the grand march, one of the belles of the evening. Yet while Miss Addams didn't grace the floor, some of the other Hull-House residents did, and they were as lively as the Italians themselves, for whose benefit the ball was given.

"Hull House, you know, is right in the midst of Chicago's congested district. It has become an 'institution' from a small beginning something over 10 years ago, until now it embraces a considerable number of buildings scattered over the best part of a small block. There are now nearly 30 regular settlement workers within its walls, and their duties include a kindergarten, day nursery, classes in sewing, cooking, handwork instruction, and—balls.

"That is the funny part of it. This Settlement, supported by good church people, in the main, who frown upon balls, masked or unmasked—and particularly masked—find it one of the best ways to interest the residents of the locality in settlement work. The Italians are a fun-loving lot of people, and those in Chicago seem to have been transplanted from the open air of sunny Italy to the dark, dirty, and narrow quarters of Chicago's poor population. They need to be amused if anybody does, and these balls, freed from the influence of saloons and indecent surroundings, are an

aid, at least, in helping these rackrented and sweated Italians to live happier lives. And those at this particular ball certainly had a 'real good time.'

"One of the former residents of Hull House told me of her first ball in the slum district. The hall was over a saloon, and there was a constant stream of dancers going to and returning from the bar. There were not enough chairs for all, and so the common way was for the girls to sit on their partners' knees, generally 'held firmly down' to prevent slipping, with two masculine arms around them, while waiting for the music to begin for the next dance. Not having brought an escort with her, my informant naively remarked that she 'was compelled to stand.' "

Jane Addams Invites Me In

Philip Davis

Hull-House residents tried to understand and help the immigrant groups in their neighborhood; but in spite of all their good intent and compassion, they often failed. Language was often a barrier and, although the settlement workers prided themselves on being "neighbors," the relationship they were able to establish with the immigrants was often artificial at best. "No one but a member of our own race can really understand us," one immigrant remarked. Many living near Hull-House found the settlement workers' reform apparatus, committees, and investigations annoying and meaningless. Worst of all, with few exceptions, the settlement failed to reach ethnic leaders, for Hull-House did not attract the men in the neighborhood.

Yet the settlement did serve a useful purpose for many immigrants, especially the young and ambitious. Many young men and women were inspired to get an education and break out of the dreary slum-sweatshop pattern. One of these "transfigured few," as Jane Addams called them, was Philip Davis (b. 1876), a Russian immigrant who found only bewilderment and discouragement until he discovered Hull-House. After attending college, he became a settlement worker himself at Civic Service House in Boston and the author of a number of books on Americanization. The following is from his little-known autobiography, And Crown Thy Good. *[Philip Davis,* And Crown Thy Good *(New York, 1952), 85–93.]*

Halsted Street, running thirty-two miles, is the longest street in Chicago, if not in America. Just as Californians take pride in their weather, so did boosters of the Windy City dwell on the length of Halsted Street.

More than anything else, Halsted Street was famous for Hull-House, planted in the middle of it. In my neighborhood it was frequently mentioned as a kind of school which extended a helping hand to the immigrant. Upon making inquiries about it among the neighbors I found that everyone assessed it favorably, according to his needs and lights: The newsboy on the corner—"Oh yeah. Nice place. We play ball there." . . . The old woman selling oranges on the sidewalk: "It's kind of a 'suspensary' " (dispensary). . . . A working girl passing by: "Oh sure. I belong to the Choral Society. We sing there every Sunday." . . . An Italian vegetable peddler: " 'Whole' House? Sure—she is open to everyone!" . . . The policeman on the beat: "It's O. K. Takes the kids off the street!"

My brother Frank didn't know Miss Addams personally but knew of her interest in the trade union movement and the immigrant, and sang her praises to me all the time. I felt that I already knew her.

The first time I approached Hull House the door was open and I walked in. No one was in the reception hall so I sat down near a table, eyeing the books and magazines. Presently Jane Addams appeared. From many pictures I had seen in the newspapers, I recognized her instantly. She greeted me cordially, then said: "Don't you want to read the *Atlantic Monthly* just out?" The *Atlantic Monthly* proved tough reading. After all, I came to see Jane Addams and Hull House, not to read the *Atlantic Monthly!* Miss Addams passed through several times. Realizing I was lingering rather than reading, she tried conversation:

"Living around here?" she ventured.

"On DeKoven Street," I answered.

"Oh, then we are neighbors. You must come often," she said warmly. That was what I had hoped for.

Such was my introduction to Hull House, the university of good will, good English, good citizenship—in brief, everything good that America stands for. All my subsequent training at Lewis Institute Prep School, University of Chicago, and even Harvard, was best interpreted by Hull House and exalted by it. . . .

Jane Addams had the happy faculty of liking people of diverse backgrounds. Unlike critics of the immigrants of that day, she encouraged us to build proudly on what was most valuable in our heritage. I remember her listening sympathetically to the account of my boyhood in Motol, of my Aunt Weizmann, my little village, and the wedding ceremony. Through such personal conversations with her neighbors on Halsted Street (with Greeks, Italians, Poles, Russians, and many others) she acquired an impressive knowledge of old-world cultures transplanted in part to this nation. . . .

Although very busy with the duties of the House, she always managed to talk with me and others like me. I have to smile now at the nature of those conversations, for she knew so much more about the subjects we discussed than I did. Gracious person that she was, she acted as if I were the authority on the subject and she an interested but unconvinced amateur. She explained to me that she was not a socialist because she thought that Americans were not class-conscious, that class hatred was wrong, that it was folly to work for a potentially perfect society in the distant future without giving thought to ameliorating immediate current evils.

Much more important for my future career were our discussions on trade unionism. Once when I described my New York sweatshop experiences to Miss Addams, she asked: "What do you want to do about it?"

"Miss Addams," I solemnly replied, "I would like to educate myself so that I may return to the garment industry!"

"Philip," she said, "I'm for it! Our country needs young educated men and women who wish to help others." Shortly after this conversation,

Jane Addams started me on the road to self-education.

Gerard Swope, a volunteer worker at Hull House, was second only to Jane Addams in my esteem. He taught me English and arithmetic, and at every opportunity corrected my speech. Oftentimes we went to his laboratory at Western Electric, where he showed me how to conduct experiments in physics and chemistry. These gave me my first taste of these sciences and helped me later in my college entrance examinations.

Occasionally he took me out to dinner. We chatted about my future. Once in awhile we had welsh rarebit, which to me was a treat. Jane Addams, Dr. Hamilton, Swope, and Mary Hill (whom he later married) introduced me to bicycling Sunday mornings. I learned to enjoy the American countryside as well as the American country home. Prior to this I had seen the countryside only once, while on the train going from New York to Chicago.

Why he, a busy and famous man, took so much interest in me, an immigrant boy, I shall never know. As I look back over the years I realize that Swope himself forced a change in my political beliefs. He was an example of the future industrialist, at ease with labor men like Bisno, Hillman, and others of his day, as well as with the prominent figures representing management. Although a man of means, he was active in the cause of reform, in playgrounds, bath houses, and, above all, housing.

Up to the time that I met Swope, I had associated only with workers and trade-unionists. Their doctrine that all bosses were evil men and, by inference, that all trade-unionists were righteous, appeared absurd when I saw what sort of individual Swope was. Like Miss Addams, he encouraged me to take an interest in labor.

In the summer, when school was over, Miss Addams suggested that I could study better if I went to the country where it was quiet and relaxing. Through her recommendation I was able to get a room for July and August at the Rockford Female Seminary at Rockford, Illinois, her Alma Mater. The few women there during the vacation period took an interest in me and helped me in every way they could.

When I returned to Hull House in the fall one of the residents said, "I hear you are going to Lewis Institute!" This was a preparatory school for boys from twelve to twenty-two years of age. I do not know who enrolled me, but I suspect the unseen hand of Jane Addams or Gerard Swope... .

While attending the Institute I used to frequent Hull House to listen to the distinguished speakers on social reform. Jane Addams, subscribing to no single ism, created a clearing house for American liberalism.

Up to that time I never could visualize an author in the flesh. To me a writer seemed some sort of superman, built on the style of Moses. Then I met one, my first one, at Hull House, a man whose name I cannot recall now, but who had just written a book. I could not understand how a human being, with all his limitations, could put so many words together. But there he was, in the flesh, and he was not a Moses, either. If Mr. "X" could write a book, why couldn't I? I asked myself. The idea intrigued me and I kept mulling it over in my mind. I mentioned it to my family. "Nonsense!" said Frank, "Philip writing a book! Just sheer nonsense. Dismiss it from your mind!" But it kept coming back to my mind, again and again. "All right," said I to myself, "we shall see. Now, quiet down and do your lessons!"

Several months later a miracle happened at Hull House. I met another author and a prince— all in one! We were sitting by the fire in the living-room about eight o'clock one evening—Jane Addams, her associates, and I. They were questioning me about sweatshop conditions which were as bad in Chicago as they were in New York, when in walked the miracle—Prince Kropotkin.

I had just finished reading his new book, *Mutual Aid,* and was not surprised to learn that he was a simple, sincere, and jolly person. He drew up a chair near the fire and was very soon the joy of the company. Later that evening he gave a lecture to a typical Hull House audience. I wish I could describe him now as I saw him then: an elderly man dressed in black, with a rich, bushy, grayish-black beard. His huge forehead impressed me most. After a brief introduction by Jane Addams, and the prolonged applause that followed, he passed his hand over his head in slight embarrassment. Then he clasped his hands in front of him and, with a peculiar Slavic accent, slowly began. He spoke of the young girls laboring in the English coal mines.

After describing their working conditions he said: "Now I ask you, ladies and gentlemen, by undermining the lives of these young women and wasting their energy, what kind of a race is England preparing for the great future before her?"

Afterwards, when I was introduced to Prince Kropotkin he asked about my life in Motol. I described my feelings as best I could. "A great country, Russia," he said, "a very great country—as soon as the people come into their own."

The Prince had written with great admiration of the famous Russian writer, Levitoff,* whose habits might have been his own. Whenever Levitoff stayed at St. Petersburg or at Moscow he always lived in the poorest quarters on the outskirts of the town. They reminded him of his native village. And when he thus settled in the lowest financial stratum of the population, he did so to run away from the artifices of the life of the educated. He could not live, even for a couple of months in the summer, in relative well-being. He would begin to feel the gnawing of conscience and it ended in his leaving and going somewhere, anywhere, where he could be still poorer.

In much the same way Jane Addams deliberately chose the poorest quarters of Chicago's slums and remained there for the rest of her life. . . .

I met many people at Hull House who inspired me with a desire to learn and serve. Gradually the words of Jane Addams took root in my mind: "The things which make men alike are finer and better than the things which keep them apart."

*Aleksandr Ivanovich Levitov (1853?–1877).—Eds.

Votes for "Ignorant Women"

Jane Addams

While many supporters of woman suffrage advocated votes for middle- and upper-class women and approved votes for working women and immigrants reluctantly if at all, Addams consistently *maintained that immigrant women would vote intelligently, and, what is more important, they needed the vote to protect themselves and their families from exploitation by government and society. Unlike some suffrage advocates, however, she stressed women's traditional role. In an urban and industrial age, she argued, because of their homemaking role, women needed to have the vote in order to become municipal housekeepers to ensure a clean water supply and a safe environment.*

Here Jane Addams answered the critics of woman suffrage, who did not want to give the vote to the ignorant women of the ghetto, by showing how shrewd these supposedly ignorant women could be. The Hull-House residents sought not only to understand their immigrant neighbors but to interpret them to a public which had fears and doubts about those "un-American types" who lived in the slums. [Survey (October 23, 1915), 85.]

I recall an experience I had last year which did much to dispel any lingering doubts I may have had regarding the vote of the so-called "ignorant woman." Serving as a judge of election in the Hull House precinct, one of my duties was to enter the polling booth with any woman who could not read and write in order to read the ballot to her. I was constantly impressed with the shrewdness and direct common-sense with which most of these women marked their ballots.

In the long lists of public policy questions an Irish woman whom I knew very well marked her ballot with only one exception according to the advice given by the specialists of the City Club, reaching her conclusions wholly and solely through her own experiences, for although I was powerless to advise her she gave me a running comment of her reasons.

For instance, she voted against the bonds for an extension to the county hospital "if the same bunch have the spending of it who built it the first time without enough room for beds"; she voted against the proposed subway until "they try clearing the streets a bit"; she voted for a contagious disease hospital under the city health department for "sure the only time a mother is willing to let a sick child go out of the house is when she is scared to death about the others, but the hospitals always took in every other disease but the catching ones." She promptly voted against the bathing beaches on the lake front, in this differing from the expert advice, because "boys have so little sense anyway that there was no use tempting them to the lake to get drowned."

As she left the room passing through the lines of waiting men she gave me a delicious wink. "It galls the men some to have us voting, but from the questions put up to me it seems pretty much a woman's job."

What Kind of a Home I Would Like to Have

An Anonymous Greek Immigrant and Carmella Gustaferre

As part of its program to help immigrants become useful American citizens more quickly, Hull-House held classes in English and in American government. The settlement teachers, some of whom had been immigrants themselves, tried to make the lessons as easy and interesting as possible for their students, who ranged in age from children to grandmothers and grandfathers. "What Kind of a Home I Would Like to Have" was the text given for compositions in one of the Hull-House English classes. These two papers, one by an anonymous Greek immigrant and one by a little Italian girl named Carmella Gustaferre, were among those turned in to complete the assignment. ["Ideals of Life and Living," Survey (July 18, 1914), 420.]

By an Immigrant Greek

If I had money enough (a few thousand dollars would be sufficient) I would go to a farm somewhere in the United States and I would stay there

for a year to learn farming. Then I would directly to my native country.

When I should go there I would make some repairs on my old house in order to make it more comfortable, then I would by more land, conect it with that I have already and mak a big farm. Then I would have some people work at it, and I would teach them to treat the land like American people do.

Early in the morning I would mount my best horse and accompanied by my two fauvorite dogs I would go the the farm, wish good morning to the people, give advice if needed, say something about this or that, and I would go and have a look at the cattle. After that I would go to the nearest town on business, on rout I would shot a few hares or rabbits if by chance they would be discovered by my dogs.

On Sundays and holidays in winter time after church I would invite some other people to my house, I would ask them to sit down around my ready table. At that time the little lambs would be pulled off from the oven and everybody would start to eate and drink. After we would start to sing and dance, while we could see the large flaks of falling snow through the windows and hear the merry sound of the burning woods.

In spring and summer time I would once in a while go on the mountains, then I would climb on the top of a landscape [mountain peak]. There I would stay for hours looking at the splendid panoram which would lay before my eyes, smell the delicious odors of the gay flours and breathe deeply the pure breeze of the mountains. After I would come down again and if I was tired I would saat down under the shade of an old tree at the edge of the little river, and while my horse would peck here and there some mouthfuls of fresh grass, and my dogs would lay down looking at me, I would enjoy the joyful and happy singing of the birds. This is only part of my edeal home and edeal life and that is what I am always dreaming. May God let the dream be a reality.

By Carmella Gustaferre

I should like to have a nice looking house with a garden like I had it at my old home in Italy. I would like to have a nice educated house and I like

A citizenship naturalization class conducted by Jessie Binford in the settlement Coffee House.

to have all the things that I have not got in my house. I would like to have a piano, a parlor and a room full of flowers. I would like to have a empty room in my house so that I could fix it into a stage so that my friends and I could have acting. We have made customs all ready, we played once and all our friends came to see it so that we made fifty cents and we were happy after that. I would like to have a back yard with a swing in it and a sink, and a large tree with branches that I would seat on the bench and read in the summer.

The Colored People of Chicago

Louise deKoven Bowen

Hull-House was surrounded by a shifting ethnic mixture of people, but there were never many black families in the neighborhood. Those few blacks who did appear at a Hull-House club or class were not always welcomed warmly, for though Hull-House was not exactly segregated many of its residents felt that the presence of blacks might discourage other groups from coming. The settlement seemed unwilling to come to grips with the "black problem" in its own environs, yet Hull-House was willing to be concerned with the same "problem" elsewhere in the city. A group of residents helped found the Wendell Phillips Settlement in a black district on the West Side. Jane Addams helped to raise money for that project as well as for the Frederick Douglass Center, begun on the fringe of the black ghetto on the South Side by Celia Parker Wooley in 1905. The Juvenile Protective Association and the Immigrants' Protective League also helped the black population, especially the new migrants from the South and those in trouble. Jane Addams served on the board of the Chicago Urban League as well as on the board of the National Association for the Advancement of Colored People which she helped found. More than most of their generation, Hull-House residents were troubled by the unequal lot of the blacks and certainly more than most, they tried to do something about it. But because there were not many blacks in their neighborhood, because there were so many other problems, and because of the racist attitudes of their day, Hull-House residents, in the period before World War I, devoted a rather small amount of time to the situation of black people.

Louise deKoven Bowen (1859–1953), the author of the following article, which is a section from the pamphlet The Colored People of Chicago, *published by the Juvenile Protective Association in 1913, was one of the most vigorous and active of the impressive group of society women who helped to support Hull-House. Bowen gave money to build a number of the Hull-House buildings, she donated the summer camp, Bowen Country Club, in memory of her husband, Joseph T. Bowen, and she could be depended upon to rescue the settlement from any financial crisis. But Bowen gave more than her money to Hull-House; she was an active leader in the Hull-House Woman's Club, president of the Juvenile Protective Association, and a long-time trustee, treasurer, and finally president of the Hull-House Association board of trustees. Her study of blacks in Chicago, the first such study attempted for the city, was stimulated by her work with the Juvenile Protective Association. Her findings in 1913 seem all too familiar. The story of blacks in Chicago was one of limited opportunity, segregation, discrimination, and poor working conditions. The outlook for blacks in 1913 was one of little hope. Notice that Bowen used the term "Colored People," which was fashionable in her day, but she also capitalized "Negro," which was not common until the late 1930's.*

Although Bowen reveals a paternalistic attitude toward the black community and never suggests social equality as a solution to the race problem, her pamphlet represented a progressive and advanced position for its day. [Louise deKoven Bowen, "The Colored People of Chicago," Survey (November 1, 1913), 117–120.]

In the course of an investigation recently made by the Juvenile Protective Association of Chicago into the condition of boys in the County Jail, the association was much startled by the disproportionate number of colored boys and young men there. Although the colored people of Chicago approximate one-fortieth of the entire population, one-eighth of the boys and young men, and nearly one-third of the girls and young women, who had been confined in the jail during the year, were Negroes.

The association had previously been impressed with the fact that most of the maids employed in houses of prostitution were colored girls and that many employment agencies quite openly sent them there, although they would not take the risk of sending a white girl to a place where, if she was forced into a life of prostitution, the agency would be liable to a charge of pandering.

In an attempt to ascertain the causes which would account for a greater amount of delinquency among colored boys and for the public opinion which so carelessly places the virtue of a colored girl in jeopardy, the Juvenile Protective Association found itself involved in a study of the industrial and social status of the colored people of Chicago.

Home Environment and School

While the morality of every young person is closely bound up with that of his family and his immediate environment, this is especially true of the sons and daughters of colored families who, because they continually find the door of opportunity shut in their faces, are more easily forced back into their early environment, however vicious it may have been. The enterprising young people in immigrant families who have passed through the public schools and are earning good wages continually succeed in moving their entire households into more prosperous neighborhoods where they gradually lose all trace of their early tenement house experiences. On the contrary, the colored young people, however ambitious, find it extremely difficult to move their families or even themselves into desirable parts of the city and to make friends in these surroundings.

Although no separate schools have ever been established in Chicago, it was found that many colored young people become discouraged in regard to a "high school education" because of the tendency of employers who use colored persons at all in their business to assign to them the most menial labor.

Many a case on record in the Juvenile Protective Association tells a tale of an educated young Negro who failed to find employment as stenographer, bookkeeper, or clerk. One rather pathetic story is that of a boy graduated from a technical high school last spring. He was sent with other graduates of his class to a big electric company where in the presence of all his classmates he was told that "niggers are not wanted here."

The association has on record another instance where a graduate of a business college was refused a position under similar circumstances. This young man, in response to an advertisement, went to a large firm to ask for a position as clerk. "We take colored help only as laborers," he was told by the manager of a firm supposed to be friendly to the Negroes.

Business College Barred

All the leading business colleges in Chicago, except one, frankly discriminate against Negro students. The one friendly school at present, among twelve hundred white students, has only two colored students, but its records show as many as thirty colored students in the past, although the manager claims that his business has suffered in consequence of his friendliness to the Negro.

After an ambitious boy has been refused employment again and again in the larger mercantile and industrial establishments and comes to the conclusion that there is no use in trying to get a decent job, he is in a very dangerous state of mind. Idle and discouraged, his neighborhood environment vicious, such a boy quickly shows the first symptoms of delinquency. Even the superintendent of the Illinois Industrial School for Boys at St. Charles complains that it is not worthwhile to teach trades to colored boys in his institution because it is so very difficult for a skilled colored man to secure employment. The colored people themselves believe that the employers object to treating the colored man with the respect which a skilled mechanic would command. As a result of this attitude, the colored laborer is being driven to lower kinds of occupation which are gradually being discarded by the white men.

Certainly the investigators found that the great corporations, for one reason or another, refused to employ Negroes. Department stores, express companies, and the public utility companies employ very few colored people. Out of the 3,795 men employed in Chicago by the eight leading express companies, only twenty-one were colored men. Fifteen of these were porters.

Restriction of Occupation

The investigators found no colored men employed as boot-and-shoe-makers, glove-makers, bindery workers, garment workers in factories, cigar box makers, elevated railroad employes, neckwear workers, suspender-makers, or printers. No colored women are employed in dress-making, cap-making, lingerie, and corset-making. The two reasons given for this non-employment by the employers are: first, the refusal of the white employes to work with colored people; second, [that] the "colored help" is slower and not so efficient as the white. Some employers solve the latter difficulty by paying the colored help less. In the laundries, for instance, where colored people do the same work as white people, the latter average a dollar a week more.

The effect of these restrictions upon Negroes is, first, that they are crowded into undesirable and underpaid occupations. As an example, about 12 per cent of the colored men in Chicago work in saloons and poolrooms. Second, there is greater competition in a limited field with consequent tendency to lower the already low wages. Third, the colored women are forced to go to work to help earn the family living. This occurs so universally as to affect the entire family and social life of the Negro colony.

A large number of Negroes are employed on the railroads, largely due to the influence of the Pullman Palace Car Company. There is a tradition among colored people that Mr. Pullman inserted a clause in his will urging the company to employ colored men on trains whenever possible, but while the investigators found 1,849 Pullman porters living in Chicago, they counted 7,625 colored men working in saloons and poolrooms. There is also a high percentage employed in theaters; more than one-fourth of all the employes in the leading theaters of Chicago are colored.

Government Employ

The federal government has always been a large employer of colored labor; 9 per cent of the force in all the federal departments are Negroes. In Chicago the percentage of colored men is higher. Out of a total of 8,012 men, 755 are colored, being 10.61 per cent of the whole, approximately their just share in proportion to the population. The Negroes, however, do not fare so well in local government. A study made of the city departments in Chicago showed the percentage of colored employes to be 1.87 per cent; in Cook County, 1.88 per cent. Three colored men have also been elected as county commissioners, but there is said to be no instance on record in Chicago of a Negro office holder having betrayed his trust.

The investigators found, in regard to the colored men in business: (1) that the greater number of their enterprises are the outgrowth of domestic and personal service occupations; (2) that they are in branches of business which call for small capital and little previous experience.

In the colored belt on the South Side of Chicago a number of business houses are managed by colored people. There is also one bank located in a fine building, of which a colored man is president, but 80 per cent of the depositors are white. According to the evidence confirmed by the figures of the United States census, there is little possibility for a colored business man to make a living solely from the patronage of his own people. The census report holds that he succeeds in business only when two-thirds of his customers are white. This affords another explanation of the fact that most of his business is of such a character that a white man is willing to patronize it—barber

shops, expressing, restaurants, and others suggesting personal service.

There is a large proportion of real estate dealers among colored men, many of whom do business with white people, the Negro dealer often becoming the agent for houses which the white dealers refuse to handle. Colored people are eager to own their homes and many of them are buying small houses, divided into two flats, living in one and collecting rent from the other. The contract system prevails in Chicago, making it possible for a man with two or three hundred dollars for the first payment to enter into a contract for the purchase of a piece of property, the deed being held by the real estate man until the purchaser pays the amount stipulated in the contract.

The largest district in Chicago in which colored people have resided for a number of years is the section on the south side, known as the "black belt" which includes a segregated vice district. In this so-called "belt," the number of children is remarkably small, forming only a little more than one-tenth of the population, and an investigation made by the School of Civics showed that only 26 per cent of the houses on the South Side and 36 per cent of the houses in the West Side colored district, were in good repair. Colored tenants reported that they found it impossible to persuade their landlords either to make the necessary repairs or to release them from their contracts, but that it was so hard to find places in which to live that they were forced to endure insanitary conditions.

High rents among the colored people, as everywhere else, force the families to take in lodgers. Nearly one-third of the population in the district investigated on the South Side and one-seventh of the population in the district investigated on the West Side were lodgers. This practice is always found dangerous to family life; it is particularly so to the boys and girls of colored families who, because they so often live near the vice districts, are obliged to have the house filled with "floaters" of a very undesirable class, so that the children witness all kinds of offenses against decency within the home as well as on the streets.

It was found that the rent paid by a Negro is appreciably higher than that paid by any other nationality. In a flat building formerly occupied by white people, the white families paid a rent of twelve dollars for a six-room apartment for which a Negro family is now paying sixteen dollars; a white family paid seventeen dollars for an apartment of seven rooms for which the Negroes are now paying twenty dollars.

The Negro real estate dealer frequently offers to the owner of an apartment house, which is no longer renting advantageously to white tenants, cash payment for a year's lease on the property, thus guaranteeing the owner against loss, and then he fills the building with colored tenants. It is said, however, that the agent does not put out the white tenants unless he can get 10 per cent more from the colored people. By this method the Negroes now occupy many large apartment buildings but the Negro real estate agents obtain the reputation of exploiting their own race.

When it becomes possible for the colored people of a better class to buy property in a good neighborhood, so that they may take care of their children and live respectably, there are often protest meetings among the white people in the vicinity and sometimes even riots. A striking example of the latter occurred recently on the west side of Chicago; a colored woman bought a lot near a small park upon which she built a cottage. It was not until she moved into the completed house that the neighbors discovered that a colored family had acquired property there. They immediately began a crusade of insults and threats. When this brought no results a "night raid" company was organized. In the middle of the night a masked band broke into the house, told the family to keep quiet or they would be murdered; then they tore down the newly built house, destroying everything in it. This is, of course, an extreme instance, but there have been many similar cases. Recently in a suburb of Chicago, animosity against Negro residents resulted in the organization of an anti-Negro committee, which requested the dismissal of all Negroes who were employed in the town as gardeners, janitors, etc., because the necessity of housing their families depressed real estate values.

Conditions in Fifty Households

Supplementary to the previous housing investigations, the Juvenile Protective Association studied the conditions of fifty of the better homes occupied by the colored people of Chicago, those

in the so-called "black belts" in the city, those in a suburban district, and other houses situated in blocks in which only one or two colored families lived. The size of the houses varied from five to fourteen rooms, averaging eight rooms each. The conditions of the houses inside and out compared favorably with similar houses occupied by white families.

Classified according to occupation, the heads of the household in nine cases were railroad porters, the next largest number were janitors, then waiters, but among them were found lawyers, clergymen, and physicians. In only four instances was the woman of the house working outside the home. Only four of the homes took in lodgers, and children were found in only fifteen out of the fifty families studied.

The total of thirty-three children found in the fifty homes averages but two-thirds of a child for each family and but for one family—a janitor living in a ten-room house and possessing eight children—the average would have been but half a child for a family. This confirms the statement often made that while the poorer colored people in the agricultural districts of the South, like the poor Italians in rural Italy, have very large families, when they move to the city and become more prosperous, the birth rate among colored people falls below that of the average prosperous American family.

From the homes situated in white neighborhoods, only two reported "indignation meetings when they moved in" and added "quiet now." One other reported "No affiliation with white neighbors"; another "white neighbors visit in time of sickness" and the third was able to say "neighbors friendly." Of the ownership of the fifty homes, thirty-five were owned by colored men, twelve by white landlords, and the ownership of three was not ascertained. Thirty-four of the houses were occupied by their owners.

According to the Juvenile Protective Association records, it was found that out of one hundred poor families, eighty-six of the women went out to work. Though there is no doubt that this number is abnormally high, it is always easier for a colored woman to find work than it is for a man, partly because white people have the traditions of colored servants and partly because there is a steadier demand for and a smaller supply of household workers, wash and scrub women, than there is for the kind of unskilled work done by men. Even here they are discriminated against and although many are employed in highly respectable families, there is a tendency to engage them in low-class hotels and other places where white women do not care to go.

Working Mothers

Investigators found from consultation with the principals of the schools largely attended by colored children that they are irregular in attendance and often tardy; that they are eager to leave school at an early age, although in one school where there is a great deal of manual work this tendency is less pronounced.

Colored children more than any others are kept at home to care for younger members of the family while the mother is away at work. A persistent violation of the compulsory education law recently tried in the Juvenile Court disclosed the fact that a colored brother and sister had been refused admittance in a day nursery, the old woman who cared for the little household for twenty-five cents a day was ill, and the mother had been obliged to keep the older children at home in order to retain her place in a laundry. At the best the school attendance of her five children had been most unsatisfactory, for she left home every morning at half past six, and the illiterate old woman in charge of the children took little interest in school. The lack of home training and the fact that many colored families are obliged to live in or near the vice districts perhaps accounts for the indifference to all school interests on the part of many colored children, although this complaint is not made of those in the high schools who come from more prosperous families.

The most striking difference in the health of the colored children compared to that of the white children in the same neighborhood was the larger proportion of the cases of rickets, due of course to malnutrition and neglect. The colored people themselves believe the school authorities are more interested in a school whose patronage is predominantly white.

It was found that young colored girls, like the boys, often become desperately discouraged in their efforts to find employment other than domestic or personal service. High school girls of refined appearance, after looking for weeks, will find nothing open to them in department stores, office buildings, or manufacturing establishments, save a few positions as maids placed in the women's waiting rooms. Such girls find it continually assumed by the employment agencies to whom they apply for positions that they are willing to serve as domestics in low-class hotels and disreputable houses. Of course, the agency does not explain the character of the place to which it sends the girl, but going to one address after another the girl herself finds that the places are all of one kind.

Recently an intelligent colored girl who had kept a careful record of her experiences with three employment agencies came to the office of the Juvenile Protective Association to see what might be done to protect colored girls less experienced and self-reliant than herself against similar temptations. Another young colored girl who, at the age of fifteen, had been sent to a house of prostitution by an employment agency, was rescued from the house, treated in a hospital, and sent to her sister in a western state. She there married a respectable man and is now living in a little home "almost paid for."

The case of Eliza M., who has worked as a cook in a disreputable house for ten years, is that of a woman forced into vicious surroundings. In addition to her wages of five dollars a week and food which she is permitted to take home every evening to her family, she has been able to save her generous "tips" for the education of her three children for whom she is very ambitious.

Colored young women who are manicurists and hair dressers find it continually assumed that they will be willing to go to hotels under compromising conditions, and when a decent girl refuses to go, she is told that that is all that she can expect. There is not doubt that the few colored girls who find positions as stenographers or bookkeepers are much more open to insult than white girls in similar positions.

All these experiences tend to discourage the young people from that "education" which their parents so eagerly desire for them and also makes it extremely difficult for them to maintain their standards of self-respect.

Crime and the Negro "Suspect"

In spite of various efforts on the part of colored people themselves to found homes for dependent and semi-delinquent colored children the accommodations are totally inadequate, which is the more remarkable as the public records all give a high percentage of Negro criminals. In Chicago the police department gives 7.7 per cent, the Juvenile Court 6.5 per cent, the county jail 10 per cent.

Those familiar with the police and the courts believe that Negroes are often arrested on excuses too flimsy to hold a white man, that any Negro who happens to be near the scene of a crime or disorder is promptly arrested and often convicted on evidence upon which a white man would be discharged. Certainly the Juvenile Protective Association has on record cases in which a Negro has been arrested without sufficient cause and convicted on inadequate evidence. A certain type of policeman, of juryman, and of prosecuting attorney has apparently no scruples in sending a "nigger up the road" on mere suspicion.

There is the record in the files of the association of the case of George W., a colored boy, nineteen years old, who was born in Chicago and who had attended the public schools through one year at high school. He lived with his mother and had worked steadily for three years as a porter in a large grocery store, when one day he was arrested on a charge of rape.

In the late afternoon of that day a woman eighty-three years old was assaulted by a Negro and was saved from the horrible attack only by the timely arrival of her daughter, who so frightened the assailant that he jumped out of a window. Two days later George was arrested, charged with the crime. At the police station, he was not allowed to sleep, was beaten, cuffed, and kicked, and finally, battered and frightened, he confessed that he had committed the crime.

When he appeared in court, his lawyer advised him to plead guilty, although the boy explained that he had not committed the crime and had confessed simply because he was forced to do so. The evidence against him was so flimsy that the judge referred to it in his instructions to the jury. The state's attorney had failed to establish the ownership of the cap dropped by the fleeing assailant and the time of the attempted act was changed during the testimony. The description given by the people who saw the colored man running away did not correspond to George's appearance. Nevertheless the jury brought in a verdict of guilty, and the judge sentenced the boy to fourteen years in the penitentiary. When one of the men who had seen the guilty man running away from the old woman's house was asked why he did not make his testimony more explicit, he replied, "Oh, well, he's only a nigger anyway."

The case was brought to the Juvenile Protective Association by the employer of George W., who, convinced of the boy's good character, felt that he had not had a fair trial. The association, finding that the boy could absolutely prove an alibi at the time of the crime, is making every effort to get him out of the penitentiary.

As remedies for the unjust discrimination against the colored man suspected of crime, a leading attorney of the race in Chicago suggests that:

Generalizing against the Negro should cease. The fact that one Negro is bad should not fix criminality upon the race. The race should be judged by its best as well as by its worst types.

The public press never associates the nationality of a criminal so markedly in its account of crime as in the case of a Negro. This exception is most unjust and harmful and should not obtain.

The Negro should not be made the universal scapegoat. When a crime is committed, the slightest pretext starts the rumor of a "Negro suspect" and flaming headlines prejudice the public mind long after the white criminal is found. . . .

In suggesting remedies for this state of affairs, the broken family life, the surroundings of a vicious neighborhood, the dearth of adequate employment, the lack of preventive institutional care, and proper recreation for Negro youth, the Juvenile Protective Association finds itself confronted with the situation stated at the beginning of the investigation—that the life of the colored boy and girl is so circumscribed on every hand by race limitations that they can be helped only as the entire colored population in Chicago is understood and fairly treated.

For many years Chicago, keeping to the tradition of its early history, had the reputation among colored people of according them fair treatment. Even now it is free from the outward signs of "segregation," but unless the city realizes more fully than it does at present the great injustice which discrimination against any class of citizens entails, it will suffer for this indifference in an ever-increasing number of idle and criminal youth, which must eventually vitiate both the black and white citizenship of Chicago.

Poverty

Robert Hunter

The Hull-House residents, with their investigations of sweating labor, tenement houses, and wage scales, did not really need graphs, charts, or statistics to convince them of the horror and consequences of poverty. They knew personally the children who died of disease or malnutrition, or whose intellectual and physical growth was stunted by having to work at an early age. They knew the discouraged men and the sullen, silent women who could not provide for their families. These people were their neighbors. Settlement residents realized that circumstances and environment, not laziness and drunkenness, were the major causes of poverty. Among the first to come to this conclusion, they helped to enlighten the American public about poverty. Hull-House residents also had faith that the environment could be changed, and that with change poverty would be eliminated.

Robert Hunter's book Poverty, *published in 1904, but based largely on his experience while a resident of Hull-House from 1899 to 1902, shocked the American people, much as Michael Harrington's* The Other America *did sixty years later. Using $460 as a minimum subsistence family income, Hunter announced that there were at least ten million and perhaps twenty million poor in America. He made a distinction between paupers and the working poor, demonstrating with overwhelming evidence that many who worked full time or who*

were willing to work still fell below the poverty line.

Robert Hunter (1874–1942) was born in Terre Haute, Indiana, and graduated from Indiana University in 1896. Disturbed by the tragedy and poverty caused by the depression of 1893, he went to Chicago after graduation and lived in settlement houses, first at Northwestern University Settlement, then at Hull-House. Not satisfied with charity, he worked in many reform movements. He was a member of the Chicago Small Parks Commission and chairman of the investigating committee of the City Homes Association (organized by Hull-House) which studied housing conditions in the city. Hunter was the author of Tenement Conditions in Chicago *(1901) which described horrible housing conditions and called for legislation to correct them.*

One of many Hull-House graduates who became leaders in the settlement movement elsewhere, Hunter moved to New York in 1902 as the head resident of University Settlement. There he helped organize a massive effort against child labor. In 1905, a year after Poverty *was published, he joined the Socialist party because he was discouraged with the meager results of progressive reform measures. He was a leading member of the party until he resigned in 1914, but in* Poverty *he displayed the faith of the American progressive who felt better laws and greater public concern could end the evils of poverty. [Robert Hunter,* Poverty *(New York, 1904), 318–325, 327–328, 337–340.]*

We are perhaps too prone to think of those in poverty as effortless beings, who make no fight for themselves and wait in misery until someone comes to assist them. Such an opinion is without any foundation. It is based upon knowledge gained by acquaintance with the pauper and vagrant, and is in no wise applicable to the workers in poverty. It is small wonder that workers who are underfed, underclothed, and poorly housed, are sometimes won from their hard and almost hopeless toil by sensual pleasures. Nor is it surprising that they are driven to despair by the brutal power of the economic forces which dominate their lives.

Without the security which comes only with the ownership of property, without a home from which they may not be evicted, without any assurance of regular employment, without tools with which they may employ themselves, they are pathetically dependent upon their physical efficiency—their health and strength, and upon the activity of machinery, owned by others, and worked or left idle as the owners consider it wise or profitable. In their weak and unorganized condition, they are unlike the skilled workers, made powerful by their unions and by their methods of collective bargaining; they are fighting alone, each one against another. . . .

Having been drawn, about twelve years ago, to some interest in the problems of poverty, there happened to me the common experience of all those of like interests. The poor in the broader sense of that word were busily at work and trying rather to conceal than to make evidence of their poverty; while the beggars, vagrants, idlers, and dependents of all sorts were more or less always pressing forward their necessities. It was natural, therefore, for me to confuse the problem of poverty with that of pauperism and to take up with some enthusiasm the ideas which are a part of the propaganda of many useful charitable organizations. To the charitable workers these problems of vagrancy and pauperism seem possible of solution. Many reforms—among which wise giving, friendly visiting, work-rooms, work-tests, model lodging-houses, rent-collecting, etc., are a few— were, in the early nineties, making rapid headway. They were, at that time, ranked first in importance in the category of organized movements for diminishing the evils of pauperism. Many committees were at work promoting these reforms, and in different cities I was able to help in their efforts. The result of their work was not discouraging, but in every instance they came hard up against one almost insurmountable obstacle. The pauper and the vagrant were not dissatisfied; they clamored for alms, but they did not wish to alter their way of living. Even those who possessed the capacity for industrial usefulness and who might have become self-supporting did not wish to go back again into the factories, mills, or mines. In fact, so far as one could see, they were as unwilling as the others to alter their ways of living. However miserable their lot seemed to those

of us on the Committees, to them it seemed to be, on the whole, acceptable enough to bring a certain sort of content. However malarious and poisonous and undrained, they loved their valley of idleness and quiet; they hated the hill upon which they were constrained to toil; they shrank from its disappointments, its bruises, its weariness and bitterness, while its meanness and ugliness of life were but slightly less mean and ugly than their own. The children, bred into the ways of pauperism, nearly always took up the vices of their parents. They were pleasure-loving, and whatever was toilsome seemed abhorrent to them. The girls took the easier path; it appeared unquestionably more desirable to their childish standards, and for a time at least it gave them more of everything for which most human beings seem to hunger—finery, leisure, and a kind of pleasure. The men and boys liked vagrancy, and those who were not attracted to these ways settled down into a satisfied, imperturbable pauperism. They lived in God only knows what misery. They ate when there were things to eat; they starved when there was lack of food. But, on the whole, although they swore and beat each other and got drunk, they were more contented than any other class I have happened to know. It took a long time to understand them. Our Committees were busy from morning until night in giving them opportunities to take up the fight again, and to become independent of relief. They always took what we gave them; they always promised to try; but as soon as we expected them to fulfill any promises, they gave up in despair, and either wept or looked ashamed, and took to misery and drink again—almost, so it seemed to me at times, with a sense of relief. . . .

But as long as one works with, or observes only, the dependent classes, the true, or at least what seems to me the true, explanation of this apparent satisfaction of vagrants and paupers remains in the dark. It was not until I had lived for several years among the toilers in a great industrial community that the reason for the content of the dependent classes became clear to me. In this community of workers several thousand human beings were struggling fiercely against want. Day after day, year after year, they toiled with marvellous persistency and perseverance. Obnoxious as the simile is, they worked from dawn until nightfall, or from sunset until dawn, like galley slaves under the sting of want and under the whip of hunger. On cold, rainy mornings, at the dusk of dawn, I have been awakened, two hours before my rising time, by the monotonous clatter of hobnailed boots on the plank sidewalks, as the procession to the factory passed under my window. Heavy, brooding men, tired, anxious women, thinly dressed, unkempt little girls, and frail, joyless little lads passed along, half awake, not one uttering a word as they hurried to the great factory. From all directions thousands were entering the various gates—children of every nation of Europe. Hundreds of others—obviously a hungrier, poorer lot than those entering the gates; some were most ragged and almost shoeless, but all with eager faces—waited in front of a closed gate until finally a great red-bearded man came out and selected twenty-three of the strongest, best-looking of the men. For these the gates were opened, and the others, with downcast eyes, marched off to seek employment elsewhere or to sit at home, or in a saloon, or in a lodging-house, until the following morning, when they came wistfully again to some factory gate. In this community, the saddest in which I have ever lived, fully fifty thousand men, women, and children were all the time either in poverty or on the verge of poverty. It would not be possible to describe how they worked and starved and ached to rise out of it. They broke their health down; the men acquired in this particular trade a painful and disabling rheumatism, and consumption was very common. The girls and boys followed in the paths of their parents. The wages were so low that the men alone often could not support their families, and mothers with babies toiled in order to add to the income. They gave up all thought of joyful living, probably in the hope that by tremendous exertion they could overcome their poverty; but they gained while at work only enough to keep their bodies alive. Theirs was a sort of treadmill existence with no prospect of anything else in life but more treadmill. When they were not given work in the mill, they starved; and when they grew desperate, they came to my office and asked for charity. Here was a mass of men whose ways of living were violently opposed to those of the vagrant or the pauper. They were distorting themselves in the struggle to be independent of charity and to overcome poverty. That they hated charity must be taken without question. The

Newsboys and messengers shooting dice on a street corner in the settlement neighborhood.

testimony of scores of men is proof of it, even if, indeed, their very lives were not. But despite all their efforts they lived in houses but little, if any, better than those of the paupers; they were almost as poorly dressed; they were hardly better fed. . . .

. . . When the working people, by reason of whatever misery poverty brings, once fall into the abyss, they so hate the life of their former struggles and disappointments and sorrows that almost no one, however well-intentioned or kindly, can induce them to take it up again. In the abyss they become merely breeders of children, who persist in the degeneration into which their fathers have fallen; and . . . they have neither the willingness nor the capacity to respond to the efforts of those who would help, or force, them back again into the struggle.

However merciful and kind and valuable the works of the charitable and the efforts of those who would raise up again the pauper and the vagrant, they are not remedial. In so far as the work of the charitable is devoted to reclamation and not to prevention, it is a failure. Not that anyone could wish that less were done in the direction of reclamation. The fact only is important that effort is less powerful there than in overcoming the forces which undermine the workers and those who are struggling against insurmountable difficulties. It is an almost hopeless task to regenerate the degenerate, especially when, if the latter are to succeed, they must be made to take up again the battle with those very destructive forces which are all the time undermining stronger, more capable, and more self-reliant men than they. The all-necessary work to be done is not so much to reclaim a class which social forces are ever active in producing, as it is to battle with the social or economic forces which are continuously producing recruits to that class. The forces producing the miseries of pauperism and vagrancy are many, but none are so important as those conditions of work and of living which are so unjust and degrading that men are driven by them into degeneracy. When the uncertainties, hardships, trials, sorrows, and miseries of a self-supporting existence become so painful that good, strong, self-reliant men and women are forced into pauperism, then there is but little use in trying to force the paupers and the vagrants back into the struggle. . . .

. . . There are probably in fairly prosperous years no less than 10,000,000 persons in poverty; that is to say, underfed, underclothed, and poorly housed. Of these about 4,000,000 persons are public paupers. Over 2,000,000 working-men are unemployed from four to six months in the year. About 500,000 male immigrants arrive yearly and seek work in the very districts where unemployment is greatest. Nearly half of the families in the country are propertyless. Over 1,700,000 little children are forced to become wage-earners when they should still be in school. About 5,000,000 women find it necessary to work and about 2,000,000 are employed in factories, mills, etc. Probably no less than 10,000,000 workers are injured or killed each year while doing their work, . . . and about 10,000,000 of the persons now living will, if the present ratio is kept up, die of the preventable disease, tuberculosis. We know that many workmen are overworked and underpaid. We know in a general way that unnecessary disease is far too prevalent. We know some of the insanitary evils of tenements and factories; we know of the neglect of the street child, the aged, the infirm, the crippled. Furthermore, we are beginning to realize the monstrous injustice of compelling those who are unemployed, who are injured in industry, who have acquired diseases due to their occupation, or who have been made widows or orphans by industrial accidents, to become paupers in order that they may be housed, fed, and clothed. Something is known concerning these problems of poverty, and some of them at least are possible of remedy.

To deal with these specific problems, I have elsewhere mentioned some reforms which seem to me preventive in their nature. They contemplate mainly such legislative action as may enforce upon the entire country certain minimum standards of working and of living conditions. They would make all tenements and factories sanitary; they would regulate the hours of work, especially for women and children; they would regulate and thoroughly supervise dangerous trades; they would institute all necessary measures to stamp out unnecessary disease and to prevent unnecessary death; they would prohibit entirely child labor; they would institute all necessary educational and recreational institutions to replace the social and educational losses of the home and the domestic workshop; they would perfect, as far as possible, legislation and institutions to make industry pay the necessary and legitimate cost of producing and maintaining efficient laborers; they would institute, on the lines of foreign experience, measures to compensate labor for enforced seasons of idleness, due to sickness, old age, lack of work, or other causes beyond the control of the workman; they would prevent parasitism on the part of either the consumer or the producer and charge up the full costs of labor in production to the beneficiary, instead of compelling the worker at certain times to enforce his demand for maintenance through the tax rate and by becoming a pauper; they would restrict the power of employer and of ship-owner to stimulate for purely selfish ends an excessive immigration, and in this way to beat down wages and to increase unemployment.

Reforms such as these are not ones which will destroy incentive, but rather they will increase incentive by more nearly equalizing opportunity.

They will make propertied interests less predatory, and sensuality, by contrast with misery, less attractive to the poor. . . . This does not mean that there is to be no struggle . . . but rather that the life of the poorest toiler shall not be a hopeless thing from which many must turn in despair. In other words, the process of Justice is to lift stony barriers, against which the noblest beat their brains out, and from which the ignoble (but who shall say not more sensible?) turn away in despair. Let it be this, rather than a barren relief system, administered by those who must stand by, watching the struggle, lifting no hand to aid the toilers, but ever succoring those who flee and those who are bruised and beaten.

The Hull-House War on Cocaine

Charities and The Commons

The use of drugs by young and old in American cities seems like a peculiarly modern phenomenon. Yet Hull-House residents faced the problem in their neighborhood in 1904. During the summer, the mother of a thirteen-year-old boy, who was rapidly losing his health because of his use of cocaine, came to Hull-House for help. The residents investigated the mother's complaint and discovered that the drug was being sold illegally throughout their neighborhood. They launched a full-scale study of the situation and, based on their findings, began to press for the passage of stricter legal controls which they optimistically believed would solve the problem. ["The Hull-House War on Cocaine," Charities and The Commons (February 1907), 1034–1035.]

Through the strong stand taken by the new municipal court judges in Chicago and the provisions of a bill which it is hoped the present Illinois legislature will pass, Hull House is expecting to get the upper hand in the hard-fought struggle of two years to stop the sale of cocaine to boys. The beginning of the fight was in the summer of 1904, when an investigation of the illegal sale of cocaine and the use of it, especially by boys, was undertaken by residents of Hull House. The occasion of the investigation was the discovery that a group of about fifteen neighborhood boys, from thirteen to eighteen years of age, had become habitual users of this drug. The cocaine habit had spread to an alarming extent. It was sold in many drug stores, openly and with no discretion as to the buyers; in saloons, pool rooms, and the low Chinese joints. Agents also peddled it on the streets, offering it freely to the boys who would snuff it at first from mere curiosity and then, as they became addicted to the habit, paid exorbitant prices to these men to get it for them. After the confidence of the boys had been gained, evidence was secured and prosecutions were begun at once under the city ordinance and the state law, both of which prohibit the sale of cocaine, except on the written prescription of a licensed physician. These prosecutions have been vigorously carried on up to the present time with the co-operation of the juvenile court committee, the Legal Aid Society, and the State Board of Pharmacy. The results hitherto have not been satisfactory and this is due, in great part, to two causes. The validity of the city ordinance has always been questioned, and for several months one of the judges had this question under consideration, during which time all of the work was at a stand-still. Another great obstacle was the lack of trustworthy witnesses and inability to have them on hand after months of delay in appealed cases. Few final convictions could be secured, and because of this and the enormous profit made on cocaine the druggists have been able and willing to run the risk of prosecution. If the new state law under consideration by the legislature is passed, it will certainly be possible to prevent the illegal sale of this and similar drugs. Pending this legislation, however, much better results are being secured than ever before, as the judges of the new municipal courts have taken a strong stand for the enforcement of the present law, and in case a conviction is secured the cost of an appeal is now so great that it probably will not be taken.

Working with the Juvenile Delinquent

Sara L. Hart

The concern of Hull-House residents for children led them to organize a kindergarten, work for child labor laws, and establish the first public playground in Chicago in 1893. It also influenced the residents to support the creation of the first Juvenile Court in the nation, and to organize the Juvenile Psychopathic Institute and the Juvenile Protective Association.

The Juvenile Court was not a criminal court; the judge was expected to rule with the interests of the juvenile offenders uppermost in mind. He could put the delinquent on probation, make him a ward of the state, or assign him to an institution. While the main idea was to help rather than penalize the child, it did not always work out that way, for the judge had enormous power while the offender enjoyed none of the rights of due process. Not until 1967 did a U.S. Supreme Court decision recognize that even juvenile offenders were entitled to procedural rights. Yet in 1899 the Juvenile Court represented a major breakthrough in the treatment of boys and girls in trouble.

The Hull-House group was not content to reform the court system alone. They also believed they could discover why young people got into trouble, and they had faith that most juvenile delinquency could be prevented. In 1909 they founded the Juvenile Psychopathic Institute with funds provided by Ethel Sturgis Dummer, a Chicago philanthropist and Hull-House supporter. Under the direction of Dr. William Healy (b. 1869) it became a leading center for research into the causes of delinquency. Healy's careful studies, which led to such books as The Individual Delinquent (1915), rejected theories that attributed delinquency to heredity. He emphasized that delinquency had many causes, environment being most important. The Juvenile Protective Association, organized the same year as the Psychopathic Institute, sought to control or eliminate poolrooms, bars, dance halls, theaters, and other in-stitutions which were, from its point of view, breeders of crime and vice.

The following account of Hull-House efforts to work with young people in trouble is from a section in Sara Hart's autobiography, The Pleasure Is Mine. Hart (b. 1869), whose husband Harry Hart (1850–1929) was one of the partners of Hart, Schaffner & Marx clothiers, was one of the many well-to-do Chicago women who gave their time and money to Hull-House. [Sara L. Hart, The Pleasure Is Mine: An Autobiography (Chicago, 1947), 95–105.]

My slogan has always been, "A happy childhood for every child." When youngsters are thwarted and their lives are crippled I feel that not they, but we, the citizens of the city, county, state, and nation, have failed. I was not a pioneer in child welfare, but I have given more than half of my lifetime to it. The young are our future. In them lie our hopes for a better world. That is why we must seek the best for them. . . .

It was in Illinois—in Chicago, in Cook County—that the first Juvenile Court was established. Jane Addams pointed out that

> The year 1899 was distinguished by the open-ing of *two* courts, *each the first of its kind in the world*. The first Juvenile Court was opened in the conviction that the existing court procedure was not fitted to a child's needs; and a court was established at The Hague in Holland, dedicated to the concili-ation and arbitration of all difficulties arising be-tween nations. These widely separated courts are not so unlike, if we take the point of view of man-kind's long spiritual struggle to maintain and purify the reign of justice in the world, with the obligation laid upon each generation to find the means by which justice may be extended into new fields.

Prior to July 1, 1899, children who fell afoul of the law, and they frequently did on the least complaint and at the caprice of any adult, were treated like ordinary felons. Even those who did not come from the slums were often led into a life of crime by the cruel treatment they suffered from unfeel-ing police officers, judges, and prison authori-ties. . . .

The basic principle of the Law of 1899 was

that no child under sixteen years of age should be considered or treated as a criminal; that, under that age, he should not be arrested, indicted, convicted, imprisoned, or punished as one. The age of criminal responsibility was ten. . . .

But the law failed to provide either a place of detention, or for the salaries of the probation officers who would exercise parental care. The first may have been an oversight; the second was probably to discourage patronage seekers. Politicians do not vie for jobs that offer no pay.

The Court could not operate without the probation officer who "in a juvenile court is like a master in chancery. He is the supervising agent of the court."

At the first session Lucy M. Flower* appeared and declared that she would raise the salary for a probation officer if the Court would appoint Mrs. Alzina P. Stevens of Hull-House. Judge Richard S. Tuthill, who was the first justice assigned from the Circuit Court bench, eagerly accepted the offer.

The early work was done by about a dozen volunteers, but professional people were also needed. Whenever a suitable person was located, additional funds were necessary. Lucy Flower, who could be called the "Mother of the first Juvenile Court," carried the burden until she left for California. Before she moved she made sure that the movement would continue, by organizing, on September 30, 1902, "The Juvenile Court Committee."

For the probation system had proved itself. In 1897, 1898, and 1899, 1,705 children had been sent to the County Jail. For an equal period after the establishment of the Court, in the years 1900, 1901, and 1902, only 60 children were jailed. Of course, an understanding judge and the faithful and patient officers had made that possible.

The women whom Mrs. Flower called together included Ellen M. Henrotin, Hannah Solomon, Alice S. Tracy, Elizabeth Bass, and Julia C. Lathrop. As soon as the Committee was formed, the latter was elected chairman.

They decided to invite every interested organization to join, for the annual budget would be at least ten thousand dollars. The clubs were asked to place the court program on their agendas.

There were times when there was not money enough to pay all the salaries. But as the public became aware of the Committee literally dozens of outlying clubs and, later, churches came in with us. One year the Chicago Tribune urged editorially, "A probation officer in time saves nine policemen. Help the Juvenile Court Committee to maintain an adequate staff."

The labors of these officers were often heroic but generally unsung. Even when they were paid, they received only $60.00 a month, $720.00 a year, a pitiful remuneration. As Chief Justice Charles Evans Hughes of the Supreme Court of the United States once said, "There is no room here for mere place-hunters or political derelicts."

To this day the conscientious officer is literally worth his weight in gold, considering what he or she saves the community.

Timothy D. Hurley, who was with the City Attorney, was loaned to the Court to be the first chief probation officer. The next selections, John H. Witter, Henry J. Lynch, and Henry N. Thurston, who was chief until 1913, were made by the County Civil Service Commission.

At that time Judge Merritt W. Pinckney asked the Juvenile Court Committee to hold the first merit examination. I was among those who framed the questions, gave the tests, and marked the papers. Joel Hunter, who passed with the highest grades, was appointed. That set a precedent for merit selections. In 1918 Joseph L. Moss succeeded Mr. Hunter, who left to become the superintendent of the United Charities. When Mr. Moss resigned to direct the Cook County Bureau of Public Welfare, Colonel Harry Hill received the post. He has held it ever since.†

The original law had not only lacked provision for the payment of the officers, it had even failed to provide a place of detention for the children.

At first the Illinois Industrial Association‡

---

*Lucy Louisa Coues Flower (1837–1921), active in the Chicago Woman's Club, also helped found the Illinois Training School for Nurses.—Eds.

†Colonel Hill held the position from 1927 until January 1954.—Eds.

‡The Illinois Industrial Association was incorporated on May 27, 1894, by William S. Potwin, Alonzo K. Parker, Benjamin M. Butler, George F. Fiske, Joseph Schneider, Charles W. Storey, and Adam C. Dodds. Its general purpose was: "To aid discharged prisoners in efforts to reform and to obtain an honest living; to employ temporarily such persons in some suitable kind of work, and to obtain work for them."

took care of the youngsters in a house at 233 Honore Street, which was donated by Mr. and Mrs. Potter Palmer. On November 30, 1902, the home was moved to 625 West Adams Street (now 1726 West Adams Street). Adam C. Dodds was superintendent. He remained until October, 1903, when Mrs. Sarah Franklin succeeded him.

That fall the Association proposed to our Committee that we assume the care of the Home. On October 24 we agreed to take over.

I became a member in early 1903, about eight months after I returned to Chicago. My first job was as a volunteer officer. One day, as Julia Lathrop and I were attending a court session, she whispered to me, "How would you like to take care of the Detention Home?"

I shrugged. "I know nothing about it."

She retorted, "Neither does anyone else!"

I decided to do it. My household was ably run by Mother and the maid, Hilda* was at school, and I had the leisure.

I was in the midst of this new assignment— "Chairman of the Detention Home Committee" was my title—when Julia Lathrop told me that because of the pressure of her other duties she was resigning from the chairmanship of the Juvenile Court Committee and had asked Mrs. Bowen to take it.

I was thunderstruck. I was still a little greenhorn from Louisiana, and any change was alarming. "Cousin Julia," I wept, "I don't know Mrs. Bowen! I don't know anything about her."

With a twinkle of amusement she assured me that the new chairman was a splendid woman, forthright and able, and that I would be just as happy under her leadership.

On October 30, 1903, Mrs. Bowen formally reappointed me chairman of this Committee. I discharged the duties of that position for the next four years. Cousin Julia proved to be right: I was just as happy with Mrs. Bowen. Indeed, although I used to ride the elevated train from the South Side, Mrs. Bowen frequently had her carriage waiting for me at the Twelfth Street Station to drive me to the Detention Home.

The first directors of the Juvenile Court Committee, after the incorporation, were Mrs. Joseph T. Bowen, president; Julia C. Lathrop, first vice-president and chairman of the Conference Committee; Judge Leroy D. Thoman, second vice-president; Mrs. Charles Henrotin, third vice-president; Mrs. Frederick K. Tracy, secretary; Mr. James H. Eckels, treasurer; Mrs. Theodore B. Wells, assistant treasurer; Mrs. George Bass, chairman of the Court Committee, and myself (then Sadie T. Wald), chairman of the Detention Home Committee.

That year we raised ten thousand dollars. The following year we needed fifteen thousand, to maintain fifteen officers. With each additional expansion we required more money. Among the civic-minded Chicagoans who joined us were Mrs. George R. Dean, who was later secretary of the Committee and followed Mrs. Bowen as president (from 1938 to the present time), Jane Addams, who was one of our directors, the Very Reverend Dean Sumner, Father Andrew Spetz, Rabbi Joseph Stolz, Mrs. William Dummer, and Mrs. Julius Rosenwald. Roscoe Pound was on the Committee until the Fall of 1909, when he left to become professor of law at Harvard. The Detention Home was a three-story brick and frame building. Two floors were set aside for dependent children. The top story was left vacant, except for the superintendent's quarters, because we feared its safety in case of fire. The stable, which was a two-story brick structure, was used for the delinquent boys. On the first floor were the kitchen and the sitting room, which was also used for play and study quarters. On the second floor fifty boys slept. The delinquent girls were housed in the Harrison Street Police Station.†

In my report of November 23, 1906—that was the year the Board of Education sent Florence Scully to teach our children—I wrote, not without feeling, that our Detention Home was a unique institution:

It shelters all sorts and conditions of children and, with the prophet of old, exclaims "Enter all ye

---

*Hilda Wald (b. 1889) the daughter of Sara Hart by her first husband, Adam Wald (1853–1901).—Eds.

†From November, 1904 to November, 1905, we received 2,667 children. From November, 1905 to November, 1906, we cared for 2,413 children. 32,046 meals were served. 1,663 of these children were delinquents, 579 were dependents, 100 were runaways, and 71 were truants. The largest total for any month was 315, in May; in September there were 26 runaways, from nearly every state. Truants remained the longest. The usual charge against the delinquents was larceny. "Larceny" meant the flipping of street cars, and the stealing of newspapers and milk bottles, the usual offenses in those days.

who knock.'' Children knock at the door of the Orphan Asylum, the Home of the Friendless, the Hospital, but they must pass muster before they can enter. Not so at the Detention Home. Do you know the method of procedure at 625 West Adams Street? Arrives the patrol wagon, accompanied by one or more police officers. Enters a boy. The police officer on duty records the name, address, and offense of the newcomer. Then the lad is searched, given a bath and clean clothes, and is privileged to mingle with the other so-called delinquents that constitute the family in the ''Annex.'' The next day when the physician calls, the youngster receives a casual examination. In the Home proper, among the dependent children, the danger of contagion is aggravated, but provision is made for an isolation room. The little ones have suffered from cold, hunger, disease. Scarcely a family crosses the threshold but one or more of the children are ill.

I had a free hand. I bought the food and the clothing, seeking only the best within our means.

It was evident that many citizens were willing to help if they were called upon and could give without inconvenience. Soon we had quantities of merchandise and provision flowing to our storeroom. We needed those gifts, for we received only a modest appropriation from Henry G. Foreman, president of the County Board, and a small one from the city. The balance was raised by Mrs. Bowen.

As the public learned about our work it became easier to obtain funds. The County Board took increasing interest and by 1910 the probation officers were being paid from the treasury. At that time Judge Pinckney called in the badges which had been issued to the volunteer officers. I confess now that I could not resist keeping mine as a souvenir; I still have it among my most treasured mementoes.

First, last, and always, we considered the children. We had taken them from poor surroundings. They were underprivileged and undernourished. I cared for them as I would have wished any child of my own to be treated. Christmas, New Year, Fourth of July, Halloween, and Thanksgiving, we held special celebrations. I could devote full time, so I presided.

Running the Home was not as simple as it may seem forty years later. Not all of our children were truants or dependents. Many were psychological misfits of unruly temperament, and presented serious problems even to kindly disposed women.

For their amusement I secured a pool table and other recreational equipment. (I used to play pool with them myself.) One day I discovered that the boys had used the cues in a fight. We could have ranted and stormed and punished, but they would have enough trouble without our discipline. When the pool table was ripped up I furnished another through the generosity of friends.

Once they realized that we were on their side, even the delinquents were anxious to do right. We were fortunate to have sympathetic assistants, who were, in no small measure, responsible for the genial atmosphere.

As I wrote in one report, ''We have always recognized the rights of the child, and supplied, for the moment, at least, that clean, sanitary, moral, loving home of which society had perhaps robbed it.''

When the children went to Court they rode in a discarded patrol-wagon, which was so ramshackle and unsteady that it was unfit for police use. We made every effort that the youngsters should not look upon the trip as a disgrace. Our horse was called ''Dan.'' Even the fact that they knew his name helped to make the rides a little more pleasant. The vehicle had a black oil-cloth drop. The youngsters poked their fingers through to peep out at the passing scenes.

That wagon was in use until the boards were falling out of the bottom, and it was too dilapidated even for us. Then, after six weeks of trying to get the authorities to give us a new one, Mrs. Bowen secured a yellow rubber-tired bus. But it was too heavy for our little horse. The only animal we could get to help him pull was a large creature from the fire department. Dan was a puny beast. These two, not always in step, were an unforgettable sight. One day the fire horse, hearing the distant clang of a bell, made a mad dash down the street, and lifted the pony off its feet. So we had to buy a new pair of horses after all.

The Detention Home became crowded. Clean though we kept our quarters, they were still shabby, compared to what a great metropolis ought to have for its children. When Edward J. Brundage was president of the Cook County Board a movement was started to build a new County Building. As I recall it, he urged that what-

Hull-House supported the Elizabeth McCormick Open Air School, held on the roof of the Mary Crane Nursery building, to help combat tuberculosis and disease. At its opening on November 5, 1911, were (standing, left to right): Mrs. Ella Flagg Young, Superintendent of City Schools; Sherman C. Kingsley; Walter T. Sumner, Board of Education; Dr. George B. Young, Health Commissioner; Kate Kellogg, District Superintendent of Schools; Dr. Theodore B. Sachs of the Municipal Sanitarium; Cyrus Hall McCormick; T. A. Allinson; Harry A. Lipsky of the Board of Education; Mrs. Cyrus Hall McCormick and Mrs. McCormick, Jr.; and Jane Addams.

ever was saved from that construction fund be set aside for another Detention Home.

We asked for a three-story fireproof brick structure with separate facilities for delinquent and dependent children, space for a court-room, and offices for the probation department. At last the plans were drawn, and the bids were received and awarded.

On October 15, 1907, we moved into the fine Juvenile Court Building and Detention Home— the two under one roof, as they should have been from the very first—at 202 Ewing Street . . . [site absorbed by the University of Illinois Chicago campus]. The Court and the executive quarters, including the receiving rooms for the mothers and the children, were on the first floor. The second floor was for the dependents. The east room of the third floor was for the delinquent girls, the west room for the delinquent boys. On the lot back of the home the Board of Education built a neat two-story school.

Up to this time the Juvenile Court Committee had expended over $100,000 for probation officers and minor court personnel, and to supplement the budget. Astonishing as it may seem, nearly ninety percent of this sum was raised by Mrs. Bowen.

At this juncture the Committee relinquished its advisory role in the Juvenile Court and in the Home. Our board believed that with the Court firmly established and with the probation system upon the payrolls of the County, the basic reason for our position as counsellor and friendly critic had disappeared.

To my mind that was a tactical error. I said so when we withdrew, and I still think that it was wrong to step out. I will not say that we could have avoided all the mistakes since made. But the Committee had earned the right to represent the public. The County Board listened to us, the judges respected our opinions, and the community relied on our experience. Eternal vigilance is not merely, as Benjamin Franklin said, the price of liberty, it is absolutely necessary to prevent official agencies from slipping.

Because our program was no longer limited to probation work and to the Detention Home, the Juvenile Court Committee changed its name, on June 4, 1909, to "The Juvenile Protective Association of Chicago." Our primary purpose was to remove the temptations and dangers which carelessness and greed placed before the children. The city had earlier been divided into districts, in each of which a Protective League tried to alleviate or remove conditions which bred delinquency. Officers and investigators policed the neighborhoods to prevent cocaine-selling and "can-rushing," and to keep the youngsters from disreputable dance halls and photographic galleries, real dangers in that day.

The Association went further than that. It investigated the five-and-ten cents theaters, the youthful newspaper merchants who were out at all hours of the night, the hazards confronting girls who worked in hotels and restaurants, and children employed in industry. Where angels feared to tread because of the economic interests involved the Juvenile Protective Association dared to go, and, furthermore, dared to publish its findings and indictments.

Originally we relied on Harry Smoot, our attorney when we were still the Juvenile Court Committee, to supervise us. Gertrude Howe Britton was the first to have a title along with the re-

sponsibilities. After many years of service Mrs. Britton left and Amelia Sears took over. Elizabeth Webster followed. Jessie F. Binford, who came to us in 1906 as a case worker, later became our executive director. (She has held that post, with but one leave during World War I, for thirty years.) Under her the Association grew to be the outstanding agency for the protection of children.

Today the "J. P. A." duplicates the work of no other organization, for it accepts every type of complaint, including those forwarded anonymously. Despite its outspoken criticism of lax public officials it is highly regarded even by those whom it so frequently censures. . . .

The Devil Baby
at Hull House

Jane Addams

Hull-House was an exciting, even—in some circles—a prestigious place to live. "The best club in Chicago," Henry Demarest Lloyd called it. Though the food was never especially good and living conditions were often overcrowded, there were always interesting guests, stimulating conversation, and sometimes impassioned arguments lasting well into the night. It was possible to live at Hull-House and become so involved with the intellectual fellowship of dedicated people that one forgot momentarily about the people who lived just down the street or around the block. Then something happened, something like the mythical visit of a devil baby, to reveal again the tragedy and pathos, the utter terror and fear faced daily by those outside the walls of Hull-House. This essay, perhaps because it touched on the supernatural and exposed a primitive side of human nature, was one of the most popular ever written by Jane Addams. She repeated the story in The Long Road of Women's Memory, *published in 1916, and in the Second Twenty Years at Hull-House, published in 1930; the following is the original version which appeared in the* Atlantic Monthly, *October 1916. [Jane Addams, "The Devil Baby at Hull-House,"*

Atlantic Monthly *(October 1916), 441–448, 451.]*

I

The knowledge of the existence of the Devil Baby burst upon the residents of Hull-House one day when three Italian women, with an excited rush through the door, demanded that he be shown to them. No amount of denial convinced them that he was not there, for they knew exactly what he was like, with his cloven hoofs, his pointed ears and diminutive tail; moreover, the Devil Baby had been able to speak as soon as he was born and was most shockingly profane.

The three women were but the forerunners of a veritable multitude; for six weeks the streams of visitors from every part of the city and suburbs to this mythical baby poured in all day long, and so far into the night that the regular activities of the settlement were almost swamped.

The Italian version, with a hundred variations, dealt with a pious Italian girl married to an atheist. Her husband vehemently tore a holy picture from the bedroom wall, saying that he would quite as soon have a devil in the house as that; whereupon the devil incarnated himself in her coming child. As soon as the Devil Baby was born, he ran about the table shaking his finger in deep reproach at his father, who finally caught him and in fear and trembling brought him to Hull-House. When the residents there, in spite of the baby's shocking appearance, wishing to save his soul, took him to church for baptism, they found that the shawl was empty and the Devil Baby, fleeing from the holy water, ran lightly over the backs of the pews.

The Jewish version, again with variations, was to the effect that the father of six daughters had said before the birth of a seventh child that he would rather have a devil in the house than another girl, whereupon the Devil Baby promptly appeared.

Save for a red automobile which occasionally figured in the story, and a stray cigar which, in some versions, the newborn child snatched from his father's lips, the tale might have been fashioned a thousand years ago.

Although the visitors to the Devil Baby included people of every degree of prosperity and education, even physicians and trained nurses who assured us of their scientific interest, the story constantly demonstrated the power of an old wives' tale among thousands of people in modern society who are living in a corner of their own, their vision fixed, their intelligence held by some iron chain of silent habit. To such primitive people the metaphor apparently is still the very "stuff of life"; or, rather, no other form of statement reaches them, and the tremendous tonnage of current writing for them has no existence. It was in keeping with their simple habits that the reputed presence of the Devil Baby at Hull-House did not reach the newspapers until the fifth week of his sojourn—after thousands of people had already been informed of his whereabouts by the old method of passing news from mouth to mouth.

During the weeks of excitement it was the old women who really seemed to have come into their own, and perhaps the most significant result of the incident was the reaction of the story upon them. It stirred their minds and memories as with a magic tough; it loosened their tongues and revealed the inner life and thoughts of those who are so often inarticulate. These old women enjoyed a moment of triumph, as if they had made good at last and had come into a region of sanctions and punishments which they understood.

Throughout six weeks, as I went about Hull-House, I would hear a voice at the telephone repeating for the hundredth time that day, "No, there is no such baby"; "No, we never had it here"; "No, he couldn't have seen it for fifty cents"; "We didn't send it anywhere because we never had it"; "I don't mean to say that your sister-in-law lied, but there must be some mistake"; "There is no use getting up an excursion from Milwaukee, for there isn't any Devil Baby at Hull-House"; "We can't give reduced rates because we are not exhibiting anything"; and so on and on. As I came near the front door, I would catch snatches of arguments that were often acrimonious: "Why do you let so many people believe it, if it isn't here?" "We have taken three lines of cars to come, and we have as much right to see it as anybody else"; "This is a pretty big place, of course you could hide it easy enough"; "What you saying that for—are you going to raise the price of admission?" We had doubtless struck a case of what the psychologists call the "contagion of emotion," added to that "aesthetic sociability" which impels any one of us to drag the entire household to the window when a procession comes into the street or a rainbow appears in the sky.

But the Devil Baby of course was worth many processions and rainbows, and I will confess that, as the empty show went on day after day, I quite revolted against such a vapid manifestation of an admirable human trait. There was always one exception, however: whenever I heard the high eager voices of old women, I was irresistibly interested and left anything I might be doing in order to listen to them.

II

Perhaps my many talks with these aged visitors crystallized thoughts and impressions that I had been receiving through years; or the tale itself may have ignited a fire, as it were, whose light illumined some of my darkest memories of neglected and uncomfortable old age, of old peasant women who had ruthlessly probed into the ugly depths of human nature in themselves and others. Many of them who came to see the Devil Baby had been forced to face tragic human experiences; the powers of brutality and horror had had full scope in their lives, and for years they had had acquaintance with disaster and death. Such old women do not shirk life's misery by feeble idealism, for they are long past the stage of make-believe. They relate without flinching the most hideous experiences. "My face has had this queer twist for now nearly sixty years; I was ten when it got that way, the night after I saw my father do my mother to death with his knife." "Yes, I had fourteen children; only two grew to be men and both of them were killed in the same explosion. I was never sure they brought home the right bodies." But even the most hideous sorrows which the old women related had apparently subsided into the paler emotion of ineffectual regret, after Memory had long done her work upon them; the old people seemed, in some unaccountable way, to lose all bitterness and resentment against life, or rather they were so completely without it that they must have lost it long since.

Perhaps those women, because they had come to expect nothing more from life and had perforce ceased from grasping and striving, had obtained, if not renunciation, at least that quiet endurance which allows the wounds of the spirit to heal. Through their stored-up habit of acquiescence, they vouchsafed a fleeting glimpse of that translucent wisdom so often embodied in old women, but so difficult to portray. I recall a conversation with one of them, a woman whose fine mind and indomitable spirit I had long admired; I had known her for years, and yet the recital of her sufferings, added to those the Devil Baby had already induced other women to tell me, pierced me afresh.

"I had eleven children, some born in Bohemia and some born here; nine of them boys; all of the children died when they were little, but my dear Liboucha, you know all about her. She died last winter in the insane asylum. She was only twelve years old when her father, in a fit of delirium tremens, killed himself after he had chased us around the room trying to kill us first. She saw it all; the blood splashed on the wall stayed in her mind the worst; she shivered and shook all that night through, and the next morning she had lost her voice, couldn't speak out loud for terror. After a while her voice came back, although it was never very natural, and she went to school again. She seemed to do as well as ever and was awful pleased when she got into High School. All the money we had, I earned scrubbing in a public dispensary, although sometimes I got a little more by interpreting for the patients, for I know three languages, one as well as the other. But I was determined that, whatever happened to me, Liboucha was to be educated. My husband's father was a doctor in the old country, and Liboucha was always a clever child. I wouldn't have her live the kind of life I had, with no use for my mind except to make me restless and bitter. I was pretty old and worn out for such hard work, but when I used to see Liboucha on a Sunday morning, ready for church in her white dress with her long yellow hair braided round her beautiful pale face, lying there in bed as I was—being brought up a freethinker and needing to rest my aching bones for the next week's work—I'd feel almost happy, in spite of everything.

"But of course no such peace could last in my life; the second year at High School, Liboucha began to seem different and to do strange things. You know the time she wandered away for three days and we were all wild with fright, although a kind woman had taken her in and no harm came to her. I could never be easy after that; she was always gentle, but she was awful sly about running away, and at last I had to send her to the asylum. She stayed there off and on for five years, but I saw her every week of my life and she was always company for me, what with sewing for her, washing and ironing her clothes, cooking little things to take out to her and saving a bit of money to buy fruit for her. At any rate, I had stopped feeling so bitter, and got some comfort out of seeing the one thing that belonged to me on this side of the water, when all of a sudden she died of heart failure, and they never took the trouble to send for me until the next day.'' . . .

Among the visitors were pitiful old women who, although they had already reconciled themselves to much misery, were still enduring more. ''You might say it's a disgrace to have your son beat you up for the sake of a bit of money you've earned by scrubbing—your own man is different—but I haven't the heart to blame the boy for doing what he's seen all his life; his father forever went wild when the drink was in him and struck me to the very day of his death. The ugliness was born in the boy as the marks of the devil was born in the poor child upstairs.''

This more primitive type embodies the eternal patience of those humble toiling women who through the generations have been held of little value, save as their drudgery ministered to their men. One of them related her habit of going through the pockets of her drunken son every pay-day, and complained that she had never got so little as the night before, only twenty-five cents out of fifteen dollars he had promised for the rent long over-due. ''I had to get that as he lay in the alley before the door; I couldn't pull him in, and the copper who helped him home left as soon as he heard me coming and pretended he didn't see me. I have no food in the house nor coffee to sober him up with. I know perfectly well that you will ask me to eat something here, but if I can't carry it home, I won't take a bite nor a sup. I have never told you so much before. Since one of the nurses said he could be arrested for my non-support, I have been awfully close-mouthed. It's the foolish way all the women in our street are talking about the Devil Baby that's loosened my tongue—more shame to me.''

There are those, if possible more piteous still, who have become absolutely helpless and can therefore no longer perform the household services exacted from them. One last wish has been denied them. ''I hoped to go before I became a burden, but it was not to be''; and the long days of unwonted idleness are darkened by the haunting fear that ''they'' will come to think the burden too heavy and decide that the poorhouse is ''the best.'' Even then there is no word of blame for un-dutiful children or heedless grandchildren, for apparently all that is petty and transitory falls away from austere old age; the fires are burnt out, resentments, hatreds, and even cherished sorrows have become actually unintelligible. It is as if the horrors through which these old people had passed had never existed for them, and, facing death as they are, they seem anxious to speak only such words of groping wisdom as they are able. . . .

The vivid interest of so many old women in the story of the Devil Baby may have been an unconscious, although powerful testimony that tragic experiences gradually become dressed in such trappings in order that their spent agony may prove of some use to a world which learns at the hardest; and that the strivings and sufferings of men and women long since dead, their emotions no longer connected with flesh and blood, are thus transmuted into legendary wisdom. The young are forced to heed the warning in such a tale, although for the most part it is so easy for them to disregard the words of the aged. That the old women who came to visit the Devil Baby believed that the story would secure them a hearing at home, was evident, and as they prepared themselves with every detail of it, their old faces shone with a timid satisfaction. Their features, worn and scarred by harsh living, even as effigies built into the floor of an old church become dim and defaced by rough-shod feet, grew poignant and solemn. In the midst of their double bewilderment, both that the younger generation were walking in such strange paths and that no one would listen to them, for one moment there flickered up that last hope of a disappointed life, that it may at least serve as a warning while affording material for exciting narrations. . . .

As our visitors to the Devil Baby came day by day, it was gradually evident that the simpler women were moved not wholly by curiosity, but that many of them prized the story as a valuable instrument in the business of living.

The legend exhibited all the persistence of one of those tales which have doubtless been preserved through the centuries because of their taming effects upon recalcitrant husbands and fathers. Shamefaced men brought by their women-folk to see the baby but ill-concealed their triumph when there proved to be no such visible sign of retribution for domestic derelictions. On the other hand, numbers of men came by themselves. One group from a neighboring factory, on their "own time," offered to pay twenty-five cents, a half dollar, two dollars apiece to see the child, insisting that it must be at Hull-House because "the women folks had seen it." To my query as to whether they supposed we would exhibit for money a poor little deformed baby, if one had been born in the neighborhood, they replied, "Sure, why not?" and, "It teaches a good lesson, too," they added as an afterthought, or perhaps as a concession to the strange moral standards of a place like Hull-House. All the members in this group of hard-working men, in spite of a certain swagger toward one another and a tendency to bully the derelict showman, wore that hang-dog look betraying the sense of unfair treatment which a man is so apt to feel when his womankind makes an appeal to the supernatural. In their determination to see the child, the men recklessly divulged much more concerning their motives than they had meant to do, and their talk confirmed my impression that such a story may still act as a restraining influence in that sphere of marital conduct which, next to primitive religion itself, we are told, has always afforded the most fertile field for irrational tabus and savage punishments. . . .

IV

The story evidently held some special comfort for hundreds of forlorn women, representatives of that vast horde of the denied and proscribed, who had long found themselves confronted by those mysterious and impersonal wrongs which are apparently nobody's fault but seem to be inherent in the very nature of things.

Because the Devil Baby embodied an undeserved wrong to a poor mother, whose tender child had been claimed by the forces of evil, his merely reputed presence had power to attract to Hull-House hundreds of women who had been humbled and disgraced by their children; mothers of the feebleminded, of the vicious, of the criminal, of the prostitute. In their talk it was as if their long role of maternal apology and protective reticence had at last broken down; as if they could speak out freely because for once a man responsible for an ill-begotten child had been "met up with" and had received his deserts. Their sinister version of the story was that the father of the Devil Baby had married without confessing a hideous crime committed years before, thus basely deceiving both his innocent young bride and the good priest who performed the solemn ceremony; that the sin had become incarnate in his child which, to the horror of the young and trusting mother, had been born with all the outward aspects of the devil himself.

As if drawn by a magnet, week after week, a procession of forlorn women in search of the Devil Baby came to Hull-House from every part of the city, issuing forth from the many homes in which dwelt "the two unprofitable goddesses, Poverty and Impossibility." With an understanding quickened perhaps through my own acquaintance with the mysterious child, I listened to many tragic tales from the visiting women: of premature births, "because he kicked me in the side"; of children maimed and burned because "I had no one to leave them with when I went to work." These women had seen the tender flesh of growing little bodies given over to death because "he wouldn't let me send for the doctor," or because "there was no money to pay for the medicine." . . .

This imposing revelation of maternal solicitude was an instance of what continually happened in connection with the Devil Baby. In the midst of the most tragic recitals there remained that something in the souls of these mothers which has been called the great revelation of tragedy, or sometimes the great illusion of tragedy—that which has power in its own right to make life acceptable and at rare moments even beautiful.

At least, during the weeks when the Devil

Baby seemed to occupy every room in Hull-House, one was conscious that all human vicissitudes are in the end melted down into reminiscence, and that a metaphorical statement of those profound experiences which are implicit in human nature itself, however crude in form the story may be, has a singular power of healing the distracted spirit. . . .

MATURITY
1914–1935

LIKE MOST AMERICANS, HULL-HOUSE RESIDENTS WERE shocked by the outbreak of war in Europe in 1914. Somehow, during the years of peace and progress they had come to assume that war, like child labor and poverty, could be outlawed. Jane Addams, who had been active in the peace movement for many years, now became a leader in the movement to end the European war by arbitration, and to make the United States an active force for promoting world peace. Only a few weeks after the fighting started, she presided at a meeting in New York which was attended by social workers and reformers (including many Hull-House graduates) who were concerned about their proper role in wartime. Out of this meeting came the organization of the American Union Against Militarism, and eventually the American Civil Liberties Union. Addams also became president of the Woman's Peace Party, later a part of the Women's International League for Peace and Freedom. In 1915, with Alice Hamilton, Grace Abbott, and other peace advocates, she traveled to The Hague for an international congress of women. There she became part of a small delegation of women which sought out the leaders of the warring countries, urging them to end hostilities through arbitration.

Addams claimed her pacifism was an outgrowth of her Hull-House experiences living among the many neighborhood nationality groups. While she was ridiculed by some for her excessive idealism, even naiveté, for believing that a group of women could end the war, almost everyone applauded her efforts to keep the United States out of the fighting. To be for peace was popular as late as 1916. But when Jane Addams, with Alice Hamilton and Jeannette Rankin of Montana, a Hull-House graduate and the first woman in Congress, continued to oppose the war and America's part in it even after April 1917, this was a different matter. Jane Addams, who a few years before had been virtually deified and called a saint, was now declared a traitor.

Hull-House suffered during the war. Some donors withdrew their support because of Jane Addams' pacifism, while campaigns for the Red Cross and other glamorous wartime causes also syphoned money away from the settlement. Yet, despite Addams' peace activity, Hull-House vigorously supported the war effort. Many of the younger residents volunteered for the Army; a contingent of the Hull-House band went overseas to entertain the troops; and a Selective Service recruiting station was opened at Hull-House. The residents conducted special campaigns to collect funds for war relief. They added more educational and recreational classes for youth, and gave special lessons in food and fuel conservation for the mothers in the neighborhood. Even Jane Addams, terribly isolated and alone, toured the country for the U.S. Department of Food Administration and spoke in favor of food conservation.

At first the war seemed to spell the end of the social movement; but as time went on the Hull-House group reluctantly concluded that, despite its horrors, war created an opportunity for social advance. It led to the first experiments in public housing and to increased benefits for organized labor; it stimulated the movement for social insurance, accelerated the drive for woman suffrage, and speeded the move to prohibition (which many, but not all, of the residents viewed as a progressive measure). But the wartime social advance was short-lived; most of the programs which held so much promise in 1918 had disappeared a year later.

While some of the social progress of the war years survived, a more immediate result of the war was the "Red Scare." In part because of the nationalism generated by America's participation in the war, in part because of the terror of the Russian Revolution and the fear of its consequences, the nation launched a massive hunt for "communists," "Bolsheviks," pacifists, foreigners, and other supposedly dangerous types. Hull-House, which had always provided an open forum for all kinds of political positions, and had once been denounced as a "hotbed of anarchism," now became a prime target for those who saw a great communist conspiracy in the nation. The worst of the Red Scare was over by 1921, but the irrational fear of communism lingered on. Even in the 1930s Jane Addams remained, for some superpatriots, "the most dangerous woman in America," and Hull-House a major link in a subversive red network.

The Hull-House neighborhood, which never remained static, was transformed again. The war and the new immigration laws reduced the flow of European immigrants into America and the Hull-House neighborhoods, while the prosperity of the war years allowed many old residents to escape to the suburbs. They were replaced by Mexicans and, gradually, by blacks who came from the South in the great migration stimulated by the war. Blacks settled to the south and west of the Hull-House area. The immediate neighborhood became largely Mexican, Italian, and Greek, with a few Irish and Jews left over from an earlier time. It was a volatile mixture: the Italians feuded with the Mexicans, and both groups attacked the blacks. Ethnic tension was not new at Hull-House, but the racial conflict that erupted in the 1920s was more bitter than anything in the past, and it cast doubt on the settlement idea of communication and neighborhood cooperation.

The black population of Chicago more than doubled in the five years after 1915, but the great migration of blacks in search of jobs and a better life raised racial tensions in the city to a fever pitch. There were minor clashes and acts of violence initiated by whites of almost every ethnic background who feared the incursion of blacks into their neighborhood and their city. A major riot erupted on July 27, 1919, when white youths attacked and drowned a black youngster who had strayed across an imaginary line while swimming in Lake Michigan. Before it was over 38 people were dead, 23 black; over 500 were injured and more than 1,000 left homeless. One of the most vicious murders of the riot took place only a few blocks from Hull-House. A rumor circulated through the neighborhood that a black had killed an Italian girl. When a black youth came riding by on a bicycle a mob attacked him with stones and clubs before finally firing fourteen bullets into his body. Jane Addams and the Hull-House group were shocked by the riot and the bloodshed. They tried to calm the situation, and they helped to write the report of the Commisssion on Race Relations appointed after the riot. Among the reformers in the city the Hull-House group were the most progressive in their attitudes toward race relations, but even Jane Addams and her co-workers never suggested social equality or complete integration as part of the solution at that time.

The decade after the war was a time of "political and social sag," in the words of Jane Addams. Hull-House continued to work for child labor laws, better housing, and more opportunity for the disadvantaged, but the group's enthusiasm, confidence, and success waned. It became more and more difficult for Hull-House to attract bright, energetic young reformers; in the twenties the young rebel was more likely to choose Paris or Greenwich Village. Those who did become residents in the decade after the war usually had a degree in social work and looked on settlement work as a profession, not a crusade. Though it became professionalized more slowly than most settlements, even Hull-House was influenced after the war by the rise of psychiatric social work, which paid more attention to the individual's adjustment than to the process of changing society. Those who came to the settlement often were treated as clients rather than neighbors. Hull-House also had to withstand the loss of some of its most important and innovative residents. Julia Lathrop and Grace Abbott went to Washington to take important federal jobs; Alice Hamilton departed for Harvard Medical School; and Ellen Starr entered a Catholic convent. Of course, any institution ultimately faces the departure of its founding generation, but in the 1920s it was difficult to replace the settlement pioneers.

Not the least of Hull-House's problems in the twenties was financial. The settlement was a large operation with an annual budget of about $100,000. An endowment of nearly half a million dollars seldom covered the expenses, so that at least $50,000 had to be raised each year. After the war this became a difficult task. Some contributors died and others refused to give because the settlement seemed "controversial." One answer, adopted by many settlements, was to join the new federated fund drives, or the community chests, as they came to be called; but Jane Addams was opposed to this on the grounds that Hull-House would lose its individuality and the right to guide its own destiny.

After the war, because of her peace activity and her failing health, Jane Addams spent much less time at Hull-House. Yet she was still the recognized leader, both head resident and president of the board of trustees. She was also much more that that; she was "Miss Addams," never Jane, treated with awe and almost reverence by the other residents. Occasionally she may have been resented, but she had the compelling ability to rise above resentments, to settle differences, to put the pieces back together when something seemed to be falling apart. She was almost a genius at raising money, and, although there were some narrow escapes, she kept Hull-House solvent. Her management of the settlement was personal in the extreme, and she prepared badly, or not at all, for the day when Hull-House would have to operate without her.

To say that Hull-House was not as vital an institution in the 1920s as it had been earlier is not to say that it did not continue to do useful work. New and able residents came, and many of the old guard remained. Jessie Binford still managed the Juvenile Protective Association; Eleanor Smith continued to direct the music school; George Hooker, Victor Yarros, Ethel Dewey, and many others remained, as did many of the powerful women who supported the settlement from the outside, especially Louise deKoven Bowen. The number of people who came to settlement functions actually increased, and the clubs and classes, lectures and country outings served a widening circle of neighbors and friends. Art, music,

A Greek merchant's shop on the corner of Polk and Halsted Streets, across from Hull-House, at Greek Easter time. The Greeks became prominent in the neighborhood early in the 1900s.

and drama, always important at the settlement, now took the center stage away from social surveys and political agitation. A number of talented young men and women were discovered and developed at Hull-House.

Clarinetist Benny Goodman and jazz pianist Art Hodes took lessons at the music school. Norah Hamilton, sister of Alice Hamilton, and Enella Benedict, director of the art school, had such talented students as William Jacobs and Michael Gamboney, who later became teachers at the same settlement art school. Morris Topchevsky, another neighborhood boy, gained fame with his still lifes and studies of Mexican people. He spent two years in Mexico studying under Diego Rivera. All these young men discovered that the settlement neighborhood and its buildings were fascinating subjects to record in woodcuts, block prints, pastels, watercolors, and oils. Hull-House kilns, under the direction of Myrtle and Beals French, were especially creative. Pottery making and ceramics were particularly popular with the settlement's Mexican neighbors, who turned out some interesting and experimental objects. Another talented artist was Wallace Kirkland, who learned photography while he was director of the Boys' Club. He left the settlement to become a professional photographer for *Life* magazine. Kirkland recorded the people, the buildings, and the activities of Hull-House in unforgettable photographs taken as he learned his trade during the 1920s and early 1930s.

The depression which followed the stock market crash of 1929 caused a new crisis for Hull-House. The residents were forced to restrict their activities for lack of funds, and all ideas of reform and change gave way to thoughts of relieving the terrible suffering that surrounded the settlement. Yet no one institution, not even the federal government, could alleviate the distress. Despair turned to hope in 1933 with the arrival of Franklin Roosevelt and the New Deal, and Hull-House residents cooperated with the Federal Emergency Relief Administration, the Works Progress Administration, and other New Deal agencies. A number of residents, including Jane Addams who served as head of the advisory committee on public housing in Chicago, held local positions in the various organizations, and Hull-House graduates held significant positions of power on the national level during the New Deal. Frances Perkins, a former volunteer, and Harold Ickes, a long-time friend of the settlement, were both in the cabinet, while Hull-House graduates Gerard Swope and Sidney Hillman were advisers of the President. Among many others who had been influenced directly or indirectly by Hull-House, Harry Hopkins, Mary Dewson, and Eleanor Roosevelt were the most obvious. But even more important than the individuals who served was the legislation that, in a sense, vindicated the long struggle at Hull-House for social justice, better housing, rights for organized labor, and social insurance. It would be an exaggeration to say that the New Deal translated the Hull-House social philosophy into national legislation, for there were many strands of influence—but it would only be a slight exaggeration.

Though the thirties brought the New Deal, which seemed to provide for the social justice Hull-House had been fighting for over the years, this period also brought a note of nostalgia and remorse, for Hull-House was no longer the vital institution it once had been— its pioneering days seemed over. Jane Addams' death in 1935 truly marked the end of an era for a remarkable institution.

War and Red Scare

Jane Addams,
United States Congressional Record,
and Elizabeth Dilling

When Jane Addams refused to support the United States' entry into the war in April 1917, she incurred the wrath of many who had long been her supporters and admirers. Addams was not alone in opposing the war, but most of the residents at Hull-House supported the American action. Still, mainly because of Jane Addams, Hull-House was branded a pacifist institution. After the war, the settlement, like a number of liberal causes, fell victim to the red hysteria which swept the country. This irrational attack on Hull-House continued well into the thirties.

Following is Jane Addams' own calm description of the war years at Hull-House, taken from her book The Second Twenty Years at Hull-House, published in 1930. This second volume of her autobiography did not sell as well as the first, perhaps because by 1930 settlement work did not seem as exciting to the reading public as it had twenty years before, or perhaps because the second volume did not have the same kind of unity and sense of purpose that marked the earlier book. Despite this dispassionate appraisal of the war years, Addams was terribly hurt and baffled by the irrational attacks leveled at her and at Hull-House.

Just how irrational these attacks were is illustrated by the two selections following that by Jane Addams. The first is from a long essay published originally in a radical right magazine, The Woman Patriot. It was read into the Congressional Record in 1926, ostensibly to oppose an amendment to the Sheppard-Towner Maternity Benefits Act, which with the U.S. Children's Bureau and Hull-House were seen as part of a great communist conspiracy. Florence Kelley became the special target of this attack, because she was a socialist and the translator of a work by Engels; but few Hull-House residents or friends escaped the charge of communism and disloyalty.

The last selection is from the pen of Elizabeth Dilling (b. 1894), a self-styled patriot and master of innuendo and half-truth, whose book, The Red Network, published the year before Jane Addams' death, demonstrated that not even the New Deal and the depression killed the red hysteria. Her denunciation of Jane Addams was really an attack on Hull-House, too, for in most people's minds the settlement and its founder were one and the same. [Jane Addams, Second Twenty Years at Hull-House (New York, 1930), 140–143; Congressional Record, 69th Cong., 1st sess. (1926), 12946–12947; Elizabeth Dilling, The Red Network (Chicago, 1934), 51–53.]

Jane Addams

Chicago with its diversified population, inevitably displayed many symptoms of an inflamed nationalism, perhaps the most conspicuous were the deportations and trials of "Reds." Throughout the period of the war we were very anxious that Hull-House should afford such refuge as was legitimate to harassed immigrants. Organizations whose headquarters were constantly being raided brought us their libraries—pitiful little collections of battered books—to keep for them until the war was over. I always said that we would not hide them, but if they wanted to put the books in our open reading room we would be glad to lend them the use of our shelves. There would be an occasional copy of Karl Marx or Bakunin, more often Herbert Spencer, but almost always there were Shakespeare's complete works and a library of American Literature. One Sunday afternoon I received a call from a man from the Secret Service Department, who asked me if I knew that Bulgarian communists were holding a meeting in our largest public hall. I told him that I knew some Bulgarians were having a concert in Bowen Hall—what better could "the alien enemy" do, I queried, than to spend a Sunday afternoon in a decent place listening to good music. He replied that his orders were to arrest the leaders, and he went back to the hall for that purpose. He returned in an hour to say that he couldn't find the leading communists for not one had said a word, and because he was young and perplexed he asked me what I would do in his place. I replied that I was afraid that I should return to headquarters and resign because I happened to feel very strongly in regard to arresting people without warrants. He answered that it wouldn't be necessary to resign because he "would be fired fast enough." I never heard of his fate but I was thankful that we got through the entire period of the war and post-war without a single arrest at Hull-House, if only because it gave a certain refuge to those who were surrounded by the suspicions and animosities inevitably engendered by the war toward all aliens. I remember one excited man who came into Hull-House to report that he was sure that "the Roumanians north of Madison Street were hatching a plot against the government" and who was very much disconcerted when I reminded him that the Roumanians were on the side of the Allies. "I never can get those Balkan countries straightened out" was his apology, and I was in no position to remind him that it was not his geography that was at fault but his state of mind.

As to the attitude of Hull-House during the war, perhaps I may again be permitted to quote from an outside source:

> The Hull-House residents were far from being unanimously pacifist. In fact, most of the residents were for the war. Eight young men who were in residence volunteered, and six of them went overseas. A contingent of the Hull-House Boys Band, with their bandmaster, went to the Front, and were afterwards taken into the occupied territory. Soldiers from the district were given their last meal at Hull-House before they left for France, with their families and sweethearts standing outside the door until the meal should be finished and they could give their last farewells in the Hull-House courtyard.

A description of Hull-House in wartime, written for the *World Tomorrow,* states the following:

> But the distinguishing characteristic of this settlement, its unshakable tolerance, is the fundamental respect its members have for one another's firm beliefs. The specific thing which sets Hull-House apart from others, which has carried its name around the world as a generic title, is this atmosphere of chivalry, so hard to describe, so much harder to achieve. . . .

I should not have ventured to have written the following words myself, though I will confess to a certain sense of their fitness. The writer continues:

> How is it that this company preserves its ranks so staunchly unbroken? The reason is their profound conviction of the worth and sanctity of the opinions of other people. Few Socialists, no Communists have it; few reformers, few doctrinaires, few radicals, few uplifters. Only heart-whole democrats, who believe the Kingdom of God is a republic in which the Sovereign dwells equally within each citizen, can possess it. These things explain perhaps how Hull-House has been able to hold so long its great company of valiant souls, slacking neither their valor nor their comradeship. It is the complete respect with which widely severed convictions are regarded by every member of the group. They differ violently but with great fellowship, like knights who battle in the tourney but drink to one another's prowess before and after.

The writer did not mention the professional services given by one of the residents, Doctor James Britton, who served in the Medical Corps in Washington, for many months; Mr. George Hooker, who was head of the Draft Board in the Hull-House district with a corps of volunteers from the residential force of men and women; Dr. Rachel[le] Yar[r]os carrying on the Social Hygiene instruction throughout the country; Mrs. Kenneth Rich and Jessie Binford, officials in protective work for young girls in the environs of the training camps; the inspection of munition factories for the elimination of poisonous gases by Doctor Alice Hamilton; the innumerable groups of women, sewing and knitting for the Red Cross, the classes in war cooking, canning, and food saving, and many another activity similar to those carried out throughout the length and breadth of the land.

The Woman Patriot

. . . Mrs. Florence Kelley has not only preached communism and urged a study of the fundamental communist books by college women taking up philanthropic or social work, but as president of the Intercollegiate Socialist League—the organization chiefly responsible for socialist propaganda in American schools and colleges—Mrs. Kelley has had great influence for a number of years in promoting radicalism among youth while in school.

The Intercollegiate Socialist League changed its name in 1922 to the "League for Industrial Democracy," but continues its socialist propaganda.

As chief factory inspector in Chicago (1893–1897) she obtained leadership among industrial women; as a resident of Hull House, Chicago, and subsequently of Henry Street Nurses' Settlement, New York, she obtained leadership among social workers, public-health nurses, etc., and as a university woman, a lawyer specializing in social legislation, and as general secretary of the National Consumers' League she has obtained other opportunities for communist propaganda and influence upon legislation.

It is of the utmost significance that practically all the radicalism started among women in the United States centers about Hull House, Chicago, and the Children's Bureau, at Washington, with a dynasty of Hull House graduates in charge of it since its creation.

It has been shown that both the legislative program and the economic program—"social-welfare" legislation and "bread-and-peace" propaganda for internationalization of the food, farms, and raw materials of the world—find their chief expression in persons, organizations, and bureaus connected with Hull House.

And Hull House itself has been able to cover its tracks quite effectively under the nationally advertised reputation of Miss Jane Addams as a social worker—who has so often been painted by magazine and newspaper writers as a sort of modern Saint of the Slums—that both she and Hull House can campaign for the most radical measures and lead the most radical movements, with hardly a breath of public suspicion. . . .

Thus while all the pacifism, internationalism, and socialist legislative schemes among women in America, together with the Women's International League, the National Women's Trade Union League, the International Federation of Working Women, the United States Children's Bureau, and the United States Women's Bureau have been cradled at Hull House, we find that Hull House itself was first taught to walk the socialist road by the ubiquitous Mrs. Florence Kelley.

The second-hand radicalism of Miss Addams, Mrs. Robins,* Miss Lathrop, Miss Abbott, Mrs. [Carrie] Catt, etc., is none the less important to show, because they "build communism with noncommunist hands" in working for Mrs. Kelley's program. . . .

Elizabeth Dilling

Greatly beloved because of her kindly intentions toward the poor, Jane Addams has been able to do more probably than any other living woman (as she tells in her own books) to popularize pacifism and to introduce radicalism into colleges, settlements, and respectable circles. The influence of her radical protegées, who consider Hull House their home center, reaches out all over the world. One knowing of her consistent aid of the Red movement can only marvel at the smooth and charming way she at the same time disguises this aid and reigns as "queen" on both sides of the fence.

I was impressed with her charm and ability (and subterfuge) at my only meeting with her, which was at a Legislative Hearing held at the Chicago City Hall, May 29, 1933. She was there to testify against the passage of the Baker Bills, which aimed only at penalizing the seditious communistic teaching of overthrow of this government in Illinois colleges. One would not have believed any person wishing to appear decently law abiding could have objected to these Bills which easily had passed the Senate; but the vehement fight the college presidents (Hutchins, Scott, McClelland, and McGuire of St. Viator's)† put up against them at the first Hearing in Springfield was in itself a revelation.

At the second Hearing in Chicago, in reply to a gentleman's testimony concerning Prof. Lov-

*Margaret Dreier Robins (1869–1945 [Mrs. Raymond]) was a reformer and a leading member of the National Women's Trade Union League.—Eds.

†Robert Hutchins of the University of Chicago, 1929–1945; Walker Dill Scott, president of Northwestern University, 1920–1939; Clarence Paul McClelland, president of MacMurray College, Jacksonville, 1925–1952; and Very Rev. John W. R. Maguire, president of St. Viator's, 1929–1934.—Eds.

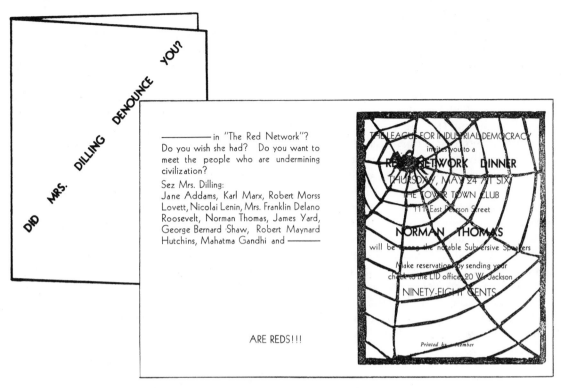

Those listed by Mrs. Dilling in her "exposé," The Red Network, *gathered at a dinner honoring their notoriety.*

ett's* revolutionary speeches, Miss Addams, after pleading for freedom to teach Socialism and Communism in schools because these are world movements, said she was sure Prof. Lovett (who lives at Hull-House) had never advocated the overthrow of this government by force and violence; in fact, said she, "I don't believe I ever heard of any member of the Communist Party doing so! Of course you all know I am a pacifist and would not advocate the overthrow of *anything* by force and violence." (Lovett writes the introduction of "Recovery Through Revolution.") . . .

I arose to remark that Communists *do* advocate such overthrow as she should know since she had been associated with enough of them, reminding her that she had spoken only in December on the same program with Communist Scott Nearing† at

---

*Robert Morss Lovett (1870–1956) English professor at the University of Chicago and Hull-House resident.—Eds.

†Scott Nearing (1883–1983), peace and environmental activist.—Eds.

the Student Congress Against War at the University of Chicago. She started to deny this, but I held up the program of the Congress with her name on it. Then she said: "But Prof. Nearing is not a member of the Party any more." I replied: "He is lecturing under the auspices of the Friends of the Soviet Union and for the benefit of the communist Chicago Workers School of revolution at 2822 S. Michigan Ave." "O, I didn't know," she murmured. (I had the announcement card with me.) . . .

Roland Libonati, chairman of the Legislative committee holding the Hearings, was impressed no doubt by the array of talent ("important" personages such as college presidents and Jane Addams) which opposed the Baker Bills and favored freedom for communistic teaching in our schools. Living as he does within a block of Hull-House, he must also realize the influence Jane Addams wields in his political district. At any rate, the Bills were killed, as he then intimated to reporters that they would be.

Miss Addams wields great influence also at the Chicago Woman's Club, where the communist Chicago Workers Theatre play "Precedent" was given in May, 1933. Its Feb. 1934 play was presented at Hull House.

The communist Daily Worker, Saturday, Oct. 21, 1933, said: "Today the John Reed Club will hold a banquet for Henri Barbusse at the Chicago Woman's Club, 72 E. 11th St. . . . Jane Addams internationally known social worker, winner of the Nobel Peace Prize and head of the Women's International League for Peace and Freedom, writes that although illness will prevent her from attending the mass meeting, she expects to be present at the banquet and is anxious to meet M. Barbusse. . . . B. K. Gebert, district organizer of the Communist Party, and Herbert Newton, editor of the Workers Voice, are also scheduled to speak at the banquet. . . . Barbusse will be accompanied by Joseph Freeman, editor of the New Masses, and Prof. H. W. L. Dana, noted author."

One of those who began his long residence shortly after the war was Robert Morss Lovett (1870–1956), literary critic, novelist, defender of liberal causes, and a professor of English at the University of Chicago. The following is an excerpt from his autobiography, All Our Years, *which demonstrates that even in the period after the war Hull-House continued to be a haven for unpopular causes and an exciting place to live—a place where one could be a scoutmaster to a boys' gang, or teach an immigrant youngster how to write, or support a strike and land in jail. That Lovett was successful—at least in his writing class—is demonstrated by a letter from his prized pupil, Oscar Ludmann (b. 1900), who suggested that Hull-House also remained a place of hope and opportunity for the immigrant. [Robert M. Lovett,* All Our Years *(New York, 1948), 225–234; Oscar Ludmann to Jane Addams, May 21, 1931, Jane Addams Papers, Swarthmore College Peace Collection.]*

Hull-House, 1921–1937

Robert Morss Lovett and Oscar Ludmann

Most people did not take seriously the attacks of the superpatriots on Hull-House, but the settlement did suffer in the postwar period. It became difficult to raise money to support Hull-House activities, and even more difficult to attract those students who before the war had clamored for the opportunity to spend a year or two at the settlement. All liberal and reform causes were in retreat, and Hull-House, like similar institutions, lost ground in the political and social atmosphere. Yet the Hull-House programs went on; the clubs and classes, the music school and the theatre, the lectures and the summer outings in the country all continued to serve the neighborhood boys and girls, and occasionally their parents. Talented and dedicated men and women continued to live at the settlement.

Robert Morss Lovett

In the spring of 1921 when I joined the staff of the *New Republic* for part of the year it became necessary to provide a home for my family in Chicago, where my older daughter* was to study medicine at the Rush Medical School on the West Side. I consulted Miss Addams as to the possibility of finding an apartment. With her usual quiet modesty Miss Addams indicated that there were apartments at Hull House, and thus in a moment we were enrolled as social workers. Ida as a girl at Radcliffe had heard Jane Addams speak, and from then on had felt drawn to that gentle and lovable person. In our earlier years in Chicago we had often enjoyed the hospitality of the House, but we had not thought of ourselves as meeting the requirements of actual residents. Ida found at once a field for an executive ability which made her successful as a lieutenant. She became one of Miss Addams' close companions, sharing her company

*Beatrice R. Lovett, who, with Lovett's wife, Ida Mott-Smith, helped direct Hull-House in Jane Addams' absences during the 1930s.—Eds.

on journeys and giving her always the watchful care which became more necessary as the years passed.

My connection with the House was less constant, but I was well satisfied to exchange the stratified suburb of Hyde Park for the amorphous neighborhood of Halsted Street, even at the expense of a long daily journey to the university. I never changed cars at the corner of Halsted Street, on returning, without a sense that here was life, something incredibly vital though its stigmata were grim enough—poverty, squalor, crime.

The residents of Hull House were a group of strikingly original characters engaged in a common enterprise. The Hull House Players were directed by Mrs. Laura Dainty Pelham, supplemented by juvenile groups under Miss Edith de Nancrede. They staged the plays of Yeats and Lady Gregory, of Hauptmann, of Galsworthy and Phillpotts. Several of the players graduated to the professional stage. Miss Eleanor and Miss Gertrude Smith directed the Music School with the assistance of Miss Pillsbury and Miss Birmingham.* Miss Benedict, the oldest resident, presided over the Art School. These activities stimulated cultural interests in the neighborhood and gave opportunities for young talent to develop. Two important organizations grew up at Hull-House—the Juvenile Protective Association, directed by Miss Jessie Binford, and the Immigrants' Protective League under Mrs. Kenneth Rich.

Dean of the House was George Hooker, who had been Secretary of the City Club. Victor Yarros, partner of Clarence Darrow and editorial writer for the *Chicago Daily News,* and his wife Dr. Rachel Yarros, chief exponent of birth-control and director of clinics, were among the most vivid personalities. Dr. and Mrs. [James] Britton were among the most important, the doctor acting as house physician and supervising the boys' athletics and gymnasium directed by Messrs. [Wallace] Kirkland and [Robert] Hicks, Mrs. [Gertrude] Britton having the kindergarten.

Miss Ethel Dewey, Miss Mary Gleason, Miss Rose Gyles, and Mrs. [Ada] Hicks were in charge of classes in English and citizenship. Mrs. Alfred Kohn and Miss Ella Waite were concerned with the general problems, especially financial, of running the establishment. Frank Keyser had been engineer from the beginning. There were many young people who took care of various clubs and classes. Altogether, when we went to Hull House, it comprised a family of about seventy people, residents of the block from Polk Street to Gilpin Place, which was occupied by a somewhat heterogeneous but well-adapted group of buildings designed by Allen and Irving Pond.

Hull-House rendered a service to Chicago by offering philanthropic men and women an opportunity to take part in a practical solution of the social problem. First should be mentioned Mrs. Louise deKoven Bowen, who acted as treasurer of the Board of Trustees. Among many gifts she gave a beautiful estate at Waukegan for a country resort for mothers and children. Though differing in politics, especially in the matter of the war, from Miss Addams and most of the residents, she never wavered in her loyalty and faith. Mrs. Mary H. Wilmarth, Miss Mary Rozet Smith, Mr. Frederick Deknatel, Mr. Julius Rosenwald, gave not only money but time and thought to the House. Miss Helen Culver, the heir of General Hull,† gave the original house and adjacent land, and started an endowment fund with a gift of one hundred thousand dollars. . . .

The residents of Hull House were not necessarily exclusively social workers. Nearly all had vocations outside and gave as a minimum two evenings a week to the House. The humblest task of all was attending to the door and telephone in the evening, and this properly fell to my lot as initiation. It was interesting because it brought one close to the life of the neighborhood—everyone who was in trouble came in person, and news of fires, crimes, and arrests came by prompt report. Miss Addams thought that I was fitted for higher things. She had always believed in lectures as a contribution to the intellectual life of the neighborhood, and she looked back to earlier days when the lecture room was crowded with audiences to hear of science, art, and poetry from professors of the university or other gifted persons.

---

*Agnes Pillsbury (d. 1937) and Alma Birmingham (d. 1973). Both were long-time Hull-House residents. Eleanor Smith was director of the Music School.—Eds.

†Charles J. Hull, who built the original house in 1856, was never a general.—Eds.

I pointed out that the community had changed. Instead of Germans, Irish, and Russians we had Italians, Greeks, and Mexicans, but I thought that a course on contemporary social and political topics might go over. I had excellent speakers, capturing as many as possible on their way to or from Washington or New York, and filling in with local talent, but the neighbors were not interested. Several times Ida raided the reading room, turned out the lights, and shepherded the ''readers'' into the lecture room, where they slept. Gradually the reading room lost custom on lecture nights.

My first real assignment was as a sort of scoutmaster to a hard gang of boys who had seceded from the regular administration of the gymnasium and clubs. I was cowardly enough to be glad when, after looking me over, they disappeared. I did, however, make an attempt at individual salvation. On a visit to the reformatory at Pontiac I met a boy whose ingenuous tale impressed me. He had been sentenced to a year, he explained, by an amiable judge who wanted to save him from bad company. I thought badly of his honor's judgment in choosing Pontiac for its uplifting influence and promised to have some job in sight for the boy as a condition of his release at the end of his term. Unemployment was then at its height and educational institutions were taking up the slack. I asked President [Robert M.] Hutchins if he would favor admitting a student from the excellent preparatory school of Pontiac. ''Certainly,'' he said, ''if he can get by the examiner.'' I asked Miss Addams if she would object to a youthful delinquent becoming a resident of Hull House. Of course she welcomed the addition to our human curiosity shop. So all was well. The boy capitalized on his prison experience with the Department of Sociology. An interesting social experiment was being conducted known as the Area Project, by which a neighborhood notable for juvenile delinquency was delimited for intensive study of conditions and the introduction of remedial measures. After graduation my protégé was given a place at South Chicago. He was successful in his work. Again his prison experience was capitalized on to win the admiration of his young clients. He married a summer resident at Hull House and had a daughter. He betrayed them. I felt that if I had continued to watch him and hold him to his work and his family

I might have saved him, but South Chicago is a long way from Hull House. I realized then that you can't launch a human being like a ship, and that you can do a lot of mischief by assuming a responsibility that you aren't willing to see through. I failed as badly as did the poor lad.

My chief activity at the House came to be meeting once a week with a group of young writers whose manuscripts I read for criticism in class, and corrected outside. Residents, neighbors, and even recruits from distant parts of the city made up a highly miscellaneous company whose writing, without benefit of academic influence, made up in spontaneity for what it lacked in conventional form. I remember especially a long narrative of exciting and dangerous experiences by Billy Ortiz, a waiter in the Coffee House, which might have been called ''Up from Mexico.'' Wallace Kirkland, who directed boys' activities and spent his vacations exploring north of the Great Lakes, wrote articles on wild life which were published in various magazines. Our chief triumph was that of Oscar Ludmann, an Alsatian, who had been forced into service in the German Navy, had participated in the mutiny at Kronstadt, had marched with the sailors on Berlin, and later joined the abortive movement for the independence of his native province. His book, *A Stepchild of the Rhine*, remains in my mind as one of the most vital records of experience in the war. The account of the cruel fate of Alsace, torn by conflicting loyalties and crushed between opposing powers, deserves to be better known as another of the age-long tragedies of nationalism.

Hull House was emphatically the refuge of lost causes. The anarchist agitation had died out, but the fear of it was maintained by press and police to haunt the slumbers of the best people. Miss Addams was attacked for entertaining Peter Kropotkin at Hull House. The celebration of his birthday was an occasion for the visit to Chicago of the mild ghost of anarchism. I was always glad to speak in memory of that innocent and noble figure, a genuine humanitarian, whose doctrine Miss Addams revived in her book *Peace and Bread in Time of War.* I also enjoyed meeting the aged widows of the victims of Judge Gary's betrayal of justice, especially the Negro wife of Albert R. Parsons, a hero who voluntarily surrendered to join his comrades in court and on the scaffold.*

Another dying cause was that of the I. W. W.† More than a hundred I. W. W.'s had joined the conscientious objectors and Indian patriots in Leavenworth, and it became the function of the surviving members of the order to help their families and work for their pardon. This was refused long after the war was over. There seems to have been a streak of malignity in Wilson's character which showed itself in his refusal to release even Eugene Debs, whose original offense, of a technical nature in opposing the draft, had lost its meaning. Hull House was a center of the movement for clemency and pardon.

It was inevitable that the case of Tom Mooney should become a fixation of liberals. An aggressive labor leader in San Francisco, he was deliberately "framed" as having caused an explosion which resulted in the death of several participants in a "preparedness" parade. Felix Frankfurter, on a mission to examine and report to President Wilson on labor difficulties in the West, saw through the plot and warned the President of the danger in the execution of an innocent man whose fate was exciting workers all over the world. After commutation of the sentence to imprisonment for life, the long struggle began. One by one the folds of perjury were peeled away until the nucleus of the noxious growth was reached. The bluff cattle buyer "who had seen Mooney plant the bomb" was shown to have been miles away from the scene. He was also revealed as having written to a friend in Ohio to come to California to add another lie. Was he prosecuted for perjury? To ask the question is naïve. Year after year governors and the Supreme Court of California wriggled like snakes to avoid a formal admission of the criminality of the state. It was not until the Christmas of 1938 that Tom Mooney was pardoned.

The interest in the Mooney case waxed and waned until the Communists took it up. They arranged a conference with trade-union support in Chicago on April 30–May 1, 1933. I know it is usual for my friends to resent the efforts of Communists in such cases, and to argue that their advocacy serves to stiffen the opposition of the tories, yet it cannot be denied that Communist activity gave an impetus to a cause that had long challenged the impotence of liberals. If the Communists are charged with exploiting such cases for the prestige of their party, and with condemnation of the government and public which permits them, the answer is that government and public deserve all that the Communists can do to them.

Hull House at Polk and Halsted Streets stands almost at the exact center of the population of Chicago. It is near the eastern frontier of the vast hinterlands of Czech, Ukrainian, Italian, Greek, Hungarian, and Lithuanian settlements. Only the Poles on the far South Side are remote. Both the local and national interests of these groups were constantly before us. During the war there had been held in Chicago a congress of oppressed nationalities, in which the Poles played a leading part. It was somewhat disconcerting to have a subgroup, suffering oppression from the oppressed, appear in the case of the Ruthenians and Ukrainians, represented by Mr. Sichinsky, who had himself assassinated the Polish governor of Galicia where the Poles enjoyed the favor of the Austrian imperialism. One Sunday afternoon at Sichinsky's invitation I spoke to a gathering of Ukrainians called in protest against the atrocities of the Pilsudski government of Poland in 1934. I told the Ukrainians that they had the right to put the case of their fellow nationals before the State Department, since the inclusion of the minority of Ukrainians within the boundaries of Poland had been secured at the Peace Conference by the eminent Polophile, Professor A. M. Lord of Harvard, according to his own account. The other speakers did not speak in English, so that I do not know what they advised, but I judged from the applause that they proposed more radical action.

Among the residents at Hull House was Dr. [Lajos] Steiner, a Hungarian, the leader of the radical wing of his countrymen in Chicago. He invited me to speak at a mass meeting held in antic-

*Lovett refers to Lucy Parsons and to the aftermath of the Haymarket Riot of May 1886. Judge Joseph E. Gary sentenced seven of the rioters to death and one to prison. Albert Richard Parsons (1848–1887), editor of the anarchist newspaper *The Alarm,* was one of those executed.—Eds.

†Industrial Workers of the World, often called "wobblies."—Eds.

ipation of the visit of Count Károlyi,* whom the State Department after ten years of anxious deliberation finally decided to admit to our sacred shores. Mr. Hoover should have had a bad conscience in regard to Károlyi. As a liberal nobleman he had been made premier of Hungary, as had Prince Max von Baden of Germany, on the collapse of the Hapsburg and Hohenzollern regimes, in order to facilitate negotiations with the triumphant Allies. In Hungary the people starved while the American Relief Administration played politics. Although, as Count Károlyi told me, his government tendered a million dollars in gold, no food was forthcoming. The liberal government was forced to yield to the Communists; the Rumanians were permitted by the Allies to overrun the country and loot it, even carrying off the black earth of the Hungarian plain on flat cars; and Admiral Horthy took over as regent to the accompaniment of a White terror which lasted for years.

I saw much of Count Károlyi during his few days in Chicago. He seemed like an English peer, kindly, courteous, rather formal. He always apologized for an impediment in his speech, but when he was roused he spoke with eloquence. He was reasonable in talking of the future of his country, to which he had sacrificed his privileged position and estates, while his relatives and colleagues of the Magyar nobility continued to flourish in their feudalism under favor of the erstwhile Allies. Nowhere in Europe was the peace more decisively lost than in Hungary.

Toward labor Hull House was boldly sympathetic. It gave aid to strikers in industries whose owners were contributors to the support of the House. This was notably the case in strikes against the great packing firms, some of which, however, remained friendly. In the organization of the needle trades into the Amalgamated Clothing Workers by Sidney Hillman, Hull House played a significant part. When Ellen Gates Starr went on the picket line with the strikers and was arrested and jailed, I am convinced that the public interest excited brought support to the strike, and that her action was a powerful stimulus to that change of policy which made Hart, Schaffner and Marx, the leading clothing firm in Chicago, formulate the agreement which, followed perforce by other firms, brought stability into one of the industries most subject to fluctuations by reason of season or caprice. I have heard Joseph Schaffner refer to Sidney Hillman as "my partner."

Having been so often a spectator and critic of the police, I could hardly claim immunity from their personal attention. A strike of Negro girls at an apron factory on Michigan Avenue was attracting attention because of alleged police cruelty to the strikers on the picket line. A number of social workers agreed to go to the scene as observers. Jessie Binford, executive secretary of the Juvenile Protective Association, was ill on the day fixed and asked me to go in her place. Accordingly I joined a party, chiefly of ladies, at six in the morning, June 26, 1933, and saw the attempt of the management to import strikebreakers against the persuasion and protest of the pickets. Everything was peaceful until the arrival of the police. They ordered the pickets off the block in one direction, and the spectators off in the other. As we paused on the opposite corner for consultation the police suddenly charged us across the intervening street, waving clubs and shouting war cries. I stepped up to the leader of the chase and asked to speak to his superior officer. "You'll speak to him in the wagon," he shouted, and in a moment I was sitting in the Black Maria along with Tom McKenna, secretary of the Chicago Civil Liberties Committee.

It was Monday morning, and in the cell into which we were hustled were forty or fifty Negroes who had been taken up for crap-shooting, bad language, or other offenses; they had spent a foodless Sunday, but were nonetheless cheerful and happy to see us. McKenna telephoned the press, and within half an hour cameras were directed at us through the bars, whereupon the captain of the station moved us into a private cell, not wishing, perhaps, to have the malign secrets of his prison house exposed. Dean Woodward† telephoned to know if the university could do anything for me. but Miss Binford had already sent twenty-five dollars for my bail. The papers enjoyed the paradox

---

*Count Mihály Károlyi (1875–1955) was president of the newly organized Hungarian People's Republic immediately after World War I.—Eds.

†Frederic Campbell Woodward (1874–1956) was a professor of law at the University of Chicago and acting president there, 1928–1929.—Eds.

Hull House residents gather for supper in the Residents' Dining Hall. Jane Addams is seated at the head of the middle table. To her right are Dr. Alice Hamilton, Robert Morss Lovett, Agnes Pillsbury, George Hooker, and Victor Yarros. To Jane Addams' left are Dr. Rachelle Yarros, Edith de Narcrede, and Esther Kohn.

of ''the elderly professor'' being rescued by the Juvenile Protective Association. . . .

Oscar Ludmann

5809 Warwick Avenue
Chicago, Ill.
May 21, 1931.

My dear Miss Addams,

As an immigrant coming to this country three years ago, I want to thank you for the help I received at Hull House. The encouragement I found has torn me out of a fatalistic stupor and proved to me that there are still such things as idealism and unselfish attempt to better the destiny of others.

When I came to America, mentally and physically dull, I passed through the bitter experiences of every immigrant. I had studied many things at home in Alsace-Lorraine but very soon I lost faith in my knowledge, and like many foreigners I realized more and more that there was but one trade I knew thoroughly—the trade which had been forced upon me in the military camps, the trade of the gun. Friendless, homesick, and terribly alone, who cared if I grew desperate?

At just that moment I was introduced into Mr. Lovett's writing class by Mrs. Evelyn Byron,* and there at last I found understanding. All the

*A Hull-House resident with her husband, William F. Byron. He sometimes served as secretary to Jane Addams.—Eds.

horrors of my past life came before me as I wrote and when, one evening, Mr. Lovett suggested, "Why don't you write these stories in a book?" for once I was happy, ready to smile upon the world I had hated. I had found a fatherland, a home—a peaceful one, I should say. Up to then Fatherland had meant some kind of a flag for me, either the imperial black-white-red, the French blue-white-red, or the flag of the revolution. Home had meant my parents' house, a family of patriots, either passionate French or loyal Germans. They were all victims of their education from before 1870 and after.

In my book "Step-child of the Rhine" I have written about Alsace-Lorraine before and after the War. Thanks to the criticisms of Mr. Lovett, and to the help of Jane Hiller who later became my American wife, I have been able to finish this work. It will be published during the coming year. I sincerely hope that it may have some value in educating, in showing people the ridicule of so-called patriotism and the helplessness of international understanding so long as children are taught to hate not men but miserable uniforms.

If my countrymen could have seen at the Christmas exercises at Hull House the little negro boy beside the Mexicans and Italians, all singing together, they would ask, "Why has my youth been poisoned? Why did we have to live through hunger, disease, constant yellow fear of death?" when children of all colors can sing to the same Lord of Peace, at Hull House.

In the name of an Alsatian immigrant I thank you sincerely, Miss Addams, for the help I have received in the institution of Hull House.

Gratefully yours,
OSCAR LUDMANN

Hull-House Photographs

Wallace Kirkland

*Wallace Kirkland (1891–1979) and his wife, Ethel, moved to Hull-House in 1921, while Wal-*lace was a student at George Williams College in Chicago. After graduation, he accepted a full-time job at the settlement as director of the Men's and Boys' Clubs. His interest in photography began when the manager of the Eastman Kodak store in Chicago gave the Boys' Club a 5 × 7 view camera. Kirkland developed his talent by taking photographs of wild flowers on weekend trips to the Indiana dunes on Lake Michigan, and by capturing the settlement neighborhood, programs, and people on film. Gradually, his photographic hobby became his vocation. "I was thinking more of composition and development than of delinquency and regeneration," he wrote in his autobiography, Reflections of a Life Photographer. He began to take professional assignments, and by 1935 he had left Hull-House. He joined* Life *magazine the year it was founded and became famous as a staff photographer there.*

Kirkland left a rich photographic record of his years at the settlement. Better than anyone in the 1920s and 1930s, he captured the humanity, the diversity, and the street-wise resiliency of Hull-House children. His photographs have been used throughout this book; the ones following reveal the joys of going to Bowen Country Club. [Wallace Kirkland Photographs, Jane Addams Memorial Collection, University of Illinois at Chicago.]

Gypsies in Halsted Street

Clare Edgar McLure

From the very early days of Hull-House, investigation and research occupied a large portion of the residents' time. They studied and surveyed their neighborhood over and over again; they wrote dozens of books and hundreds of articles based on their findings, and they often used their charts, graphs, and statistics to help make their

Bowen Country Club camp, Waukegan, Illinois.

case for new legislation. Hull-House became an outpost for the study of the city and a pioneer in the development of urban sociology.

After World War I there was a decline in interest in social research. With reform in retreat, few had the same confidence that statistics would lead to legislation and social change. And in the 1920s the settlement attracted fewer of the young, aggressive college graduates eager to study the problems of the city. Yet despite the decline of interest in research, the residents continued to observe and document their changing neighborhood. They cooperated with a national investigation on the effects of prohibition and the extent of unemployment, and they made their own investigations of the shifting ethnic mixture of people—the Greeks, the Italians, and the Mexicans—who lived near them. They even discovered gypsies nearby. Here is a sympathetic essay written by a Hull-House resident based upon her study of life among a special group of immigrants who refused to be Americanized. [Clare Edgar McLure, "Gypsies in Halsted Street," Survey (October 1, 1927), 13–16.]

In the environs of Hull House, Chicago, on that colorful stretch of Halsted Street between the ghetto of Maxwell and the cheap white way of Madison, we have come to appreciate the survival of the Gypsies in our American life and to see how they adapt themselves outwardly just enough to enable them to keep inwardly the integrity of their racial language and customs. As neighbors we want to understand them, and to do that it is necessary to study them from within and from without, as individuals and in contrast to the people and peoples among whom they find themselves. As neighbors, what have we to give them—and what have they to give us?

It is from the Russian steppes that most of our Gypsy neighbors in Halsted Street have come. Many of them came first to Canada, and from Canada to the States, and more and more they have wintered in Chicago. From year to year they may drift from one block to another, but along Halsted Street one can always be within a stone's throw of a Gypsy doorway. Into these mystic hallways, hung with gay draperies, these Gypsies have

brought much of Russian along with them—the Russian Easter with a festival and exchanging of eggs, some of the balalaika steps, a smattering of Russian lingo, a fondness for brass and copper utensils, a liking for well-brewed tea. But they have carried over much more that is distinctively Gypsy—Romani language, the foretelling of the future, a host of traditions as old as time, that indefinable quality recognized the world over as Gypsy culture.

It is a culture which refuses to be standardized into regular American moulds. Our Jewish and Italian neighbors in Chicago are quickly assimilated, wear Hart, Schaffner and Marx clothes, and read the popular magazines. The Mexicans, despite a naïve, primitive charm, soon melt into the background of American life. The Greeks are stern and stolid, and mingle little with the currents of life; but withal, they have very little with which to hold themselves apart besides the church, coffee-house political gossip, and a scarcity of Greek women. Negroes and Nordics fall into line and soon become good Chicagoans, good Americans. The Gypsies, on the other hand, remain in the midst of seething, consciously adaptive groups, a people apart, so far apart that most people overlook their having any connection at all with contemporary life. Indeed, so fine a mesh has been woven about the Gypsy that the real Rom is as difficult to grasp as is the leprechaun. . . .

But what, then, is the Rom as we find him in Chicago? We have been taught that he is immoral or, at best, unmoral; a thief; a filthy carrier of disease; lazy, shiftless, living on his women; a child snatcher and, in short, an undesirable citizen. It is true that the Gypsy is far from being a hundred-and-six-per-cent American; but those of us who lack faith in the results of a Buddha-like contemplation of the navel of our own perfection find in this want of sameness in the Gypsy a moral virtue which may be turned in the future to the advantage of America.

It is as untrue to say that the Gypsy is immoral as it would be to say that all United States cabinet officials, without exception, are grafters or morons. Of all the races which have reached the shores of America there is none which has a more rigid code of sexual behavior than the Gypsy. What race has been able to maintain its racial purity, in the midst of a constant intermarrying of people, as has the Romani? Among what people are there so few husband or wife desertions? . . .

The Gypsy is the proverbial thief; and yet during a seven months' association with Mexican and Gypsy boys the leader of a club encountered just one attempt at thieving, and this in spite of the fact that her coat, containing a small purse with change, was always placed on the same table as the boy's caps, sweaters, and overcoats. The one mishap occurred in this way: a Mexican boy asked the leader to hold his gold watch for him while he boxed. She kept the watch under one hand while playing checkers with a small Gypsy, but left it when she got up to rule on a point of boxing. When she returned an older Mexican was saying to a Gypsy, "Come on—give it up!" And the watch was just vanishing into the blouse of the Gypsy. Without a word he handed it over and burst into a laugh when he saw the *Gajo's* face. No doubt he would have kept the watch, had he been successful in his thieving, but being caught turned the whole affair into a huge joke; a joke, not on the members of the club or the leader, but on himself, and he was the first to see it. All evening he kept chuckling over his own misfortune.

If one means by shiftlessness the inability to provide for old age by accumulating a surplus of wealth during youth and middle age, then the Rom can never be accused of shiftlessness. Almost all of them are wealthier than are the teachers of the same age in our schools and universities. . . .

Whence comes this wealth; from palm reading alone? By no means, for the Gypsy woman has other occult powers beside that of telling the future; many of them are "cures" and brew magic messes, which, if they don't cure, at least satisfy those who come to be helped. One boy's mother was famous as a "cure" and when asked what she used he replied, "Oh, a black mass of something which she brought from Russia and two chestnuts." The men have their own means of livelihood. There is still in Chicago a group of Gypsy coppersmiths who are noted for their expertness and who command large sums for their work. And in the summer the men still do a bit of horse and automobile trading in rural districts.

The life of the Rom as we find it amid city surroundings is still tribal in form and consequently close-knit and loyal in spirit. The women hold the family wealth in jewelry, silks, shawls, and eider-down mattresses which can be easily transported and personally guarded in camp or on the road. There is close understanding among the members of the tribe. The father is loved and respected, and the honor of the women of the tribe is the concern of all the members—a boy will go to any ends to defend the names of his mother and sisters. But he won't hesitate to fool them about how often he plays truant from school. He obeys his elders in most matters, and to the "head of the wagons," usually an older Gypsy woman, he gives unquestioning and devoted obedience. It is the chosen "head of the wagons" who decides when they will move and where, and it is this "head of the wagons," among the true Roms, who discovers the dawning of that mysterious day when they shall depart for the summer wandering. The men talk, boast, and make a great show of authority, but the tribal head has the final word. She is usually a quiet person, very quiet, whom the onlooker would never suspect of any unusual powers.

Though living under the domination of the one over the group, with rare exceptions the women

A gypsy girl in the Hull-House courtyard.

are content. Their interests center about their children, and the children return this devotion with a fidelity and loyalty often lacking in other racial groups. For instance, the only fight of the year that occurred in the Mexican-Gypsy boys' club started because a sixteen-year-old Mexican made a slighting remark about the mother of a thirteen-year-old Gypsy. Although the Mexican was twice the size of the Gypsy, he flew at him with such ferocity that to stop the fight the entire club had to be sent home. And it took two weeks of patient and tactful explaining to convince the Gypsies that the rest of us did not look with scorn on their mothers and sisters.

Another example of family loyalty and also of self-control was shown by three Gypsy boys varying in age from seven to fifteen. It is the custom among the Gypsies that when a member of an immediate family dies the family goes into mourning for a certain period, during which time they cannot attend feasts nor take part in any gaiety. There is at Hull House a group of Gypsies who meet once a week to paint; the first night these three boys were there, they refused to use colors in any form though, thinking they might not like water-colors, the director offered them chalks and pastels. They said they might use white chalk on black paper or black chalk on white paper. The smallest boy, particularly, seemed to be experiencing slow torture while watching the other boys paint, and at last his brother was induced to explain their dilemma: "You see, our brother died and for three mon' we can't dance, sing, or whistle; we can't paint. No colors, only black or white or maybe dark brown chalk."

Several weeks later a party was given to which all the mothers, fathers, and sisters of the boys were invited. More than forty people came, and although the little girls danced and several Mexicans sang their songs, and a group of Romani children sang in Romani, the three boys in mourning took no part in the general fun. Toward the end of the evening when they were playing Going to Jerusalem, the excitement proved too much for the seven-year-old Gypsy, and he fought with his older brother to be allowed to join in the games. When he finally did take part the older brother wept and went home disgraced. . . .

During seven months contact with ten and more Gypsy boys one of the residents of Hull House found only one with an inclination to cheat in games. Another resident spent many afternoons playing ball with small Romani children on the stone terrace. He afterwards remarked that he had never encountered in any children such an acute sense of fair play.

One of the most absurd traditions about the Gypsy is that he is a child snatcher. As it has been pointed out somewhere, the idea is illogical and ridiculous on the face of it. Any pale-faced child would be conspicuous among the dark children of a Rom, and would subject him to that inquiry by the police which many people find inconvenient if not hampering. Moreover, why should he go out of the way to steal a child of the despised *Gajo* when he always has more than plenty of his own?

Despite the limitations of Gypsy nomadic habits, there is much in their happy and colorful life from which hectic America could learn. Already, with the coming of the automobile we have picked up the travelling trait and all summer long one can hear in loud, proud American tones at almost any stopping place from the Adirondacks to Glacier National Park, "Yes, we're just gypsying across the country. Just packed up and started out for the summer."

When one considers that the people who live in this naif and chaste fashion are extremely passionate, full of the joy of life, virile and strong, one acknowledges that at least in their own case, innocence and tribal discipline work and work very well. . . .

A Decade of Prohibition

Jane Addams

Johnny Powers, the Irish ward boss, had ruled the 19th Ward since 1888, but as the ethnic balance in his area shifted from Irish to Italian, Powers' control was threatened. He was able to retain his position through favors granted to some politically ambitious Italians, but by 1921 the Italians held a clear majority in the ward and Powers faced a challenge for his position as alderman from An-

thony D'Andrea. The election campaign was accompanied by a rash of bombings and killings. On February 7, 1921, a bomb exploded in a meeting hall where a rally for D'Andrea was in progress. Earlier, Powers' house had been bombed, and a few days before the election one of D'Andrea's chief lieutenants was killed by an explosion. Powers managed to win the election by a few hundred votes, but that did not end the violence. A few days later two of his best known supporters were gunned down, one of them only a few blocks from Hull-House. The climax to this wave of terror came on May 11, 1921, when D'Andrea himself was killed by a blast from a sawed-off shotgun. Several more murders followed before peace was restored. Powers had won the election, but it was to be his last, for the bloody election battle effectively ended his control of the ward. He retired at the end of his term in 1921 and, in an effort—largely unsuccessful—to neutralize the Italian strength, the 19th Ward was split up and divided among four other wards.

One element in the community was not dependent on the ward structure for its source of power. That was the gang, which could steal and murder while forcing politicians and police alike to defer to it. The Prohibition Era, ushered in in 1919 by the passage of the Eighteenth Amendment to the Constitution, banning the manufacture, sale, or transportation of liquor, presented the gang with possibilities for new illicit activities which were highly lucrative and added to its power base. Congress could not legislate the thirst of the man in the street. Since the demand for liquor could not be satisfied legally, gangs sought to fill the demand illegally—making huge sums of money in the process and gaining political and economic control over large areas of Chicago.

Yet there were those, particularly in the early days of prohibition, who were sure the Eighteenth Amendment was the answer to a pressing social problem. Jane Addams was one of these. Like most of the residents of Hull-House, she favored prohibition. She viewed it as another progressive measure which, like child labor laws, would help preserve human resources. Living as they did in a largely immigrant neighborhood, the residents appreciated the natural place that drinking occupied in the social life of many ethnic groups; but they also saw the disasters caused by alcoholism. During the first two years of prohibition, the settlement workers thought they detected improvement in the living conditions of the neighborhood, but then the problems of enforcement and the bootlegging and gang warfare connected with the liquor traffic began to outweigh the good results.

In this essay Jane Addams described some of the problems and activities that earned Chicago its worldwide reputation as a haven for gangsters—a reputation it is still trying to live down. Hull-House had an interesting relationship with some of the gangland figures of the twenties in Chicago. Many men who led notorious lives in the underworld were faithful participants in one or another Hull-House activity; some were actors at the theatre or creative members of the art classes. It was rumored that these men protected Hull-House from gangland disruption. At Jane Addams' funeral some of the most famous hijackers, bootleggers, and gang leaders in the city were observed paying their respects. [Jane Addams, ''A Decade of Prohibition,'' Survey Graphic (October 1, 1929), 5–8, 10.]

A neighborhood such as ours affords an epitome of the results of general unenforcement of the prohibition regulations in Chicago, as in other American cities. Very interesting experiences in the last ten years at Hull House center about the Eighteenth Amendment. Our neighborhood has sheltered the bootlegger in his earliest activities, witnessing his rapid rise into power. It knew the adventurous hi-jacker and can trace the humble origin of the political liquor rings. . . .

The building conditions of our neighborhood easily lend themselves to [bootlegging]. . . . Along the south branch of the Chicago River the property owners are waiting to sell their old houses and barns, disused stores, and small factory buildings, believing that the sites will be used for railroad terminals, garages, and warehouses, which are already displacing the old buildings. These dilapidated houses and the somewhat casual population now tenanting them—Mexicans and gypsies—afford good hiding places both for the manufacturing and storing of liquor and for the hi-jackers and others who openly prey upon the illicit industry. A hi-jacker is one who holds up a truck of booze, frightening the driver with his gun until he induces him to desert his load. The driver dare not call upon the police to protect his illicit freight, and when he is obliged to abandon it, can only telephone to his gang and try to intercept the hi-jacker later and in turn terrify him with guns in order to recover the precious stuff. If the original owner of the "booze" later calls upon the police at all, he can make a charge only for the stealing of the truck without daring to mention what was loaded upon it, for of course "booze" is not legitimate property. From time to time we have found abandoned trucks in the alley back of Hull House which have evidently been left there because it was dangerous for the hi-jacker to keep them near his own house. Of course, the profession of a hi-jacker is highly lucrative. He obtains his booze with all the profit it stands for without even the difficulty and expense of manufacturing it. He sometimes operates directly upon the manufacturing still and empties the store room of its contents. Such places are also easy victims of the regular hold-up men, and this accounts for the fact that many of them are equipped like small arsenals. Of course, the owners of places which have been robbed are filled with vengeance, and unending raids are thus started. There is in all this warfare an element of old-fashioned business rivalry, what used to be called "cut-throat" competition.

Bootlegging, in its economic aspect, is a great industry. Production, formerly carried on in factories, if we may thus designate the distilleries and breweries, has become decentralized and has gone back into the home industry stage. This is just the reverse of what has happened in other industries. But we find the exploiter trying to get control of all the stills within a given area, creating a situation comparable to that in the Pennsylvania oil fields years ago. Almost any man who had a piece of land where a well could be dug, could produce oil after a fashion, but for selling it he was dependent upon rival companies. Unless one company could gain control of a given section, it was at a great disadvantage because the mere collecting of the oil meant crossing and recrossing a given territory and because of the necessity of focusing the oil at a given point for final transportation into the outside world. As one company gained control of a certain section, and impinged upon the territory belonging to a rival, the competition became more

and more intense, until one company won the field. The bootlegging situation came to resemble that in the early Pennsylvania oil fields not only in its economic structure but in its ruthlessness and widespread terrorism.

The production of alcoholic drinks, by going back from the factory to its domestic beginnings, quite naturally first fell into the hands of those who had never gotten very far from the domestic type of industry. These actual producers exhibit many of the characteristics of simple people, but the new industry, in the selling end, from the very first attached to itself shrewd business men, trained in an age of complicated commercialism, who also understood the necessity for political protection. We had grown accustomed during the last decades to the idea that great vested interests connected with the manufacturing of alcoholic drinks were bringing to bear continuous pressure on Congress and very often on the state legislatures as well. We had at one time our own "whiskey ring" in Illinois with headquarters at Peoria. But the pressure formerly brought to bear on Washington and upon state capitals has now been transferred to the simplest unit of government, the patrolman on his beat. The federal officials detailed to enforce an unpopular law are subjected to temptations of the most flagrant sort.

The development of political corruption in connection with the manufacture and sale of liquor follows a direction the reverse of that of the industrial change from factory to decentralized small-scale production. The old national "whiskey ring" came first, for it was in General Grant's administration that the secretary of the treasury unearthed frauds in the collection of internal revenues for certain distilleries which were operating in collusion with high officials, who throve upon the profits. The wholesale corruption of petty government officials came much later with the decentralization of the industry when business opportunities on an unprecedented scale had been opened to simple peasants who have an opportunity to make money such as they had never even dreamed of before. It is not difficult to understand that the barrier of illegality was a frail one and easily went down before this onrush of avarice.

In the first days of the home-brewing and kitchen-distilling, rival bootleggers found it essential to control a given area, and they made to anyone discovered operating within that area a fifty-fifty proposition. They gave police protection and selling advantages in return for half the output. If a man resisted, his still was broken up, and if he was persistent, he would suffer personal violence. But he was in the end obliged to conform or to go out of business. In fact, however violent his opposition to the monopoly, he could not go on without protection, and there was the added danger that his neighbors would ''squeal to the police'' if he were selling to a rival. From the beginning these home-producers realized that it was the transporting and selling end of the business which was difficult and perilous, and so there inevitably developed a hostile rivalry between two sets of men who were not producers, but sellers. They were not, of course, carrying on a purely economic rivalry, for the situation was enormously complicated by the fact that both the manufacturing and selling were illegal and absolutely dependent upon successful corruption. Even if the federal official did not collect money for protection, someone would probably do it in his name, and if the policeman on the beat was perfectly honest, politicians who pretended to control police organizations, collected for him. The law-breaker, of course, always subjects himself to an unending series of blackmail. There is also the grave situation when bootleggers come to count upon immunity from the very people whose business it is to report them. In a very real sense, the people who represented the administration of the law became as much a part of the criminal situation as the so-called criminals themselves.

In the very earliest days of the 1920s, the illicit making of liquor entered the stage of the small factory or shop, although small copper stills were piled high for sale in the outdoor markets of the neighborhood. Strictly family manufacturing was going out, and larger stills were owned by groups of bootleggers who employed men from the neighborhood. The enterprises housed in old barns and basements used gasoline for heating the mash and operating the still, the whole outfit rather expensive and requiring a man capable of running it as well as one who would be courageous if the police appeared. There was also a real danger from escaping fumes if the matter were carelessly handled. Sometimes the volume of business was quite large—a still recently raided in our neighborhood was producing 200 gallons a day. The building housing it was a comparatively small barn, for the vats were in the basement sunk into the ground itself. The ''stuff'' is moved sometimes in a dilapidated old grocery wagon, sometimes in a motor truck. In our neighborhood it is usually handled in two-gallon cans. The inhabitants of a street near the Settlement were accustomed to seeing a man sitting on a front seat beside the driver of an old Ford truck with a shotgun wrapped up in newspaper lying across his knees; another armed man would walk casually along the pavement. This was to secure protection from hi-jackers as well as from police interference. During one half-year our neighborhood was filled with bootleggers coming from various parts of the city, added to those from our own vicinity, because the local police captain had the reputation of being easy to deal with.

This political protection produces great cynicism among the immigrants who say quite openly, ''You can do anything in America if you pay for it.'' What must be the effect of an incident like the following? An Italian drinking with his gang one evening came home late at night and was shot in his own kitchen by a drunken companion. There was sufficient proof to indict the wife for complicity in the murder. She acknowledged that she was ''fed up'' with the abuse of herself and her family, and had promised to divide the insurance money with anyone who would get rid of her husband, who was himself supposed to be something of a gunman. Although it was shown in court that the insurance money had been divided with the gang, she was acquitted through the political power of the gang in a determination to save itself from exposure. A year later, the city was astounded when an assistant state's attorney was shot and killed in an automobile in company with a man whom he had tried for murder but who had been acquitted. The assumption was that the assistant state's attorney had been collecting from the gang of men with whom the criminal was connected. Two juries failed to convict the murderer. It was said that the official had been ''bumped off'' for political reasons totally unconnected with bootlegging. Without a verdict, it is impossible to know the situation, but there was no doubt that the incident gave an increased consciousness of political power to the bootlegging community.

The Sicilians in Chicago have an unsavory

reputation for desperate measures in connection with bootlegging, partly because of the dramatic history of six Sicilian brothers,* three of whom lost their lives in a prolonged war with a rival gang. The story, which in many respects is a typical one, may be outlined as follows:

Jim, the oldest of the six brothers, who came to the United States fifty years ago, operated a restaurant and a speakeasy; Angelo quickly reached the heights of an extortionist, and when Sicilian turned against Sicilian, in an aldermanic election, he killed his man, and thereafter had a standing as a gunman. Sam, more diplomatic in training and temperament, acted as a political agent for his brothers. Antonio was the gentleman of the family, the opera patron, and man about town. Peter was a saloonkeeper, and Michael was well fitted to do the rough bidding of his brothers. They formed a united family and gained a foothold in the alcohol business. The put stills in the home of every Sicilian whom they were able to dominate. In a short time they controlled much of the home-made alcohol in the city and were able to undersell all competitors. The combined credit rating of the family at one time was five million dollars, each one of the brothers almost a millionaire. Indeed, it was necessary to have capital in this business. In the fall of 1923 it was discovered that one Italian bootlegger had a payroll for chauffeurs, truckmen, bootleggers, guards, killers, lawyers, and general handymen, of $2500 a week.

The troubles of the brothers came at length from a savage outbreak with the rival gang, in which three of their men killed the hated leader of their competitors. Swift vengeance followed. Angelo was the first of the brothers to be killed, and Mike was next, although he was actually shot by the police as he was running away from a rival who had tried to kill him. Then, a few weeks later, Tony was shot down as he grasped the hand of a supposed friend who lured him "to the spot." These brothers had the reputation, even in the old country, we were often told, of being able to live without working, a remark very sinister in its implications. A certain type of Sicilian for centuries had a training in taking care of his own affairs outside of the law. The island was full of banditry and the vendetta survived there more than in any other part of the world. A man so trained easily goes over into the selling of booze, ready for all the desperate measures which may be involved. If a rival "muscles in," as the bootleggers laconically phrase it, on the territory and trade of his gang, he is ready to punish him. His very training in illegal activity and in dealing with his enemies for himself, becomes economically useful in the peculiar situation obtaining in Chicago in "the third decade of the twentieth century," as our newspapers put it. If he can go through the form of a trial and "walk smilingly out of court," so much the better. These two gangs of Sicilians† almost exterminated each other, and the entire Sicilian population of helpless immigrants, living in Chicago, suffered in the process.

But in the last analysis, it is big money that makes Chicago gang wars so murderous. The city holds the key to the rich trade of the West and Northwest in whiskey, wine, gin, and beer, exactly as it does in wheat, hogs, furniture, and more staple commodities. Bourbon now comes from Canada and is cleared through Chicago, arriving on motor trucks, steamers, freight cars, and aeroplanes, from Detroit and other points along the border. Supplementing the Canadian ale and beer with the product of its own breweries, Chicago redistributes the lighter beverages as well. Certain Chicago citizens point out, almost with pride, that if other cities have escaped the bootleg wars, it is because they are less strategically located than Chicago in the scheme of liquor distribution. The most optimistic citizens, however, could scarcely be proud of the role the police play in the Chicago situation, and their connection with the massacre of February 14 in which seven men were killed is but a flagrant example.

The residents in a settlement, like other good citizens, are much concerned as to the effect of all this law-breaking upon the young. There is no doubt that a spirit of adventure natural to boys in adolescence has been tremendously aroused by the bootlegging and hi-jacking situation. It is as if this adventurous spirit were transferred from the wild west into the city streets. A boy was recently arrested in Chicago, who had come from Indiana for the express purpose of seeing "the brave men

---

*Genna brothers.—Eds.

†Johnny Torrio—Al Capone versus the Genna brothers.—Eds.

who were able to keep the police at bay." City boys in bootlegging neighborhoods have many opportunities to participate and even to collect hush money or at least to help by guarding secrets as to location of bootlegging outfits. They are quite often used as outposts, and are expected to give an alarm if a policeman or a hi-jacker appears to "be wise" as to the location of the hidden activity. If word is given that the police are on the trail, everything is set in readiness for protecting the plant. Everything depends upon who shoots first, for shooting is inevitable and a matter of self-protection on both sides. How general the carrying of arms by boys, for one reason or another, has become is shown by the recent killing of a police officer when he was arresting five boys who had been drinking and were evidently out for mischief. They told him to let them off or they would shoot him, and they finally succeeded in doing it because they outnumbered him in firearms.

Bootleg liquor is integrated with vice and crime quite as liquor always has been. Roadhouses where liquor is sold are notorious for their prostitution, and automobiles make it possible to transport patrons quickly to these disorderly roadhouses, also affording concealment for the intoxicated young people returning together. In addition to a boy's natural love of automobiles is the association of banditry. An automobile bandit is more successful and more dangerous than the romantic wild west robbers of fifty years ago, or the bands so recently to be found in remote parts of Sicily, Spain, and of Mexico. A boy in the state reformatory tells how easily he and his gang, who owned a Ford, used to hold up young people who were returning from the roadhouses, finding it easy to take their money because they were always more or less intoxicated.

How inextricably this new type of crime and indeed the whole prohibition question are involved with the development of the automobile it is impossible to describe. Chicago, with only one-third of the population of New York, covers four times as much territory—prairie territory opening by hundreds of outlets into the country on every side—and this too affects the local situation.

In pre-Volstead days happiness and release from reality were associated with drinking, and much of the social life for men centered around drinking together. There is no doubt that more wholesome outlets are gradually being substituted in spite of the fact that many young men are very eager to demonstrate their superiority to law, and consider this demonstration a very sporty thing. We know indeed that a great many young people are drinking at the present moment solely from a sense of bravado. Each generation looks for a method with which it may defy the conventions and startle its elders. The present generation seems to have settled upon the obtaining and consuming of illicit liquor. The motive is so cheap and superficial that it is almost impossible to place the situation in the area of morals or any other human field. Unhappily their elders often imitate and abet them, although they live in homes in which liquor was never used in the pre-war days.

There is a general impression, however, that this braggadocio movement is spending itself and that a reaction has set in among the young people themselves. Many flappers are afraid to drive with men who carry hip flasks. Automobile accidents are multiplied, not only by the man who is intoxicated but even more by the man whose few drinks have made him recklessly eager to take chances and evoked within him a certain exhibitionism of dare-devil courage. If it ever comes to a forced choice between automobiles and liquor, there would be a little doubt, I imagine, as to which would be preferred. . . .

The Story of a Gang Member

John Landesco

In the 1920s, the Hull-House neighborhood and the surrounding region on the West Side became the center for much of the crime and underworld activity in Chicago. Al Capone, the Genna brothers, and the "42 Gang" all operated in the area. Prohibition and bootlegging were responsible for some of the criminal activity, but there were many other factors, including ethnic tensions and the struggle for political power.

Jane Addams and other Hull-House residents

appreciated even in the 1890s the relationship of the boys' gang to politics and to adult gangster activities. They also understood some of the appeal, some of the sense of belonging, and the feeling of being important that went with membership in a gang. But despite boys' clubs, classes, handicrafts, sports, excursions to the country, and the Juvenile Protective Association, the Hull-House group was never able to counteract and control the gang activity in its own neighborhood. The schools and churches in the area had no better luck.

The following is the story of one member of the "42 Gang" who came from a "good" family. He grew up in the Hull-House neighborhood, and despite settlement influences drifted into a life of crime. The story, told in the boy's own words, describes some of the attractions of gang life, shows how petty theft led to more serious offenses, and makes clear the compliance of the police, business interests, and private citizens in the gang's activities. John Landesco (1890–1954), the author, was born in Rumania. He came to this country with his parents at the age of ten and lived five years on the West Side of Chicago before moving to Milwaukee. He attended the University of Wisconsin, held a succession of jobs, including that of director of the Abraham Lincoln Settlement in Milwaukee, before becoming a student at the University of Chicago in 1922. There he studied sociology and was strongly influenced by Ernest Burgess and other urban sociologists at the University. His background and training enabled him to study crime and the criminal with a rare sympathy. He sought to understand rather than condemn. [John Landesco, "Member of the 42 Gang," Journal of Criminal Law and Criminology *(March 1933), 967–980.]*

The life history of Rocco [Marcantonio], 21 years of age, life-long participant in the gang activities of the West Taylor street area, known to police and the law as a gun robber, is introduced as the core of the history of the "42" gang.

"I was born on Ewing Street, a little east of Desplaines Street. Ewing Street is a street south of Polk Street. Our house was located one block from the Guardian Angel church. I lived there through my infancy, and when I was old enough to go to

school I was enrolled at the Dante public school. At the age seven I became an altar boy at the Guardian Angel church.

"One year later we moved to De Koven and Halsted, which is only three blocks away, and I continued at the Dante school. We lived there only one year and then moved to Taylor and Sibley. Sibley is one block east of Loomis, and our house was just across the way from the Hebrew Institute.

"Here I attended Rees School at Elburn and Throop. I entered this school when I was about nine years old and continued there until I was in the seventh grade and about fourteen years of age.

"My childhood was simple and happy. My record at the Dante school would prove that I attended school regularly, passed in my grades. After school I ran eagerly to the Guardian Angel church where I played with the altar boys in a clubroom under the church, and on warm days played baseball with these boys in the street or in the school yard.

"My father has been in America for 32 years. He was married before he arrived here, came to live in Ewing Street with my mother before their first child was born. His home town was Montfalcone, situated in about central Italy. He began then as a railroad laborer and has continued in the same work since. He is now a track foreman and is always employed.

"I was the sixth child. Seven of us were born and all are alive today. Phyllis is now 31 and married, Connie is 29 and married, Pete 27, Tony 25, Albert 23, myself about 21, and Gerald 13. My grandmother, that is my father's mother, has lived with us for many years. She is now about 97 and still alive and well. . . .

"My schooling at Dante was regular, and I attended to my work while I was at Dante. I always, from a very small child, wanted to be an altar boy, and one day when one of the altar boys came and told me that I was chosen for an altar boy, I was very happy. I went to church every morning, arose at 6 and served the 7 to 8 o'clock mass—on Sunday the 8 to 9 mass. The altar boys were my playmates. There was a little club-like room in the basement where we played games, checkers, and read books. Even before I was chosen they took me in to play with them and they asked the priest to take me and talked to me to try to be an altar boy. After school we used to play ball in the school

A littered alleyway near the settlement.

yard. In the winter time we went to Hull House sometimes and spent some time in a play room or tried to attend the club. Sometimes I went on hikes. I was never truant from school. When we moved to De Koven and Halsted there was no changes in my schooling. I kept on being altar boy and played with the same boys.

"When we moved to Taylor and Sibley I had to transfer to the Rees school. At first I didn't like it because I didn't know anybody. When I passed into the 6th grade I began to know them all. Even before I became acquainted with the gang pals just out of lonesomeness, I would sometimes bum school of an afternoon to run back to Dante school and be at the gate when my old friends, the altar boys, came out of school.

"Something happened toward the last months while I was still an altar boy that made me lose faith in the church, and I wasn't so religious after that. I came running in to the priest and found him eating chicken on Friday. He reached for a towel and hurried to cover the chicken before I could see it, but I saw it. When we moved I stopped altar work and stopped going to church. My grandmother, who all of her life has gone to church every morning, always scolded me for that. But I have attended church once in a while even since and now, since I live in this new neighborhood where people know each other and watch each other, out on the northwest side, I go to church so people won't talk about us. I have to be seen at church, and I like to go to light a candle for my mother.

"I always cared more for my mother and brother Albert, but Albert and I never played together. He had other boys. He not only liked sports but he played himself on teams at the Hebrew Institute. My crowd always went to see the Cubs play. We would watch games of professional ball. Very early, as soon as our first racket began to bring us in money, we always wanted to go out with women, and drink.

"While at the Rees school I began selling papers after school to about 6 p.m. in the lobby of a loop building. I gave it up because of trouble with the customers and with the building. Some customers would pick up a paper daily and would forget to pay me at the end of the week, and the building wanted the space so they gave me a lot of trouble about keeping the lobby clean. Also I began to run around with the fellows that first introduced me to rackets.

"About in the 6th grade, when I was 14 years old, I began to have trouble in school and it began to be reported to my father. It was time, too, for my lessons for confirmation, and my father transferred me to Pompeii school (parochial). At Pompeii school I behaved a little better. The principal took me in and gave me a talking-to right at the beginning. Later I began to find my old friends again, and I was kicked out of Pompeii and went back to Rees where I quit in the seventh grade. By this time we were bumming and stealing.

"We first started stealing from clothes lines while bumming from school. Pete, Louie, and Babe Ruth were all in Rees school then. Of that racket we had been hearing a lot. The first day we went out west, near Oak Park. We took the street car with a little sack under our arm and filled it and came home. We picked silk shirts and would sell

them for only a dollar or two dollars apiece. We sold them to our friends and our cousins and our cousins' friends. And they always told other people, but I never would sell to my own brothers and tell them anything about it. We quit school and began to hang out at Throop and Elburn, shooting dice.

"Beginning at about this time and for 7 years to follow, we always had the basement of the delicatessen store for our hangout. Here we stored out loot. We would shoot craps on the sidewalk, and buy delicatessen, go to shows and worry the girls.

"For 2 years we were in the shirt-stealing racket and we were never caught once. If somebody ran after us we would just run away, take the street car home when we were chased.

"Our next racket was 'robbing pennies.' One of us would take a small sledge hammer and with a partner start down Roosevelt Road, looking for peanut machines. One smash and the pennies would come rolling out. We would get four or five slot machines an evening. We could even get some in the daytime. If we were chased we would quit. It was before the pistol was around and if the Jew came out of the store the fellow with the sledge hammer would threaten him. We knew the streets like a book, would run through the alley like lightning, or over the fence into the open lot and were gone. We used to study getaways day and night. We were never caught. Sometimes these owners would trace us and come around, or even the police. When they came we would duck.

"There were about 15 fellows in our near neighborhood in the original shirt racket, and about that many around the peanut racket, but our own little bunch was only three or four.

"A little later we began to steal bicycles, as did others in the neighborhood. We would go out to Oak Park or to some other west side or Hyde Park residence district on the street car, take the bicycles, and ride back home on them. We were the same partners; we would use the same basement. We would sell these bicycles, sometimes worth $55 or $65, for four, ten, or fifteen dollars. We always had a half-dozen bikes in the basement. This went on until 1924, the same basement at Throop and Elburn.

"One day a man came around and said he'd give us $9 for a 29x.4 tire. He told us it was easy. He explained to us that we could get a bar clip in a hardware store which we did, and with that bar clip we took that spare tire off the car. We delivered the tire and he gave us the $9. Through him another and another customer heard of us, and these passed us on to others. We soon got a list of 'phone numbers of tire customers. Later a single trucking firm would buy many tires from us, leaving orders in advance for what they wanted.

"We weren't the only ones in the neighborhood, but there were a few little bunches like ours working at stealing tires.

"This same trucking firm, the owners of which are young men strong in politics and with money, were for a long while general fences for anything stolen and would be willing to buy anything from boys of the neighborhood, but not from anyone outside of the neighborhood. Many of our customers were legitimate working people. We stole tires all over the city and outside of our neighborhood. I soon owned a little Ford coupe, and in it we cruised around until we found what we wanted.

"In the delicatessen store we 'stoshed' some of our money. I suppose the four of us in some good weeks would make as high as $200, $250, or even $300 the best weeks.

Members of the Boys' Club at Hull-House in the 1920s.

"Our biggest expense then was shooting craps, and we wanted to go with girls like the older fellows. We picked up with two broads, one Mildred and the other Marie. One was a German and the other was a Polak. They lived in a hotel. When it got a little hot for us we would go there to stay. We were suckers for these girls, bought them clothes and gave them money, and they took us around to beer flats and hotels. They were much older than we, 24. I think that it was because we didn't know how to dress then and didn't know how to talk to girls. I'd call up over the 'phone and say, 'Say, broad, we're out to a joint west. You want to come out here?' And they'd come out. But we saved some of our money and, as I said, we stoshed in the delicatessen store.

"We got into our first jam when I was about 16 years of age and we had been a few months in the tire business. We had our little basement hangout fixed up with shelves and marked tire sizes on the shelves. When a customer wanted a tire we would take him down to the basement, switch on the light, and pull down the right tire. Getting into a jam with the police was new to us but not so new because we heard a lot from other fellows about getting into jams, ducking the police, 'fixing,' springing writs, and getting bail. Others in the neighborhood were in many jams before us, especially the older fellows. We were picked up around the old Empire theater, at Union and Madison street, by the old Marmon squad that used to have a gong on each side. They took us down to the Desplaines street station. At the time of this first jam we had about $900 saved in the hands of the delicatessen man. They thought that the Ford I was driving was a stolen Ford, and they had us under suspicion for stealing tires.

"They gave us some beatings. We didn't 'know anything about stealing tires nor machines.' We knew even then that we must take a beating and keep our mouth shut. They let the other fellow out the same evening because I claimed the car was mine. They wouldn't give me permission to 'phone my cousin, but the other fellow reached him the next day and he came down and identified me, himself, and claimed the car was his and he let me use it. We were booked for disorderly, and the court discharged the case.

"After that we began to be watched and the coppers began to pick us up because once or twice they found stolen tires in our little car. I learned that when you are picked up and you have money in your pocket you can fix the copper.

"For all of these four or five years Pete, known as 'Mibs,' and Louie, of a well-known pair of brothers, and I were the close partners in the little hangout under the delicatessen store. Even though we were four or five years in the rackets it looked like we would never see the inside of a police station. When we were arrested that one time we felt pretty bad about it, but it was pretty easy. I can't explain how we were safe so long. We had no 'fix' in anywhere. We used to hear of the older crowd getting pinched all the time but we knew nothing of any station, squad, or fix.

"Then Red, who was about 17 or 18 years old, and lived in the neighborhood of 12th and Lytell, wanted to come with us. He had a Chevy '24 even before I had a Ford coupe. He was Irish but always hung around in the neighborhood. He came with us only after we were in the tire racket a while. We used to see him around with Babe Ruth, Vito, and some of the big fellows. They used to gip him too much, he said. We used to see him coming in with whole loads of merchandise in his Chevy, or tires. We would ask him 'How much would you get for the load?' 'Oh, a couple of dollars.' 'Who did you sell it to?' 'I don't know. They sold it for me.'

"Twenty-five dollars would fix it on the spot. I can say that up to my 18th year I was in very little trouble with the police. We hardly figured even on getting pinched. We had little to do either with lawyers or bondsmen.

"Then we started getting in with the older clique. They hijacked us into their gang but we, too, wanted to be with them. Vito's house was the hangout for the older crowd. I lived across the alley from him and I would see him often, and his pals, Salvi, Babe Ruth, Sharkey, Sam. They were 20 and 21 years of age. At Vito's house it was different than at mine. His family knew what was going on. How could they help it with so many well-dressed young fellows around doing nothing? If they had a spot for hot stuff of their own they never told us. They were afraid we would steal from them. The weren't exactly afraid; they just didn't trust us. We might have liked to be with these older fellows, the big shots, only if they didn't gip us so much.

"They were in the big money, after butter and

egg trucks, dry goods, shoes in loads. They were driving Chryslers; they were having better and bigger times—cabarets, shows, beer joints. We were too small to go around, we didn't know how to dress, and we felt that they were smarter.

"They found out that we were hanging around the delicatessen store and that we had money there. One day four of five of us were shooting craps on the corner on the sidewalk. We each had ten or twenty dollars in our hands. Whatever you wanted to shoot for that was the stakes. They saw money! All of them were in a Ford—Babe, Vito, Salvi, Patsy, Frankie. They stopped to ask us for money—'We're broke. Give us some money.' We gave them some, afraid they'd take all. That wasn't enough so they started taking more. We ran away. Then for a while we always tried to duck them, for about 2 or 3 weeks. But it was the only place we knew where to hang out. So they came around and hijacked us for our money.

"Then one day they told us that if we wanted to go along with them, 'making' trucks and merchandise, they'd take us, and we says, 'all right.'

"Those fellows were like coppers. Anyway they'd come around and shake us down and hijack us for our money, steal it from us, take it from us.

"They showed us a way where we could make more money, go out 'making' trucks, butter and eggs, merchandise, making more money.

"The last six months in the tire business we would go out after 1 p.m. We averaged about $75 a week, all sweet—nobody to bother us, nobody to pay off, but I thought, 'If I went out with the big fellows I'd be a big shot.' We were helped out by a teaming company and their friends with lists of customers. We sold to users and to other contractors and to men in the teaming union. These neighborhood trucking men thought we were all right. We showed them that we had a reasonable price, and we never stole from them.

"I have told you how the older fellows, there were only four, hung around Vito's house. We were four younger fellows hanging around our 'spot' at the delicatessen. They first hijacked us and then took us into a business with bigger money, butter and eggs and trucks. At first they did take us for suckers. They did all the selling. Later we learned the buyers when they let it slip while they were talking. We went to the buyers and asked about the prices. Then we learned about the true prices. Then we told 'em that if they didn't play square with us, no more going out together. We were doing the dirty work, they sat in the machine; 'an even split or nothing.' By this time we had guns. They fitted us out with them, and they said, 'yes.' . . .

"We were down in the basement at Figlio's. Vito asked me if I wanted to try to use a pistol, showed me how to aim. Pointing to the target he demonstrated how a pistol must be aimed lower than the object to allow for the jump (recoil). Later he sold me a 36 Colt (break open).

"The older fellows were in the pistol racket even then. They went into the pistol racket just as the butter and egg racket was waning. The gang had started to 'crack up' into cliques of four and three.

"The older fellows knew how to wear their clothes. They taught me how to match ties and suits, what color shoes and hats to wear. For a long time I used to wear the suits my mother bought me to go away and come home in, or to do a job with, but used to keep swell suits at Archie Cappozi's house to dress up when I went out with the fellows. . . .

"Both for tires and trucks later we worked all over town but brought the stuff 'in' (into the neighborhood). With the trucks we had to begin to carry pistols. I don't remember the first time we went out after a truck. I can give you instances though.

"We met one morning at an appointed time at Edgemont and Loomis. . . . 'Let's go out and see if we can get some money,' said Salvi, I don't remember his last name. He was killed in an auto accident on the outer drive two years ago. We got into his Ford and cruised around, north, south, and west. This cruising before we found anything sometimes took an hour or even a half-hour, till we met up with something. At Kedzie and Flournoy there stands a truck, butter and eggs. The driver is in the store. I jumped in the truck and drove it east, he and the Ford behind me. His work was to cut off anybody following me in a machine by crowding him to the curb.

"We had our own garage in the neighborhood. Once we got there we would unload the stuff and take the truck out of the district. We would only drive the truck out of the police district (about 4 blocks into the Marquette district, out of the Maxwell St. district). How could we keep the truck? We'd only get caught with it. (We took butter and eggs because there was more money in it and easier to get rid of.) We found out the places where they disposed of the stuff. We knew the places and knew the prices received.

"I would be in on 'making' a truck every 2 or 3 days, but in the crowd they made a truck a day and brought it always to this same place. Twice we had to take the truck when the driver was on it (not in a store). There was so much value in it that we wanted the truck badly enough.

"Once, the driver was in the store doorway watching the truck. I started toward it. He came up. I stuck a gun in his ribs. 'Stick 'em up!' 'Quiet!' He obeyed and drove around the corner with me. 'Get out,' I ordered, and I drove away. In the machine behind me was Salvi and either Babe or some other fellow.

"For the trucks we always were with one of the big fellows. We thought they knew more about driving a machine in a pinch. Anyone could drive the truck away.

"If the party belonging to the truck chased us in a machine, the big fellow in the machine behind cut him off.

"The coppers used to come around once in a while. The older fellows told us they paid them off, did the dealing with the police. We used to give them money to pay them off, ten or fifteen dollars at a time. Either Vito, Babe, or Salvi used to come around for 'dough' to pay off coppers at certain times—about once a month.

"I used to always carry my money on me. I couldn't take it home to give to my folks, so they always knew I had a lot with me. They'd ask me for ten or fifteen dollars for the coppers once a month about. I didn't mind it. The other young fellows sometimes didn't have it or didn't have enough and they would beg off or 'jew' them down or come and ask me for some.

"The prices were, for cases of eggs ten dollars, tubs of butter fifteen dollars (to the dealer legitimate the tubs were worth about $25, the cases of eggs six to ten dollars). Out of a load as my share I got as high as $300. About $100 or $150 twice a week was my share. This racket lasted a year when I was 19 years old. I only went for butter and eggs, the other guys, the older fellows, took other merchandise, silks, shoes, suits. They were all taken to the same garage. I have seen the goods and I have worn it—suits and shoes. . . .

"Once in a while I would get picked up, never was caught red-handed until lately. When picked up they would stop our machine, call us out, take one of us in the squad car, allow the other fellow to drive our own machine with a copper at his side. The first chance is to talk to the copper himself. I keep quiet till the copper begins to talk: 'I know you guys, west side teeves, after butter and eggs or tires. You're with so-and-so, ain't you? With Babe, Patsy, Sharkey, and Vito?'

" 'No, we don't know 'em from Adam and Eve. How about talking business?'

" 'How much you got on you?'

" 'We got so much. Talk business or take us to the station.'

"Our big money we kept in our watch pockets. The police money we kept in our pants pocket. After we got in with the big fellows and were making big money, we were stopped two or three times a week like that. For a stretch of time you could buy yourself out one after another. Other times were hotter, after they started to know us, and then we were taken into the station one after another.

"One time I was pinched seven Sundays in a row. I would be on the streets, riding around in a machine or on the corner. They'd come along and pinch the mob and lock us up. . . .

"We never talked; no confessions. In some cases they'd take us down, bring us up every two or three hours, question us, and beat us up. At Desplaines street one time a young copper came down, first talked tough to us, slapped me in the face, could get nothing out of us. He came down later and in a kinder mood told us he was an ex-hood himself. He did some small favors for me, and I met him later when I was out and took him out to a good Italian dinner.

"I can say that we were always thrown in when we had no money in our pockets. Money buys any copper in this city. Any time when we were picked up on the street it was $25 to $100 for the two. If you didn't have it, you'd go down. In four years, the last four years, I can say I have been arrested forty times. I can say I have paid out to coppers $7,000 or $8,000.

"Then Figlio opened his poolroom in the neighborhood, the eight of us started hanging out there, the four older fellows and the four of us.

The poolroom drew more fellows from around the neighborhood who were also in little mobs of two and four and eight in the racket, and the mobs got close, got acquainted that way. Then came this fellow's neighbor and that fellow's brother and that fellow's cousin. Everybody had a racket—some came in little cliques that had their spots, like we had the basement or the garage later. No one could be called head. The "older fellows" of our mob didn't shake them all down because they had their own mobs.

"Then Figlio, about two months later, moved to 'Mary's,' a restaurant, around the corner from the poolroom, and the mob started hanging out there.

"It was there the name '42' sprang up.

"The bunch were all acquainted. I could approach any fellow if they were two or five or twenty, whether they were eating on the inside or hanging around on the outside, and ask him to go on a job. 'Do you want to go on a job? I got something *good.*'

"There was an elderly man we all trusted there. We left our guns, left our money to bank, whoever kept stuff there would drop him a fin or a sawbuck if you had it when you had it. You could eat there, sleep there; you could receive your 'phone calls—call up lawyers.

"If you were 'in' (under arrest) the lawyer knew the that mob boys were good. He'd spring a writ for you or do anything for you and collect afterwards because he knew where to find you and that you'd pay if you were of the mob. If you didn't have it the boys would take up a collection for you for springing a writ anyway. McConnell was the lawyer. We all had one lawyer who would beat any case for us, could do anything for us. He beat one case for us like an angel. I'll tell you about it later. I suppose I have spent $3,000 or $4,000 for lawyers between 1927 and today.

"My biggest raps were suspect for manslaughter in a hit-and-run case, burglary of a cigar store, theft of an auto, shooting through windows of a school in the neighborhood, Mann act (Chicago to Benton Harbor). I have been convicted only once, but I have been held for trial in the county jail several times. Of the last time I was in the county jail just after I was shot in the back while trying to stick up a dope cache—of that time you know. There have been a few times like that.

"In this one conviction I got an 18-months' sentence. It was a Federal case, but my partners got nothing, were never found out, and I got St. Charles* even though I was 17 years old then and had had long experience as a thief.

*Illinois State Training Schools for Boys, at St. Charles. —Eds.

Twice Twenty Years at Hull-House

Paul Kellogg

The Hull-House residents, ever conscious of their pioneering position in the social settlement movement and always aware of the significance of their own accomplishments, loved to celebrate the anniversaries of the founding of the settlement. But when twenty years at Hull-House became forty years, the celebration—as usual a year late—found the country in the depth of the depression, with the residents and former residents no longer confident that the settlement movement held the answer to the nation's problems. Thus the party took on the nature of nostalgic reminiscences of the good old days. There was, of course, much to be proud of and a great deal to look back upon. Paul Kellogg (1879–1958), editor of The Survey *(the principal journal of social work) and longtime friend of Hull-House, captured the mood of the occasion. Kellogg also tried to look bravely toward the future, but in 1930 it was obviously more fun to look back. [Paul Kellogg, "Twice Twenty Years at Hull-House,"* Survey *(June 15, 1930), 265–267.]*

The premiers of Canada and Great Britain sent messages. They had themselves known the shelter of Hull-House. Old residents and friends turned out in force—our foremost American philosopher for example, the upbuilder of Sears-Roebuck and the ranking American expert in occupational diseases, the president of the General Electric Company, and the first chief of the Children's Bureau, the editor of Collier's and the pioneer of child labor reform,* a galaxy of men and women of all vocations, all faiths, all parts of the country. And for three days they held holiday with the people of Halsted Street with the zest of a college reunion and something beside.

But the picture I took away in my memory was one which has since been spread by press and screen throughout the country—of Jane Addams and three of her small neighbors as they sat at the end of the Hull-House dining room. One small child was Mexican, another Jewish, the third Italian, and without premeditation or grooming they had been whisked over from one of the children's rooms when the talkie people arrived with their cameras, their reproducing apparatus, and their glaring lights. Miss Addams was asked to speak 200 words; but that brief commission ran into an hour or more, because of the delays and finesse of this new method for recording current history. And those children—did they get tired and fret and wriggle? Quite the contrary. She made it a game for them. They played it with a pastmaster who meets the spirit of youth on its own ground, as she has met the vicissitudes of city streets and become our great interpreter of the common life. They might have been in a garden, talking of cockleshells and pretty maids all in a row. For Hull-House and its mistress are something new and vibrant in those corridors of time long given over to quiescent saints in their niches and dour sages in their retreats.

Hull-House was established in September, 1889, but the fortieth anniversary was observed in conjunction with the annual spring exhibit in early May. While the year has been in process, Miss Addams has been writing the chapters of her Second Twenty Years at Hull-House. . . .

The spring exhibits afforded a colorful setting for the anniversary. The proverbial joyous echoes of the boys' club and gymnasium were matched by the quiet nursery school in the Mary Crane building, where the advances in nutrition, education, psychology, and psychiatry interplay uniquely in the work of a preschool clinic. The Harlequins

presented Creatures of Impulse in the Hull-House Theater, a Gypsy orchestra played for the social dance of the Inter-Club Council, the Punch and Judys put on Conrad the Gooseherd, and the Hull-House Players had The Farmer's Wife for their bill. The Music School presented Reineke's Elfrieda and the Swans, and three of its pupils assisted at the Sunday afternoon concert of the Women's Symphony Orchestra. There were etchings, wood blocks and batiks, paintings, drawings, and photographs in the studios; spinning and weaving in the textile room; pottery, the product of the Hull-House kilns; wood-carving, handiwork, embroideries, printing, and other going exhibits that emphasized the cultural overture to life which has been such a marked development of neighborhood work in recent years and which Hull-House long ago pioneered. The Coffee House, the octagon room in the original building, the quadrangle, the corridors were overrun with the throngs of neighborhood folk and guests, and every nook and corner yielded up its stories. There was supper for old residents Saturday night and breakfast Sunday at the Bowen Country Club, where the shaded lawns and deep ravines of the old lake bluffs have healed the bruises of many hard-pressed city dwellers and where Mrs. Bowen was at her hospitable best.

The celebration started with an afternoon meeting, under the auspices of the Chicago Federation of Settlements, where Graham Taylor† of Chicago Commons told of those early impulses which reached back to the realization that culture is an obligation, education a debt which those who have had leisure to learn owe to their generation.

Saturday evening came the formal meeting with Miss Addams presiding at Bowen Hall, and deftly foiling the attempts of one speaker or another to drift into "panegyrics." But it was all so unpretentious, so genuine, so filled with the unspoiled spirit of neighborliness which has characterized the Hull-House group from the beginning, that "formal" is a misnomer. Miss Addams countered the applause that greeted her entrance by spending the first few moments singling out old-timers in the audience and beckoning them to

*In order, Mackenzie King, Ramsay MacDonald, John Dewey, Julius Rosenwald, Dr. Alice Hamilton, Gerard Swope, Julia Lathrop, William L. Chenery, and Florence Kelley.—Eds.

†In 1884, Graham Taylor (1851–1938) founded Chicago Commons, a settlement not far from Hull-House. He worked with Hull-House residents in many reform campaigns.—Eds.

Indians at Hull-House? One of the boys' clubs.

come to the platform. John Dewey was the first speaker, member of the first board of trustees, and in introducing him Miss Addams explained its make-up. There were women of sentiment, afraid they were going to be sentimental and so tending to be hard-boiled; and there were hard-headed business men, afraid they were going to be hard-boiled and so tending to be sentimental. No wonder she had welcomed a philosopher as a lubricant; and Dr. Dewey retorted in kind by saying their responsibilities were simple—to say to Miss Addams, what her friends have always said, "You are all right; go ahead."

"But Dr. Dewey has forgotten how—" broke in the chairman.

"Nevertheless, whether we said it or not," said the author of Experience and Nature, "you did go ahead and if you would see the results, look around you." And then he went on to tell how Hull-House had become an institution—without becoming institutionalized. He liked to think of it as a way of living—a companionship that had extended from the neighborhood to the world. It was not founded to do the neighborhood good. It had done that—but that was not its object; rather its

genius lay in its essential human contacts, its give and take. "In these days of criticism of democracy as a political institution," he said, "Miss Addams has reminded us that democracy is not a form but a way of living together and working together. I doubt if any other one agency can be found which has touched so many people and brought to them a conception of the real meaning of the spirit of the common life."

Now Dr. Dewey was the first of a long string of speakers who had nine minutes apiece into which to crush the import of four decades. There is no space to set down the pith of what they said: how Julia Lathrop told of that awful winter of unemployment following the World's Fair, and the night the horse stables burned. "Everything is valuable for what it creates and hands on," she said. "What Miss Addams and Hull-House have achieved that is new is that they have woven human sympathy with the scientific method." How William L. Chenery* traced social legislation from its roots in neighborly contact. How Dr. Al-

*William Ludlow Chenery (1884–1970), journalist, editor of *Collier's Weekly*, 1925–1943.—Eds.

ice Hamilton acknowledged the debt of the industrial hygienist. ''Hull-House gave me my method.'' How Gerard Swope acknowledged that of the business executive. ''I came here thirty-four years ago after working in a factory and studying in a school of engineering; but knew absolutely nothing of what employment meant in terms of human beings. Hull-House gave me that insight.'' How Mary Kenney O'Sullivan, state factory inspector of Massachusetts, told of her early encounter as a working-girl with Miss Addams, the first person outside her class not only to understand but to stand ready to do something about it. There were others who carried the arc of settlement interests through its full range.

But if there was one thing more than another that this anniversary revealed, as in a pageant, it was the extraordinary group of women associated with Hull-House and their contribution to American life. Warm greetings were sent to Ellen Gates Starr, who with Miss Addams took up residence on Halsted Street in '89, and who was prevented by illness from being present. There was instant applause when Mrs. Bowen cited the thirty-eight years of disinterested service of Mary Rozet Smith as there was when mention was made of the three Hull-House women who have served under the League of Nations—Julia Lathrop, Dr. Hamilton, and Grace Abbott, chief of the Children's Bureau. There were ripples of applause on Friday when Mary McDowell* of the University of Chicago Settlement called Hull-House the Mother House—''It belongs to all of us''—and when Saturday evening, Mrs. Florence Kelley, secretary of the National Consumers' League, ran true to form in her challenge to resist current attacks in the federal Children's Bureau. She was a resident at Hull-House in the '90's when she was made the first woman factory inspector in the United States.

I can see four of them as they stood together, Miss Addams in grey—serene, dauntless; Miss Lathrop in bonnet and cape which the profane called Dunkard but which could not extinguish the parry and thrust of her wit; Mrs. Kelley, alight with the resurgent flame of her zeal; Miss McDowell, palm-leaf fan in hand, and with a crest of cornflowers on her hat, and that engaging smile that has broached a hundred insurgencies. Was there ever their like as a team? By what rare stroke of fortune were they brought together in the days when Chicago was a great focus of our mounting industrialism and when if ever there was need for that rare combination of insight, innovation, and group leadership which has characterized Hull-House and the settlement movement? They have taken risks of ill health and strain, have given their strength and their courage open-handedly. Witness Miss Addams' valiance for peace and what it cost her.

Perhaps their very endurance and the span of their service has given color to the notion in some quarters that such neighborhood work must lapse with their generation. Ten years ago it was frequently said that the settlements were back numbers. Time in its swift pacings has outflanked such forecasts. In the decade since, for one settlement which has dropped out a score of modern neighborhood houses, equipped as never before for their organic tasks, have been reared in American cities on foundations laid by the pioneers. Young leaders have joined their ranks. Objectives have changed and moved forward with the years. Decentralized as they are, no social agencies show greater contrasts. But the old blend of intuition and instigative energy is there. The earlier achievements have in themselves unfolded new opportunities.

Such an anniversary affords occasion for gauging this trend, with *time* itself as a unit for measurement. For example, during the forty years of the settlement movement, we have made marked gains in overcoming preventable diseases. The settlements have played a role in this process, beginning with the early campaigns against the sweatshops, and for better housing, for nursing (as at Henry Street†), for advances all along the line of improved living conditions. As result of scientific discoveries, and health measures which applied them, during these decades to which the settlement has thus contributed its early spirit of inquiry and ministration, we are lengthening the span of the effective years of human beings. We have more time. What to do with those years? How

---

*Mary McDowell (1854–1936), an early Hull-House volunteer, became the head of the University of Chicago Settlement, 1894–1929.—Eds.

†The Henry Street Settlement was founded in New York City in 1893 by Lillian Wald.—Eds.

to enable grown men and women to keep abreast of their changing world? In the new epoch the settlements are helping find an answer as educational centers for grown men and women. Moreover, go to California, the one American state with a state-wide scheme for adult education, and the leaders will tell you they drew their inspiration originally from the early settlement work with immigrants.

With child labor laws and modern schooling we are prolonging American childhood—conserving the most precious time of all—and here again the settlements have been at the fore in our movements to these ends. For one thing, we owe them the United States Children's Bureau. And again, with the new epoch, the settlement is foraging. Those prolonged years of childhood unfold talents which would have been crushed and

cramped under the old conditions. The music rooms, studios, and workshops of the settlements are so many trellises up which these aptitudes may climb. Their demonstrations help promote kindred developments throughout the schools.

With the accident hazard in industry countered in the last twenty-five years by the advances in safety engineering and the spread of compensation laws, we are now taking up the hazard to all-year-round households on part-year incomes. Again the settlements are pioneering, a committee of the National Federation carrying forward during the last eighteen months our first appraisal of the human consequences of irregular employment. Neighborhood workers have long known what broken working-time and broken pay mean in terms of misery; their study will help arouse the

Long-time Hull-House residents on the 40th anniversary of the settlement. Seated, left to right: Dr. Alice Hamilton, Rose Gyles, Jane Addams, Enella Benedict, and Edith de Nancrede. Standing, left to right: Jessie Binford, Rachelle Yarros, Esther Kohn, Victor Yarros, Ethel Dewey, George Hooker, and Adena Miller Rich.

public conscience and break through to the imagination of the business world with the realization
that wage-earning-time is money and that we have
been wasting it outrageously.

Nevertheless, with reduction of hours of
work, with increased prosperity, we have leisure
such as no people in the world has ever had, but
we know less about what to do with it. The settlements have ever been a force in persuading the
public to humanize the conditions of industry—to
grapple with the evils of overwork. In this new epoch they are, in a special sense, harbingers of the
new time. In their recreational and cultural activities they are breaking new roads for the new freedom which goes with a leisured democracy. They
see this new freed time for what it is—a great lode
of opportunity. They are experimenting in its joyous use.

William Bolitho, in his book, Twelve Against
the Gods, has a chapter on Mahomet as the adven-
turer of the East. He points out that in instituting
the new religion, the prophet was baffled by the
fact that the Jew had the horn, the Christian the
bell, to call his co-religionists to worship. So in his
dilemma he turned to his black follower who had
a rich baritone voice, and hence the first muezzin.
Horn and bell and muezzin—they were not only
calls to worship. They marked time; people told it
by them through the centuries. Even unto Chicago. I have seen a desert dance go forward for
three days in a basement in Pittsburgh. No doubt
Halsted Street with its polyglot population has
often matched it. Our synagogues cherish the old
ram's horn of the Hebrew ritual. Certain it is that
our American urban centers have rung to the bells
of the Christian churches of all denominations.

But in a way modern Chicago—if by that we
mean the Chicago of the stockyards and the steel
mills and the great manufacturing plants—grew
up to the strident tones of another challenge to
time and action—the whistles of industrialism,
which released energies, organized great team
plays of production, but have been impatient and
often ruthless in their demands on household and
community.

Now we enter a new day—a day of the radio
that starts us off with setting-up exercises in the
morning and lays us down with bed-time stories.
It is more than a contrivance—it is a symbol of
applied science brought to the household as well

as the factory, of telescoped distance, of swifter
tempo. Its antennae spread over the housetops of
Halsted Street and of every home district of Chicago; of every American city. It is the sign of the
new, democratized leisure-time—with the touch
of art as never before in our means for communication among men.

The settlement served its times in the gruelling
years of development when America sought to humanize work. It has more of that service to perform in our half-achieved industrial civilization.
Its spiritual contributions of protest and affirma-
tion are not over. But we are on the threshold of a
new time—of greater leisure, more adventurous
culture—and Hull-House and the other settlements of America are here to help us to enter upon
them.

Hull-House in 1932

Edmund Wilson

*The depression that followed the stock market
crash in 1929 got a head start in neighborhoods
like those near Hull-House. Unemployment began
to increase long before the speculative bubble
burst, and the ordinary workingmen and their
families, who had never really profited from the
prosperity of the twenties, faced starvation and
despair by 1932. Hull-House, long concerned with
reform, became little more than a relief agency
during the dark years after 1929. The settlement
residents raised emergency funds for those who
could not qualify for regular charity; they loaned
rent money to those faced with eviction; they provided free milk for infants and lunch money for
schoolchildren. Over 100,000 families appealed
to the settlement for food during the first two
months of 1932. To meet this demand the residents
spent much of their time collecting money, buying
food wholesale, and distributing it to those in
need; but there was never enough to go around.
Hull-House also sponsored special art classes,
lectures, and discussions for the unemployed, but
they were no substitute for a job and enough to eat.
Edmund Wilson (1895–1972), novelist, essay-*

ist, poet, and already in 1932 on his way to becoming the nation's leading literary critic, here captures some of the hopelessness and despair in Chicago at the depth of the depression. [Edmund Wilson, The American Earthquake (Garden City, 1958), 447–464.]

The landscape has turned gray: the snow-fields gray like newspaper, the sky gray like paste-board—then darkness; just a crack of gray, distinct as a break in a boiler, that separates darkening clouds—a black fortress with one smokestack: the Northern Indiana Public Utility Company—darkness, with light at long intervals—a sudden street with lighted stores and streetcars—then the darkness again: dim front of a frame house, dim signboards—a red electric globe on a barber's pole—bridges in the blackness, a shore?—black factories—long streets, with rows of lights that stretch away into darkness—a large blunt tower embroidered in coarse beadwork of red, green, and gold lights—then the endless succession of cars speeding along the dark lake-front, with the lights at shorter intervals now—then a thing like a red-hot electric toaster as big as an office building, which turns out to be one of the features of next summer's World Fair.*

But mostly black midland darkness. Chicago is one of the darkest of great cities. In the morning, the winter sun does not seem to give any light: it leaves the streets dull. It is more like a forge which has just been started up, with its fires just burning red, in an atmosphere darkened by coalfumes. All the world seems made of gray fog—gray fog and white smoke—the great square white-and-gray buildings seem to have been pressed out of the saturated atmosphere. The smooth asphalt of the lake-side road seems solidified polished smoke. The lake itself, in the dawn, is of a strange stagnant substance like pearl that is becoming faintly liquid and luminous—opaque like everything else but more sensitive than asphalt or stone. The Merchandise Mart—the *biggest* building in the world, as the Empire State Building is the *highest*—is no tower, in the fog, but a mountain, to brood upon whose cubic content is to be amazed, desolated,

*A Century of Progress Exposition, 1933 and 1934.—Eds.

stunned. The Chicago River, dull green, itself a work of engineering, runs backward along its original course, buckled with black iron bridges, which unclose, one after the other, each in two short fragments, as a tug drags car-barges under them, like the peristaltic movement of the stomach pushing a tough piece of food along. The sun for a time half-reveals these scenes, but its energies are only brief. The afternoon has scarcely established itself as an identifiable phenomenon when light succumbs to dullness, and the day lapses back into dark. The buildings seem mounds of soft darkness caked and carved out of swamp-mud and rubber-stamped here and there with red neon signs. A good many of the streets, one finds, aside from the thoroughfares, are dimly lighted or not at all; and even those that are adequately lighted lose themselves in blurred vistas of coal-smoke.

In that dull air, among those long low straight streets—the deadened civilization of industry, where people are kept just alive enough to see that the machines are running—the almost neutral brick walls of Hull-House have themselves an industrial plainness. The old big square high-windowed mansion of earlier family grandeur, embedded in the dormitories, eating halls, gymnasiums, nurseries, and laundries that today pack a city block, has been chastened as well as expanded: it has something of both the monastery and the factory. The high Victorian rooms that open into one another through enormous arched and corniced doorways, though they still contain mahogany tables, sofas, and faded Turkish rugs, are in general scantily and serviceably furnished. The white woodwork and the marble fireplace have been painted a sort of neutral drab green, so that the use of the house may not soil them. In the little polygon room, in which one imagines hanging pots of ferns and a comfortable window-seat, one sees a typewriter and a set of colored charts showing the shift of nationalities around Hull-House. Yet one finds also traces of a cult of art: copies of paintings and statues, a fragment of a Greek frieze. Behind the glass doors of bookcases are nineteenth-century sets of Ruskin and Augustus Hare's *Walks in Rome*. The hallway is lined with photographs of residents and friends of the house; and on the walls of the polygon room hang the patron saints and heroes of Hull-House: Kropotkin and Catherine Breshkovsky, Arnold Toynbee and Jacob Riis*—and Jane Addams's father. Over the desk by the front door is a picture of Jane Addams herself, in a big-sleeved and high-collared gown of the nineties, a young woman, slender and winning and almost like an illustration for some old serial by William Dean Howells or Mrs. Burton Harrison in the *Century Magazine*.

A little girl with curvature of the spine, whose mother had died when she was a baby, she abjectly admired her father, a man of consequence in frontier Illinois, a friend of Lincoln and a member of the state legislature, who had a flour mill and a lumber mill on his place. Whenever there were strangers at Sunday school, she would try to walk out with her uncle so that her father should not be disgraced by people's knowing that such a fine man had a daughter with a crooked spine. When he took her one day to a mill which was surrounded by horrid little houses and explained to her, in answer to her questions, that the reason people lived in such houses was that they couldn't afford anything better, she told her father that, when she grew up, she should herself continue to live in a big house but that it should stand among the houses of poor people.

At college, in the late seventies, she belonged to a group of girls who vowed before they parted for their summer vacation that each would have read the whole of Gibbon before they met again in the fall. In a Greek oration she delivered, Bellerophon figured as the Idealism which alone could slay the Chimera of Social Evils; and for her graduation essay she chose Cassandra, doomed "always to be in the right and always disbelieved and rejected." She heard rumors of the doctrines of Darwin and borrowed scientific books from a brother-in-law who had studied medicine in Germany; and she resisted with invincible stubbornness the pressure brought to bear by her teachers to make her go into the missionary field. The year that she graduated from college, she inherited a part of her father's estate and gave the college a thousand dollars to spend on a scientific library.

*Catherine Breshkovsky (1844–1934), known as the "Grandmother of the Russian Revolution"; Arnold Toynbee (1852–1883), English sociologist and economist for whom Toynbee Hall, London, was named; Jacob Riis (1849–1914), journalist who helped popularize the plight of the poor.—Eds.

She herself went to medical school; but her spinal trouble got worse, and she had to stop. She spent six months strapped to a bed. This gave her a lot of time for reading, with no uncomfortable feeling that she ought to be doing something else, and she was very glad to have it; but when she was able to get about again, she felt dreadfully fatigued and depressed. She tried Europe; but one day, in London, she went out for a bus-ride in the East End. As she looked down on the misery and squalor, she remembered De Quincey's *Vision of Sudden Death:* how, when confronted with a pair of lovers about to be run over by the mail coach in which he was traveling, he had found himself powerless to warn them till he had remembered the exact lines in the *Iliad* which describe the shout of Achilles; and she was suddenly filled with disgust for the artificial middle-class culture upon which she had been trying to nourish herself and which had equipped her to meet this horror with nothing but a literary allusion, and that derived from an opium-eater as far removed from life as herself.

What was the good of enjoying German operas and the pictures in Italian galleries? In the interval between two trips to Europe, she visited a Western farm on which she held a mortgage—it was one of the American investments which made her traveling possible. She found there a woman and her children almost starved by the drought and attempting to raise money on a promissory note for which she could offer as collateral nothing but a penful of pigs. The pigs were starved, too, and horrible: one was being eaten by the others, all hunched up and crowded together.

She gave the mortgages up and went back to Europe again, and there she saw some striking match-girls suffering from phossy jaw. She decided to return to Chicago and to found a settlement house—there had never yet been one in America. The "subjective necessity" for settlement work she analyzes as follows: "first, the desire to interpret democracy in social terms; secondly, the impulse beating at the very source of our lives, urging us to aid in the race progress; and thirdly, the Christian movement toward humanitarianism." But she did not exclude "the desire for a new form of social success due to the nicety of imagination, which refuses worldly pleasures unmixed with the joys of self-sacrifice" and "a love of approbation so vast that it is not content with the treble clapping of delicate hands, but wishes also to hear the bass notes from toughened palms.'' Her father had impressed upon her early that scrupulous mental integrity, the unwillingness to make pretenses which one knew inside one did not live up to, was practically the whole of morality.

In South Halsted Street in Chicago, where there were Italians, Germans, Russians and Jews, she tried to help relieve their difficulties; to teach English to those who had immigrated as well as to give the young generation some idea of the European tradition from which they had been cut off. But this led to looking into their living conditions; and the problems of their living conditions led to the industrial system. When it was a question of children of four spending their whole day indoors pulling out basting threads or pasting labels on boxes, she found that she felt it her duty to get some labor legislation put through. She got one of the Hull-House residents appointed factory inspector.

At the time of the Pullman strike in 1894, Miss Addams was surprised and dismayed to find Chicago split up into two fiercely antagonistic camps. She had known Mr. Pullman and had been impressed by the excellence of his intentions in building a model town for his employees. She tried to maintain relations with both camps; but by the time the strike was over, it turned out the she and Pullman were on different sides of the fence, and that he was highly indignant with her. The Socialist and other radicals tried to convince her that she ought to be one of them; but, though she carefully looked up to socialism, she resisted them as she had the teachers who had tried to make her become a missionary. She could not bind herself to parties and principles: what she did had to be done independently, on a basis of day-by-day experience. And she had still so vivid an impression of the classless democracy of the Western frontier that it was difficult for her to imagine a general class conflict in the United States.

Yet the winter after the World's Fair Chicago was full of people left stranded with no employment; and she was assailed by a new sense of shame at being comfortable in the midst of misery. The activities carried on at Hull-House now began to seem to her futile; its philanthropy a specious way of reconciling one's own conscience to the social injustice from which one profited. She remembered that the effect on Tolstoy of a similar period of suffering in Moscow had been to make him degrade his own standard of living to that of the poor themselves. She was again incapacitated by a serious illness, but got well and decided to travel to Russia and discuss the problem with Tolstoy himself.

Miss Addams found the great moralist working in the hayfields with the peasants and eating their black bread and porridge, while the Countess with her children and their governess had a regular upper-class dinner. He pulled out one of Miss Addams' big sleeves and said that there was enough material in it to make a frock for a little girl; and he asked whether she did not find ''such a dress'' a ''barrier to the people.'' She tried to explain that, since big sleeves were the fashion, the working girls in Chicago were wearing even bigger ones than hers, and that you could hardly dress like a peasant on South Halsted Street, since the peasants there wore middle-class clothes. But she was abashed when he asked her who ''fed'' her and how she got her ''shelter,'' and she had to confess that her income was derived from a large farm a hundred miles away from Chicago. ''So you are an absentee landlord?'' he said scathingly. ''Do you think you will help the people more by adding yourself to the crowded city than you would by tilling your own soil?''

She went away feeling humbled, and, before she arrived at Bayreuth and could allow herself to enjoy the *Ring,* she resolved that when she got back to Hull-House, she would spend two hours every day in the bakery. Yet as soon as she was actually at home again and found the piles of correspondence and the people waiting to see her, she decided that this and not baking was the proper work of her life, and she forgot her Tolstoyan scruples.

Her efforts for labor legislation embittered the manufacturers against her; her attempts to get garbage and dead animals that had been left in the street removed embroiled her with the political machine: garbage-collecting was a racket, and the rackets seemed to go right on up. She was astonished to find that her opposition to reëlecting a corrupt alderman roused both pulpit and press against her. When Czolgosz assassinated Mc-

Kinley, the editor of an anarchist paper was arrested and held incommunicado, not allowed to see even a lawyer. She protested, with the result that Hull-House was denounced as a hotbed of anarchy. When the agents of the Tsar succeeded in making Gorky a pariah in America by circulating the news that he and his companion were not properly married, she asked a Chicago paper to print an article in his defense and found that she was at once accused of being an immoral woman herself by interests that wanted to get her off the school board.

At last, when, in 1900, she saw the Passion Play at Oberammergau, it struck her for the first time that the real enemy of Jesus was the money power. The young agitator had antagonized the merchants by interfering with their trade in the temple, and hence the Pharisees, whose racket depended on the temple, too. Church and State had stood solid with the Pharisees; and the money power had bribed Judas to betray him.

When she avocated peace at the time of the war, she found that President Wilson bowed her out and that she was presently being trailed by detectives. And then, when the war was over, people were more intolerant than ever.

Hull-House had always stood for tolerance: all the parties and all the faiths had found asylum there and lived pretty harmoniously together. And it still stands planted with a proud irrelevance in the midst of those long dark streets—where its residents occasionally get beaten and robbed—only a few blocks from a corner made famous by a succession of gang murders. With its strong walls, its enclosed staircased courts, and a power plant of its own, it stands like a medieval château protected by a moat and portcullis.

Inside there is peace and a sort of sanctity. Jane Addams at seventy-two still dominates her big house among the little ones—though she is supposed to have been forbidden by the doctors to spend more than four hours a day there—with her singular combination of the authority of a great lady and the humility of a saint. In the large refectory-like dining room with its copper and brass and bare brick, the quick glances of the "seeing eye" which fascinated young women in the nineties and excited them to go in for settlement work—that glance at once penetrating and shy—still lights its responses around her table. Through her vitality, Hull-House still lives—the expression of both pride and humility: the pride of a moral vision which cannot accept as its habitat any one of the little worlds of social and intellectual groupings; the humility of a spirit which, seeing so far, sees beyond itself, too, and feels itself lost amid the same uncertainties, thwarted by the same cross-purposes, as all of those struggling others.

All around the social workers of Hull-House there today stretches a sea of misery more appalling even than that which discouraged Miss Addams in the nineties. This winter even those families who had managed to hang on by their savings and earnings have been forced to apply for relief.

A relief worker's cross-section of an industrial suburb shows the sinking of the standard of living. The people here are mostly Poles. Every pressure has been brought to bear on them to induce them to spend their money on motor-cars, radios, over-stuffed furniture, and other unattractive luxuries; and they are caught now between two worlds, with no way of living comfortably in either. The most urgent problem, however, is how to be sure of living at all.

In one house, a girl of seventeen is interpreter for her mother, in whom the girl's stocky figure has expanded to enormous amorphous bulk, and she changes not only her language but her expression and gestures, her personality, in passing from English to Polish. She had till lately, at $2 a week, been doing all the housework for a real-estate man; but she decided he was imposing on her and quit. She is handsome and evidently high-spirited—Americanized during the whoopee period. Her brother had had a job on the conveyer at a book-bindery; but, due to a mechanical improvement, this job no longer exists: the boy has been laid off, with no prospect of reëmployment. The girl takes us up from the downstairs kitchen, where the family mostly live, and shows you the little-used floor above, which is papered with big blue, pink, and magenta blossoms and furnished with all the things that the salesmen of the boom have sold them: a victrola and wadded chairs and couches, spotted with a pattern of oranges, which nobody seems ever to have sat in. On the walls, as in all these houses, exhibited in ornate gold frames, hang Slavic saints and Madonnas, bristling with spiky gold crowns, Byzantine embroidery, and Polish inscriptions.

Elsewhere an old man is dying of a tumor, with no heat in the house, on a cold day. His pale bones of arms lie crooked like bent pins; nothing is heard in the house but his gasping. His old wife, her sharp Polish nose sticking out from under a bonnet-like cap, stands beside him, as silent as a ghost. Their granddaughter, who is married and wears well-fitting American street-clothes—an American middle-class woman, but today as badly off as they are—has just been to the relief station for coal.

In another place, a family of five have three small rooms in a basement, and they have sunk below any standard: the father grinningly and glaringly drunk in the middle of the morning, the mother stunned and discouraged by her struggle against poverty and filth. They live around the stove with their small dirty children, in the close sweetish sickish smell of cooking and boiling clothes. Where they sleep on two narrow cots, the bedclothes are old twisted gray rags that have not even been smoothed out flat. They do not know very much English, and they cannot explain to the relief worker what they have done about relief and insurance; they do not understand, themselves. All they know is that they are living in that dirty hole, from which they have not yet been expelled, and where the man, with a little liquor in him, can imagine himself the shrewd and sound father of a family, with the situation well under control. In another basement, however, the young husband has carpentered and painted the big cellar room which, with a tiny bedroom, is all they have, so that it almost resembles a human dwelling. He used to work for the Fruit-Growers' Express, but has been laid off a long time. The stout blond girl to whom he is married has had to be on her feet all day and, from the strain on her heart, has just had a collapse. They do not have any children, but they keep a canary in a cage. The young wife in another household has put kewpie dolls around in an otherwise bare apartment, and has made blue curtains for the cot in which her two children sleep. She and her husband are very fond of one another and very fond of the children. They are the kind of people who do not like to ask for relief, and they have put it off as long as they could, with the result

that, though goodlooking and youthful, they are now pale and thin with undernourishment.

A pink clear-eyed innocent-eyed woman, alone in an immaculately kept kitchen, all white oilcloth and green-and-white linoleum and with the latest thing in big gleaming gas-ranges, flushes at the relief worker's questions. She is going to have a baby and has applied for money to pay the midwife. The relief worker offers her a doctor but she is used to having the midwife. An elderly couple from Zurich are living in an apartment equally immaculate, though far less completely equipped, amid blue-and-green chromolithographs of Swiss waterfalls and mountains and lakes. The woman is cooking a few slivers of onions on a tiny coal-stove, which was intended primarily for heat. The husband is out on the railroad tracks picking up pieces of coal in order to keep it going. The woman suddenly begins to cry as she is answering the relief worker's queries, then as suddenly stops. The husband, a little smiling man with Kaiser Wilhelm mustaches, comes back with a few pieces of coal: the railroad detectives have chased him away. He was formerly an industrial chemist and has recently turned his ingenuity to inventing little gambling toys. One of them, he says, he has a fair prospect of selling: you shoot a marble which drops into a hole and knocks up a little tin flap; "Swiss Navy" counts lowest and "America" a hundred per cent. In another place, the bookbinder who has lost his job through a technological improvement has a fellow in the musical field—a young violinist whose profession has been partly abolished by the talkies.

Above the straight criss-cross streets the small houses of brick and gray boards, the newer little two-story Noah's Arks, prick the sharp Roman Catholic spire and the bulbs of the Orthodox Church.

The single men are driven to flophouses. During the last year—September 30, 1931–September 30, 1932—50,000 have registered at the clearing house. Those who are not residents of Chicago are ordered to leave the city: if they got there by paying their fare, they are given a half-fare which will take them home. Others are sent to the asylum, the poorhouse, the veterans' home; referred to the blind pension, the juvenile court. About 500 men a month are disposed of in this way. The Oak Forest poorhouse, called "the

Graveyard,'' has people sleeping in the corridors and turned 19,000 away last year. The rest are directed to the shelters, where they get two meals a day and a bed.

Among the high whitewashed walls of an obsolete furniture factory, the soiled yellow plaster and the scrawled and punctured blackboards of an old public school, the scraped-out offices and pompous paneling of a ghastly old disused courthouse; on the floors befouled with spittle, in the peppery-sweetish stink of food cooking, sulphur fumigation, bug exterminators, rank urinals doctored with creosote—ingredients of the general fetor that more or less prominently figure as one goes from floor to floor, from room to room, but all fuse in the predominant odor of stagnant and huddled humanity—these men eat their chicken-feed and slum amid the deafening clanking of trays and dump the slops in g.i. cans; wait for prize-fights or movies of Tarzan (provided to keep them out of the hands of the Communists or from holding meetings themselves) in so-called ''recreation halls,'' on the walls of which they have chalked up ''Hoover's Hotel''—big bare chambers smothered with smoke, strewn with newspapers like vacant lots, smeared like the pavements with phlegm. Here they sit in the lecture seats, squat on the steps of the platform, stretch out on the floor on old papers. In one room a great wall-legend reminds them: ''The Blood of God Can Make the Vilest Clean,'' and they get routed to mess through a prayer meeting. When they come back to the recreation hall, they discover that a cheerful waltz has served merely as a bait to draw them to the harangue by an old Cicero policeman who says that he has been saved. They are obliged to send their clothes to be fumigated, and, if they are wet with the winter rain, ruined. They herd into steaming showers, the young men still building some flesh on straight frames, the old with flat chests, skinny arms and round sagging bellies; and they flop at last on the army cots or in the bunks in double tiers, where the windows which are shut to keep out the cold keep in the sour smell—men in slit union suits and holey socks, men tattooed with fancy pictures or the emblems of some service they have left—resting their bunioned feet taken out of flattened shoes or flat arches wound around with adhesive tape—lying with newspapers for pillows, their arms behind their heads or with a sheet pulled over their faces or wrapped up in blankets, rigid on their backs, their skin stretched tight over their jawbones so that these look like the jaws of the dead.

There is a clinic which does what it can to head off venereal diseases. There is also a great deal of t.b., to which the Negroes have a fatal susceptibility; and in one shelter spinal meningitis got out of hand for a while and broke nine backs on its rack. Another common complaint of the flophouses is the poisoning that results from drinking a dilution of wood alcohol which the inmates buy for fifteen cents a pint, which looks and tastes, as somebody says, like a mixture of benzine, kerosene and milk, and which usually lands them in the infirmary or the psychopathic ward. And yet one man, given his choice between his bottle and admission to the shelter, refused to give up the bottle: he preferred to spend the night in the cold rather than surrender his only support in a life so aimless and hopeless. In the Salvation Army shelter, they will not take in steady drinkers, but the others do the best they can with them. In one, there is a hobbling cripple who comes in drunk every night. ''I wouldn't be surprised,'' says the manager, ''if a hearse drove up and a dead man got up and walked out and asked for a flop.'' One man turned up ''lousy as a pet coon—so lousy nobody would go near-um and they put-um in the stable with the horse for the night, and the horse tried to get away. The next morning they gave-um a shower and scrubbed-um with a long-handled brush.'' But most of the cases in the infirmaries—from exhaustion to bad kidneys and body sores—come down to the same basic disease: starvation.

Razor-slashings and shootings bring in other patients—though the prospect of a day of work a week, with its brief liberation from the shelters, is said to have diminished these. The bad characters are sent to the bull-pens in the basement, where, crowded together, in fetid air, they sleep on hard benches with their coats under their heads. Newcomers for whom there is no room have to be dumped down among them.

Yet Chicago has apparently been particularly efficient in providing and running these shelters. At best, it is not unlike the life of barracks—but without the common work and purpose which give a certain momentum to even a dull campaign. In the shelters, there is nothing to coöperate on and nothing to look forward to, no developments, no chance of success. The old man is ending his life without a home and with no hope of one; the wage-earner who has hitherto been self-dependent now finds himself dropped down among casuals and gradually acquires their attitude; the young man who comes to maturity during the workless period of the depression never learns the habit of work. (There are few actual hoboes here: the hobo can do better by begging or stealing.)

In so far as they are unable to adapt themselves, they must live under a continual oppression of fear or guilt or despair. One sees among them faces that are shocking in their contrast to their environment here: men who look as if they had never had a day's ill health or done a day's careless work in their lives. Now they jump at the opportunity of spending a day a week clearing the rubbish off vacant lots or cleaning the streets underneath the Loop tracks. This is the only thing that stands between them and that complete loss of independence which can obliterate personality itself—which degrades them to the primal dismal undifferentiated city grayness, depriving them even of the glow of life that has formerly set them off from the fog and the pavements and the sodden old newspapers, rubbing them down to nothing, forcing them out of life.

Yet none of these single-men's shelters produces such an impression of horror as the Angelus Building on South Wabash Avenue, where families of homeless Negroes have taken refuge. This neighborhood was once fairly well-to-do; but at the present time, left behind by the city's growth in other directions, it presents a desolation that is worse than the slums. When the snow in the darkening afternoon has come to seem as dingy as the dusk and the sky as cold and tangible as the snow—as if the neutral general medium of the city were condensing in such a way as to make it hard to move and exist—the houses, interminably scattered along the straight miles of the street, monotonous without being uniform, awkward or cheap attempts at various types of respectable architecture in gray limestone, colorless boards or red brick, all seem—whether inhabited or not—equally abandoned now. The windowless slots of one open into a hollow shell: it has been gutted of even its partitions; the Romanesque prongs of an-

other make it look like a blackened pulled tooth; on the brownstone façade of a third, some distance above the ground, is stuck a pretentious doorway, from under which, like a lower jaw, the flight of front steps has been knocked. And, as a suitable climax to this, the Angelus Building looms blackly on the corner of its block: seven stories, thick with dark windows, caged in a dingy mesh of fire-escapes like mattress-springs on a junk-heap, hunched up, hunchback-proportioned, jam-crammed in its dumbness and darkness with miserable wriggling life.

It was built in 1892 and was once the Ozark Hotel, popular at the time of the old World's Fair. In the dim little entrance hall, the smudged and roughened mosaic, the plaster pattern of molding, the fancy black grill of the elevator, most of it broken off, do not recall former splendor—they are abject, mere chips and shreds of the finery of a section now dead, trodden down into the waste where they lie. There is darkness in the hundred cells: the tenants cannot pay for light; and cold: the heating system no longer works. It is a firetrap which has burned several times—the last time several people were burned to death. And, now, since it is not good for anything else, its owner has turned it over to the Negroes, who flock into the tight-packed apartments and get along there as best they can on such money as they collect from the charities.

There are former domestic servants and porters, former mill-hands and stockyard workers; there are prostitutes and hoodlums next door to respectable former laundresses and Baptist preachers. One veteran of the war, once foreman of the Sunkist Pie Company, now lives in cold and darkness with his widowed mother, even the furniture which he had been buying for $285 the outfit and on which he had paid all but the last installment of $50.20, taken away by the furniture company. For light, they burn kerosene lamps, and for warmth, small coal-stoves and charcoal buckets. The water-closets do not flush, and the water stands in the bathtubs.

The children go to play in the dark halls or along the narrow iron galleries of an abysmal central shaft, which, lighted faintly through glass at the top, is foggy and stifling with coal-smoke like a nightmare of jail or Hell. In the silence of this dreadful shaft, sudden breakages and bangs occur—then all is deathly still again. The two top floors have been stripped by fire and by the tenants' tearing things out to burn or sell: apartments have lost their doors and plumbing pipes lie uncovered. These two floors have been condemned and deserted. Relief workers who have visited the Angelus Building have come away so overwhelmed with horror that they have made efforts to have the whole place condemned—to the piteous distress of the occupants, who consider it an all-right-enough place when you've got nowhere else to go. And where to send these sixty-seven Negro families? Brought to America in the holds of slave-ships and afterwards released from their slavery with the chance of improving their lot, they are now being driven back into the black cavern of the Angelus Building, where differing standards of living, won sometimes by the hard work of generations, are all being reduced to zero.

Those who want to keep clear of the jail-like shelters get along as they can in the streets and huddle at night under the Loop or build shacks on empty lots. On whatever waste-places they are permitted to live, the scabby-looking barnacles appear, knocked together from old tar-paper and tin, old car-bodies, old packing boxes, with old stovepipes leaning askew, amid the blackened weeds in the snow and the bones of old rubbish piles. One "Hooverville" on Harrison Street flies a tattered black rag like the flag of despair.

The inhabitants of these wretched settlements chiefly forage from the city dumps, as do many of those whom charity will not help or who for one reason or another will not go to it or for whom the relief they get is inadequate. There is not a garbage-dump in Chicago which is not diligently haunted by the hungry. Last summer in the hot weather, when the smell was sickening and the flies were thick, there were a hundred people a day coming to one of the dumps, falling on the heap of refuse as soon as the truck had pulled out and digging in it with sticks and hands. They would devour all the pulp that was left on the old slices of watermelon and cantaloupe till the rinds were as thin as paper; and they would take away and wash and cook discarded turnips, onions and potatoes. Meat is a more difficult matter, but they salvage a good deal of that, too. The best is the butcher's meat which has been frozen and has not spoiled. If

they can find only meat that is spoiled, they can sometimes cut out the worst parts, or they scald it and sprinkle it with soda to neutralize the taste and the smell. Fish spoils too quickly, so it is likely to be impossible—though some people have made fish-head soup. Soup has also been made out of chicken claws.

A private incinerator at Thirty-fifth and La Salle Streets, which disposes of the garbage from restaurants and hotels, has been regularly visited by people, in groups of as many as twenty at a time, who pounce upon anything that looks edible before it is thrown into the furnace. The women complained to investigators that the men took an unfair advantage by jumping on the truck before it was unloaded; but a code was eventually established which provided that different sets of people should come at different times every day, so that everybody would be given a chance. Another dump at Thirty-first Street and Cicero Avenue has been the center of a Hooverville of three hundred people.

The family of a laid-off dishwasher lived on food from the dump for two years. They had to cook it on the gas of the people downstairs, since their own had been shut off. Their little girl got ptomaine poisoning. Two veterans of the war, who had been expelled from Washington with the bonus army and made their homes in the fireboxes of an old kiln, were dependent on the dump for some time, though a buddy of theirs found he could do better by panhandling at people's doors. One widow with a child of nine, who had formerly made $18 a week in a factory and who has since been living on $4 a week relief and two or three hours' work a day at fifty cents an hour, has tried to get along without garbage but has had to fall back on it frequently during a period of three years. Another widow, who used to do housework and laundry but who was finally left without any work, fed herself and her fourteen-year-old son on garbage. Before she picked up the meat, she would always take off her glasses so that she would not be able to see the maggots; but it sometimes made the boy so sick to look at this offal and smell it that he could not bring himself to eat. He weighed only eighty-two pounds.

Many people in the Hooverville on Cicero Avenue have been poisoned from eating the garbage. One man ate a can of bad crab-meat thrown away by a chain store, and was later found putrefying.

On the endlessly stretching latitude of West Congress Street—lit only on one side at long intervals by livid low-power lamps—along which huge cubes of buildings are infrequently belted by lighted-up floors and where black and blind ranks of trucks stand posted in front of dark factories, some anonymous hand has chalked up on a wall: "VOTE RED. THE PEOPLE ARE GOOFY."

The Death of Jane Addams

Louise deKoven Bowen

After World War I, because of her commitments to the Women's International League for Peace and Freedom and her declining health, Jane Addams spent less and less time at Hull-House, where the various settlement activities went on without her. But even while she was away, Addams was the unchallenged leader of the settlement. She was both head resident and president of the board of trustees, and—much more—she was the conciliator, the mediator who could settle conflicts and disagreements which inevitably arose among the staff. She was the financial genius who could make a few phone calls to rich friends and rescue the settlement from its ever-increasing financial crisis. Even more, she was the role model, a charismatic figure revered as a patron saint and talked about in hushed tones by the younger residents, though sometimes she was secretly resented.

In a real sense, Jane Addams was Hull-House. And because of her personality and the special aura that surrounded her, the house was run in a personal manner. Addams' goal was a flexible program responsive to the ever-changing needs of her neighbors. She encouraged investigation and creative solutions to problems, and made it possible for individual settlement residents and workers to learn, innovate, and grow in relative safety.

Hull-House was the product of an overpowering personality, and though Jane Addams had casually asked both Grace Abbott and Alice Hamilton to take the reins of leadership if anything happened to her, both had declined. When she died in 1935, no arrangements had been made for the transfer of command. Her death was mourned by thousands, but for Hull-House it caused a major organizational crisis.

Throughout her life Jane Addams suffered from a variety of illnesses and submitted to a number of operations. In Tokyo in 1923, she underwent a mastectomy, and in 1931, at The Johns Hopkins in Baltimore, surgery for an ovarian cyst. In 1926, she suffered her first attack of angina, and for the remainder of her life the threat of heart disease affected her activities. She died immediately following surgery to remove an intestinal blockage caused by cancer. Louise deKoven Bowen wrote the following note for some of Jane Addams' friends who wanted particulars of her last illness. [Esther Kohn Papers, Jane Addams Memorial Collection, University of Illinois at Chicago Circle.]

May 27, 1935.

Jane Addams spent the winter in Phoenix, Arizona. She was extremely well, and devoted most of her time to writing a book on the life of Julia Lathrop which she finished before she returned to Chicago.

While in the West, she had a Degree of LL. D. conferred upon her by the University of California at Berkeley. She returned to Chicago in extremely good health, and soon after went down to Washington to take part in the Twenty-Fifth Anniversary of the International League for Peace and Freedom. She had a very good time there, enjoyed her visit immensely, and came home in excellent spirits.

On the 14th of May she was taken ill, but improved during the following two days. It was then found, however, that an immediate operation was necessary and she went to the Passavant Hospital on the 18th of May. The operation was performed on that day but it was found that she had an incurable disease. On the 20th she sank into unconsciousness, and she died very quietly on the

Jane Addams' funeral in the Hull-House courtyard.

evening of the 21st. May 22nd and 23d Miss Addams lay in state in Bowen Hall at Hull-House. She looked very lovely and very natural, and during the twenty-four hours she was there thousands of people passed through the Hall. The Hull-House Woman's Club formed a guard of honor and stood on either side of the hall, while the older boys and girls in the Clubs with white ribbons tied around their arms acted as ushers and everything was conducted in a most orderly way. She lay in a casket with a loose light blue robe around her, her hair pushed back from her forehead as she always wore it. On either side of the casket were bright colored tulips, so that it looked as though she were resting on a bed of flowers. The hall was opened at five o'clock in the morning, and working men on their way to their jobs came in with lunch boxes in their hands, many of them kneeling on a little stool in front of the casket and saying a prayer. Thousands of people—it is not know exactly how many—passed through the Hall. Little children bearing tiny bouquets laid them upon the casket, while groups of school children, wearing black or white ribbons around their arms, brought floral tokens to lay beside her. The street outside was crowded and thousands of people from all over the city and from her own neighborhood thronged to see her, and say a last goodbye.

There were telegrams in hundreds from all over the world—the President of the United States, the Premiers of England and Canada, the President of Czechoslovakia, and notables from almost every European country and even from the Sandwich Islands, Japan and India. In contrast to these telegrams from all over the world were those from the King of the Hoboes, the Lady Garment Workers' Union, the Cooks', the Waiters', and the Waitresses' Unions and even the Bar Tenders' Union—all sent their expressions of sorrow at her passing. People poured into Hull-House by the thousands before the funeral to say how she had been the inspiration of their lives and how they felt bereft that she was no longer with them.

The morning of the funeral—and it was a beautiful day—she was taken from Bowen Hall and placed upon the terrace in Hull-House Court. This Court is surrounded by the various Hull-House buildings. The funeral was at 2:30 in the afternoon. Dr. Gilkey* of the University of Chicago officiating, and the benediction being pronounced by Dr. Graham Taylor, her lifelong friend. As early as ten o'clock in the morning the Court Yard was crowded with people, one or two thousand standing there all day in order to be present at the services. When the funeral began, the music . . . which was furnished by the Hull-House Music School, every window in the Court was filled with people, there were flowers in every window and wreaths hanging below the windows, while the terrace was banked with lilacs and apple blossoms with bright colored tulips around the

*Charles W. Gilkey (b. 1882), professor of preaching and dean of Chapel, University of Chicago.—Eds.

edges. It was a most touching and democratic gathering. Strong men and women with children in their arms all stood weeping for the friend they had lost. The casket was covered with a pall of lilies of the valley given by the residents and they with the pall bearers sat upon the terrace.

Dr. Gilkey, in his opening sentence, spoke of the epitaph to Sir Christopher Wren in St. Paul's cathedral—"If thou seekest a monument, look about thee," adding that if you would see Jane Addams' monuments you had only to look about you. Those who looked saw the weeping people, for Jane Addams has entered always into the life of the community, advising here and directing there, welcoming with equal cordiality and courtesy a distinguished visitor or some unfortunate who had come to ask for help. They saw the men she had made decent and self-respecting—the women whose burdens she had lifted; the youth she had guided to useful manhood and the little children to whom she had given the opportunity to play.

The people in the Court Yard lingered almost until it was dark. They could not bear to go away. The next morning she was taken to Cedarville, her childhood home, and as the hearse bearing her went through the town of Freeport a few miles from Cedarville, all the bells were tolling, and at the grave the little children formed in lines as the casket was taken between them up to her last resting place, and sang, "America, the Beautiful."

The Jane Addams Memorial Fund for continuing her work at Hull-House is in process of formation, and it is hoped that her influence and her spirit will live on through the years to come.

MRS. JOSEPH . . . [T.] BOWEN

CONFUSION AND RECOVERY: 1935–1962

WHAT HAPPENS TO AN INSTITUTION WHEN ITS FOUNDER AND charismatic leader dies? When Jane Addams died in 1935 Hull-House almost collapsed, but after a period of confusion and despair the settlement survived and looked to the future. Still, the transition was not easy, and the situation was complicated by the aftermath of the depression, personality conflicts, and the general sense of drift in the settlement movement. Through the period of readjustment and reorganization the spirit of Jane Addams continued to inspire and to haunt those who tried to follow in her footsteps.

In the weeks after Jane Addams' death, when the shock and disbelief at her passing had not worn off, many people debated the future of Hull-House. Then Louise deKoven Bowen took over. She had been a close personal friend of Addams and a devoted supporter of the settlement for more than thirty years. She replaced Addams as president of the board of trustees and set out to solve the two most pressing problems faced by the settlement: the need for more funds and a new head resident.

At the urging of Hull-House residents, Bowen and the board offered the position of head resident to Adena Miller Rich, who, with her husband, Kenneth Rich, had been a resident of the settlement for more than fifteen years. Since 1926 she had been director of the Immigrants' Protective League located at Hull-House. Rich had been a devoted associate of Jane Addams; she was well known to the residents and to the board; and she was familiar with Hull-House programs and activities. A bright woman, well organized, with a gentle though queenly bearing, she seemed the ideal choice as Addams' successor. Like Jane Addams, Rich, by her own choosing, received no salary. She worked only half time as settlement head resident, devoting the remainder to the Immigrants Protective League, where she remained director.

207

Louise deKoven Bowen

The second major problem, that of financial crisis, had been facing Hull-House for some time. No one knew this better than Bowen, who had for many years been treasurer of the board of trustees. The loss of Jane Addams only made the crisis more acute, for approximately one-third of the settlement's yearly income had come from funds she was personally able to raise. The depression complicated the settlement's financial problems. Hull-House now had to compete for funds with many other charitable institutions. Expenses were greater than ever; social work had become a profession, and Hull-House, in order to get trained people, had to pay them.

The Jane Addams Memorial Fund was one of Bowen's solutions to financial problems. She hoped that the interest from it would duplicate Addams' yearly contribution. To run its first professional fund-raising campaign, Hull-House hired Kennicott Brenton, a social worker with money-raising experience. By the end of 1935 more than $53,000 had been collected for the settlement.

In conjunction with this money-raising effort, Bowen and the board decided to seek support from the Community Fund. Jane Addams had never allowed Hull-House to participate in any group fund-raising effort, for she believed that if the settlement received money from such an organization it would also have to accept the possibility of regulation by that organization. Addams thought Hull-House should be free to establish its own goals and activities. But without her there to object, Hull-House committed itself to the Chicago Community Fund, from which it received $15,000 in 1936 and $15,160 in 1937.

In another scheme to raise money the settlement board put the rental of Hull-House rooms and apartments on a more businesslike basis. Rents ranged from $15 per month for some rooms to $40 to $65 for apartments. In some years this represented a third of the settlement's income. After Jane Addams' death the board dropped the six-month probation period and actively sought residents. The result was that the number of residents increased from 65 in 1935 to more than 100 in 1939. But for many of the new residents, Hull-House was merely a place to live. They had no commitment to the settlement programs and no knowledge of the settlement heritage.

When Adena Rich took over as head resident, she began immediately to reassure staff and neighbors that there would be no drastic changes at Hull-House. The basic programs at the settlement continued. There were the usual clubs and classes, art and music lessons as well as dances, plays, parties, and basketball in the gym. Yet there was a difference in emphasis. With her background and interest in immigrant problems, Rich organized a new Department of Naturalization and Citizenship, focusing more of the settlement's efforts on educating the immigrant and cooperating with the Immigrants' Protective League. She formed two new committees. The Committee on International Relations, headed by resident George Hooker, was to sound out neighborhood ethnic groups whose national problems in homelands abroad affected situations in the United States and the Hull-House area. Professor Wayne McMillen of the University of Chicago headed the new Housing and Sanitation Committee, which sought to improve living conditions in the surrounding area. Before Jane Addams died, the Hull-House group was responsible for locating one of the first public housing projects in the city, in the settlement neighborhood. But the Jane Addams Homes, named for her after her death, did not solve the housing problem in the area. Only 21 of 533 families moved from the site could afford to live in the new federal housing project when it was completed.

During the 1930s Hull-House residents, like settlement workers everywhere, devoted a great deal of time and energy to the overwhelming problem of poverty and despair. It was a discouraging and ultimately hopeless task, but the election of Franklin Roosevelt, as well as the presence of Hull-House graduates and friends in Washington, encouraged the settlement residents. The most important New Deal measure as far as Hull-House was concerned was the Works Progress Administration, passed in 1935. It provided 66 government-paid workers at the settlement. Most of these people supervised clubs and recreational activities; but some taught art classes or painted murals, and others took part in the Federal Writers Project. The presence of the WPA workers, even though temporary, helped to revitalize Hull-House in the late 1930s.

Yet all was not going smoothly at the settlement. The two Hull-House positions of leadership and power originally vested in Jane Addams, as founder, creator, and person who demanded the complete respect of the settlement family, were now held by two people. Louise deKoven Bowen was president of the board of trustees of Hull-House Association, and Adena Miller Rich was head resident of the settlement. Each felt a deep sense of responsibility to preserve Hull-House in the spirit of Jane Addams, performing the duties and services Addams had performed as the settlement leader. But Jane Addams' responsibilities had never been defined, especially as to which decision-making powers accrued to each position. As long as Addams or one person held both jobs, the overlapping areas of responsibility were not impractical or important; but when two people, especially two strong-minded individuals with different ideas about settlement goals, held the two jobs, the duties and responsibilities of each needed to be clearly defined. They were not clarified, and this situation led to a power struggle which lasted more than eight years between the president and board of trustees on the one hand, and the head resident on the other, for control of the settlement.

Bowen and Rich disagreed almost daily over staff positions, use of funds, and program priorities, as each sought to impose her leadership on the settlement in the manner of Jane Addams. Most of these conflicts were ultimately won by Bowen and the board of trustees who held the purse strings. While the inability to resolve this executive conflict seemed to cause the most friction between Rich and Bowen, a major personality clash was also responsible. These factors, coupled with others, particularly the demand of the Community Fund for a full-time salaried head resident—a stipulation which Rich would not accept—led the members of the board of trustees who agreed with the Fund's demand and felt Hull-House needed Community Fund support, to accept Rich's resignation in April 1937.

The struggle for power did not end with the resignation of Adena Rich. It continued to haunt the next head resident, though she was hand-picked by Louise Bowen. Charlotte E. Carr had been in no way associated with Jane Addams and seemed very little like her in personality. Carr, who was described by one writer as "large and gusty, with a hearty laugh," had never lived in a social settlement before. Yet Bowen felt she was just the "practical idealist" to direct Hull-House.

While Jane Addams had been a pioneer in the settlement movement and Rich well known to settlement people, Charlotte Carr was an unknown quality in the social settlement world. That Carr had had plenty of experience with large and complex organizations was one of the reasons Bowen thought she would succeed in the settlement. To come to Hull-House she left the directorship of New York City's Emergency Relief Bureau, where she spent more than $9 million a month to feed New York's starving thousands. Yet her experience with federal relief in New York and with labor problems in that state as well as in Connecticut and Pennsylvania had prepared her for working with men in a man's world. She was more at home arguing with striking workers, organizing unions, or demanding and passing out relief funds than making speeches at women's clubs, sipping tea, and enticing probable donors.

Charlotte Carr began immediately to put her stamp on operations at Hull-House. She reorganized the settlement administrative structure, making it more formal than it had been under Jane Addams. She consolidated some programs and eliminated others. She replaced volunteers with paid workers, and, in a move that angered many of the old residents, but which symbolized her business approach, she changed her title from "head resident" to "director." She did continue many of the traditional settlement programs and activities, however. Bowen Country Club was active; dancing, basketball, and social clubs at Hull-House now came under the heading of recreation, and recreation meant the "club house," the name now associated with the Boys' Club Building. The Mary Crane Nursery at Hull-House continued its association with the settlement. Supported by the National College of Education, the Infant Welfare Society of Chicago, and the United Charities of Chicago, it provided one of the best programs in Chicago for pre-school children. Two new sections appeared on the settlement organization chart: a Community Service Department and a Workers' Education Department.

During the fifty years since the founding of the settlement, contact with neighborhood and ethnic groups near Hull-House had been maintained. Hull-House residents had led many a fight on behalf of their neighbors; but there was no Hull-House department that dealt specifically with the complicated relationships of neighbors and nationality groups to one another, to their environment, and to Hull-House. Carr organized a Community Service Department to do just that. Among other things, this department mounted a successful campaign to clean up the neighborhood alleys. Under the leadership of resident Bert Boerner and his neighborhood assistant, community clubs were organized as outposts for Hull-House in its fight against slums. Two such clubs, the Tay-Mor Neighborhood Club and the Sholto-Eleventh Club, supported by an Italian population, served juveniles and adults. On the west side another neighborhood center sponsored by the Hull-House Community Club, a group of black women who met regularly at the settlement, provided recreation facilities for a largely black district. The center, to which the Negro Business Men's Club contributed substantially, sponsored activities that included afternoon game periods for children, pre-school play groups, weekly dances, and English classes for adults.

Yet few blacks came to Hull-House, even though in the 1930s the second largest concentration of blacks in the city was just to the west of the settlement. Three Hull-House yearbooks were issued in the 1930s; all contained photographs depicting some integrated settlement programs. But Dewey Jones, with his wife, Faith, the only black residents during the late 1930s, decided that although there was no conscious policy of segregation, blacks did not feel welcome at the settlement. Charlotte Carr tried to rectify the situation, but many of the regular participants did not want blacks in their clubs and classes. Jones's death in 1939 left the settlement without a black staff member. On the eve of World War II, Hull-House was far from integrated.

Carr believed in integration; she believed even more in the Workers Education Department, which she had created out of the Naturalization and Citizenship Department. She realized that with the foreign-born in the Hull-House community there was still a need for emphasis on citizenship and English; but she also felt that the settlement curriculum should be broadened to include other subjects to help community workers who were first-generation Americans get ahead in the world of management and labor. Carr believed that the establishment of such a worker's school was the primary function of the settlement.

By 1939 the Hull-House community consisted of eighteen ethnic groups—Italian, Greek, Mexican, British, Scandinavian, Polish, German, Russian, Czechoslovakian, French, Lithuanian, Hungarian, Swiss, Rumanian, Yugoslavian, Belgian, Finnish, and Dutch—including the largest Italian, Greek, and Mexican population in Chicago, in addition to the black community. Usually these four large groups did things separately, but Hull-House attempted to get them to work together. In 1938 they cooperated for the first time to present the Christmas tableaux. It embraced the Italian conception of the birth of Christ; the Blessing of Christ in the church according to Greek tradition; "Pasada," the entrance into Bethlehem according to Mexican conception; and the Adoration of the Magi from the black point of view. The play was accompanied by songs rendered by the group whose tableau was on view at the time.

This kind of cooperation remained rare, however. Had Hull-House been able to achieve more trust between ethnic and racial groups, had it firmly established a precedent for cooperation and compromise during this and earlier times, the neighborhood planning efforts of the 1940s and 1950s, which lacked a coordinated approach, might have been more successful.

Bowen's "practical idealist" lasted five years as director of Hull-House. By January 1943 Charlotte Carr had resigned. She had brought upheaval and change to Hull-House. Bowen and particularly the older residents, who had loved Jane Addams and her style, were happy to see Charlotte Carr leave. The old ways of doing things were gone; old familiar furnishings and pictures were also gone. Carr had been difficult to talk with; she seemed to prefer discussing labor problems with men in saloons, drinking and smoking, to discussing Hull-House problems with residents. Her personality and ideas were completely foreign to Hull-House tradition. The chaos and confusion she left in the wake of her resignation were accented by the financial condition of the settlement, which under Carr made up its almost yearly deficit from capital endowment funds.

To replace Carr, the Hull-House Board of Trustees selected a man for the first time. Russell Ward Ballard was also the first married head of the settlement. His wife, Ethel, worked in the settlement; and they had two sons. For almost twenty years, until his retirement in 1962, Ballard led Hull-House back to prominence as a social and cultural force in the Chicago community, but his tenure was not without its problems. Eighty-four-year-old Louise deKoven Bowen was shocked by the choice. She could not accept the idea of having a man in Jane Addams' place. But even she finally agreed, for Ballard had an impressive background in social work. He came highly recommended by those at the University of Chicago School of Social Service Administration, where he had done his graduate work, and he had an extensive background as an administrator and as a social worker. Before he came to Hull-House he had been director of the Illinois State Training School for Boys at St. Charles, and before that, he had taught school in Indiana Harbor, Indiana, and headed the Lake County (Indiana) Board of Public Welfare. His experience with juvenile delinquents and his knowledge of the conditions in Hull-House neighborhoods led Ballard to attempt to make the welfare of children and youth a major settlement objective and return the focus of Hull-House to its traditional role of service to its neighborhood and community.

The first task facing Ballard was to enlist the cooperation of the residents and volunteers still at Hull-House and to secure new staff to fill the many vacancies that existed because of wartime personnel demands and the Carr years. He needed staff to develop settlement programs. Ballard insisted that the opportunity to learn athletic skills, the chance to play a band instrument, to model in clay, to sew, to weave, to print, to construct useful objects which could be taken home, gave a child status, a sense of belonging, and helped combat delinquency. The Music School, the largest of its kind in Chicago, under the direction of Nesta Smith had an enrollment of 160. There were 685 children registered for daytime recreation activities and 275 for evening programs at the settlement. Yet, Ballard knew that Hull-House, because of lack of funds and personnel, was offering a minimum program.

Conflict between the new director and the president of the board was resolved when Louise deKoven Bowen became honorary president in 1944. Although her influence continued until her death in 1953, her retirement left the way open for a new generation of board members. The new trustees, without the experience of the Jane Addams years, were content to leave the decision making to Ballard and to act only in an advisory and policy-making capacity. Yet Ballard's relationship with the board and the institution was not smooth. He created a crisis for the settlement in 1947, when he requested that he be allowed to live away from the settlement. The board voted unanimously to dismiss him if he gave up living in the settlement, but the board did offer him an apartment at Hull-House rent-free. Ballard never threatened to move out again, and Hull-House did not give up residency until its original buildings were torn down.

Ballard made progress on other fronts. In an interview in the *Chicago Daily News* of August 6, 1943, Ballard said: "Hull-House, with its human contacts with folks of many racial and national backgrounds, symbolizes the world neighborhood. . . . The institution that Jane Addams reared is a proving ground for amity among so-called racial groups, where all comers are treated like fellow Americans, equals in democracy." By the time Ballard came to Hull-House, the settlement neighborhood consisted of a large Italian, Greek, Mexican, and—just to the west—a black population. Most of the Italians and Greeks were second-generation Americans of naturalized parents. Their problems, like those of the blacks, were not those of immigrants in a strange land, unable to read or speak English and unfamiliar with American customs; rather, they had family and economic problems and a need for better housing. While the settlement catered to its Spanish-speaking neighbors, with classes in English and citizenship, it also began to spend more time and money for trained social workers who could help with the problems of the other groups. More and more emphasis was placed on neighborhood services.

After World War II, other ethnic and racial groups came into the settlement neighborhood. The hospitality of Hull-House was offered to Japanese-Americans as they came from relocation camps. Lithuanian, Hungarian, and Greek displaced persons also sought out Hull-House and its neighborhood. In addition to more blacks and Mexicans, by the 1950s Puerto Ricans had begun to come into the Hull-House area in sizable numbers. Ballard insisted that his staff include representatives of each group. He encouraged all established residents and new arrivals to get acquainted with Hull-House and with each other. But he could not prevent the gang warfare and the racial strife that existed in the settlement neighborhood and occasionally influenced the settlement directly. In 1952, for example, a male settlement resident was attacked and stabbed by a gang of white teenagers as he escorted some black youngsters to their home.

Russell Ballard optimistically believed that he could overcome the poverty and the violence in the neighborhood. He was convinced that delinquency grew out of poor housing, and that one of the major settlement priorities should be improving housing and community conditions. "Our whole society should be indicted for permitting people to live in basements with rats running over their children while they sleep," he said. He thought the people who lived in such areas would take more pride in improvements and be more interested in bettering their conditions if they were actively involved in planning and campaigning for the improvements. Thus when the settlement discovered in 1947 that the city was going to declare the Hull-House neighborhood a blighted area and begin redevelopment, Russell Ballard encouraged an interested group of area inhabitants—mostly Italian veterans of World War II—to take part.

Working with the West Side Community Committee of Chicago, Hull-House helped form and finance a Temporary Organizing Committee headed by Eri Hulbert, great-nephew of Jane Addams, long a resident of Hull-House and the neighborhood and an expert on housing. After eighteen months of intensive work, the T. O. C., consisting of sixty-five working members representing all groups in the area—industry; business; social, civic, religious, educational, and recreational agencies; property owners; and residents—held a public meeting on June 15, 1949, at which the Near West Side Planning Board was established. Its stated purpose was to serve the people of the near west side of Chicago by planning and carrying out a program of conservation, rehabilitation, and development based on facts submitted by the area's residents and institutions. In the venture the Planning Board and Hulbert, its executive director, promised to integrate their redevelopment plans with those of the wider Chicago community.

With the help of Hull-House and money from several Chicago foundations and institutions, work on the plan got under way. Between 1949 and 1961, the Planning Board struggled to find financing to keep the operation going, meanwhile fighting ward politicians, the designs of city planners, and apathetic ward citizens who seemed to feel that planning meant blacks. The Planning Board had to create its own plan, which would be acceptable not only to its community but also to the various governmental agencies which controlled the final disposition of the area. All these problems were accentuated by friction between the neighborhood ethnic groups, who seemed unable to work together.

During the late 1950s the University of Illinois began looking for a site for a new four-year campus within the Chicago metropolitan area. The University finally identified four possible locations. When none of those selected proved acceptable to both the city and the university, the city suggested the Harrison-Halsted area. In its formal report, September 1960, the city indicated that "no great difficulty" was expected in acquiring the local, newly built Holy Guardian Angel School and Hull-House.

The neighborhood people, especially those involved in the planning effort, felt they had been stabbed in the back by the city and its politicians, and by the very people they had looked to for support and guidance through the difficult planning years—the Catholic archdiocese and the Hull-House board. The people were sure these two institutions must have known of the impending disaster, because the city had evidently conferred with them while it was making its study. Yet neither group had warned the neighborhood.

On February 15, 1961, Dr. David Dodds Henry, president of the University of Illinois, accepted the proposed Harrison-Halsted site. The near west side was to have a large and wealthy institution, one of the requirements usually listed by planners as a necessity for neighborhood rejuvenation and growth. But it was not the institution the people wanted.

During thirteen long years of struggling and planning, the neighborhood had fought for its right of self-determination and preservation. "The local Planning Board, and that means the people," Russell Ballard said, "cooperated with city officials and supported the city council ordinance that provided for clearance of 55 acres of deteriorated property near Hull-House—and with the understanding that the cleared land would be utilized for HOME CONSTRUCTION. . . . So when a completely changed plan, namely a site for the university campus, was proposed [and passed] in the city council ordinance (of May 10, 1961), the PROTEST WAS LONG AND LOUD AND BITTER."

A neighborhood group, the nucleus of which was the Near West Side Planning Board, began to campaign against the city's decision. Florence Scala, sister of Ernie Giovangelo, who after Hulbert's death in 1955, directed the Planning Board, led the fight with Hull-House resident Jessie Binford. They fought the city's decision with screaming and tearful placard-festooned marches, with speeches, and with legal suits. When their elected ward officials deserted them, Florence Scala ran for alderman herself. Though she was defeated, her unusual campaign brought city-wide recognition and support, underlined the grim reality of machine politics, and helped intensify efforts to preserve Hull-House. Scala went into battle in much the same crusading, reforming way that Jane Addams and the Hull-House residents of the 1890s had in their attempt to depose Johnny Powers. The frustrating results were the same, too: defeat at the hands of politicians with more clout and more jobs to hand out.

Hull-House was caught in the midst of all the furor, for it was through its encouragement that the Planning Board and the attempt at planning had come to life. Yet when Scala and her followers approached the settlement board for help, they were ignored. The board had decided not to fight City Hall. Scala and her co-chairman, Jessie Binford, continued their fight against the city and the University of Illinois in the courts. But when the Illinois Supreme Court decided in favor of the University in 1963, all hope was gone. The battle had lost the University of Illinois one year on its completion date and had cost the Hull-House neighbors thousands of dollars.

On March 5, 1963, the Board of Trustees of Hull-House accepted an offer of $875,000 for the settlement buildings from the city of Chicago. Hull-House had found new quarters on North Broadway near Belmont and promised to vacate the old buildings by April 1. The last dinner, held at Hull-House on March 28, was followed on March 29 and 30 by a sale of settlement furnishings that could not be taken to the new location.

Though the neighborhood struggle to plan and maintain its homes, businesses, and institutions seemed to overshadow all settlement programs, activities went on at Hull-House as usual. Dramas were presented by the Hull-House Players. Art, music, and dance classes were given. Children's and adults' clubs continued to meet; Bowen Country Club ran at capacity; and visitors in large numbers came for tours of the historic settlement buildings. By 1961, between seven thousand and eight thousand visitors toured its premises annually. At least five agencies whose work complemented that of the settlement were located there: the Juvenile Protective Association, the Retarded Children's Training Center, the Mary Crane Nursery School, the Infant Welfare Nursing Center and Well Baby Clinic, and the National Training Center for Settlement Workers. Traditional settlement programs had obviously lost none of their appeal.

Yet, as soon as the city plan for rehabilitation of the Hull-House neighborhood began, the settlement and Russell Ballard realized that a redefinition of settlement aims and goals was demanded. Urban redevelopment would destroy the homes of the neighbors, resettle them in other locals, and leave Hull-House without a neighborhood to serve. After a study conducted in 1957–1958, the settlement discovered that though Hull-House was just as busy as ever, a greater percentage of those who participated in settlement activities were not from the neighborhood but had traveled some distance to get there. On the basis of this discovery the board of trustees began to formulate long-range plans leading to the eventual decentralization of Hull-House operations.

The outcome of a symposium on the future of the settlement held June 24–25, 1961, at Bowen Country Club, after the loss of the Hull-House site to the University of Illinois, seemed to underscore the idea of decentralization. Based on discussions with political and social scientists, the Hull-House board of trustees agreed that Hull-House would continue to operate "one or more multi-function neighborhood centers." In 1962 Russell Ballard retired and the next year the wrecking balls and bulldozers knocked down the Hull-House buildings and reduced the Harrison–Halsted Street neighborhood to rubble. Studs Terkel, interviewer and raconteur of Chicago lore, had a last word: "When they destroyed the old Hull-House area with its polyglot talkers and poly-cultures and the old world and new world breathing together, it was done in the name of a university in the city. Not to mention the names of cement contractors and brokers and all sorts of breakers."

Mrs. Rich Takes Command

Louise deKoven Bowen and
Adena Miller Rich

"I just feel as if Hull-House had been dumped in my lap. Jane had her finger so on all the details, and in the last few years had wanted to run everything herself, so much so that many of us did not even know what was going on. . . . The Trustees have made me Acting President of the Board, and everyone comes to me now to know what shall be done." When Louise deKoven Bowen wrote these words to Ellen Gates Starr just two weeks after Jane Addams died, she realized more than many associated with the settlement the enormity of the task ahead. She had been a close personal friend of Addams and knew first hand the major problems the settlement faced—reaffirming its usefulness and goals at a time when the effectiveness of the whole settlement movement was in question, and dealing forcefully and adequately with conditions resulting from the depression. But these problems could begin to be solved only if a more pressing one could be dealt with.

As treasurer of the settlement and one of its major benefactors, Bowen was aware of the financial crisis that had been creeping up on Hull-House. She knew that in order to survive the settlement needed leadership, and she set out to find it.

Hull-House residents, just as concerned as Bowen and the board of trustees, held their own meetings to discuss possible candidates for head resident. Their suggestion was Adena Miller Rich (1888–1967), a resident who had been a close associate of Jane Addams and an advocate of her ideas and work. At least thirty-three Hull-House residents who officially petitioned the board to consider Rich as a candidate felt that she would "represent Hull-House with dignity and effectiveness in public, and in the intimate domestic relations of this family, she will carry on the fine tradition of Miss Addams in maintaining harmony and cooperation among the residents, in making Hull-House a pleasant and inspiring place in which to live." The board and Bowen took the resi-

dents' suggestion seriously and offered Rich the position which she finally accepted.

From the following exchange of letters it was already evident, even before Rich was hired, that Bowen and Rich, two intelligent, strong-willed leaders, had different ideas about the future of the settlement. [Louise deKoven Bowen to Adena Miller Rich, June 28, 1935; Adena Miller Rich to Louise deKoven Bowen, July 9, 1935, both in Adena Miller Rich Papers, Jane Addams Memorial Collection, University of Illinois at Chicago Circle.]

Baymeath
Bar Harbor, Maine
June 28, 1935.

Mrs. Kenneth Rich,
Hull-House,
800 South Halsted Street,
Chicago, Illinois.

Dear Mrs. Rich:

I cannot tell you how disturbed and regretful I was to receive your husband's letter saying that you both were leaving Hull-House in the fall. Miss Addams depended upon you so much, and was so enthusiastic about your ability that I feel we need you now more than ever. Miss Addams told me several times that she had asked you to become Head Resident of Hull-House, but that you had always said you couldn't do it; that it would take you away from your family life; that you were busy in the Immigrants' Protective League, and that altogether it was out of the question. She told me this before she first asked Grace Abbott to become Head Resident.

Of course Miss Addams' death has changed everything. Perhaps the work of the House will have to be curtailed. It is certain that we will have to be economical and take great care to husband our resources. I have no right to ask you if you would reconsider and become Head Resident now. I feel sure, however, that when I get back in the fall if I presented your name to the trustees there would be no doubt but that they would extend the call to you at a salary to be agreed upon. Even if the arrangement was not a permanent one but could last for a year or two until we had time to look about us it would be of great advantage to the House. I am so afraid that if you and Mr. Rich leave us some of the other residents may feel that some of the prestige of the House is departing and they will want to go to more comfortable quarters. If a large number of residents desert it our income would be cut very materially, and it would be difficult for us to build it up again. Also, we might not be able without a Head to get residents as valuable as those who are with us now. I am writing you this to ask if you would consider some kind of a proposition such as I have stated. I know that the day we were at the hospital together you felt there must be some radical changes. If I remember correctly you suggested the House should be a center for the social agencies for the city. I do not agree with you about this because I don't think the social agencies would care to leave the Loop and go to the West side. I am very anxious to try to maintain the House as it is now. Possibly, as I have said before, decreasing some of its activities. I am not unmindful, however, that there must be changes. We must have the vision to plan and to try new experiments in the social service field, but I do want to keep it as a neighborhood center, a place where the poor and the troubled and the sick may get advice and be comforted. If we do not conduct it in this manner it might look as if we were not playing fair to the contributors to the Jane Addams Memorial Fund.

I am aware that Halsted Street is not the pleasantest place in the world to live; that it is hot and noisy in summer, difficult to approach, and the air is not of the purest, but we all think that the people who live there are leading unselfish lives, and we are grateful to them for giving up many material comforts in order to be of service to the people of the neighborhood.

I have written you a long letter, but I do wish you would think it over seriously. Of course your family always comes first, but Mr. Rich can be so valuable to the House with his business ideas and suggestions that it would be a great pity to lose him as well as you. Do think favorably of my suggestion.

Sincerely yours,
LOUISE deKOVEN BOWEN

July 9th, 1935.

Mrs. Joseph T. Bowen,
Baymeath,
Bar Harbor, Maine.

Dear Mrs. Bowen:

Your letter of June 28th was received yesterday. While your message was en route and while I was away, the Residents now at Hull-House had met and passed a Resolution asking permission to submit my name to the Trustees as their choice of leadership. After much reconsideration of our plan to move away, I have finally told them they might do so, but explained some of the conditions under which I could act. I have asked that they use the right of recall, if my entanglements offset what they think are my qualifications.

I am glad that you have raised the point as to my suggestions regarding the centering of more social services here in the Settlement. I am afraid that I failed to tell you, on that saddest of days— the time I had desperately hoped might never come—that Miss Addams herself had suggested the idea that Hull-House might become a home of the social agencies. Various considerations make it an interesting possibility, although perhaps not for years to come, and certainly not one to force. One does know, however, how great an advantage it is for the poor, or the sick, or the stranger to our tongue, or for the parents of children who need special guidance and protection to feel that there is a skilled agency right at the Settlement upon which they can call for help. These are not the only types to whom we must minister in a more than casual fashion. Well operated social agencies benefit the neighborhood more than mediocre new Residents. It is very important I think, for the Settlement to supplement the work of those agencies, perhaps by a neighborhood visitor, and certainly by availability of assistance in those emergencies which so often arise after the day of an ordinary office has closed.

One remembers too, the Plan of the Chicago Plan Commission, which placed the Civic Center for Chicago practically on the Hull-House doorstep, and the fact that Polk and Halsted Streets have subsequently been determined as the center of the City's population.

And in the third place, because Hull-House has mothered so many of the movements now expressed in the professional services of social and civic agencies, it seems appropriate that they should continue to regard it as a natural center of operation.

But this may be laboring the point instead of explaining it. Although there is no immediate occasion for expressing it, I am anxious that my feeling should not be misunderstood.

I am sure you are right about the scrutiny of expenditures. The Coffee House, for instance, must either be operated without loss or closed. The Residents' Dining Room must be operated without cost to the Settlement, and if a deficit occurs, it must be met by those who dine there.

I could write of many other problems of the House but the length of this letter has already intruded unduly upon your summer's rest. I have written you very frankly, and shall expect the same frankness from you, if there is any fear on your part in which the future of the Settlement is involved.

I have come to my decision with considerable reluctance, because I had wished to do some other things; because I know my own limitations; and because none of us wish to face the changes I suppose must come in the life of the Settlement. But I can see that these are days in which we must all stand together. You would be very happy, just as Miss Addams would be, if you could see the way in which the Residents have drawn together with a new courage and morale. They can make Hull-House worthy of Miss Addams' memory. You have no idea how much your own presence over here that night comforted them and contributed toward this spirit.

Faithfully yours,
ADENA RICH

The Rich Years

Adena Miller Rich

Adena Miller Rich became the head resident of Hull-House on October 1, 1935. After graduating from Oberlin College in Ohio and attending and working at the Chicago School of Civics and Philanthropy, she went to Cincinnati in 1916 as civic director of the Woman's City Club. She returned to Chicago to live at Hull-House as a resident, with her broker husband Kenneth Rich, and became executive vice president of the Illinois League of Women Voters from 1923 to 1926. Her early and continued interest and expertise in immigrant problems led to her becoming director of the Immigrants' Protective League in 1926, a position she continued to hold even after she resigned the head residency of Hull-House in 1937.

Adena Rich set out to establish order and stability from the confusion and bewilderment that reigned at Hull-House in the wake of Jane Addams' passing. She reassured the residents and staff, declaring, "I shall follow Miss Addams' idea that the house be conducted on a family basis rather than institutional." She saw that the traditional Hull-House programs were continued as usual; and she tried to emphasize areas in which the settlement programs might grow.

The following report was made by Rich to Hull-House residents on March 15, 1937, just two weeks before her resignation became effective. It recounts her activities and accomplishments at Hull-House during her brief tenure as head resident and presents her reasons for resigning. Some of the major problems facing the settlement, especially those concerning division of responsibility between the head resident and the board of trustees and its president, were carefully examined by Mrs. Rich. [Adena Miller Rich, "Head Resident's Work During Transition Since the Death of Miss Jane Addams," unpublished manuscript, March 15, 1937, Adena Miller Rich Papers, Jane Addams Memorial Collection, University of Illinois at Chicago Circle.]

When the Head Resident took over the reins of Hull-House on October 1, 1935, there were many vacancies in the Resident group. There were six vacant apartments and suites. . . . The Men's Quarters had very few occupants. There were vacancies in the Women's Quarters.

It seemed evident that immediate action was required to build up the Resident group. . . .

Many communications with the "outside world" were undertaken at that time, and since, with a view to this up-building of the Resident group. The result is that the House is full. There are at present, including the three children in the House (and including the Superintendent of Buildings and his wife, the Bookkeeper, Postmistress, and their mother; but *not* counting the Jane Club), 71 persons living under the roof of Hull-House. . . .

A pressing problem, the management of the Dining Room and Coffee House, came to a head in the busiest month of the year, last December, when Miss Sara Potter felt that she could no longer continue her duties in that capacity. . . . The Home Economics Departments of 8 universities and other schools were canvassed; the Managers of 6 successful loop restaurants were consulted. One of the latter secured for Hull-House, the present Manager. . . .

The Residents of Hull-House know that Miss Blanche Joseph has devoted herself first of all to making the Dining Room as irresistible as she can from a standpoint of food and service. She, too, believes that the Dining Room is a center of the esprit de corps of the House and that the more the Residents dine together here, the more successful will their joint efforts in the Settlement become. . . .

The Residents know that there have frequently been oysters, turkey, mushrooms, canapes! Attendance has been increased. The real secret to making the Coffee House and Dining Room pay is, however, a much larger attendance in the Coffee House, primarily by special parties at night, in which the direct cooperation of the Residents is needed. Through their contacts, some very successful dinners have already taken place in the last three months, which have made new friends for Hull-House and its work. . . .

Hull-House received a body blow when it lost Miss Edith de Nancrede last May. Her work was built deeply into the heart of Hull-House and of the Hull-House neighborhood. Hundreds of children and young people were turning to her as their avenue to life and happiness. . . .

All through the summer, the Head Resident and the President of the Board were in communication upon the question of a successor. It seemed providential that at last Miss Helen Tieken (Mrs. Maurice P. Geraghty) was found to be here in the City, and so situated that she could devote part of her time to Hull-House. She has won distinction by her exquisite productions, not only in this community but in other cities of the United States and abroad. She came eager to take up the direction of these young groups in the Hull-House Theatre, and eager to reach out to the groups in the community, such as the Italians, the Greeks, the Mexicans, and the colored people, who have had even fewer opportunities than the young people who had been coming to Hull-House for years. . . .

There have been, as usual, three plays by the Guild, Christmas Performances by the children, the Living Pictures at the Music School Christmas Concert, and now, interesting and original new plans for the Spring. The Hull-House Actors' Guild is now again on its feet, far more rapidly than might have been expected, rallying about the new Director.

Their performance of "Green Grow the Lilacs" for the Chicago Chemists' Club in the Hull-House Theatre, on March 3rd, following the Club's Annual Dinner in the Coffee House, with reception at the evening's end for both Club and Guild, was in the best Hull-House tradition. Two groups, educationally and economically diverse, met personally on common ground. Miss Tieken has brought many new connections and made many new and important friends for Hull-House and its young people. . . .

Before her death, Miss Addams had expressed the hope that as the depression passed, Hull-House might again claim the services of a regular Director for the Social Clubs. Miss Edna Rowe had carried that responsibility for a number of years on a full-time salary basis, until it became necessary to make drastic reductions in the Hull-House budget. Two years ago, the Social Clubs operated as best they could with the supervision of about one-fourth of the time of one of the Residents. Last year, that part time was increased to half time under Mrs. Helen Frew, who was, however, not a Resident, and therefore not in so advantageous a position.

Last summer, faced with the necessity of substituting for Miss de Nancrede's work also among the Social Clubs and Folk Dancing Classes, the President of the Board agreed that the full time of a Director of Social Clubs was possible. Upon the strongest kind of recommendations from Northwestern University, Miss Mildred Richards, who graduated last year with Phi Beta Kappa honors, not only in group work courses but in case work courses in the School of Sociology, was appointed to this position at Hull-House on a full-time basis. Miss Richards carries with ability a very substantial responsibility in the program of the House—the groups under her direction numbering approximately five hundred young people. In the nature of things, they do not come to Hull-House "ready made," either in manners or interests. . . .

The blows which have fallen upon Hull-House since that tragic day, May 23, 1935, have been particularly severe for the Music School. . . . The year before it had lost its best friend, Miss Mary Smith. . . . Within the same year the serious illness of the Founder of the Music School, Miss Eleanor Smith, withdrew her from the scene. . . . In February 1937, the Music School lost a third ardent supporter and friend, Miss Agnes Pillsbury. She had helped to raise money for its support; had initiated and carried forward the Annual Concert of the Chicago Woman's Symphony at Hull-House so that young pupils might have the opportunity of concerto work with the Orchestra. . . .

The Music School Faculty, on a part-time basis—with personal expenses barely covered (at a rate lower than W.P.A.)—goes valiantly onward. Residents who attend the Recitals and Concerts of the pupils are well aware of their exquisite quality and promise. The Music School needs the interest of the outside friends of the Residents and Trustees.

The Head Resident believes that it would lift the spirit in this Department at this time, and throughout the House, if the Endowment bequest of $10,000 from Miss Mary Smith, who was so deeply interested, could be designated as income toward the maintenance of the Music School. . . .

The Art School and Industrial Arts Department has also suffered serious losses. It is a tribute to the last immigrant group, the Mexican, to be constantly reminded by the Art School Committee that the return of the Mexicans to their homeland during the depression "took the heart out of the classes in clay modeling, sculpture, and pottery." The loss of their original work has been perhaps one of the chief factors in the necessity felt by the Hull-House pottery "Factory," separately incorporated by Mr. and Mrs. Beals French, to close its Shop in the Italian Court Building on North Michigan Avenue. The pottery made in the "Factory" in moulds "cannot run the Shop alone." . . .

The second blow suffered by the Art School was the loss of the work of Miss Adeline Titsworth in the Labor Museum and Weaving Classes, when she was discharged by the Treasurer of the Board in June 1935. . . . The third blow has been the serious illness of Mrs. French.

Last Spring, the Art School Committee drafted an excellent statement for the Hull-House Board of Trustees, setting out the value of the School to the neighborhood and urging the point that if it were not to be supported, it should be entirely discontinued. The Board felt decidedly that its work should be rebuilt. The Committee and the Head Resident were authorized to find a Director for the Hull-House Art School. Mrs. French devoted a great deal of attention to this need last Summer. Then Miss Enella Benedict rediscovered Emily Edwards, a former Hull-House Resident with the best of training, who was persuaded to return. She is well known in the world outside Chicago, through her canvasses and through her writings on the Frescoes of Mexico.

The classrooms for Industrial Arts have been redecorated; student teachers have been discovered; the looms are again at work; and the enrollment has increased from approximately 60 as before Christmas, to 225 adults and children. The new Director is a magnet for the neighborhood, and the Art School is blossoming out. It holds much of the key, with the other Arts at Hull-House, to the whole purpose and aim of the Settlement.

Jesus Gonzales, a Mexican pottery worker, creates a vase to be sold in the Hull-House pottery shop.

This is not an attempt to draw a picture of the work of Departments that have not been struck by loss in this transition period. Work is going on in others, in quality of which any institution may be very proud. . . .

But I must turn to a more personal matter. . . .

When the Residents of Hull-House in June 1935 graciously requested permission to place my name in nomination as Head Resident, they will remember that I pointed out personal limitations. My reluctance to accept this responsibility was deep seated.

I knew the pitfalls and some of the dangers. I had expected difficulties. I had not expected so many *unnecessary* difficulties. It is the unnecessary difficulties which are so ruinous to initiative, and so wearing upon morale. . . .

I had no idea that the right to *contribute* one's time and efforts to Hull-House would become so much a ''bone of contention,'' nor that the exact hours one devoted to it would be so challenged, and so held in question.

I have always made it a point to be ''better than my word'' in a contractual relationship. No agency with which I have been associated in a responsible way has had full time *only*, or half time *only*. One becomes associated only with those which hold deep personal interest, and in such, one works without keeping one's eye on the clock. Hull-House has had much more than half of my time. . . .

If I were considering the matter all over again . . . , I would still not be willing at this time (even if I were free to do so) to pledge more than half of my time to Hull-House. . . . Other ''outside contacts'' are too important to the Settlement itself. Under some interpretations of controlled time, they are precluded. . . . A specialty of one's own lends confidence and perspective to the carrying of responsibilities of more general nature. . . .

Miss Jane Addams set an example, as Head Resident, in making herself a specialist in leadership in certain social problems, and in devoting a large share of her time to those special needs or movements. . . .

The feeling of the Board of Directors that the Head Residency should be placed upon a paid basis has been enormously aggravated by certain communications from the Chicago Council of Social Agencies, following the granting of the Budget allocation of $15,000.00 to Hull-House from the Community Fund of Chicago.

The Community Fund vehemently protested against anyone's assumption that there should be any such condition to the payment of this grant to Hull-House. The Fund sharply criticized the Chicago Council of Social Agencies, moreover, for writing the President of the Hull-House Board of Trustees upon this matter—the Fund maintaining that this is an internal matter of administration and quite outside the Council's province.

The Hull-House Board of Trustees devoted its January 1937 meeting, at which the Head Resident was not present, to a discussion of this question.

It rankles (at least in the President's mind) that the Head Resident cannot subscribe to these two conditions—full time, and a salary.

The fact that they were pressed upon the governing body of Hull-House is a striking illustration, however, of Miss Addams' strong and often expressed belief that participation in the Fund might mean attempted or actual dictation to Hull-House by an outside body. . . .

With respect to my occupancy of this position without a salary, I should like to make it very clear that I am not personally insensible to the advantages of a salary. I am fully aware that the professional status of social work is partly measured by its ability to command substantial salaries. I am aware also, that if the position of Head Resident of Hull-House were placed upon a salary basis, it would fall within the higher brackets of the profession. There are many considerations, however, which have made me feel, in this transition period of weakness, when the consolidation of forces is so important, that the position is a stronger one without a salary. . . .

It seemed very necessary that the basis upon which I accepted the offer of this position should be clear to my fellow Residents—that it was *not for personal financial gain*. Relationships are far more personal and intimate in Settlement life than in an ordinary office staff. The Residents of Hull-House have a strong feeling, built up through all these years, that it is not only a medium through which there is opportunity for their own self-expression, development, and usefulness in social and civic affairs, but that it is home to them. The morale could, however, easily be lost, especially without Miss Addams, and the Settlement easily become institutionalized and commercialized.

. . . Because I knew that there might be other persons who would like to have occupied this position, it seemed to me that my responsibility upon a no-salary basis would make for harmony.

. . . Within the large group of Hull-House Residents, mostly volunteer but partly paid, some workers upon a part-time basis and some upon a full-time basis, it seemed to me that the volunteer nature of the Head Resident's service would build up the esprit de corps of the *unpaid workers,* whose value in the Settlement's program and activities is of the greatest importance. And most especially, . . . instead of adding to the Executive overhead in this first year or two of transition, I have been eager to build up the *paid staff* at points at which Department work was weak. . . . And in the third place, I am poignantly aware that among the paid technical workers within our number, *salaries,* with one exception or possibly two exceptions, *are too low.* With the passing of the depression, Hull-House owes to its staff members an increase in salaries, or a restoration of cuts. The Head Resident believes that the Budget should be so set up. There are moments when such action tremendously lifts morale! The Head Resident has been repeatedly told, however, that she is ''to have nothing to do with funds.'' She feels strongly, on the other hand, that Hull-House cannot be administered by a Head Resident without the right to make policy in this respect.

. . . One more consideration has weighed heavily. An Executive's salary sometimes means the *sacrifice of freedom and initiative.* The position of a paid agent to execute orders is completely distasteful to me. This Head Resident's freedom is not for sale. Freedom for initiative and experiment is a precious Hull-House heritage. I have had no intention, however, of abusing initiative and freedom. Miss Addams' leadership has opened up a future path, both in interests and in methods, that points the way for years to come. She constantly refused, however, to make the future program either rigid or too definite. A Head Resident who cannot be trusted with freedom of action and initiative should not be entrusted with the office at all.

Since these two conditions within which this service seems possible to me—*half time and no salary*—appear unacceptable (to the President of the Board and to certain of its members), the only course for me is to step aside and make way for a paid Head Resident on full time.

It is the President's expressed belief that *''unless the Head Resident accepts a salary, the Board has no control over her.''* The relationship desired with that body by the Head Resident would be *not control, but cooperation.* . . .

In an institution organized as Miss Addams organized Hull-House, with Departments, Schools, and Committees, it has seemed sound to this Head Resident to continue the delegation of initiative and responsibility to the Heads of those Departments and others. Without Miss Addams, we have all known that *more responsibility devolved upon each Resident.*

That the division of executive responsibility and its assumption by various House Committees should be questioned by members of the governing body, has been a great surprise. The Head Resident did not agree to do all there is to be done at Hull-House. But far more important even than that, she believes that the *strength of the Settlement Program depends upon the responsible operation of it by all the Residents* as a group. It *has always been the Residents of Hull-House who gave its work character, and quality, and distinction.* Upon them its real future depends (far more than upon its Board of Trustees). . . .

A Trustee told a Resident recently, that ''It is the function of the Board of Trustees to hire the staff, raise the money, and run the institution.''

It would seem to one living at Hull-House that such a definition ignores several very important factors in the situation:

. . . *The so-called ''staff'' are not all ''hired.''* Some of the most important work done at Hull-House has always been by persons who are not ''hired.''

. . . *A Settlement, as is indicated by its very name, is more than an office or an agency.* It is not only home and a residence, but as Dr. [Graham] Taylor and Miss Addams often pointed out, it is *a way of life.* Its efforts in the past have often counted in the community because of that fact first of all, as week day trips to an office might never count. One can hardly ''run''—''a way of life.''

. . . The third consideration which that definition ignores is the *danger of absentee dictatorship*. Facts are known best by those living on the spot. Policies which appear desirable in theory are often far from practical when situations are met close at hand.

Miss Addams' wisdom in providing in the Hull-House By-Laws (Article VIII) that "at least one of the members of the Board of Trustees shall reside at Hull-House" seems almost self-evident. This stipulation was omitted from the By-Laws, when amended by the Hull-House Trustees at a meeting on November 27, 1935. The fact that there *was no Trustee living at Hull-House when it was so amended* raises of course a legal question. It is believed that Miss Addams' plan in this respect was not accidental; that her counsel should again guide in this respect; and that a Trustee in residence should be restored to the Board.

All these considerations are far more basic than the mere question as to who is Head Resident at the moment. Misunderstandings that are so costly to the spirit, torn initiative, and checkmated efforts cannot be avoided until there is a dispassionate examination and analysis of the respective functions and province and autonomy of the Trustees and of the Residents; and similarly of the President and of the Head Resident. In stepping out of the latter position at this time, I shall be helping to clear the air, and so permit the question to be faced, uncomplicated, upon impersonal merits alone. . . .

We shall both miss you very deeply. Hull-House has been home to us for a long time. We met here. But Hull-House has now passed the first stage of this internal transition period. The next step ahead will not be so difficult as that through which we have passed.

Charlotte Carr— Settlement Lady

Milton Mayer

After Adena Rich's resignation, Louise Bowen and the board began to search for a new head resident. They found her in New York. Charlotte E. Carr (1890–1956) had had no settlement experience and admitted freely that she had little reverence for Hull-House or Jane Addams. With her cursing, smoking, drinking, and disdain for the past, she was nothing like "saintly Jane." Carr wanted to lift Hull-House out of its tradition-worn path and to create something new and vital, but she wanted to do it in her own style. Her interest in relief problems and the labor movement led her to shift the emphasis of programs and activities at Hull-House. It did not take Carr long to alienate the residents and workers who revered Jane Addams. She also angered Hull-House contributors with her manner and political activities, and she pushed the board of trustees to the limit of their endurance with her financial excesses and changes in the settlement's program. A major confrontation with Bowen and the board was inevitable. Milton Mayer (b. 1908) did not know all this when he described Carr and her hopes and ideas in December 1938. [Milton Mayer, "Charlotte Carr—Settlement Lady," Atlantic Monthly (December 1938), 741–748.]

I

A few months ago a "fat Irishwoman" (as she describes herself) decided she'd seen enough front-line service for a while. For twenty years she had manned the barricades, as a policewoman under Brooklyn Bridge, as Secretary of Labor of war-torn Pennsylvania, and as director of relief in New York City. Now she was tired and forty-seven (though she looked neither) and she wanted a furlough. What she got was one of the toughest assignments in America.

When Charlotte Carr hit town to succeed Jane Addams as head of Hull House, Chicago couldn't quite make her out. For the new boss of the world's most famous settlement did not resemble the old in any superficial respect except total displacement. Charlotte Carr is probably the only graduate of boarding school and Vassar who ever walked a beat. To-night she dominates a drawing-room with native grace; to-morrow she dominates a relief demonstration with native persuasion. Her long service in behalf of the hard-bitten under-privileged has awakened in this well-born woman the traits of her ancestors. They, seven or eight generations back, were meat-and-potatoes Irish.

Chicago was a little afraid of the rugged successor of the "angel of Hull House." That was partly because Chicago didn't know Charlotte Carr, and partly because it had forgotten that it once called Jane Addams all the dirty names it could think of. But Charlotte Carr wasn't worried. She knew Chicago; she had seen Pittsburgh and Philadelphia and New York fighting and stumbling and afraid, and the picture was the same everywhere. At the moment Chicago happened to be stumbling worst.

The settlement house as an institution, as Jane Addams knew it and made it great, was as dead as Austria. It had fulfilled its early purposes, outlived its original usefulness. The settlements may not have been aware of their unhappy state—few corpses are. But Charlotte Carr has a facility for sizing things up. The result, at Hull House, has been audit and upheaval, to the end that the glorious landmark of an old era may be a living agency for a new.

For many years Hull House had a community doll that the children of the neighboring tenements came and played with. "What Hull House is interested in doing now," says the new Head Resident, "is making the homes of those children fit to have a doll in, and enabling their parents to buy them one."

The first heresy was the de-emphasis of such Hull-House prides as pottery and weaving. Work in the arts and crafts was shifted from a production basis to an educational one. Hull House got out of the bric-a-brac business. "Why should working people weave rugs in 1938?" Charlotte Carr wanted to know. "Let's ship these looms to a mental hospital and send the weavers down to City Hall in a nice, orderly committee to tell the Mayor what their neighborhood needs."

Charlotte Carr put carpenters to work inside the ancient buildings of Hull-House, and classrooms took shape in such holy relics as the Jane Club. Founded by Miss Addams as a cooperative home for working women who were dispossessed when they went out on strike, the Jane Club had become just a good cheap place to live.

When Jane Addams moved into it, forty-eight years ago, Chicago's nineteenth ward was one of the plague spots of America—an unrelieved slum, rotting and stinking within and eating its way into the rest of the careless city. In the square mile between Hull House and the river there was one bathtub. There were no parks or playgrounds. For every pickpocket clubbed by the police there were twenty maturing in every poolroom. The children of the immigrants earned four cents an hour at piecework on garments.

Hull House had two jobs, from the first. One was to make the poor less miserable in their poverty. The other was to make them less poor. The first had the blessings of Chicago's "leading citizens"; the second did not. Jane Addams and Hull House fought the city. They forced Chicago to establish a juvenile court, to build small parks and playgrounds where the children of the poor could get at them. They forced Illinois to pass factory inspection laws, the eight-hour day for women, and a workmen's compensation act. By their example, they carried these reforms to many another city and state.

Hull House was the haven of every unpopular movement of its time. Its halls were open to every new idea, its heart to every losing cause. Young mavericks of every shade took refuge under its wings. The early residents of Hull House included Ellen Gates Starr, Walter S. Gifford,* Sidney Hillman, Dr. Alice Hamilton, Julia Lathrop, Gerard Swope, Robert Morss Lovett, Florence Kelley, Frances Perkins, John Dewey—yes, and Benny Goodman. Young Crown Prince Leopold was there, looking out from his window onto Polk Street and observing that in all of Belgium there was no street quite so wretched.

The battles of the early years were ultimately won. The sweatshop was shamed. Trade-unions were accepted. Bathtubs and forums were no longer oddities. The University of Chicago, which had spurned Jane Addams in the early days, was only one of the respectable institutions which fell over themselves trying to honor her. At seventy she was still known, in some quaint circles, as "the most dangerous woman in America," but John D. Rockefeller, Jr., echoed the sentiment of

---

*Walter S. Gifford (1885–1966) became chairman of the board of AT&T, 1948–1950, and U.S. Ambassador to Great Britain, 1950–1953.—Eds.

Rooftops of Hull-House.

the world when he called her "the most Christlike of all living human beings."

II

Its battles won, Hull House, like the rest of the settlements, rested on its oars. The result was that it came to a standstill. When Charlotte Carr took over, the place was a museum, a shrine to Jane Addams. The thousands who still poured through its doors came to see not what Hull House was doing but what it had done. The bloody battleground had become a "must" item for out-of-town tourists. Tinted memories overlay the scenes of Jane Addams' struggles. The crusaders were gone. Pottery, weaving, and dramatics attracted bored young matrons from other sections of the city. Hull House had become Chicago's toy.

There stood $800,000 worth of property, occupying a city block, in the center of a neighborhood that had begun to forget it was there. Its usefulness as a refuge and rallying ground for the immigrant had disappeared as the foreign-born got the feel of the new country and learned its language and its ways. Immigration had dried up. Hull House was a place for "foreigners," and the foreigners were no longer foreign.

The wealthy trustees of the institution dumped their problem child in the lap of a spinster who had never been a social worker. They asked her to come to Chicago and find the place of the settlement house in a new age. Charlotte Carr gave them fair warning. She told them she was considering accepting an executive job with the CIO. She told them that in certain circles she was known as "Scarlet" Carr.

They didn't bat an eye. Their chairman, Mrs. Joseph T. Bowen, had abandoned her patrician role in Chicago society half a century before to follow the thorny path of Jane Addams. Seventy-nine-year-old Mrs. Bowen had gone to the trustees and asked them if "Hull House was going to stand still and go on making tams, taffies, and tidies." Only one of them answered yes, and he resigned. Then the board told Charlotte Carr to pitch in. The place was hers.

The biggest obstacle in the way of the "Irish policewoman" was the dead hand of her predecessor. In Charlotte Carr, Chicago wanted another Jane Addams not the Jane Addams who was misunderstood, despised, and even hated while she lived, but the "Saint Jane" of blessed memory. One look at the newcomer, who offers her guests a drink and can cuss in a crisis, and Chicago whistled with mixed amazement and respect.

But to those who know the No. 1 Settlement Lady of 1938 and the life of the No. 1 Settlement Lady of fifty years ago, their differences are superficial. Jane Addams was "no lady" in her day. She organized trade-unions, lobbied for social legislation, defied the railroad barons, and sheltered the "anarchists"—in an era when decent women rustled modestly between kitchen and drawing-room and never, never read the newspapers. Beneath her mantle of serenity was the spirit of a fierce fighter, defying the thunder of the mobs and the millionaires alike.

Miss Addams is remembered widely but inaccurately for the last ten years of her life, which, painfully ill as she was, she devoted to frantic efforts to save the world from another war. As a peace worker she assumed a relatively harmless aspect in the eyes of solid citizens. But in the last year of her life the enfeebled founder of Hull House took to the battlements again to fight for a system of old-age pensions and government-subsidized housing. Ten days before she died she appeared before the Cook County Commissioners and demanded public relief for the jobless and suffering.

Jane Addams was a Quaker and a product of the nineteenth century. Charlotte Carr is Irish, and a product of the twentieth. The new head of Hull House is an enveloping personality, a strong executive, an eager, adventurous nature. If her thinking falls short of profundity, it abounds in facility. Between action and contemplation her choice of action is invariable. Externally, and in the little, she is politic and canny; in the large she is imprudent and uncalculating, an emotionalist with an incidental knack for administration. She was meant to be the hard-headed, soft-hearted mother of about fourteen unmanageable kids.

She looks her duality, too. Like Hull House, she finds it equally natural to be stately and informal. Her dominating height reduces her heft to dignified, yet potentially genial, proportion. Her eyes are at once jovial and belligerent. And while her nose and mouth are small and unobtrusively businesslike, her heap of black hair, slightly graying, rides off in a dozen directions and gives her big Irish face an Ossa-on-Pelion look. Jane Addams hated to be called "sweet"; no one will make the same mistake with the laughing, scrapping woman who has taken her place.

Miss Carr's lifelong struggle for the betterment of industrial conditions is her qualification for the backbreaking job of restoring life to an institution which was established to improve the lot of the "lower third." The nation that was still handicraft and pioneer fifty years ago is to-day industrialized. Charlotte Carr's career has convinced her—and this may be a clue to the future of Hull House—that enlightened organization among industrial workers is a modern bulwark of the democracy to which she is wholly devoted. But first, she insists, workers must be educated in democracy if they are to save their organizations from exploitation. And that may be another clue to the future of Hull House.

As Jane Addams saw the danger signals of democracy in the squalid back streets of Freeport, Illinois, and became a social worker, so Charlotte Carr saw them, as a girl, in the mills and factories of Dayton. The half-century that separated these two girlhoods saw the national economy expand so rapidly that it had no time to solve the problems it created. Charlotte Carr was still in her teens when she decided to go into industrial work; to bridge, if she could, the widening gap between honest labor and honest capital in an assembly-line age. Her father owned a collection agency, and she learned what hard times did to the poor who bought luxuries on the installment plan. She saw

the breakdown of paternalism when the unorganized workers of a Dayton factory walked out because a genuinely benevolent employer, who happened to be "bugs" on health, refused them salt and pepper in the company dining room.

Her parents had refused to send her to college. She was (she says) unpopular, and they wanted to assure her of social success by "bringing her out" as soon as she left boarding school. So she ran away and got a job in Pittsburgh. Mama and papa relented and let her go to Vassar. There, she recalls, she learned very little, but as the fat girl of the dramatic association she starred in the roles of Falstaff, President Taft, and Friar Tuck.

Out of Vassar, she became the $18-a-month matron of an orphan asylum; then a "kidnapper" for a child placement agency in New York, delegated to bring back children who got into the wrong homes; then a policewoman in New York during the war, patrolling Brooklyn Bridge and Sand Street from 6 P.M. to 6 A.M.; then the personnel manager successively of a printing plant in New York, a hat factory in Brooklyn, and a textile mill in New Hampshire.

It was in these years, in the world of lower conflicts, that Charlotte Carr got her higher education. She already had the superficial equipment for Park Avenue dinner parties—dignity (which she turns on and off, mostly off, at will), ease of bearing, and the social conversational graces befitting a daughter of Vassar. But it was in "bumming around," as she puts it, that she picked up a stone here and a stone there for the foundation of what is now a full-blown social philosophy.

"Charity," she says, "costs more than unions." Again: "Child labor is cheap—until you have to build penitentiaries and county hospitals." These Carrisms fall casually from her lips, but they are grounded in long experience. Behind them lie more than theories. As a personnel manager she discovered that 85 per cent of the factory workers to whom charity had to minister were nonunionists. A few years later, when she worked under Al Smith and Frances Perkins in the New York woman's bureau, she made a survey revealing that more than 50 per cent of the children under seventeen working in factories had physical afflictions that were being aggravated by the kind of work they were doing.

It was Governor Gifford Pinchot who called

her to Pennsylvania to start a woman's bureau. The state had never known civil service, but heard about it from Charlotte Carr. Pinchot's successor fired her because she refused to contribute to a campaign fund, and Pinchot then made Charlotte Carr a campaign issue. He promised to bring her back to Pennsylvania, and the people elected him. She was appointed Secretary of Labor.

While Pinchot was out of office, Miss Carr was industrial consultant for the Charity Organization Society of New York, headed by that old Hull-House boy, President Walter S. Gifford of the American Telephone and Telegraph Company. Representing organized philanthropy's efforts to cope with depression, she added another stone or two to the foundation of her philosophy. Private charity was still bearing the relief load, and Miss Carr made a survey which demonstrated the impossibility of absorbing the growing numbers of able-bodied men and women thrown out of work. She learned too that when private charity releases its clients to employers at substandard wages it is simply creating more charity cases.

III

. . .

When Pinchot's second term expired, his Secretary of Labor went back to home base—New York—to look for a job. Governor [Herbert H.] Lehman immediately appointed her to his unemployment commission. A few months later she was hired by Mayor La Guardia—whom she had never seen or talked to—as assistant director of home relief for New York City. It wasn't long before the director, a member of the stronger sex, had retired, and Charlotte Carr was feeding New York's million hungry with a staff of 18,000 and a budget of $9,000,000 a month.

Guided by all her past experience, she ran the big town's relief administration not on the basis of "humane" treatment of the individual but with the single aim of doing nothing that would make worse the kind of conditions she was trying to cure. Typical of her clashes with the social workers was her insistence upon deducting the earnings of children from a family's relief allotment, though her colleagues pointed out that children whose wages were taken by their families to run the household sometimes ran away from home. Agreeing heartily that this was unfortunate, Director Carr pointed out that unless children's wages were deducted from the relief allotment, parents would keep their children at work and stay home themselves, thus getting a full allotment and the children's wages besides. Her job was to spend available funds intelligently, not "humanely." . . .

IV

Breaking away from New York and La Guardia wasn't easy. The Little Flower stormed and pounded and told her he'd never speak to her again. But she just laughed—and so did he. She wanted to see how the other half lives—not the other half of the people, but the other half of those who represent the people. For twenty years Charlotte Carr had been a public official. Now she was going to be one of those who go to the public officials and try to get things done. She was going to be—horror of horrors—a social worker.

When she told her friends why she was resigning as New York's relief director, they suggested she get ready to write her memoirs—only, instead of *Twenty Years at Hull House,* the title would be *Twenty Days.* She wouldn't last a month, they told her. Settlement houses and social work were not for the likes of Charlotte Carr. She wasn't ready, they said, for the old lady's home. But she went. And she's still there. And it's a fair guess that she'll be there a long time.

The settlement house is dead. That's as it should be. "The very job of the settlement," says Charlotte Carr, "is to keep putting itself out of business. It can't cure the ills of society, but it can point the way. As the public awakens to the settlement's example, public agencies absorb its functions. Then the settlement writes the past off the books and moves on to new frontiers."

The new frontiers of Hull House are two, and Charlotte Carr is formulating her plans to cross them.

The first, she believes, is adult education, and something more than the kind of adult education that consists of instruction in English and that nebulous something called citizenship. The new classrooms at Hull House are filled with workers of the lowest wage groups, and they are studying labor law and collective bargaining. As long as workers are going to organize—and England, France, and Sweden convince her that they are— Miss Carr thinks they might as well know how to organize intelligently and democratically. In addition to the workers' education programme, the famous Hull House forum, dormant for several years, has been revived, and it is packing 'em in.

The second frontier that Charlotte Carr wants to put behind her is the elimination of nationalistic barriers and racial lines that serve the machine politicians of a big city and perpetuate irrational antagonisms that divide groups which have common interests. When she arrived at Hull House, Miss Carr found that there wasn't a Negro in residence—in a heavily Negro neighborhood. She persuaded Dewey and Faith Jones, distinguished Negro social workers, to move in and set up an education programme. To stimulate the thinking of Negroes, Mexicans, Italians, Poles, along neighborhood instead of national and racial lines, she has begun opening community centers in an ever-widening radius from Hull House.

This woman who has made so many surveys in her time has a consuming contempt for talk and a consuming faith in facts. She has established a research staff, putting her own investigative ability and the man power of Hull House to work on such foggy problems as public health service and city planning for blighted areas. She wants Hull House to be once more what it was in the old days—a sounding board for Chicago's needs, a center for educating not only its neighbors but its city.

Strangely enough, she isn't raising the roof. Defying her own impetuous Irish nature, she has begun scientifically on the foundations. She knows what she wants, she thinks she knows what the settlement house needs, but, like any good builder, she gets the lay of the land before she turns a shovel. The months she's been at Hull House have been devoted, for the most part, to some arduous listening. She is new at the settlement game; she knows she is new; and she insists that experts, including people who don't like her, tell her what they think of her notions.

Chicago is beginning to cotton to this Jane-Addams-geared-to-a-new-age. She speaks its language. She listens to its troubles. She isn't "high-hat." She is, as she says herself, a "sentimental Irishman," and the boys in the City Hall

will listen to her where they laugh at the professional reformers. Already she's been called in on Chicago's tangled relief situation as chairman of an emergency committee appointed by the mayor. She keeps a fire going under the committee and makes the mayor like it.

The settlement house isn't going to turn twentieth-century overnight. It's a long pull, and Charlotte Carr knows it. That's why she's taking her time. But one of these days you'll hear the eggs being broken for the new omelette on Halsted Street. Mossy memories are going to be shattered and a few old hats crushed. There will be plenty of squawks from the tenders of the sacred shrine.

Well, Jane Addams could take it, as they didn't say in those days, and Charlotte Carr is not what you'd call a violet. She's forgotten all about that vacation she had to have. It's heavy duty from here on in.

Integration at Hull-House

Dewey R. Jones

The settlement movement, as a general rule seemed ambivalent about integration; Hull-House was no exception, but it was better than most. Prior to World War I there were few blacks living in the Hull-House neighborhood. Black leaders came to the settlement as speakers and visitors. Residents were supportive of local and national black organizations like the Chicago Urban League and the National Association for the Advancement of Colored People. Celia Parker Woolley, who founded the Frederick Douglass settlement in 1905 on the Chicago's southside to promote integration, found ready and active assistance at Hull-House.

By the 1930s, however, blacks formed a large segment of the Hull-House neighborhood, and the settlement began to respond. The minutes of the Hull-House board of trustees for January 21, 1938, indicate: "Miss Carr declared that she felt quite strongly that Hull-House has not been giving adequate service to the negroes, who are com-

The Hull-House Community Club organized about 1927 meets at the Bowen Country Club.

paratively new neighbors, nor does the House have the contacts which would enable it to ascertain the type of services needed." She recommended Dewey R. Jones to conduct a study of black needs and to come into residence with his wife, Faith. Jones had been a journalist and had served until 1938 as a special assistant on black issues to Secretary of the Interior Harold Ickes. He had been involved on the Secretary's behalf in efforts to guarantee integrated public housing in Chicago.

Jones took up his project at the settlement early in 1938, but his work was cut short by his death in April 1939. The following excerpt from the March 15, 1939, minutes of the executive committee, Division on Education and Recreation, Welfare Council of Metropolitan Chicago, was no doubt based not only on Jones's survey research but also on his experience as one of the first black Hull-House residents. Faith Jefferson Jones became director of Parkway Community Center and the first

black to sit on the board of the Chicago Commons. [Minutes, March 15, 1939, Executive Committee, Division on Education and Recreation, TMs, 7–9. Welfare Council of Metropolitan Chicago Papers, Box 145, Folder 1: Minorities. Manuscript Collection, Chicago Historical Society.]

Most of you know something of the Hull House area, and something of the tradition of the House. It will be 50 years old in October. The area includes the largest Italian population in Chicago, the largest Mexican colony and the second largest Negro colony. If anyone is interested in doing inter-racial work you have an ideal set-up in which to start. I think, however, the facts have shown that Hull House has not done very much in an inter-racial sense as far as Negroes are concerned. I do not believe this was because of any policy of the

House or any decision on anyone's part but just because of a sort of taking for granted that if an institution was in the heart of the community and had facilities, everyone who needed them would take advantage of them. That didn't happen in the case of the Negro because the experience of Negroes has been that when they assume too quickly that whatever facilities are available, are available to them, they have found they are not intended to participate at all. They are sometimes told in subtle fashion and sometimes in brutal fashion that they are not wanted.

Hull House has gone on serving as a melting pot and clearing house and center for bringing children in off the streets, developing recreational facilities for them, classes, almost anything you could think of, with absolutely no Negro participation in the program. That started because no direct invitation was made to them to come in. I believe that very attitude set up a policy which made new workers who came into the settlement assume the attitude that since they found no Negroes it wasn't their job to bring them in, or that it might be dangerous. I found in talking with a number of the staff about this particular question that there is a definite feeling that it is dangerous to attempt to break precedents. Everyone said this is an Italian community and Italians are Fascist inclined and we cannot afford to upset the good an institution of this kind can do by injecting matters which some members of the staff consider extraneous. That idea developed to such a place where it was almost an established policy.

Twelve years ago a Negro mothers' club was organized, at the expressed invitation of Miss Addams. Most of the mothers did not live in the immediate vicinity. They attended meetings regularly. Every year the Hull House yearbook showed this Negro club and stated that Negroes were taking part in the program. I had occasion last year to talk with one of the original founders of this organization who told me that they had been meeting there for twelve years but as far as getting anything out of the Hull House program, that did not happen. They weren't invited to take part in any of the activities that had been set up for the general community. They were not on any mailing list. They had their meetings only. Their children came the same night, and when the Federal Government began to assist in this type of program

Hull House acquired some W. P. A. and N.Y. A. workers and one of them was assigned the job of corralling the Negro children and keeping them busy. This continued for some time and suddenly Miss Carr looked around and knowing there were so many Negroes and none taking part brought the question into the open. Within the last three years some attention has been given to the problem. It is more difficult to do anything about it now because there have been so many traditions and such a long span of activity when no attempt was made to solve the problem. Efforts now are definitely frowned upon by certain people in the community.

It does create a problem. The community workers have found resentment among the neighbors against any program that had for its objective the integration of Negroes into the House activities. Bowen Country Club, which is a well-equipped camp, had just absolutely ignored the Negro as far as the camp was concerned. Last summer 21 Negroes attended the camp, which is a very small proportion but they considered it a beginning.* Last year Hull House began to organize community centers. Two centers were set up in dense Italian communities and the people in that community were asked to take over the actual management, the idea being that these could serve as outposts for Hull House and develop community leaders and a community spirit right in the neighborhood where people could come together who had problems in common. These two centers were started and seemed to be quite successful. Another attempt was made to go into the near Negro neighborhood on Blue Island Avenue and a worker was secured to work with these children, the idea being that in time they could start a center there. This was attempted about three years ago, after the other two centers were started, and the worker did a fairly good job of getting these people together and playing, but when they attempted to get a building to house this group it was found impossible. The matter was finally given up.

The worker stayed there for some time, and would take these youngsters and teach them games; but eventually that was given up, so that now the two Italian centers are still flourishing but

*There is photographic evidence that black children attended Hull-House summer camp in 1906 (see p. 82).—Eds.

the attempt to form a Negro center hasn't made any progress at all. The worker isn't there any longer and the children have gone back to whatever they were doing before the worker came.

The Hull House music school draws no lines and makes everyone welcome who cares to come in. The same is true with the art department. It just happens that thus far very few have come into these activities. The game room, which was just opened this year, began drawing in the boys who had been using Hull House and immediately became filled to capacity by children who came in after school. An embarrassing thing came up. People who had heard about Hull-House saw Negroes in the street but not in the House and began to ask questions and wondered if Negroes were barred.

It was thought the best way to start on this program would be to introduce some Negroes to the game room where the children came. We felt they shouldn't be surprised or resentful at finding Negroes in the game room with them after school if they went to school with them. After a while, just by consciously being aware of the problem and watching it from every point of view and telling the other children, "This boy is one of your neighborhood boys and he wants to play here; we are trying to help him as we are trying to help you," it didn't take very long for the boys to forget whatever resentment they had. Now there are a number of Negro boys in the game room. They aren't registered by clubs, but register as individuals.

An interesting offshoot happened last week. One of the groups had been going to the Duncan Y. M. C. A. for swimming. There was one Negro in the group. The worker made no comment on the racial situation. The first day the boy in charge of the pool seemed surprised but did not say anything. When the swimming period was over he told the worker that he hoped one of the boys would not be back but did not name the boy. The worker pretended not to understand. The next time the boy came again. The worker in charge of the boys was told that the Negro boy could not come back. That matter was adjusted very quietly, when Miss Carr got in touch with the executive secretary, who stated that the matter should never have been brought up and he considered the incident closed. He did say there were rules which prevented Negroes in the Y. M. C. A. pool. The boy went yesterday and there was no question at all. We feel something has been done there at least to carry the same idea a little farther than Hull House itself.

It has been my experience that a very large part of the difficulty that Negroes have in trying to fit into these programs is traceable directly to those people in charge of the programs who assume there will be trouble if they attempt to bring about integration. They have certain ideas about Negroes and Whites and they feel it would cause trouble if they attempt to do it. Wherever we have found it possible to break down that idea among the leaders we have found that 90 per cent of the problem was solved and that there was no trouble after the people understood that the leaders wanted it done that way.

When the Jane Addams Housing Project was about to open the question was discussed among the leaders of the [Chicago Housing] Authority as to whether it would be wise to permit Negroes to live in the project. They overlooked the fact that Negroes had lived in the neighborhood for years side by side with Whites; yet I heard officials say it would be a dangerous thing. Those objections were broken down, the Negroes were taken into the project, and there have not been any disturbances yet as far as I know. If the leaders and workers make up their minds that this should be done and feel that it can be done, and then undertake the job of doing it, you yourself will go a long way toward helping to solve the problem. That has worked out to a very large extent. As far as the inter-racial problem goes at Hull House some definite steps have been taken toward bringing about a kind of melting pot, the kind of agency the House has stood for in theory all these years. There are one hundred Negro families almost within a block of Hull House. About 20 per cent of the people who participate in the Hull House program no longer live in the Hull House area. Hull House is not particularly a local institution any longer.

Rug Cutters at Hull-House

Todd Hunter

One of the most famous jazz musicians of the twentieth century studied clarinet at Hull-House and played in the settlement boys' band. Benny Goodman (1909–1986), the "King of Swing," grew up in the Hull-House neighborhood and took music lessons from band leader James V. Sylvester during the early 1920s. In 1938, an enormous success, he returned to play a concert at Hull-House for the neighborhood children. He brought the other members of the famed Goodman group, jazz pianist Teddy Wilson and drummer Gene Krupa. This edited version of a radio broadcast by Todd Hunter on September 15, 1938, describes the concert scene at Hull-House and the settlement's reception for one of its own. [Todd Hunter, "Rug Cutters at Hull-House," Hull-House Yearbook (1939), 45–47.]

On the way down to Hull-House late today, the cab driver turned around and said, "That must be SOME place. Something's always going on down there." "What makes you think so?" I asked him. "Well," the cab driver said, "I get quite a bit of business down there—a lot of people from the Gold Coast. Say," he continued, "what kind of a place is it?" But before I had a chance to tell him, we were there—800 South Halsted. I jumped out of the cab and dashed into Bowen Hall where—

Over one thousand five hundred children of all nationalities, big and little—boys and girls—were packed and jammed . . . yelling, cheering, chattering, and whistling . . . a perfect Bedlam of noise. A woman was upon the stage blowing a whistle for silence, but it was of no use. A colored boy came out on the stage and went into a tap dance—with kids yelling louder than ever. . . .

Finally, the big hall in Hull-House quieted down—it was then about four-fifteen—and the speaker on the stage was heard to say, "Boys and girls, we have just learned that Benny Goodman won't be here until five o'clock." A mighty groan went up, then boos and stamping of feet. Shortly, someone turned out the lights and an old, animated cartoon of "Felix the Cat" was flashed on the screen and the boos changed to wild applause as Felix got his revenge on a mean old man by baiting his house with a big piece of cheese that served to call the mice from all over town—Felix the while pacing back and forth, his hands behind his back, chuckling at the old man's distress.

At last the lights went up . . . Miss Charlotte Carr, the head resident of Hull-House, appeared on the stage . . . she smiled and waved . . . and instantly, such a screaming and yelling you never heard in your life! For she had with her none other than Benny Goodman, the King of Swing. You couldn't hear yourself think as he put his clarinet together and as one of his men sat down at the piano and another assembled his drums.

Benny Goodman just stood there in the center of the stage for a moment, a big smile as he looked out into the faces of the neighborhood kids of Hull-House . . . and his mind probably went back to the days *he* was a neighborhood kid of Hull-House . . . the days years ago when as a boy he, Benny Goodman, used to go to Hull-House, take music lessons from James V. Sylvester, and play in the Hull-House boys band. But only for a moment did he pause. . . .

The King of Swing put his clarinet to his mouth and swung out with "Some of These Days" and "Chinatown." In the middle of a number he sat down on the edge of the stage surrounded by a seething, swaying mass of boys and girls . . . it was THEIR Benny Goodman, if only for a few all-too-short moments. Soon he was gone and the party was over . . . the children to go back to their homes in the Hull-House neighborhood . . . Benny Goodman back to his theatre engagement and his career as the most popular band leader of the day.

I never go down to Hull-House but what I come away with a feeling that *there* is one place where ideals really appear to work . . . a cross-section of many of the racial groups of the world were there this afternoon listening to Benny Goodman. One little girl was dressed in the Old World style, her ear lobes pierced with ear rings, a shawl about her head, and her little baby brother in her arms . . . there were Jews, Negroes, Italians, Greeks, and Mexicans . . . all jammed in together, singing and laughing in a place that is famous the world over as a haven for the underprivileged. . . .

And at the end of one of the motion pictures which was flashed on the screen while they were waiting for Benny Goodman—at the very end of the picture, the American Flag came into view together with these words: ''For true liberty, respect the rights of others.'' Instantly, a cheer went up. . . .

Yes, as the cab driver said—there's always something going on at Hull-House!

Fiftieth Birthday Party

Lloyd Lewis

Hull-House celebrated its fiftieth birthday in 1940. Between May 17 and 26, at the usual spring festival time, the settlement held open house to display its progress and development since its founding in 1889. The residents and neighbors presented plays, dances, and exhibits and held forums, neighborhood parties, a street fair, a parade, and a concert. Both Mayor Edward J. Kelly of Chi-

Charlotte Carr, settlement director, introduces Benny Goodman to his Hull-House audience.

cago and Fiorello H. LaGuardia of New York City participated in the ceremonies. Robert M. Hutchins and Gerard Swope were there, as were University of Chicago Professor of Social Work Wayne McMillen and Dr. Alice Hamilton. The group of former residents attending was almost as impressive as that which had attended the fortieth anniversary commemoration. There was one big difference, though: Jane Addams was not there; instead, the week of ceremonies was held as a tribute to her life and service.

Lloyd Lewis (1891–1949), a journalist who was to become managing editor of the Chicago Daily News, *used the occasion to write a story on Hull-House for the* New York Times Magazine. *His article, "The House That Jane Addams Built," evoked a nostalgic view of the settlement's glorious past while almost ignoring its present. The attitude was typical during this interim period when Hull-House was not only searching for stable leadership but also trying to establish a genuine purpose and direction in a field in which settlements were no longer the leaders. [Lloyd Lewis, "The House That Jane Addams Built,"* New York Times Magazine *(May 19, 1940), 12, 22.]*

When Jane Addams rented the old Hull mansion, the unskilled laborers around Halsted and Taylor Streets were earning from $9 to $12 a week, and little children were coming home with pennies earned at the rate of 4 cents an hour in sweatshop toil.

Miss Addams was mad about this, but not boiling—she was too tolerant to boil even when hammering the hardest at the "oppressors" of her people—as on Sept. 14, 1889,* she and Miss Starr moved into the Hull mansion, and, with one housekeeper to help with the domestic duties, opened the first "social settlement house" in America, though the term wasn't applied to the venture for some years to come. Their aim, they said in the incorporation papers of Hull-House, was "to provide a center for a higher social life; to institute and maintain educational and philanthropic enterprises, and to investigate and im-

*Jane Addams always said she and Ellen Starr opened the settlement on September 18, 1889.—Eds.

prove the conditions in the industrial districts of Chicago."

Aristocratic friends, members of the old Yankee ruling class of the city, had advised Jane Addams not to make this plunge into the slums. They said it would make her inacceptable in the homes of the "best people." And as she and Hull-House fought their way down through the next two score years, there was always to be heard a protest—sometimes a blast, sometimes a growl—about their perilous fostering of radicalism. That certain reactionaries always wanted "to run Jane Addams out of town" was true from 1889 until her death in 1935.

But she remained socially eligible and able to hobnob with the city's rich; she went everywhere in those pioneering days, enlisting money and influence. And she could talk well, as William Jennings Bryan had discovered in 1881 when, representing Illinois College in a debate, he measured words with a Miss Addams representing Rockford College.

Miss Starr also was eligible in the fashionable sector, which had by the Eighteen Nineties shifted from the West to the South Side. Another Hull-House resident, Mary Rozet Smith, daughter of the oldest local aristocracy, went about sweetly dragooning donations from the groaning industrialists.

Often in subsequent years wealthy donors would writhe when Mrs. Florence Kelley, one of Miss Addams's first recruits, went campaigning against sweatshops, or when she clubbed legislators into passing a child-labor law, or when Miss Addams disturbed the even tenor of life by agitating for garbage removal to save children's lives. Such things were all very well and should come in time, but Hull-House moved too fast.

The warfare was bitter. When Governor Altgeld died in 1902 nobody but Clarence Darrow and Jane Addams spoke at his little funeral. Altgeld had moved all the power of the Governor's office to help Miss Addams and Mrs. Kelley in their fight to get humane laws for the protection of women and children in factories and sweatshops, and had stood with them for that radical proposal, the eight-hour day.

Since the turn of the century the fame of Hull-House has become world-wide. The strenuous T. R., with his zeal for reform, poured hosannas

The Hull-House Boys' Band on Polk Street.

upon Miss Addams and the whole social settlement movement, which by that time had become important in most of the large American cities. A whole school of settlement houses had grown up in imitation of Hull-House, and the University of Chicago had, by its marked friendship, given Miss Addams's idea high academic and scientific approval.

Some of the university's most celebrated professors gave time to the settlement's citizenship, poetry and English-language classes; for early Hull-House had arranged to give quarters to a certain number of "residents," persons who paid their own expenses and gave their leisure time to the manifold projects of the institution.

The influence of Hull-House upon many of its residents of the past fifty years has been highly apparent. It is to be seen in the social-mindedness of Harold Ickes, John Dewey, Professor Robert Morss Lovett, Frances Perkins, Walter S. Gifford, Gerard Swope, W. L. Mackenzie King, Prime Minister of Canada; Julia Lathrop, social settlement authority; Sidney Hillman, union-labor leader; Harriet Monroe, the poet; Francis Hackett, the novelist; William L. Chenery, the editor; Stuart Chase, writer on economics; Alice Hamilton, the scientist of the Harvard Medical School, and Ramsay MacDonald, British statesman, not to mention less-famous educators who dot American colleges and high schools.

The days of the settlement's unorthodoxy are now long gone. Chicago hears about the Hull-House Theatre and its amateur dramatics now more than about Hull-House radicalism. Under Miss Charlotte Carr, who took the directorship in 1937, the settlement goes its busy course, teaching a myriad of things to a myriad of persons, and escaping criticism from the conservative forces of the city.

In its first year Hull-House counted 50,000 persons entering its doors, most of them curious at first, then gradually gaining confidence. Last year over 320,000 persons were served, and more than 30,000 visitors were counted. Now it is estimated that an average of 1,500 persons enter Hull-House daily.

First to arrive on a typical day are the lusty-voiced Negro girls training for household service under a WPA domestic science project. To the rolling tunes of "Wagon Wheels" or "America the Beautiful," they are wielding their mops and brooms by 8 o'clock, wiping away the dust of yesterday's myriad of footprints.

Close on their heels come the white mothers, bringing their babies for a morning's play in the pre-school nursery maintained by the Mary Crane

League, or to be examined in the health service clinics which the league maintains at Hull-House.

While these groups assemble, a constant stream of people flows past the information desk, where a trained worker sits all day answering questions and endeavoring to help. First come men from the neighborhood's several flophouses, asking suggestions as to how to spend their time until the shelters take them in again.

Other neighbors come to ask about the labor laws, the relief laws, and the tenement laws, about personal problems, how to find a missing son, how to get a divorce, what to do about a fire escape that won't work, why the milkman did not deliver milk this morning, or piteously how to make arrangements to bury a child.

Others in trouble call on the telephone. Upstairs in her office Miss Carr and her secretary take care of still another stream of people.

By mid-morning at least one group of tourists has come to Hull-House and must be shown through the settlement, for it has often been said that, after the stockyards, Hull-House is a Chicago visitor's first stopping place.

At 1 o'clock the library opens, and older boys and girls without jobs come in to spend the afternoon with books. Adult classes in art begin, too, at 1 o'clock, and the workers' education classes get under way.

From Monday through Friday this department has an average of ten classes every day, the first at 9 o'clock in the morning; during the evening hours several meet simultaneously. A typical day's schedule includes four classes in English and citizenship, two camera clubs, a class in lip reading, another in creative writing, one in speech improvement, another in beginning economics, and a discussion of current events.

Hull-House really becomes a beehive of activity after school hours. From 3 o'clock until 10:30 in the evening there is hardly a nook or corner which is not occupied by a class or a committee. Boys and girls pour into the game rooms, the gymnasium and the clubrooms, the music-lesson rooms, the art department, the printing shop, where they publish their own newspaper, the Hull-House Star.

In the afternoons junior clubs share the settlement's clubrooms with mothers' groups. One of these is the Stop-Light Mothers' Club, so named because it was organized to campaign for a stoplight at one of the neighborhood's busy intersections, in order that children could come to the settlement by themselves. They obtained the stoplight many months ago, but they have found other things to campaign for, so they have kept their organization alive.

Theatricals attract both children and adults to Hull-House for nightly rehearsals. Just now the major activity of the older group is the creation of "Halsted Street—1940," a living newspaper of community life.

Hull-House, amid its new and manifold activities, is still hammering away upon its old subject of sanitation, with committees of neighbors helping to spread the gospel. The awful slums are still there, but they are not so awful as they once were, and pressure from the United States Government is helping.

One reason why the world hears less of Hull-House today than it did twenty or forty years ago is that the Federal power has now taken over, on a national scale, the social betterment campaign. But Hull-House is still there, just as it was when its flag was the only one in the dawn's early light.

Charlotte Carr Departs

Howard Vincent O'Brien and Time Magazine

Charlotte Carr lasted five years as head resident of Hull-House. Her devotion to the cause of labor, while she ignored other social issues and settlement programs, rankled Hull-House board members and residents. They felt she was leading the settlement in a direction too far from its traditional role and from the ideas of Jane Addams. Carr alienated residents and board members with her personal habits, one of which was smoking and drinking in local saloons with neighborhood men—something they knew Addams would not have done! Carr also angered residents, staff, and neighbors, for whom the settlement house itself was a shrine to Jane Addams, by discarding fur-

nishings and Hull-House memorabilia associated with Addams' life there, and by rearranging the interiors of some buildings so that they little resembled the Hull-House of Addams' day.

As Hull-House braced itself to meet the wartime needs of the 1940s, it was evident that some change would have to be made. Carr did abandon her labor college idea, for which there was little need during the war. But her attempt to return to more traditional settlement programs to meet the challenges of the 1940s came too late. The settlement had lost many of its residents. With World War II, new social workers were hard to find. Money, which Carr had spent with ease, was in desperately short supply at a time when the settlement needed it most to cover wartime expenses. Bowen was vividly aware of this shortage. Priorities had to be set, and by the end of December 1942, Charlotte Carr was gone. She said she quit because she no longer was permitted to be active in political and economic issues "where they related to Hull-House." The board denied Carr's version, saying the dispute arose over wartime cuts in budget.

Here are two brief explanations of her departure. The first appeared in "All Things Considered," a column written by Howard Vincent O'Brien (1888–1947) in a January 1943 issue of the Chicago Daily News. *His observations were based on an interview with a member of the West Side Community Committee of Hull-House neighborhood. The second article appeared in* Time *magazine on January 11, 1943, and is based on an interview with Miss Carr. It needs no explanation. [*Chicago Daily News, *January 1943;* Time, *January 11, 1943.]*

All Things Considered

Charlotte Carr and the trustees of Hull House have parted company. As for all divorces, there are many explanations.

Here is one, offered by a citizen who is a member of the West Side Community Committee and who has spent his life in the neighborhood of Halsted and West Polk.

"The fundamental point is: who shall formu-

late the policies of Hull House? Does Hull House belong to the people it serves, or to the trustees? Shall it be an 'agency' superimposed from above; or shall it be an instrument of the people themselves?

"Only by involving the people significantly in the management of Hull House can it ever become a real part of the attitudes, sentiments and thinking of the people." . . .

Continues this man: "Formerly the largest proportion of our adult population was foreign-born. But our community has now come of age. Most of the adults are native-born, were educated in American schools and act and think as Americans. We believe that our people are capable of participating in the management of our educational and social welfare institutions. Only five years ago there were no parent-teacher associations in our area. Today there are five.

"Because Charlotte Carr was thoroughly familiar with conditions as they are, and was in complete accord with our aspirations for democracy, we consider her resignation an irreparable loss to our community. And we hope that the trustees will reconsider it." . . .

And there you have another example of the ancient idea that he who pays the piper has the right to call the tunes.

The trustees of Hull House pay the bills. Therefore it is their show. Charlotte Carr is a hired hand, and if she wants to take part in politics, she should do it on her own time. And if the people who use the facilities of Hull House insist on participating in its management, they are forgetting their place.

So, I imagine, runs the reasoning of the trustees. And if I were a trustee, I would probably feel that way myself. When you give a dog a bone it's no fun having him snap at you. . . .

That, alas, is the unhappy fate of the charitable. As La Rochefoucauld and other cynics have pointed out, we dislike nobody so much as our benefactors.

Those people on lower Halsted st.—Greeks, Negroes, Mexicans, Italians, and what not—are really serious about "democracy." They want to practice it as well as have it preached at them. They believe in self-government and the community spirit. And that is extremely disconcerting to Mr. and Mrs. Bountiful, who cannot break them-

A gymnasium class at Hull-House.

selves of the habit of looking on a settlement house as a glorified Christmas basket.

Folk dances and classes in pottery are all right. Programs of "Americanization" are uplifting. But what are you going to do when the Americanized become Americans? Then you really are in a fix; and the benevolence in your blood is likely to curdle.

It is vexing indeed when the thing you run turns around and tries to run you.

Haunted Hull House

"Hell, I was fired!" exclaimed Charlotte Carr last week at reports that she had "resigned" after five years as director of Chicago's world-famed slum settlement, Hull House. For many reasons, Charlotte Carr's position at Hull House had become shaky. Some trustees and philanthropists in particular did not like her outspoken political ac-

tivity, her affiliation with the Union for Democratic Action.

Hull House's founder, Jane Addams, in the 19th Century spirit, believed in the social adjustment and education of the alien poor. Miss Carr thought that times had changed, that organization and political pressure were now the best ways for slum dwellers to better their lot.

She deliberately tried to make Hull House take a back seat in the affairs of the Halsted Street slums. "The very job of a settlement is to keep putting itself out of business," she announced, to the horror of Hull House traditionalists who not only wanted to keep the place as a going concern but fixed in the course Jane Addams had set. They were also shocked by Miss Carr's smoking and cocktailing, by her taking Jane Addams' bedroom as her office. Charlotte Carr often mourned that Hull House was in danger of becoming a shrine.

When contributions fell off, Miss Carr inevitably had budget trouble. Running in the red for years, Hull House had used up all its surplus funds. A Carr protégée, Mary Wing, offered to make up further deficits of some $20,000—on condition that her friend Charlotte be given a free hand in shaping Hull House policy. The Board of Trustees found the condition unacceptable, and Charlotte Carr refused to work on a smaller budget.

Hull House's budget of some $110,000 a year was peanuts to Charlotte Carr. "Miss Carr is a big-time operator with a flair for the spectacular," said a trustee last week. In her former job, as director of New York City's Emergency Relief Board (1935–37), she had $9,000,000 a month to spend to feed more people than live in all Milwaukee. Before that, she was Secretary of Labor & Industry in teeming, brawling Pennsylvania.

One of her first jobs after Vassar ('15) was as a policewoman in the tough Navy Yard section of Brooklyn. Tall, heavy, and gusty, Charlotte Carr calls herself "a fat Irishwoman" and is a female counterpart of John L. Lewis—more a labor leader than a social worker. Last week she had been offered a job with the Rosenwald Fund (race relations).

Confusion and Despair

Jessie F. Binford

Hull-House was again without a leader. Everyone knew it was necessary to find someone to take over the activities immediately; yet former residents, residents, staff, and board members alike felt a great deal of care should be taken in choosing a new director. They did not want confusion and indecision, but they did not want another Charlotte Carr either. They hoped to find someone who could revive Hull-House in the tradition of Jane Addams, establish the settlement again as a community force and a leader in the social welfare movement. All knew it had to be someone with a background in social work who could appreciate the problems that had to be faced at Hull-House.

One group of former residents, including Sophonisba P. Breckinridge, Edith Abbott, Esther Kohn, Eri Hulbert, Mr. and Mrs. William F. Byron, and Mr. and Mrs. Kenneth F. Rich, made a suggestion—almost a plea—to the board. They thought the staff, former residents, and neighborhood would cooperate with the board and the new director if the choice of head resident resulted from a search for available people "by a group of friendly, impartial, specially trained and experienced individuals whose knowledge of settlement activities provides a background for a fair appraisal of candidates." All were concerned that Bowen and her board might select someone who would be completely unacceptable.

A letter from Jessie F. Binford (1876–1966) to Bowen best describes the despair at Hull-House, the lack of direction and doubt about the settlement's future that assailed the residents and friends of the settlement on Carr's departure. Binford had come to Hull-House as a resident in 1906; she stayed until 1963. From 1916 until 1952 she was director of the Juvenile Protective Association, and during the early 1960s she was one of a group of neighborhood people who campaigned to save the settlement and its neighborhood from destruction to make way for the University of Illinois' Chicago campus. She was clearly aware of the enormous problems that faced the next director of Hull-House. [Jessie Binford to Louise deKoven Bowen, July 23, 1943, Russell W. Ballard Papers, Jane Addams Memorial Collection, University of Illinois at Chicago Circle.]

Juvenile Protective Association
816 So. Halsted Street
Chicago
July 23, 1943

Mrs. Joseph T. Bowen, President
Hull-House
Bowen Country Club
Waukegan, Illinois

Dear Mrs. Bowen:

Some of us who live at Hull House are vitally interested not only in Hull House, but in the settlement movement, and we have been thinking and talking together these last months about the future of Hull House.

As important as the selection of a new Director is and that it should be made as soon as possible, we sincerely believe that the Board has before it even more important decisions and problems that should be thought over before anyone is asked to come here.

We cannot believe that anyone who is qualified to direct this great institution would consider coming until this has been done.

Many other groups—the Chicago Council of Social Agencies, the Community Fund, the Area Project, and the West Side Community Council and its so called Hull House Citizens Committee—have all been discussing and even taking action on very vital policies in relation to what Hull House should do and what place it is to have in the community.

There is a great deal of discussion today, not only in Chicago but in all cities in which settlements exist, as to their future. Time has changed since their inception; public and private agencies have developed and increased in number; neighborhoods in which they were built have completely changed.

Hull House faces not only these conditions, but an almost complete change and dis-organization in its own services; in its personnel; in its influence in the neighborhood and the attitude of our neighbors to us.

We must be clear as to what we want to do— what programs we are to have.

Closely allied to this is the problem of financing. We have an enormous plant, the upkeep of which is out of all proportion to the program budget, and it is difficult now to raise our share of our budget. No new Director will want, or should be expected, to raise money, but he or she will have to know in the very beginning just what the Board can promise in a budget for services.

We like to think that Residents will again, as in the past, be considered as a most vital part of the settlement and contribute their services. Here too there has been a change, and settlements do not get the type of residents they formerly did or the services.

Our Board should help us face this question of residents now; the question of negro residents and whether they will be accepted by certain racial groups who come here; the question of Japanese-American residents, one of whom has just applied; the question of the residence of other racial groups; the question of certain residents we now have who by their own statements have signified that they can take no part in our program.

The Boys' Club is a great problem. We now have in close proximity the C. Y. O. Club House, the West Side Area Project, the new Mexican Center, and many other centers for boys' work. Is our Club needed, or is that one building which might be rented for some valuable service in this community?

The Race question: More and more negroes are moving into this district. How can we serve them, and what effect does their participation have on our neighbors of other races and colors? How can this settlement contribute the most to this great and imminent problem in Chicago, and especially our own neighborhood?

A new Director here faces a disorganized Hull House.

Some of the old activities have gone on through the changes of the last five years and seem still to be of the greatest value, especially the Art Department and the Music School. And yet, I am told, these have received the least financial support, comparatively. The Boys' Club will have to be completely re-planned. Adult Education Classes, of course, continue.

Dramatics, Clubs for adults, activities for girls, community work, all need to be studied and re-evaluated.

There is only a small staff left, somewhat increased for the Summer program.

The Residents represent—a few who have lived here for some time, some who came during Miss Carr's regime, others who are new and have never known Hull House except during this interim period. Others are applying for residence, but before decisions are made it is difficult to know which should be accepted as future residents.

Mrs. Camp* came the first of the year to fill a most needed position. With the immediate changes that came when Miss Carr resigned, she

*Mrs. Ruth Orton Camp (b. 1896) was acting director of Hull-House from June to September 1943.—Eds.

Jessie Binford and two friends.

helped in every possible way, and I do not know what we would have done without her. We were very glad when she was made Interim Director.

It is for these reasons and others that we have hoped that a great deal of "ground work," so to speak, could be done before a new Director came. We realize that it is impossible for members of the Board, especially those who are comparatively new, to realize, as we do, the problems that all settlements face today, and Hull House especially, and that the appointment of a Director is only one of the responsibilities which we must all shoulder.

Very sincerely yours,
JESSIE F. BINFORD

An Evening at Hull-House

Russell Ward Ballard

Russell Ballard (1893–1980), the director who followed Charlotte Carr, believed Hull-House should exemplify the idea that people of all races, nationalities, and creeds could live and work together in democratic freedom. In theory, that was what American men were trying to establish on the battlefronts in Europe and in the Pacific; the least Hull-House could do was to try at home. The new director was proud that Hull-House was a place "where people of differing backgrounds could be brought together naturally in social intercourse, where fears could be dispelled and human personality dignified," as he explained in his account entitled "An Evening at Hull-House" in February 1945. The principles of equality and freedom that Ballard expressed in this description of Hull-House activities during the war continued to be one of the guiding precepts of the settlement. The reality fell short of the ideal, but for the next fifteen years, Ballard encouraged Italians, Greeks, Mexicans, and blacks to work together for a better neighborhood with the Latvians, Hungarians, and Japanese who sought refuge at Hull-House as displaced persons after the war.

Upon receiving her copy of Ballard's account, Dr. Alice Hamilton wrote to him: "I read with great interest the description of a single evening at Hull-House and thought how much it would have pleased Miss Addams, for that is just the sort of work she planned for Hull-House. Her interests were many, of course, but I believe that closest to her heart was the use of the House as a refuge and a meeting place for the foreign-born, with people of understanding and sympathy living in the House and acting as a bridge between the foreign immigration and the old American stock. You are certainly carrying out this program beautifully, and I congratulate you." At least one of the former residents felt that Hull-House was in good hands again. [Russell W. Ballard, "An Evening at Hull-House" (Chicago, 1945).]

For some time I have felt the urge to share with you my reflections upon a recent evening's experience at Hull-House. There was drama in it, though it does not sound dramatic in the telling and less so in reading about it.

What I shall relate seems commonplace, since it conforms so completely to the Hull-House tradition, indeed to the settlement tradition, that it may seem of little consequence. This reporting could be a partial answer, however, to the uninformed as to what happens in the atmosphere of a settlement.

I cannot begin my narrative without reflecting upon the present sacrifices and suffering of the youth of different races and religions with whom I spent so many years as they were growing up. I learned early from intimate contact with them of their hurts and their fears. As there must now be sacrifices, I passionately want them to be for a purpose. And those of us who utterly failed a generation of youth; those of us who are smug and complacent and comfortable, have laid upon us a distinct obligation to labor at home for what our boys fight for abroad, namely, the perpetuation of a society in which the individual with his rights and responsibilities is superior to the state and in which all men have the right to enjoy liberty protected by law.

As one considers the failures in human relationships after the civilizing process has gone on for centuries; when one surveys the current social scene—cities in shambles, nations at the crossroads, a million casualties among our finest youth with more to follow—perhaps it is not inappropriate to attempt to relate an evening's experience at Hull-House, which brings into focus an interplay of individuals of various cultural backgrounds and which reflects, in my judgment, a demonstration of democracy in action.

On this particular evening, the two classes in English for Mexican railroad workers were to begin. Preparation and planning had been carried on in cooperation with the Pan-American Good Neighbor Forum. How many of these soldier-workers brought to the States under government contract would respond was problematical. I invited the German-born executive secretary of the Forum to have dinner with the residents and to interpret the importance of making friendly contact with at least some of the 4,000 Mexican workers living in work camps on the fringes of Chicago.

I should like to comment upon my guest of the evening. He is a doctor of philosophy and was connected with the diplomatic service in Berlin until the rise of Hitler. His father had already died in a concentration camp. When with the help of Ambassador Dodd he escaped from German persecutions and entered the United States, he came directly to Hull-House at the suggestion of Dr. Dodd. He knows fascism in all of its manifestations.

As we came through the doors of Hull-House that evening, a Chinese girl on duty at the switchboard greeted us. The school in Shanghai where she was teaching was bombed by the enemy; and she had the responsibility of guiding 300 children to a place of safety. Enroute they were machine-gunned while trying to hide in the rice fields, and many children were wounded or killed. Later she reached Hong Kong; and after recovery from an illness aggravated by her emotional experience, she made her way back to her home in America. She is enrolled in our music school and finds release and relaxation in music. She enjoys coming to Hull-House, and though she works for the Navy, she is glad to help out at the switchboard between five and seven o'clock each evening.

At dinner an interest in our "new immigrants" was aroused and found expression in a volunteer committee of residents who proposed to develop occasional social events at the House for the Mexican workers.

The classes were to open at seven o'clock, and my guest and I were impatient to learn the results of our efforts to recruit attendance. As we left for the classes, I observed in passing that a Negro resident, who is engaged in social work, was seated in the reception room acting as hostess for evening visitors. A young woman of Swedish-born parents was now operating the switchboard.

At the desk next to her sat a young Japanese girl, American born, who had found residence at Hull-House after leaving the camp where she had lived for two years following the evacuation from California. She was addressing invitations for her club, which was to give a dance in honor of the servicemen of Japanese ancestry, recently returned from the European war theatre. (Incidentally, 150 servicemen attended this dance, and it appeared that most of them were wearing the purple heart. For those handicapped soldiers who were unable to dance because of infirmity, other means of entertainment were provided. I shall never forget those purple hearts.)

When we reached the classes, we were delighted to find the two rooms filled with men at work on their first lessons in English. My guest greeted each group in Spanish, and commented that beyond teaching English, we desired to extend hospitality and friendship to our neighbors from the South. I was introduced to the classes and to the teachers, one of whom was an American young man of Japanese ancestry. Though my Spanish is limited, the felicitations and good will expressed were understood and reciprocated. Before I left one of the classes, I was asked by two of the students and by the teacher if they might see me later in the evening.

Now to report on my conferences. One young railroad worker inquired about the possibility of enrolling in the music school for voice lessons. It was arranged. His friend eager to learn English wanted to know if he could attend school four evenings each week instead of two. He was accommodated.

The young teacher of Japanese ancestry had arrived recently in Chicago from Harvard Law School. He wanted to know if it would be possible for him to live at Hull-House for two weeks until he could find a small apartment, so that his mother could leave the Government relocation center in the West. I learned that this twenty-two-year-old young man was a Phi Beta Kappa from Haverford, his father's alma mater, and that he had been granted an honor scholarship at Harvard. His brother was overseas, and because he himself was unacceptable to the armed services for physical reasons, he stated that he left law school to work in a war industry because, to quote him, "there is a war to be won."

As the interview progressed it was interesting to observe how this rather perplexed young man responded to my understanding and cordiality. I told him that I would be delighted to have him come to Hull-House and that I could make it possible for his mother to join him and thus be removed from the abnormal life of an evacuation center. Fortunately, a small apartment was to be vacant within a month.

After he had gone and I closed the doors for the night, there was a feeling of satisfaction as the events of the evening passed rapidly in review before my mind: A German Refugee Jew, a Chinese-American girl, a Negro resident volunteer, the young woman of Swedish extraction, a Japanese-American girl preparing to entertain wounded servicemen, Mexican nationals being taught a new language by an American-born Japanese, as typically American as my own two sons.

I reflected upon the limited opportunities in America, where people of differing backgrounds could be brought together naturally in social intercourse, where fears could be dispelled and human personality dignified. I admit it was gratifying to be a part of such a company and to have the opportunity here at home to demonstrate the dynamics of democracy.

This very evening, as our young men of many cultural backgrounds were fighting in strange lands, I was overwhelmed with the obligation to help in dispelling prejudices among us and to labor to keep America safe for differences. Because of the courage of these young men, I have faith to believe that the eternal spirit of man will, in the end, prevail over the paganism of the false prophets of a "master-race" philosophy; and that men of all races and creeds can live together without fear. The events of the evening were stimulating and thought-provoking and brought hope and encouragement.

Hull-House has work to do today. Over and beyond the day-to-day contacts with growing youth and the chance of influencing them for creative living; besides helping people as they come daily with their troubles; in addition to providing a stimulating and reassuring atmosphere for adults over whom the sorrow of war has cast its shadows, Hull-House today, if it keeps faith with its illustrious founder, has an obligation to be counted among those who would promote unity and advance the cause of human freedom, to help remove the causes of inequities, and to assist in extending equality of opportunity, so that the promises of our democracy may be more fully realized.

Hull-House in the Late 1940s

Elaine Switzer

By 1943, because of the loss of trained personnel and wartime activities at Hull-House, regular settlement programs had been disrupted. Two major problems faced Russell Ballard when he took over as director: to rebuild a solid settlement staff, and to emphasize programs that would again involve the whole neighborhood community at the settlement. Ballard arrived at the settlement in September 1943. During the summer, all program staff members except those of the music school and Bowen Country Club camp had resigned. In the midst of war, trained personnel were unavailable, but Ballard was able to hire a part-time male worker and volunteer neighborhood men for the physical education department. Fortunately, a woman experienced in settlement work came to Hull-House in 1945. Ballard appointed her program director. Her name was Elaine Switzer, and according to Ballard she had a "major role in reestablishing the Hull-House program." The new program policies that were planned and carried out over a four-year period, 1945–1949, while Elaine Switzer was program director, were significant. They were to be the basis of all Hull-House activities until the early 1960s and signaled the rise of renewed influence and power for the settlement in the neighborhood community.

Switzer's report of her activities, published in the National Federation of Settlements and Neighborhood Centers' newsletter, Round Table, *gives a vivid picture of conditions at Hull-House when she came, problems she faced in initiating programs, and activities she carefully planned to meet those conditions and problems. After staying with Hull-House for several years, Switzer returned to the University of Illinois where she received a masters degree in social work and began teaching at the University of Chicago. [Elaine Switzer, "Four Years of Program Planning: A Report, 1945–1949,"* Round Table *(March–April 1950), 1–4.]*

This story is not too different from many agency programs as they have been rehabilitated after the war years when leadership was at a low ebb everywhere. It is a story of a big agency, with much tradition and important past history. . . .

My first two weeks were spent in making observations, wondering how I could leave with professional dignity. . . . I even spent some time at a self-imposed switchboard hour to help me learn things I needed to know about questions I couldn't even formulate. Some of the foolish queries that came over the phone helped me to better understand both the community and agency. . . . The summer membership was the sternest, least friendly of any group of children I had ever met, and this was even more true of the teen-agers, young adults, and adult women whom I met in the fall. Unmindful of past traditions, there were stormy days and calm days. For example, on hot summer mornings we sprinkled the children with a hose in the Halsted Street courtyard, which shocked old residents who had never seen the courtyard so used before but delighted passersby. Some of the parents who watched eagerly let their children join the fun. We told stories in the resident courtyard, where the only neighborhood grass is seen, to the horror of some who thought "all would be destroyed," but it never was. And by sheer luck the weaving was moved to its old "weaving room," delighting the oldest neighborhood residents who commented, "This is like the old Hull-House." I must confess I had never known the location of the old weaving room; it was to me just a large well-lighted space suitable

for the activity, and recently vacated by a rationing board. . . .

After the summer program, where we made a few feeble beginnings, much thought was given to readjusting staff and staff schedules. A group-work degree as a requirement for employment was out of the question, but as an agency we were certainly interested in the experience and the type of person of each individual interviewed. We wanted a staff that was honest in their relationships with people, not afraid to face whatever might beset us: cooperative to the extent of seeing the "whole Hull-House" and not just buildings nor the overstress of their activity; understanding of people and situations; a sense of humor if possible; a liking for people for what they are, and not because of their color or national origin; one who would not carry grudges from day to day; one who could relate facts to a situation with the least amount of emotion and whose eyes had a keenness for the job they would be hired to do. We hoped this staff would be interracial, but we were going to employ personnel on the basis of the best for the job and not on a racial quota. We had faith there would be qualified Mexican-American and Negro as well as white workers, and of course there were!

The staff had to work with a complex community. The oldest settlers were concerned about a lack of the "old Hull-House" as well as the effect upon them of a changing community of mixed racial population. The Greeks and Italians who had lived in the neighborhood a long time with their feeling of prior rights to Hull-House were objecting to the Mexicans and Negroes who were moving in rapidly. Religiously the community is Catholic, although some evangelistic Mexican churches are increasingly in evidence.

We started the fall with a series of staff meetings and training sessions, including orientation to both the agency and the community, and the purpose and plan of program. We decided not to use any of the rooms that were too badly in need of decoration and repair. We hung curtains wherever appropriate, making the buildings as clean and homelike as possible. We set a minimum of rules, such as places to smoke, no spitting on the floor, cleaning up after groups were through, hats off for men and boys, and that was about all. The rules were the same for all six buildings, and all staff had concern for each. All staff worked with

Neighborhood children leaving Hull-House.

all age groups and both sexes, so that there was, and is, no teen-age worker, no boys worker, etc. All staff attended and still attend a weekly staff meeting to maintain this cohesiveness and to change, regulate, and evaluate program with its assets and faults in relationship to a creative program and a stimulated membership.

Children six to fourteen years of age come to program during the afternoon and those fifteen and over come in the evening. Fourteen-year-olds choose which part of the program they prefer so as not to separate them from friends. Adults come whenever they have free time, mornings, afternoons, or evenings for clubs and educational classes. The agency is open for any who want to participate! Classes are differentiated from clubs in that clubs choose their own membership and plan their own programs; classes have no membership selection except on the basis of interest, skill, or age as best suits the activity, such as sewing for advanced or beginning sewers; and the leader does most of the planning, preparation of materials, etc. All activities are co-educational with the exception of some of the gym program— but not many girls come in the evening. Publicity this first year as well as every year since, is taken to all neighborhood schools. It is simple and pictorial, so even those that can't read can understand. . . .

Younger children from the very first autumn

enrolled early, most evening participants came more out of curiosity than interest, and were mostly boys and young men, a sprinkling of Mexican and Greeks, no Negroes, but mostly Italians. They'd sit, arms folded, and demand to be entertained. They were assured there were things to do if they wanted to do them. The staff often suggested that the kids go to a movie for entertainment, often repeating, "Nobody has to come to Hull-House, and why come if you don't want to?" This seemed quite a shock to the burliest, and one night we hit a crisis. All prearranged at a given signal, the entire game room went up for grabs. Tables, chairs, wastebasket—everything but the floor sailed through the air. With as little emotion as possible I signaled with the lights and declared the game room closed and saw to it that everyone left. A chair or two that had been lowered out of a window sat on the street, and the room itself was in chaos. The staff stayed as usual until the regular closing time. No doors were locked nor rooms barred, but those entering were told things were closed. A few suggested coming back and straightening the mess, but nobody wanted to make the first overt motion and be a sissy. Within an hour or so all had gone down the street. The next night the doors were open as usual, but we met each person on the steps as he came up, announcing that everything was open but the game room. This went on for four nights, each night a bigger and bigger crowd gathering in the hallway, which made for much conversation and discussion about when we'd reopen and how. Persons who had not participated in the mess, but had been there that night complained the hardest about being kept out when they "hadn't done anything." The "not doing anything" was explained as the very reason. We began to know each other pretty well night after night, and finally some ventured as to what would they have to do to get the game room open again. "Use it as a game room," was all they were told, and a date was set for the reopening, and it has stayed open.

While this went on in one building, basketball looked like football scrimmage in another. Biting, fighting, kicking, scalding in the showers was thought by them to be part of the game. Kids were taken out of the game for rough playing night after night. Rules of the game were posted everywhere, and each player was told that this was how we were going to play, nobody had to play this way, and they had free choice of either doing so or not playing at all. It took a whole season of the best refereeing obtainable to teach those playing that fouls weren't called because of the one who did it, but because it was the rule, and that rules held for everybody, no matter whom. We played the expected trophy tournament the first season with the accompanying fights, and every known deceptive device used. After two years of this we boldly abolished trophies and let the teams decide if they wanted a tournament, and so we have continued with new decisions made each season. Each season there has been a tournament played hard, with extreme regularity and nothing for the winners. Other agencies in the neighborhood are adopting this same pattern. This helps considerably, but there are still complaints from winners and losers about a "cheap Hull-House," though we can laugh and joke it through *now*. The winners this past year were going to buy trophies for themselves out of their club money, but were too lazy to do the shopping. Another group that participated also paid $20 membership to a "Y" so as to join their trophy tournament, but not enough teams registered so the tournament defaulted. We know, however, that our gym atmosphere has changed completely. We know that they are playing only because they *want* to play, and that the game is good enough to stand up without a bribe. None of the competition has been withdrawn and we like it that way.

. . . While activities formed the greater part of our early program and still are an opening wedge for the developing of new interests and varied contacts, now clubs are the nucleus of evening program and a large portion of that in the afternoon. Because groups were difficult, we have used staff as leaders, with but few volunteers. Now we are able to widen this leadership, particularly with resident help. . . . The club idea and its own possibilities is still new to many.

The management of the afternoon basketball tournament through their own club council of participating teams was a revelation. Rules established by the council were more strict than any we as staff would have imposed, and the idea of the responsibility for carrying them through by group demand and insistence was a stimulating experience.

Afternoon clubs are almost without exception mixed racially, as are all activity groups. One Negro boy was fought for by two clubs in addition to a group of Negro boys who wanted him for their team, "because he's a good guy." An all-Negro and a mixed club considered the possibility of a merger for weeks and weeks, not on the basis of color, but on which of the two presidents would then preside—how would the treasury have to be split where one club maintained dues and the other had not; and whose club rules would be followed?

. . . Racial friction in evening program is more tense. Boys who go to high school where there is mixed enrollment are often afraid to acknowledge recognition in the game room for fear of losing face with some neighborhood friends who dislike anybody but those of their own nationality background. Mothers groups have professed, "Sure we're prejudiced. We like it that way."

Staff is forever alerted in activity as well as hallways and shower-room. Fortunately we have been able to avert major difficulties by always bringing the conflict back to the point of difference, rather than of color or national origin on both sides; but this is not an easy job. One hallway conflict which led to a punching and spitting fight between some Italian and Mexican boys and a group of Negro girls needed solving on the point that sides were even, blow for spitting, before we could talk about the reason for the sudden flare between teen-age kids that didn't even know each other. It evolved that Joe, a Mexican boy's brother, had been beat up by a Negro the night before—but nowhere in the neighborhood. After questions we found that none of the girls were related to the Negro boy at all, so we asked Joe if his brother was ever in a fight with a Mexican. "Sure," he said. "Did you go down the street punching every Mexican girl you saw after that fight?" we asked. "That's silly," he commented. "How's that different from this?" he was asked. "Aw, skip it," and the gang, led by Joe, walked out of the building. Later four windows were broken, and we had a fairly good idea this could have been done by Joe and his friends. Before we could even make comment about it the next night, the boys came in and Joe handed me some money. "For what?" I asked. "The windows," said Joe. "We felt so dumb last night we had to do something, but we're sorry—it won't happen again."

And to date it hasn't. . . . The many areas of progress make all those bad nights look fairly good now. Some of the so-called toughest find things to do. We talk about employment—and whether it takes more "guts" to work every day or jack-roll; what movies make them cry; girl and boy friends; neighborhood filth and whose responsibility it is; how we can have more dances; what it felt like to be in jail or parental school; take-home pay and salaries; almost everything and anything. We have never set up situations where these fellows or girls have had to maintain their degree of toughness for us to be impressed.

. . . Yet but four years ago, and it takes a number of years, for programs like this move slowly if they are to move solidly, our first dance [in] the fall of 1945 attracted only 25, and all of them were boys. This was to be a gala Hallowe'en dance the staff had planned, for at this time nobody was ready to plan with us. With members and staff planning together, by now the dances are regular monthly affairs, 175 strong, with neighborhood orchestra and a tone of dressing up. Stumbling feet are learning security in ballroom dancing sessions every week. Refreshments are sold at cost, and the orchestra plays in exchange for weekly rehearsal space.

Because there are no expenses involved, no admission is charged. Membership cards are the tickets of admission, and each member may get two guest cards for friends he or she may wish to invite.

Besides these monthly dances, teen-age dances can be held only by Hull-House clubs. This way we have recourse to the tone of dances and maintaining a consistent house policy.

Parties and buffet tables are always in style with perfect order, membership assists with minor repair and paint jobs, the radio has had no outside mechanic for two years, women have helped with special parties without any feeling of need to be paid, young adults and women are participating in the area-redevelopment program in every possible way, and even more startling are the kids who stop us on the street just to say hello and chat for a while.

A club council is ripe for evening clubs, but evening Negro clubs still being a minority makes the council a future plan. A women's club council will be started this fall, upon their request for some things they would like to do that they can't do as individual clubs. Temporary councils are the beginnings. A Hull-House carnival for the past two years operated through council planning. In January representatives from all clubs, from children to the aged, laid basic plans and then met twice a month. Each club participating assumed its own responsibility for a part in the great day and finally in May the Carnival was born, operating simultaneously in five buildings, with 29 clubs participating and some 2,300 visitors, of all races, colors, and creeds enjoying a glorious affair. The council's last meeting was held after the Carnival to make some evaluations and to make suggestions to the director for the use of the $660 made on three-cent tickets. Discussion was lively and varied, with much conceding on the part of some of the boys who started by asking for personal things like trophies to others who thought of the decorating of Bowen Hall which the entire membership uses. The latter became the final recommendation. Bowen Hall was decorated in a beautiful Chinese red ceiling and refinished wood walls.

As a little girl said in inquiring as to whether Hull-House was open before program began one fall, "Hull-House is?" "No," said I, "not yet." "Oh, I thought Hull-House was." It not only was, but we are happy to say, it is! with the music school, art school, dramatics, gym, and every other activity . . . , through staff meeting planning, understanding, and participation. We know there will be more problems to face both within the agency and with our relationships to the community because such is the case wherever people are involved, but we feel we have developed a basic direction. If in reading this, any of it has seemed like a simple one, two, three process, this is furthest from the truth. We have planned and won, as well as planned again. . . .

Public Housing in Chicago

Robert C. Weaver

The National Industrial Recovery Act in June 1933 established the Public Works Administration. This agency, under the direction of Secretary of the Interior Harold L. Ickes, a long-time Hull-House supporter and friend, established a Housing Division with the principle objective of stimulating the building industry. Jane Addams and Hull-House residents who had struggled so long to meet the problems of slum housing now felt they had an agency through which to work to improve their neighborhood. What better place to encourage building than in slum areas?

By February 1934 the Housing Division of the PWA, with Colonel Horatio B. Hackett of Chicago as director, began to initiate projects. With the influence of Ickes, Jane Addams, and the settlement workers, the PWA located one of the three projects designated for Chicago in the Hull-House area. The project, a complex of apartments to be built southwest of the settlement, would be of modern construction, fireproof and sanitary, with hot and cold running water, central heating, bath facilities, and gas stoves and electric refrigerators in the kitchens. The apartments were to be "rented to deserving families whose incomes do not enable them to secure proper accommodations in privately owned dwellings." Named the Jane Addams Homes, the project was completed in the summer of 1937 and occupied shortly thereafter, as were the two other federal projects in the Chicago area.

Yet occupancy of these federal housing projects, supported by public tax monies, was not based on economic need alone, for space was not available to all regardless of race or color. Robert C. Weaver (b. 1907), who became Lyndon B. Johnson's Secretary of Housing and Urban Development, 1966–1969, pointed out this fact in his book The Negro Ghetto *(1948), a study of residential segregation in the North. Weaver wrote the book when he lived at Hull-House and served as director of Community Services of the American*

Council on Race Relations in Chicago. Much of the information he reported was developed as Weaver prepared the socio-economic memorandum used in arguments before the United States Supreme Court in successfully challenging the validity of restrictive housing covenants in 1948. [Robert C. Weaver, The Negro Ghetto *(New York, 1948), 191–196.]*

No local housing authority has faced more difficult problems in establishing democratic patterns of racial occupancy than the one in Chicago. The high degree of Negro concentration in Black Belts, continuing migration of Negroes to the city, the active support of residential segregation by real estate and organized property owners' inter-

ests, community acceptance of ghetto living, and the pattern of violence, all complicated the issue. By 1946 the local authority operated under a clear-cut ruling that all public housing projects must be open to all races. This policy was vigorously pressed; but it has not always existed nor has it always been implemented.

Like New York, Detroit, Buffalo, and several other northern cities, Chicago was the location of 3 PWA housing division projects that were restricted to white occupancy. Consequently, the local authority had not only to establish a liberal racial policy but also had to undo practices which it inherited. This was a real difficulty since residential segregation engenders vested interests, and the occupants of an all-white housing development soon come to consider it as a white project, objecting strongly to the admission of colored

Citizen participation in urban renewal—a meeting in the Residents' Dining Hall at Hull-House.

people. Jane Addams Homes in Chicago was the PWA project, located in an area where Negroes had lived, that had established a pattern of racial exclusion in the low-rent program of the city. The practice of Negro exclusion in this project was to haunt and harass the local Authority as it expended its program. The first job, obviously, was to get a few colored families into Jane Addams Homes. After much hesitancy, the Authority accomplished this and cleared the first hurdle. Meanwhile, the much-disputed Ida B. Wells project on the South Side was completed and opened. Because of its location and the controversy preceding its development, it was foredoomed as a Negro project. For the same reason, other public housing within the Black Belt is Negro housing despite the announced policy of the Chicago Housing Authority.

During the war several in-lying projects were constructed by the Authority. They were and are open to all racial groups; some of them, such as Robert Brooks Homes, were rapidly filled by colored migrants who were more numerous and in greater need of shelter than whites, since public war housing was one of the few sources of decent living space open to colored war workers. Vacancies occasioned by the slight turnover of initial tenants (92 per cent of the original tenants were still in the project in the summer of 1947) were quickly absorbed by Negroes, who, on the basis of need, were at the top of the list. The complexion of Robert Brooks Homes remained dark. In addition, the larger area, of which the project is a part, extending south of Roosevelt Road, is almost solidly Negro. Across Roosevelt Road, Jane Addams Homes stands. It has a few colored residents, and, according to the Housing Authority, about 5 per cent of the units were occupied by Negroes in 1947; but it is, from appearances, as much a white project as Brooks is Negro. Similarly, the surrounding area north of Roosevelt Road is solidly white. One of the factors that has led to racial stability in Jane Addams Homes is the fact that as a low-rent project catering to established residents in Chicago, tenant turnover has been low. Also, there is evidence that prior to the time of the severe housing shortage in the city which, of course, operated to reduce tenant turnover to a minimum, the Authority paid little more than lip service to its non-segregation policy. Since the war, reasonable

compliance would not have resulted in many Negroes entering Jane Addams Homes, since, as we have indicated, there have been few vacancies in the project.

At Cabrini Homes, a low-rent project opened for occupancy about the same time as Robert Brooks, the Authority established and has maintained bi-racial occupancy. In the face of organized neighborhood hostility, the Authority included 20 per cent Negroes among the initial tenants. There was no segregation in the project, and the management staff was made up of colored and white persons. This policy has been maintained, amid difficulties from time to time, in an area long known for its high incidence of racial tension. The project was bi-racial, with a minority of Negro tenants and without segregation, in 1947.*

As the Chicago Housing Authority faces the problem of finding shelter for migrant war workers, it became convinced of two things: the principal need was among Negroes, and the existing Black Belt should not and could not take care of the additional colored people who were coming into the city. The Authority rightly opposed the construction of small clusters of war housing in areas of blight and dangerously high densities. It also stood out for permanent units on the ground that the deficiency in the supply of shelter for Negroes was of long standing and would be serious after the emergency of war had passed. The war program in the city included 4,881 units, of which 4,147 were programmed for or occupied by Negroes as of July 31, 1945. This program involved and required the use of sites outside the Black Belts. The Authority, therefore, selected a location far removed from the ghetto but near to industry. On this site, it constructed 1,500 units of permanent war housing known as Altgeld Gardens. Despite the attractiveness of the project and the efforts of the Authority to attract white applicants, almost all of the tenants were and are Negroes. This project, completed in 1944–45, marks

*As of October 30, 1947, there were 984 white and 43 Negro families in Jane Addams Homes. Cabrini Homes had 415 white, 137 Negro, and 32 other families. Altgeld and Wentworth Homes were exclusively Negro, while Lathrop, Trumbull, Bridgeport, and Lawndale Homes were exclusively white. Ida B. Wells and Robert Brooks Homes had one white family each. Almost half the units in the permanent low-rent and war housing developments of the local authority were occupied by Negroes.

the half-way point in the Authority's approach to housing for Negroes. In planning and developing Altgeld Gardens, the Chicago Housing Authority faced resolutely the problem of space and provided housing for Negroes outside the established areas for colored people.* The resulting project failed to become truly interracial for many reasons, the most important of which were the entrenched acceptance of residential segregation in the city, the disproportionately greater need for housing among Negroes, and a certain hesitancy and ineptitude on the part of the Housing Authority.†

The relatively progressive racial policies of the Chicago Housing Authority have not been effected without resistance all the way. In some instances there has been open hostility. This was dramatically illustrated in 1946 when the Authority attempted to carry out its non-segregation policy in the veterans housing program of temporary dwelling units. Bi-racial occupancy was accomplished without incident in the first project opened. Not so with the second. The Authority planned a 180-unit development on a site which came to be known as the Airport Homes. About 18 Negro tenants were expected to be included. Just as the buildings were completed, however, well-organized white squatters swept in, taking over all units. Police and community politicians co-operated with them. And when the Authority started eviction proceedings, word was passed that the squatters would leave voluntarily if the Authority would abandon its announced plan of renting some of the units to Negroes. The Authority refused to do so; it was supported by Mayor Kelly‡ and liberal groups, and managed to move in two Negro families. A few months later, when the police (at last activated by the mayor) relaxed their vigilance, shots were fired into the apartment of one of the Negro families. The Authority, however, met this move by planning to introduce a few more colored families into the area.

The Airport Homes difficulties were not without their good effects. The Chicago Housing Authority found itself in deep water and, with the assistance of the Mayor's Commission on Human Relations and associated agencies, began to marshal the active support of liberal groups for its policy of nonsegregation. The approach paid off. When, in February, 1947, the first of three North Side trailer projects was completed, a group of residents in the area remembered Airport Homes. They accepted the racial policy of the Authority and decided that there should be no disturbances incident to Negro occupancy in their community. Under the leadership of the North Side Association members, a welcoming committee laid plans for greeting the incoming veterans of all races. On the day the tenants arrived, they were invited to a trailer on the back of which was a sign reading, "Welcome Neighbor," and, inside the trailer, ladies from several neighborhood churches served the new arrivals, white and black alike, with coffee, sandwiches, and doughnuts. Colored occupancy was effected without incident or great concern.**

In the midst of all these problems—problems not so much of democratic racial policy pronouncements as practical matters of changing from a segregated to an unsegregated pattern in a vast public program—there were evidences that white and Negro tenants adjusted to bi-racial living in Chicago low-rent housing projects. By 1947, Cabrini Homes, despite its early difficulties, had settled down to a more normal existence, and in many

*Another attempt to solve the space problem during the war was additional permanent war housing developed by the Authority on a vacant site contiguous to a Negro neighborhood of middle-class owners of new homes. . . .

†One instance of the latter will suffice. The tenant selection office was established in the heart of the Black Belt, where it became a symbol of ghetto living and discouraged white tenants from following up on their applications for admittance.

‡Edward J. Kelly, Mayor, 1933–1947.—Eds.

**A new mayor [Martin Kennelly] who took office in the spring of 1947 has been impressed by the fact that Negro veterans, as individuals, have not pushed to go into new and often hostile neighborhoods. Consequently, he is questioning whether or not the Housing Authority and the Commission on Human Relations were not "creating" unnecessary trouble by encouraging such a move. Neighborhood opposition to the entrance of colored veterans still existed, too. "That the residents of the Fernwood-Bellevue communities are definitely opposed to having Negro families assigned to the Veterans Emergency Housing Project now nearing completion at 106th and Union was clearly indicated Tuesday evening at a public meeting held at Fernwood Park fieldhouse under the sponsorship of the Fernwood-Bellevue Civil Assn." The alderman of the ward urged that white veterans only be assigned to the project. (*Calumet Index*, May 19, 1947.) This was the beginning of further post-World War II major racial tension over housing. Negro veterans were admitted, despite neighborhood opposition. Although municipal and civic organizations succeeded in keeping the situation from erupting into open conflict during the summer and early fall of 1947, tensions were still high in the area in October.

veterans' projects, black and white families lived together in a spirit of co-operation. In one instance where Negro veterans in a public project were the first colored residents in a hostile community, their white neighbors in the project took the initiative in appealing to the local merchants and delivery services to serve the colored veterans. The appeal was successful. In its recent publication, *The Tenth Year of the Chicago Housing Authority,* the local Authority observed

> In contrast to the attitudes displayed . . . [in opposition to the presence of Negroes in veterans' projects outside the Black Belt], there were other biracial veterans' projects whose tenants were eager to demonstrate that families of all races and creeds could live peaceably together. . . .

Teeming with Problems
The Hull-House
Neighborhood

Paul B. Johnson

Between 1947 and 1961, Hull-House and its neighborhood, through the Near West Side Planning Board and its derivatives, were partners in one of the pioneer citizen-participation-in-urban-renewal efforts in America. As it developed a coordinated neighborhood plan, the Planning Board worked hard to achieve cooperation and support among its neighbors as well as official recognition from governmental agencies responsible for final plan approval. Financial backing for the Planning Board came from Hull-House, individuals, industry, business, and foundations. The Field Foundation helped finance its early operation, and for a four-year period until 1953, Hull-House received an annual grant from the Wieboldt Foundation to support citizen participation in the Planning Board. The Emil Schwarzhaupt Foundation subsequently made a grant to Hull-House in November 1954 to finance a more intensive effort to alert neighborhood people to the possibilities of participation in city plans for their area.

To report on the results of these expenditures, Hull-House hired Paul B. Johnson (b. 1918), Associate Professor of History at Roosevelt University, to prepare a study of citizen participation in urban renewal. The report, Citizens Participation in Urban Renewal: The History of the Near West Side Planning Board and a Citizen Participation Project, *was published by Hull-House in 1960. Before it could be widely distributed it was quietly submitted to the Schwarzhaupt Foundation in fulfillment of the requirements of the grant. Then, just as quietly, it was set aside by the Hull-House board of trustees who by that time had decided to cooperate with the city in providing the settlement neighborhood and the settlement buildings themselves as the site for the University of Illinois' new Chicago campus. Citizen participation in planning had evidently counted for very little. Professor Johnson, who made an intensive study of the twelve-year planning effort, was skeptical of the Planning Board's accomplishments even before the city threw all its renewal and conservation plans out the window in favor of the University of Illinois: "The Near West Side Planning Board's work . . . did not fix the details of the community's future; but it tremendously affected the choice between action and total inaction. The greatest tribute to the twelve-year effort . . . is that, without it, the whole area would have been neglected while agencies turned to other neighborhoods clamoring for clearance and for renewal funds."*

The following segment from the Johnson report describes the settlement neighborhood in the 1950s. Some of the reasons the citizen planning effort met with little success is evident in this description. Professor Johnson obviously believed the primary one was a lack of neighborhood unity. In any event, the neighborhood would be gone forever after construction began on the University of Illinois' campus. [Paul B. Johnson, Citizens Participation in Urban Renewal: The History of the Near West Side Planning Board and a Citizen Participation Project *(Chicago, 1960), 3–16, 22–23.]*

The term "Near West Side" itself may be misleading, if it implies the slightest unity. Here Chicago's newest residents have come, in almost incredible variety, since the 1880's. The brilliant variegation of the 1893 census maps gave early evidence of this diversity. From that day to this, few regions in Chicago have contained more different ethnic groups simultaneously, or more of them in rapid succession.

A visit in 1954, before the latest changes, would have underscored the point. The stroller from Harrison and Halsted down Blue Island Avenue could not have failed to note the Kaffeneion houses, their elderly customers reading *Hellenikos Typos* over their Turkish coffee; for this is the "Greek Delta." Elsewhere on Blue Island or Halsted Street, the Tienda Vera Cruz or the Farmacia Latina bespeaks the presence of Mexicans and Puerto Ricans. Nowhere in the entire area could one find more than a handful descended from Slavic or North European stocks. But across the north tier of the arch, from the western boundary of the area at Ashland to Morgan and Miller Streets on the east, one notes a solid, populous, better-housed group, the third- and fourth-generation Italians. Reaching almost south to Roosevelt Road, this section comprises the northwest part of the Near West Side. Between them and Roosevelt Road, in the Chicago Housing Authority's "Jane Addams" housing project, live many Negroes. South of Roosevelt Road and to the west are two more projects, the two-story Robert Brooks homes and the high-rise Grace Abbott homes; their residents are Negroes. To the south and east, between Halsted and Loomis, an almost entirely Negro population occupies Chicago's worst slums.

The "nationality" groups do not differ in nationality alone. In age, the average member of the Negro groups was young; the Italian community was diversified; the Greek population was unusually old. Surprised investigators reported that there was "no second generation" of Greeks living in the area; only the elderly, from the first immigrant generation, lingered on, while the others moved throughout the city. Furthermore, continuity of residence was extremely varied: those of Italian descent had the deepest roots; the Spanish-speaking population was much newer and constantly changing; transients and new arrivals were most numerous in the south-of-Roosevelt population of Negroes. From the consequent differences in rate of growth, there resulted population move-

ments and changes in neighborhoods; upon them, as we shall see, friction and suspicion fed, and disunity increased.

More than nationality, race, and descent enter into the diversity of the Near West Side. There are enormous differences in education. The young Greek student at Roosevelt University, or the Italian-descended city employee with a Master of Arts degree from the University of Illinois, stand out at one extreme; at the other extreme are those families who, though their children are crowding into run-down, understaffed schools, see no problem at all because the Southern states, their most recent home, gave them so much less.

There are cleavages along denominational lines among the area's twenty-nine churches. Relatively few are the Catholics south of Roosevelt Road; but the Italian community in the northwest is almost solidly Catholic, loyal to Holy Family Church or to Our Lady of Pompeii Church. The Greeks represent yet another faith; occasionally their newspapers ring with indignant protest at the familiar formula "Protestant, Catholic, and Jew"—which omits them! Clergymen have, however, repeatedly, consciously, personally transcended denominational lines and taken the lead in all-community work. Thus the weight of the religious organizations sometimes is thrown against the divisive effect of nationality or race. But sometimes a clergyman does the opposite: there was the bishop who publicly expressed the hope that the new Land Clearance Commission project, west of Halsted, would chiefly be populated by those of his own faith—the Italian families who were being relocated from blocks east of Halsted; there was the priest who denounced Hull-House as secular and non-Catholic, . . . and the bishop of another faith who protested against its non-participation in a religious parade.

Great are the differences in income, as well. Some few of the Greek businessmen could offer to put up $25,000 each toward a "Greek shopping center"; some of the wealthier Negroes around Newberry Avenue and 13th Street earned $6,000 a year. Appearances, moreover, were often deceptive. Income of some Negro tenants in public housing projects was so great that, under the law, they had to be evicted by the [Chicago Housing Authority]. Similarly, within the "Italian community" to the northwest, unprepossessing porch steps or artificial-brick siding told little of the excellent, even luxurious, interior furnishings—as many a surprised visitor has attested. Only 30 per cent of the Near West Side people were eligible for pubic housing. The general average of income for the area, of course, was low.

How shall we answer the question, "Was the Near West Side one city—or none?"

If the test is *quantitative,* then the Near West Side is easily large enough. It was far larger than most incorporated separate cities of Illinois. With its 1,200 stores, 200 community establishments, 47 major plants, 13 community centers, 9,000 parcels of land, and 55,000 people—all jammed into *one and seven-tenths of a square mile**—the Near West Side met the quantitative test of a city.

Yet there is another test, and seemingly the Near West Side failed it: it was penned by St. Augustine in his *Civitas Dei.* In that view, a city, or republic, or community, was a body of men "united by the object of their love." St. Augustine stressed genuine community and true unity of moral purpose.

But by that test the Near West Side seemed too disunified—and too racked by distrust and hostility—to be any city at all. Every one of the major racial, national, and religious differences bred fear and distrust. One merchant declared himself for a Greek merchants' center but told the Hull-House Neighbors director that "it would never work to include the Mexicans. . . . They are only trouble-makers"; personally, he did not allow them in his store. An Italian neighbor of Hull-House complained about the Mexican children next door. Within Hull-House itself, one "Mothers Club" spoke in such terms of disapproval at seeing Negroes and Mexicans at a dinner, and bandied so many "old worn-out arguments for keeping Negroes and others 'in their place,' " that one settlement worker was moved to despair:

> It is the oldest club in Hull-House and was started by Miss Addams. . . . Miss Addams would have cried had she heard their comments.

Suspicion and fear between groups were matched by suspicion within groups. Late in our story, in 1959, a group of homeowners just south of Hull-House began to confer with the Citizens Participation Project director. One evening, one of the ladies who had shown most interest and had participated most actively announced why she had missed a recent meeting: she could not attend because of the suspicions of her neighbors; they were bound to misinterpret her visiting Hull-House! In the same vein, a Mexican merchant complained:

> . . . we lack someone in our group with leadership. Within our group there is much suspicion and lack of confidence.

In this pattern of conflict, memory sometimes added its part. Thus, in the 1930's a memorable experience for the Italian community had been the establishment of the Jane Addams Homes. America's first federal housing project had been carved out of "their" area in the days of Harold Ickes' administration; and, though it was pledged that the whites would have first choice and would reoccupy the area in the new housing, in fact Negroes moved in. The story, passed from parent to child, formed part of the mental outlook of thousands. This folk memory reinforced others, stemming from forty or more years of turmoil and fighting for recognition and survival; the result was a cohesion, a sense of identity, that all observers remarked.

Not that there were no differences among Italian residents! When one expressed satisfaction that proposed new high-rise buildings would be so costly as to exclude Negro tenants, her neighbor expressed disapproval in the sharpest terms. Orientation toward Hull-House—both for and against—was another difference. Generations made a difference, too. The *West Side Community News*—organ of the predominantly Italian West Side Community Committee—printed a column in Italian for older residents; but most of its copy was in English. To some of the older family heads, those young Italians who had worked or studied at Hull-House were suspected of modernism and

---

*I once worked out the "farm equivalent" of the Near West Side. The typical American farm, east of the Great Plains, occupied 160 acres (the classic "quarter section"); the area's 1.7 square miles would hold seven such farms, at the most. One may assume an average farm population of five persons. The result is that, as farm area, the Near West Side's population should have been about thirty-four people!

ethnic disloyalty in ways that harked back to Miss Addams' arrival in the area.

How Many Problems?

Poverty and discord were handicaps enough. But one newspaper reporter found more. M. W. Newman told readers of the *Chicago Daily News* in April 1959 to

Look around . . . and see all of Chicago's best hopes and worst nightmares, in one overpowering chunk.

Look down and you see garbage-strewn streets, gaping slums, big-eyed kids shuffling among the fishbones and filth in soiled alleys. Even some manhole covers in the streets are missing.

It is being torn down and rebuilt. Parts of it look as if it had been bombed.

It is a patchy mixture of vile slums and good old homes, massive public housing, Italian, Mexican, and Greek neighborhoods, colorful "foreign" groceries where fascinating cheeses hang in the windows, warring street gangs, settlement houses, crime, racial tensions—a melting pot that never quite melted, Chicago's Old World and port of entry.

Slums? Near West Side has acres of 'em, in the Maxwell St. area. Some of the houses were so shaky they almost caved in by themselves.

Walk on Miller St., in eye-shot of the Loop, and see Chicago's disgrace—a Negro slum jungle second to none.

And yet, it's a place where flower pots brighten a rickety porch.

"Sometimes I feel the only thing to do is to move the people out and clean up the place with bombs," said William Jones feelingly. He is executive director of the interracial Near West Side Community Council, neighborhood affairs group.

A backward glimpse revealed early deterioration and more recent absolute decline. Eri Hulbert told this to a Hull-House audience in 1949:

The Near West Side is an old and historic section of Chicago. When Charles Hull, a Chicago Real Estate man, built the house in which we are now meeting, in 1856, the area represented the outskirts of Chicago, the suburbs, if you please. When my father was born a few blocks from here in 1880, it was an area of new but congested housing similar to those areas the Chicago Plan Commission now

calls "Conservation Areas." Only nine years later, when Jane Addams asked city officials where the most congested area in Chicago was, they told her to go to Halsted and Blue Island and there she would find it.

By that time the area was already overcrowded and homes were running down. By that time it was what it has been ever since, the temporary haven Chicago offered new arrivals while they tried to adjust themselves to urban life and prepared for the day when economic and social success would enable them to move on to the other sections. Irish citizens lived here while becoming American citizens and then moved on; Russian, Jewish, Greek, and Polish citizens paused to transfer their citizenship and become familiar with "American ways." Italian citizens came next. Many of these have moved, to be followed by Mexican citizens and by American citizens from the rural South. Some of the original settlers have remained, and many Americans whose parents belong to one or another of these groups have been born here and to many the neighborhood is still home. . . .

In general terms, what is the picture at present? Almost half of the families have lived here more than thirty years, and most of the rest have been here from ten to twenty years. . . . Population decreased markedly from 1920–30 (by from 20–25%) and between 1930–40 (by another 10–20%). The decrease in population has been halted only by the depression of 18 years ago, the war of three years ago, and the current housing shortage.

How many problems? Another answer was given by building surveys. Eri Hulbert reported in 1949:

The housing, too, has been here a long, long time. It is mostly old and worn out, some of it built 75 years ago, much of it built over 50 years ago.

All the public schools were built before 1900. A Near West Side Community Council summed things up in 1951:

Fifty-six per cent of our homes lack a private bath and/or are dilapidated. Overcrowding is found in 18% of our dwelling units, as contrasted with six per cent for the city as a whole. Our tuberculosis morbidity and mortality rate is among the highest in the city. The Family Court has more delinquency referrals from our community than any other in the city.

A 12-year-old neighborhood boy entered this letter in a contest sponsored by the Catholic Youth Organization:

> I don't like the area because the streets are too dirty. You can't play football in the streets because you might fall down and get cut or hurt. If you go in an empty lot to play, there are house bricks. If you go to the park someone might steal your ball. Instead of the people putting the garbage inside of the can where it belongs, they throw it around the cans so the rats, cats, and dogs could scatter it all over the alley.

If a boy in the somewhat better northwestern area could write that, what words might be found to express the problems "south of Roosevelt?" Here, amidst many small businesses and large factories, close by the Maxwell Street market and the South Water produce market with their destroying effect upon normal community life, lived 11,400 persons in "Chicago's most abject slum area." Of 2,516 buildings in the area, 68 per cent were officially termed dilapidated. Only 12 per cent had central heating (77 per cent was the Chicago average). Overcrowding in these wretched tenements contrasted sharply with the vacancy of fully one-third of the region's land: the average population per dwelling unit was 30 per cent above the city norm; 20 per cent of the dwellings had over 1.5 persons per room. An owner-occupancy rate of 5 per cent deviated far from the city average of 29 per cent.

Ninety per cent of the 11,407 persons were Negroes; many of the remainder were Mexicans and Puerto Ricans. Both groups were isolated; to quote one observer, the unurbanized, uneducated new arrivals from the South were "cut off from the mainstream of Negro community life." Socially disorganized and facing discrimination everywhere in employment, these groups scraped the economic bottom. Unemployment was considerably higher for them than for the city in general. Each person who was working had to support *two* persons other than himself, whereas the Chicago typical worker supported *one* other than himself; yet this area's Negroes held almost none of the better-paid jobs, and their median income was *half* that of typical Chicago families. Home ownership and business ownership alike were very low.

The proportion of adult males was low, whereas the ratio of children to adults was disproportionately high. This, commented planner Lewis Elston, "implies problems of family finances, education, recreation, social hygiene, public health, medical care, and juvenile delinquency—all out of proportion to the economic capabilities of a depressed area such as this."

Community self-organization was nil. The churches (save the two Catholic churches, which had some social concern and activity) were otherworldly, offering emotional release, avoiding or strongly opposing participation in community affairs. Activities of the five social agencies were partially offset by the tendency, and sometimes the active effort, of poolrooms and junk shops to harbor or attract hoodlums. The Institute for Juvenile Research found the area had almost the highest juvenile delinquency rate in Chicago. Schools furnished few remedies. Physically antiquated, they suffered because teachers and principals struggled to get transferred out of the area.

The result of it all, wrote social worker J. A. Hargraves, was that the "basic psychology" of the Negro group was "to withdraw, take the role of non-participation," and wait to move farther west.

Meanwhile the area's firetraps contributed to an annual toll of deaths in agony; meanwhile the stories of rat attacks upon children came from the area with horrifying frequency.

Eri Hulbert once listed all these who find something wrong with the Near West Side. The city's Tax Collector "knows we don't pay our way and over a thousand parcels in the area are forfeited"; the Federal Housing Agency "won't insure mortgages in the area"; the banks "are reluctant to loan money for repair and construction"; insurance companies "charge us higher rates"; employers "see excessive costs for insurance, cleaning and decorating, special guards, high labor turnover"; schools "have many broken windows—students can't keep clean and are too tired to do their homework"; children "have no place to play"; the list went on, and on, and on. Eri Hulbert dubbed it all *blight* and drew a contrast with Kenwood and Hyde Park:

> . . . in South East Chicago the place is teeming with resources, including political resources. In our

area we are teeming with problems, including political problems.

Such comparisons, in fact, were painful. The West Side was more renowned for its "West Side bloc," known as a "bipartisan combination of machine politicians." It conspicuously lacked that professionally skilled population which abounded in the region of Michael Reese Hospital, the University of Chicago, the north-side "Magnificent Mile," or Illinois Institute of Technology.

Local Factors, and Others

What were the causes? Excessive, ceaseless *change* may have contributed to some of these problems. Change made it always problematical, for instance, that any kind of attachment to community would develop; when civic organizations were founded, the pattern of change menaced continuity in leadership and membership alike.

Above all, change reduced potential neighbors to actual strangers. And the result was not a community—and certainly not a city by St. Augustine's definition. Alvin Eichholz phrased it aptly in 1959:

> . . . the Near West Side, as it exists today, is an agglomeration of individuals primarily concerned with individual survival. This kind of existence is a major reason for deterioration in the area.

*Area 28.**—The whole region of which our Near West Side was a part—Area 28, to the social worker—was witnessing rapid transformation. Between 1940 and 1950, native-born whites in

*"Community Area 28," to give Chicago's Near West Side its official name, was considered to extend from the Chicago River, eastward about to Western Avenue (2400 West), and from Kinzie Street at 400 North down to 16th Street on the south; this is about 6.5 square miles and 160,000 persons, as contrasted with the 1.7 square miles and 55,000 persons which is the "Near West Side" of our story.

Hull-House as it looked before it was razed by the University of Illinois in 1963. The front of Hull-House. From left to right: the Immigrants' Protective League and the Juvenile Protective Association, with resident apartments above; the Butler Building; the original Hull residence; and the Smith or Children's Building.

The north side of Hull-House. From left: the Smith or Children's Building; the Hull-House Theatre and Coffee House; the Gymnasium; Bowen Hall for the Woman's Club Building; and the Boys' Club Building.

Area 28 declined from 60 per cent to 47 per cent; and of this group, the proportion of newcomers of Mexican descent was rising rapidly. In the same period, the proportion of Negroes to the whole population doubled; and Negroes, once concentrated in the northwest and southeast sections of the area, began to move westward south of Roosevelt Road, and to the north of Roosevelt Road west of Ashland. In 1940, sixteen of the sixty-eight census tracts in Area 28 had no Negroes; ten years later, only six tracts contained no Negroes. The increase in dwelling units (4 per cent) was no match for the population increase (17 per cent) of the same decade; and in fact, the increase in dwelling units was due almost entirely to subdivision of old dwelling units. Except for construction of one housing project, there was virtually no new residential construction in the forties. One report linked the low amount of owner-occupancy significantly to population change:

In 1950, 12 per cent of the dwelling units were owner occupied as compared with 30 per cent for the City. The proportion of owner occupancy is lower than . . . one would expect in view of the fact that over one-half of the dwelling units were in structures of four dwelling units or less. The transient population pays premium rents for the services provided, which makes absentee ownership profitable even for small buildings and tends to reduce . . . owner occupancy.

The occupational pattern of Area 28 also requires notice. In contrast with the city-wide pattern, in 1950 one-third of employed persons in Community Area 28 were employed as laborers or domestic workers; in 5 census tracts, over 50 per cent of the workers were so employed. The city-wide average in these lowest-paid jobs was one out of six workers, not one out of three. Another one-third of the workers in the area were semi-skilled workers, as compared with one-fourth of all work-

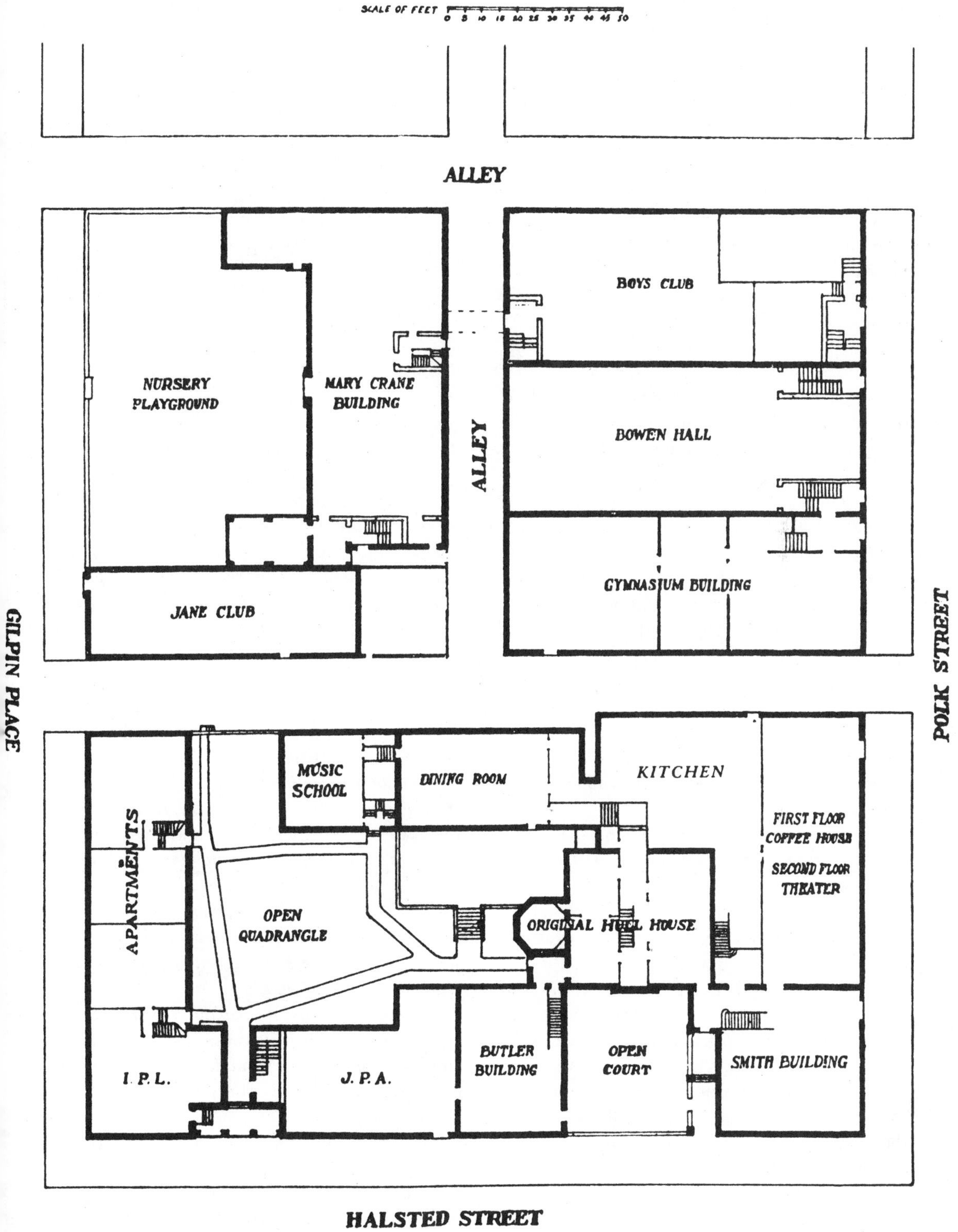

SCALE OF FEET
0 5 10 15 20 25 30 35 40 45 50
ALLEY
NURSERY PLAYGROUND
MARY CRANE BUILDING
ALLEY
BOYS CLUB
BOWEN HALL
GYMNASIUM BUILDING
JANE CLUB
GILPIN PLACE
POLK STREET
MUSIC SCHOOL
DINING ROOM
KITCHEN
FIRST FLOOR COFFEE HOUSE
SECOND FLOOR THEATER
APARTMENTS
OPEN QUADRANGLE
ORIGINAL HULL HOUSE
I. P. L.
J. P. A.
BUTLER BUILDING
OPEN COURT
SMITH BUILDING
HALSTED STREET

Plan of the Hull-House buildings in 1963.

ers in the city. In the top occupational groupings were 9 per cent of Area 28's workers, contrasting with 17 per cent for the city. In 1949, the median income for residents in Area 28 was at least one-third lower than the city average. Some 27 per cent of all families and unrelated persons in Area 28 had annual incomes of less than $1,000—twice the proportion for the city. Yet the median rental paid by residents of Area 28 was 75 per cent of the city-wide median rental; "families in this area obviously spend a higher proportion of their income for rent," concluded one analysis—and, we might add, "for inferior housing." In general, the economic level of the community was declining, and the downward spiral of the whole was speeded by the plight of its parts: the low economic level of recent immigrants, the low income of those in public housing projects, even the unusually great proportion of broken homes, contributed their depressing effect.

Area 28 was hardly a favorable matrix. . . .

Was there someone who could seize this bundle of contradictions and make the best of it? Was there, somewhere, a force for improvement? Was there anyone who, beyond "the people of the moment"—with their hatreds, divisions, and demoralization—could see the future people of a true community—a Near West Side united, self-conscious, self-determining, and proud? Among all the many peoples of the Near West Side itself, where were the men and women who cared and dared to act?

A statistician might compile his data endlessly, a surveyor pore over his maps, a traffic analyst study the streets, and see only the problems, never the human beings who could rise above them. One gifted with the fabled cloak of invisibility might glide from room to room, from the "Ta-Mor Social and Athletic Club" to the Kaffeneion Peloponnessos to the Newberry Avenue center, pausing along Maxwell Street or peering in store windows and church doors, and never guess which of all these humans might take arms against this sea of troubles. Observers see the actual, not the potential. What the neighborhood *was*, was known; but what could it *become*?

It would take a stimulus, and it would take a special moment—and, yes, it would take a special leadership—to bring out what was possible and what was necessary.

The crucial thing was to take all these ingredients and to make the attempt. . . .

The Fight to Save Hull-House

Nancy Craver, Charlene Dalpiaz, Helen Z. Fedoryn, the Debonairs, and Russell W. Ballard

When it became evident in February 1961 that the city of Chicago had decided to allocate urban renewal property in the Harrison-Halsted area to the University of Illinois for a new campus, a long, loud, and bitter protest arose. Hull-House, the historic institution founded by Jane Addams and Ellen Gates Starr, would be destroyed. An immediate campaign to save the settlement and its neighborhood was launched. Florence Scala, a neighborhood woman who with her brother Ernie Giovangelo had been a leader in the Near West Side Planning Board, and Hull-House resident Jessie Binford took up the fight against the city of Chicago, the University of Illinois, and the Hull-House board, which did not actively support the neighborhood's struggle.

The settlement board realized the futility of fighting the city and the University. It also realized the uselessness of preserving a settlement in an area where it would have no neighborhood to serve. As William F. Deknatel, architect and one time Hull-House board president, put it, "When the slums around us were cleared and rebuilt, there would be only one slum left, and that would be Hull-House." It would have taken an enormous amount of money to refurbish the settlement buildings, money which the trustees would have had to raise. It would be more practical to sell the settlement property for funds with which to begin anew in another area.

Yet throughout Chicago, Illinois, the United States, and the world, people found it hard to believe that the destruction of the famous institution could even be considered. Letters of protest to Mayor Richard J. Daley and to Dr. David D. Henry, president of the University of Illinois, and letters of encouragement to Hull-House Director Russell Ballard came from the great and the small. Some of these messages were mimeographed by those fighting to preserve Hull-House and its neighborhood, and were sent to the press and others influential in making the final decision.

Following are three letters that reflect the feelings of ordinary people whose lives had been touched in some way by Hull-House. One letter was written by two sixteen-year-old girls from Pennsylvania, one by a Chicago housewife who called Hull-House her "second home," and one by a settlement teen-age club.

Following the letters is the text of Russell Ballard's presentation before the Committee on Housing and Planning of the Chicago City Council at the public hearing it conducted on April 12, 1961, before the Council approved the ordinances making possible the transfer of property to the University. [Russell W. Ballard Papers, Jane Addams Memorial Collection, University of Illinois at Chicago Circle.]

83 School Lane
Conyngham, Pennsylvania
February 25, 1961

Dear People of Hull-House,

Last night we saw on the newsreel that they are going to destroy Hull-House for the purpose of building new buildings. Destroying it is just like destroying part of America itself.

We just bet that the people who want to do this are rich, or not very old, or have no feeling at all for great things, because if they were they wouldn't want to tear it down.

We speak for those of us left in the United States who cherish fine old things. We are not against progress, but are definitely against those who would prohibit fine work.

On the newsreel they showed the old people who make things to occupy their time and seek hospitality, and of the mentally retarded people who try their best to express themselves. May God have mercy on the people who will be turned away from here from now on if Hull-House is destroyed.

Over 70 years ago Jane Addams cared enough for humanity to start an institution such as this. She was surely promted by God to start it. If we

had more buildings like the Hull-House it would be a *FINE* credit to America. She started it with very good intentions and they want to destroy it. Tell them that there is other land to build their old building on.

Good Luck and Best Wishes to those who have carried on her work through the years, and to their present fight to preserve this fine national institution.

Yours truly,
NANCY CRAVER and
CHARLENE DALPIAZ

P. S. We are only 16 years old.

2100 West Chicago Avenue
Chicago 22, Illinois
February 27, 1961

Dear Sir:

I am pleading with you and hope that they will not tear down Hull-House.

I was a student in the weaving and sewing classes. I enjoyed being there and hope to come back again, as so many of my friends are there.

I often said it was my second home.

Hull-House has done a lot of good to the community as well as the outsiders. Very well known historical place.

It is still in good condition for a long time to come.

I hope they can build a campus elsewhere, where there is lot of vacant places such as on the lake front (if it is intended to build near the loop).

I sure hope it will not happen to us here in Chicago.

Thank you.

MRS. HELEN (ZOCHOCKIEWIZ) FEDORYN

March 17, 1961

Dear Mayor Daley,

I am writing you on behalf of a group of 18 girls who at the present are enjoying many of the Hull-House's benefits. We hold our club meetings here at Hull-House once a week. There are many young teen clubs here, and each one is grateful that there is a place in which friends can gather and be safe. This is what Hull-House means to us; for almost in every case our parents have also gone to Hull-House.

I, myself, went to Hull-House when I was very young. It was there that I learned how to mix with all different types of children. It was there that I was taught to be a humble winner and a good loser. This is true in each child's case—no matter his religion or color.

It seems to me, therefore, Mr. Mayor, that it would be a silly thing to destroy Hull-House, and the Harrison-Halsted district, when the people of the Garfield district are begging for the University! Why should a great establishment such as Hull-House be destroyed to build a University that is greatly desired by another district? I wish I knew the answer, for maybe then it wouldn't be such a heartbreak for us teens to give up Hull-House. Perhaps you may feel that this district is a so-called slum district, and thus a better place to reconstruct. Well, Mr. Mayor, our houses might be old buildings; but three fourths of their insides are remodeled with the modern facilities that any other district of Chicago could offer. If there wasn't any other place to build the University, I would then go along with the city's present plans. However, why not please the Garfield district by building the University there, and also make the Harrison-Halsted district very happy by permitting them to remain in their life-long homes that they love so much?

Although this letter might not change a single thing, you will have some idea how the teens of this district feel, and what your present plans mean to us. We love this neighborhood and we love Hull-House. We wish very much to keep Hull-House active here in Chicago so that it might have the chance to help many more boys and girls become good citizens of this great city.

Respectfully yours,
THE DEBONAIRS
A teen-age club
at Hull-House

To: THE COMMITTEE ON HOUSING & PLANNING OF THE CHICAGO CITY COUNCIL
PUBLIC HEARING, APRIL 12, 1961
STATEMENT OF: RUSSELL W. BALLARD,
Director of Hull-House

Mr. Chairman, members of the Committee on Planning and Housing:

In November 1947, a group of young men who were born and reared in the Halsted-Harrison neighborhood came to me in fear that the area would be cleared. They came to enlist the help of Hull-House in organizing a community effort to work for community improvement and to have some part in planning decisions concerning the area.

In June of 1949 the Near West Side Planning Board was organized as a grass-roots enterprise with membership open to all interested individuals, agencies and businesses in the area. A real citizen participation effort was born pre-dating the urban renewal legislation in which was incorporated provision for and encouragement of citizen participation in physical changes and renewal and rehabilitation.

During the intervening years, much time, effort and money was spent in this people's movement to upgrade a neighborhood. They supported Industrial Project #3 east of Halsted Street in the hope and with the promise that the area west of Halsted would remain residential, where workers could live close to their employment. They stimulated city agencies to clear abandoned buildings that had stood for years as monuments to neglect. Community esprit de corps was built up and many property owners were stimulated to repair and rehabilitate their homes.

Eri Hulbert, the leader of the Planning Board, and I went early to call on His Eminence, the late Cardinal Stritch, to enlist his interest and in turn that of the local clergy. A cooperative spirit among all groups pervaded the Planning Board. Our Lady of Pompeii parish, with renewed faith in the area, enlarged its school and other facilities.

One outgrowth of the people's effort was the designation of an urban renewal project from Morgan to Ashland and the land clearance project of some 55 acres surrounding Hull-House. I appeared at a public hearing before a Council committee in support of the land clearance area in the belief that new homes and shopping centers would be built.

I now appear with my neighbors in protest at the proposed change in land use. If the land use was to be changed from homes, WHY, will someone tell me, was the Guardian Angel parish permitted to spend $600,000 of hard-earned money to build a new school and sanctuary in the area—completed only two years ago?

Federal money is involved in these urban renewal and land clearance projects. Federal statutes recognize the value of citizen participation which gives the people affected some voice, some part in the contemplated changes. Hull-House and its neighbors have been planning together for neighborhood rehabilitation for the past 13 years. During this time we have had many contacts with public planning officials of the city who have encouraged the people to organize and express themselves as members of a democratic society. Former Mayor Kennelly spoke in January 1949 to a community group at Hull-House and emphasized the value of gaining neighborhood acceptance of physical changes. Mr. Follin, administrator of the Housing and Home Finance agency, came out from Washington to meet with our Planning Board staff. He told us at a Hull-House meeting in 1954 that our early efforts constituted the type of activity anticipated in effective urban renewal.

Until recent months no suggestion was ever made of a change in plans for the area. The fact is that within the past 18 months a group of our neighbors were encouraged by the land clearance officials to select a builder to construct their individual homes in the area. Businessmen of Greek, Italian and Mexican background have been planning and advising with city planning officials concerning their joint efforts in establishing a nationality shopping center. Planning officials did not discourage them. These people were told by land clearance officials that if they themselves did not make plans to build and remain in the area, the land would be sold to a developer who would plan and build without any special thought for their needs. A group of neighbors explored the possibility of building housing for the aged and were well received by land clearance officials. Is it any wonder that the people are now disillusioned, dissatisfied and angry, as a major change in plans for the area is presented to the city council? Those of us who live and work at Hull-House are supporting our neighbors in their protest. We feel, as they do, that a promise has been broken. Even the children in these families with whom we work know that a promise has not been kept. How can we then instill in these children a respect for law and government?

FINALLY, the ordinance calls for total clearance of the area, including Hull-House. I want to express a vigorous protest at the proposed ruthless destruction of a historic landmark in Chicago. We hear references to the "greater good." WHO can judge what is the "GREATER GOOD"?

The Committee on Preservation of Historic Buildings of the Chicago Chapter of the American Institute of Architects voted unanimously in favor of preserving Hull-House as "perhaps Chicago's most important historic structure." The national committee of this organization has taken similar action.

In March we received 1162 visitors who came for a "tour" of Hull-House. Many of them expressed dismay at the proposed destruction. A national protest is building up. Observe this file of letters which is added to by every mail.

Bessie Hillman, the widow of Sidney Hillman, writes from the New York office of the Amalgamated Clothing Workers of America, AFL-CIO, to Mayor Daley:

> To those of us who recall the work of Jane Addams and Hull-House in the early years of this century, the institution is not only hallowed and venerable, it is sacred. It should be sacred to every American with the slightest understanding of the social forces that have given America its internal strength and vitality.
>
> The groping, searching immigrants, yearning for dignity and hungry for learning, the fiery, idealistic trade-union organizers, and the thousands of plain people merely looking for relaxation or inspiration—all these were part of Hull-House, and Hull-House was part of them. In the fullest sense, it is woven into the fabric of America. If it dies, a vital part of America dies.
>
> I am sure that if my husband were alive today he would join me in this plea to you. I know that thousands of men and women who are better citizens and better human beings because of Hull-House, and thousands of children who are better children because their parents were inspired by Hull-House, do join me when I say:
>
> Please, Mayor Daley, do everything in your power to save Hull-House.

Senator Paul H. Douglas wires President Henry of the University of Illinois as follows:

> May I urge with all the strength at my command that you do not allow Hull-House to be destroyed but that you keep it in its major form as part of your new campus. As Irving Dilliard says: Hull-House and

Lincoln's home are the two great inspiration centers in Illinois. It would be an act of vandalism—complete and unadulterated—to bulldoze it. Can it not serve as the headquarters for the School of Social Service or for some other purpose?

Yes, a national protest is mounting, and the multitude of friends of Hull-House are not going to be satisfied with a bronze plaque mounted on a brand new modern building and reading "JANE ADDAMS SLEPT HERE."

I am sure of another thing. If the Holy Guardian Angel School and our neighbors and our businessmen were as well known nationally as is the historic home of Jane Addams, a similar protest would be heard in their behalf against the passage of this ordinance.

Jane Addams' Hull-House

David Dodds Henry

By the summer of 1961, David D. Henry (b. 1905), president of the University of Illinois, had announced that a portion of Hull-House would be preserved and integrated with the University's new campus on Chicago's near west side. Of the thirteen structures, the first settlement building, which had been built in 1856 as the home of Charles Hull, and the Hull-House Residents' Dining Hall, designed by the Pond brothers in 1905, were chosen to be saved. As the new university buildings rose around them, these two structures were restored under the direction of architects Frazer, Raftery, Orr, and Fairbank. The exterior of the Hull home, which had undergone many renovations during Jane Addams' day, was restored to its original two-story size, and the piazza surround at ground level was reconstructed. The size and design of the Residents' Dining Hall was maintained, but the building was moved to a new location south of the residence to make room for a student union behind the two structures.

In the spring of 1967, both buildings were ready to receive visitors. They were officially

opened and declared a national historic landmark by the federal government on June 14, as a memorial to Jane Addams and her associates, and to their contribution to social welfare. Since then, thousands of people from all over the world have visited the memorial to see displays depicting the growth, development, and importance of the settlement; to walk through rooms restored with furniture from the settlement; to use a library of materials relating to Hull-House, its founder, residents, and programs; and to hold meetings in its conference center. From 1975 until 1983, a project designed to gather, organize, and publish the papers and writings of Jane Addams was located there.

On January 23, 1964, David Henry outlined the University's hopes—chiefly realized—for this memorial. He was the principal speaker at the unveiling of a bust of Jane Addams that had been commissioned by the State of Illinois to commemorate the centennial of her birth. [David Dodds Henry, "Remarks," Ceremony on the Unveiling of the Jane Addams Bust, Springfield, Illinois, January 23, 1964.]

In the light of her place in history, it is most appropriate that the General Assembly of Illinois should have provided for the execution of this bronze bust of Jane Addams—in acknowledgment of a cherished citizen of this State.*

In the same spirit the University of Illinois is restoring Hull-House on its new Chicago campus. On the day that the Congress Circle site was selected for the new University of Illinois campus in Chicago, the Jane Addams Memorial Fund was born. For on that 102-acre site was located the complex of buildings which had grown up around the original Hull Mansion since 1889, when Jane Addams and her college classmate, Ellen Gates Starr, selected the neighborhood at Polk and Halsted streets for the beginning of what proved to be notable efforts on behalf of mankind.

I say the Jane Addams Memorial Fund was born on that day because it was immediately obvious to the administration of the University of Il-

*The sculptor was Lawrence Taylor, a black Chicago artist who had attended the Hull-House art school.—Eds.

linois that public sentiment was strong—even demanding—that Hull-House be retained in its original setting in memory of this remarkable woman.

Since funds for the project would of necessity have to come from non-University sources, the Trustees and the University of Illinois Foundation undertook a fund campaign in the belief that the restoration of Hull-House would be accepted as a civic responsibility.

Thus, the Trustees approved a plan to restore the original Hull Mansion constructed in 1856, and the historic dining room, where so many fateful decisions were made, to provide both a me-morial and a useful facility on the new campus at Congress Circle, at an estimated cost of $350,000. About $200,000 has been contributed or pledged.

The Mansion, when restored, is to house memorabilia, art objects, important papers, and library works related to Miss Addams, to her career, and to the story of social work, the history of labor unions, industrial relations, and other fields of study closely tied to her efforts. The Dining Room, now to be known as a Conference Center, will offer meeting places for students, for faculty and staff, and for citizen groups.

As the restoration of one of the few surviving residential structures pre-dating the Great Chicago

Russell Ballard (left) shows Hull-House and its neighborhood to Senator Paul H. Douglas. With them is Mrs. Robert H. McCormick, Jr., a leader in the fight to save Hull-House from demolition.

Fire, Hull-House will lend a traditional touch to the new campus. It will link both architecturally and spiritually a proud chapter of Illinois history with the modern steel and concrete structures in which young citizens will be educated for hundreds of years to come.

All who admire Jane Addams, all who have been touched by her influence, and all who would sustain her ideals in our time are invited to assist in the Hull-House restoration. For years Hull-House has been a stopping place for those who have sought the inspiration of a physical reminder of Jane Addams' career and spirit. The restored Hull Mansion will be an important landmark of Illinois history.

Florence Scala's Story

Studs Terkel

Some felt that a victory of a sort had been won when David Henry indicated in the summer of 1961 that a portion of the settlement would be saved to become part of the University of Illinois' new campus. But there were others who were determined to win a complete victory. They fought on through the U.S. Court of Appeals and in the Illinois Supreme Court, and with demonstrations and in the press, even after Mayor Richard J. Daley indicated quite strongly in a letter published in the Chicago Tribune's *"Voice of the People" column on October 15, 1962, that: "The city will not sacrifice the branch of the University of Illinois, which will meet the needs of thousands of young men and women for an unequaled opportunity for higher education."*

The leader of those who fought longest and hardest was Florence Scala, a young woman who had grown up in the neighborhood with Hull-House a part of her daily life. From the beginning of the Near West Side Planning Board, she assumed an active role in her community's problems with her brother Ernie Giovangelo, who eventually became the leader of the Planning Board. As a Catholic Youth Organization Community Center

worker, she gained experience working with her neighbors and carried it over to her Planning Board duties, which finally blossomed into leadership of the Harrison-Halsted neighborhood group protesting the coming of the University. Twice she ran for alderman in her ward. Though she was defeated in both attempts, her candidacy brought attention to the plight of Hull-House and the neighborhood, and pointed out the weakness of machine politics. When the citizens of the Harrison-Halsted group lost their fight in the federal and state courts, where they had pleaded unfairness in condemnation proceedings in 1963, the construction of the new University of Illinois campus was inevitable. Scala and her supporters were bitterly disappointed. Studs Terkel (b. 1912), noted Chicago interviewer and author, caught this quality in the courageous woman in a section in his book Division Street: America. *Scala remained in her neighborhood and by the mid-1980s she was operating a successful neighborhood restaurant, called appropriately Florence Restaurant. [Studs Terkel,* Division Street: America *(New York, 1967), 1–9.]*

Florence Scala, 47

I was born in Chicago, and I've always loved the city. I'm not sure any more. I love it and I hate it every day. What I hate is that so much of it is ugly, you see? And you really can't do very much about it. I hate the fact that so much of it is inhuman in the way we don't pay attention to each other. And we can do very little about making it human ourselves.

What I love is the excitement of the city. There are things happening in the city every day that make you feel dependent on your neighbor. But there's detachment, too. You don't really feel part of Chicago today, 1965. Any more. I don't feel any.

I grew up around Hull House, one of the oldest sections of the city. In those early days I wore blinders. I wasn't hurt by anything very much. When you become involved, you begin to feel the hurt, the anger. You begin to think of people like Jane Addams and Jessie Binford and you realize why they were able to live on. They understood how weak we really are and how we could strive for something better if we understood the way.

My father was a tailor, and we were just getting along in a very poor neighborhood. He never had money to send us to school; but we were not impoverished. When one of the teachers suggested that our mother send us to Hull House, life began to open up. At the time, the neighborhood was dominated by gangsters and hoodlums. They were men from the old country, who lorded it over the people in the area. It was the day of moonshine. The influence of Hull House saved the neighborhood. It never really purified it, you know what I mean? I don't think Hull House intended to do that. But it gave us . . . well, for the first time my mother left that darn old shop to attend Mother's Club once a week. She was very shy, I remember. Hull House gave you a little insight into another world. There was something else to life besides sewing and pressing.

Sometimes as a kid I used to feel ashamed of where I came from because at Hull House I met young girls from another background. Even the kinds of food we ate sometimes . . . you know, we didn't eat roast beef, we had macaroni. I always remember the neighborhood as a place that was alive. I wouldn't want to see it back again, but I'd like to retain the being together that we felt in those days.

There were Negroes living in the neighborhood even then, but there was not the tension. I've read about those riots in Chicago in the twenties—the race riots. But in our neighborhood it never did come to any kind of crisis. We used to treat each other as neighbors then. Now we look at each other differently. I think it's good and bad in a way. What we're doing is not understanding, some of us, what it was like then. I think that the American-born—the first generation, the second generation—has not hung on to what his mother and father had. Accepting someone naturally as a man. We don't do that today.

I think that the man who came over from Europe, the southern European especially, who was poor, could understand and see the same kind of struggle and have immediate sympathy for it. He accepted the Negro in the community as a man who is just trying to make a way for himself, to make a living. He didn't look upon him as a threat.

I think it was the understanding that both were striving. Not out of some great cause, but just in a human way.

I'm convinced that the first and second generation hasn't any concern about the other person's situation. I think money and position are hard to come by today and mean an awful lot, and now they see the Negro as a threat. Though they may say he's inferior, they know darn well he's not. He's as clever as we are and does many things better than we can. The American-born won't accept this, the first and second generation family, especially among the Italians and Poles, and the Irish, too. Remember Trumbull Park?*

Through my teens I had been a volunteer at Hull-House. After the War, Eri Hulbert, Jane Addams' [great] nephew, told me of a dream he had. The Near West Side, our area, could become the kind of place people would *want* to live in, close to the city. Did I think this was possible? I said no, people didn't care enough about the neighborhood to rebuild it. But he introduced me to the idea of city planning. He felt the only hope for big cities, in these communities that were in danger of being bulldozed, was to sit down and look and say we have a responsibility here. He convinced me that you could have a tree on the West Side, see?

That's where my life changed. I became involved with a real idea and talking to people like the banker, the social worker, and the Board of Trustees at Hull House. But I suddenly realized my inadequacy. I simply couldn't understand their language, you know? I had to go back to school.

This is where I began to lose the feeling of idolatry you have about people. I think that's bad. I idolized the people that were involved in Hull House. I thought they could never make a mistake. I was later to find out they were the ones who could hurt me the most. I feel that people have to be prepared always for imperfections in everyone, and we have to feel equal, really, to everyone. This is one of the things lots of slum kids, people who came out of poor areas, don't have. Not to be afraid to say something even though it may be way off base. I did this many times and I'd be embarrassed, realizing I had said something that had

*Several years ago, a Negro family, having bought a home in Trumbull Park, was stoned out of the neighborhood.

Hull-House comes down.

nothing to do with what they were talking about. But Eri Hulbert kept saying it makes no difference. Just keep at it. You're as good as they are.

Miss Binford and Jane Addams resented being treated as special persons. This was the kind of thing they had to cut through all the time. Yet we insisted on treating them as special people, in an uncomfortable kind of way. These feelings of confidence, you know, ego, so necessary—most of us in the neighborhood didn't have it. Most of us hung back, see.

In those days it was a new idea. You had to fight the politician who saw clearance and change as a threat to his power, his clout. He likes the kind of situation now around Maxwell Street, full of policy and hot goods being sold on the market and this kind of stuff that could go on and on without too much interference from authority because it's so oppressed. The rotten housing and no enforce-

ment of codes and all that business. We had a tough time selling the Catholic Church, too. From '47 to '56 were rough years. It was tough selling people on the idea that they could do it for themselves, that it was the only way it could be done. Their immediate reaction was: You're crazy, you know? Do you really think this neighborhood is worth saving?

All the meetings we had were so much frustration. Eri Hulbert was trying to lead us in a democratic way of doing something about our city. The misunderstandings never came from the neighborhood people. It arose out of the Hull House Board's unwillingness to understand. He couldn't get his point across.

Eri Hulbert committed suicide before our plan was accepted by the city. His death, more than anything else, opened a door which I never dreamed could open. You know, there's a real kind of ugliness among nice people. You know, the dirty stuff that you think only hoodlums pull off. They can really destroy you, the nice people. I think this is what happened to Eri, the way he was deserted by his own. I think it really broke his heart. What disturbs me is that I was a grown woman, close to thirty, before I could see. Sometimes I want to defend the rotten politicians in my neighborhood. I sometimes want to defend even gangsters. They don't pretend to be anything but what they are. You can see what they are. They're not fooling anybody, see? But nice people fool you.

I'm talking about the Board of Trustees, the people who control the money. Downtown bankers, factory owners, architects, people in the stock market. The jet set, too. The young people, grandchildren of old-timers on the Board, who were not really like their elders, if you know what I mean. They were not with us. There were also some very good people, those from the old days. But they didn't count so much any more. This new crowd, this new tough kind of board members, who didn't mind being on such a board for the prestige it gave them, dominated. These were the people closely aligned to the city government, in real estate and planning. And some very fine families, old Chicago families. (Laughs.) The nicest people in Chicago.

Except for one or two of the older people, they made you feel that you had to know your place. You always felt this. That's the big argument about the poverty program today. You cannot have the nice rich people at the top passing on a program for the poor, because they simply *don't* understand, they *can't* understand. These people meet in board meetings once a month. They come by the main street into the building and out they go. They've never had anybody swear at them or cry or ask for help or complain the kind of way people do in our neighborhood. They just don't know.

In the early sixties, the city realized it had to have a campus, a Chicago branch of the University of Illinois. (There was a makeshift one at the pier out on the lake.) There were several excellent areas to choose from, where people were not living: a railroad site, an industrial island near the river, an airport used by businessmen, a park, a golf course. But there was no give. The Mayor

looked for advice. One of his advisers suggested our neighborhood as the ideal site for the campus. We were dispensable. He was a member of the Hull House Board. It was a strange thing, a very strange thing. Our alderman, he's not what I'd call a good man—even he tried to convince the Mayor this was wrong. But the Mayor was hearing other voices. The nice people.

The alderman alerted us to the danger. Nobody believed it. The priest himself didn't believe it. They had just opened the parish, a new church, a new school. Late in the summer of 1960, the community could have been touched off. But the people were in the dark. When the announcement came in 1961, it was a bombshell. What shocked us was the amount of land they decided to take. They were out to demolish the entire community.

I didn't react in any belligerent way until little kids came knocking at the door, asking me to attend a meeting. That's where the thing got off the ground. It was exciting to see that meeting, the way people felt and the way they talked and the way they hurt—to hear our Italian priest, who had just become an American. This was in February, we had just celebrated Lincoln's birthday. He had just become a citizen, he couldn't understand.

Though we called the Mayor our enemy, we didn't know he was serving others. It was a faceless thing. I think he'd just as soon have had the University elsewhere. But the pressures were on. We felt it as soon as our protests began.

A member of the Hull House Board took me to lunch a couple of times at the University Club. The University Club—lunch—me! My husband said, go, go, have a free lunch and see what it is she wants. What she wanted to do, really, was to dissuade me from protesting. There was no hope, no chance, she said. I had had a high regard for her. I've been thinking she's probably one of those on the Board who would have fought the people's end. But she was elected to convince me not to go on. The first time I went, I thought this was a friend through whom we could work. But I could see, you know, that she allowed me to be just so friendly, and there was a place beyond which I couldn't go. There was a difference now. I stayed in my place, but I said what I wanted to say. There was a place beyond which she couldn't go, either. See? I was glad to experience it anyway.

I think I understand her. She had strong ties

with old Hull-House and she was really a good person who ought not have allowed this to happen and she knew it. When the lunches failed to bring anything off, I had no more contact with any of them on that level. We reached the letter-writing stage. We no longer used the phone.

I shall never forget one board meeting. It hurt Miss Binford more than all the others. That afternoon, we came with a committee, five of us, and with a plea. We reminded them of the past, what we meant to each other. From the moment we entered the room to the time we left, not one board member said a word to us. No one got up to greet Miss Binford nor to speak to her. No one asked her a question. The chairman came forward, he was a gentleman, and showed us where to sit.

Miss Binford was in her late eighties, you know. Small, birdlike in appearance. She sat there listening to our plea and then she reminded them of what Hull House meant. She went back and talked, not in a sentimental way, about principles that must never waver. No one answered her. Or acknowledged her. Or in any way showed any recognition of what she was talking about. It's as though we were talking to a stone wall, a mountain.

It was pouring rain and we walked out of the room the way people walk out who feel defeat. I mean we walked out trying to appear secure, but we didn't have much to say to each other. Miss Binford could hardly speak at all. The shock of not being able to have any conversation with the board members never really left her. She felt completely rejected. She knew then there would be no help anywhere. In the past, whenever there was a serious problem in the juvenile courts, she could walk into the Mayor's office and have a talk with him, whoever he was. Kelly, for instance, or Kennelly, or Cermak. And never fail to get a commitment from him. Never. But she knew after this meeting, she'd never find that kind of response again. And sure enough, to test herself, she made the rounds. Of all the people who had any influence in town, with whom she had real contact, not one responded. They expressed sympathy, but it was hands off. Something was crushed inside her. The Chicago she knew had died.

I don't think we realized the stakes involved in this whole urban renewal system. The money it brings in, the clout necessary to condemn

land . . . a new Catholic Church was demolished, too. It had opened in '59, built near Hull House with the city's approval. The Church was encouraged to go ahead and build, so as to form the nucleus for the new environment, see? It cost the people of the area a half-million dollars. The Archdiocese lends the parish money, but the parish has to repay. It's a real business arrangement.

Now the people of the area have learned a good deal, but it was a bitter education. The politicians' actions didn't bother us as much. We hated it, we argued about it, we screamed about it out loud. Daley gave the orders and the alderman followed it. This kind of thing we could understand. But we could never understand the silence of the others. A group wanted to picket the Archdiocese, but I felt it was wrong, because we were put into a position of fighting education, the University being built, you know.

Here we were in a big Roman Catholic city, we'd be looked upon as a bunch of fanatics. As I think back on it now, the instinctive responses of the people, who are thought of as being uneducated, were better than my own. I was very anxious we should not be looked upon as people from the slums, many of us Italians and Mexicans. We

The restored Jane Addams' Hull-House at the University of Illinois at Chicago was opened as a museum and conference center in 1967.

had to proceed in an orderly manner. We overdid that. We should have picketed the Archdiocese. We should have been tough with Hull House. We should have spoken the truth from the beginning.

Most of the people who left the area were deeply embittered. They said never again will they ever become involved about anything in their city. They'd had it. This was a natural kind of thing because it was a pretty brutal two and a half years. But I don't know now. This is a big question to ask: whether that experience gave any meaning to their lives? If they turn their backs on it, it's been a failure as far as I'm concerned. There's a danger of their becoming extremists in the self-indulgent sense. They'll be concerned with themselves and their own safety and nothing else. It has happened with some of them.

I don't believe so much any more. I don't believe so much in people as I used to. I believe in *some* people but not in all people any more. I feel I have to be careful about this business of believing in all people. That's the number-one change, I think. And I've found there are certain kinds of liberals who'll sell you out, who make life miser-

able for great numbers of people when they will not see beyond their narrow views. I'm thinking of Urban Renewal, and the huge Negro ghettos that have sprung up and have your heart break at the kind of overcrowding and rotten environment that's developed. It's an evil thing the liberal community does: it wants to see the slums cleared but doesn't fight to see housing for lower-income groups built first. It reinforces all the terrible things we're talking about in the big cities. Segregates the poor people, particularly the Negro people, and this goes on and on.

In an area like ours, the uprooting is of another kind. I lived on the same block for over forty-five years; my father was there before me. It takes away a kind of stability big cities need. Lots of the people have moved into housing no better than the kind they lived in. Some have moved into public housing. The old people have really had it worse. Some have moved into "nicer" neighborhoods, but they're terribly unhappy, those I've spoken with. Here, downtown in the Loop, everything is clearing and building and going up. And the social workers in this town, boy! I can hardly look at them with respect any more. The way they've knuckled down to the system themselves, because everybody wants a Federal grant or something. They don't want to be counted out. I'm sick of the whole mess and I don't know which way to go.

There are the little blessings that come out of struggle. I never knew Jessie Binford as a kid at Hull House. I used to see her walking through the rooms. She had such dignity, she just strode through the rooms and we were all kind of scared of her. In the past four or five years, we became close friends. I really knew the woman. It means something to her, too. She began to know the people in the way she knew them when she first came to Hull House as a young girl. It really gave her life, this fight. It made clear to her that all the things she really believed in, she believed in all the more. Honor among people and honor between government and people. All that the teacher tells the kids in school. And beauty.

There was a Japanese elm in the courtyard that came up to Miss Binford's window. It used to blossom in the springtime. They were destroying that tree, the wrecking crew. We saw it together. She asked the man whether it could be saved. No, he had a job to do and was doing it. I screamed and cried out. The old janitor, Joe, was standing out there crying to himself. Those trees were beautiful trees that had shaded the courtyard and sheltered the birds. At night the sparrows used to roost in those trees and it was something to hear, the singing of those sparrows. All that was soft and beautiful was destroyed. You saw no meaning in anything any more. There's a college campus on the site now. It will perform a needed function in our life. Yet there is nothing quite beautiful about the thing. They'll plant trees there, sure, but it's walled off from the community. You can't get in. The kids, the students, will have to make a big effort to leave the campus and walk down the streets of the area. Another kind of walling off. . . .

To keep us out. To keep the kids out who might be vandals. I don't see that as such a problem, you know. It wasn't the way Jane Addams saw it, either. She believed in a neighborhood with all kinds of people, who lived together with some little hostility, sure, but nevertheless lived together. In peace. She wondered if this couldn't be extended to the world. Either Jane Addams brought something to Chicago and the world or she didn't.

THE END AND A NEW BEGINNING: 1963–1989

EVEN BEFORE 1963, AS THE SETTLEMENT BUILDINGS AT 800 South Halsted stood vacant and waiting for the wrecker's ball, Hull-House began to lay the foundation for a new and different social welfare organization that would provide programs in several different neighborhoods throughout the Chicago metropolitan area. Hull-House abandoned the settlement idea of residence, left its old neighborhood, and became Hull-House Association, a loosely organized confederation of affiliated organizations, including former settlements, newly created community centers, and other programs. The number, variety, and location of the agencies changed over the next twenty-five years, and there was conflict and disagreement, budget crises and personality clashes. Yet for all the turmoil and change, the new Hull-House continued many of the programs and purposes, and maintained the same focus on responding to neighborhood need with creativity and flexibility begun by Jane Addams and her co-workers in the early days of the settlement.

The person presiding over the transformation of Hull-House was Paul Jans, who had been hired by the board to replace Russell Ballard. Jans was a seasoned settlement worker with experience in St. Louis, Detroit, and Philadelphia, where he headed the Lighthouse settlement, before coming to Chicago. The process of building the new association began in 1962, shortly after Jans arrived. It was fostered by the settlement's need to relocate and by the desire of the Community Fund of Chicago to encourage mergers among settlements for the purpose of creating larger, stronger, and more financially sound neighborhood organizations.

The first new Hull-House Association affiliates were two settlements serving largely black neighborhoods: Henry Booth House, founded in 1898 and operating in the 1960s from Harold L. Ickes Housing project at 2328 South Dearborn; and Parkway Community House, a twenty-four-year-old settlement at 500 East 67th in West Woodlawn, on the south side. Hull-House itself founded two new centers on the north side, one in the Lakeview area and eventually headquartered in the Jane Addams Center, a former American Legion hall at 3212 North Broadway; the other in the Uptown area, finally located at 4520 North Beacon in a building especially constructed for it and named the Uptown Center.

In addition, Abraham Lincoln Center, 700 Oakwood Boulevard, founded in 1905, affiliated in 1966; and Clarence Darrow Community Center, organized in 1953 and operating in LeClaire Courts at 4340 South Lamon, joined in 1967. Des Plaines Valley Community Center, founded in 1943 as a teen center in Summit, a western suburb, also affiliated in 1967. The next year, the Senior Centers of Metropolitan Chicago, a group of facilities offering services to older adults, joined Hull-House Association. Most of these eight major centers also had an assortment of satellite programs. Some were lodged in store fronts, others in rooms in housing projects, and a few in separate buildings. These locations tended to change as the population moved or as the funding and personnel shifted. In 1968, Hull-House listed eleven program centers (seven major affiliates and four senior centers) in its association. By 1985, it had twenty-nine program sites, including major centers and outposts, even though Abraham Lincoln Center disaffiliated in 1970 and Henry Booth House in 1985.

One problem with decentralization and this new and somewhat artificial grouping of organizations was the matter of identity. For seventy-five years Hull-House meant Jane Addams (even after her death) and a jumbled group of buildings on Halsted Street. Hull-House also meant helping the poor. It stood for a variety of programs and publications and a fascinating and important group of residents and graduates whose names were instantly recognizable. Much of that identity was lost when its connection with its historic buildings was severed.

No longer a single organization, Hull-House Association was becoming an administrative entity helping to promote programs in a variety of affiliated institutions. When the original Hull-House existed, there was a sense of place and residents who lived in the buildings. Now there was a growing cadre of professional social workers, men and women from all ethnic and racial backgrounds with masters degrees in social work, some of whom lived outside the neighborhood where they worked, and all keeping nine-to-five hours, five days a week. There was an assortment of dissimilar program centers loosely and often unwillingly associated for funding purposes. Many of the affiliated agencies did not want to relinquish their own histories and identities. Without the settlement base and without residents in a particular neighborhood, Hull-House lacked a special method to differentiate its approach to social problems from that of many other agencies operating in the city.

Adding to the confusion over exactly what Hull-House meant was the fact that beginning in 1966 there were two separate and different programs with the same name. On its new Chicago campus, the University of Illinois developed a memorial to Jane Addams in restored versions of two of the original settlement buildings. Though the University called its site Hull Mansion and eventually Jane Addams' Hull-House, to the public it was still Hull-House; yet these two buildings were no longer connected with Hull-House Association, and Paul Jans wanted no connection. He tried during the 1960s to distance his new agency from the settlement's past. His focus was not on Jane Addams and certainly not on the former settlement buildings. He set out to chart a new course.

The rapid expansion of Hull-House Association in the 1960s coincided with the passage of federal legislation that resulted in the War on Poverty programs and the massive expenditure of federal funds to solve social problems, especially in the cities. The War on Poverty (the phrase came from Lyndon Johnson's 1964 inaugural address, but the concept was invented by John Kennedy) did not eliminate poverty, end discrimination, or remove the stigma attached to welfare, but it did help to revive the settlements.

The settlements' special method of neighborhood work, in disrepute in the 1950s even among social workers, seemed vindicated in the 1960s. No settlement profited more than Hull-House from the new federal programs and the rediscovery of poverty as an issue. By 1965, Hull-House had received nine federal grants totaling more than a million dollars, which allowed the various Hull-House agencies to double their services and to add over 150 staff members. The VISTA program (Volunteers in Service to America), sometimes called the domestic Peace Corps, which sent volunteers to live and work in poor neighborhoods, was very much in the settlement tradition. Hull-House trained more volunteers (371 in one year) and accepted more program graduates on their staff (61 were employed in the fall of 1966) than any other settlement. Most of the VISTAS served in useful ways, but the social work professionals sometimes resented the extra time and resources it took to prepare and supervise them; and Hull-House had to dismiss three volunteers for allowing a group of youngsters to smoke marijuana. One or another of the Hull-House centers also had federally funded Head Start programs, Neighborhood Resources Projects, Meals on Wheels, Work Study and STREETS (Socialization, Training, Recreation, Education and Employment Technical Services) projects. Suddenly there was activity everywhere, new programs to administer, forms to fill out, new staff to hire.

Paul Jans had his hands full. He often seemed dictatorial and uncompromising as he tried to control the increasing number of affiliated centers, the bewildering mixture of new and traditional programs, and the budget. The administrative relationships among the affiliates—each with its own director, staff, and board—and between the affiliates and the

Paul Jans developed a new Bowen Country Club camp near East Troy, Wisconsin, with a performing arts focus. The camp also served as a training center for VISTA *volunteers and a work camp for teaching hard-to-employ inner-city youth construction skills. Here a* VISTA *worker and a trainee work on a camp building.*

In the 1960s, programs in storefronts became an important mechanism for reaching groups who might not easily be attracted to the settlement building. Hull-House established Una Puerta Abierta in 1967, to reach an increasingly large Spanish-speaking population in its Lakeview neighborhood.

central agency—with its director; public relations, fund raising, and financial management staff; and board—were never adequately defined. The uncertainty this caused often led to mistrust, misunderstanding, and charges of discrimination.

But any director would have run into conflict during the 1960s because many of the projects created through the War on Poverty were philosophically opposed to the settlement idea. Many of the anti-poverty agencies were based, at least in part, on the idea that the poor should have policy-making roles in programs established to assist them. The underlying philosophy was that one needed to be black to understand and help blacks, or Italian to help Italians. A masters degree in social work was not nearly as important as the proper ethnic or racial background. This inevitably led to conflict and confusion, though it was also true that Hull-House, like most settlements, was slow to appreciate the power of race and ethnic consciousness in the 1960s. It was not until 1968 that the Hull-House Board of Trustees adopted a public policy supporting blacks' efforts ''to achieve their rightful place in society.'' During the 1960s, however, Jans placed black staff in black neighborhood centers and left them to develop their own programming in response to community needs.

Paul Jans' consuming passion at Hull-House was the development of a performing arts and theatre program. He brought Robert Sickinger, an innovative theatre director, with him from Philadelphia, and by the end of the decade almost all the Hull-House centers had theatre of one kind or another. There were four community theatres, a writer's workshop and studio, a children's theatre, a short-lived touring theatre, and acting classes. The settlement became famous for its imaginative and experimental theatre. In 1967, the year the theatre program received a grant of $30,000 from the National Foundation on the Arts and Humanities, 20,000 people attended productions in the Jane Addams Center Theatre alone.

In 1963, at Jans' urging, the Association sold the Bowen Country Club to Waukegan for a public park. Created from an initial gift of property by Louise deKoven Bowen, it had served as the settlement summer camp since 1912. With the proceeds from the sale, Jans directed the purchase of 400 acres of land around Peter's Lake, near East Troy, Wisconsin. It became the new summer camp facility with dormitories, a concert shell, and music, art, dance, sculpture, and woodworking studios designed by former Hull-House resident and student of Frank Lloyd Wright, architect William F. Deknatel. The Art and Music Camp opened in the summer of 1964. The same facility also served as a work camp for urban youth, as a VISTA training center, and as a year-round recreation center.

The Jans era at Hull-House was a time of explosive growth and change, not only because of the new arts programming, but even more because of the affiliation process and federal funding. By 1968, the Association's budget had swelled to over $3,000,000, primarily from federal grants. While Hull-House profited from the diversity and amount of government support, the new infusion of federal money led to problems, too. Instead of identifying a community need and finding funds to develop a program to address it, there was an increasing tendency to launch programs because government money was available. But Hull-House learned that government funding could fluctuate. Program support, here today, could be gone tomorrow depending upon the actions of Congress and the President. Recognizing this, Hull-House eventually began to design programs to achieve goals in a limited time.

Unfortunately, in the late 1960s, Hull-House had not yet learned that strategy. The Hull-House Association deficit in 1967 was over $200,000, and it was larger in each of the next two years. Center directors competed with one another, and with Jans himself, for increasingly scarce money. The mix of performing arts, special government programs, and center-supported projects had become too much for the agency's resources. In 1969, the board asked for Jans' resignation.

Robert T. Adams came to Chicago in September 1969, to assume the position of Hull-House executive director. Graduating with a masters degree in social work from the University of Buffalo in 1957, he had been a clergyman, social worker, and administrator in Rochester and Buffalo, New York, and in Kansas City, Missouri. Since 1963, he had been executive director of Friendship House Association in Washington D.C. Even before he appeared, the tasks with which the Hull-House board charged him were being tackled by someone else. Homer C. Bishop, who retired from Hull-House in 1977 after eleven years as associate director, was acting executive director of the agency from January 1969 until Adams arrived. Bishop successfully began reducing and establishing program priorities in order to achieve a balanced budget, and he initiated the sale of the East Troy, Wisconsin camp, which was barely five years old. Adams was able to use the proceeds from the sale to strengthen programming and to rebuild the endowment, another one of the tasks he was given by the board. Sickinger resigned shortly after Jans left, and with the support of board leadership, Bishop began an effort continued by Adams to reduce the theatre and performing arts programs drastically. The Board of Trustees returned control of all theatre programs to center directors, in effect giving each center permission to abolish its theatre program if it chose. Remnants of a performing arts program survived in many of the centers, but near-professional theatre at Hull-House disappeared.

Adams was a manager not an entrepreneur, and the board hoped he would bring administrative order. He moved into the Hull-House headquarters at 3139 North Broadway, diagonally across the street and just south of the Jane Addams Center. Adams and Bishop halted the deficits and gave each center more responsibility for developing program ideas in response to the needs of its particular neighborhood. They urged centers to concentrate on helping local citizens improve the quality of their lives.

Recognizing that the whole agency needed to address the issue of its public image, Adams believed that Jane Addams' Hull-House at the University of Illinois could benefit

Hull-House became famous in Chicago in the mid-1960s for its near-professional theatre. A scene from a play performed at Jane Addams Center and directed by Robert Sickinger.

Hull-House Association. With its restored rooms and exhibits explaining the history of the settlement, the museum could serve an outreach function for Hull-House Association, connecting Hull-House past, present, and future in the public mind. With the help of the museum staff, Adams developed a list of settlement firsts which he frequently used in public statements and press releases. He formed an organization of former residents, hoping that they would give the agency a sense of connection with its past; and he began to use pictures of Jane Addams and the old Hull-House buildings in association publications.

Under Adams the agency did not look back nostalgically to the glory days of the settlement; it began to concentrate its energies, once again, on solving social problems throughout the city. The task was not easy. The various centers served their neighborhoods in different ways through child care facilities, counseling and job referral, recreation, and art classes. They were involved in neighborhood development and organization and served as hosts for other useful services. By 1976, the Department of Public Aid Food Stamps Registration and IRS Income Tax Counseling operated from Clarence Darrow Center and Des Plaines Valley Center; the Illinois Department of Corrections' Community Advancement Program was associated with the Jane Addams Center; and the Chicago Department of Human Resources Runaway Program was lodged in Parkway Community House. During the 1970s, Hull-House increased its work with senior citizens, as that part of Chicago's population increased dramatically. Patricia Sharpe, who became Associate Director of the agency in 1973, received funding for the first Retired Seniors Volunteer Program (RSVP) in Chicago. Eventually responsibility for it was transferred to the Senior Centers of Metropolitan Chicago. In various centers new and innovative program ideas were developing, such as the Housing Resources Center at Uptown Center and the Constance Morris Center for battered women and children at Des Plaines Valley Community Center.

The 1970s were a difficult time for the settlement movement. The War on Poverty and a variety of government programs had breathed new life into the settlements in the 1960s, but had also changed them irrevocably. They became more dependent on grants, not only from federal and state governments, but also from private foundations. They also became more attuned to the needs of their neighborhoods, sometimes to the extent of putting neighborhood leaders on their boards and hiring local people as staff members and paraprofessionals. Even the words "settlement house" began to be replaced by "neighborhood center," because "settlement" had too much of a paternalistic ring. Another development in many settlements in the 1970s was the emergence of a group of black male leaders. This trend was symbolized in 1971, when Margaret Berry resigned as executive director of the National Federation of Settlements and was replaced by Walter Smart, a black social worker from Alabama who had had a variety of settlement experience in Philadelphia and Boston.

One major problem faced by Hull-House and other settlements in the 1970s was the cutback and, in some cases, the elimination of federal programs. By 1971, government support at Hull-House had been reduced by $700,000 from the 1968 level. Office of Economic Opportunity funding ended in 1974; the VISTA program had been canceled several years earlier. But Hull-House, better than most institutions, retained its federal support through other programs. The 1974 revisions of the Social Security Act, especially Titles IV and XX, allowed the government to purchase service from private agencies. Title III of the Older Americans Act, under which RSVP was initiated, was also important for the Association, although during the 1970s day care attracted the largest percentage of federal funds. In 1977, with the total revenue at various Hull-House centers at just under $3,000,000, 57 percent came from the federal government. Funding from the United Way increased during the decade from $385,000 to $865,000, barely keeping up with inflation.

Hull-House shared other problems and tensions of the settlement movement in the 1970s, but because of its organization as a loose confederation the effect was somewhat different. Neighborhood leaders often served on the boards of the affiliated centers. Sometimes they found themselves sitting on the central Hull-House board, which counted among its membership two representatives from the board of each affiliated center. In contrast to other former settlements, the Hull-House board never lost its upper middle-class bias or its potential access to traditional sources of financial support. Stanley Horn is an example of a black leader who emerged from one of the neighborhoods Hull-House served. He grew up in the Parkway Center neighborhood and worked part-time in a work-study program at the center, while completing a degree in Urban Ethnic Studies at Loyola University. He was program director at Parkway before becoming director at Darrow in 1977.

Robert Adams, the executive director of Hull-House during the 1970s, was a white male. During his ten years as director of the Association, Adams had success in reducing the budget deficit and in standardizing some administrative practices, but there was still confusion about the distribution of responsibilities and authority among the various center directors and boards and the Association's director and central board. Disgruntled employees seeking a larger share in the direction of the agency and better pay formed a union which later affiliated with the UAW. The refeminization of the agency, which continued into the 1980s, also began under Adams. In 1970, there were three female and ten male managers in the Association. By 1980, the numbers were reversed, with nine female and five male managers. When Adams resigned in November 1979, the board did not appoint a black male, but rather a white female in his place. Patricia Sharpe became director of the agency in January 1980.

Sharpe was the first woman to lead the agency since 1943 and the first Hull-House employee to hold the post since Adena Miller Rich, in 1935–1937. She was born in Canada and was a naturalized U.S. citizen. She received her masters degree in social work from the University of British Columbia in the late 1950s and had worked at Hull-House in a number of positions since 1968, joining the settlement when the Senior Centers of Metropolitan Chicago affiliated. In addition to working with the elderly, Sharpe had served as Director of Social Services and as Associate Director of Hull-House. Long familiar with the organizational and administrative flaws in the agency, she organized a long-range planning committee of agency, staff, and board members to untangle and define the relationships among central administration and the affiliated centers and to chart a course for the next decade. There would be many accomplishments, despite further cuts in federal programs during the Reagan administration's war on welfare and the deteriorization of the urban environment in Chicago.

In the 1980s, the poor got poorer and were filled with a greater sense of despair. Unemployment, drug abuse, homelessness, teenage pregnancy, illiteracy, and violence all increased, putting more pressure on the social agencies. Despite long-range planning committees, Sharpe continued to face a cumbersome administrative structure. Though funding from government and private sources increased, sufficient support for the growing Hull-House program remained a problem. As a general rule, grants provided funds for program but not for administrative expense. Support for the administrative expertise that made the grants possible was difficult to find. Budget deficits began to appear again. Sharpe also had to contend with the agency's first strike. "Hull-House Workers Call Strike," the Chicago newspapers announced in the fall of 1982. Over 200 members of the union picketed to protest the board's wage freeze. The strike did not last long, but the presence of a union and the very idea of a strike at Hull-House was a certain indication that times had changed since the days of Jane Addams.

Settlement founders might have been surprised by other developments at Hull-House in the 1980s, but there were many programs that would have seemed familiar. In the early days of the century the rooms at Hull-House were strewn with books, papers, and partly completed reports, for many of the residents were writing books, preparing speeches, or doing research on social problems. In that same tradition, and at the urging of Patricia Sharpe, in 1980 the Hull-House Board of Trustees created a Department of Research and Advocacy in the central administrative office. The new department was directed by Ann Seng, who had been community development director at Uptown Center since 1971. She was charged with conducting research, making presentations, and organizing conferences on city-wide social issues. The department chose three issues on which to focus: creation and retention of jobs for the poor; capital formation to support the creation and expansion of businesses; and advocating women's rights to reduce the number of women at or below poverty level. In the next few years the department organized the Jane Addams Conference on Security in the Nuclear Age, and ran forums on employment, women in poverty, and starting business ventures. It issued more than ten studies, including *Illinois Women and the Block Grant Cuts* (1981), *Child Support Enforcement: A Citizen Issue* (1982), and *Women, Work and Welfare* (1984). The department was also a co-convener, with the Chicago League of Women Voters, of the Chicago Jobs Coalition in 1981. By 1987, the group had become the Chicago Jobs Council, successfully carrying out pilot projects aimed at employing the hard to employ and in promoting access to jobs for Chicago residents, especially minorities and women, whenever tax dollars were used to finance or subsidize economic development. The Research and Advocacy Department also helped to create the Chicago Capital Fund (CCF), an organization to provide venture capital for small businesses located in Chicago neighborhoods. Successful neighborhood businesses created more neighborhood jobs. By 1988, the CCF had access to $7,000,000 and had made some initial investments.

Since the days of the Hull-House Labor Bureau, begun in the early 1890s under the guidance of Florence Kelley, the settlement had been concerned with unemployment. During the 1980s, unemployment continued to be a program focus. Hull-House placed emphasis on organizations and programming that would create jobs, educate for jobs, and promote access to jobs. In addition to the activities of the Research and Advocacy Department, the central office and the centers initiated a variety of programs to address unemployment. The First Aid Care Team (FACT), the first program of its kind in the nation, provided employment and sorely needed medical services for residents in an increasing number of Chicago public housing projects. The Clarence Darrow Catering Service, established in 1981, and the Pre-Building Maintenance Program at Darrow provided training and jobs for residents in LeClaire Courts. Uptown Center maintained Project TEAM (Training and Employment of Auto Mechanics), Telephone Answering Service with private clients, and Health Care Job Link through its Economic Development and Training Unit, which was designed to improve economic conditions in the neighborhoods it served. A similar program at Jane Addams Center, called Jane Addams Resource Corporation, developed Spread the News Mailing and Distribution Service, founded in 1982; carried out special economic studies; and created programs to provide basic and special skills education. A component of almost all of the agency's employment programs was education to promote literacy.

Jane Addams and her associates worked hard to improve the housing of their Chicago neighbors early in the century. They conducted surveys, wrote reports, lobbied for legislation, and even tried to teach their immigrant neighbors the proper way to organize their apartments. They had faith that better houses would help produce better citizens. The Hull-House staff in the 1980s did not have quite the same faith in housing reform, but they continued to work to improve housing for the poor people in Chicago.

At Clarence Darrow Center, Stanley Horn helped the residents of LeClaire Courts establish a resident management corporation. It contracted with the Chicago Housing Authority to allow the residents to manage the project themselves. In 1988, LeClaire Courts became the first tenant-managed public housing project in Chicago. Meanwhile, in 1983, at Uptown Center, where Brooks Miller was director, the Housing Resource Center received approval from the Chicago Housing Authority and the United States Department of Urban Development to manage scattered public housing units in its neighborhood. This was the first time that a community-based, non-profit group had received that authority. The Housing Resource Center also organized a two-year Resident Managers Training Program, whose design and training material were used across the country.

The early residents of Hull-House, many of them the first generation of college-educated women, felt a special responsibility to help improve the lives of women and children.

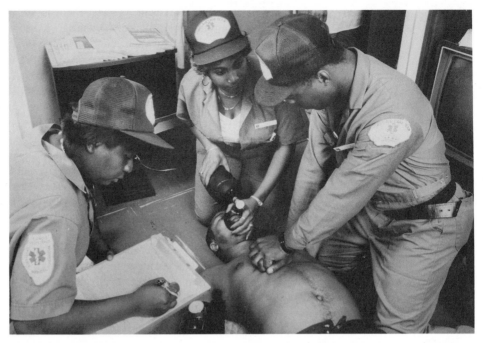

The award-winning First Aid Care Team program (FACT), the first of its kind in the U.S., has been developed at Hull-House to provide skills, employment, and on-site emergency care for residents of the Robert Taylor and Henry Horner housing developments. During a simulated drill two FACT members apply CPR and oxygen, while a third staffer charts the patient's age, medical history, blood pressure, and pulse.

They campaigned for child labor laws and for protective legislation for working women. They helped to found the first juvenile court in the United States, and they sought to promote women's rights in other ways. They were the pioneer generation of feminists. In the 1980s, Hull-House, led by a woman executive director and by female board presidents, still fought to promote the rights of women and children. At Jane Addams Center, Lina Cramer, who became director in 1979, and her staff developed Child Care Initiative, a unique day-care provider training program.

Recognized nationally, the program was selected by the U.S. Department of Health and Human Services, the Mayor's Office of Employment and Training, the Chicago Board of Education, and Child Care Systems of Philadelphia to provide either child-care programs or referral and placement services. By 1987, Jane Addams Center, with its new director, Nancy McCullar, was teaching seven other agencies in diverse communities how to duplicate its innovative model. Des Plaines Valley Center pioneered in helping women who were the victims of family violence, and created one of the first residential shelters for battered women and children in Illinois. The Women's Abuse Action Project of Uptown Center helped to organize the Domestic Violence Court of Cook County in 1984, the first such court in the United States. Ann Seng represented Hull-House through the Research and Advocacy Department in a number of statewide programs relating to women's issues. Her work drew attention to the feminization of poverty in the 1980s. At the same time, Patricia Sharpe, the only female head of a neighborhood-based social welfare organization in Chicago and one of the most prominent women settlement executives in the country, was a leader in many women's organizations and coalitions.

Hull-House one hundred years after its founding, is still an evolving institution, responding to neighborhood need with flexibility and creativity. In many ways it is very different from the world-famous Hull-House of the early decades of the century, but it still seeks to improve the lot of the poor; to make life more meaningful for all kinds of people; to conduct research, organize, and publish in order to help the helpless; and to give inspiration to the young and old. In 1989, Hull-House, again directed by a woman, looked back to its illustrious past in order to chart a course for the future. In an act perhaps symbolic of this rediscovery of its history, the central office of Hull-House Association moved in February 1984 to leased space on the second floor of a converted loft building at 118 North Clinton Street, less than a mile from the original Hull-House site on Halsted Street.

Hull-House, a New Face

Richard Gosswiller

By April 1963, social work programs which had been located for so long at the original Hull-House site were moved to new headquarters at 3212 North Broadway and to several neighborhood centers throughout Chicago. The settlement board of trustees and its new director, Paul Jans, began to implement decentralization and expansion plans. In some instances, social settlements already in existence merged with the Hull-House Association in search of a broader financial base, more sophisticated and varied programs, and larger professional staff. In other instances, Hull-House created its own neighborhood settlement facilities.

Paul Jans, innovator and developer, brought new ideas to the association of settlements and led it into government-supported programs with money allocated through the War on Poverty and state revenues. Jans hoped the settlement could be flexible enough to meet the problems of poverty and cultural and educational depravity in the inner city. Richard Gosswiller, a journalist, describes some of the diverse programs sponsored by the Hull-House Association in 1967, four years after the closing of the original buildings. [Richard Gosswiller, "Hull-House, A New Face," Chicago (Autumn 1967), 52–59.]

As rec rooms go it wouldn't have cut the mustard in Flossmoor, or even in Stickney, but it was better than nothing. And nothing is what people who live near the "L" tracks in Uptown Chicago these days have a lot of. It was just a basement room, unpaneled, with a bare, concrete floor. There were a few chairs and rickety tables scattered about, a pile of much used children's toys, and near the center of the room a half-size pool table with only seven balls and a slant like a putting green.

Tonight, however, the Clifton Street Recreation Center, created and staffed by the Hull House Association, was to be used as a meeting place. Two VISTA volunteers, young social workers paid by the War on Poverty program and operating through Hull House, had formed a tenants' council among residents of the two Clifton Street apartment buildings served by the rec room. For this meeting the VISTA workers had rounded up 14 tenants to hold a discussion with their landlord's representative. And the fact that this landlord, the Kate Maremont Foundation, was a benevolent one didn't prevent the tenants from griping:

"What about that crack in my apartment?" "We've still got cockroaches." "Sometimes there's no hot water." "We've got no keys for the basement."

Dick Bentley, the Maremont rep, smiled gamely and answered each complaint, usually with the suggestion that the tenant fill out a service request. As for the basement keys, he said, "We've given out dozens of keys. Where do you suppose they go?"

"I don't know where they go. I know I haven't got one," said one tenant.

"Ask the janitor," replied Bentley.

"He hasn't got any, either."

"We gave him plenty of keys."

"Well he hasn't got any now."

Then a woman tenant said, "Why don't we put down a $2 deposit for each key we get?"

Bentley looked at the woman, smiled and replied, "It will certainly surprise them downtown if I tell them that the tenant council recommends we have a key deposit system."

And that is what was done, except that Bentley reduced the amount suggested to $1 per key. "At the end of the year if there's any profit, it will go back to the tenant council," he added.

It wasn't much, but it was a kind of moment that helps keep the Hull House social program going. In the past six years, as Hull House has expanded from one to six locations in Chicago and from a paid staff of 37 to more than 200, there have been more such moments. Paul Jans, the graying, pipe-smoking ex–social worker who as director has brought Hull House to its present eminence, tells of a boy who suddenly became a disciplinary case at school. A Hull House case worker visited the boy's home and learned that his father and mother were quarreling savagely. The father made

$48 a week as a parking lot attendant. He gave his check to his wife, asked only for a quart of beer and the TV set in the evening. When the TV set broke down the father spent 27 precious dollars to have it fixed. His wife exploded. But because the man was a reliable employee, the case worker soon found him a job for $60 a week and the turmoil subsided in the home.

Last year Hull House services touched an estimated 12,000 Chicagoans, some of them with problems more serious than that of the parking lot attendant, others with none at all in the social work sense. For Hull House is a settlement, and a settlement, says Webster's, is "an institution, maintained amidst congested city population, to render educational, recreational, and other services to the community." Nothing in this definition suggests that all of these people need be welfare cases. Hull House, in fact, goes out of its way to be a "bridge between people who have and people who have not," sometimes with success, sometimes without. When the Jane Addams Center at Broadway and Belmont opened its gym in the morning as a play area and sitter space for mothers with young children, hoping in the process to bring together people of different classes, the ladies on Lake Shore Drive were quick to make use of it; mothers who lived in low-income areas west of Broadway stayed away.

But Hull House goes on the theory that if you have enough to offer, sooner or later you'll attract nearly everyone. Its six centers provide, at little or no charge, classes in swimming, basketball, dance, acting, singing, art, sculpture, and sewing. There are game rooms, swimming pools, and gymnasiums; a club for film addicts; workshops for opera singers and aspiring playwrights; community theaters and a children's theater; and a full scale camp. Plus, of course, an extensive social work program headed by professional social workers.

Hull House, in short, is today reminiscent of its most dynamic period under Jane Addams, the years between 1890 and 1910. In physical facilities and personnel it has far surpassed that Hull House. Certainly much of its social work is more sophisticated. But it will have to go some to achieve the fame and admiration of that earlier Hull House, where settlement work in America began. Still, Jane Addams would have been proud of her offspring. And seeing the malaise that hangs over the city in 1967—the strangling traffic, air pollution, the crime rate, the middle-class desertion to the suburbs—she might have said that the Hull House revival is happening none too soon. . . .

The almost simultaneous loss of the Hull House mansion and buildings, coupled with the necessity for hiring a new director, proved a blessing in disguise. For the Harrison-Halsted area had long since ceased to need Hull-House in the way many other parts of the city needed a settlement. And though Ballard had put Hull-House back on its feet, 20 years later he was saying to the Hull House Board, "What is Hull House in 1961? Hull House is a character building agency. It if isn't I don't know what is."

"Character building," with its connotation of a wrong and right way, of good guys and bad guys, is not quite what Paul Jans, a professional social worker, had in mind when he left his job as director of Philadelphia's Lighthouse Settlement to head Hull House in 1962. Intensive case and group social work instead became the foundation of his program at Hull House. This meant helping people—especially children—to overcome problems caused by poverty, dependency, and emotional deprivation. Jans knew that for such people games, classes, summer camps, fine arts programs—even heart-to-heart talks—weren't enough. However, he also knew that in many Chicago communities the need for the traditional settlement house activities was immense. So, after acquiring a former American Legion post on Broadway near Belmont as its home base, the Hull House Association quickly added the Henry Booth House, in the Harold Ickes Housing Project at 22d and State, a Woodlawn branch (which later moved into the new $250,000 Parkway Community House at 67th near South Park Way), and the Uptown Center which moved into a new $572,000 building last June. Recently Hull House has opened two more centers, Abraham Lincoln at 700 East Oakwood and Clarence Darrow, which is located in a housing project at Cicero and 43d Street.

Today, each of these centers includes professional social workers on its staff. Their instructions from Jans are to help the people who need help most for as long as they need it. "For example," says Jans, "four or five workers in a neigh-

By the 1970s, street art began to appear as murals on many public buildings and walls in Chicago. This 1970s portrayal of Jane Addams was created by Hull-House art students at street level near the entrance to Jane Addams Center.

borhood might be assigned to work with third-grade kids. They look for kids who might become delinquents later. Six to eight such youngsters are taken into a group. The problem for the social worker in this group is to help these kids make a social adjustment to other people. At the same time we give casework support to the family. We counsel with the parents, bring them together to discuss their problems under the guidance of the social worker. Of course,'' adds Jans, ''Hull House alone can't solve the delinquency problem, but we are trying to document what could be done if large numbers of social workers were assigned to such activities.''

I visited an after-school ''class'' of Gene Aronowitz, who is head of social services for Hull House. Aronowitz explained, before the boys arrived, that of the six 8- and 9-year-olds who would be present, only two had both a mother and father at home. Most were Southern immigrants and all had been referred by schools or hospitals because they were too aggressive—showoffs and bullies (a word Aronowitz doesn't like)—or, at the other extreme, passive and uncommunicative. ''Most

of these kids are highly aggressive,'' Aronowitz explained. ''The norm is aggressiveness, rebellion, and fighting.''

Actually, they seemed at first glance much like a spirited group of normal youngsters. They shoved and punched one another, but how many 8-year-olds don't? Aronowitz tried to interest them in games. One boy began to play with a dilapidated erector set, but the others continued pushing and shoving and hiding in the adjoining washroom until Gene, as they all called him, summoned them out. After 20 minutes, behavior that at first had seemed normal seemed not so normal. The pushing and shoving—always with smiles on their faces—hadn't let up. One boy finally crawled behind a mattress stored in the room and remained there until the session ended and the others left.

This group meets twice a week. ''One boy hasn't missed a meeting in three months,'' said Aronowitz. ''The others have missed two or three.'' From the playroom they go to the ice cream store across the street, where a different kind of behavior is expected. Then they walk back to the center (the boys cross in the middle of the block; Aronowitz always walks to the corner) and downstairs to the recreation room. There the social worker can talk with some boys individually while the others play table tennis or pool.

I asked Aronowitz whether the methods he is using get results. "How do you know?" he answered. "You're working with people and people are so complex. You do things. You watch. There's no way to say, 'I did this. I helped.' You can never say, 'I was responsible for this.' People change. People are dynamic. If you work with a group for a year, there's a temptation to say, 'I did so and so.' But if you do you're nuts. What's basically important is whether the kid moves." Some kids do seem to "move." One boy in Aronowitz's younger group was sent to him because he wouldn't speak—to anyone. But after a few sessions with the group the boy was calling out numbers in games of musical chairs. Later on he was able to name the flavor of the ice cream he wanted. Then he talked to Aronowitz "in a limited way." Now he is beginning to speak to his teachers. But Aronowitz says, "He might have come out of it anyway."

At Henry Booth House, on the Near South Side, group social workers deal primarily with teenagers. One group of 14 high school boys who call themselves the Gay Caballeros has been meeting once a week for several years. The social worker encourages the boys to make decisions and act on them—not an easy task for Negro youngsters whose principal responsibility in life has been self-defense. I watched one evening as a social worker tried to persuade the boys to accept coatroom and ticket-selling assignments for a dance the group had planned. At first it was difficult to get their attention. Then came comments such as "I'll check a girl's coat, but I ain't gonna check any boy's coat," and "Don't make no sense to sell tickets." Finally, though, after 45 minutes of mayhem, and as the time for a favorite television program approached, several boys volunteered. After the meeting, the social worker said, without irony, "When they came to us three years ago they were drinkers and fighters. Today they are the most influential teenage group in the community."

Hull House casework takes a slightly different turn. Jeanne Rose, a pretty redhead with a master's degree from Denver University, occasionally guides discussion groups for parents with problem children, but her principal work is with individual families in Lakeview and Uptown. One family referred to her back in 1963 was particularly distraught. The father was in jail, the mother jobless and with four children on her hands. Jeanne arranged for the mother to receive food from Hull-House until the welfare check came, then began biweekly visits that continued for ten months. When the father was released from jail, Jeanne found him a job. He soon lost it, found another, lost that, found another, and so on through four jobs in eight months. With frequent "crises" between man and wife, the oldest daughter began failing in school. "When there was a crisis," says Jeanne, "he'd belt her one."

Gradually, however, Jeanne's frequent talks with both parents seemed to take effect. They began to discuss their problems rather than fight about them. Meanwhile Jeanne worked individually with the daughter.

In time the mother began to do volunteer work with Hull House, distributing clothes and food. The father held his job. Later on they referred to Jeanne other families who needed help. Today, in an almost fairy-tale ending to the story, the mother is a full-time social worker, the father works part time with teenage boys in the War on Poverty program and has enrolled in college, and the oldest daughter is studying music on a scholarship.

Hull House tries to strengthen not only the individual and the family unit but the community as a whole. Toward this end each center employs at least one worker to handle community organization. The tenant council mentioned earlier is an example. Campaigning with local citizens for a new high school is another. At Henry Booth House volunteers have established a small library while effort is made to solicit a public library branch.

Last fall at Parkway Center in Woodlawn, staff members knocked on doors throughout the community, asking people what they needed. One result of this informal poll was the formation of a group of eight mothers on public assistance. The group met once a week and formed a Knowhow Swap Club, discussing money-saving techniques for the household. At the same time the group began raising funds by baking pies and selling them.

By Christmas last year they had saved $170, which was used to buy presents for their children. The group is supervised by a Hull House staff worker who was on public assistance herself until she was hired with War on Poverty funds. Previously she had been unemployed for eight years. Now, according to social worker Jerome Stevenson, "She says that she's sure she would never be without a job again."

The War on Poverty program enabled Hull House to almost double its services in 1965 and 1966. Not only is Hull-House commissioned to train VISTA volunteers, young men and women who are engaged to do social work and are paid by the government ($210 a month), but Hull House centers have 62 full-time VISTA workers assisting with their program—two-thirds of all the VISTA workers in Chicago. Federal money also pays for a Neighborhood Resources Program, in which VISTA volunteers and other Hull-House workers go into poor neighborhoods and attempt to engage people in useful activities—job training, group meetings, and so forth. In addition, Hull House operates several Head Start programs, teaching such subjects as language rudiments to "kindergarten dropouts"; a home-delivered meals program, providing home-cooked meals for 60 elderly people; and a STREETS program, in which government-paid young people go into the neighborhoods of the city to work with various problem teenagers.

Hull House's newest enterprise is a senior citizens' center at Hilliard Homes, 54 West Cermak Road. The center, staffed by two full-time workers and several VISTA volunteers, offers a recreational and educational program for people in the homes. And at East Troy, Wisconsin, 70 miles north of Chicago, is the oldest continuous Hull House establishment, the Bowen Country Club, acquired in 1909* as a summer camp. In 1966, at the summer camp 883 boys and girls, 10 to 18, from both poor and well-to-do Chicago neighborhoods, used the camp's recreation facilities and took part in art, music, and drama programs.

Bowen's chief function today, however, is social work. It serves as a training camp for high school dropouts. Each week during the spring,

*The original BCC, acquired in 1912, was replaced in 1964 by a camp with the same name near East Troy, WI.—Eds.

fall, and winter months an average of 20 high-school-age boys live at Bowen five days a week, for 4 to 15 weeks, until they are ready for employment. Most of the boys are Spanish speaking or Negro. "We don't teach them trades, we teach them how to work," says Jans, and he tells about the boy for whom Hull House found a job at Riverview amusement part several years ago. Though the boy liked his job, he quit because, as he told it, he was being "pushed around." Actually his boss, satisfied with his work, had promoted him to a job with greater responsibility. "This boy," says Jans, "didn't have the vaguest idea of what a boss's prerogatives are. Middle-class concepts of work are simply not known to housing project kids. The boss is considered an exploiter." At the camp the boys build roads, plant trees, do laundry. They learn to meet schedules and understand authority.

Jans said his biggest disappointment in the social work program concerned the work camp. "I would think that businessmen would be interested in the camp," he said. "It costs $50 a week per boy. We're trying to get some group of firms to help us support this operation. It would be a source of unskilled labor for them. But we haven't been able to connect."

If social work is the heart of Paul Jans's program, fine arts is its head. And at Hull House the theater has traditionally been foremost among the arts. In 1899 Jane Addams erected a combination theater and coffee shop. Plays of Ibsen, Shaw, and Strindberg were performed there for the first time in the United States.

Though Bob Sickinger worked with Paul Jans at the Lighthouse in Philadelphia, Jans could hardly have anticipated the effect this intense young man would have on Chicago. Even before his first Hull House production (*Who'll Save the Plowboy?*), Sickinger's unpretentiousness, his uncanny ability to remember names, and above all his prodigious capacity for work and dedication to theatre had won him scores of friends. Then came the plays, and they won him—and Hull House—more. Here at last was a Chicago director who recognized the importance of contemporary off-Broadway plays, most of which had never been produced in Chicago. So into a small, 102-seat theater (later expanded to 158), built to the director's specifications so that the audience sits on

Since 1980, more than 300 former welfare recipients have graduated from Project TEAM (Training Employment of Automotive Mechanics). Supported by leaders of the auto aftermarket industry, government, and private foundations, this successful program is an excellent example of the Hull-House approach to program development. Here TEAM instructor Jose Ontaneda shows Gerald Lloyd how to use a timing light.

three sides of the stage, Sickinger brought the works of Albee, Arrabal, Beckett, Brecht, Gelber, Gilroy, Jones, Pinter, Snyder, and others. . . .

Hull House is a vastly different enterprise today from the institution Jane Addams founded. Jane made her Hull House unique in the world, and Chicagoans—and the world—will never forget her. But the new Hull House deserves their attention fully as much as Jane's did. Not only is it working on a grander scale than Jane could have imagined, it is dedicated, efficient, and, like Jane's Hull House, a small ship in a stormy sea of need. As past riots and lootings show, there is great tension in the city, always seeking release. Hull House and agencies like it provide some, but far too little.

After the tenant's council meeting on Clifton Street, I walked upstairs to his apartment with Ed Majewski, a 25-year-old VISTA volunteer. Though far from sumptuous, it was a typical bachelor flat in other ways: beds unmade, dishes in the sink, *Playboy* calendar on the wall. Ed's roommate, a STREETS worker, was present but didn't say much. Ed explained that his roomy was feeling pretty low; he expected to lose his job because of the War on Poverty cutbacks that had gone into effect.

Ed said that he had come to Chicago from his home state, New Jersey, nine months earlier. After taking his degree in chemistry at Seaton Hall he had served in the Army, then found a job as a $700-a-month chemist. Six months later he quit and joined VISTA for $210 a month.

"Kids are really disturbed here," Ed was saying, referring to the pre-teen youngsters who live in his Clifton Street building. "They smoke, drink, fool around with girls. I caught four of them sniffing glue. Some miss school 70 per cent of the time. You try different things with them. We have games in the rec room, but with the really disturbed ones nothing happens. We're going to have drama, so the kids can have some emotional outlet.

"Most of the families here are on ADC. They live in Chicago but think of Kentucky and Tennessee as their homes. A lot of them are good people in many ways. They invite me to supper now and then. We get along fine."

Ed paused for a moment, cut a peach he was eating with his spoon, then looked up.

"We're a billion-dollar nation," he said, qui-etly. "Why do we have to have this? Screw the moon!"

Jane Addams may not have said it quite that way, but she would have liked the idea.

Hull-House Theatre: Capital *C*, Small *s*

Peter Jacobi

Jane Addams supported a strong theatre program at Hull-House. She saw theatre as a mechanism for promoting self-expression and socialization. From the late 1930s through the 1950s, however, the role theatre played in the Hull-House program dwindled to almost nothing. Under the leadership of Paul Jans (1916–1984), Hull-House theatre experienced a rebirth.

Jans brought Robert Sickinger and his wife, Selma, to Hull-House to develop and administer a theatre program. Jans had known Sickinger in Philadelphia, where Sickinger had been a full-time English teacher but used his free time to develop his own acting and directing skills and to promote community theatre. He was so successful that in 1961 he received a two-year grant from the Plumstock Foundation of the Lilly Pharmaceutical Company. With it he opened the Cricket Playhouse in Philadelphia, developed acting classes, and established an experimental studio called Theatre Workshop, which was located in the Lighthouse Settlement, where Jans was director.

Sickinger became Hull-House Theatre Director on February 1, 1963. He began to implement a program approved by the Hull-House Board, the backbone of which was the creation of a theatre center in each of the four affiliates associated with Hull-House at that time. Theatres were established in Henry Booth House by September 1963; Jane Addams Center, October 1963; Parkway Community Center, July 1965; and Uptown Community Center, November 1967. In addition, there were a playwrights' workshop, a chamber theatre, a touring theatre, acting classes for people of all ages, a childrens' theatre, and a magazine pro-

moting Hull-House theatre called Intermission, which was published between 1965 and 1968. A new Hull-House summer camp, replacing Bowen Country Club in 1964, also emphasized training in the performing arts.

The Board of Trustees granted Sickinger complete artistic freedom. His theatre program at Hull-House during the 1960s paved the way for the renaissance of experimental neighborhood theatre in Chicago during the 1970s and 1980s. Jim Jacobs, author of the long-running musical Grease, and David Mamet, author of American Buffalo and other award-winning plays and screen stories and one of the founders of the St. Nicholas Theatre, prototype of Chicago theatres to follow, were part of the Hull-House theatre group.

Unfortunately, Hull-House theatre did not pay for itself. By 1967, parts of the program had begun to falter and collapse. First to go, in 1967, was the year-old touring theatre. Then, in 1968, Parkway Community Center and Henry Booth House theatres, located in black neighborhoods, closed their doors. In 1968, many blacks had priorities other than supporting black theatre. In addition, whites were afraid to venture into black neighborhoods to support black theatre, which often focused its performing efforts on experimental plays promoting black power.

Social workers at Hull-House also protested the expanding theatre program on the ground that it was spending money that could better be used for social programs and welfare services. Finally, the Hull-House board acted. Jans was one of the first casualties of the monetary crisis caused, at least in part, by the rapid expansion of the performing arts program. After Jans left in April 1969, Robert Sickinger found himself vulnerable without his mentor's protection. Hull-House announced Sickinger's resignation on May 28, 1969. The next day, the Hull-House Board of Trustees returned control of all theatre facilities and programs to each center director, effectively giving each affiliate permission to dismantle its theatre program.

Peter P. Jacobi, Professor of Journalism at Indiana University, was a faculty member of the Medill School of Journalism at Northwestern University and a drama critic when he followed the rise and fall of Robert Sickinger and Hull-House theatre in a number of articles in Chicago area publications. Here he offers a glimpse of the theatre's development to 1965 and suggests that the Sickinger theatre was not the neighborhood theatre that traditionally had been associated with the settlement. This lack of neighborhood focus was one of the criticisms leveled by the Hull-House trustees at the Sickinger program. [Peter P. Jacobi, "Capital C, Small s." New City [Magazine] (June 15 1965), 5–9.]

Hull House Theatre walks a tightrope between capital C Culture and lower case s sociology. It is striving to supply two Chicago needs, one to provide long absent theatre of an experimental and avant-garde nature, the other to follow in the tradition of Jane Addams and her settlement house ideas.

The legendary Jane Addams was devoted to the arts and felt their efficacy in expanding the limited lives of deprived people. She wrote:

The very first day I saw Halsted Street, a long line of young men and boys stood outside the gallery entrance of the Bijou Theatre, waiting for the Sunday matinee to begin at two o'clock, although it was only high noon. This waiting crowd might have been seen every Sunday afternoon during the 20 years which have elapsed since then. Our first Sunday evening in Hull-House, when a group of small boys sat on our piazza and told us "about things around here," their talk was all of the theatre and of the astonishing things they had seen that afternoon . . . the young men told us their ambitions in the phrases of stage heroes, and the girls, so far as their romantic dreams could be shyly put into words, possessed no others but those soiled by long use in the melodrama. All of these young people looked upon an afternoon a week in the gallery of a Halsted Street theatre as their one opportunity to see life. The sort of melodrama they see there has recently been described as "the ten commandments written in red fire." Certainly the villain always comes to a violent end, and the young and handsome hero is rewarded by marriage with a beautiful girl, usually the daughter of a millionaire, but after all that is not a portrayal of the morality of the ten commandments any more than of life itself.

Nevertheless the theatre, such as it was, appeared to be the one agency which freed the boys and girls from that destructive isolation of those who drag themselves up to maturity by themselves, and it gave them a glimpse of that order and beauty into which even the poorest drama endeavors to restore the bewildering facts of life.

And so there was theatre at Hull House right from the start, even before an auditorium could be built. There were plays in the drawing room and later in the gymnasium. The young people rehearsed and performed tirelessly. So did the older folks of the neighborhoods around the settlement house. The immigrants staged works of their own national pasts.

Drama was an expression of emotional need. It was something to do and something to think about. It was separation from drabness and tedium and drudgery.

Thus, with the development of Hull House as a settlement, as a center for social work, came the evolvement of the nation's oldest community theatre. Jane Addams had her Hull House provide drama in classes, drama in writing workshops, drama in public performance. Her theatre—and, of course, others did most of its running for her—looked for plays that would mean something to its needy participants and its needy audiences. Some plays were very close to the tradition of old-fashioned melodrama. Others were of more challenging scope.

John Galsworthy had four of his American premieres at Hull House. He was so pleased with the results of one production that he gave the Addams establishment permission to produce any future plays of his without royalty.

Hull House Theatre introduced eight Shaw plays to Chicago. Alongside these were seen the works of Ben Jonson, Arthur Wing Pinero, John Masefield, James Barrie, Elmer Rice and quite a few hopefuls from Chicago.

At one time Hull House Theatre toured Europe and this continent as well. William Butler Yeats, Eleanor Duse, Theodore Roosevelt spoke or visited.

But always, with Jane Addams looking on, the major emphasis was on participation, by those on stage and those just viewing, by those who needed to participate. She felt, Jane Addams did, that theatre should fill a longing. So the youngsters performed and were enchanted by fairy tales and puppeteers. The teens and the oldsters and those

between put on their own shows and dramas, and those who didn't watched and laughed and lost for at least a little while the shadows of loneliness and pain which so darkened their lives on the outside.

The Russians developed their own theatre group at Hull House. So did the Greeks. So did the Latvians. So did, at one time or another, several other nationality groups.

It was theatre for the people, theatre of a sociological purpose.

Now the original Hull House is turning into several centers. The concept is spreading to serve more neighborhoods. And with the social help goes theatre, just as Jane Addams would have wished.

Hull House Theatre, under its current guide and director, Robert Sickinger, has the old thoughts in mind and operation. Yet, part of the current story is different. Different not because Bob Sickinger wants to have Hull House Theatre in various neighborhoods of the city, but because the most flourishing example of Hull House Theatre 1965—at the Jane Addams Center, 3212 North Broadway—differs somewhat from tradition.

It is *avant-garde* theatre, brilliantly performed in almost professional (and sometimes better than professional) style. It is theatre that attracts not the people who need but the *cogniscenti* from all over the Chicago area who have yearned for more than touring companies of Broadway musicals and farces. It is theatre of actors who do not need, who have good jobs for the most part and security, but who want the opportunity to use an unused talent.

Hull House Theatre would seem to be moving in the wrong direction, doing Pinter, Beckett, Leroi Jones, and Gelber at ticket prices of just under and somewhat over three dollars, for people who can afford paying for intellectual stimulation.

Chicago needs such theatre, you might say, and I would agree. But should Hull House be the scene of such activity? I pondered the matter for some months and questioned the value of certain plays to the Hull House cause in some of my reviews.

I've changed my mind and now believe Hull House Theatre may be doing just the right thing, that Hull House Theatre is seeking to accomplish just what Jane Addams wanted all along. The manner is different, hence the tightrope. But Hull-House 1965 has a goal right in the old and honored tradition of servicing the deprived.

"No, we don't attract many from the neighborhood with our far-out plays," says Bob Sickinger. "But we are using our success with such plays to support what will be a more conventional theatre of service in other Hull House drama centers now in operation or soon to go.

"We are not forgetting the Addams goal. By charging sizeable prices for a product which the intellectual elite of the area cannot get anywhere else, we are making possible—or going to make possible—the introduction of theatre into the lives of those who cannot afford it, who should have it as an outlet of escape and for whom theatre could be a mental and emotional opportunity. I want our success at the Hattie Callner Theatre to mean theatrical exposure at Henry Booth House, at the Parkway Community Center and before long in the Uptown neighborhood where transients need ties and cultural chance so desperately."

So the controversially excellent Hull House Theatre at 3212 North Broadway is the feeding place, and sociology with the small *s* is to meet Culture with the capital *C* in that little hundred-seat house which has created a stir. *Avant-garde* drama is to bring the many into a cultural present, offering some of that hope which Jane Addams always believed theatre could provide. Soon the North Broadway theatre will have 30 more seats to help raise money; a two-row balcony is being added.

Sickinger has put on more than a dozen plays for Hull House. The results have been remarkable, would have been remarkable for a professional resident group. Sickinger has worked with amateurs, which means people who may have just as much talent as professionals but who work at something else for a living and get nothing but dramatic kicks for their work at Hull House. There are students of drama and education, teachers, free-lance writers, a cabdriver, a dentist, a free-lance model, a media director and an account executive, an exterminator, a public relations man, a free-lance photographer, a newsman, quite a few housewives, a sales representative or two, an auditor, an auto salesman. They meet on theatrical terms at 3212 North Broadway and create for Chi-

cago uniquely good theatre, and with it create a number of socially worthy by-products.

Recently the name of Hull House Theatre spread eastward when Sickinger and company at the request of David Susskind taped a presentation of Pinter's *The Dumbwaiter*. Thirteen regional acting companies were selected by Susskind for a series of television programs. Hull House was the only nonprofessional troupe. The Arena Stage of Washington, D.C., and the Actors' Workshop of San Francisco were among the professional groups. The Hull House production was highly praised, with acclaim coming even from *Time*, which usually rejects any artistic products from west of the Hudson River.

The plays done locally have had something to say to us, not always in terms that Jane Addams' boys from Halsted Street would have understood. But the Sickinger repertoire—if sometimes of questionable choice at least on first study—has always spoken of today and of problems which face us.

Frank Gilroy's *Who'll Save the Plowboy?* speaks of broken dreams, of man and wife destroying themselves and each other.

Samuel Beckett's *Happy Days* is of the woman buried first to her waist and then to her neck in sand, the woman who mirrors a confined emptiness seen by author Beckett in life today.

The Connection by Chicagoan Jack Gelber moves away from symbolism to ultra realism in picturing beats and addicts waiting for, then receiving, the needle of dreams and nightmares.

William Snyder's *The Days and Nights of Beebee Fenstermaker* tells us we might have more dreams than we should have, that too much expectation leads to disaster.

Murray Schisgal, the acclaimed new hope of the American theatre, or so he's been called by some New York theatre people, was an early choice for Hull House. His *The Typists* and *The Tiger* were pin sharp, heady mixtures of humor and tragedy, the former striking particularly hard with its theme of a lifetime being wished away.

Edward Albee's *The American Dream* and *The Death of Bessie Smith* bit into the absurdity of American conventions and the brutality of prejudice.

Three Penny Opera—that Brecht-Weill collaboration on a theme of Gay's—has become a classic and reminded the viewers that all's not well with a world which allows beggary and poverty, which makes people believe, as the denizens of the story shout, "What keeps a man alive? He lives on others. First feed your face, then talk right from wrong."

Beckett's *Endgame* was the most far out of the Hull House productions to date, an almost endless torture, like nails scraping against the blackboard, a paean of hate for life, a puzzling denial that we can be human and that we can understand existence. Hull House paired this two-hour agony with *Play,* also by Beckett, about two women and a man reviewing their triangular relationship in life after death.

Kenneth Brown's *The Brig* is of Marine life at its bitter worst, a documentary of man's cruelty to man.

Harold Pinter has been the most recent addition to the repertory. His *The Collection* and *The Lover* tell of marriage and human relationships gone awry, but in marvelously humorous terms.

This has not been Broadway-type theatre. It has not been Bijou melodrama. Perhaps the *avant-garde* should have been mixed with some of the more palatable, something along the line of Drury Lane fare which makes neighborhood people laugh and have harmless fun. Certainly more of the Drury Lane diet would reach those people in the deprived areas around and near 3212 North Broadway, those who do not need more bitterness on stage, those who might not even understand the vague profundities of several playwrights offered there.

But Sickinger claims he is reaching some— some who come to dress rehearsal nights free of charge, some who work backstage to aid in the classy productions of Hull House plays, and many in other neighborhoods who will be able to see drama through the efforts of his showcase theatre.

"We haven't forgotten those who need it," he says. "Take Henry Booth House—in a deprived area on the South Side. There we offer theatre to would-be actors and to audiences, theatre that means something to them and which they can have for close to nothing, moneywise. If a person can pay a penny, and that's all, then that's what he has to pay to enter the theatre world at Henry Booth House. How can we do it there? We do it through our Hattie Callner Theatre right here on Broad-

way. We do it through our *avant-garde* selections which tempt people who can pay to do so.

"And we do it through more *avant-garde* theatre than that." Sickinger refers to the Hull House Chamber Theatre which gives readings of "out" plays in homes of the well-to-do. There have been hundreds of these readings, of Pinter, Ionesco, Albee, and the result has been money for Hull House theatre activities which cannot and will not be able to support themselves.

At Henry Booth House the plays are of a lighter, brighter hue, good plays, but of a level which less-educated people can understand. *Clandestine on the Morning Line* is interracial and earthy; it's been done there. So have four short plays by Edward Albee, William Inge, Norman Walsit and Conrad Seiler billed together as *The American Scene.* These touched on comedy and the serious in their look at foibles in neighborhood living, life in a beatnik pad, the problems of the artist in a materialistic society, the trial of boarding-house living.

"There's a heavy emphasis on workshops and classes at Henry Booth House," says Sickinger. "We do a little less public performing and a little more training of children, teenagers and adults. The children, for instance, go to acting classes for no charge, and they work on plays to give at Christmas and Thanksgiving, on variety shows. Hull House Broadway supports this, supports the penny tickets, the six-for-a-quarter tickets, the tickets which never go higher than a dollar-fifty for anyone. People down there are seeing theatre for the first time, experiencing joy and escape."

Hull House Broadway also will help support the third Hull House theatre, scheduled to open the early part of June, this one at the Parkway Community Center on 67th street. Here is a basement hall for 120, not yet finished, but preparing—under director Elaine Goldman—to do interracial theatre. "We want," says Miss Goldman, "to set the image of all races working together. So we will cast interracially, and we will seek plays, whenever possible, that involve all people. In our area many folks will not have been exposed to any drama. So we could not do LeRoi Jones' *Dutchman* even though it is an interracial play. We must seek new plays and good old plays that will mean something and add something to the lives of our patrons."

Again at Parkway there will be acting classes and a writers' workshop, patterned after a highly successful one established by Sickinger at his North Side headquarters.

Tickets at Parkway will be about two dollars, lower than at Hull House Broadway, higher than at Henry Booth. "But we'll have virtual give-away tickets, too, for those who cannot pay," says Miss Goldman. "And the funds for this will come from Bob Sickinger's haven up north."

In a year or so, hopes Sickinger, his fourth theatre will be getting underway in the Uptown area of Chicago, where Indians, southern whites, Puerto Ricans, and other ethnic and social groups are merging into what as yet is still an unstable neighborhood. "Here, too, we still have to plan to suit a different people. We must select carefully because our major task at Hull-House is to bring theatre into the lives of people. For that we've got to hit them right and hit them hard. We cannot go over their heads. We cannot give them just what they can get on television."

What else is planned? Sickinger mentions a touring theatre to reach small towns in the Chicago area and the midwest which haven't any of their own, and to colleges that need exposure to new theatre and the concept of social work. The status of a professional Hull House theatrical group is up in the air; the status of Hull House Sheridan—supported in part by the Maremont Foundation to present short arts festivals and professional off-Broadway plays—also is currently in doubt.

In the meantime—while planning for expansion and future—Sickinger continues to produce and direct his rather futuristic repertory. But there is more to Hull House Broadway than the *avant-garde* which meets the eye. There is a thriving children's theatre, available to any and all for 25 cents. A dramatic serial called *Captain Marbles* excites the children every second week, and in weeks between they have opportunity to see the likes of Japanese dancers, Northwestern University speech students doing *Peter Pan,* magicians, folk singers, puppets, ventriloquists.

"These kids are gaining theatrical exposure," says Sickinger. "If things go well, we'll tour our children's theatre to reach other areas where Hull House does not have a direct contact. Of course,

children's theatre will be a part of each of our theatre centers."

Sickinger speaks of other children at his Broadway theatre, of those from the streets of the neighborhood who are taking acting classes, of 10 to 12-year-olds who now come in each afternoon to work on scenery, props and lighting rather than drift on the street.

Youngsters who have been in the Audy Home and in trouble come in and feel they've become part of something.

Sickinger finds it harder to reach the teenage crowd than the younger ones. Teenage acting classes are smaller. But there are some who do come and who with the younger ones build virtually all the sets, under supervision.

"We work with Threshhold, too," says Sickinger. "That means with people who have had mental breakdowns and are now trying to return to normality of work and home. Several Threshhold people help us here. One fellow cleans seats, windows, does carpentry work. Another, a former psychiatrist, does bookkeeping for us three or four hours a day. About six of these people work for us. So in this way, too, we provide service."

Of all activities Sickinger is proudest of the Writers' Studio, which attracts hopeful writers from all parts of the metropolitan area and from all professions and backgrounds. "Here is where we will find future playwrights; here is where we hope a future Chicago school of dramatic writing may be born. One hundred-twenty authors attend our Broadway writers' workshop. There'll be others who go to Parkway. And we'll work with these people, have professionals show them how. The best products will be performed at our special Writers' Studio shows."

One Writers' Studio production was seen last year on television. WTTW presented the Hull House players in Joe Esselin's full-length *The Bookstore.* Esselin is an advertising man.

A recent showing of Writers' Studio products included the play of a dentist and one of a young writer just setting up shop.

"We're going to work with the writers. I'm sure we're going to have really stageworthy plays before long. A few of the writers already are approaching realization of talent."

Hull House theatre has accomplished much, sometimes skirting that original Jane Addams precept of reaching the people of a deprived neighborhood through theatre they can understand. But it has not departed from the Addams goal. It is using its own modern methods, raising money where it can to bring theatre to those who need it.

"What's wrong with our giving unusual theatre fare if with it we can build theatre in deprived areas?" asks Sickinger. "Giving Chicago what it hasn't got otherwise in theatre is an added plus. But we're interested primarily in culturally and economically deprived areas," he explains. "That's what we're here for. I may seem to be going in other directions. Yet, going that way, we are making money for what we must eventually do, grassroots theatre in neighborhoods of the poor.

"And someday I'd like to have a performing arts center under the Hull House name, an arts center for underprivileged people with theatre, music, dance. This is what we at Hull House would be happiest about. It will need to be something dynamic, something for the underprivileged which the world would know of. We've really just started."

It has been a good start, on a tightrope but with a broader ground level path ahead.

People Power

La Gente

In 1967, Jane Addams Center opened Una Puerta Abierta *(An Open Door), a storefront site in the 3300 block of North Halsted Street. It was an attempt to help the rapidly growing Hispanic population in the Uptown and Lakeview neighborhoods bridge the gap between their rural homeland experience and English-speaking, urban Chicago. The program, carried out by a bilingual staff, offered English classes, tutoring, pre-school activities, personal and family counseling, a referral service for job and educational opportunities, social clubs, community meetings, a day camp, arts and crafts, and a bilingual newspaper. By the*

late 1970s, its focus was jobs; and from 3952 North Ashland Avenue, it served its heavily Hispanic population as a non-profit employment agency.

In 1969, Bruce Young became the director at Jane Addams Center. He immediately started to move the center away from its heavy emphasis on theatre and the arts toward serving the neighborhood poor. He was so successful that in 1978 he was elected neighborhood alderman to the Chicago City Council. He encouraged La Gente (the People), an outgrowth of a neighborhood gang, to meet at the settlement, and they did so for a year before moving to a storefront nearby. Urban gangs had always been part of the Hull-House neighborhood environment. At least one other gang tried to use the settlement as its headquarters. In 1932, Jane Addams became embroiled in a conflict between Hull-House and the West Side Sportsman's Athletic Association, a group of young neighborhood men who met regularly at the settlement. Apparently, several members of the group kept weapons in their clubroom. After investigation and negotiation, Addams, mindful of the importance of community relations, tactfully encouraged them to find another meeting place, and eventually they did so.

But the world has changed since Jane Addams' day. Settlements in the 1960s and 1970s had to contend with angry neighbors who talked about black power or Hispanic power and confrontation with the establishment. Often they saw the neighborhood center as part of the establishment. These three brief essays from the first newsletter issued by La Gente, printed in English and Spanish, suggest some of the possibilities and problems raised by neighborhood power. [All Power to the People, *(October 1969), mimeographed newsletter, 2, 6, 8.]*

What Is La Gente?

La Gente–The People is a community organization made up of mainly the poor people of Lakeview. It is composed of people of various races and ethnic backgrounds, with an emphasis on those who have been largely ignored by those in positions of power. Although we developed from several of the local gangs, we want to stress the fact that we are an organization and not a gang.

We do not believe in gang fighting. We urge all members of gangs or clubs to stop fighting each other and work for changes needed in the community. One of our strongest beliefs is in the brotherhood of man, and we are striving together as brothers and sisters to combat the ignorance and indifference and racism that has been directed at our community.

Another belief of La Gente is that narcotic addiction is harmful . . . , and any member found shooting drugs is expelled. All members are expected to be ready and in condition for duty at any time of day, which means that we discourage even those members over twenty-one from getting drunk. Although there must be some flexibility with this, we can only serve the community well if we exercise some restraint on drinking.

In four months that La Gente has existed (it was originally known as the Latin Eagle Organization), we have established programs in these areas: a drug program at Illinois Masonic Hospital; a free lunch program several times a week at the Northern District Public Aid Office; a youth center at Jane Addams Hull House; a food pantry for the needy at the Hull House Spanish Outpost; legal aid, including bail money; community representation on local boards and committes; education workshops; a community-based program for presentation to the Urban Renewal authorities; and tutoring for schoolchildren. Some of these programs are well under way, and others are in their early stages. In addition, we are working on programs for improvements of Public Aid policies for welfare recipients, a day-care and pre-school training center, housing improvements, school improvements, and garbage and rat control.

All of this is being done on a gradually increasing level with one main purpose in mind: to give the community back to the people. La Gente feels that the people of Lakeview do not have enough voice in the way that their community is run. Experience has shown that the only way the people can determine the nature of local institutions and agencies is to make specific demands, and to make them firmly and forcefully. We know that we must demonstrate determination and unity before our voice will be listened to, but we believe that the people *can* be joined together into a body powerful enough to insist that the people of Lakeview determine themselves what kind of a community they want and how it is to be organized and run. This we call "Peopleism," and a belief in this underlies everything we do, every action we take. *Participatory* democracy is the only answer to our problems, a democracy in which every member of the community has a meaningful chance to take part. This means *community* control of police, schools, hospitals and other community institutions and agencies. Human rights are *always* more important than property rights, but many of our institutions and agencies have lost sight of this. We intend to remind them, again and again and again, until this is accepted *and acted upon*. The name of our organization is testimony to our belief that the people are the back-bone of everything that is great not only in this country but in all the world.

BILL HARRIS

An Open Letter to Clubs

You have been calling yourselves a club member and strutting down the street with your sweater so everyone looks at you and you feel proud. You drink your boze and smoke grass an maybe shoot up heroin and beat hell out of your girl cause you a tough mother-fucker. You say your "club" never looks for trouble but if trouble comes you ain't backing down. Then for some little petty bullshit mickey mouse excuse blam!—you fighting 3 or 4 different clubs. But you didn't start it, no, "they" started it when they winked at one of your girls who was just "scared to death" and by the time the rumor comes to you she was raped-shot-inahiliated-siscopated-fragmitized and these words don't mean anything just like your sissy-ass rumor excuse for fighting don't mean anything and you know it fool! You know, your problem is that the people call you a gang kid and the Polise say they will stop you because you're just a punk and fool, with no thinking power except to kill, rape and steal old lady's purses cause you don't work or go to school and your social-worker goes to court with you and takes you on bus trips and sets up dances and bassball games to keep you out of trouble while you laugh at him behind his back calling him a fool. But you the fool, fool! You depend on him for everything just like he's pulling those puppett strings to make you act just the way he wants you to. He don't want you to think. He don't want you to educate yourself and learn of what's really going on with the struggle of poor people. He don't want you to know about the poor people getting together all over the city to stop the brutality and death, beatings and pride stealing that's been going on for years. He don't want you to know that everytime he beats shit out of you he's wrong but he enjoys it, because he's a sick product of a sick society. He don't want you to know that there's pride in your heritage whether you're purple, blue or orange and that there's another identity you were born into. Don't tell me everytime you gang-bob or pull a trigger to kill another young blood you don't feel bad inside. No matter how stone face tough you suppose to be. Think. What do you think of poor people getting together to stop from getting killed. Fool! You *are* the poor people. It doesn't take guts to fight another club of brothers. It takes guts to get together with them and solve things out. Think. If you break those puppet strings and stand together to help "resolve the problem" with other poor people then brother, you'll feel like the proud human being you always wanted to be. You'll be doing somethin of your own free will and no bitter taste in your mouth such as the taste you *always* got after gang bopping and you were home alone washing off the blood and fear as your mother watched with tears in her eyes and your little brother was already getting ideas to be just like *you!*

Think. The man *wants* you to hate and fight so that you will *never* get together, but destroy each other, and all the more power to him!

It's a hard fight brother. Harder than the puppett sissy-ass little fights you're use to. Ten thousand times harder, but if you join in, then you're no longer a fool and the poor people like you can get Mickey Mouse off your back. You will smell that fresh air after the rains.

All Power to You!

All Power to the People!

DAVID HERNÁNDEZ

Why Revolutionaries

La Gente Organization is a revolutionary organization. The members of La Gente are revolutionaries. We see the need for change, and we are going to do something to bring about the necessary changes. We are going to get those changes now.

We see our community as we see our city and our country ruled by, for and in the interest of the wealthy capitalistic imperialistic minority.

We know the police protect and serve the interests of the wealthy. We call them pigs because to the poor, to the Latin, to the black, to the oppressed majority of this city and country the police are pigs. They act like pigs to us; they think like pigs. And we, the people, say that if they don't stop being pigs they are going to die like pigs. Because the people want to be served and protected and not used and beaten. We have been used and beaten too long. There must be a change now!

We know that all people can work together. All people can learn together and all people can live together in peace and harmony.

But the pigs and the imperialistic pig system does not want you to know this. The system wants the Latin brother to hate and fight the White brother. The system wants the Black brother to hate and fight the White and Latin brothers. The system wants the Latin brothers to fight other Latin brothers—Why? Because just as soon as we stop fighting our brothers, just as soon as we get ourselves together, Latin, Black, White and others, the Pig knows we'll see who our real enemy is. When we're together, we'll stop fighting and take a good look at the courts and judges, at the pigs and the mayor, at the school system and welfare and we're going to see something worth fighting against.

The La Gente Organization sees how the government agencies neglect the poor and how the wealthy use the poor, and how the courts treat the poor. We intend to set an example for the people, to show the people what they can do when they get themselves together.

Our programs reflect the needs of the people in our community and our organization is responsive to the people in the community.

There is nothing too large to change if only people get together. We will make ourselves as a fist and smash the oppressor. We are black, brown, yellow, white, and red, we are people of every race and we know our enemy is this imperialistic state ruled by, and for the wealthy minority.

All Power to the People
Free All Political Prisoners

JACK GAMNEL
Minister of Information

Domestic Violence

Susan Lewis

In the 1970s and 80s Hull-House Association pioneered in Chicago in helping the victims of family violence. At Des Plaines Valley Community Center (DVCC), in the southwestern suburb of Summit, Director Tom Yeager began organizing a shelter, support, and counseling program in 1977. The Constance Morris Shelter for Battered Women and Children was opened in Brookfield in April 1979. It was one of the state's first residential shelters for abused women, and unique in Illinois because of the backup services it provided for dealing with all aspects of domestic violence. The DVCC program offered immediate protection while providing therapy, counseling, court advocacy, outreach to the abusive partner, and employment assistance, as well as a twenty-four-hour hotline counseling and referral service. After a campaign that secured $400,000 from private sources and an array of organizations, the Constance Morris Center was replaced by a modern 4,200 sq. ft., three-story structure. The new center, in LaGrange, opened on March 6, 1988 and can shelter thirty occupants. Florence Forshey, director of Des Plaines Valley since 1984, guided the project to completion.

On the southeast side of Chicago, the Southeast Council on Domestic Violence and Family Rescue, which became a Hull-House sponsored program in February 1981, initiated a bilingual counseling and information service for families experiencing domestic violence. It was associated with Ada S. McKinley Community Services, which provided space in its south Chicago Neighborhood House as an interim site for the shelter, making it the first shelter operating in the city south of 600 State Street.

Meanwhile, on the north side of Chicago, the Uptown Center Family Violence Task Force, which evolved into the Woman Abuse Action Program, was established in April 1978 to organize a neighborhood network of resources helpful to an abused woman. A self-help group of women met regularly at Uptown Center for referral, assistance, counseling, and mutual support. Their children met in a separate, special group organized to help them understand that negotiation was a reasonable substitute for physical power. Program staff focused on making the problem of domestic violence public, and encouraged hospitals, schools, clergy, and other community institutions to recognize and deal with domestic violence.

The Domestic Violence Court Advocacy Project, a model effort to provide information and assistance to women who wish to press criminal charges against their abusers, grew out of the Uptown Center program. By 1987, staff who served as court advocates for victims had assisted more than 4,000 women in obtaining protection. The project was a result of an attempt to influence the court system in Cook County in its treatment of domestic violence. The response has been the nation's first Domestic Violence Court, described in this newspaper article by Susan Lewis. [Susan Lewis, "Unique Court Makes Difference to Victims of Domestic Violence," Chicago Tribune (November 10, 1985), Section III, 4.]

Unique Court Makes Difference to Victims of Domestic Violence

A man and a woman sit shoulder to shoulder on the courtroom bench, holding hands and sharing whispers. Within the hour they will stand in front of the judge, adversaries separated by a state's attorney and a sheriff's deputy as a safety precaution.

"It was only a lover's quarrel," the young woman tells the judge on the night her boyfriend beat her and destroyed the livingroom furniture. "He was a little drunk, but it don't mean nothing now." Without her willingness to prosecute, the state's case is closed.

It's another afternoon at the Domestic Violence Court at 930 N. Wood St., where men, women and children open the intimate wounds of violence at home for the proceedings of a public hearing. The court—the only one of its kind in the nation—was started as an experimental program serving the North Side in 1984 but will be expanded to a citywide program by the end of the year. Judges and victims' advocates say the expanded court will help achieve uniform treatment of domestic violence cases and encourage victims to follow through with prosecution.

"No system is perfect, but this court has made a difference," said Connie Vulkan, an Uptown Hull House supervisor and one of the victims' advocates at the court. "We still have a long way to go," she said, noting that 50 to 70 percent of the charges brought against abusers eventually are dropped.

Each day from 11 A.M. until the docket is cleared, the accused and the accusers stand before Associate Judge Brent Carlson. Some wear expensive suits and bring high-priced lawyers. Other wear paint-splashed T-shirts. Some don't speak English. Some arms are in casts, some faces black and blue.

"This court cuts across society completely," said Carlson, who has presided over the Domestic Violence Court for about six months. "It is not just husband and wife, but brother and brother, sister and sister, mother and son, the Gold Coast rich, the Appalachian poor and the West Side unemployed." Carlson is quick to point out that no matter how heart-wrenching the case, his purpose is to preside over a criminal court. "I am not a social worker," he said. "The attorneys aren't social workers. But I do believe the law can have some social impact in this area."

Although most victims here are women, Carlson estimates that about 10 percent of the cases involve a man who claims to be brutalized by a wife

or girlfriend. And other trials reveal home lives riddled with other crimes, including the sexual abuse of children. Carlson recalls the case of a Chicago businessman brought to court on charges that he abused his wife. Through hours of testimony, Carlson learned the man had molested his teenage stepdaughter for years while the girl's mother, afraid of losing the material comforts of his household, looked the other way. "It is difficult to fathom what lives like that are like," he said, shaking his head.

The Wood Street court can be a mysterious and discouraging spectacle to someone who has agonized over whether to ask for protection, according to the women's advocates who work with the victims. In two cramped offices just outside the courtroom lobby, counselors from the Uptown Hull House and the Chicago Metropolitan Battered Women's Network take the cases of about 25 women each day.

"Battered women are not in themselves inadequate or stupid or unwilling to follow through," said Margaret Luft of the Chicago Battered Women's Network. "The system simply does not respond to women or encourage them, because of its size and its purpose."

Most victims don't understand the court system and rely on the advocate's guidance each step of the way, Vulkan said, but many also need referrals to shelters and counseling programs. Vulkan said victims who are economically and emotionally dependent on their abusers and lack support from friends or family are more likely to give up their prosecution, which may require many court appearances. "Sometimes it is simply the fear," she said. "The fear is very real and can keep a woman in a precarious situation."

The Domestic Violence Court has the power to ease a victim's fear with an order of protection, a document made available to victims of domestic violence by the Illinois General Assembly in its 1982 Domestic Violence Act. If the judge believes a victim would be in physical danger without one, he issues the protection order solely on the basis of the victim's testimony. The order of protection can be used to evict a family member, most often the man, from his home, require him to seek counseling, take away custody of children and prohibit him from striking or harassing the recipient of the order. Women's advocates consider the protection order an advance in the fight for victim's rights. Vulkan said that if violence occurs in the home after the order is issued, police can arrest the offender and charge him with violation of the order.

Carlson, however, is careful to point out that the rights of the accused are equally important. "The order of protection is an extraordinary remedy for extraordinary cases," he said. "Who is to say if, just because a woman is holding two sheets of paper in her hand, a man in a passion is going to refrain from hitting her? How do we measure that?"

"The haunting thought I have every day when I walk into that courtroom is that this may be the case where, if I don't issue an order of protection, he or she will go back to that household and something horrible will happen. When I hear of a terrible incident on the radio I think to myself, 'When was he in my court?' I just listen for the name."

Housing Reform in the 1980s

Grant Pick and Stevenson O. Swanson

"*America is increasingly becoming a nation of housing haves and havenots,*" *announced William Apgar and H. James Brown, co-authors of a study from the Joint Center for Housing Studies of Harvard University called* The State of the Nation's Housing, 1988. *Between 1970 and 1986, Chicago demolished 83,484 housing units while building only 72,296, for a net loss of 11,188. This number is misleadingly small. Demolition removed the oldest, least-expensive units, and new construction, most of which had been concentrated downtown, and on the near north side, tended to be luxury units, in effect drastically reducing the affordable housing stock. In addition, the gentrification of older neighborhoods, some of which Hull-House served, forced poorer residents out of their houses.*

Hull-House Association recognized that adequate, affordable housing for low- and middle-income families in Chicago was a major community problem, and they tried to find solutions. The

Clarence Darrow Center is located at 44th Street and Cicero Ave. in a thirty-year-old, 615-unit, low-rise housing project called LeClaire Courts. One of the Chicago Housing Authority's oldest and most successful public housing projects, with a relatively stable population of 3,000 residents that included senior citizens, low-income families, and single mothers, began a gradual, but perceptible decline in the early 1980s. Upkeep and rent collections were becoming lax; stolen cars and drug deals in the project were proliferating. Something had to be done.

Stanley Horn, a black who had grown up in the Parkway Center program and became director of Clarence Darrow Center in 1977, took up the challenge. He began working with Irene Johnson, a twenty-year resident of the housing project and leader of a residential group seeking positive change. Together they asked for help from Bill Peterman, an academic entrepreneur at the Nathalie P. Voorhees Center for Neighborhood and Community Improvement, on the Chicago campus of the University of Illinois.

After considerable discussion and investigating of alternatives, the LeClaire Center residents, with the advice and help of Horn and Peterman, decided to call for the right to manage their project. In a formal proposal that the LeClaire Courts Resident Management Corporation submitted to the Chicago Housing Authority (CHA), residents requested responsibility for budgeting, screening new tenants, hiring staff, maintaining grounds and apartments, and overseeing repairs.

In the spring of 1986, the CHA agreed to the proposal. LeClaire Courts became the first tenant-managed public housing project in Chicago. On May 27, 1986, Mayor Harold Washington and CHA Chairman Renault Robinson presented a check for $1,000,000 in CHA capital improvement funds to be used at the residents' discretion for rehabilitation, and they publicly announced their permission for the LeClaire Courts Resident Management Corporation to work toward assuming responsibility for the project. After management training, the transfer took place in 1988, with Hull-House continuing to provide management training and technical assistance through the transition phase.

Uptown Center has long recognized housing as a major problem for its neighborhoods. Staff

there, particularly Ann Seng, who had joined Uptown Center in 1971 as its community development director, was instrumental in helping to
organize the Uptown Peoples Federal Credit
Union, chartered in 1974 with 400 members, as a
response to the red-lining of their neighborhood by
Chicago mortgage bankers. By 1985, after being
located for a time in space provided by Hull-
House, it had become the North Side Community
Federal Credit Union with assets of $600,000 and
over $2,000,000 loaned out, serving not only Up-
town, but also Lakeview, Edgewater, and Rogers
Park. Neighborhood people continued to have an
opportunity to invest in their own community.

In the summer of 1976, Uptown Center Director Brooks Miller was arrested along with five
other persons who tried to prevent the demolition
of a three-story apartment building at 4425 N. Racine. Their demonstration argued that the structure could have been rehabilitated. Besides this
attempt to bring public awareness to the housing
problems of the Uptown area, the Uptown Center
created the Housing Resource Center (HRC); from
1975 to 1981 it operated a technical assistance
program aimed at reducing tension between tenants and landlords. Landlords received counseling on building maintenance and rehabilitation
and could cut costs by buying materials and supplies through a buying club. Staff at the center
helped secure public money for rehabilitation
work and weatherization; they also screened tenants and developed a program to train neighborhood residents as building janitors. One of the
goals of the program was to find housing for the
poor in the private market.

The HRC, initiated by Ann Seng with the assistance of Kathy Devine, Jim Green, and six volunteers, was operated by Sue Brady, Janice Byron,
and Andre Phillips. In 1982, because of the gentrification of the area and the speculation described in the Swanson article in the Chicago
Tribune, the HRC closed its program in order to
take a different approach. Becoming a community-based management firm, it sought to gain
even more control over housing on Chicago's north
side.

In 1983, the HRC received the first private
management contract from the CHA to oversee
scattered-site housing in its area. By 1987, it was
managing over 200 units in 43 buildings. The HRC

developed a model management strategy to integrate public housing into neighborhoods and involve residents in decisions affecting their housing
through a Tenant Council.

Hull-House and Uptown Center were also supportive of the Lakefront SRO Corporation in its
successful effort to develop single-room occupancy housing for low-income residents. After
three years of negotiation and planning supported
by Hull-House, the Moreland Hotel, 4949 N. Sheridan Road, was renovated at a cost of nearly
$2,000,000 and renamed the Harold Washington
SRO Apartments. Hull-House acted as fiscal agent
and provided a loan of $5,000 dollars to get the
project underway.

The following articles suggest some of the
problems and pitfalls in trying to improve urban
housing in the 1980s. [Grant Pick, "Neighborhood News: Is the CHA Ready to Try Tenant Management?" The Reader (May 2, 1986), 3–4;
Stevenson O. Swanson, "The Failure of Uptown
Housing Resource Center," Chicago Tribune
(March 4, 1982).]

Is the CHA Ready to Try
Tenant Management

By Grant Pick

The Ickes Homes, a public housing project at
23rd and South Dearborn, played host to the regular meeting of the Chicago Housing Authority
(CHA) commissioners on the morning of April 23
[1986]. The meeting was held in a gym, dressed
up for the occasion. The table up front, where the
commissioners sat, was draped in yellow bunting.

And this was an occasion! Not only was there
a big crowd in the gym, but CHA chairman Renault Robinson had an initial announcement "of
great importance" to make.

"The Chicago Housing Authority has decided
to embark on a new and more positive direction,"
Robinson began. He said the commissioners were
going to set up a committee, under attorney Allison Davis, to explore joint "public-private initia-
tives" to shore up a sagging CHA. According to

Robinson, those ventures might include private forays into both scattered-site housing and development of the CHA's lakefront lands, the sale of "some of our properties" to residents, and "experiments in tenant management."

When Robinson was done, commissioner Leon Finney couldn't contain himself. "I can't remember when I was so encouraged at coming to a meeting," he exclaimed.

In the back of the gym, however, there was a mixed reaction by leaders from LeClaire Courts, a CHA development on the southwest side. Irene Johnson, president of a newly formed nonprofit corporation designed to allow LeClaire tenants one day to run their project themselves, was heartened; she felt the Allison Davis committee marked a commitment to the concept of tenant management.

But Stanley Horn's blood pressure rose. The director of the Clarence Darrow Community Center, a social service agency that ministers to LeClaire Courts, Stan Horn has worked strenuously to bring tenant management to the development. He thought he was being put off.

The concept of tenant management—the empowerment of residents of a public housing development to take over all or part of its administration—has been applied in several cities, with considerable success. The community leadership at LeClaire Courts had long wanted to bring tenant management to Chicago, but was still waiting for the CHA to get firmly behind the idea. To Horn, the Davis committee sounded like further study— a stall. "We want something in writing," Horn huffed after the CHA commissioners voted unanimously to establish the Davis committee.

But that was last Wednesday. Since then, the residents and Stan Horn all have had new reason to feel their time has come.

LeClaire Courts is a complex of two-story brick row houses tucked off Cicero Avenue south of the Stevenson Expressway. Its 615 units of one-to four-bedroom apartments were constructed in two sections in the early 1950s. The first section was built with city and state funding, the second with federal financing; today there is still a division, as LeClaire Courts is operated by two different CHA offices. LeClaire is home to 3,700 people, nearly all of them black.

Irene Johnson, who is 45, moved into LeClaire Courts 20 years ago with her family. She and her husband raised two children in a three-bedroom town house, and Irene is now the clerk for LeClaire's local advisory council (or LAC), the CHA's resident arm on site.

"This has been an ideal place to bring up children," Johnson says. "There has always been a spirit about this place, like here we are in the city but it's almost like the suburbs. People grow grass, flowers, and they care about their homes. There is crime; I wish it were zero, but it isn't. Still, we have a neighborhood watch program and though cars get stripped in our parking lots a good deal, the gangs have never taken hold."

The problems at LeClaire Courts center on inferior upkeep, according to Johnson. "In general we don't have good maintenance," she says. "Orders are not filled fast enough, and when they are they involve only little repairs to the property." Even now, says Johnson, the federally financed section of LeClaire needs its gutters painted and downspouts replaced; apartment walls are cracked, and many cabinets are in lousy condition. Johnson claims the city-state side of LeClaire suffers from shoddy roofs, plumbing, and window seals. (The CHA, which generally complains of not having enough money to make repairs, did not comment on Johnson's complaints.)

Beginning in the spring of 1983, the residents of LeClaire began to do more than complain. The LAC, joined with a couple of other community groups, approached the Clarence Darrow Community Center, an affiliate of the Hull-House Association, for help. The Darrow Center's then director, Stan Horn, invited the Nathalie P. Voorhees Center for Neighborhood and Community Improvement at the University of Illinois at Chicago to look over the possibilities.

In time the Voorhees Center developed what it felt were five sensible alternatives. The residents could merely get more involved as what they were, CHA tenants. Or LeClaire could be converted into a cooperative, along the lines of Racine Courts, a row house development on the south side that the CHA turned over to its occupants on a limited-equity basis in 1968. By another option—called "mutual association"—the residents would own their units in an arrangement underwritten by private investors. Or a development corporation

In 1988, with the help of Clarence Darrow Center of Hull-House, LeClaire Courts became the first resident-managed public housing project in Chicago. Irene Johnson, President, Clarence Darrow Resident Management Project, clasps hands with Mayor Harold Washington while holding a check from the Chicago Housing Authority for operations and improvements to mark the new status of LeClaire Courts. Others present are (from left) Zirl Smith, Executive Director, CHA; Renault Robinson, Chairman, CHA; and CHA Commissioners Lettia Nevill, Earl Neal, and (seated) Artensa Randolph.

could be created by the tenants and private interests to buy the development and operate it.

Then there was tenant management, the operation of LeClaire by its inhabitants. Everyone decided it justified more research. In February of 1985, 16 LeClaire residents and representatives from the Darrow and Voorhees centers traveled to Saint Louis to check out the experience at Cochran Gardens, an 800-unit development near the downtown there.

In 1976, the residents of Cochran Gardens had obtained a Ford Foundation grant, received training in how to run their development, and set up a nonprofit tenant management corporation (or TMC) to do just that. Under its energetic president, a tough-talking activist named Bertha Gilkey, the Cochran TMC has applied a firm hand to its domain. Each of Cochran's 12 buildings has its own council and floor captains, relates Gilkey, "and they deal with the problem families, so we have no graffiti, no garbage, no hanging around the halls." The councils enforce sweeping, laundry-room schedules, and playground curfews. Persons who bid to live in Cochran are carefully

screened (no one with a criminal background need apply), and those who do gain residency find their rent collected by the TMC, which accepts no excuses for tardiness.

According to Gilkey, life is grand at Cochran Gardens. "Crime is down to nothing, vandalism is down to nothing," she says. "If you live here you think you have a condo." When the TMC took over, reports Gilkey, half of the apartments stood vacant; now there are only nine empty units. Monthly rent collections have risen from an average of $24 a month per unit to $103. To Gilkey's mind, this is all because the Cochran managers have a stake in the place: "If the elevator doesn't work, *they* walk up the steps, just like everybody else. When there's crime, they get mugged, too. When a pipe breaks, the water falls on them just like the next person."

Irene Johnson and the LeClaire delegation were mightily impressed with Cochran Gardens, right down to the glassy entryway that no young tough had dared shatter with a rock. "What struck us most," says Johnson, "was the pride we found at Cochran Gardens."

Bill Peterman, the director of the Voorhees Center who was along on the trip, discovered in talking to Saint Louis housing officials that resident management had its limits. The Saint Louis Housing Authority has sparred with the TMCs ("It's very difficult when they look on us as the enemy," one housing authority official told Peterman), and today only two local projects feature resident management at all. Moreover, it is "soft management," meaning the housing authority retains ultimate control of the purse strings. Cochran Gardens has a $2 million annual budget, but a mere $120,000 falls within the direct purview of Bertha Gilkey's TMC.

Still, the LeClaire Courts contingent returned to Chicago sold on the self-worth and efficiency resident management brings, and over the next few months their conviction only became more total. Bertha Gilkey came to Chicago to present a slide show on Cochran Gardens, "and that got our community really fired up," reports Irene Johnson. At the end of last summer, another, larger delegation from LeClaire paid a visit to the Kenilworth-Parkside housing project in Washington D.C., where a TMC under a dynamo named Kimi Gray is allowed to practice "hard management." The TMC keeps the books, writes the checks, and does even more sponsoring a health clinic, a food co-op, a beauty shop, and a day-care center.

The LeClaire residents also forged a link with the National Center for Neighborhood Enterprise (NCNE), a group founded by black conservative Robert Woodson in 1981 under the credo "self-help is the best help." NCNE, believing so strongly that the poor can rise by their own bootstraps, has been instrumental in assisting TMCs in Saint Louis, Washington, Boston, and New Orleans. The group is also a force behind federal legislation, introduced in the House by the odd couple of black Democrat Walter Fauntroy of Washington D.C., and white Republican Jack Kemp of New York, that would create incentives for resident control. NCNE has agreed to devote $85,000 of a $1.9 million grant from the Amoco Foundation to train LeClaire residents in tenant management. LeClaire has now incorporated its own TMC, Irene Johnson being its president, that desires to run LeClaire under a regime of hard rather than soft management.

The problem was—and remains—to get the CHA to go along. Though the CHA leadership is acquainted with resident management, their public response so far has been lukewarm. Zirl Smith, the authority's executive director, was heard to hail resident management as a good concept at a meeting held in March of 1985. Yet since last December, when the LeClaire residents formally petitioned the CHA for its OK, they have failed to get so much as a note back in writing. On the other hand, NCNE in Washington received a letter recently from Renault Robinson, in which he said the CHA "has endorsed the concept of tenant management and the efforts of residents to enter into a partnership with the authority to operate LeClaire Courts." And some informal conversations were promising.

So when Irene Johnson, Stan Horn, and others from LeClaire showed up at the April 23 CHA board meeting, they expected Robinson to embrace tenant management at LeClaire. Instead, Robinson and his fellow commissioners unfurled Allison Davis's privatization committee. That satisfied Johnson, but not Horn.

Davis, the former law partner of Acting Corporation Counsel Judson Miner, is known for fostering community development corporations throughout the city. Davis says his committee, to be composed of an as-yet-unnamed collection of architects, engineers, and developers, will consider tenant management among a range of items. But CHA commissioner Leon Finney concedes the panel's primary charge is to figure out how to leverage private dollars to help fix up the authority's decaying housing stock. "Right now," says Finney, "we're $700 million short of what it takes."

The CHA's reluctance to embark on tenant management puzzles the people from LeClaire, but other observers, who speak off the record, think they understand: If the CHA placed the $895,000 LeClaire budget in the hands of the residents, the residents might screw up. Worse yet, they might succeed, and the CHA would be out a substantial amount of turf. In addition, granting autonomy to LeClaire could increase pressure for more independence from CHA residents across the city. All a spokesman for the CHA would say is that the issue of tenant management "is still in negotiation with the residents."

But Stan Horn was assured last Friday by CHA

planning director Robert Scott that a written compact with the authority is imminent. Horn and Irene Johnson have an appointment with Zirl Smith this coming Monday at 9 AM. Smith is said to be "ready to go." Horn and Johnson sure hope so.

The Failure of Uptown Housing Resource Center

By Stevenson O. Swanson

When a nonprofit program closes these days, observers are likely to speculate that the cause was a shortage of funding brought about by the changes the Reagan administration has wrought. The failure of Uptown's Housing Resource Center was indeed an economic failure, but the culprit was subtler than a government cutback. "We closed after five years because we couldn't find affordable housing for low- and moderate-income people," said Sue Brady, the center's director.

Unlike most community housing organizations, the resource center, which was a branch of the Hull House Association, tried to find housing for the poor in the private market. Most groups have relied on such government programs as the Section 8 housing subsidy. The center's failure has ominous overtones, Brady said, because it indicates that the private market is not able to help the poor—at least not in Uptown.

The Center started with an emphasis on organizing tenants and landlords, with the goal of reducing tension between the two traditionally hostile groups. "We decided at first that we couldn't save the world," Brady said. "We didn't deal with irresponsible families and we didn't provide emergency housing." Although the center's services changed during its five years, it continued to help both tenants and landlords. Landlords who joined the center received discounts through a buying club and counseling on building maintenance and rehabilitation. The center helped with budgeting and financing, acquired public money for weatherization and rehabilitation work, screened tenants, and even set up a program to train neighborhood residents as building janitors.

Staff members mediated landlord-tenant disputes and made loans to tenants for security de-

posits and moving expenses. The center, which ceased full operations in September [1982], also tried to cut red tape in tenants' dealings with public aid or pension offices. At its peak, the center had nine staff members and a $200,000 budget. Now only Brady remains, although two former staff members help part time with the task of running the center's sole remaining program, training resident managers, and tying up loose ends at the center.

The center's money came in equal parts from the government, foundations and Hull House. "I'm not saying that Reaganomics wouldn't have affected us, too," Brady said. "But at the time we decided to close, we had the funding." The center's remaining staff say that gentrification and rising rents killed the program. The symptoms, as Brady explained, were an increasing number of calls from tenants looking for a new place to live and an ever-decreasing number of apartments for them.

"There are apartments out there," said Janice Byron, who headed the center's management program and tried to drum up new landlords for the center. "But our goal is decent, affordable housing. How could we refer tenants to a run-down building with high rents?" The staffers said they dealt with three kinds of landlords. A core of "sincere" landlords wanted to help poor and lower–middle-class tenants, but market forces drove them to raise rents and shut them out of the building-improvement-loan market. Other landlords were speculators, Byron said, who thought an Uptown building was a good buy. These landlords were generally undercapitalized, she said, so their buildings continued to deteriorate.

The third group of landlords hold the future of Uptown in their hands, Brady said. These are the developers who have condominium conversions in mind. "I can think of five developers who each own more than 12 buildings," she said. "The buildings are in terrible condition, but the basic decisions have been made."

Blaming gentrification might seem premature in Uptown, which looks very little like the commonly recognized gentrified areas of Lincoln Park and Lake View, but, Byron said, appearances are deceiving because the economy has stalled the developers' plans. "The economy has frozen everything," she said. "In the meantime, people are in these buildings and they're paying higher rents all the time while the buildings deteriorate because the developer doesn't want to put any money into them until he's ready to convert."

Large apartments, which the poor people of Uptown need most because of their large families, are extremely hard to find, said Andre Phillips, the center's housing counselor. Rents are from $300 to $400. As an example of the dilemma, Brady cited the case of a single mother with a child. She received, before the Reagan cuts, about $300 a month in welfare and food stamps, but the cheapest one-bedroom apartment in the neighborhood would rent for about $225, leaving little more than $70 to live on per month.

"When we started, the vacancy rate in Uptown was pretty good, about 5 percent," Brady said. "Landlords needed us. When the vacancy rate went down, rents went up, and the landlords didn't need us. We surveyed them, and they said that they liked us but that they wouldn't really miss us." The staff considered its future for many months. The center might have become a management agency for low-income buildings, but the staff felt that the buildings would be in such bad shape to begin with that they would be beyond help or that the staff would manage a building so well that the landlord would sell it to make a profit. The center did not want to become a neighborhood housing development organization because the Voice of the People is already developing low and moderate income housing in Uptown. "We couldn't come up with any strategies except the resident manager training program, which is still going on," Brady said. "We only hope we don't discourage other agencies from trying other strategies."

The staff conducted a study of the center's failings, and concluded that the center failed as much because of it location as any other cause. "It's not that it's a bad program, but when you've got a combination of high rents and costs, gentrification and speculation, a housing program like ours won't work," said Byron, who wrote an 83-page report about the center's closing. "Perhaps it would work in a neighborhood like Bridgeport, where the people who own and the people who rent are all about the same," Byron said.

Although a somewhat similar program in South Shore also closed recently, the Housing Services Center in the North-of-Howard Street neighborhood of Rogers Park is still working. "The answer seems to be that the program will work only in narrowly defined types of neighborhoods—probably only a small percentage of all U.S. neighborhoods," Brady said.

In the absence of any attempt to make the private housing market work for the poor, families double up, move to cheaper apartments, or pay as much as 70 percent of their incomes in rent, she said. One indication of the problem did not occur to staff until after the center's closing: All of the tenants who were members of the center's board during the five years eventually moved from Uptown.

After the closing, Phillips spent about a week calling around the city to find out if a program existed to refer families to landlords. "There's nothing around to help put people in contact or make a referral," he said. "Families were still calling us, and we'd tell them we couldn't help. Then, they'd say, 'What do you suggest?' And all you can say is, 'I don't know.' "

Working with the Elderly

Patricia L. Sharpe, Jane F. Connolly, Ruby L. Schmidt, and Marjorie W. Lundy

In 1956, the year that the Senior Centers of Metropolitan Chicago (SCMC) was organized, Patricia Sharpe, who later became director of Hull-House, was entering the School of Social Work in Vancouver, B. C. In a speech on the occasion of the thirtieth anniversary of Senior Centers, she recalled, "At that time, in the social work world, concerning yourself with problems of older persons was not high status." While her curriculum focused on child development and parent-child relationships, her thesis topic, "Housing Projects for Old People," opened a new and fascinating segment of society for her. She spent the first years of her professional life in child welfare service, but in 1966 she went to work for Senior

Centers, even though "The profession of social work still seemed to regard work with the elderly as somehow low status."

That perspective was about to change. By the 1960s, it was becoming clear that the American population was aging and that much of it was in need of social services. In 1968, when it was forced to affiliate with Hull-House, Senior Citizens of Metropolitan Chicago operated a number of centers offering a variety of activities for older adults, including opportunities to socialize, to make new friends, and to learn new skills. Through the 1970s and the 1980s, as the older adult population and its needs grew, the program achieved a more prominent role in the agency, in part because federal funds became available to serve the elderly.

The Retired Senior Volunteer Program (RSVP), which began as a nationwide effort to develop a corps of persons over age sixty for volunteer service, was initiated in Chicago in 1972, when Hull-House received funds from the federal agency ACTION to administer the program in the city. At first its administration was lodged in Hull-House headquarters, but by 1985 the program was being operated through Senior Citizens of Metropolitan Chicago with more than 1,300 volunteers contributing over 300,000 hours in 250 different non-profit organizations.

In the 1980s Senior Centers tried to deal with the problem of adequate housing for the elderly through its Board and Care Program. It trained persons to care for older adults who need a protective environment while receiving assistance with basic housekeeping, laundry, meal preparation, or emotional support. Since guidelines and regulations in this area had not been created, SCMC assumed a leadership role in developing them and enlisted the cooperation of state and local health departments in creating regulations that would ensure quality care.

By the late 1980s, through its Home Delivered Meals Program, the Senior Centers provided two meals a day, five days a week, to an average of forty-eight older adults each month. Support came from the recipients and funds raised by SCMC. This concept originally came to Hull-House from Philadelphia with Paul Jans as the American version of the English program Meals on Wheels. For

a time, the program received federal funding as well as assistance from a number of other Chicago welfare agencies, among them Olivet Community Center, Catholic Charities of Chicago, and Lutheran Welfare Services of Illinois.

Other Hull-House centers also worked with the elderly. Jane Addams Center initiated a United Senior Citizens Program, which provided an outlet for seniors to meet socially, attend educational and recreational workshops, and benefit from a variety of activities and services. Many who participate eventually become members of the center's Senior Caucus, which focuses on health care issues and the operation of White Crane Senior Health Center, a national prototype for consumer-driven health care for senior citizens.

Uptown Center created a program to link latchkey children with older adults, resulting in the nationally recognized "Grandma Please" Hotline. Youngsters five to twelve years old make 500–900 telephone calls each month to talk to someone about their problems and experiences. Older adults are the "Grandmas" and "Grandpas," able to share their wisdom, help with school work, or simply listen. Begun in January 1985, through funding received from the Retirement Research Foundation, the program features a training workshop for participants to ensure quality and consistency. This successful and needed program has been featured on Cable News Network, WBEZ Radio, the Voice of America, and CBS Weekend News. Fifteen agencies across the country have become associate members of the program by establishing it in their own states, and legislation pending in Illinois would allow the program to operate statewide.

Uptown Center was one of the first to design an outreach program for the ill or housebound elderly. Lakeview Uptown Senior Citizens Project was so successful that it became a model for other Hull-House outreach efforts and for other senior programs throughout the country. It underlined the pivotal role that neighborhood workers, with little or no formal training in social work, could play in providing service; and it used storefronts to attract many older people who would not go to the centers.

By 1986, Patricia Sharpe pointed to a number of Hull-House programs for older adults and to

"Grandma Please," a program to connect latchkey children with older adults, was developed at Uptown Center of Hull-House and has won national recognition. Left to right, volunteer Grandmas Betty Garfinkle and Mary Ellen Dileonardis; Pauline Miller, administrative assistant; Patricia L. Sharpe, executive director of Hull-House Association; Grandma Frances Weisberg; Christine Williams, President, Uptown Center Board of Trustees; and Beverly Nash, program director, accept the United Way/Crusade of Mercy "Voluntary Action Award" for 1988.

specific improvements in living conditions for the elderly. Yet she recognized that much remained to be done:

> SCMC [and Hull-House] in the future will continue to address particular and general needs of the elderly, to be flexible in changing and to be influential in bringing about change. We can celebrate improvements, and know that we participated actively. As we move into the next decade, demographics are on our side—the over age sixty-five group is the fastest growing segment of our population. SCMC, and all of us who share their values, will strive to ensure that the new political power of the elderly is used in ways that will unite and improve the whole, and will break down age barriers and age segregation and stereotyped social roles.

This excerpt from an essay describing a successful outreach program for seniors suggests the pioneer role played by Hull-House in working with the elderly, but it also demonstrates how massive the problem is and how inadequate is the funding. [Patricia L. Sharpe, Jane F. Connolly, Ruby L. Schmidt, and Marjorie W. Lundy, "Outreach: Bringing Services to the Elderly Senior Centers of Metropolitan Chicago," in Organization and Ad-

ministration of Service Programs for the Older Adult, *edited by Rubard E. Hardy and John G. Cull (Springfield, Il.: Charles C. Thomas, 1974).]*

The Elderly . . . Lost in the Shuffle

In this affluent, opportunity-rich country, one growing segment of the population has been dealt a losing hand. America's elderly have somehow been lost in the shuffle of minority groups struggling for equal rights and a decent standard of living. The reasons for this are numerous and complex, but the result is singularly poignant—the crying needs of many aging Americans, whose productive years have gone to making their country great, are not being met. Aggravating the situation and presaging grave problems for the future, is the fact that the number of elderly is increasing at nearly twice the rate of the general population.*

*McCarthy, Colman, "Politics and Helping the Aging," *The Washington Post*, July 29, 1971, editorial page.

Needed . . . A New Approach

Although public and private concern about the plight of the aged has accelerated in recent years, constructive remedial action has been slow in coming. Legislation lags. Social services remain fragmented, and social workers persist in assigning the elderly a low priority. Many senior centers cater to the "well" aged, serving those fortunate few able to attend center functions and often failing to look beyond their walls to the ill, impoverished, and isolated—the so-called "invisible elderly." We have reached a point where the rhetoric of concern and piecemeal action are no longer accepted. Critically needed is a new approach—a realistic approach, geared to the multiple problems of aging and to delivering tangible, essential services NOW to all aging Americans in need of help, wherever they may be.

An Early Start in Chicago

In the mid-1960's, Hull House of Chicago began exploring ways to reach out to the community elderly. This role was altogether appropriate for Hull House with its settlement house tradition and long history of active involvement with the problems of local neighborhood residents, young and old. A small-scale outreach program was initiated in the Uptown area of Chicago's north side, where census figures and personal observation indicated an extremely high concentration of elderly people. Many of the aged there were ill, malnourished, alone, and barely able to make ends meet. Many were utterly confused by the myriad public and private welfare agencies confronting them or were completely unaware that sources of help existed. It was these people that Hull House particularly wanted to reach and serve, by placing the highest priority on outreach into the community and on rehabilitation through services and activities provided by neighborhood senior centers.

The tremendous and immediate human needs revealed by this pilot program in Uptown, and the equally serious plight of the elderly in the adjoining neighborhood of Lakeview, prompted Hull House social planners to begin searching for ways to expand outreach services. This search was ended with the acceptance by the Illinois State Council on Aging of a proposal for a demonstration project in outreach to the elderly, submitted under provisions of the Older Americans Act. With the authorization of government funds in March 1967, the Lakeview–Uptown Senior Citizens Project officially came into being. Experimenting with new but basically simple techniques and concepts—most importantly the use of neighborhood workers—the Project staff succeeded in implementing a system for effective delivery of individualized services to the aged on a neighborhood level.

Readily usable written material on how to set up and sustain a program of outreach to senior citizens is, at this point, a scarce commodity. In the following pages, members of the Lakeview–Uptown Project staff have outlined some of their methods and experiences in the hope that these may be of use to others engaged in the important work of helping aging Americans. . . .

A Central Resource for the Elderly

The priorities of the Lakeview–Uptown Senior Citizens Project have been clear from its inception: to reach out to the invisible neighborhood elderly and to provide them with services to meet their needs. In approaching these objectives, Hull House planners recognized that the needs of the aged are frequently multiple, desperate, and immediate. They envisioned the establishment of a central neighborhood resource equipped to sort out the innumerable social service agencies that the elderly individual encounters, to act as his broker and advocate, to interpret his needs, and to provide or arrange for the appropriate service as quickly as possible. The multi-purpose neighborhood senior center seemed uniquely suited for this task.

In March 1967, two such senior centers were established, one in Lakeview and another in Uptown. These centers provided a congenial place where older people could casually drop in, gather to socialize, engage in recreational activity, or just get away from dreary home environments. But they were service-oriented facilities as well—bases of operation for neighborhood outreach workers and for a small professionally-trained back-up staff.

A participant in the ceramics class receives guidance from an instructor. The arts and crafts program is only one aspect of the services provided by the Senior Centers of Metropolitan Chicago, a Hull-House affiliated program.

A Model for Effective Service Delivery

As these centers began serving the community and gaining experience, it became clear that a workable system for maximizing the delivery of available services to the elderly could be achieved on the neighborhood level. The successful functioning of this system depended on coordination of three essential types of services—those of neighborhood/outreach workers, center professional personnel, and related community agencies. By combining its own services and those of other vital programs and organizations into an integrated whole, the center could cope with the multi-problem situations presented by the aging person and not only provide him with services to meet current needs but also help him formulate an overall plan for future years.

Neighborhood Worker Services: The senior center was the axis of the service delivery system. From the center, neighborhood workers moved out into the community, finding isolated elderly, forming friendships, regularly helping the aged with personal tasks, and referring to the center

professionals those problems requiring their attention. The neighborhood workers became the center's link with the people of the community, informing local residents about center activities and services, and feeding back information about the neighborhood into the center. Perhaps most important, they provided the tangible supportive services as well as the personal interest and concern which helped make it possible for many homebound elderly to continue living independently.

Center Professional Services: Backing up the neighborhood workers were in-center personnel from a variety of professional disciplines—a social worker, a public health nurse, and a recreation worker. These staff members contributed not only substantive knowledge and direct services in their respective fields, but also know-how in dealing with the many related community organizations and programs. They provided the center's link with outside resources from which aged clients might need assistance. A basic social casework procedure was the professionals' rule of thumb: establish contact with the client, develop an assessment/diagnosis to identify the problem, and formulate a service intervention plan. A strong effort was made to maintain flexibility so that the client's needs would not be lost sight of in a rigid, institutionalized plan of action.

Related Outside Resources: A broad spectrum of outside resources was tapped by the Project's professional workers for the benefit of their elderly clients. The advocacy skills of the workers were regularly used in dealing with such agencies as the Chicago Housing Authority, local Social Security offices, and the Cook County Department of Public Aid. Ongoing relationships with nursing homes, hospitals, and clinics were maintained. Perhaps most interesting and productive, however, was the use of two other Hull House-sponsored programs, specifically designed—like outreach—to provide tangible supportive services for disabled, homebound elderly. The first program, Home Delivered Meals,* supplied an essential service for physically handicapped older people who might not otherwise have gotten the proper food or perhaps might not have eaten at all. The second, the "Get Together Bus,"† met another vital need by providing special, free transportation for the aged. The bus was regularly used to distribute Home Delivered Meals and also to transport elderly people to clinics, shopping, and occasionally on pleasure outings. The Lakeview–Uptown Project successfully coordinated its outreach effort with the Meals and Bus services, thereby enhancing the effects of all three programs. Consequently, it has been possible to provide an integrated and quite comprehensive service which has allowed many elderly people to remain in their own homes and to avoid a dreaded alternative—institutionalization.‡

The successful functioning of the service delivery system is best illustrated through a case example such as that which follows:

*Originally a demonstration project, funded in part by the U.S. Public Health Service and the Department of Health, Education and Welfare; when the government grant terminated on July 31, 1968, Hull House continued the service with private funds.

†A government-funded demonstration project administered by Hull House Association under Title III, Older Americans Act.

‡Connolly, Jane F., Director, Senior Centers of Metropolitan Chicago, in testimony in Chicago on November 2, 1971, before the Select Sub-Committee on Education, Committee on Education and Labor, House of Representatives, U.S. Congress.

Mrs. H., a frightened, insecure elderly woman, was discovered by a neighborhood worker who was canvassing a dilapidated building in search of older people who might need help. Mrs. H. was living alone and had completely lost track of her family. After several visits with the worker, Mrs. H. began coming to the Uptown Senior Center for recreational activities. At first she seemed somewhat retarded, but as staff members became better acquainted with her, they realized that she had severe visual and hearing difficulties. Mrs. H. was examined and treated at a clinic, where she was taken by a neighborhood worker. Subsequently, she was admitted to a hospital for cataract surgery, and was fitted with a pair of special glasses. A hearing aid was also secured for her. At about the same time, the Project staff provided another important service by relocating her to better housing. Although her vision and hearing were still impaired, Mrs. H. became more independent, resumed her sewing, and began talking about going back to work. It was as if she had gained a new lease on life because someone cared. Eventually, at the urging of the Project social worker, Mrs. H. decided to return to school; she had dropped out many years earlier at age ten. She entered adult classes at the Urban Progress Center and, in six months of hard work, graduated from the eighth grade. Project staff members—"her family"—attended the graduation and helped Mrs. H. celebrate the happy occasion.

Mrs. H. is planning to continue her education and has enrolled in high school classes. She has literally blossomed and has become an accomplished hostess, frequently entertaining staff and center members in her home. She is still not ready to handle the strains and frustrations of a job, but with social worker guidance and support, Mrs. H. may someday achieve this goal or at least find an acceptable substitute.

The Storefront Center

Over the years, the Lakeview–Uptown Project has had experience with various types of center facilities—facilities within a community center, in a church, in a storefront, and within a senior citizen housing project. Staff and elderly alike agree that by far the most successful has been the storefront center located on a busy street—"where the action is!" The advantages of a storefront are many: it is easily accessible to older people who may be in wheelchairs or have difficulty navigating steps; its large, street-level window is inviting to elderly passers-by; and center participants are able to watch the busy street activity from a secure vantage point but in close enough proximity to feel a part of the community life. The storefront is also beneficial to the outreach effort. This aspect was brought out by a neighborhood worker, who noted,

> The center members loved the storefront, and it was nice for the neighborhood workers too. I felt very comfortable approaching people on the street just outside the center, telling them about our activities and services and then inviting them in. But now that the storefront center is no longer there. I wouldn't *think* of just going up to a strange person on the street like that!

The visible, accessible base of operation afforded by the storefront gave neighborhood workers the confidence and assurance to spread word about the center to local residents, although they were complete strangers, and to actively promote their involvement. The storefront center in Lakeview eventually had to be closed because of inadequate funds. If the needed financial support could be found, the Project staff would strongly favor its restoration.

Senior Center Staff

Facilities are important but people are more so. One of the key factors in the Lakeview–Uptown Project's successful effort has been the cooperative, team approach taken by all staff members. From the outset, center personnel, professional and nonprofessional alike, joined forces as equals working toward common goals, exhibiting a mutual respect for each individual's contribution to the effort. This situation generated a free and creative exchange of ideas which has greatly facilitated outreach and the delivery of services. The moral support the workers gained from each other was also invaluable. All these factors contributed to the congenial atmosphere within the senior centers themselves.

The Lakeview–Uptown staff has not been able to do everything the Project's planners suggested in their original proposal. Their priority has been

on individual services and in-center activities have accordingly played a subordinate role. The Project might have been strengthened if funds had permitted an expansion of staff, particularly the employment of a trained group worker who could have stimulated and developed more group activities for center members—a vital aspect of rehabilitation for many older people.

The Hull-House Neighborhoods

Hull-House Association

For seventy-five years Hull-House was located in one neighborhood on the Near West Side. The ethnic composition of the area changed over the years, but the Hull-House residents not only served the neighborhood but also studied it and analyzed it and then used their knowledge to lead dozens of reform movements. For the last twenty-five years, Hull-House has been located in many neighborhoods. The following map from the 1984 Hull-House Association Annual Report and the description of the diverse neighborhoods (prepared in 1983 as part of a long-range planning effort) indicate the complexity and the overwhelming nature of urban social problems at the end of the twentieth century. But the Hull-House staff was still studying human needs at the local level and trying to devise programs to meet them. [Hull-House Association 95th Year (1984), 24; Hull-House Association Long Range Planning Committee, ''Environmental Analysis Overview'' (February 28, 1983), mimeographed, 3 pages.]

Environmental Analysis Overview

1. Henry Booth House

The community is comprised of three Chicago Housing Authority low-income housing developments—Dearborn, Hilliard, and Ickes homes.

Center Locations

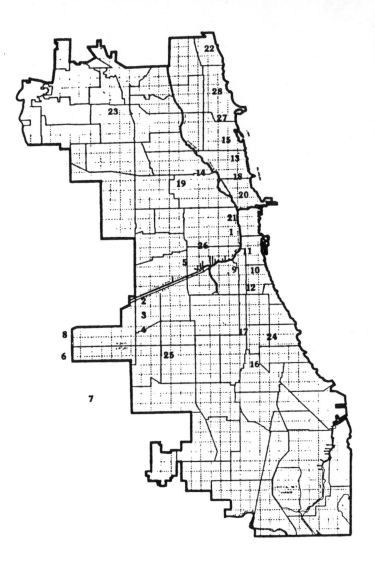

1. **HULL HOUSE ASSOCIATION**
   118 N. Clinton 60606
   726–1526

2. **CLARENCE DARROW
   COMMUNITY CENTER**
   4340 S. Lamon 60638
   767–1516

3. **Adolescent Clinic**
   4714 S. Cicero 60638
   585–3773

4. **Ryder Day Care Center**
   4410 S. LaPorte 60638
   767–5170 or 767–4867

5. **Lawndale Headstart**
   2641 W. 12th Pl. 60608
   521–5559

6. **DES PLAINES VALLEY
   COMMUNITY CENTER**
   6125 S. Archer Rd.
   Summit, IL 60501
   458–6920

7. **Child Development Center**
   8600 Roberts Rd.
   Justice, IL 60458
   430–3055

8. **Constance Morris Crisis Center
   Shelter for women and children**
   HOTLINE: 485–5254

9. **HENRY BOOTH HOUSE**
   2328 S. Dearborn 60616
   225–0800

10. **Adolescent Family Life Center**
    2320 S. State, #102 60616
    842–5507

11. **Hilliard Day Care Center**
    2031 S. Clark 60616
    663–9450

12. **World's Fair Employment Project**
    c/o Quinn Chapel Church
    2400 S. Wabash 60616
    225–8941 or 225–8276

13. **JANE ADDAMS CENTER**
    3212 N. Broadway 60657
    549–1631

14. **Lifelines**
    c/o Church of the Good News
    2900 N. Damen 60618
    549–5025

15. **Sheridan Day Care Center**
    912 W. Sheridan 60613
    528–8885 or 528–8815

16. **PARKWAY COMMUNITY
    HOUSE**
    500 E. 67th Street 60637
    493–1306

17. **First Aid Care Team**
    4844 S. State 60609
    493–1306

18. **SENIOR CENTERS OF
    METROPOLITAN CHICAGO**
    501 W. Surf 60657
    525–3480

19. **Conrad Senior Center**
    2717 N. Leavitt 60647
    248–1093

20. **Green Senior Center**
    2838 N. Pine Grove 60657
    525–2135

21. **Retired Senior Volunteer Program**
    118 N. Clinton 60606
    726–1526

22. **Northeast Office**
    1545 W. Morse 60626
    338–4456 or 338–7973

23. **Northwest Office**
    5320 W. Giddings 60630
    545–0111 or 545–0112

24. **Southeast Office**
    514 E. 50th Pl. 60629
    373–4820 or 3730–5043

25. **Southwest Office**
    3506 W. 63rd Pl. 60629
    434–4977

26. **West Side Office**
    750 S. Wolcott 60612
    226–5490

27. **UPTOWN CENTER**
    4520 N. Beacon 60640
    561–3500

28. **Uptown Child Care Center**
    1020 W. Bryn Mawr 60660
    769–5753

Combined, these developments have 2,000 apartments and over 29 buildings, which range from 7 to 22 stories.

80% of the population is under the age of 30. 50% of the heads of household are women, the majority of whom are single. The trend has been toward younger heads of household. Adolescent pregnancy has been on the increase. 35%–40% of the unmarried women in the community experience one live birth prior to the age of 18.

The unemployment rate is at 80% to 95%. The majority of the population is on public aid. The median income is $4,455.

The public schools in the area have been rated in the lower 10%. There has been an increase in disruptive behavior among youth and in crime.

II. Clarence Darrow Community Center

The community served is LeClaire Courts, a low-rise Chicago Housing Authority housing development. The community is comprised of low-income Black families that are primarily single-parent familes with young [children].

There is a high level of unemployment, particularly among youth. There is a high level of poverty, and many families are on public aid.

Public schools are not meeting the needs of the students. Gang problems exist and there is a high crime rate.

III. Jane Addams Center

The community served include Lakeview and North Center. There has been a declining population overall, although the refugee population is increasing.

There is a large percentage of single member households in Lakeview, including a significant number of people aged 65 and over. There is a shortage of housing for the elderly, even though Lakeview has the most people over 65 living in it in the city.

There is increasing unemployment in the area, but it is lower than the city average. There has been a slight increase in welfare participation in Lakeview, but less than the city rate. There has been a significant increase in the welfare rolls in North Center, especially in General Assistance.

Although North Center has a poverty level 50% lower than the average for the city, its infant mortality rate is a little higher than the city's.

The ethnic distribution is 33% Hispanic, 33% Black, 33% White, and 1% other.

IV. Parkway Community House

Blacks comprise 99% of the West Woodlawn population. The age breakdown is 27% under 18 years, 11% between 18 and 24 years, 32% between 25 and 54, and 30% over 55 years of age. 55% of the population is female. 47% of all the households are female-headed.

There was a 14% decrease in the population from 1970 to 1980. At the same time, there was a 10% decrease in available housing units. In 1980, 92% of housing units were occupied, and 8% were vacant. The number of abandoned and condemned housing units is continuing to grow.

The unemployment rate is at 28% to 32%, and rising. 64% of the population is on public assistance or receiving Social Security.

The quality of public school education is at an all-time low. Medical facilities in the community are inadequate.

West Woodlawn has a large drug-alcohol induced population. The youth have to deal daily with gang pressure.

There is a high rate of infant mortality, particularly among teen mothers. Senior citizens are the most vulnerable population segment.

V. Uptown Center

Prior to 1980, Uptown and Edgewater were considered one community area. In 1980, the city's historical boundaries for Uptown were altered.

Uptown has lost 14% of its population since 1970, and Edgewater has lost 5% of its population. In 1980, Whites were 57.2% of the Uptown population, Blacks were 15%, and Mexicans were 12.1%. In 1980, Whites were 72% of the Edgewater population, Blacks were 11.1%, and Mexicans were .05%. Other ethnic groups with a high percent of population are Filipino and Puerto Rican, with a rapid[ly rising] number of Southeast Asians in Uptown. Other groups in Edgewater are Japanese and Cuban.

The unemployment rate in Uptown-Edgewater is at 20%. Hispanic unemployment is at 10%, Black at 15%, and other (recent arrivals) at 24%. There were 121% more people on public assistance in Uptown between 1970 and 1980, and 556% more in Edgewater.

There was a total loss of 8.5% of housing units in Uptown betwen 1970 and 1980, and a gain of 7% in Edgewater. There were 2551% more condominiums and co-ops in Uptown in 1980, and 345% more in Edgewater. There is not enough housing available for the poor.

The public schools produce very low test scores and poorly trained students. There is a high crime rate and a high rate of woman abuse.

VI. Senior Centers of Metropolitan Chicago and Retired Senior Volunteer Program

There is an increase in poverty among the elderly, and a high level of unemployment. 70% of the elderly poor are women. Minorities are heavily represented among the elderly poor. Women over 65, living alone (or with unrelated individuals) are the poorest of the poor. New elderly poor are becoming more prevalent as incomes and savings dwindle.

Affordable housing for the elderly is scarce. More homeless individuals are beginning to surface.

The elderly are often victimized. Fear of crime is a pervasive attitude among the elderly-victimized and non-victimized. Elder abuse in on the rise.

77% of the over 65 population are independent and managing. 23% are impaired and need at least one support service. 5% will need to be institutionalized (some of those could make it in the community with more support).

Contributions over One Hundred Years

Patricia Sharpe

By the time Patricia Sharpe became Executive Director in 1980, she knew the organization well. She had worked at Hull-House in various capacities for sixteen years and had served Robert Adams as Associate Director after Homer Bishop retired in 1977. She knew first-hand the administrative and funding problems that the agency faced; she was part of its history.

Not since the appointment of Adena Rich, who became the first head resident after Jane Addams died, had the board approved someone from the Hull-House staff. Sharpe became the first woman to direct the association of affiliated programs and the first since Charlotte Carr to serve as director of Hull-House.

During the Midwest American Settlement House Centennial Conference, May 1–2, 1986, in Minneapolis, Sharpe offered a perspective on what Hull-House had accomplished, what it should do, and the type of people she believed could best carry out its mission. Her pragmatism, her sense that reform should be based in the neighborhood, her distrust of professional methodology, and her faith in the future, all have roots in a tradition at Hull-House that has lasted for a hundred years. [Patricia Sharpe, ''Contributions over One Hundred Years,'' [Speech] (1986), mimeographed, 6 pages.]

Earlier this week, back at the office, we had a staff meeting at which a number of department heads each brought the others up to date on their programs and activities. In that group of seven, I was the only professional social worker. The reports included these activities:

A program called F. A. C. T.: First Aid Care Team. A group of trained Emergency Medical Technicians has an office in a large high rise public housing proj-

Hull-House celebrated 100 years of service in 1989 under the direction of Patricia Sharpe, seen here with an Ed Weiss portrait of the first head resident, Jane Addams.

ect. Their job is to respond instantly to medical crisis or trauma, and to provide first aid until the Paramedics arrive. Sometimes they might need to escort the Paramedics. Why are we, Hull House, engaged in that activity? Because it is needed, useful, valuable to that community. And I believe that because we are doing it, rather than the fire department or the Housing Authority, it becomes a more human service. But is it social work?

The Chicago Capital Fund, a Community Equity Corporation for Business Development. The purpose of this project is to provide long term capital and management assistance to small and emerging businesses. The success of the portfolio will enhance the process of creating and maintaining jobs in Chicago. Why are we, Hull House, engaged in that activity? Because jobs in the inner city are desparately needed, and businesses too often move out to the suburbs. And because we bring to it a value that is not only profit. We believe we can make a difference in neighborhood development and still have reasonable earnings which will go back into the neighborhood.

The Jane Addams Conference, a Woman's Leadership Program for Peace and Security. Why are we, Hull House, involved in such a broad program? Because it is our conviction that problems of security in this nuclear age are problems which affect everyone. We have lived in the shadow of nuclear disaster for fifty years. And because Jane Addams said ''So we have fallen back into warfare, and perhaps will fall back again and again, until in self-pity, in self-defense, in self-assertion of the right of life . . . the whole people of the world will brook this thing no longer.''

Community-based Training in Literacy, in which we are applying the research done by Early Childhood Education specialists to the inner city communities in which we have day care and Headstart programs. Again, why are we doing this? Because we believe that in the area of literacy development,

Child welfare remains a major focus of Hull-House program. Betty Archibald (right) is one of more than 300 women who have been trained through the Jane Addams Center's Day Care Home Provider Program. Participants receive assistance with job placement, state licensing, and business skills development as well as ongoing support and training.

a parent, teacher or administrator cannot effect lasting change in a child single-handedly, but a system-wide effort that aims to build continuity in adults' efforts can make a difference. In the communities we serve, we know that many of the parents of our young children are themselves illiterate and we suspect they may therefore de-value the efforts to teach and to learn. That has dire implications for the future, and we want to make a difference for the children and their parents.

In these examples I have cited, the role of social workers or social work education, is not specific. Not necessarily included nor excluded.

We believe that our neighborhood centers must be responsive to the problems and people in those neighborhoods. To be properly responsive, we need to develop a wide variety of interventions. Some of those interventions may in fact be consistent with social work training, but many are not. We try to focus our efforts in those communities most in need, and the overwhelming need as expressed by the community is for relief from poverty, for opportunity to be self-sufficient, for ways to influence institutions and systems in areas of education, health, economics, and housing.

Further, we believe that those of us who work in neighborhood centers are in a position to work for change and reform in institutions and systems. We try to move from the particular problem to the general, and to make sure we are really in touch with the particular. For example, jobs are a major particular concern for an individual, for a community, and a general concern for policy-makers. We can design programs for counseling and placement, but we need also to look at economic systems and structures and politics.

When I talked about a variety of interventions, I did not mention counseling or casework, and I believe that a neighborhood center should have counseling service available.

Schools of social work do a good job of teach-

Carrying on the tradition begun by Jane Addams in 1889, Hull-House continued to focus much of its program on child welfare. Today, Hull-House helps build a foundation for learning through early childhood development programs like Head Start and after-school activities. A special literacy program, developed with the Erikson Institute of Early Childhood Education, reaches almost 1,000 pre-school children.

ing casework; the combination of field work and classroom work is a valuable system of teaching. But what I see, and what staff members tell me, is that students are mostly prepared to work in mental health centers and family service agencies, where income and status are likely to be higher. It may be that students themselves determine this kind of direction. It may be that the push by the profession toward third party payment sets up a certain expectation about clientele. I can't imagine third party payment being an issue in our neighborhoods.

While I believe that casework services should be part of the mix of programs and services in a neighborhood center, my experience is that it is not a comfortable mix. Settlement workers and professional social workers make each other uncomfortable. Settlement workers tend to be viewed as undisciplined, too ready to jump in and get involved. Professional social workers tend to be viewed as too bound by their professional discipline, not ready enough to involve themselves in practical realities. And it does seem that in the preparation of social workers there is not a lot of attention paid to problems of poverty, to the realities of the inner city neighborhoods.

Where does a settlement worker receive training? Where do we look in our hiring for people who can work out the variety of interventions we want? There is no one particular source. We find a number of "maverick" social workers, those who are perhaps somewhat dissatisfied with what they see as an overemphasis on casework, or who get impatient with casework and start looking beyond individual problems to institutional or political contributions to solve the problems. We like a background in sociology, or history, or economics.

I am uneasy about the "Future Relationship between Neighborhood Centers and Social Work Professional Academia."* I sense that we are drifting apart, that fewer students are placed in neighborhood centers now than in the past. I think we are becoming more uncomfortable with each other, thus more critical and less likely to see where our interests and talents are complementary.

When I try to come up with specific recommendations, I have trouble. Perhaps part of the difficulty has to do with methodology. Believing that we need a variety of interventions means we are not committed to a particular methodology. In general, neighborhood centers have derived strength from their ability to use a variety of methodologies, to borrow from other fields, or to create, or to somehow muddle through without any particular methodology. To quote Alice Hamilton, "Getting things done mattered more than methodology." But when we talk about schools of social work, and training students, do we get trapped in worrying about methodology?

As centers involved in human services, we need people who can think, analyze, and also bring a set of specific values to solving social and civic problems. Neighborhood centers seem well suited to being both a training ground and a base for action. I would like to see schools of social work more broadly involved, and hope we can get involved in how we become more comfortable with each other.

*The title of the conference session at which Sharpe spoke.—Eds.

AFTERWORD

TWO MONTHS AFTER WE SENT THE MANUSCRIPT FOR THIS edition to our publisher, we began to get hints from Chicago that Hull-House Association might be experiencing more reorganization. We were aware that the administrative structure was artificial and cumbersome and that financial support, especially for the central office, was totally inadequate. In 1989, the agency expected a shortfall of $200,000, primarily from operating costs for its central office. After ten years as executive director, Patricia Sharpe planned to retire effective with the appointment of a replacement.

It also appeared likely that the movement toward disaffiliation would continue after the centennial year. Darrow Center, with its director, Stanley Horne, planned to go its own way. In addition, the site of the Jane Addams Center, one of the two facilities opened by Hull-House Association when it moved from its original neighborhood in 1963, might be sold; its program might be dismantled and perhaps moved elsewhere. By June 1989, center director Nancy McCullar was pointing out that over the past few years the Lakeview neighborhood, which the Center served, had become gentrified with middle-class residents. They paid fees for services like photography and ceramics classes and used the swimming pool; they were supportive of civic endeavor; but, they did not require or want the social services that had also long been part of the Hull-House tradition.

The central Hull-House board made plans to undertake a national search for a new director and began developing an agenda for a retreat to consider the agency's future. Hull-House seemed on the verge of yet another new era. For us, as editors, there were lots of questions and few answers. For example, what would happen to the Hull-House name and 100 years of tradition and service in Chicago? Would the agency totally be restructured, giving up some or all of its affiliates and central office? Would more of the centers move to

323

locations where their services would be more in demand? And what would those services be? Should centers focus on basic social welfare services primarily for those in need of food, shelter, jobs, education, and health care; or should they concentrate on social reform and civic improvement, trying to change circumstances and attitudes in society? Would there be adequate community support for both approaches?

Jane Addams always admonished the settlement movement to strive for flexibility, to be ready to respond creatively, quickly, and positively to changing environment, needs, and population. It seems likely that once again the leadership at Hull-House is facing that challenge.

MLB
AFD

August 1989

INDEX

MARY LYNN McCREE BRYAN is former Curator of Jane Addams' Hull-House and is Editor of *The Jane Addams' Papers*.

ALLEN F. DAVIS, Professor of History at Temple University, is author of several books including *American Heroine: The Life and Legend of Jane Addams, Spearheads for Reform: The Social Settlements and the Progressive Movement, Conflict and Consensus in Modern American History*.